REA's Test Prep Books Are The Best!

(a sample of the <u>hundreds of letters</u> REA receives each year)

" This book is an excellent preparation for the PSAT... Get this book if you're serious. "

Student, Laguna Beach, CA

" My students report your chapters of review as the most valuable single resource they used for review and preparation. "

Teacher, American Fork, UT

" Your book was such a better value and was so much more complete than anything your competition has produced (and I have them all!). "

Teacher, Virginia Beach, VA

" Compared to the other books that my fellow students had, your book was the most useful in helping me get a great score. "

Student, North Hollywood, CA

" Your book was responsible for my success on the exam, which helped me get into the college of my choice... I will look for REA the next time I need help. "

Student, Chesterfield, MO

" Just a short note to say thanks for the great support your book gave me in helping me pass the test... I'm on my way to a B.S. degree because of you! "

Student, Orlando, FL

(more on next page)

(continued from front page)

" I am writing to congratulate you on preparing an exceptional study guide. In five years of teaching this course, I have never encountered a more thorough, comprehensive, concise and realistic preparation for this examination. "

Teacher, Davie, FL

" I have found your publications, *The Best Test Preparation...*, to be exactly that. "

Teacher, Aptos, CA

" I used your book to prepare for the test and found that the advice and the sample tests were highly relevant... Without using any other material, I earned very high scores and will be going to the graduate school of my choice. "

Student, New Orleans, LA

" I used your *CLEP Introductory Sociology* book and rank it 99% – thank you! "

Student, Jerusalem, Israel

" Your GMAT book greatly helped me on the test. Thank you. "

Student, Oxford, OH

" I recently got the French SAT II Exam book from REA. I congratulate you on first-rate French practice tests."

Instructor, Los Angeles, CA

" Your AP English Literature and Composition book is most impressive."

Student, Montgomery, AL

" The REA LSAT Test Preparation guide is a winner! "

Instructor, Spartanburg, SC

The Best Coaching and Study Course for the

PSAT/NMSQT

*Preliminary Scholastic Assessment Test/
National Merit Scholarship Qualifying Test*

Robert A. Bell, Ph.D.
SAT Skills Consultant
Mathematics Professor
The Cooper Union School of Engineering
New York, NY

Suzanne Coffield, M.A.
SAT Preparation Instructor
Aurora, IL

Anita Price Davis, Ed.D.
SAT Skills Consultant
Chair, Education Department
Converse College, Spartanburg, SC

George DeLuca, J.D.
SAT Skills Consultant
New Rochelle, NY

Christopher Dreisbach, Ph.D.
Department of Philosophy
College of Notre Dame of Maryland
Baltimore, MD

Joseph D. Fili, M.A.T.
Director, Verbal "PrepSAT" Program
English Department
Christian Brothers Academy
Lincroft, NJ

Marilyn B. Gilbert, M.A.
SAT Skills Consultant
Hampton, NJ

Bernice E. Goldberg, Ph.D.
SAT Skills Consultant
Former Adjunct Professor
Seton Hall University, South Orange, NJ

Leonard A. Kenner
SAT Preparation Instructor
Math Instructor
Island Trees Junior High School
Levittown, NY

Gary Lemco, Ph.D.
SAT Preparation Instructor
Atlanta, GA

Maxine Morrin, Ph.D.
SAT Skills Consultant
New York, NY

Marcia Mungenast
SAT Preparation Instructor and
Educational Consultant
Upper Montclair, NJ

Sandra B. Newman, M.A.
SAT Skills Consultant
Research Associate
Queens College / CUNY, Flushing, NY

Richard C. Schmidt, Ph.D.
SAT Skills Consultant
Instructor, Department of English
Roosevelt University, Chicago, IL

Archibald Sia, Ph.D.
Department of Mathematics
California State University-Northridge
Northridge, CA

Research & Education Association
61 Ethel Road West
Piscataway, New Jersey 08854

The Best Coaching and Study Course for the
PSAT/NMSQT™
Preliminary Scholastic Assessment Test/
National Merit Scholarship Qualifying Test

Year 2002 Printing

Printed in the United States of America

Library of Congress Control Number 00-130641

International Standard Book Number 0-87891-936-8

Research & Education Association
61 Ethel Road West
Piscataway, New Jersey 08854

REA supports the effort to conserve and
protect environmental resources by
printing on recycled papers.

CONTENTS

CHAPTER 8
ATTACKING REGULAR MATH QUESTIONS

CHAPTER 9
ATTACKING QUANTITATIVE COMPARISON
QUESTIONS

CHAPTER 10
ATTACKING STUDENT-PRODUCED RESPONSE
QUESTIONS

ABOUT RESEARCH & EDUCATION ASSOCIATION

Research & Education Association (REA) is an organization of educators, scientists, and engineers specializing in various academic fields. Founded in 1959 with the purpose of disseminating the most recently developed scientific information to groups in industry, government, high schools, and universities, REA has since become a successful and highly respected publisher of study aids, test preps, handbooks, and reference works.

REA's Test Preparation series includes study guides for all academic levels in almost all disciplines. Research & Education Association publishes test preps for students who have not yet completed high school, as well as high school students preparing to enter college. Students from countries around the world seeking to attend college in the United States will find the assistance they need in REA's publications. For college students seeking advanced degrees, REA publishes test preps for many major graduate school admission examinations in a wide variety of disciplines, including engineering, law, and medicine. Students at every level, in every field, with every ambition can find what they are looking for among REA's publications.

Unlike most test preparation books—which present only a few practice tests that bear little resemblance to the actual exams—REA's series presents tests that accurately depict the official exams in both degree of difficulty and types of questions. REA's practice tests are always based upon the most recently administered exams, and include every type of question that can be expected on the actual exams.

REA's publications and educational materials are highly regarded and continually receive an unprecedented amount of praise from professionals, instructors, librarians, parents, and students. Our authors are as diverse as the fields represented in the books we publish. They are well-known in their respective disciplines and serve on the faculties of prestigious high schools, colleges, and universities throughout the United States and Canada.

ACKNOWLEDGMENTS

In addition to our authors, we would like to thank Dr. Max Fogiel, President, for his overall guidance, which brought this publication to completion; Larry B. Kling, Quality Control Manager of Books in Print, and John Paul Cording, Manager of Educational Software, for their editorial supervision; Michael Tomolonis, Editorial Assistant, for coordinating revisions; Christine Saul, Graphic Designer, for designing our cover; and Martin Perzan for typesetting the manuscript for this revised edition.

PSAT/ NMSQT

Independent Study Schedule

PSAT/NMSQT INDEPENDENT STUDY SCHEDULE

The following study schedule allows for thorough preparation for the PSAT/NMSQT. Although it is designed for nine weeks, it can be condensed to about half that long by collapsing two weeks into one. If you are not enrolled in a structured course, be sure to set aside enough time, at least two hours each day, to study. But no matter which study schedule works best for you, the more time you spend studying, the more prepared and relaxed you will feel on the day of the exam.

Week	Activity
Week 1	Read and study Chapter 1, which will introduce you to the PSAT/NMSQT. Take the Diagnostic Test to determine your strengths and weaknesses. Score each section by using the score chart found in Chapter 1. You can then determine the subjects in which you need to strengthen your skills by using the cross-referencing chart provided at the end of the Diagnostic Test.
Week 2	Study the Basic Verbal Skills Review. Be sure to thoroughly work through the Vocabulary Enhancer and complete all the drills. If you have particular trouble with any of the drill questions, go back and study the corresponding section of the review.
Week 3	Study the three reviews on Attacking Analogy Questions, Sentence Completion Questions, and Critical Reading Questions. Complete all drills using the tips and techniques you have learned.
Week 4	Study the Basic Math Skills Review, and be sure to complete all drill questions. If any particular type of question gives you trouble, review that section again.
Week 5	Study the three separate reviews on Attacking Regular Math, Quantitative Comparison, and Student-Produced Response questions. Answer each drill using the methods you have learned in the review.

Week	Activity
Week 6	Study the Writing Skills Review in Chapter 11. Be sure to complete all the drills. If you have trouble with a particular type of question, be sure to revisit the corresponding section in the review.
Week 7	Take Practice Test 1, and after scoring your exam, review carefully all incorrect answer explanations. If there are any types of questions that are particularly difficult for you, review those subjects by studying again the appropriate section.
Week 8	Take Practice Test 2, and after scoring your exam, review carefully all incorrect answer explanations. If there are any types of questions that are particularly difficult for you, review those subjects by studying again the appropriate section.
Week 9	Take Practice Test 3, and after scoring your exam, review carefully all incorrect answer explanations. If there are any types of questions that are particularly difficult for you, review those subjects by studying again the appropriate section.

PSAT/ NMSQT

CHAPTER 1

About the PSAT/NMSQT

Chapter 1

ABOUT THE PSAT/NMSQT

ABOUT THIS BOOK

This book provides you with an accurate and complete representation of the Preliminary Scholastic Assessment Test/National Merit Scholarship Qualifying Test (PSAT/NMSQT™). Inside you will find reviews that are designed to provide you with the information and strategies needed to do well on the exam, and four practice tests based on the format of the most recently administered PSAT/NMSQT. The practice tests contain every type of question that you may expect to appear on the PSAT/NMSQT. Following each test, you will find an answer key with detailed explanations designed to help you more completely understand the test material.

ABOUT THE TEST

Who Takes the Test and What Is It Used for?

The PSAT/NMSQT is usually taken by high school sophomores and juniors for three main reasons: (1) practice for the SAT I, (2) to compete for scholarships offered through the National Merit Scholarship Corporation and other programs, and (3) to participate in the Student Search Service (SSS). Nearly 1.5 million students take the PSAT/NMSQT each year. This means there is a great deal of competition for scholarship money and the opportunity to be considered by colleges.

National Merit Scholarships are given to outstanding college-bound students. Qualifying criteria include performance on the PSAT. The top scorers on the PSAT in each state become semifinalists and compete for college scholarships.

The Student Search Service is a program that matches your academic background and interests to appropriate colleges and scholarship services. Once your data is processed, you will receive information from the schools and scholarship services you have chosen.

How Important Are My PSAT/NMSQT Scores?

If you don't do well on the PSAT/NMSQT, don't panic! The test can be taken again if you are a sophomore, or you can work on improving your score in preparation for the SAT I. The PSAT/NMSQT is not a requirement for entering college, so if you do poorly, it does not mean you will not get into college or that you will not do well on the SAT I. Colleges you apply to do not need to know your PSAT/NMSQT scores. A score on the PSAT/NMSQT that does not match your expectations does not mean you should change your plans about attending college. It is, after all, only a *preliminary* test.

Who Administers the Test?

The PSAT/NMSQT is developed and administered by the Educational Testing Service (ETS) and involves the assistance of educators throughout the country. The test development process is designed and implemented to ensure that the content and difficulty level of the test are appropriate.

When Should the PSAT/NMSQT Be Taken?

You should take the PSAT/NMSQT during your sophomore or junior year of high school. The test provides you with the opportunity to register for scholarship competition, to enter the Student Search Service, and to practice for the all-important SAT I as well as the SAT II: Writing Test. Taking the PSAT/NMSQT will familiarize you with the types of questions and format of the actual SAT I. If you are thinking of attending college, you should take the PSAT/NMSQT because it will give you practice for the SAT I, provide an opportunity to obtain scholarships to help pay for college, and give colleges a chance to see your potential for success as a college student.

When and Where Is the Test Given?

The PSAT/NMSQT is administered once a year in October at many locations, including high schools, throughout the United States. A school may choose one of two days on which to administer the test.

To receive information on upcoming administrations of the PSAT/NMSQT, consult the *PSAT/NMSQT Student Bulletin,* which can be obtained from your guidance counselor or by contacting the following:

PSAT/NMSQT Office
P.O. Box 6720
Princeton, NJ 08541-6720   *or*
Telephone: (609) 771-7070
Website: www.collegeboard.org

National Merit Scholarship Corp.
1560 Sherman Ave., Suite 200
Evanston, IL 60201-4897
Telephone: (847) 866-5100
Website: www.nationalmerit.org

Is there a Registration Fee?

To take the PSAT/NMSQT, you must pay a registration fee. Financial assistance may be granted in certain situations. To find out if you qualify and to register for assistance, contact your academic advisor.

HOW TO USE THIS BOOK

What Do I Study First?

Remember that the PSAT/NMSQT is designed to test knowledge acquired throughout your education. Therefore, taking the sample tests provided in this book will familiarize you with the types of questions, directions, and format of the PSAT/NMSQT. In addition, our practice tests will help you establish a feel for the time frame within which each section must be completed. Read over the reviews and the suggestions for test-taking, take the Diagnostic Test to determine your area(s) of weakness, and then go back and focus on your specific problem areas. The reviews include the information you need to know when taking the exam. Make sure to take the remaining practice tests to further familiarize yourself with the format and procedures of the actual PSAT/NMSQT.

One final point: Brushing up on the areas you did *well* on couldn't hurt, either.

When Should I Start Studying?

It is never too early to start studying for the PSAT/NMSQT. The earlier you begin, the more time you will have to sharpen your skills. Do not procrastinate! Cramming is *not* an effective way to study, since it does not allow you the time needed to learn the test material. The sooner you learn the format of the exam, the more time you have to make yourself comfortable with it. Come test day, you may find that this can be at least as important as knowing the material.

FORMAT OF THE PSAT/NMSQT

Section	Number of Questions	Skills/Areas Covered
Verbal	13 multiple-choice 13 multiple-choice 26 multiple-choice	Sentence Completions Analogies Critical Reading
Mathematics	20 Regular Math multiple- choice 12 Quantitative Comparisons 8 Student-Produced Response	Arithmetic Algebra Geometry
Writing Skills	19 multiple-choice 14 multiple-choice 6 multiple-choice	Error Identifications Sentence Improvements Paragraph Improvements

Total Testing Time: 130 minutes (plus instructions and break period)

All of the questions on the PSAT/NMSQT are in multiple-choice format except for the Student-Produced Response mathematics questions. No answer choices will be provided for these questions. You must enter your answer in a special grid. Most of the multiple-choice questions will have five options lettered (A) through (E), but the Quantitative Comparison questions will only have four options lettered (A) through (D). Be aware that there is a time limit for each section, so you should keep track of how long you have left in each section. Using the practice tests will help you prepare for this task.

SECTIONS OF THE PSAT/NMSQT

Verbal Sections

There are two separate verbal sections on the PSAT/NMSQT which contain a mix of three different question types: Sentence Completions, Analogies, and Critical Reading.

- Sentence Completions: A sentence will be given with either one or two words omitted. You will have to choose the word or words which best complete the sentence.

- Analogies: These questions test your ability to identify the relationship between two words and choose another pair which shows a similar connection.

- Critical Reading: There are four reading passages on the PSAT/NMSQT, including one double passage which consists of two related selections. The questions will test your critical reading skills– that is, how well you can analyze the material rather than simply recall factual information from what you have read.

The breakdown of the 52 verbal questions may be as follows:

Section 1:   7 Sentence Completion questions
                            6 Analogy questions
(25 minutes)   Reading passage #1 with 5 Critical Reading
                            questions
                            Reading passage #2 with 8 Critical Reading questions

Section 3:   6 Sentence Completion questions
                            7 Analogy questions
(25 minutes)   Reading passage #3 with 5 Critical Reading
                            questions
                            Double passage with 8 Critical Reading questions

Mathematics Sections

You will encounter three different types of math questions on the PSAT/NMSQT; they will test your arithmetic, algebra, and geometry skills.

- Regular Math: These are questions of the usual multiple-choice format which will ask you to perform basic mathematics.

- Quantitative Comparisons: Here you will be given two quantities and asked to compare them in terms given in the question. The two quantities will be represented in separate columns. Four answers for comparing the values will be presented at the beginning of the questions, and these four choices will be used to answer all of these questions.

- Student-Produced Response: These questions require you to solve a problem and enter the solution into a grid, instead of choosing the correct answer from among the provided answer choices.

The 40 math questions may be arranged as follows:

Section 2:   20 Regular Math questions
(25 minutes)

Section 4:   12 Quantitative Comparisons questions
(25 minutes)   8 Student-Produced Response questions

Writing Skills Section

There are three different types of Writing Skills questions on the PSAT/NMSQT: Error Identifications, Sentence Improvements and Paragraph Improvements.

Identifying Sentence Errors: These questions test your ability to find errors of structure and usage in sentences. Several words and phrases in the sentence will be underlined; you must choose the incorrect word or phrase or, if the sentence is correct as is, choose "No error."

Improving Sentences: These questions ask you to revise the part of a sentence that is underlined. The question gives you five choices—answer (A) is the same as the underlined part, which is to say the sentence needs no revision. Choices B-E are alternate phrasings of the underlined section. You should choose the phrase that most clearly communicates the original idea of the sentence.

Improving Paragraphs: Some of these questions are essentially the same as the Sentence Improvement questions except that they ask you to ensure that the revised sentence makes sense in the context of the entire passage. Some questions ask you about the structure and meaning of the reading as a whole.

The breakdown of the 39 writing skills questions may be as follows:

Section 5:   19 Error Identification questions
(30 minutes)   14 Sentence Improvement questions
                    6 Paragraph Improvement questions

ABOUT THE REVIEW SECTIONS

The reviews in this book will not only teach you the skills needed to approach PSAT/NMSQT questions, but also provide strategies for attacking each type of question. Drills are provided to help reinforce what you have learned. By using the reviews in conjunction with the practice tests, you will sharpen your skills for the PSAT/NMSQT.

Verbal Reviews

In the Basic Verbal Skills Review, you will find advice for building your verbal skills, as well as an extensive vocabulary enhancer which contains a list of words commonly found on the PSAT/NMSQT. There are also separate reviews for each type of verbal question: Analogies, Sentence Completions, and Critical Reading. In these reviews, the types of questions you will encounter on the PSAT/NMSQT will be presented, along with step-by-step strategies for answering them.

Mathematics Reviews

The Basic Math Skills Review will help to reinforce the arithmetic, algebra, and geometry concepts you need to know in order to succeed on the PSAT/NMSQT. Included are drills with questions that will help reinforce these skills. Next, you will find separate reviews for Regular Math, Quantitative Comparison, and Student-Produced Response questions. These reviews will present every possible question type that will be encountered on the math test, and will also provide step-by-step strategies and tips for solving the problems.

Writing Skills Review

The Writing Skills review will hone your English Language skills. It reviews and drills many grammar points that you will find useful for the writing skills questions on the exam.

SCORING THE PSAT/NMSQT

How Do I Score My Practice Test?

Verbal Sections

Count the number of correct responses in the verbal sections (Section 1 and Section 3). Next, count up the number of incorrect responses. Enter these numbers into the corresponding blanks on the provided scoring worksheet. Next, multiply the number of incorrect answers by one-fourth (this is the penalty for answering incorrectly). Subtract this product from the total number of correct answers. Fractions should be rounded off: round up for one-half or more and round down for less than one-half. Add the subtotals for Sections 1 and 3 together; this will yield your total number of points for the verbal section.

Mathematics Sections

Count the number of correct responses in the math sections (Section 2 and Section 4). Count up the number of incorrect responses for the regular math questions (Section 2). Enter this number in the worksheet, multiply by one-fourth, and subtract the product from the total number of correct answers in that section. Next, count up the number of incorrect responses for the Quantitative Comparisons questions (Section 4, questions 1-15). Enter this number in the worksheet, multiply this by one-third, and subtract the product from the number of correct answers in that section. You do not need to count the number of incorrect answers for the Student-Produced questions (Section 4, questions 16-25) because there is no penalty for incorrect answers to this question type. Once again, fractions should be rounded off. Add all of the subtotals together to yield the total of mathematics points.

Writing Skills Section

Count the number of correct responses in the writing section. Next, count the number of incorrect responses. Enter these numbers into the corresponding blanks on the provided scoring worksheet. Then multiply the number of incorrect answers by one-fourth and subtract this product from the total number of correct answers. If the number is a fraction, round it off– this is your number of points for the writing section.

How Do I Calculate My Scaled Score?

Scores on the PSAT/NMSQT range from 20 to 80. Take the total number of points for each section, your Raw Score, and check the following chart for its corresponding Scaled Score. To convert your PSAT/NMSQT score to an SAT I score, just add a zero to the end of your score. This will give you a general idea of where your score would fall in terms of SAT I scores. Remember, the questions on the PSAT/NMSQT are taken from a pool of SAT I questions, but the more difficult questions are excluded from the PSAT/NMSQT. Therefore, your estimated SAT I score is not completely accurate. If your performance is not as good as you had expected, don't worry. With each practice test you are building skills to do well on the PSAT/NMSQT and the SAT I. (See the Conversion Table for Total Scores on page sixteen.)

SCORING WORKSHEET

Verbal Sections

Section 1   _____ − 1/4 (_____) = _____
            correct   incorrect   subtotal

                                                    +

Section 3   _____ − 1/4 (_____) = _____
            correct   incorrect   subtotal

Total Verbal Raw Score   _____
                                  total

Mathematics Sections

Section 2   _____ − 1/4 (_____) = _____
            correct   incorrect   subtotal

                                                    +

Section 4,   _____ − 1/3 (_____) = _____
Quantitatives   correct   incorrect   subtotal

                                                    +

Section 4   _____   = _____
Grid-ins   correct   subtotal

Total Mathematics Raw Score   _____
                                      total

Writing Skills Section

Section 5   _____ − 1/4 (_____) = _____
            correct   incorrect   total

STUDYING FOR THE PSAT/NMSQT

It is very important for you to choose the time and place for studying that work best for you. Some students may set aside a certain number of hours every morning to study, while others may choose to study at night before going to sleep. Other students may study during the day, while waiting on a line, or even while eating lunch. Only you can determine when and where your study time will be most effective. But be consistent and use your time wisely. Work out a study routine and stick to it!

When you take the practice tests, try to make your testing conditions as much like the actual test as possible. Turn your television and radio off, and sit down at a quiet table free from distraction. Make sure to time yourself with a timer.

As you complete each practice test, score your test and thoroughly review the explanations to the question you answered incorrectly; however, do not review too much at any one time. Concentrate on one problem area at a time by reviewing the questions and explanations, and by studying our review until you are confident you completely understand the material.

Keep track of your scores and mark them on the Scoring Worksheet. By doing so, you will be able to gauge your progress and discover general weaknesses in particular sections. You should carefully study the reviews that cover your areas of difficulty, as this will build your skills in those areas.

PSAT/NMSQT TEST-TAKING TIPS

Although you may be unfamiliar with standardized tests such as the PSAT/NMSQT, there are many ways to acquaint yourself with this type of examination and help alleviate your test-taking anxieties. Listed below are ways to help you become accustomed to the PSAT/NMSQT, some of which may apply to other standardized tests as well.

Become comfortable with the format of the PSAT/NMSQT. When you are practicing to take the PSAT/NMSQT, simulate the conditions under which you will be taking the actual test. Stay calm and pace yourself. After simulating the test only a couple of times, you will boost your chances of doing well, and you will be able to sit down for the actual PSAT/NMSQT much more confidently.

Know the directions and format for each section of the test. Familiarizing yourself with the directions and format of the different test sections will not only save you time, but will also ensure that you are familiar enough with the PSAT/NMSQT to avoid nervousness (and the mistakes caused by being nervous).

Work on the easier questions first. If you find yourself working too long on one question, make a mark next to it in your test booklet and continue. After you have answered all of the questions that you can, go back to the ones you have skipped.

If you are unsure of an answer, guess. But if you do guess, guess wisely. Use the process of elimination by going through each answer to a question and eliminating as many of the answer choices as possible. By eliminating three answer choices, you give yourself a fifty-fifty chance of getting the item correct since there will only be two choices left from which to make your guess.

Be sure that you are making your answer in the oval that corresponds to the number of the question in the test booklet. Since your test is graded by machine, marking one answer in the wrong space will throw off the rest of your test. Do your scratchwork in the test booklet only.

Read all of the possible answers. Just because you think you have found the correct response, do not automatically assume that it is the best answer. You should read through each choice before marking your answer on the sheet to be sure that you are not making a mistake by jumping to conclusions.

You don't have to answer every question. You are not penalized if you do not answer every question. The only penalty you receive is if you answer a question incorrectly. Try to use the guessing strategy, but if you are truly stumped by a question, do not answer it.

Work quickly and steadily. You will have only twenty-five minutes to work on each verbal and math section and only thirty minutes for the writing skills questions, so you will need to work as quickly as possible and work steadily to avoid focusing on one problem too long. Taking the practice tests in this book will help you to budget your precious time.

THE DAY OF THE TEST

Before the Test

On the day of the test, you should wake up early (it is hoped after a decent night's rest) and have a good breakfast. Make sure to dress comfortably so that you are not distracted by being too hot or too cold while taking the test. Also, plan to arrive at the test center early. This will allow you to collect your thoughts and relax before the test, and will also spare you the anguish that comes with being late. If you arrive after the test begins, you will not be admitted, and will not receive a refund.

If you would like, you may wear a watch to the test center, but do not wear one that makes noise; this may disturb other test-takers. You are also permitted to use a calculator on the test. You can use any programmable or non-programmable four-function, scientific, or graphing calculator. No pocket organizers, hand-held minicomputers, paper tape, or noisy calculators may be used. In addition, no calculator requiring an external power source will be allowed. Finally, no sharing of calculators will be permitted; you must bring your own.

During the Test

When you arrive at the test center, try to find a seat where you feel you will be comfortable. Once you enter the test center, follow all of the rules and instructions given by the test supervisor. If you do not, you risk being dismissed from the test and having your scores canceled.

When all of the test materials have been passed out, the test instructor will give you directions for filling out your answer sheet. You must fill this sheet out carefully since this information will be printed on your score report.

Remember that you can write in your test booklet, as no scratch paper will be provided. Mark your answers in the appropriate spaces on the answer sheet. Each numbered row will contain five ovals corresponding to each answer choice for that question. Fill in the circle which corresponds to your answer darkly, completely, and neatly. You can change your answer, but remember to completely erase your old answer. Only one answer should be marked. This is very important, as your answer sheet will be machine-scored and stray lines or unnecessary marks may cause the machine to score your answer incorrectly. When you have finished working on a section, you may want to go back and check your answers.

After the Test

When you have completed the PSAT/NMSQT, you may hand in your test materials and leave. Then, go home and relax!

When Will I Receive My Score Report and What Will It Look Like?

You will not receive your score for quite a few weeks because your school gets them first so that they may compile data about students' performances. Aside from your school, you and the National Merit Scholarship Corporation (co-sponsors of the test) are the only other people to see your score, unless you sign up for entrance into the scholarship competitions. You can do this simply by indicating on your PSAT/NMSQT answer form that you would like to be entered into the competition and by answering a few additional questions.

When you do receive your scores, a test book and a PSAT/NMSQT score report will be included. This is so you can review the questions you answered incorrectly and figure out why you chose the wrong answer. Included on the PSAT/NMSQT score report are:

- your scores for the verbal, math and writing skills sections
- a percentile of where your score falls in relation to others taking the PSAT/NMSQT
- the answers you gave on the exam
- the correct answers to the exam
- the difficulty level of each question on the exam
- a summary of your performance on the varying levels of question difficulty
- information about your grade average and future plans
- recommendations for high school courses in your field of interest
- typical courses in your indicated college major
- alternative majors to consider
- careers associated with your indicated major
- skills associated with doing well in the major
- an estimated SAT I score
- selection index number
- eligibility for NMSC programs

For those students who choose to participate in the scholarship programs, the top-scoring students are assigned a selection index number. This number is then used, along with other information, to screen out potential scholarship recipients. To determine the selection index number, add together your verbal, math and writing skills scores. The pool of eligible students is reduced to about 14,000 individuals who compete for 6,500 monetary awards. These awards can be given out by colleges, corporations, or the government. Students must individually pursue the scholarships sponsored by corporations and colleges, but all finalists are automatically enrolled for the National Merit Scholarship competition. Special scholarships are also available for minority students. If you would like more information about these scholarships, see your advisor.

The Student Selection Service provides information to colleges about PSAT/NMSQT test takers and gives the schools a first look at potential students. Colleges can enroll in this service and receive information about students, especially those who express an interest in a certain school.

Conversion Table for Total Scores

Verbal

P	S	P	S	P	S	P	S
52	80	39	68	26	56	13	44
51	80	38	67	25	55	12	43
50	79	37	66	24	54	11	42
49	78	36	65	23	53	10	41
48	77	35	64	22	53	9	40
47	76	34	64	21	52	8	38
46	75	33	63	20	51	7	36
45	74	32	62	19	50	6	34
44	73	31	61	18	49	5	33
43	72	30	60	17	48	4	32
42	71	29	59	16	47	3	31
41	70	28	58	15	46	2	30
40	68	27	57	14	45	1	29

Mathematics

P	S	P	S	P	S	P	S
40	80	30	66	20	54	10	42
39	80	29	65	19	53	9	41
38	79	28	64	18	52	8	40
37	77	27	62	17	51	7	38
36	75	26	60	16	50	6	37
35	73	25	59	15	48	5	36
34	71	24	58	14	47	4	35
33	70	23	57	13	46	3	34
32	68	22	56	12	45	2	33
31	67	21	55	11	44	1	32

Writing Skills

P	S	P	S	P	S	P	S
39	80	29	67	19	55	9	45
38	79	28	66	18	54	8	44
37	78	27	64	17	53	7	43
36	77	26	63	16	52	6	42
35	76	25	62	15	50	5	40
34	75	24	61	14	49	4	39
33	73	23	60	13	48	3	38
32	71	22	58	12	48	2	37
31	70	21	57	11	47	1	36
30	68	20	56	10	46		

PSAT/ NMSQT

CHAPTER 2

A Diagnostic Test

Chapter 2

A DIAGNOSTIC TEST

Now that you have some background information concerning the PSAT/NMSQT, you are ready to take the diagnostic test. This test is designed to help you identify where your strengths and weaknesses lie. You will want to use this information to help you study for the PSAT/NMSQT. It is a complete test, so take this diagnostic test in the same way you would take the actual PSAT/NMSQT. Situate yourself in a quiet room so that there will be no interruptions and keep track of the time allotted for each section. When you are finished with the test, refer to the charts that follow to evaluate your performance. The entries in the chart refer to the questions you answered incorrectly and where to look in the book for a discussion of material covered in that type of problem.

PSAT/NMSQT DIAGNOSTIC TEST

Section 1

(Answer sheets appear in the back of this book.)

TIME: 25 Minutes
  26 Questions

For each question in this section, select the best answer from among the given choices and fill in the corresponding oval on the answer sheet.

DIRECTIONS: Each sentence below has one or two blanks, each blank indicating that something has been omitted. Beneath the sentence are five lettered words or sets of words. Choose the word or set of words that **BEST** fits the meaning of the sentence as a whole.

EXAMPLE:

Although the critics found the book _____, many of the readers found it rather _____.

(A) obnoxious . . . perfect   (D) comical . . . persuasive

(B) spectacular . . . interesting   (E) popular . . . rare

(C) boring . . . intriguing   Ⓐ Ⓑ ● Ⓓ Ⓔ

---

1. The teacher told the class to pay close attention to the lecture because it was _____ , and they would be tested on the information it contained.

    (A) significant   (D) expedited

    (B) unseemly   (E) superfluous

    (C) highlighted

2. It was difficult to approach the author and congratulate him because his attitude was so _____ .

    (A) gaudy   (B) swaggering

(C) courteous   (D) retaliatory

(E) indirect

3. Max Planck, a physicist, discovered a constant by which to measure the amount of energy _____ by light particles.

(A) extracted   (D) collapsing

(B) implanted   (E) aligned

(C) radiated

4. Herodotus and Thucydides were both ancient Greek _____ , but their styles of recording and analyzing events differed greatly.

(A) dramatists   (D) scientists

(B) historians   (E) politicians

(C) psychoanalysts

5. Many religions use _____ as an expression of faith and _____ .

(A) prayer . . . blasphemy   (D) belief . . . asceticism

(B) atonement . . . heresy   (E) fasting . . . discipline

(C) animism . . . monotheism

6. Everyone has had the experience of hearing a line of reasoning which sounds _____, but which one still wants to _____ .

(A) logical . . . dispute   (D) murky . . . classify

(B) topical . . . believe   (E) rational . . . apprehend

(C) recent . . . fabricate

7. The _____ attitude of the administrator was worsened by her _____ questions.

(A) contemptuous . . . compassionate

(B) condescending . . . superficial

(C) punitive . . . fascinating

(D) refreshing . . . haranguing

(E) culpable . . . humbling

8. The class was _____ with the mathematical theorems, but had not yet been taught how to _____ the proofs.

   (A) ecstatic . . . right

   (B) enlightened . . . discount

   (C) cautious . . . dismiss

   (D) familiar . . . demonstrate

   (E) satisfied . . . circumvent

9. Although the diplomat was a wily negotiator, she had difficulty convincing people of that because of her _____ manner of relating to them.

   (A) devious

   (B) Machiavellian

   (C) ingenuous

   (D) mutinous

   (E) titular

10. When the class went to the zoo on a trip, they learned that cats are more _____ related to lions than dogs are to each other.

    (A) intrinsically

    (B) intimidatingly

    (C) intimately

    (D) imminently

    (E) immanently

11. When the company is ready to hold interviews for new employees, the personnel office _____ hiring notices to the local newspapers.

    (A) terminates

    (B) seeks

    (C) overlooks

    (D) directs

    (E) decreases

12. The theory of evolution, among other things, _____ that human beings are descended from a line of animals that originally belonged to the biological classification of apes.

    (A) teaches

    (B) believes

    (C) posits

    (D) hovers

    (E) ponders

13. Tile manufacturers need high-quality clay; this is why brickyards are invariably located in places where high-quality clay is _____ and can be readily _____ .

(A) present . . . verified

(D) abundant . . . accessed

(B) evident . . . procured

(E) visible . . . utilized

(C) nearby . . . obtained

DIRECTIONS: Read each passage and answer the questions that follow. Each question will be based on the information stated or implied in the passage or its introduction.

Questions 14–18 are based on the following passage.

The following passage discusses the development and early study of Roman archaeology.

1   The emergence of archaeology as a subject worthy in its own right was to come . . . in the late seventeenth and eighteenth centuries. The origins of modern archaeology are . . . to be seen in [the] shift away from . . . texts alone to the physical remains as well. Mercati in the sixteenth century was
5   the first to write a treatise on what we would regard today as archaeology. At the same time, academic societies were being founded to promote the investigation of natural phenomena, including archaeology.

The next stage in the emergence of Roman archaeology was the development of an aesthetic appreciation of ancient art and architecture. Artists
10   such as Palladio, Piranesi, and Winkelmann drew and recorded surviving buildings and sculptures. Out of Palladio's architectural work came much of the inspiration for the neoclassical revival of the eighteenth century. Winkelmann is best known as an art historian, whose judgments on ancient art were to color opinions about the Greeks and Romans for most of
15   the neoclassical period. He maintained that Roman art was inferior to Greek as it slavishly copied the Greek originals. . . . This may be true up to a point, but at the time it prejudiced many people against Roman art, and Roman archaeology became less popular as a result.

Excavations of ancient sites started in the eighteenth century with the
20   ransacking of Herculaneum and Pompeii for statues and other works of art. At the same time, expeditions were being organized by such groups as the Society of Dilettanti for the purpose of carrying off sculpture and ancient art objects for private and public collections in northern Europe. Museums such as the British Museum were founded and soon filled to
25   bursting with material of all kinds, including Roman finds. The accumula-

tion of artifacts, and the increasingly enthusiastic appreciation of the ancient world by the leisured classes, led to a more rigorous historical approach on the part of scholars, exemplified by Edward Gibbons' *Decline and Fall of the Roman Empire* (1788). More scientific excavations started
30 with the planned program of King Murat to uncover all of Pompeii in the 1810s, which he decided to do not only to recover works of art, but also to discover the ancient town plan. Upstanding monuments elsewhere started to be conserved and treasured as part of Europe's heritage.

After the early years of the nineteenth century, public interest in the
35 ancient world changed. No longer were the Greeks and Romans used as the inspiration of contemporary writings, architecture and art, for fashions were changing from the neoclassical to the romantic and the Gothic revival. Roman history and archaeology became a more academic discipline, with such great scholars as Theodor Mommsen laying the foundations of
40 the modern study of the subject. The archaeological contribution to Roman history began to realize its true potential, especially in the provinces outside Italy, where large-scale excavations at the end of the nineteenth century led to a much clearer understanding of the great differences between the various regions of the Empire. A good example is the complete
45 excavation of the Roman town of Calleva (Silchester, Hampshire, England) by the Society of Antiquaries.

14. The original inspiration to excavate Pompeii arose from

    (A) a spirit of piracy and looting.

    (B) the admiration for Palladio's work.

    (C) the influence of Winkelmann on a generation of scholars.

    (D) Gibbons' work on the history of Rome.

    (E) the neoclassical concern with methods of preservation.

15. The author treats Winkelmann as an art historian

    (A) whose authority still resists criticism or question.

    (B) who single-handedly altered tastes towards the Gothic.

    (C) whose prejudices tended to devalue the Roman contributions.

    (D) responsible for the Society of Dilettanti.

    (E) directly influential on the work of Theodor Mommsen.

16. The "more rigorous historical approach" (lines 27–28) of scholars was brought about

    (A) in the middle of the nineteenth century.

    (B) by the excavations at Calleva.

    (C) by the definitive work by Mercati.

    (D) partly by the influence of collectors, like the British Museum.

    (E) by the repeated efforts of King Murat.

17. The author indicates that archaeology can provide

    (A) few clues as to the sources of ancient civilizations.

    (B) no real relationship between the Roman and Greek cultures.

    (C) little insight beyond which Winkelmann has already given us.

    (D) an explanation for the disasters at Pompeii and Herculaneum.

    (E) a distinct cultural character in a national and a regional sense.

18. The author interprets King Murat's efforts at Pompeii

    (A) as part of a continued line of plundering ancient sites.

    (B) in the tradition of personal aggrandizement and greed.

    (C) as expanding the role of archaeology in European life.

    (D) as limiting the involvement of science to mere theory.

    (E) as an expression of resistance to Gibbons' theories.

Questions 19–26 are based on the following passage.

The following passage addresses individual rights and the justification for government to abridge those rights.

1   Although democratic nations are founded on the principle of individual liberties and rights, there clearly must be a balance between the scope of individual freedom and the needs of government. Theoretically, individual rights must be curtailed where their exercise constitutes a threat to the very
5   preservation of the nation or of the states and local communities within it. Whether a nation, a state, or a locality, the community at large does have a

From Peter Woll and Robert H. Binstock, *America's Political System,* 4th edition. Reprinted by permission of McGraw-Hill, Inc. ©1991.

public interest that it can and should pursue with diligence. In the broadest sense, the decisions made by legislative majorities reflect community interests, although such interests are also represented by the executive and
10 the judiciary. Only at the federal level is the judiciary independent of direct political control, under the system of separation of powers and checks and balances. At the state and local levels, judges are still mostly elected, making them directly accountable to the people. An elected judiciary is less likely to stand apart from the political process in making its
15 decisions on the scope of individual liberties and rights. Such rights therefore are more likely to be limited if there is a public clamor for their restriction (as, for example, where the elected officials of localities respond to local public opinion by demanding controls over "obscene" magazines, movies, and books.)
20 While there may be political excesses that threaten to limit civil liberties and rights, there are also legitimate governmental needs that may call for a modification of individual freedoms. This occurs when these civil freedoms are used, or misused, to attack the very foundations of the system itself. This problem becomes most acute during times of war or
25 civil unrest. During such times the Supreme Court has given the government wide powers to curb individual freedom.

Perhaps the most extraordinary abridgment of the rights of citizens occurred in 1941, when a Japanese attack was considered by large numbers of people within and outside the government, including military lead-
30 ers, to be an imminent possibility on the West Coast. An even more likely probability considered was sabotage and subversion by Japanese infiltrators. These fears eventually led to the establishment of concentration camps for Japanese-Americans, largely based upon an executive order by President Roosevelt, a decision that was upheld by the Supreme Court,
35 against constitutional challenges in *Korematsu v. United States* in 1944. Writing for the majority of the Court, Justice Hugo Black said that during wartime, military necessity justified the order, which excluded Japanese-Americans from the West Coast. Did the exclusionary order constitute racial discrimination? No. The Court said that although only the Japanese-
40 Americans were excluded, the reason was not of race but of military necessity. *Korematsu* was an extreme case, but it illustrates the degree to which civil rights have been denied on the basis of the public interest.

In drawing the line between public interest and individual freedom, the Supreme Court has relied upon the "balancing test," which attempts to
45 weigh the needs of government against the rights of individuals to determine the proper balance between permissible government restraints and individual freedom. One of the most important spheres of civil liberties, where the balancing test has been applied, regards the civil liberties and

rights enumerated in the First Amendment, particularly the liberties of
50 speech, press, and the right of assembly. In addition to the balancing test,
the "clear and present danger" test is used in determining the permissible
scope of political speech, press, and assembly. In this political sphere the
clear and present danger test is used to judge the extent to which Congress
or the state legislatures may regulate and control the expression of politi-
55 cal ideas.

19. Based on the passage, with which of the following statements would
the authors be most likely to agree?

(A) Individual rights are superior to governmental needs.

(B) Governmental needs are superior to individual rights.

(C) A balance must be struck between individual rights and governmental needs.

(D) Political excesses can never limit civil liberties.

(E) The balance of individual rights and governmental needs is irrelevant to democracy.

20. Based on the passage, we can reasonably infer which of the following?

(A) Local judges are mostly elected.

(B) Federal judges are mostly elected.

(C) State judges are not accountable to the people.

(D) Federal judges are not elected.

(E) State judges are not elected.

21. According to the authors, which of the following are in a better
position to protect individual liberties?

(A) Members of Congress   (D) The President

(B) Federal judges   (E) The Supreme Court

(C) State judges

22. Based on the passage, what type of governmental needs can justify
limitations on individual liberties?

(A) Any type of governmental needs

(B) Those needs which restrict civil rights

(C) Those which threaten the nation

(D) No governmental need justifies limitations on individual liberties.

(E) Those which threaten individuals of other nations

23. According to the authors, what was the justification for the abridgment of rights in *Korematsu*?

    (A) Fear of Japanese invasion

    (B) Racial discrimination

    (C) Public opinion

    (D) Electoral pressures

    (E) Legal precedent

24. Based on the passage, the establishment of concentration camps for Japanese-Americans was found to be which of the following?

    (A) Justified   (D) Unnecessary

    (B) Illegal   (E) Unjustified

    (C) Unconstitutional

25. Which of the following liberties is not specifically mentioned in the passage as a First Amendment liberty?

    (A) Speech   (D) Assembly

    (B) Press   (E) Right to bear arms

    (C) Religion

26. Based on the passage, which of the following tests may allow restrictions on civil rights and liberties?

    I.   Balancing test

    II. Rational basis test

    III. Clear and present danger test

(A) I and II

(B) I and III

(C) II and III

(D) I, II, and III

(E) None of the above.

Section 2

TIME: 25 Minutes
20 Questions

DIRECTIONS: Solve each problem, using any available space on the page for scratch work. Then decide which answer choice is the best and fill in the corresponding oval on the answer sheet.

NOTES:

(1) The use of a calculator is permitted. All numbers used are real numbers.

(2) Figures that accompany problems in this test are intended to provide information useful in solving the problems. They are drawn as accurately as possible EXCEPT when it is stated in a specific problem that the figure is not drawn to scale. All figures lie in a plane unless otherwise indicated.

REFERENCE INFORMATION:

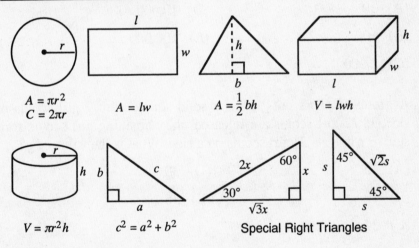

$A = \pi r^2$
$C = 2\pi r$

$A = lw$

$A = \frac{1}{2}bh$

$V = lwh$

$V = \pi r^2 h$

$c^2 = a^2 + b^2$

Special Right Triangles

The number of degrees of arc in a circle is 360.
The measure in degrees of a straight angle is 180.
The sum of the measures in degrees of the angles of a triangle is 180.

1. A solid block 1' × 2' × 3' weighs 6 kg. What is the weight (in kg) of a solid block of the same material 4' × 5' × 6'?

   (A) 36 kg
   (B) 120 kg
   (C) 20 kg
   (D) 90 kg
   (E) 720 kg

2. The first of five morning classes begins at 8 a.m. The last class ends at 11:40 a.m. Allowing 5 minutes between classes, how many minutes are there in each class period?

   (A) 40
   (B) 45
   (C) 50
   (D) 55
   (E) 60

3. How many one-cm cubes can be put in a box 10 cm wide, 10 cm long, and 10 cm deep?

   (A) 30
   (B) 100
   (C) 1,000
   (D) 10,000
   (E) 100,000

4. A group of girl scouts forms a solid square with g girl scouts on a side. If 72 girl scouts are released, the remaining girl scouts form a square with $(g-2)$ girl scouts on a side. What is the value of g?

   (A) 15
   (B) 19
   (C) 24
   (D) 30
   (E) 36

5. How many 10-gallon cans of milk will be needed to fill 160 pint containers?

   (A) 1
   (B) 2
   (C) 3
   (D) 16
   (E) 20

6. The area of a circle is 298. What is the diameter of the circle? (Use $\pi = {}^{22}/_7$.)

   (A) 3.14   (D) 25

   (B) 7   (E) 49

   (C) 19.47

7. If $x + y = {}^1/_k$ and $x - y = k$, what is the value of $x^2 - y^2$?

   (A) 4   (D) k^2

   (B) 1   (E) $\dfrac{1}{k^2}$

   (C) 0

8. If $3^{a-b} = {}^1/_9$ and $3^{a+b} = 9$, then $a =$

   (A) – 2.   (D) 2.

   (B) 0.   (E) 3.

   (C) 1.

9. If $2X + Y = 2$ and $X + 3Y > 6$, then

   (A) $Y \geq 2$.   (D) $Y \leq 2$.

   (B) $Y > 2$.   (E) $Y = 2$.

   (C) $Y < 2$.

10. A man paid $3,500 for a used car. At the end of five years he was given $500 for it toward the purchase of a new car. What was the average amount of depreciation?

   (A) $250   (D) $650

   (B) $500   (E) $3,000

   (C) $600

11. $\overline{KL}$ is parallel to $\overline{MN}$. $\overline{OPQR}$ is a straight line. If $\angle KPO$ is 4 times $\angle MQR$, what is the measure of $\angle RQN$?

(A) 36

(B) 120

(C) 135

(D) 144

(E) 160

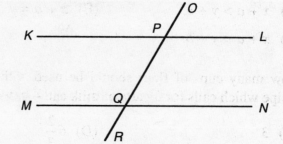

12. Pam drives 25 miles from home to her college at the average rate of 25 miles per hour. She returns on a better road that is 50% longer but she can increase her rate by 100%. How much time does she save by taking the better road on her return trip?

(A) 5 minutes   (D) 30 minutes

(B) 10 minutes   (E) 45 minutes

(C) 15 minutes

13. Flight #100 left Los Angeles at 8:00 a.m. and travelled north at an average rate of 250 miles per hour. Flight #200 left from the same point an hour later and travelled south at 300 miles per hour. How far apart are these planes at 12 noon?

(A) 900 miles   (D) 1,300 miles

(B) 1,000 miles   (E) 3,800 miles

(C) 1,900 miles

14. What does $5 + \dfrac{5}{0.5}$ equal?

(A) 12   (D) 15

(B) 13   (E) 16

(C) 14

15. If $a = b$ and $x < y$, then

    (A) $x + a = y + b$.   (D) $x + a = b$.

    (B) $x + a > y + b$.   (E) $x + a = y$.

    (C) $x + a < y + b$.

16. How many cups of flour should be used with 5 cups of milk in a recipe which calls for 3 parts of milk and 4 parts of flour?

    (A) 3   (D) $6\dfrac{2}{3}$

    (B) 4   (E) 7

    (C) 5

17. While giving lemonade to a group of children, it is found that a jug of lemonade will fill either 4 large plastic cups or 7 small plastic cups. How many small plastic cups can be filled with one large plastic cup?

    (A) $\dfrac{4}{7}$ (D) 2

    (B) $1\dfrac{1}{2}$ (E) $2\dfrac{4}{7}$

    (C) $1\dfrac{3}{4}$

18. During what period did the sharpest increase in profits occur?

    (A) 1987–1988

    (B) 1988–1989

    (C) 1989–1990

    (D) 1990–1991

    (E) 1992–1993

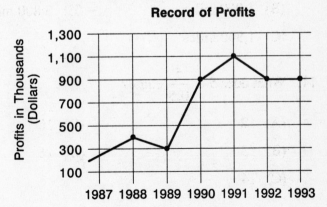

Record of Profits

19. Four associates own a business establishment in the ratio of 16:10:6:2. What part of the total business does the person with the smallest interest control?

    (A) 2%   (D) 29%

    (B) 6%   (E) 47%

    (C) 8%

20. A prime number is an integer greater than 1 that is evenly divisible only by itself and 1. Which of the following represents a prime number when $n = 4$?

    (A) $n^2 + 2$ (D) $5n$

    (B) $n^2 + 2n$ (E) $n^2 - 4$

    (C) $3n + 1$

Section 3

TIME: 25 Minutes
26 Questions

For each question in this section, select the best answer from among the given choices and fill in the corresponding oval on the answer sheet.

DIRECTIONS: Each question below consists of a related pair of words or phrases, followed by five lettered pairs of words or phrases. Select the lettered pair that best expresses a relationship similar to that expressed in the original pair.

EXAMPLE:

SMILE : MOUTH ::

(A) wink : eye

(B) teeth : face

(C) voice : speech

(D) tan : skin

(E) food : gums

● Ⓑ Ⓒ Ⓓ Ⓔ

---

27. HINDER : OBSTRUCT ::

(A) arrange : begin

(B) duplicate : follow

(C) deduct : subtract

(D) renew : establish

(E) inhabit : distort

28. EMBATTLED : CONFLICT ::

(A) witty : humor

(B) bored : activity

(C) generous : courage

(D) smart : riddles

(E) weary : sickness

29. DISORDER : ARRANGEMENT ::

(A) humble : personality

(B) limits : freedom

(C) altruism : charity

(D) credit : interest

(E) remorse : humility

30. BEGINNING : INCEPTION ::
    (A) origin : sequence   (D) delay : clock
    (B) end : conclusion   (E) duration : exchange
    (C) term : season

31. UNIFORM : CHANGEABLE ::
    (A) immutable : permanent   (D) durable : coherent
    (B) brittle : shape   (E) savory : tasteless
    (C) absent : delayed

32. PETITE : DIMINUTIVE ::
    (A) placid : resigned   (D) false : document
    (B) decayed : buried   (E) noxious : harmful
    (C) glib : voice

33. CAPTIVE : ENSLAVED ::
    (A) monster : scaly   (D) hero : revered
    (B) soldier : fierce   (E) reporter : biased
    (C) neighbor : gossip

34. SLANG : INFORMAL ::
    (A) bush : forest   (D) bauble : worthless
    (B) globe : world   (E) horse : wagon
    (C) language : person

35. PANE : SHARD ::
    (A) wood : splinter   (D) food : meat
    (B) chair : comfort   (E) omen : fortune
    (C) raindrop : moisture

36. SCRIPT : WORDS ::
    (A) house : stairs   (B) opera : notes

(C) sport : tennis

(D) garment : collar

(E) photo : camera

37. MISSILE : PROJECTILE ::

(A) doctor : medicine

(D) cage : animal

(B) merchandise : currency

(E) taxes : government

(C) sculpture : art

38. SMUGGLE : CONTRABAND ::

(A) learn : express

(D) celebrate : holiday

(B) destroy : building

(E) share : silence

(C) reveal : note

39. HEIGHT : ELEVATION ::

(A) summit : mountain

(D) overhang : caliber

(B) pitch : potential

(E) depth : depression

(C) diameter : arc

DIRECTIONS: Read the passage and answer the questions that follow. Each question will be based on the information stated or implied in the passage or its introduction.

Questions 40–43 are based on the following passage.

In the following passage, written in 1849, Henry David Thoreau discusses his philosophy of government.

1   I heartily accept the motto,—"That government is best which governs least"; and I should like to see it acted up to more rapidly and systematically. Carried out, it finally amounts to this, which also I believe,—"That government is best which governs not at all"; and when men are prepared
5   for it, that will be the kind of government which they will have. Government is at best but an expedient; but most governments are usually, and all governments are sometimes, inexpedient. The objections which have been brought against a standing army, and they are many and weighty, and deserve to prevail, may also at last be brought against a standing govern-
10 ment. The government itself, which is only the mode which the people have chosen to execute their will, is equally liable to be abused and per-

verted before the people can act through it. Witness the present Mexican war, the work of comparatively a few individuals using the standing government as their tool; for, in the outset, the people would not have con-
15 sented to this measure.

This American government,—what is it but a tradition, though a recent one, endeavoring to transmit itself unimpaired to posterity, but each instant losing some of its integrity? It has not the vitality and force of a single living man; for a single man can bend it to his will. It is a sort of
20 wooden gun to the people themselves. But it is not the less necessary for this; for the people must have that idea of government which they have. Governments show thus how successfully men can be imposed on, even impose on themselves, for their own advantage. It is excellent, we must all allow. Yet this government never of itself furthered any enterprise, but by
25 the alacrity with which it got out of its way. It does not keep the country free. It does not settle the West. It does not educate. The character inherent in the American people has done all that has been accomplished; and it would have done somewhat more, if the government had not sometimes got in its way. For government is an expedient by which man would fain
30 succeed in letting one another alone; and, as has been said, when it is most expedient, the governed are most let alone by it. Trade and commerce, if they were not made of India rubber, would never manage to bounce over the obstacles which legislators are continually putting in their way; and, if one were to judge these men wholly by the effects of their action and not
35 partly by their intentions, they would deserve to be classed and punished with those mischievous persons who put obstructions on the railroads.

But to speak practically and as a citizen, unlike those who call themselves no-government men, I ask for, not at once no government, but at once a better government. Let every man make known what kind of gov-
40 ernment would command his respect, and that will be one step toward obtaining it.

40. Generally speaking, Thoreau believes that

    (A) individual men assert more real force in the world than governments.

    (B) only governments make the contributions of individual men possible.

    (C) the future of America lies in its corporations.

    (D) governments are resistant to change and rarely improve.

    (E) individual men impede the progress of government too often.

41. The term "alacrity" (line 25) means

   (A) determination.   (D) quickness.

   (B) sensitivity.   (E) ruthlessness.

   (C) secrecy.

42. The fact that Thoreau sees government as a "wooden gun" (line 20)

   (A) reduces the notion of government to a mere "toy," something useless.

   (B) suggests that government is a relatively new institution.

   (C) is his way of mocking the inexperience of the legislators.

   (D) does not veil his rather sinister perception of government.

   (E) does not negate the force that government exerts on its citizens.

43. Thoreau's objections to a standing government

   (A) derive from his clear call to abolish government.

   (B) are motivated by his fear of anarchy.

   (C) find representation in his example of the Mexican war.

   (D) are in direct contrast to his views on standing armies.

   (E) are based on the impractical uses that business makes of established parties.

DIRECTIONS: Read the passages and answer the questions that follow. Each question will be based on the information stated or implied in the selections or the introduction, and may be based on the relationship between the passages.

Questions 44–52 are based on the following passages.

Each passage considers the proposition that dreams can be immoral. Passage 2 offers a critique of the arguments offered in Passage 1.

Passage 1

1   If in a dream I commit a murder, have I acted immorally? Many answer "no" since the dreamer has no control over the contents of the dream and since those contents are imaginary, not real. Yet the question persists as to

whether dreams can have moral significance, so further discussion of these
5   answers seems worthwhile.

The kind of control a dreamer would have to exercise in order to give
the dream moral significance would have to involve free will, otherwise it
would be unfair to punish him for something which was not his fault. But
two facts demonstrate the unlikelihood that dreamers have free will. First,
10   the source of the dream clearly acts independent of our control. If the
source is external to us—such as God or demons, as monotheistic scrip-
tures suggest—then it is obvious that we receive the dream without having
the freedom not to. If the source is within us, which is the prevailing view,
it appears to act spontaneously: neurophysiologist Alan Hobson argues,
15   for example, that the dream begins with random neurochemical firings of
the brain, followed by the brain's retrieval of certain images stored in
memory in an attempt to define the neurochemical event.

Second, whatever the source of the dream, it is evident from our own
experiences that dreams take twists and turns, jump from one scene to
20   another, without our being able to predict these events or control them
once they are under way. It's almost as if the dreamer were a passive
member of the audience, even when he is one of the characters of the
dream.

The other argument against the belief that actions in dreams can be
25   immoral centers on the fact that dream contents are imaginary, not real. As
philosopher Margaret Macdonald points out, it would be absurd to regard
an imaginary murder as a real murder. And dreams are imaginary events.
What's more, the moralistic position leads to greater absurdity when we
switch the example from an "immoral" one to a "moral" one. Suppose in
30   my dream I commit an act of heroism? Ought I to be commended for
doing a morally good deed? Of course not. The imaginary act of heroism
has no more moral force in a positive way, than the imaginary act of
murder has in a negative way.

It is clear, then, that dream acts have no moral significance either posi-
35   tively or negatively.

Passage 2

On the face of it, the argument that dream acts can have no moral
significance is a good argument. Dreamers appear to have no control over
their dreams and almost certainly dreams are imaginary events. But there
are weaknesses in these claims sufficient to leave open the possibility that
40   dreamers are capable of acting morally or immorally in their dreams.

The argument from lack of control rests on the claim that dreamers lack
the free will to choose either a right or wrong action and thus are immune
to charges of immorality. One objection to this is that control over our

dreams may not be the morally significant point. As Freud points out,
45 "unless the dream is inspired by alien spirits, it is part of my own being."
For this reason, he argues, we must assume full responsibility for our
dream content—good or bad—since there is no one else to blame.

The second argument against the claim that dream acts can have moral
significance is that dreams are imaginary and just as an imaginary act of
50 murder, for example, is not a real murder, any action in a dream must not
be the real action which we might regard as immoral. This is morally
inconclusive since, as Augustine points out, the immorality of an action
lies not in the possibility or reality of that action, but in the intent to carry
it out. Now it appears that some dreams confront us with a choice of
55 actions which we can intend to do or not do. The intent in a dream to
commit murder, e.g., already indicates a morally significant character
flaw—even if the intent is not carried out. So it may be true that I cannot
commit a real murder in my dream and thus ought not to be punished for
having committed a real murder, but I nevertheless can behave morally or
60 immorally by intending to act morally or immorally. Whether or not morality really lies in the intent or on the carrying out of that intent remains a
question for another time. But we now see that the question whether
dream acts can be immoral is not settled simply by appealing to the imaginary character of dreams.
65 Given these possible objections to two of the stronger arguments against
the claim that dreams have moral significance, we must conclude that
many of them probably do have moral significance after all.

44. Which of the following statements best sums up the argument in
Passage 2?

(A) No argument against the possibility of moral dreams is a good
argument, so there are moral and immoral dreams.

(B) Two of the stronger arguments against the possibility of morally
significant dreams are weak and thus it is probable that dreams
can be moral or immoral.

(C) Given Freud's authority, it is clear that we have control over our
dreams and, therefore, arguments to the contrary fail.

(D) Given the imaginary nature of dreams and the fact that we have
no control over them, there is no moral significance to dreams.

(E) We do have control over our dreams and they are not imaginary,
so the argument in Passage 1 is invalid.

45. Which of the following, if true, would weaken the position of Passage 2?

    (A) Dreams are imaginary.

    (B) Freud believed that dreamers do have control over their dreams.

    (C) The morality of an action does not lie in the intent to carry it out.

    (D) Hobson is not a physiologist.

    (E) Dreams are neurochemical.

46. According to lines 6 through 8, what is the relationship between the moral significance of an act and the free will of the person acting?

    (A) An action has no moral significance unless it is done from free will.

    (B) All actions done from free will are morally significant actions.

    (C) If God and demons are the source of our dreams, then we have no free will.

    (D) If dreams occur in us spontaneously, then we have no free will.

    (E) All acts that are in our control are acts done from free will.

47. How does Passage 2 regard the position attributed to Margaret Macdonald in lines 25–27?

    (A) As wrong

    (B) As irrelevant to the question whether dreams can be morally significant

    (C) As consistent with Freud's position

    (D) As support for the claim that dreamers have no control over their dreams

    (E) As support for the claim that dreams are not imaginary

48. Which of the following is not a reason given in Passage 2 for the claim that dreams may have moral significance?

    (A) Dreams may confront us with a choice of actions.

    (B) Intention is more important to the morality or immorality of an action than the possibility of that action.

(C) Intention is more important to the morality or immorality of an act than the reality of that action.

(D) Dreams may not be imaginary.

(E) Given a choice of actions in dreams, we can intend or not intend to do them.

49. Which of the following statements best characterizes the underlying assumption in lines 28–31 concerning moralistic positions?

(A) If it is possible to act immorally in a dream, it must also be possible to act morally.

(B) It is possible to commit an act of heroism in a dream.

(C) It is possible to commit an act of murder in a dream.

(D) An imaginary act of murder is immoral not moral.

(E) Dream contents are imaginary, not real.

50. What is Passage 2's position on the imaginary character of dreams?

(A) It is possible that dreams are imaginary, which makes the argument that dream acts can have no moral significance a good argument.

(B) It is possible that dreams are imaginary, but even if they are, this is inconclusive as an answer to the question about a dream's moral significance.

(C) Dreams are not imaginary, since it is possible to have choices in dreams.

(D) Dreams are not imaginary, since dreams are actions and an imaginary action is not an action.

(E) Dreams are not imaginary, since they are random neurochemical events.

51. If what is said in lines 14–17 about Alan Hobson is true, which of the following must be true?

(A) Hobson believes that imagery in dreams precedes random neurochemical firings.

(B) Hobson would disagree with Freud's claim that we are morally responsible for the content of our dreams.

(C) Hobson would agree with Macdonald's statement that an imaginary murder is no murder.

(D) Hobson believes that unless dreamers have control over their dreams, the dreams are not morally significant.

(E) Hobson believes that random neurochemical firings of the brain precede imagery in a dream.

52. Which statement below best characterizes the position of Passage 1 and of Passage 2 concerning the "lack of control" argument?

(A) They disagree on whether we may have control over our dreams.

(B) They agree that we may have control over our dreams.

(C) They consider the imaginative character of dreams to be more important.

(D) Passage 2 considers this argument to be more significant than Passage 1.

(E) Passage 2 argues that Augustine's position weakens Passage 1's support of the argument.

Section 4

TIME: 25 Minutes
20 Questions

DIRECTIONS: Solve each problem, using any available space on the page for scratch work. Then decide which answer choice is the best and fill in the corresponding oval on the answer sheet.

NOTES:

(1) The use of a calculator is permitted. All numbers used are real numbers.

(2) Figures that accompany problems in this test are intended to provide information useful in solving the problems. They are drawn as accurately as possible EXCEPT when it is stated in a specific problem that the figure is not drawn to scale. All figures lie in a plane unless otherwise indicated.

REFERENCE INFORMATION:

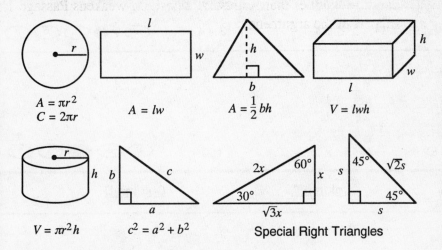

$A = \pi r^2$
$C = 2\pi r$

$A = lw$

$A = \frac{1}{2}bh$

$V = lwh$

$V = \pi r^2 h$

$c^2 = a^2 + b^2$

Special Right Triangles

The number of degrees of arc in a circle is 360.
The measure in degrees of a straight angle is 180.
The sum of the measures in degrees of the angles of a triangle is 180.

45

QUESTIONS 21–32 each consist of two quantities, one in Column A and one in Column B. You are to compare the two quantities and on the answer sheet blacken space

(A) if the quantity in Column A is greater;

(B) if the quantity in Column B is greater;

(C) if the two quantities are equal;

(D) if the relationship cannot be determined from the information given.

NOTES:

(1) In certain questions, information concerning one or both of the quantities to be compared is centered above the two columns.

(2) In a given question, a symbol that appears in both columns represents the same thing in Column A as it does in Column B.

(3) Letters such as x, n, and k stand for real numbers.

EXAMPLES:

	Column A	Column B	Answer
E1:	$3 + 4$	3×4	Ⓐ ● Ⓒ Ⓓ Ⓔ
E2:	x	150	Ⓐ Ⓑ ● Ⓓ Ⓔ

Column A	Column B
21. Round off 984 to the nearest hundred	Round off 1004 to the nearest ten
22. $.08 \times 10^3$	$8,000 \times 10^{-2}$
23. $\dfrac{3}{4} + .75 + 75\%$	$2\dfrac{1}{2}$

	Column A	**Column B**

$$x < 0$$
$$y < 0$$

| 24. | $x - y$ | 0 |

$$m < 0, n < 0, \text{ and } m > n$$

| 25. | $\dfrac{m}{n}$ | $\dfrac{n}{m}$ |

$$y = x - 2$$

| 26. | $y + 3$ | $x - 1$ |

The sum of three consecutive even numbers is 42.

| 27. | First number | 11 |

| 28. | $(1 - \sqrt{2})(1 - \sqrt{2})$ | $(1 - \sqrt{2})(1 + \sqrt{2})$ |

$$x = 5, y = -3$$

| 29. | $(x + y)^2$ | $(x - y)^2$ |

| 30. | 4.445×10^5 | 445,000 |

$$m > n > 0$$

| 31. | x^m | x^n |

| 32. | $a(a - c) + b(a - c)$ | $(a + b)(a - c)$ |

DIRECTIONS: Questions 33–40 require you to solve the problem and enter your answer in the ovals in the special grid:

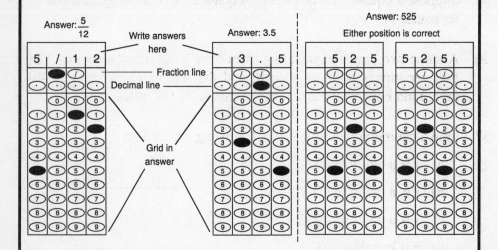

- You may begin filling in your answer in any column, space permitting. Columns not needed should be left blank.

- Answers may be entered in either decimal or fraction form. For example, $^3/_{12}$ or .25 are equally acceptable.

- A mixed number, such as $4^1/_2$, must be entered either as 4.5 or $^9/_2$. If you entered 41/2, the machine would interpret your answer as $^{41}/_2$, not $4^1/_2$.

- There may be some instances where there is more than one correct answer to a problem. Should this be the case, grid only one answer.

- Be very careful when filling in ovals. Do not fill in more than one oval in any column, and make sure to completely darken the ovals.

- It is suggested that you fill in your answer in the boxes above each column. Although you will not be graded incorrectly if you do not write in your answer, it will help you fill in the corresponding ovals.

- If your answer is a decimal, grid the most accurate value possible. For example, if you need to grid a repeating decimal such as 0.6666, enter the answer as .666 or .667. A less accurate value, such as .66 or .67, is not acceptable.

33. Simplify the fraction below.

$$\frac{2}{3} \times \frac{9}{4} \times \frac{16}{12} \times \frac{3}{8}$$

34. Let $2^x = 64$ and $2^y = 256$. Solve for 2^{y-x}.

35. Suppose x equals 10% of zy and y equals 20% of w. What fraction of wz equals x?

36. Assume two cars start traveling from New York simultaneously. The first car travels north at 30 mph and the second travels west at 40 mph. Find how long it takes for the cars to be 150 miles apart.

37. Find a natural number x with the following properties:

    a) x is a multiple of 21.

    b) x is a multiple of 15.

    c) x is a multiple of 35.

    d) x is less than 225.

38. Consider the figure given below. What is the value of $x + 2y$?

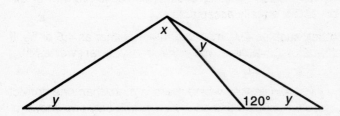

39. Final exam scores on a science exam are given below.

Score	Percentage of Students
50 – 59	9%
60 – 69	5%
70 – 79	25%
80 – 89	40%
90 – 100	21%

If there were 80 students in the class, how many students scored between 60 and 89?

40. Find a solution to the equation below.

$$\frac{1}{r^2} - 7\frac{1}{r} + 10 = 0.$$

Section 5

TIME: 30 Minutes
39 Questions

> **DIRECTIONS**: Each of the following sentences may contain an error in diction, usage, idiom, or grammar. Some sentences are correct. Some sentences contain one error. No sentence contains more than one error.
>
> If there is an error, it will appear in one of the underlined portions labeled A, B, C, or D. If there is no error, choose the portion labeled E. If there is an error, select the letter of the portion that must be changed in order to correct the sentence.
>
> **EXAMPLE:**
>
> He drove <u>slowly</u> and <u>cautiously</u> in order to <u>hopefully</u> avoid having an
>   **A**   **B**   **C**
>
> <u>accident</u>. <u>No error</u>.
>   **D**   **E**

1. Each campus appointed <u>their</u> own committee to apply the <u>findings of</u>
                                  A   **B**

    the city-wide survey concerning ways <u>in which</u> the school district <u>can</u>
                                                  C   **D**

    save money. <u>No error</u>.
                       E

2. When <u>I</u> asked Gary and John what would be <u>good</u> for dinner, the
            A   **B**

    boys said they <u>could care less</u> <u>about eating</u> liver for the main dish
                          C   **D**

    with spinach for a vegetable. <u>No error</u>.
                                          E

3. John will be <u>liable for</u> damages to Mrs. Simon's car because he was
                       A

    <u>fascinated by</u> his new red truck and driving so <u>fast</u> that he failed to
         B   **C**

conform to a law limiting the speed of any vehicle within the city
    D

limits. No error.
        E

4. I have seen, more than anything else, that self-esteem is a problem in
       A   B   C   D

    many people of all ages and nationalities. No error.
                                                E

5. Mr. Burgess made sure the ten-year-olds were accommodated with
                                                 A

    quarters for a video games party; afterwards, he declined to say how
                                                              B

    much the event cost him but allowed as how it was more than he
                                C

    had expected. No error.
        D   E

6. This afternoon's boating accident having turned out differently
                                        A   B

    through the efforts of Jack Williams, a fellow vacationer who knows
                                                                C

    CPR, so the little girl has survived. No error.
         D   E

7. Three hundred years ago John Milton protested against laws which
                    A   B

    required a government official to approve of any manuscript before it
                                     C   D

    was published. No error.
                   E

8. Often called members of the "Fourth Estate," journalists have rapidly
          A   B

    developed into powerful people, influencing public opinion and gov-
        C

    ernment policy that has a bearing on the course of history. No error.
                        D   E

9. Totaling <u>more than expected</u>, the groom's wedding expenses
                      A

   <u>included</u> hiring a limousine for the trip to the airport after the wed-
      B

   ding, <u>buying gifts</u> for his groomsmen, and <u>a tuxedo</u> for the ceremony.
         C   **D**

   <u>No error</u>.
    E

10. <u>Our viewing</u> these photographs of Dad standing in front of the throne
     A

    at Macchu Pichu <u>brings</u> back pleasant memories for <u>we</u> children,
                  B   **C**

    reminding us <u>of the need for</u> more family get-togethers. <u>No error</u>.
               D   **E**

11. Finally confessing to the <u>theft of</u> money collected for a class movie,
                      A

   Jules said <u>he only</u> stole money once in his life and <u>his</u> conscience
           B   **C**

   would not allow <u>him</u> to enjoy spending it. <u>No error</u>.
             D   **E**

12. If <u>a person</u> is a criminal, <u>he</u> should be punished for <u>it</u>; unfortunately,
     A   **B**   **C**

   many criminals are <u>never</u> caught. <u>No error</u>.
               D   **E**

13. An intriguing habit many hawks have <u>is bringing</u> a fresh green
                          A

   branch <u>daily</u> to line the nest <u>during the season</u> in which <u>they</u> are
        B   **C**   **D**

   mating and rearing their young. <u>No error</u>.
                   E

14. Hawks and owls can be seen <u>more frequent</u> in populated areas than
                        A

   <u>most people</u> <u>suppose</u>, and it is <u>possible</u> to hear screech owls at night
     B   **C**   **D**

   when the adult birds feed their chicks. <u>No error</u>.
                        E

15. The grass was <u>growing over</u> the curb and the oak tree had a branch
                     A
hanging almost <u>to</u> the ground, so we decided to trim <u>it</u> before the
             B   **C**
neighbors became <u>annoyed with us</u>. <u>No error</u>.
                    D   **E**

16. Charles Draper developed the <u>theory of</u> and invented the <u>technology</u>
                               A   **B**
<u>for</u> inertial navigation, a guidance system <u>which</u> does not <u>rely on</u>
                                        C   **D**
external sources. <u>No error</u>.
               E

17. Inertial navigation is a system of navigation <u>employed</u> in submarines
                                             A
when <u>they are</u> underwater, missiles used <u>for</u> defense purposes, air-
           B   **C**
craft, and <u>to get</u> man to the moon in the Apollo exploration series.
              D
<u>No error</u>.
   E

18. Much <u>to</u> <u>everyone's</u> surprise, the company president, <u>known for</u> his
         A   **B**   **C**
intelligence and good business judgment, <u>and enjoying</u> a hobby of
                                      D
sky diving. <u>No error</u>.
           E

19. <u>They</u> are very <u>grateful the city</u> has <u>set up</u> a special fund which <u>helps</u>
    A   **B**   **C**   **D**
pay for electric bills of the elderly and the handicapped. <u>No error</u>.
                                                     E

DIRECTIONS: In each of the following sentences, some portion of the sentence is underlined. Under each sentence are five choices. The first choice has the same wording as the original. The other four choices are reworded. Sometimes the first choice containing the original wording is the best; sometimes one of the other choices is the best. Choose the letter of the best choice. Your choice should produce a sentence which is not ambiguous or awkward and which is correct, clear, and precise.

This is a test of correct and effective English expression. Keep in mind the standards of English usage, punctuation, grammar, word choice, and construction.

EXAMPLE:

When you listen to opera, a person may not appreciate it.

(A)   a person may not appreciate it.

(B)   it may not be appreciated by a person.

(C)   which may not be appreciated by one.

(D)   you may not appreciate it.

(E)   appreciating it may be a problem for you.

20.   The new secretary proved herself to be not only capable and efficient but also a woman who was adept at working under pressure and handling irate customers.

(A)   to be not only capable and efficient but also a woman who was adept

(B)   not only to be capable or efficient but also a woman who was adept

(C)   not only to be capable and efficient but also a woman who was adept

(D)   to be not only capable and efficient but also adept

(E)   to be not only capable and efficient but also an adept woman

21. <u>Hunting, if properly managed and carefully controlled</u>, can cull excess animals, thereby producing a healthier population of wild game.

    (A) Hunting, if properly managed and carefully controlled

    (B) Managing it wisely, carefully controlled hunting

    (C) Managed properly hunting that is carefully controlled

    (D) Properly and wisely controlled, careful hunting

    (E) If properly managed, hunting, carefully controlled

22. In spite of my reservations, <u>I agreed on the next day to help her put up new wallpaper</u>.

    (A) I agreed on the next day to help her put up new wallpaper.

    (B) I agreed on the next day to help put up her new wallpaper.

    (C) I agreed to help her put up new wallpaper on the next day.

    (D) I, on the next day, agreed to help her put up new wallpaper.

    (E) I agreed to, on the next day, help her put up new wallpaper.

23. <u>We saw many of, though not nearly all, the existing Roman ruins</u> along the Mediterranean coastline of Africa.

    (A) We saw many of, though not nearly all, the existing Roman ruins

    (B) We saw many, though not nearly all, of the existing Roman ruins

    (C) Seeing many, though not nearly all, of the existing Roman ruins

    (D) Having seen many of, though not nearly all, the existing Roman ruins

    (E) Many of, though not nearly all, the existing Roman ruins we saw

24. <u>The horned owl is a carnivore who hunts a diversity of creatures, like</u> hares, grouse, and ground squirrels.

    (A) The horned owl is a carnivore who hunts a diversity of creatures, like

    (B) The horned owl, a carnivore who hunts a diversity of creatures like

(C)   A hunting carnivore, the horned owl likes a diversity of crea-
      tures

(D)   The horned owl likes a diversity of carnivorous creatures, such
      as

(E)   The horned owl is a carnivore that hunts a diversity of creatures,
      such as

25.   In many of his works Tennessee Williams, <u>of whom much has been
      written</u>, has as main characters drifters, dreamers, and those who are
      crushed by having to deal with reality.

      (A)   of whom much has been written

      (B)   of who much has been written

      (C)   of whom much has been written about

      (D)   about him much having been written

      (E)   much having been written about him

26.   The world history students wanted to know <u>where the Dead Sea was
      at and what it was famous for</u>.

      (A)   where the Dead Sea was at and what it was famous for.

      (B)   where the Dead Sea is at and for what it is famous.

      (C)   where the Dead Sea is located and why it is famous.

      (D)   at where the Dead Sea was located and what it was famous for.

      (E)   the location of the Dead Sea and what it is famous for.

27.   Literary historians <u>cannot help but admit that they do not know</u>
      whether poetry or drama is the oldest form of literature.

      (A)   cannot help but admit that they do not know

      (B)   cannot admit that they do not admit to knowing

      (C)   cannot help admitting that they do not know

      (D)   cannot help but to admit that they do not know

      (E)   cannot know but admit that they do not

28. Getting to know a person's parents <u>will often provide an insight to</u> his personality and behavior.

   (A) will often provide an insight to

   (B) will often provide an insight into

   (C) will often provide an insight for

   (D) will provide often an insight for

   (E) often will provide an insight with

29. Upon leaving the nursery, Mr. Greene, together with his wife, <u>put the plants in the trunk of the car they had just bought</u>.

   (A) put the plants in the trunk of the car they had just bought.

   (B) put in the plants to the trunk of the car they had just bought.

   (C) put into the trunk of the car they had just bought the plants.

   (D) put the plants they had just bought in the trunk of the car.

   (E) put the plants into the trunk of the car.

30. The way tensions are increasing in the Middle East, some experts <u>are afraid we may end up with a nuclear war</u>.

   (A) are afraid we may end up with a nuclear war.

   (B) being afraid we may end up with a nuclear war.

   (C) afraid that a nuclear war may end up over there.

   (D) are afraid a nuclear war may end there.

   (E) are afraid a nuclear war may occur.

31. <u>Whether Leif Erickson was the first to discover America or not</u> is still a debatable issue, but there is general agreement that there probably were a number of "discoveries" through the years.

   (A) Whether Leif Erickson was the first to discover America or not

   (B) That Leif Erickson was the first to discover America

   (C) That Leif Erickson may have been the first to have discovered America

(D) Whether Leif Erickson is the first to discover America or he is not

(E) Whether or not Leif Erickson was or was not the first discoverer of America

32. <u>People who charge too much are likely to develop</u> a bad credit rating.

(A) People who charge too much are likely to develop

(B) People's charging too much are likely to develop

(C) When people charge too much, likely to develop

(D) That people charge too much is likely to develop

(E) Charging too much is likely to develop for people

33. The museum of natural science has a special exhibit of gems and minerals, <u>and the fifth graders went to see it on a field trip</u>.

(A) and the fifth graders went to see it on a field trip.

(B) and seeing it were the fifth graders on a field trip.

(C) when the fifth graders took a field trip to see it.

(D) which the fifth graders took a field trip to see.

(E) where the fifth graders took their field trip to see it.

DIRECTIONS: The following passages are considered early draft efforts of a student. Some sentences need to be rewritten to make the ideas clearer and more precise.

Read each passage carefully and answer the questions that follow. Some of the questions are about particular sentences or parts of sentences and ask you to make decisions about sentence structure, diction, and usage. Some of the questions refer to the entire essay or parts of the essay and ask you to make decisions about organization, development, appropriateness of language, audience, and logic. Choose the answer that most effectively makes the intended meaning clear and follows the requirements of standard written English. After you have chosen your answer, fill in the corresponding oval on your answer sheet.

EXAMPLE:

(1) On the one hand, I think television is bad, But it also does some good things for all of us. (2) For instance, my little sister thought she wanted to be a policemen until she saw police shows on television.

Which of the following is the best revision of the underlined portion of sentence 1 below?

On the one hand, I think television <u>is bad, But it also</u> does some good things for all of us.

(A)   is bad; But it also

(B)   is bad. but is also

(C)   is bad, and it also

(D)   is bad, but it also

(E)   is bad because it also

Questions 34–39 are based on the following passage.

(1) Actually, the term "Native Americans" is incorrect. (2) Indians migrated to this continent from other areas, just earlier then Europeans did. (3) The ancestors of the Anasazi—Indians of the four-state area of Colorado, New Mexico, Utah, and Arizona—probably crossed from Asia into Alaska. (4) About 25,000 years ago while the continental land bridge still existed. (5) This land bridge arched across the Bering Strait in the last Ice Age. (6) About A.D. 500 the ancestors of the Anasazi moved onto the Mesa Verde a high plateau in the desert country of Colorado. (7) The Wetherills, five brothers who ranched the area, is generally given credit

Diagnostic Test

for the first exploration of the ruins in the 1870s and 1880s. (8) There were some 50,000 Anasazi thriving in the four-corners area by the 1200s. (9) At their zenith A.D. 700 to 1300, the Anasazi had established widespread communities and built thousands of sophisticated structures—cliff dwellings, pueblos, and kivas. (10) They even engaged in trade with Indians in surrounding regions by exporting pottery and other goods.

34. Which of the following best corrects the grammatical error in sentence 7?

   (A) The Wetherills, a group of five brothers who ranched in the area, is generally given credit for the first exploration of the ruins in the 1870s and 1880s.

   (B) The Wetherills, five brothers who ranched in the area, are generally given credit for the first exploration of the ruins in the 1870s and 1880s.

   (C) The Wetherills are generally given credit for the first exploration of the ruins in the 1870s and 1880s, five brothers who ranched in the area.

   (D) The Wetherills, generally given credit for the first exploration of the area, is five brothers who ranched in the area.

   (E) Best as it is.

35. Which of the following sentences would best fit between sentences 9 and 10 of the passage?

   (A) Artifacts recovered from the area suggest that the Anasazi were artistic, religious, agricultural, classless, and peaceful.

   (B) By 12,000 to 10,000 B.C., some Indians had established their unique cultures in the southwest.

   (C) The Navaho called their ancestors the Anasazi, the Ancient Ones.

   (D) I think it is unfortunate that such a unique and innovative culture should have disappeared from the country.

   (E) Before Columbus reached the New World, the Anasazi had virtually disappeared.

36. Which of the following is an incomplete sentence?

    (A) 4   (D) 7

    (B) 5   (E) 10

    (C) 6

37. Which of the following best corrects the underlined portion of sentence 9?

    <u>At their zenith A.D. 700 to 1300</u>, the Anasazi has established widespread communities and built thousands of sophisticated structures—cliff dwellings, pueblos, and kivas.

    (A) At their zenith which was from A.D. 700 to 1300

    (B) At their zenith B.C. 700 to 1300

    (C) At their zenith, from A.D. 700 to 1300,

    (D) At their zenith, being A.D. 700 to 1300,

    (E) At their zenith, of A.D. 700 to 1300,

38. Which of the following would be the best way to punctuate sentence 6?

    (A) About A.D. 500, the ancestors of the Anasazi moved onto the Mesa Verde a high plateau, in the desert country of Colorado.

    (B) About A.D. 500 the ancestors of the Anasazi moved, onto the Mesa Verde: a high plateau in the desert country of Colorado

    (C) About A.D. 500 the ancestors of the Anasazi moved onto the Mesa Verde: a high plateau, in the desert country of Colorado.

    (D) About A.D. 500, the ancestors of the Anasazi moved onto the Mesa Verde, a high plateau in the desert country of Colorado.

    (E) Best as it is.

39. Which of the following sentences contains a spelling/grammatical error?

    (A) 1   (D) 10

    (B) 2   (E) 5

    (C) 3

DIAGNOSTIC TEST

ANSWER KEY

Question Number	Correct Answer	If You Answered this Question Incorrectly, Study the Section on . . .

Section 1

Attacking Sentence Completion Questions, pp. 156–178

1.	(A)	p. 160: Dealing with Positive Value Words
2.	(B)	p. 163: Dealing with Negative Value Words
3.	(C)	p. 167: Dealing with Neutral Value Words
4.	(B)	p. 167: Dealing with Neutral Value Words
5.	(E)	p. 165: Dealing with Mixed Value Words
6.	(A)	p. 165: Dealing with Mixed Value Words
7.	(B)	p. 163: Dealing with Negative Value Words
8.	(D)	p. 167: Dealing with Neutral Value Words
9.	(C)	p. 160: Dealing with Positive Value Words
10.	(E)	p. 167: Dealing with Neutral Value Words
11.	(D)	p. 167: Dealing with Neutral Value Words
12.	(C)	p. 167: Dealing with Neutral Value Words
13.	(D)	p. 160: Dealing with Positive Value Words

Attacking Critical Reading Questions, pp. 198–240

14.	(A)	p. 209: Interpretation
15.	(C)	p. 209: Interpretation
16.	(D)	p. 209: Vocabulary-in-Context
17.	(E)	p. 209: Interpretation
18.	(C)	p. 209: Interpretation
19.	(C)	p. 209: Interpretation

Question Number	Correct Answer	If You Answered this Question Incorrectly, Study the Section on . . .
20.	(D)	p. 209: Interpretation
21.	(B)	p. 208: Synthesis/Analysis
22.	(C)	p. 208: Synthesis/Analysis
23.	(A)	p. 209: Interpretation
24.	(A)	p. 209: Interpretation
25.	(C)	p. 208: Synthesis/Analysis
26.	(B)	p. 208: Synthesis/Analysis

Section 2

Attacking Regular Math Questions, pp. 406–428

1.	(B)	p. 415: Drawing Diagrams
2.	(A)	p. 413: Word Problems
3.	(C)	p. 413: Word Problems
4.	(B)	p. 413: Word Problems
5.	(B)	p. 413: Word Problems
6.	(C)	p. 415: Drawing Diagrams
7.	(B)	p. 412: Algebraic Expressions
8.	(B)	p. 412: Algebraic Expressions
9.	(B)	p. 412: Algebraic Expressions
10.	(C)	p. 409: Averages
11.	(D)	p. 414: "If . . . Then" Reasoning
12.	(C)	p. 413: Word Problems
13.	(C)	p. 413: Word Problems
14.	(D)	p. 408: Evaluating Expressions
15.	(C)	p. 412: Algebraic Expressions
16.	(D)	p. 413: Word Problems
17.	(C)	p. 413: Word Problems
18.	(C)	p. 411: Data Interpretation
19.	(B)	p. 413: Word Problems
20.	(C)	p. 412: Algebraic Expressions

Question Number	Correct Answer	If You Answered this Question Incorrectly, Study the Section on . . .

Section 3

Attacking Analogy Questions, pp. 180–196

27.	(C)	p. 185: Word-to-Synonym
28.	(A)	p. 183: Trait-to-Example
29.	(B)	p. 185: Word-to-Antonym
30.	(B)	p. 185: Word to-Synonym
31.	(E)	p. 185: Word-to-Antonym
32.	(E)	p. 185: Word-to-Synonym
33.	(D)	p. 186: Answering Analogy Questions
34.	(D)	p. 186: Answering Analogy Questions
35.	(A)	p. 182: Part-to-Whole
36.	(B)	p. 182: Part-to-Whole
37.	(C)	p. 186: Answering Analogy Questions
38.	(D)	p. 186: Answering Analogy Questions
39.	(E)	p. 186: Answering Analogy Questions

Attacking Critical Reading Questions, pp. 198–240

40.	(A)	p. 208: Synthesis/Analysis
41.	(D)	p. 209: Vocabulary-in-Context
42.	(E)	p. 209: Evaluation
43.	(C)	p. 209: Interpretation
44.	(B)	p. 208: Synthesis/Analysis
45.	(C)	p. 209: Evaluation
46.	(A)	p. 208: Synthesis/Analysis
47.	(B)	p. 209: Interpretation
48.	(D)	p. 209: Interpretation
49.	(A)	p. 209: Interpretation
50.	(B)	p. 208: Synthesis/Analysis

Question Number	Correct Answer	If You Answered this Question Incorrectly, Study the Section on . . .
51.	(E)	p. 209: Interpretation
52.	(B)	p. 208: Synthesis/Analysis

Section 4

Attacking Quantitative Comparison Questions, pp. 430–455

21.	(C)	p. 432: Conversions
22.	(C)	p. 433: Exponents and Roots
23.	(B)	p. 432: Calculations
24.	(D)	p. 433: Variables
25.	(B)	p. 433: Variables
26.	(A)	p. 433: Variables
27.	(A)	p. 432: Calculations
28.	(A)	p. 433: Exponents and Roots
29.	(B)	p. 433: Exponents and Roots
30.	(B)	p. 433: Exponents and Roots
31.	(D)	p. 433: Variables
32.	(C)	p. 433: Variables

Attacking Student-Produced Response Questions, pp. 458-494

33.	3/4 or .75	p. 462: Simplifying Fractions
34.	4	p. 470: Systems of Non-Linear Equations
35.	1/50	p. 482: Answering Student-Produced Response Questions
36.	3	p. 482: Answering Student-Produced Response Questions
37.	105 or 210	p. 461: Properties of a Whole Number N
38.	150	p. 476: Solving for the Degree of an Angle
39.	56	p. 482: Answering Student-Produced Response Questions
40.	1/5 or 1/2	p. 482: Answering Student-Produced Response Questions

Question Number	Correct Answer	If You Answered this Question Incorrectly, Study the Section on . . .

Section 5

Attacking Writing Skills Questions, pp. 496–503

1.	(A)	p. 519: Subject-Verb Agreement
2.	(C)	p. 534: Faulty Comparisons
3.	(D)	p. 506: Word-Choice Skills
4.	(E)	p. 517: Verb Forms
5.	(C)	p. 506: Word-Choice Skills
6.	(A)	p. 513: Fragments
7.	(B)	p. 506: Word-Choice Skills
8.	(D)	p. 519: Subject-Verb Agreement
9.	(D)	p. 510: Parallelism
10.	(C)	p. 525: Pronoun Case
11.	(B)	p. 511: Misplaced Modifiers
12.	(C)	p. 527: Pronoun-Antecedent Agreement
13.	(B)	p. 533: Adjectives and Adverbs
14.	(A)	p. 533: Adjectives and Adverbs
15.	(C)	p. 527: Pronoun-Antecedent Agreement
16.	(E)	p. 510: Parallelism
17.	(D)	p. 510: Parallelism
18.	(D)	p. 513: Fragments
19.	(A)	p. 527: Pronoun-Antecedent Agreement
20.	(D)	p. 510: Parallelism
21.	(A)	p. 510: Parallelism
22.	(C)	p. 511: Misplaced Modifiers
23.	(B)	p. 511: Misplaced Modifiers
24.	(E)	p. 506: Word Choice Skills
25.	(A)	p. 525: Pronoun Case
26.	(C)	p. 515: Subordination, Coordination, and Predication

Question Number	Correct Answer	If You Answered this Question Incorrectly, Study the Section on . . .
27.	(C)	p. 517: Verb Forms
28.	(B)	p. 534: Faulty Comparisons
29.	(D)	p. 511: Misplaced Modifiers
30.	(E)	p. 506: Word Choice Skills
31.	(B)	p. 507: Wordiness and Conciseness
32.	(A)	p. 519: Subject-Verb Agreement
33.	(D)	p. 515: Subordination, Coordination, and Predication
34.	(B)	p. 519: Subject-Verb Agreement
35.	(A)	p. 506: Word Choice Skills
36.	(A)	p. 515: Subordination, Coordination, and Predication
37.	(C)	p. 515: Subordination, Coordination, and Predication
38.	(D)	p. 515: Subordination, Coordination, and Predication
39.	(B)	p. 506: Word Choice Skills

DETAILED EXPLANATIONS
OF ANSWERS

Section 1 — Verbal

1.   **(A)**   "Significant" (A) is the answer because it means important. If something is "unseemly" (B), it is disadvantageous, and a teacher would not tell a class to take notes on material that would not be to their advantage. "Highlighted" (C) is not an adjective, and therefore not a type of lesson, which this sentence calls for, and "expedited" (D) means improvised, which would have no meaning in the context of this sentence. "Superfluous" (E) means not crucial, or extra, and again, the teacher would not tell the class to take notes if the material were not crucial.

2.   **(B)**   The answer is "swaggering" (B) because that is a boastful attitude, and if a person is boastful, it is difficult to congratulate him or her. It is much easier to give praise to someone who demonstrates humility, which is the opposite of a swaggering attitude. "Gaudy" (A) means glaringly colorful, which would not describe an attitude. If someone is "courteous" (C), he or she is polite, and such a person would not be difficult to approach to congratulate. If someone is "retaliatory" (D), he or she wants to get revenge for something, and this sentence does not supply enough information for this to be the choice. While it may be difficult to talk to someone who has an "indirect" (E) manner, it is hard to say what an indirect attitude (what the sentence states) would be.

3.   **(C)**   The answer is "radiated" (C) because that means emitted, or given out. For something to be "extracted" (A), it must be pulled out, and this cannot be the answer because it would imply that something pulls energy out of light instead of light emitting energy, which is the case. "Implanted" (B) means put in, which, for similar reasons, would be faulty reasoning. For something to be "collapsing" (D) it would be falling in on itself, which is indicated nowhere else in the sentence. For something to be "aligned" (E) with something else, it must be parallel to it, which is extraneous to any meaning in this sentence.

4.   **(B)**   These men were "historians" (B) because recording and analyzing events is what historians do. "Dramatists" (A) are playwrights, who

do not record events, but create fictional works about them, expressed in plays. There could be no "psychoanalysts" (C) in ancient Greece because this method of treatment was developed in the nineteenth century A.D. These men were not "scientists" (D) either, because what scientists do is not record and analyze events, but discover the natural laws underlying them. They were also not "politicians" (E), because politicians govern people, which is not what the sentence states.

5. **(E)** Many religions in the world use "fasting" (E), going without food and/or liquids for certain periods of time, to express their faith in that religion and submit to religious "discipline." Since "blasphemy" (A) means speaking in opposition to a deity, "prayer" would not be an expression of this, but its opposite. "Atonement" is repenting for one's transgressions, and while many world religions urge people to do this, that would not amount to "heresy" (B), which is maintaining a doctrine or belief which is designed to thwart the basic tenets of a religion. "Animism" (C) is the belief that objects have souls, and no monotheistic (belief in one God) religion holds this belief. "Asceticism" (D) is self-denial in the interests of religion, but "belief" would not be an expression of self-denial.

6. **(A)** Hearing an argument which sounds "logical," but which one still does not like or agree with, and which one still wants to disagree with, or "dispute" (A) is the best choice. If an argument is "topical" (B) it is based on timely events. The sentence provides no reason that one would want to dispute such a line of reasoning, so the context of this sentence does not indicate that this is the answer. To "fabricate" (C) is to make something up, or lie. Again, the sentence provides no context for coming to this conclusion. If something is "murky" (D), it is difficult to decipher, which would not prompt a listener to try to "classify" the line of reasoning; in fact, it would make that very difficult. If a line of reasoning is "rational" (E), that means it is sensible, which would offer little resistance to understanding, or apprehension, so this choice makes no sense either.

7. **(B)** If a person has a "condescending" (B) attitude, meaning haughty and putting others down, then one would expect "superficial" (not authentic or genuine) questions to be the ones asked by such a person. If someone has a "contemptuous" (A) attitude, the questions he or she asks will not be "compassionate," which means the ability to put oneself in another's place. Contempt is looking down on someone, the opposite of feeling compassion. If an attitude is "punitive" (C), it is punishing, and questions coming from a person with this attitude would not be "fascinat-

ing," but frightening. A "refreshing" (D) attitude is one that is delightful to the people around, which would indicate no "haranguing" (critical) questioning. If an attitude is "culpable" (E), it is deserving of blame, which would indicate that no "humbling" (embarrassing) questions would be asked, so this cannot be the correct answer either.

8.   **(D)**   The answer is (D), because students "familiar" with theorems would also need to be taught how to "demonstrate" the proofs for them. It is not likely that a class would be "ecstatic" (A) about mathematics, as the heightened emotion that they would be expected to convey if they won the lottery, not if they were working on mathematics problems. Too, "right" here does not mean "write," so it is difficult to decide what this might mean. If the class is "enlightened" (B), they are taught something, but that would not lead to them discounting proofs; just the opposite would be expected. Similar reasons are those which account for rejecting (C) as the answer, since even if they were "cautious," the sentence says nothing about why they would want to "dismiss" the proofs for the theorems. In addition, a class can be "satisfied" (E) with what they are learning, but that would not account for their wanting to "circumvent" (get around) the proofs, instead of learning to do them.

9.   **(C)**   The answer is "ingenuous" (C), because that means open and sincere, both are qualities that would get people to trust her, and assist her in her roles as diplomat and negotiator. "Devious" (A) and "Machiavellian" (B) both refer to dishonest, deceitful styles. Neither would enable a diplomat to be a wily (shrewd) negotiator, where people must make constant compromises. "Mutinous" (D) means uncontrolled, which would also work against effective negotiating. "Titular" (E) means honorary, which, although she might have honorary achievements, makes no sense in the context of this sentence.

10.   **(E)**   The answer is "immanently" (E), because spelled with an "a," "immanently" means genetically, and cats are more closely genetically related to lions than different breeds of dogs are to each other. "Intrinsically" (A) means characteristically, and while this might be considered as an answer here, it is not the most precise one, so should not be chosen. "Intimidatingly" (B) means in a threatening manner, which bears no relation to the rest of the sentence. "Intimately" (C) means closely, but for reasons similar to those stated for (A), should not be chosen (it is not the most precise answer). "Imminently" (D) means approaching, which has no meaning in this context.

11. **(D)**   "Directs" (D) means sends, or forwards, so this is the correct answer. "Terminates" (A) means ends, so this would be the opposite of what the company would do if seeking new employees. The verb "seeks" (B) cannot be used to describe what the company does with hiring notices, as it means what the company does in terms of new employees (seeks them). To overlook (C) is to ignore or pass over, and to decrease (E) is to limit and pare down in number, so these, again, would not be what a company would do if it wanted to hire new employees.

12. **(C)**   The answer is "posits" (C), as that means states. A theory doesn't teach (A) anything: people do. Similarly, a theory, in itself, can't believe (B), because it is not a person. To hover (D) is to float in the air, which makes no sense in this context. To ponder (E) is to wonder about, and again, it is impossible for a theory to ponder anything, because a theory is not a living thing.

13. **(D)**   The correct answer is "abundant . . . accessed" (gain access to). The makers require a large quantity (abundant) of high-quality clay, and, once found, the clay must be accessed, or easily gotten to, in order to be of use. All of the first words in the other choices are possible answers; (A) "present," (B) "evident," (C) "nearby," and (E) "visible." However, they do not address the key words "large quantities," and are incorrect as the best answers for this question. Since we have chosen "abundant" as the correct answer, it is not necessary to address the secondary choices.

14. **(A)**   Archaeology has ignoble roots in plunder, not in admiration of Palladio (B), nor in academic response to Gibbons (D) and Winkelmann (C). (E) is a distractor.

15. **(C)**   Winkelmann belittled Roman art as merely imitative (line 16), but his opinions have not prevailed (A), as the work of Mommsen (E) attests. A neoclassicist, Winkelmann did not recommend the Gothic (C). There is no stated connection between Winkelmann and the Dilettanti (D).

16. **(D)**   Collectors, including museums, upgraded archaeology in order to provide authenticity of findings, this well before the nineteenth century (A). Calleva (B) far exceeds in time this rigor; King Murat (E), while possibly influential, is cited not for repeated efforts, but only for one, at Pompeii (line 30). Mercati (C), while a pioneer, is not credited with sixteenth century definitive "rigor."

17. **(E)** Archaeology embraces local and national traits (lines 40–44) with many clues, not few (A), and is not limited by Winkelmann's influences (C). It has reassessed the relation of Greece and Rome, negating (B). (D) is a distractor, more in the province of geology than archaeology.

18. **(C)** Whatever Murat's personal motives, which are not clearly identified as greedy (B) nor marauding (A), his excavations extended beyond loot into physical anthropology (line 32). Murat's efforts were practical, not theoretical (D). (E) is a distractor not based on the text.

19. **(C)** The authors tell us this in the first sentence of the passage when they say, "there clearly must be a balance between the scope of individual freedom and the needs of government." The authors note there may be instances when either individual rights or governmental needs dominate, but these are extreme cases (e.g., *Korematsu*) and the usual case is to strike a balance between the two. Thus, both (A) and (B) are incorrect. (D) is incorrect because the authors admit in the first sentence of the second paragraph that "there may be political excesses that threaten to limit civil liberties and rights. . . . " Although it is true that a threatened limitation is not necessarily a limitation, if it did not sometimes occur the author would have been remiss in mentioning the possibility without indicating it hasn't happened. (E) is clearly negated by the focus of the passage on these issues.

20. **(D)** In the fourth sentence of the first paragraph the authors tell us that federal judges are independent of direct political control. In the next sentence the authors contrast this by telling us most state and local judges are elected "making them directly accountable to the people." We can thus infer that federal judges are not elected (which is true). Thus, (B) is incorrect. This same statement also makes (C) incorrect. Although (A) is true, we do not have to *infer* that local judges are mostly elected. We are directly told this is the case in the fifth sentence of the first paragraph. (E) Nowhere in the passage is it mentioned that state judges are not elected.

21. **(B)** In the first sentence of the second paragraph the authors mention the concern of political excesses. In the sixth sentence of the first paragraph, the authors suggest elected judges might be influenced by the political process in making its decisions. In the fourth sentence of the first paragraph we are told federal judges are not subject to direct political control. Thus, federal judges are better able to make decisions protecting individual liberties even though such decisions may run counter to public

preferences. (A), (C), and (D) are all incorrect because each of these groups is elected and therefore subject to political influences. The Supreme Court (E), according to the authors, actually facilitated "the most extraordinary abridgment of the rights of citizens."

22. **(C)**   The authors address this question in the second paragraph when they tell us, "there are also legitimate governmental needs that may call for a modification of individual freedoms. This occurs when these civil freedoms are used or misused, to attack the very foundations of the system itself." In the third paragraph the authors discuss how World War II concentration camps for Japanese-Americans were justified on the basis of the fear the Japanese would attack the West Coast. Thus, when the nation is threatened, individual liberties may be limited. It is clear, then, that (D) is incorrect. It should be equally clear that (A) is incorrect. The third paragraph illustrates that the governmental need must be great to justify the magnitude of the restrictions placed on Japanese-Americans. In addition, in the first sentence of the second paragraph the authors note the limitation that the governmental need must be *legitimate*. (B) is incorrect because it suggests that the government may restrict civil rights when it needs to restrict civil rights. This merely restates the question and does not answer it. The rights of other nations' individuals (E) are not addressed here.

23. **(A)**   This point is made in the first sentence of the third paragraph. The fear of the Japanese invading the West Coast, along with the fear of subversive activities, justified the extraordinary limitation of the rights of the Japanese-Americans relocated to concentration camps. (B) is incorrect because we are told the Supreme Court specifically rejected the possibility that the exclusion of Japanese-Americans was racially motivated. Rather, it was based on military necessity (sixth sentence of the third paragraph). (C) and (D) are incorrect because there is no mention of electoral pressures of public opinion in the discussion of the exclusion and *Korematsu*. According to the passage there was no legal precedent (E) for the detention of Japanese-Americans.

24. **(A)**   In the third sentence of the third paragraph we are told the order excluding Japanese-Americans from the West Coast was upheld by the Supreme Court against constitutional challenges (making (C) incorrect). In the following sentences we are told the exclusion was justified by military necessity. If the exclusion was upheld and justified, it cannot be considered either unnecessary or illegal, making (B), (D), and (E) incorrect.

25. **(C)** The second sentence of the fourth paragraph indicates, "One of the most important spheres of civil liberties where the balancing test has been applied regards the civil liberties and rights enumerated in the First Amendment, particularly the liberties of *speech, press,* and *the right of assembly* (emphasis added)." Although the free exercise of religion *is* a First Amendment liberty, it is *not* specifically mentioned in the passage. Since (A), (B), and (D) are all mentioned, they are all incorrect. The passage does not address the right to bear arms (E).

26. **(B)** The fourth paragraph of the passage introduces the balancing and clear and present danger tests. Since the authors have previously indicated in both discussion and by example that restrictions on civil rights and liberties may sometimes be allowed, the purpose of these tests is to aid in the determination of when restrictions are justified. Thus, application of both the balancing test (I) and the clear and present danger test (III) may allow restrictions on civil rights and liberties. The rational basis test (II) is not mentioned in the passage, so we cannot make any judgments as to what it allows.

Section 2 – Math

1. **(B)** Use ratio and proportion.

$$1' \times 2' \times 3' = 6 \text{ kg}$$

$$4' \times 5' \times 6' = x$$

$$\frac{6}{120} = \frac{6}{x}$$

$$6x = 720$$

$$x = \frac{720}{6}$$

$$x = 120$$

2. **(A)** Time from 8:00 a.m. to 11:40 a.m. equals 220 minutes. Time allowed between the first and second class, second and third class, third and fourth class, fourth and last class equals 20 minutes. Time for instruction in all five classes is

$$220 - 20 = 200 \text{ minutes.}$$

Time for each class period is

$$200 \div 5 = 40 \text{ minutes.}$$

3. **(C)**

$$V = LWH$$

$$= 10 \times 10 \times 10 = 1,000$$

Choice (A) just added the three dimensions, (B) only considered the two dimensions, and (D) and (E) considered the fourth and fifth power, respectively.

4. **(B)**

$$g^2 - 72 = (g - 2)^2$$

$$g^2 - 72 = g^2 - 4g + 4$$

$$4g = 76$$

$$g = 19$$

5. **(B)**

    4 quarts = 1 gallon

    2 pints = 1 quart

    8 pints = 1 gallon

    80 pints = 10 gallons

    160 pints = (2) 10-gallon cans

6. **(C)**

    Area of circle = πr^2

    $$\pi r^2 = 298$$

    $$\frac{22}{7}r^2 = 298\left(\frac{7}{22}\right)$$

    $$r^2 = 94.8181$$

    $$r = 9.73$$

    Diameter = 19.47

7. **(B)** A very easy solution is: $x + y = \frac{1}{k}$, now substitute for k, its given value:

    $$x + y = \frac{1}{x-y};$$

    cross multiplying gives $x^2 - y^2 = 1$. The long way to do this problem (which would have more chance of error): Solve simultaneously, by adding the equations $x + y = \frac{1}{k}$ and $x - y = k$ getting

    $$2x = k + \frac{1}{k} \quad \text{or} \quad x = \frac{1}{2}k + \frac{1}{2k}.$$

    Then squaring both sides:

    $$x^2 = \frac{k^2}{4} + \frac{1}{2} + \frac{1}{4k^2}$$

    Finding y from $x + y = \frac{1}{k}$:

    $$y = \frac{1}{k} - \frac{1}{2}k - \frac{1}{2k} = \frac{k}{2} - \frac{1}{2k}$$

Then squaring both sides:

$$y^2 = \frac{k^2}{4} - \frac{1}{2} + \frac{1}{4k^2}$$

Therefore,

$$x^2 - y^2 = \frac{1}{2} - \left(-\frac{1}{2}\right) = 1.$$

8. **(B)**

$$(3^a + b)(3^a - b) = 9 \times \frac{1}{9}$$

$$3^{2a} = 1$$

$$3^{2a} = 3^0 \qquad\qquad \text{(since } 3^0 = 1)$$

$$2a = 0$$

$$a = 0$$

9. **(B)** If $2X + Y = 2$, then

$$2X = 2 - Y, \text{ or } X = 1 - \frac{Y}{2}$$

Substituting in $X + 3Y > 6$, we get

$$1 - \frac{Y}{2} + 3Y > 6.$$

Thus $\dfrac{5Y}{2} > 5$, or $Y > 2$.

10. **(C)**

$3,500 - \$500 = \$3,000$ (total depreciation)

$3,000 \div 5 = $ average yearly depreciation $= \$600$

11. **(D)** Let $x = \angle MQR$. Then

$$4x = \angle KPO$$

$$\angle KPO = \angle MQR \qquad \text{(corresponding angles)}$$

$$\angle MPQ = \angle RQN \qquad \text{(vertical angles)}$$

$$\therefore RQN = 4x$$

$$\angle RQN + \angle MQR = 180 \qquad \text{(supplementary angles)}$$

or
$$4x + x = 180$$
$$5x = 180$$
$$x = 36$$

Then $4x$ $(\angle RQN) = 144$.

12. **(C)** Distance ÷ rate = time

Trip to college: 25 miles ÷ 25 mph = 1 hr

Trip from college: 37.5 miles ÷ 50 mph = 0.75 hr or 45 min

Saving = 0.25 hr = 15 min

13. **(C)** Time in flight for #100 = 4 hrs

$$250 \times 4 = 1{,}000 \text{ miles}$$

Time in flight for #200 = 3 hrs

$$300 \times 3 = 900 \text{ miles}$$

Let x = distance between planes at 12:00 noon

$$= 1{,}000 + 900 = 1{,}900 \text{ miles}.$$

14. **(D)**

$$5 + \left(\frac{5}{0.5}\right) = 5 + 10 = 15$$

15. **(C)** If equal quantities are added to unequal quantities, the resulting sums are unequal in the same order. Therefore,

$$x + a < y + b.$$

16. **(D)** Let x = number of cups of flour to be used with 5 cups of milk.

$$\frac{\text{milk}}{\text{flour}} = \frac{3}{4} = \frac{5}{x}$$
$$\frac{3}{x} = 20$$
$$x = \frac{20}{3} = 6\frac{2}{3} \text{ cups of flour}$$

17. **(C)**

$$\frac{\text{content of small cup}}{\text{content of large cup}} = \frac{7}{4}$$

Let x = number of small plastic cups that can be filled with one large cup.

$$\frac{7}{4} = \frac{x}{1}$$
$$4x = 7$$
$$x = \frac{7}{4}$$
$$x = 1\frac{3}{4}$$

18. **(C)** Choice (C) shows a sharp rise. Choices (A) and (D) show a rise. Choice (B) shows a drop. Choice (E) shows neither a drop nor a rise.

19. **(B)**

Total = 34
$$\frac{2}{34} = \frac{1}{17} = 6\%$$

20. **(C)**

$$3n + 1 = 3(4) + 1 = 13 \text{ (prime number)}$$

(A) $n^2 + 2 = 4^2 + 2 = 18$

(B) $n^2 + 2n = 4^2 + 2(4) = 16 + 8 = 24$

(D) $5n = 5(4) = 20$

(E) $n^2 - 4 = 4^2 - 4 = 16 - 4 = 12$

Section 3 — Verbal

27. **(C)** The sentence that best describes the relationship between the given words is: "If you HINDER something, then you OBSTRUCT it." The words are synonymous. The best answer is (C) because "if you DEDUCT something, then you SUBTRACT it." DEDUCT and SUBTRACT are also synonyms. (A) is wrong because "if you ARRANGE something, you BEGIN it," is a false statement. The words are not synonyms. (B) "If you DUPLICATE something, you FOLLOW it," makes no sense, and is incorrect as a relationship based on the given words. (D) is wrong because "if you RENEW something, you ESTABLISH it," has no meaning. In addition, these words are not synonyms of each other. (E) "If you INHABIT (live in, occupy) something, you DISTORT it," is a meaningless sentence.

28. **(A)** "An EMBATTLED person is characterized by CONFLICT." "If a person is EMBATTLED, they have CONFLICT." These sentences best represent the relationship between the given words. The best answer is (A) "a WITTY person is characterized by HUMOR," or "if a person is WITTY, they have HUMOR." (B) is wrong because "a BORED person is characterized by ACTIVITY," is false. Usually, a BORED person is characterized by a lack of ACTIVITY. (C) is incorrect because "a GENEROUS person is characterized by COURAGE," is not an accurate analogy. A GENEROUS person is characterized by things other than COURAGE. (D) is incorrect because "a SMART person is characterized by RIDDLES," is a strange statement. (E) is wrong because "a WEARY person is characterized by SICKNESS," makes no sense. A WEARY person is a tired person.

29. **(B)** The best way to describe the relationship between the given words is: DISORDER is the opposite of ARRANGEMENT. "If something is in DISORDER, then it has no ARRANGEMENT." The words are antonyms. (B) is the best choice because LIMITS and FREEDOM are antonyms. "If something has LIMITS, then it has no FREEDOM." (A) is wrong because "if something is HUMBLE (modest), then it has no PERSONALITY," is inaccurate. HUMBLE is not the opposite of PERSONALITY. (C) is wrong because "if something has ALTRUISM, then it has no CHARITY," is an incorrect statement. ALTRUISM and CHARITY are synonyms. If something has ALTRUISM, then it is related to CHARITY. (D) is an incorrect choice because "if something has CREDIT, then it has

no INTEREST," is not accurate. CREDIT and INTEREST are not antonyms. (E) is the wrong choice because REMORSE and HUMILITY are not words with opposite meanings. "If you have no REMORSE, then you have no HUMILITY," is a meaningless statement.

30. **(B)**   The relationship between the given words is best described in the following sentence: "The BEGINNING of something is the INCEPTION." BEGINNING and INCEPTION are synonyms. (B) expresses the same kind of relationship: "The END of something is the CONCLUSION." END and CONCLUSION are synonyms. (A) is wrong because ORIGIN (beginning, cause) and SEQUENCE are not synonymous. An ORIGIN is not a SEQUENCE. (C) is incorrect because TERM and SEASON are not semantically similar. (D) is wrong because a "DELAY is a CLOCK," is a nonsense statement. (E) is incorrect because "the DURATION of something is the EXCHANGE," does not express any relationship.

31. **(E)**   The relationship between the given words can be expressed as: "Something that is UNIFORM (not varying) is not CHANGEABLE." The words are antonyms. UNIFORM means the opposite of CHANGEABLE. (E) is the best answer. SAVORY (pleasant-tasting) and TASTELESS are opposite in meaning. "Something that is SAVORY is not TASTELESS." (A) is incorrect because "something that is IMMUTABLE (unchanging) is not PERMANENT," is inaccurate. The two words are synonyms and not antonyms of each other. (B) is wrong because "something that is BRITTLE has no SHAPE," is a meaningless sentence. Whether or not something is BRITTLE (breaks easily) has nothing to do with its SHAPE. (C) is incorrect because "if something is ABSENT it is not DELAYED," doesn't make any sense. If something is ABSENT, it is not present, and might be DELAYED under the circumstances. (D) is wrong because "if something is DURABLE (long lasting), then it is COHERENT," is a nonsense statement.

32. **(E)**   The best way of describing the relation between the given words is to say: "If something is PETITE (small and trim), then it is DIMINUTIVE" (indicating small size). The words are synonyms. The most appropriate answer is (E). "If something is NOXIOUS, it is HARMFUL." These words are also synonyms. (A) is incorrect because "if something is PLACID (calm), it is RESIGNED" (give up without resistance), is not a semantically accurate sentence. (B) is wrong because "if something is DECAYED, it is BURIED," is not correct. Things can DECAY and not

be BURIED (such as teeth). (C) is incorrect because "if something is GLIB (smooth talking), it is VOICE," makes no sense. (D) is wrong because "if something is FALSE, it is DOCUMENT," is a nonsense relationship.

33. **(D)** "A CAPTIVE (prisoner) is ENSLAVED" (have no freedom) is the best way to describe the relationship between the two given words. If you are a CAPTIVE, then you are ENSLAVED. (D) expresses the same kind of relationship: "A HERO is REVERED" (honored, worshipped). If you are a HERO, then you are REVERED. (A) is wrong because "if you are a MONSTER, then you are SCALY," isn't always true. Some MONSTERS are not SCALY. (B) is incorrect because "a SOLDIER is FIERCE," does not apply to all SOLDIERS. Some SOLDIERS are not FIERCE. (C) is wrong for the same reason. "If you are a NEIGHBOR, then you GOSSIP," is an inaccurate statement. Not all NEIGHBORS are known to GOSSIP. (E) is wrong because the statement: "If you are a REPORTER, then you are BIASED," is inappropriate. REPORTERS are expected to be unbiased.

34. **(D)** The relationship between the given words can be described as: "SLANG is INFORMAL." INFORMAL is an adjective that characterizes the word SLANG. The best answer is (D) because "a BAUBLE (trinket) is WORTHLESS." WORTHLESS is an adjective that describes BAUBLE. (A) is incorrect because "a BUSH is FOREST," makes no sense. FOREST is not an adjective that describes BUSH. (B) is wrong because "a GLOBE is WORLD," is silly. Both words are nouns and their relationship is not appropriate to the given words. (C) "a LANGUAGE is PERSON," is a ridiculous statement, and does not share the relationship as the given words. (E) "A HORSE is WAGON," is wrong because the sentence makes no sense. There is no relationship between these words in this sentence.

35. **(A)** A PANE is a whole piece of glass, but a SHARD is a fragment of glass. (A) is the best choice because it contains words which form an analogy most closely resembling the relationship established by the given words: that of a whole and its part. WOOD is a whole section, but a SPLINTER is a fragment of WOOD. (B) is incorrect because "a CHAIR is a whole and COMFORT is a part of it," makes no sense. You can sit in a CHAIR for COMFORT. (C) is wrong because "a RAINDROP is a whole and MOISTURE is a part," makes no sense. A RAINDROP is MOISTURE. (D) "FOOD is a whole, and MEAT is a part," is incorrect because although MEAT is part of FOOD as a category, the required relationship

as stated by the given words is not similar. (E) "OMEN is a part and FORTUNE is a whole," is a statement with no meaningful relationship.

36. **(B)** "A SCRIPT (written matter) contains WORDS"; or "a SCRIPT is composed of WORDS," is the best way to describe the relationship between the given words. The best answer is (B). "An OPERA (drama set to music) contains NOTES." Choice (A) is wrong because although "a HOUSE contains STAIRS," the STAIRS are not the essence of a HOUSE. You could not accurately say that "a HOUSE is composed of STAIRS." (C) is incorrect because "a SPORT contains TENNIS," makes no sense. TENNIS is a SPORT. (D) is wrong because "a GARMENT is a COLLAR," is inaccurate. A GARMENT may contain a COLLAR. (E) is incorrect because "a PHOTO contains a CAMERA," is a ridiculous statement.

37. **(C)** "A MISSILE is a particular kind of PROJECTILE" (self-propelling weapon). This is the best way to relate the given words in the question. The best answer is (C). "A SCULPTURE is a particular kind of ART." Choice (A) is wrong because "a DOCTOR is a particular kind of MEDICINE," is silly. A DOCTOR prescribes MEDICINE. Choice (B) is incorrect because "a MERCHANDISE is a particular kind of CURRENCY," makes no sense. MERCHANDISE can be purchased using CURRENCY. (D) is wrong because "a CAGE is a particular kind of ANIMAL," is meaningless. You can keep an ANIMAL in a CAGE. (E) is incorrect because "TAXES is a particular kind of GOVERNMENT," is not a meaningful analogy. TAXES can be levied by a GOVERNMENT.

38. **(D)** The relationship between the given words can be expressed as: "If you SMUGGLE something, then it's CONTRABAND" (smuggled goods), or something that is SMUGGLED is CONTRABAND. (D) expresses the same kind of relationship: "If you CELEBRATE something, then it is a HOLIDAY." (A) is incorrect because "if you LEARN something, then it's EXPRESSED," is a false statement. Not everything that is LEARNED is EXPRESSED. (B) is incorrect because "if you DESTROY something, then it's BUILDING," does not make any sense. (C) "If you REVEAL something, then it is NOTE," is not a semantically meaningful statement. (E) is wrong because "if you SHARE something, then it is SILENCE," is an inaccurate relationship.

39. **(E)** "The HEIGHT of something tells you the ELEVATION," or "the HEIGHT of something is the ELEVATION," best expresses the rela-

tionship between the given words. (E) best states the same relationship: "The DEPTH of something tells you the DEPRESSION." Also, the "DEPTH of something is the DEPRESSION" into some surface. (A) is incorrect because "the SUMMIT (peak) of something tells you the MOUNTAIN," is false. A MOUNTAIN has a SUMMIT, but a SUMMIT is not a measure of a MOUNTAIN. (B) is incorrect because "the PITCH (downward slope) of something tells you the POTENTIAL," makes no sense. (C) is wrong because "the DIAMETER (straight line passing through the center of a circle) of something tells you the ARC" (part of the circumference of a circle), is an incorrect statement. (D) is wrong because "the OVERHANG of something tells you the CALIBER (degree of importance)," makes no sense as a relationship.

40. **(A)** Lines 18–19 and 24–25 tell us that men thrive when government gets out of the way, denying (B) and (E). Thoreau has no words for corporations (C); and a "better government" (line 39) is possible, negating (D).

41. **(D)** Alacrity means speed, celerity.

42. **(E)** Government is not "the less necessary" (line 20) for being an ineffective weapon, denying the literal reading of (A). Line 16's "tradition" of government denies (B), and by extension, (C). Thoreau has mitigating remarks for government (lines 29–31, 39–41), denying (D).

43. **(C)** The Mexican war (lines 12–13) provides Thoreau with an example of government acting beyond the people. He does not espouse anarchy (see line 39), denying (A). Mexico confirms his view of standing armies, negating (D). Thoreau does not see anarchy as imminent (B). Business surmounts government in Thoreau's experience (line 32), denying (E).

44. **(B)** The opening and closing paragraphs of Passage 2 state that the weakness of the stronger arguments against the moral significance of dreams makes it probable that dreams can be moral or immoral. Passage 2 addresses only two arguments against the possibility of moral dreams, it does not claim that no such argument is good (A). It acknowledges that we may have no control over our dreams (lines 37 and 38), but cites Freud (C) to show that this point might be irrelevant. Choice (D) sums up the argument of Passage 1, not of Passage 2. Passage 2 does not say that we have control over our dreams or that dreams are not imaginary (E).

45. **(C)** One of the premises in support of Passage 2 is Augustine's claim that the morality of an action lies in the intent to carry it out, thus if it is false, Passage 2's position weakens. Passage 2 accepts the possibility that dreams are imaginary (A), but regards this as morally inconclusive. It never tells us what Freud thinks about a dreamer's control over dreams (B). Since Passage 2 rests on Freud's and Augustine's positions, and since these positions might be true whether or not dreams are neurochemical, it is irrelevant whether Hobson is a neurophysiologist (D) and whether dreams are neurochemical (E).

46. **(A)** Lines 6 through 9 state explicitly that an action must be done from free will in order to have moral significance. They do not say that all actions done from free will are morally significant (B). They do not deny that we have free will altogether even if God or demons are the source of dreams (C), and even if dreams occur spontaneously (D). They talk about a certain kind of controlled act, not about all acts in our control (E).

47. **(B)** Passage 2 concedes the possibility that, as Macdonald states, imaginary acts are not real acts, but it dismisses this point as being morally inconclusive. It does not label her view as wrong (A). It says nothing about the relationship between Freud's position (C) and Macdonald's. Macdonald's position has to do with the imaginary character of dreams, not the dreamer's control (D). It makes no reference to the claim that dreams are not imaginary (E).

48. **(D)** The passage says nothing about whether dreams are imaginary. It does say dreams may confront us with choices of actions (A); intention is morally more significant to an action than the possibility (B) or the reality (C) of that action; and that given a choice of actions in dreams, we can intend or not intend to do them (E).

49. **(A)** The assumption is that if dreams can be immoral then they can also be moral. From this assumption it would be consistent to conclude that it is possible to commit an action of heroism (B) or an act of murder (C) in a dream, and that an act of murder in the dream, even if imaginary, would be immoral (D). The moralistic position, as stated in Passage 1, says nothing about the reality of dream contents (E), only about the morality of those contents.

50. **(B)** Passage 2 accepts that dreams may be imaginary (line 38) but argues that Augustine's position shows the imaginary nature of dreams to

be inconclusive as an answer to the moral question. Passage 2 denies the argument that dream acts can have no moral significance (A). Because Passage 2 accepts the possibility that dreams can be imaginary, choices (C), (D), and (E) are incorrect.

51. **(E)** Lines 14 through 17 state that, for Hobson, random neuro-chemical firings precede the dream images. This is contrary to choice (A). The passage says nothing about Hobson's position on the morality of dreams, so it is unclear whether he would agree with Freud (B) or with Macdonald (C), or with the position that dreamers must have control of their dreams in order for the dreams to be morally significant (D).

52. **(B)** Both passages do agree that we may have no control over our dreams, even though they may disagree about the significance of this point. Thus, it is incorrect to say they disagree about whether we can control our dreams (A). There is no indication that either passage considers the "imaginary character of dreams" argument to be more important than the "lack of control" argument (C). Passage 2 does not regard this argument as having the significance which Passage 1 thinks it has (D). Passage 2 uses Augustine's position against the "imaginary character of dreams" argument, not the "lack of control" argument (E).

Section 4 — Math

21. **(C)** 984 rounded to the nearest hundred is 1,000; 1004 rounded to the nearest ten is 1,000.

22. **(C)**
$$.08 \times 10^3 = .08 \times 1,000$$
$$= 80$$

$$8,000 \times 10^{-2} = 8,000 \times \frac{1}{100}$$
$$= \frac{8,000}{100}$$
$$= 80$$

23. **(B)**
$$.75 = \frac{3}{4}; 75\% = \frac{75}{100} = \frac{3}{4}$$

$$\frac{3}{4} + \frac{3}{4} + \frac{3}{4} = \frac{9}{4} = 2\frac{1}{4}$$

24. **(D)** As a first example, let $x = -3$ and $y = -4$.
$$x - y = -3 - (-4) = 1 > 0$$
As a second example, let $x = -4$ and $y = -3$.
$$x - y = -4 - (-3) = -1 < 0$$

25. **(B)** Since
$$m < 0, n < 0, \frac{m}{n} \text{ and } \frac{n}{m} > 0.$$
Also, $m > n$ gives us
$$\frac{m}{n} < 1, \frac{n}{m} > 1$$
(remember m, $n < 0$), therefore
$$\frac{n}{m} > \frac{m}{n}.$$

26. **(A)**

$$y = x - 2$$

Add 3 to both sides.

$$y + 3 = x + 1$$

For any value of x, we always have $x + 1 > x - 1$, thus,

$$y + 3 > x - 1.$$

27. **(A)**   We can define an even number as $2x$, and the following numbers will be $2x + 2$ and $2x + 4$. Therefore,

$$2x + 2x + 2 + 2x + 4 = 42$$

$$6x + 6 = 42$$

$$6x = 36$$

$$x = 6$$

Remember that the first number was $2x$, which is 12 if $x = 6$.

28. **(A)**   In Column A expand the indicated product by using the FOIL method or some other method. Thus, the product of

$$(1 - \sqrt{2})(1 - \sqrt{2}) = 1 - \sqrt{2} - \sqrt{2} + (\sqrt{2})(\sqrt{2})$$
$$= 1 - 2\sqrt{2} + \sqrt{4}$$
$$= 1 - 2\sqrt{2} + 2$$
$$= 3 - 2\sqrt{2}$$

which is positive.

Similarly, in Column B one expands the indicated product to get

$$(1 - \sqrt{2})(1 + \sqrt{2}) = 1 - \sqrt{2} + \sqrt{2} - (\sqrt{2})(\sqrt{2})$$
$$= 1 - \sqrt{4}$$
$$= 1 - 2$$
$$= -1$$

Thus, the quantity in Column A is larger.

29. **(B)**   To compare $(x + y)^2$ with $(x - y)^2$ set $x = 5$ and $y = -3$ in each expression and calculate. One gets the following:

$$(x + y)^2 = \{5 + (-3)\}^2 = (5 - 3)^2 = 2^2 = 4$$

and $(x - y)^2 = \{5 - (-3)\}^2 = (5 + 3)^2 = 8^2 = 64$

Since $64 > 4$ we can conclude that $(x - y)^2$ in Column B is larger than $(x + y)^2$ in Column A for $x = 5$ and $y = -3$.

If response (A) is chosen then perhaps an error was made in the computation after substituting the values for x and y, respectively. Or, it was wrongly assumed that $(x + y)$ is always greater than $(x - y)$ and thus

$$(x + y)^2 > (x - y)^2.$$

Response (C) implies that

$$(x + y)^2 = (x - y)^2$$

for $x = 5$ and $y = -3$ which is not possible. Finally, response (D) is incorrect.

30. **(B)** Since

$$10^5 = 100,000$$

$$4.445 \times 10^5 = 444,500$$

which is less than 445,000. Thus, the number in Column B is greater.

31. **(D)**

If $x = 0$, $\qquad\qquad\qquad x^m = x^n$

If $x > 0$, $\qquad\qquad\qquad x^m > x^n$

If $x < 0$ the results can be $x^m = x^n$

$$x^m > x^n$$

$$x^m < x^n$$

Thus, the relationship cannot be determined.

32. **(C)** Note that each term on the left contains a factor of $(a - c)$. This expression can therefore be factored to $(a + b)(a - c)$, which is identical to the expression in Column B.

33. The correct response is:

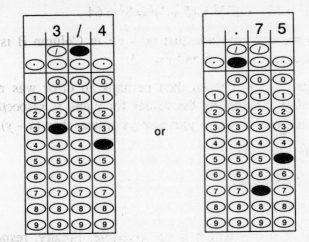

or

Cancelling factors common to both the numerator and denominator we get

$$\frac{2}{3} \times \frac{9}{4} \times \frac{16}{12} \times \frac{3}{8} = \frac{12}{16} = \frac{3}{4}$$

The answer can be entered as either 3/4 or .75.

34. The correct response is:

$$2^{y-x} = \frac{2^y}{2^x} = \frac{256}{64} = 4$$

35. The correct response is:

From the information given we have

$$10\%zy = x = \left(\frac{1}{10}\right)zy = x$$

and $\quad 20\%w = y = \left(\frac{2}{10}\right)w = y.$

Plugging the first equation into the second we obtain

$$\left(\frac{1}{10}\right)z\,(\left(\frac{2}{10}\right)w) = x$$

i.e., $\qquad \left(\frac{2}{100}\right)zw = x.$

Hence, wz is $\dfrac{2}{100} = \dfrac{1}{50}.$

36. The correct response is:

The distance the first car travels in time t is given by $d_1(t) = 30t$ and the distance the second car travels is given by $d_2(t) = 40t$. Since the cars are traveling in perpendicular directions, we use the Pythagorean Theorem via the diagram below.

We have

$$d^2(t) = d_1^2(t) + d_2^2(t)$$

hence

$$(150)^2 = (30t)^2 + (40t)^2$$

$$22{,}500 = 900t^2 + 1{,}600t^2$$

$$22{,}500 = 2{,}500t^2$$

$$\sqrt{\frac{22{,}500}{2{,}500}} = t$$

$$\frac{150}{50} = t$$

$$3 \text{ hours} = t$$

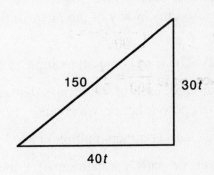

37. The correct response is:

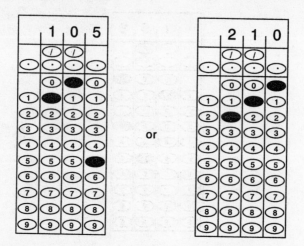

or

If x is a multiple of 21, 15, and 35 it will be a multiple of the least common multiple of 21, 15, and 35. In order to calculate the least common multiple, we look at the prime decomposition of these numbers. We have

$$21 = 3 \times 7$$

$$15 = 3 \times 5$$

$$35 = 5 \times 7$$

The least common multiple is obtained as follows;

1) For each prime, consider the highest power h to which the prime occurs in any of the factorizations. This yields a factor of the form p^h.

2) The least common multiple is the product of the above factors.

In our case, each of the primes that occur (i.e., 3, 5, and 7) only occur to the first power; hence, we obtain

least common multiple $= 3 \times 5 \times 7 = 105$.

In order to satisfy condition d) x must be less than 225; thus, the two possible solutions are 105 and 210.

38. The correct response is:

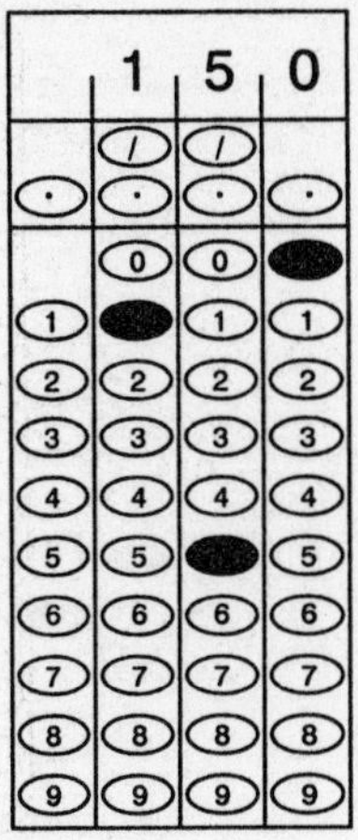

From the large triangle we have

$$y + (x + y) + y = 180.$$

From the left inner triangle we have

$$x + y + 60 = 180.$$

These equations simplify to

$$x + 3y = 180 \qquad (1)$$

and

$$x + y = 120 \qquad (2)$$

Subtracting (2) from (1) we get

$$2y = 60$$

$$y = 30$$

Plugging back into (2) we have

$$x + 30 = 120$$

$$x = 90$$

The solution is $x + 2y = 90 + 60 = 150.$

39. The correct response is:

The percentage of students who scored between 60 and 89 is equal to

$$5\% + 25\% + 40\% = 70\%;$$

hence, the number of students who scored between 60 and 89 is

$$70\%(80) = \frac{7}{10}(80) = 56.$$

40. The correct response is:

   or

Letting $\frac{1}{r} = x$ we obtain the quadratic equation

$$x^2 - 7x + 10 = 0.$$

Upon factoring we obtain

$(x-2)(x-5) = 0.$

This yields $x = 2$ and $x = 5$ and thus the solutions $r = \frac{1}{2}$ and $r = \frac{1}{5}$.

Section 5 – Writing Skills

1.   **(A)**   "Campus" is a singular noun; therefore, the pronoun referring to "campus" should be "its" so that the pronoun will agree with its antecedent. Choices (B), "findings of," and (C), "in which," both have prepositions appropriately used. Choice (D), "can," is a helping verb in the correct tense.

2.   **(C)**   Choice (C) should read, "could not care less." A person using this expression is indicating his or her total lack of interest in something; to say, "I could care less" indicates some interest, so the correct expression is "I could not care less." Choice (A) is the correct subject pronoun; choice (B), "good," is the adjective form used to follow the linking verb "be" and choice (D) is a gerund used as the object of a preposition.

3.   **(D)**   The idiom is "conform with" a law; something or someone will "conform to" an environment. Choices (A) and (B) are correctly used idioms. Choice (C) is the proper form of the adjective.

4.   **(E)**   Choice (A), "have seen," is the present perfect tense, which is used to make a statement about something occurring in the past but continuing into the present. The speaker has observed the problem of lack of self-esteem, but this problem has not stopped in the present time. Choice (B) is a comparative form, and "else" of choice (C) is necessary when comparing one thing with the group of which it is a member or part. (The observation about self-esteem is but one of several observations the speaker has made.) Choice (D) has a preposition to indicate relationship between "problem" and "people."

5.   **(C)**   "Allowed as how" is used sometimes in speaking, but the proper expression should be "allowed that." "Accommodated with," choice (A), is an idiom used to indicate "to supply with." Choice (B) is an infinitive phrase followed by a subordinate clause as the direct object. Choice (D), "had expected," is the past perfect tense to indicate previous past action: Mr. Burgess's estimate of the cost was made before the actual event.

6.   **(A)**   As this sentence reads, it is a fragment. "Having" should be eliminated, leaving "turned out" as the main verb in the proper tense. Choice (D), "so," is a coordinating conjunction relating two events of

cause-and-effect; therefore, both main clauses should be independent. Choice (B) is the adverb form modifying the verb "turned out," and choice (C), "who," is the nominative form serving as the subject of "knows."

7. **(B)** "Protested against" is redundant; "protested" is sufficient. "Ago" in choice (A) is an adjective used following the noun "years" or as an adverb following "long." Choice (C) is a correct idiom. Choice (D), "any," is an adjective.

8. **(D)** Two subjects joined by "and" require a plural verb; "public opinion and government policy" should be completed by "have." Choice (A), "called," is a participle modifying "journalists." Choice (B), "rapidly," is an adverb modifying choice (C), which is a correct idiom.

9. **(D)** The expression should read, "renting (or buying) a tuxedo," in order to complete the parallelism following choice (B) "included": "hiring a limousine" and "buying gifts," choice (C). Choice (A) is a correct expression which can also be phrased, "more than he expected," if greater clarity is desired.

10. **(C)** The object pronoun "us" should follow the preposition "for." In choice (A), "viewing" is a gerund used as the subject and therefore requires the possessive adjective "our." Choice (B) is the verb. Choice (D) is a correct idiom.

11. **(B)** The modifier "only" is misplaced. To place this word before "stole" indicates that stealing is a minor problem; also, the meaning of the sentence clearly indicates Jules has stolen money one time, so the sentence should read, "stole money only once." Choice (A) is a correct preposition; choice (C) is a possessive pronoun modifying "conscience"; and choice (D) is an object pronoun as the object of "allow."

12. **(C)** There is no antecedent for "it." Choice (A), "a person," is the subject to which "he" in choice (B) refers. "Never" in choice (D) is a correctly placed adverb. The sentence should include a phrase such as "a crime" to serve as the antecedent of "it," or the phrase "for it" could be deleted.

13. **(B)** The adverb "daily" is misplaced and should be placed with "is bringing," choice (A), or with "habit." Choice (C) is a prepositional phrase, and choice (D) is a subject pronoun for the subordinate clause.

14. **(A)**   The adverb form, "frequently," should be used to modify the verb. Choices (B) and (C) are a correct subject-verb combination. The adjective form, "possible," of choice (D) follows the linking verb "is."

15. **(C)**   The antecedent for "it" is unclear because "it" can refer to the grass or to the branch. Choice (A), "growing over," and choice (B), "to," are correct pronouns. Choice (D) is a correct idiom because we become "annoyed with" people but "annoyed at" things or situations.

16. **(E)**   The sentence is correct as written. Choices (A) and (B) are a compound structure and are in proper parallel form. Choice (C) has a clear reference to "system." Choice (D) is a correct idiom.

17. **(D)**   The preposition "in" has three objects: "submarines," "missiles," and choice (D) which must be made parallel to the previous two nouns. Choice (A) is a participle modifying "navigation." Choice (B) is a part of a subordinate clause modifying "submarines." Choice (C) is a correct preposition.

18. **(D)**   This sentence is a fragment made by the conjunction "and" linking "enjoying" with "known," the participial adjective of choice (B); "and" should be eliminated and "enjoying" changed to "enjoys" to be the subject of "president." Choice (A) is an idiom. Choice (B) is the correct possessive form to complete the idiom.

19. **(A)**   There is no antecedent for this pronoun, although it is implied that the elderly and the handicapped are the logical ones to be grateful. Choice (B) and (D) are elliptical constructions, "grateful [that] the city" and "helps [to] pay." Choice (C) is a verb.

20. **(D)**   The conjunction "not only . . . but also" must be properly placed to indicate which qualities are being discussed and to maintain proper parallelism. Choice (D) contains three adjectives to follow the verb "to be": "capable and efficient" and "adept." Choices (A), (B), (C), and (E) are not parallel. In addition, choices (B) and (C) have "to be" after the conjunction, and this construction would require another verb after the second conjunction, "but also."

21. **(A)**   This sentence contains two concepts, proper management and careful control. In choice (A) these two concepts are concisely worded and appear in parallel form. Choice (B) has no noun for "Managing" to

modify. Choice (C) would be acceptable with the addition of commas to set off the introductory phrase. Choice (D) mangles the concepts, and the wording in choice (E) is poor.

22. **(C)** Choice (A) is a "squinting" modifier: it is unclear if "on the next day" tells when "I agreed" or when "to put up." Choice (B) does not clarify this problem. Choice (D) unnecessarily splits the subject and the verb, and choice (E) unnecessarily splits an infinitive.

23. **(B)** The interrupter, "though not nearly all," should be placed so as not to split important parts of the sentence. Choices (A), (D), and (E) are incorrect because the interrupter splits a preposition and its object. Choices (C) and (D) will produce a fragment because the subject "we" is missing.

24. **(E)** To mean "for example," the expression "like" is incorrect; the correct usage is "such as." Moreover, only a person can be referred to as "who." Therefore, choices (A) and (B) are incorrect. Choices (C) and (D) incorrectly use "likes" as a verb, thereby changing the intent of the sentence.

25. **(A)** Choice (A) correctly uses the object pronoun "whom" to follow the preposition "of." Choice (B) uses the wrong pronoun. Choice (C) inserts an extraneous preposition "about" that has no object. Choice (D) is awkward wording; choice (E) is also poor wording, especially with the pronoun "him" so far away from its antecedent.

26. **(C)** Choice (C) clearly and simply deals with the location and the fame of the Dead Sea. It is incorrect to use a preposition with no object in order to end a sentence. Choices (A), (D), and (E) are incorrect because they end with "famous for." Also, in the phrase, "where the Dead Sea is at," the word *at* is redundant; it is sufficient to write "where the Dead Sea is." Therefore, choices (A) and (B) are incorrect. Finally, since the Dead Sea still exists, the verbs must be in the present tense.

27. **(C)** The phrase "cannot help" should be followed by a gerund, not by "but." Choice (C) follows "cannot help" with the gerund "admitting." Choices (A) and (E) are incorrect because they follow "cannot help" with "but." The wording of choice (B), "cannot admit," and choice (E), "cannot know," twists the meaning of the sentence.

28. **(B)** The correct idiom is to have an insight into a situation or person. While "to" in choice (A) is close in meaning, it is not exact; "for" and "with" of choices (C), (D), and (E) are unacceptable. The location of "often" in choice (D) is poor, and the location of "often" in choice (E) makes no significant change in the meaning.

29. **(D)** It is obvious that the Greenes have just purchased plants: "Upon leaving the nursery." The location of the modifying phrase, "they had just bought," should be carefully placed in the sentence so it clearly modifies "plants" and not "car." Choice (D) has the modifying phrase immediately following "plants," and the meaning is clear. The wording of choices (A), (B), and (C) makes the reader think the car has just been purchased. Choice (E) omits the concept "they had just bought."

30. **(E)** Choice (E) retains the central idea while eliminating the wording problems of the other choices. There is no antecedent for "we" in choices (A) and (B). Also, the phrase "end up" is redundant; "up" should be eliminated. Therefore, choice (C) is incorrect. Choice (D) introduces a new concept of "war may end over there," an idea clearly not intended by the original.

31. **(B)** Choice (B) clearly and precisely states the issue of debate. Choice (C) is eliminated because it is too wordy and not the precise issue under debate. The correlative conjunctions, "whether . . . or," should be followed by parallel structures. Choice (A) follows "Whether" with a subject-verb combination not seen after "not." Choice (D) is parallel but in the wrong tense. Choice (E) has "Whether or not" run together and uses poor wording in the rest of the sentence.

32. **(A)** Choice (A) has both correct agreement and clear reference. Choice (B) has a subject-verb agreement problem, "charging . . . are." Choice (C) produces a fragment. It is unclear in choice (D) who will have the bad credit rating, and the wording of choice (E) has the obvious subject, "people," in a prepositional phrase.

33. **(D)** Choice (D) correctly presents the fifth grade field trip in a subordinate clause modifying "exhibit." Choices (A) and (B) have the coordinating conjunction "and," but the first part of the sentence is not equal in meaning or importance to the second part of the sentence. Choice (C) introduces "when" with no antecedent. Choice (E) uses "where" as the subordinating conjunction, but it is too far from its antecedent and is not

the important idea of the sentence.

34. **(B)** "The Wetherills" is plural, and the verb must agree. Choice (B) correctly changes "is" to "are"; the rest of the sentence is fine. (A) adds the singular "a group" which may make the verb "is" seem right, though it still modifies "The Wetherills" and must agree accordingly. (C) corrects the verb problem, but misplaces the clause "five brothers who ranched in the area" at the end of the sentence where it is unclear. (D) fails to correct the verb disagreement and places the clause at the end of the sentence, which alters the sense.

35. **(A)** Choice (A) best continues the topic of sentence 9, which concerns the cultural achievements of the Anasazi, and provides a nice transition toward the final sentence. (B) concerns an entirely different historical epoch, and is clearly irrelevant. (C) may fit somewhere in this essay, but not between sentences 9 and 10, where this new fact would seem obtrusive. (D) introduces the personal voice of the author which is contrary to the expository tone in the passage thus far, and which would not fit between the factual content of sentences 9 and 10. (E) would be a good topic sentence for a new paragraph, but would not be good here.

36. **(A)** Sentence 4 is a dependent prepositional clause and would be best added onto sentence 3.

37. **(C)** The years of the Anasazi's zenith are best set off by commas and turned into a prepositional phrase, and of the two choices which do this, (C) uses "from," which is more appropriate than (D) "being." Without the punctuation, choice (A) is awkward; if the phrase were set off by commas, it would be acceptable, though (C) is more concise. (B) is just wrong; from the context of the passage it is clear that the Anasazi thrived in the years A.D. and not B.C.

38. **(D)** Choice (D) best utilizes commas which clarify the sense of the sentence. Choice (A) places the second comma incorrectly. (B) and (C) both utilize a colon, and each has an unnecessary comma. Choice (E) is correct as written.

39. **(B)** Sentence 2 uses "then," a temporal reference, instead of "than," which should be used for the comparison in this sentence.

PSAT/ NMSQT

CHAPTER 3

Basic Verbal Skills Review

Chapter 3

BASIC VERBAL SKILLS REVIEW

I. THE VOCABULARY ENHANCER

II. KNOWING YOUR WORD PARTS
(The most common prefixes, roots, and suffixes)

In order to perform successfully on the PSAT, you must be as familiar as possible with the different aspects of the test. One particular characteristic that becomes obvious when practicing the PSAT verbal questions is that without a strong, college-level vocabulary, it is virtually impossible to do well on the Analogies section, the Sentence Completion section, or the Critical Reading section.

But don't give up! Not all students have strong vocabularies, and if you don't, there are still ways to build on it before taking the PSAT. A game of Scrabble® will help build your vocabulary. But surely the most effective way to build your vocabulary is to read as much as you can. Reading increases your familiarity with words and their uses in different contexts. By reading every day, you can increase your chances of recognizing a word and its meaning in a question.

As you read books, newspapers, and magazines, ask yourself these questions:

- What was the main idea of this material?
- What was the author's purpose in writing this material?
- How did the author make his arguments?
- What tone did the author use?

Doing so will enhance your understanding of what you are reading. This ultimately leads to a stronger vocabulary and an increase in your reading abilities.

Unfortunately, you may not remember all the words that you read. This is why we have provided you with a necessary tool to building your vocabulary. We know that learning new words requires much time and concentration. Therefore, rather than giving you an extensive list of thousands of words, we have narrowed down our vocabulary list so that you will be able to study all the words without becoming overwhelmed. Our list consists of 600 words. The first 300 are essential vocabulary, covering the most frequently tested words on the PSAT. These words have appeared over and over again on the PSAT. In addition, we have provided a second list of 300 words that are commonly tested on the PSAT. It is very important to study all 600 words because any of them could appear on the test. Although these are not the only words you may encounter, they will give you a strong indication as to the appropriate level of vocabulary that is present on the PSAT and prevent you from wasting time studying words that will never appear on the test.

OUR VOCABULARY ENHANCER

The Vocabulary Enhancer is a list of the most frequently tested words on the PSAT. The most effective way to study these words is one section at a time. Identify the words you don't know or that are defined in unusual ways, and write them on index cards with the word on one side and the definition on the other. Test yourself on these words by completing the drills that follow each section. Doing the same for the list of additional words will also help you. In addition, studying our table of prefixes, roots, and suffixes will allow you to dissect words in order to determine the meaning of any unfamiliar words.

I. THE VOCABULARY ENHANCER
(The most frequently tested words on the PSAT)

GROUP 1

abstract – *adj.* – not easy to understand; theoretical

acclaim – *n.* – loud approval; applause

acquiesce – *v.* – to agree or consent to an opinion

adamant – *adj.* – not yielding; firm

adversary – *n.* – an enemy; foe

advocate – 1. *v.* – to plead in favor of; 2. *n.* – supporter; defender

aesthetic – *adj.* – showing good taste; artistic

alleviate – *v.* – to lessen or make easier

aloof – *adj.* – distant in interest; reserved; cool

altercation – *n.* – controversy; dispute

altruistic – *adj.* – unselfish

amass – *v.* – to collect together; to accumulate

ambiguous – *adj.* – not clear; uncertain; vague

ambivalent – *adj.* – undecided

ameliorate – *v.* – to make better; to improve

amiable – *adj.* – friendly

amorphous – *adj.* – having no determinate form

anarchist – *n.* – one who believes that a formal government is unnecessary

antagonism – *n.* – hostility; opposition

apathy – *n.* – lack of emotion or interest

appease – *v.* – to make quiet; to calm

apprehensive – *adj.* – fearful; aware; conscious

arbitrary – *adj.* – based on one's preference or judgment

arrogant – *adj.* – acting superior to others; conceited

articulate – 1. *v.* – to speak distinctly; 2. *adj.* – eloquent; fluent; 3. *adj.* – capable of speech; 4. *v.* – to hinge; to connect; 5. *v.* – to convey; to express effectively

☞ Drill: Group 1

DIRECTIONS: Match each word in the left column with the word in the right column that is most **opposite** in meaning.

Word		Match	
1.___articulate	6. ___abstract	A. hostile	F. disperse
2.___apathy	7. ___acquiesce	B. concrete	G. enthusiasm
3.___amiable	8. ___arbitrary	C. selfish	H. certain
4.___altruistic	9. ___amass	D. reasoned	I. resist
5.___ambivalent	10. ___adversary	E. ally	J. incoherent

DIRECTIONS: Match each word in the left column with the word in the right column that is most **similar** in meaning.

Word		Match	
11.___adamant	14. ___antagonism	A. afraid	D. insistent
12.___aesthetic	15. ___altercation	B. disagreement	E. hostility
13.___apprehensive		C. tasteful	

GROUP 2

assess – *v.* – to estimate the value of

astute – *adj.* – cunning; sly; crafty

atrophy – *v.* – to waste away through lack of nutrition

audacious – *adj.* – fearless; bold

augment – *v.* – to increase or add to; to make larger

austere – *adj.* – harsh; severe; strict

authentic – *adj.* – real; genuine; trustworthy

authoritarian – *adj.* – acting as a dictator; demanding obedience

banal – *adj.* – common; petty; ordinary

belittle – *v.* – to make small; to think lightly of

benefactor – *n.* – one who helps others; a donor

benevolent – *adj.* – kind; generous

benign – *adj.* – mild; harmless

biased – *adj.* – prejudiced; influenced; not neutral

blasphemous – *adj.* – irreligious; away from acceptable standards

blithe – *adj.* – happy; cheery; merry

brevity – *n.* – briefness; shortness

candid – *adj.* – honest; truthful; sincere

capricious – *adj.* – changeable; fickle

caustic – *adj.* – burning; sarcastic; harsh

censor – *v.* – to examine and delete objectionable material

censure – *v.* – to criticize or disapprove of

charlatan – *n.* – an imposter; fake

coalesce – *v.* – to combine; to come together

collaborate – *v .* – to work together; to cooperate

☞ Drill: Group 2

DIRECTIONS: Match each word in the left column with the word in the right column that is most **opposite** in meaning.

Word		Match	
1. ___augment	6. ___authentic	A. permit	F. malicious
2. ___biased	7. ___candid	B. heroine	G. neutral
3. ___banal	8. ___belittle	C. praise	H. mournful
4. ___benevolent	9. ___charlatan	D. diminish	I. unusual
5. ___censor	10. ___blithe	E. dishonest	J. fake

DIRECTIONS: Match each word in the left column with the word in the right column that is most **similar** in meaning.

Word		Match	
11. ___collaborate	14. ___censure	A. harmless	D. cooperate
12. ___benign	15. ___capricious	B. cunning	E. criticize
13. ___astute		C. changeable	

GROUP 3

compatible – *adj.* – in agreement with; harmonious

complacent – *adj.* – content; self-satisfied; smug

compliant – *adj.* – yielding; obedient

comprehensive – *adj.* – all-inclusive; complete; thorough

compromise – *v.* – to settle by mutual adjustment

concede – 1. *v.* – to acknowledge; to admit; 2. to surrender; to abandon one's position

concise – *adj.* – in few words; brief; condensed

condescend – *v.* – to come down from one's position or dignity

condone – *v.* – to overlook; to forgive

conspicuous – *adj.* – easy to see; noticeable

consternation – *n.* – amazement or terror that causes confusion

consummation – *n.* – the completion; finish

contemporary – *adj.* – living or happening at the same time; modern

contempt – *n.* – scorn; disrespect

contrite – *adj.* – regretful; sorrowful

conventional – *adj.* – traditional; common; routine

cower – *v.* – to crouch down in fear or shame

defamation – *n.* – to harm a name or reputation; to slander

deference – *adj.* – yielding to the opinion of another

deliberate 1. – *v.* – to consider carefully; to weigh in the mind; 2. *adj.* – intentional

denounce – *v.* – to speak out against; to condemn

depict – *v.* – to portray in words; to present a visual image

deplete – *v.* – to reduce; to empty

depravity – *n.* – moral corruption; badness

deride – *v.* – to ridicule; to laugh at with scorn

☞ Drill: Group 3

DIRECTIONS: Match each word in the left column with the word in the right column that is most **opposite** in meaning.

	Word		**Match**	
1. ___deplete	6. ___condone	A. unintentional	F. support	
2. ___contemporary	7. ___conspicuous	B. disapprove	G. beginning	
3. ___concise	8. ___consummation	C. invisible	H. ancient	
4. ___deliberate	9. ___denounce	D. respect	I. virtue	
5. ___depravity	10. ___contempt	E. fill	J. verbose	

DIRECTIONS: Match each word in the left column with the word in the right column that is most **similar** in meaning.

	Word		**Match**	
11. ___compatible	14. ___comprehensive	A. portray	D. thorough	
12. ___depict	15. ___complacent	B. content	E. common	
13. ___conventional		C. harmonious		

GROUP 4

desecrate – *v.* – to violate a holy place or sanctuary

detached – *adj.* – separated; not interested; standing alone

deter – *v.* – to prevent; to discourage; to hinder

didactic – *adj.* – 1. instructive; 2. dogmatic; preachy

digress – *v.* – to stray from the subject; to wander from the topic

diligence – *n.* – hard work

discerning – *adj.* – distinguishing one thing from another

discord – *n.* – disagreement; lack of harmony

discriminating – *adj.* – able to distinguish

disdain 1. – *n.* – intense dislike; 2. *v.* – to look down upon; to scorn

disparage – *v.* – to belittle; to undervalue

disparity – *n.* – difference in form, character, or degree

dispassionate – *adj.* – lack of feeling; impartial

disperse – *v.* – to scatter; to separate

disseminate – *v.* – to circulate; to scatter

dissent – *v.* – to disagree; to differ in opinion

dissonance – *n.* – harsh contradiction

diverse – *adj.* – different; dissimilar

document – 1. *n.* – official paper containing information; 2. *v.* – to support; to substantiate; to verify

dogmatic – *adj.* – stubborn; biased; opinionated

dubious – *adj.* – doubtful; uncertain; skeptical; suspicious

eccentric – *adj.* – odd; peculiar; strange

efface – *v.* – to wipe out; to erase

effervescence – *n.* – 1. liveliness; spirit; enthusiasm; 2. bubbliness

egocentric – *adj.* – self-centered

☞ Drill: Group 4

DIRECTIONS: Match each word in the left column with the word in the right column that is most **opposite** in meaning.

Word		Match	
1.___detached	6. ___dubious	A. agree	F. respect
2.___deter	7. ___diligence	B. certain	G. compliment
3.___dissent	8. ___disdain	C. lethargy	H. sanctify
4.___discord	9. ___desecrate	D. connected	I. harmony
5.___efface	10. ___disparage	E. assist	J. restore

DIRECTIONS: Match each word in the left column with the word in the right column that is most **similar** in meaning.

Word		Match	
11.___effervescence	14. ___document	A. stubborn	D. liveliness
12.___dogmatic	15. ___eccentric	B. distribute	E. odd
13.___disseminate		C. substantiate	

GROUP 5

elaboration – *n.* – clarification; addition of details

eloquence – *n.* – the ability to speak well

elusive – *adj.* – hard to catch; difficult to understand

emulate – *v.* – to imitate; to copy; to mimic

endorse – *v.* – to support; to approve of; to recommend

engender – *v.* – to create; to bring about

enhance – *v.* – to improve; to compliment; to make more attractive

enigma – *n.* – mystery; secret; perplexity

ephemeral – *adj.* – temporary; brief; short-lived

equivocal – *adj.* – doubtful; uncertain

erratic – *adj.* – unpredictable; strange

erroneous – *adj.* – untrue; inaccurate; not correct

esoteric – *adj.* – incomprehensible; obscure

euphony – *n.* – pleasant sound

execute – *v.* – 1. to put to death; to kill; 2. to carry out; to fulfill

exemplary – *adj.* – serving as an example; outstanding

exhaustive – *adj.* – thorough; complete

expedient – *adj.* – helpful; practical; worthwhile

expedite – *v.* – to speed up

explicit – *adj.* – specific; definite

extol – *v.* – to praise; to commend

extraneous – *adj.* – irrelevant; not related; not essential

facilitate – *v.* – to make easier; to simplify

fallacious – *adj.* – misleading

fanatic – *n.* – enthusiast; extremist

☞ Drill: Group 5

DIRECTIONS: Match each word in the left column with the word in the right column that is most **opposite** in meaning.

Word		Match	
1. ___extraneous	6. ___erratic	A. incomplete	F. eternal
2. ___ephemeral	7. ___explicit	B. delay	G. condemn
3. ___exhaustive	8. ___euphony	C. dependable	H. relevant
4. ___expedite	9. ___elusive	D. comprehensible	I. indefinite
5. ___erroneous	10. ___extol	E. dissonance	J. accurate

DIRECTIONS: Match each word in the left column with the word in the right column that is most **similar** in meaning.

Word		Match	
11. ___endorse	14. ___fallacious	A. enable	D. worthwhile
12. ___expedient	15. ___engender	B. recommend	E. deceptive
13. ___facilitate		C. create	

GROUP 6

fastidious – *adj.* – fussy; hard to please

fervent – *adj.* – passionate; intense

fickle – *adj.* – changeable; unpredictable

fortuitous – *adj.* – accidental; happening by chance; lucky

frivolity – *adj.* – giddiness; lack of seriousness

fundamental – *adj.* – basic; necessary

furtive – *adj.* – secretive; sly

futile – *adj.* – worthless; unprofitable

glutton – *n.* – overeater

grandiose – *adj.* – extravagant; flamboyant

gravity – *n.* – seriousness

guile – *n.* – slyness; deceit

gullible – *adj.* – easily fooled

hackneyed – *adj.* – commonplace; trite

hamper – *v.* – to interfere with; to hinder

haphazard – *adj.* – disorganized; random

hedonistic – *adj.* – pleasure seeking

heed – *v.* – to obey; to yield to

heresy – *n.* – opinion contrary to popular belief

hindrance – *n.* – blockage; obstacle

humility – *n.* – lack of pride; modesty

hypocritical – *adj.* – two-faced; deceptive

hypothetical – *adj.* – assumed; uncertain

illuminate – *v.* – to make understandable

illusory – *adj.* – unreal; false; deceptive

☞ Drill: Group 6

DIRECTIONS: Match each word in the left column with the word in the right column that is most **opposite** in meaning.

Word		Match	
1. ___ heresy	6. ___ fervent	A. predictable	F. beneficial
2. ___ fickle	7. ___ fundamental	B. dispassionate	G. orthodoxy
3. ___ illusory	8. ___ furtive	C. simple	H. organized
4. ___ frivolity	9. ___ futile	D. extraneous	I. candid
5. ___ grandiose	10. ___ haphazard	E. real	J. seriousness

DIRECTIONS: Match each word in the left column with the word in the right column that is most **similar** in meaning.

Word		Match	
11. ___ glutton	14. ___ hackneyed	A. hinder	D. overeater
12. ___ heed	15. ___ hindrance	B. obstacle	E. obey
13. ___ hamper		C. trite	

GROUP 7

immune – *adj.* – protected; unthreatened by

immutable – *adj.* – unchangeable; permanent

impartial – *adj.* – unbiased; fair

impetuous – *adj.* – 1. rash; impulsive; 2. forcible; violent

implication – *n.* – suggestion; inference

inadvertent – *adj.* – not on purpose; unintentional

incessant – *adj.* – constant; continual

incidental – *adj.* – extraneous; unexpected

inclined – *adj.* – 1. apt to; likely to; 2. angled

incoherent – *adj.* – illogical; rambling

incompatible – *adj.* – disagreeing; disharmonious

incredulous – *adj.* – unwilling to believe; skeptical

indifferent – *adj.* – unconcerned

indolent – *adj.* – lazy; inactive

indulgent – *adj.* – lenient; patient

inevitable – *adj.* – sure to happen; unavoidable

infamous – *adj.* – having a bad reputation; notorious

infer – *v.* – to form an opinion; to conclude

initiate – 1. *v.* – to begin; to admit into a group; 2. *n.* – a person who
    is in the process of being admitted into a group

innate – *adj.* – natural; inborn

innocuous – *adj.* – harmless; innocent

innovate – *v.* – to introduce a change; to depart from the old

insipid – *adj.* – uninteresting; bland

instigate – *v.* – to start; to provoke

intangible – *adj.* – incapable of being touched; immaterial

☞ Drill: Group 7

DIRECTIONS: Match each word in the left column with the word in the right column that is most **opposite** in meaning.

Word   Match

1. ___immutable   6. ___innate   A. intentional   F. changeable

2. ___impartial   7. ___incredulous   B. articulate   G. avoidable

3. ___inadvertent   8. ___inevitable   C. gullible   H. harmonious

4. ___incoherent   9. ___intangible   D. material   I. learned

5. ___incompatible   10. ___indolent   E. biased   J. energetic

DIRECTIONS: Match each word in the left column with the word in the right column that is most **similar** in meaning.

Word   Match

11. ___impetuous   14. ___instigate   A. lenient   D. conclude

12. ___incidental   15. ___indulgent   B. impulsive   E. extraneous

13. ___infer   C. provoke

GROUP 8

ironic – *adj*. – contradictory; inconsistent; sarcastic

irrational – *adj*. – not logical

jeopardy – *n*. – danger

kindle – *v*. – to ignite; to arouse

languid – *adj*. – weak; fatigued

laud – *v*. – to praise

lax – *adj*. – careless; irresponsible

lethargic – *adj*. – lazy; passive

levity – *n*. – silliness; lack of seriousness

lucid – *adj*. – 1. shining; 2. easily understood

magnanimous – *adj*. – forgiving; unselfish

malicious – *adj*. – spiteful; vindictive

marred – *adj*. – damaged

meander – *v*. – to wind on a course; to go aimlessly

melancholy – *n.* – depression; gloom

meticulous – *adj.* – exacting; precise

minute – *adj.* – extremely small; tiny

miser – *n.* – penny pincher; stingy person

mitigate – *v.* – to alleviate; to lessen; to soothe

morose – *adj.* – moody; despondent

negligence – *n.* – carelessness

neutral – *adj.* – impartial; unbiased

nostalgic – *adj.* – longing for the past; filled with bittersweet memories

novel – *adj.* – new

☞ Drill: Group 8

DIRECTIONS: Match each word in the left column with the word in the right column that is most **opposite** in meaning.

	Word				Match		
1.	___irrational	6.	___magnanimous	A.	extinguish	F.	ridicule
2.	___kindle	7.	___levity	B.	jovial	G.	kindly
3.	___meticulous	8.	___minute	C.	selfish	H.	sloppy
4.	___malicious	9.	___laud	D.	logical	I.	huge
5.	___morose	10.	___novel	E.	seriousness	J.	stale

DIRECTIONS: Match each word in the left column with the word in the right column that is most **similar** in meaning.

	Word				Match		
11.	___ironic	14.	___jeopardy	A.	lessen	D.	carelessness
12.	___marred	15.	___negligence	B.	damaged	E.	danger
13.	___mitigate			C.	sarcastic		

GROUP 9

nullify – *v.* – to cancel; to invalidate

objective – 1. *adj.* – open-minded; impartial; 2. *n.* – goal

obscure – *adj.* – not easily understood; dark

obsolete – *adj.* – out of date; no longer in fashion

ominous – *adj.* – threatening

optimist – *n.* – person who hopes for the best; one who sees the good side

orthodox – *adj.* – traditional; accepted

pagan – 1. *n* – polytheist; 2. *adj.* – polytheistic

partisan – 1. *n* – supporter; follower; 2. *adj.* – biased; one-sided

perceptive – *adj.* – full of insight; aware

peripheral – *adj.* – marginal; outer

pernicious – *adj.* – dangerous; harmful

pessimism – *n.* – gloominess; hopelessness

phenomenon – *n.* – 1. miracle; 2. occurrence

philanthropy – *n.* – charity; unselfishness

pious – *adj.* – religious; devout; dedicated

placate – *v.* – to pacify

plausible – *adj.* – probable; feasible

pragmatic – *adj.* – matter-of-fact; practical

preclude – *v.* – to inhibit; to make impossible

predecessor – *n.* – one who has occupied an office before another

prodigal – *adj.* – wasteful; lavish

prodigious – *adj.* – exceptional; tremendous

profound – *adj.* – deep; knowledgeable; thorough

profusion – *n.* – great amount; abundance

☞ Drill: Group 9

DIRECTIONS: Match each word in the left column with the word in the right column that is most **opposite** in meaning.

Word		Match	
1.___objective	6.___plausible	A. scanty	F. minute
2.___obsolete	7.___preclude	B. assist	G. anger
3.___placate	8.___prodigious	C. superficial	H. pessimism
4.___profusion	9.___profound	D. biased	I. modern
5.___peripheral	10.___optimism	E. improbable	J. central

DIRECTIONS: Match each word in the left column with the word in the right column that is most **similar** in meaning.

Word		Match	
11.___nullify	14.___pernicious	A. invalidate	D. threatening
12.___ominous	15.___prodigal	B. follower	E. harmful
13.___partisan		C. lavish	

GROUP 10

prosaic – *adj.* – tiresome; ordinary

provincial – *adj.* – regional; unsophisticated

provocative – *adj.* – 1. tempting; 2. irritating

prudent – *adj.* – wise; careful; prepared

qualified – *adj.* – experienced; indefinite

rectify – *v.* – to correct

redundant – *adj.* – repetitious; unnecessary

refute – *v.* – to challenge; to disprove

relegate – *v.* – to banish; to put to a lower position

relevant – *adj.* – of concern; significant

remorse – *n.* – guilt; sorrow

reprehensible – *adj.* – wicked; disgraceful

repudiate – *v.* – to reject; to cancel

rescind – *v.* – to retract; to discard

resignation – *n.* – 1. quitting; 2. submission

resolution – *n.* – proposal; promise; determination

respite – *n.* – recess; rest period

reticent – *adj.* – silent; reserved; shy

reverent – *adj.* – respectful

rhetorical – *adj.* – having to do with verbal communication

rigor – *n.* – severity

sagacious – *adj.* – wise; cunning

sanguine – *adj.* – 1. optimistic; cheerful; 2. red

saturate – *v.* – to soak thoroughly; to drench

scanty – *adj.* – inadequate; sparse

☞ Drill: Group 10

DIRECTIONS: Match each word in the left column with the word in the right column that is most **opposite** in meaning.

Word		Match	
1.___provincial	6. ___remorse	A. inexperienced	F. affirm
2.___reticent	7. ___repudiate	B. joy	G. extraordinary
3.___prudent	8. ___sanguine	C. pessimistic	H. sophisticated
4.___qualified	9. ___relevant	D. unrelated	I. forward
5.___relegate	10. ___prosaic	E. careless	J. promote

DIRECTIONS: Match each word in the left column with the word in the right column that is most **similar** in meaning.

Word		Match	
11.___provocative	14. ___rescind	A. drench	D. severity
12.___rigor	15. ___reprehensible	B. tempting	E. disgraceful
13.___saturate		C. retract	

GROUP 11

scrupulous – *adj.* – honorable; exact

scrutinize – *v.* – to examine closely; to study

servile – *adj.* – slavish; groveling

skeptic – *n.* – doubter

slander – *v.* – to defame; to maliciously misrepresent

solemnity – *n.* – seriousness

solicit – *v.* – to ask; to seek

stagnant – *adj.* – motionless; uncirculating

stanza – *n.* – group of lines in a poem having a definite pattern

static – *adj.* – inactive; changeless

stoic – *adj.* – detached; unruffled; calm

subtlety – *n.* – 1. understatement; 2. propensity for understatement; 3. sophistication; 4. cunning

superficial – *adj.* – on the surface; narrowminded; lacking depth

superfluous – *adj.* – unnecessary; extra

surpass – *v.* – to go beyond; to outdo

sychophant – *n.* – flatterer

symmetry – *n.* – correspondence of parts; harmony

taciturn – *adj.* – reserved; quiet; secretive

tedious – *adj.* – time-consuming; burdensome; uninteresting

temper – *v.* – to soften; to pacify; to compose

tentative – *adj.* – not confirmed; indefinite

thrifty – *adj.* – economical; pennywise

tranquility – *n.* – peace; stillness; harmony

trepidation – *n.* – apprehension; uneasiness

trivial – *adj.* – unimportant; small; worthless

☞ Drill: Group 11

DIRECTIONS: Match each word in the left column with the word in the right column that is most **opposite** in meaning.

Word

1. ___scrutinize	6. ___tentative	A. frivolity	F. skim
2. ___skeptic	7. ___thrifty	B. enjoyable	G. turbulent
3. ___solemnity	8. ___tranquility	C. prodigal	H. active
4. ___static	9. ___solicit	D. chaos	I. believer
5. ___tedious	10. ___stagnant	E. give	J. confirmed

DIRECTIONS: Match each word in the left column with the word in the right column that is most **similar** in meaning.

Word

11. ___symmetry	14. ___subtle	A. understated	D. fear
12. ___superfluous	15. ___trepidation	B. unnecessary	E. flatterer
13. ___sycophant		C. balance	

GROUP 12

tumid – *adj.* – swollen; inflated

undermine – *v.* – to weaken; to ruin

uniform – *adj.* – consistent; unvaried; unchanging

universal – *adj.* – concerning everyone; existing everywhere

unobtrusive – *adj.* – inconspicuous; reserved

unprecedented – *adj.* – unheard of; exceptional

unpretentious – *adj.* – simple; plain; modest

vacillation – *n.* – fluctuation

valid – *adj.* – acceptable; legal

vehement – *adj.* – intense; excited; enthusiastic

venerate – *v.* – to revere

verbose – *adj.* – wordy; talkative

viable – *adj.* – 1. capable of maintaining life; 2. possible; attainable

vigor – *n.* – energy; forcefulness

vilify – *v.* – to slander

virtuoso – *n.* – highly skilled artist

virulent – *adj.* – deadly; harmful; malicious

vital – *adj.* – important; spirited

volatile – *adj.* – changeable; undependable

vulnerable – *adj.* – open to attack; unprotected

wane – *v.* – to grow gradually smaller

whimsical – *adj.* – fanciful; amusing

wither – *v.* – to wilt; to shrivel; to humiliate; to cut down

zealot – *n.* – believer; enthusiast; fan

zenith – *n.* – point directly overhead in the sky; apex

☞ Drill: Group 12

DIRECTIONS: Match each word in the left column with the word in the right column that is most **opposite** in meaning.

Word   **Match**

1. ___uniform   6. ___vigor   A. amateur   F. support

2. ___virtuoso   7. ___volatile   B. trivial   G. constancy

3. ___vital   8. ___vacillation   C. visible   H. lethargy

4. ___wane   9. ___undermine   D. placid   I. wax

5. ___unobtrusive 10. ___valid   E. unacceptable   J. varied

DIRECTIONS: Match each word in the left column with the word in the right column that is most **similar** in meaning.

Word   **Match**

11. ___wither   14. ___vehement   A. intense   D. possible

12. ___whimsical   15. ___virulent   B. deadly   E. shrivel

13. ___viable   C. amusing

ADDITIONAL VOCABULARY

The following words are among the terms most commonly found on the PSAT.

abandon – 1. *v.* – to leave behind; 2. *v.* – to give something up; 3. *n.* – freedom; enthusiasm; impetuosity

abase – *v.* – to degrade; to humiliate; to disgrace

abbreviate – *v.* – to shorten; to compress; to diminish

aberrant – *adj.* – abnormal

abhor – *v.* – to hate

abominate – *v.* – to loathe; to hate

abridge – *v.* – 1. to shorten; 2. to limit; to take away

absolve – *v.* – to forgive; to acquit

abstinence – *n.* – self-control; abstention; chastity

accede – *v.* – to comply with; to consent to

accomplice – *n.* – co-conspirator; partner; partner-in-crime

accrue – *v.* – to collect; to build up

acrid – *adj.* – sharp; bitter; foul-smelling

adept – *adj.* – skilled; practiced

adverse – *adj.* – negative; hostile; antagonistic; inimical

affable – *adj.* – friendly; amiable; good-natured

aghast – *adj.* – 1. astonished; amazed; 2. horrified; terrified; appalled

alacrity – *n.* – 1. enthusiasm; fervor; 2. liveliness; sprightliness

allocate – *v.* – to set aside; to designate; to assign

allure – *v.* – 1. to attract; to entice; 2. *n.* – attraction; temptation; glamour

amiss – 1. *adj.* – wrong; awry; 2. *adv.* – wrongly; mistakenly

analogy – *n.* – similarity; correlation; parallelism; simile; metaphor

anoint – *v.* – 1. to crown; to ordain; 2. to smear with oil

anonymous – *adj.* – nameless; unidentified

arduous – *adj.* – difficult; burdensome

awry – *adj./adv.* – 1. crooked(ly); uneven(ly); 2. wrong; askew

baleful – *adj.* – sinister; threatening; evil; deadly

baroque – *adj.* – extravagant; ornate

behoove – *v.* – to be advantageous; to be necessary

berate – *v.* – to scold; to reprove; to reproach; to criticize

bereft – *adj.* – hurt by someone's death

biennial – 1. *adj.* – happening every two years; 2. *n.* – a plant which blooms every two years

blatant – *adj.* – 1. obvious; unmistakable; 2. crude; vulgar

bombastic – *adj.* – pompous; wordy; turgid

burly – *adj.* – strong; bulky; stocky

cache – *n.* – 1. stockpile; store; heap; 2. hiding place for goods

calamity – *n.* – disaster

cascade – 1. *n.* – waterfall; 2. *v.* – to pour; to rush; to fall

catalyst – *n.* – anything which creates a situation in which change can occur

chagrin – *n.* – distress; shame

charisma – *n.* – appeal; magnetism; presence

chastise – *v.* – to punish; to discipline; to admonish; to rebuke

choleric – *adj.* – cranky; cantankerous

cohesion – *n.* – the act of holding together

colloquial – *adj.*– casual; common; conversational; idiomatic

conglomeration – *n.* – mixture; collection

connoisseur – *n.* – expert; authority (usually refers to a wine or food expert)

consecrate – *v.* – to sanctify; to make sacred; to immortalize

craven – *adj.* – cowardly; fearful

dearth – *n.* – scarcity; shortage

debilitate – *v.* – to deprive of strength

deign – *v.* – to condescend; to stoop

delineate – *v.* – to outline; to describe

demur – 1. *v.* – to object; 2. *n.* – objection; misgiving

derision – *n.* – ridicule; mockery

derogatory – *adj.* – belittling; uncomplimentary

destitute – *adj.* – poor; poverty-stricken

devoid – *adj.* – lacking; empty

dichotomy – *n.* – branching into two parts

disheartened – *adj.* – discouraged; depressed

diverge – *v.* – to separate; to split

docile – *adj.* – manageable; obedient

duress – *n.* – force; constraint

ebullient – *adj.* – showing excitement

educe – *v.* – to draw forth

effervescence – *n.* – bubbliness; enthusiasm; animation

emulate – *v.* – to follow the example of

ennui – *n.* – boredom; apathy

epitome – *n.* – model; typification; representation

errant – *adj.* – wandering

ethnic – *adj.* – native; racial; cultural

evoke – *v.* – to call forth; to provoke

exotic – *adj.* – unusual; striking

facade – *n.* – front view; false appearance

facsimile – *n.* – copy; reproduction; replica

fathom – *v.* – to comprehend; to uncover

ferret – *v.* – to drive or hunt out of hiding

figment – *n.* – product; creation

finite – *adj.* – measurable; limited; not everlasting

fledgling – *n.* – inexperienced person; beginner

flinch – *v.* – to wince; to draw back; to retreat

fluency – *n.* – smoothness of speech

flux – *n.* – current; continuous change

forbearance – *n.* – patience; self-restraint

foster – *v.* – to encourage; to nurture; to support

frivolity – *n.* – lightness; folly; fun

frugality – *n.* – thrift

garbled – *adj.* – mixed up

generic – *adj.* – common; general; universal

germane – *adj.* – pertinent; related; to the point

gibber – *v.* – to speak foolishly

gloat – *v.* – to brag; to glory over

guile – *n.* – slyness; fraud

haggard – *adj.* – tired-looking; fatigued

hiatus – *n.* – interval; break; period of rest

hierarchy – *n.* – body of people, things, or concepts divided into ranks

homage – *n.* – honor; respect

hubris – *n.* – arrogance

ideology – *n.* – set of beliefs; principles

ignoble – *adj.* – shameful; dishonorable

imbue – *v.* – to inspire; to arouse

impale – *v.* – to fix on a stake; to stick; to pierce

implement – *v.* – to begin; to enact

impromptu – *adj.* – without preparation

inarticulate – *adj.* – speechless; unable to speak clearly

incessant – *adj.* – uninterrupted

incognito – *adj.* – unidentified; disguised; concealed

indict – *v.* – to charge with a crime

inept – *adj.* – incompetent; unskilled

innuendo – *n.* – hint; insinuation

intermittent – *adj.* – periodic; occasional

invoke – *v.* – to ask for; to call upon

itinerary – *n.* – travel plan; schedule; course

jovial – *adj.* – cheery; jolly; playful

juncture – *n.* – critical point; meeting

juxtapose – *v.* – to place side-by-side

knavery – *n* – rascality; trickery

knead – *v.* – to mix; to massage

labyrinth – *n.* – maze

laggard – *n.* – a lazy person; one who lags behind

larceny – *n.* – theft; stealing

lascivious – *adj.* – indecent; immoral

lecherous – *adj.* – impure in thought and act

lethal – *adj.* – deadly

liaison – *n.* – connection; link

limber – *adj.* – flexible; pliant

livid – *adj.* – 1. black-and-blue; discolored; 2. enraged; irate

lucrative – *adj.* – profitable; gainful

lustrous – *adj.* – bright; radiant

malediction – *n.* – curse; evil spell

mandate – *n.* – order; charge

manifest – *adj.* – obvious; clear

mentor – *n.* – teacher

mesmerize – *v.* – to hypnotize

metamorphosis – *n.* – change of form

mimicry – *n.* – imitation

molten – *adj.* – melted

motif – *n.* – theme

mundane – *adj.* – ordinary; commonplace

myriad – *adj.* – innumerable; countless

narcissistic – *adj.* – egotistical; self-centered

nautical – *adj.* – of the sea

neophyte – *n.* – beginner; newcomer

nettle – *v.* – to annoy; to irritate

notorious – *adj.*– infamous; renowned

obdurate – *adj.* – stubborn; inflexible

obligatory – *adj.* – mandatory; necessary

obliterate – *v.* – to destroy completely

obsequious – *adj.* – slavishly attentive; servile

obstinate – *adj.* – stubborn

occult – *adj.* – mystical; mysterious

opaque – *adj.* – dull; cloudy; nontransparent

opulence – *n.* – wealth; fortune

ornate – *adj.* – elaborate; lavish; decorated

oust – *v.* – to drive out; to eject

painstaking – *adj.* – thorough; careful; precise

pallid – *adj.* – sallow; colorless

palpable – *adj.* – tangible; apparent

paradigm – *n.* – model; example

paraphernalia – *n.* – equipment; accessories

parochial – *adj.* – religious; narrow-minded

passive – *adj.* – submissive; unassertive

pedestrian – *adj.* – mediocre; ordinary

pensive – *adj.* – reflective; contemplative

percussion – *n.* – the striking of one object against another

perjury – *n.* – the practice of lying

permeable – *adj.* – porous; allowing to pass through

perpetual – *adj.* – enduring for all time

pertinent – *adj.* – related to the matter at hand

pervade – *v.* – to occupy the whole of

petty – *adj.* – unimportant; of subordinate standing

phlegmatic – *adj.* – without emotion or interest

phobia – *n.* – morbid fear

pittance – *n.* – small allowance

plethora – *n.* – condition of going beyond what is needed; excess; overabundance

potent – *adj.* – having great power or physical strength

privy – *adj.* – private; confidential

progeny – *n.* – children; offspring

provoke – *v.* – to stir action or feeling; to arouse

pungent – *adj.* – sharp; stinging

quaint – *adj.* – old-fashioned; unusual; odd

quandary – *n.* – dilemma

quarantine – *n.* – the isolation of a person to prevent spread of disease

quiescent – *adj.* – inactive; at rest

quirk – *n.* – peculiar behavior; startling twist

rabid – *adj.* – furious; with extreme anger

rancid – *adj.* – having a bad odor

rant – *v.* – to speak in a loud, pompous manner; to rave

ratify – *v.* – to make valid; to confirm

rationalize – *v.* – to offer reasons for; to account for

raucous – *adj.* – disagreeable to the sense of hearing; harsh

realm – *n.* – an area; sphere of activity

rebuttal – *n.* – refutation

recession – *n.* – withdrawal; depression

reciprocal – *n.* – mutual; having the same relationship to each other

recluse – *n.* – solitary and shut off from society

refurbish – *v.* – to make new

regal – *adj.* – royal; grand

reiterate – *v.* – to repeat; to state again

relinquish – *v.* – to let go; to abandon

render – *v.* – to deliver; to provide; to give up a possession

replica – *n.* – copy; representation

resilient – *adj.* – flexible; capable of withstanding stress

retroaction – *n.* – an action elicited by a stimulus

reverie – *n.* – the condition of being unaware of one's surroundings; trance

rummage – *v.* – to search thoroughly

rustic – *adj.* – plain and unsophisticated; homely

saga – *n.* – a legend; story

salient – *adj.* – noticeable; prominent

salvage – *v.* – to rescue from loss

sarcasm – *n.* – ironic; bitter humor designed to wound

satire – *n.* – a novel or play that uses humor or irony to expose folly

saunter – *v.* – to walk at a leisurely pace; to stroll

savor – *v.* – to receive pleasure from; to enjoy

seethe – *v.* – to be in a state of emotional turmoil; to become angry

serrated – *adj.* – having a sawtoothed edge

shoddy – *adj.* – of inferior quality; cheap

skulk – *v.* – to move secretly

sojourn – *n.* – temporary stay; visit

solace – *n.* – hope; comfort during a time of grief

soliloquy – *n.* – a talk one has with oneself (esp. on stage)

somber – *adj.* – dark and depressing; gloomy

sordid – *adj.* – filthy; base; vile

sporadic – *adj.* – rarely occurring or appearing; intermittent

stamina – *n.* – endurance

steadfast – *adj.* – loyal

stigma – *n.* – a mark of disgrace

stipend – *n.* – payment for work done

stupor – *n.* – a stunned or bewildered condition

suave – *adj.* – effortlessly gracious

subsidiary – *adj.* – subordinate

succinct – *adj.* – consisting of few words; concise

succumb – *v.* – to give in; to yield; to collapse

sunder – *v.* – to break; to split in two

suppress – *v.* – to bring to an end; to hold back

surmise – *v.* – to draw an inference; to guess

susceptible – *adj.* – easily imposed; inclined

tacit – *adj.* – not voiced or expressed

tantalize – *v.* – to tempt; to torment

tarry – *v.* – to go or move slowly; to delay

taut – *adj.* – stretched tightly

tenacious – *adj.* – persistently holding to something

tepid – *adj.* – lacking warmth, interest, enthusiasm; lukewarm

terse – *adj.* – concise; abrupt

thwart – *v.* – to prevent from accomplishing a purpose; to frustrate

timorous – *adj.* – fearful

torpid – *adj.* – lacking alertness and activity; lethargic

toxic – *adj.* – poisonous

transpire – *v.* – to take place; to come about

traumatic – *adj.* – causing a violent injury

trek – *v.* – to make a journey

tribute – *n.* – expression of admiration

trite – *adj.* – commonplace; overused

truculent – *adj.* – aggressive; eager to fight

turbulence – *n.* – condition of being physically agitated; disturbance

turmoil – *n.* – unrest; agitation

tycoon – *n.* – wealthy leader

tyranny – *n.* – absolute power; autocracy

ubiquitous – *adj.* – ever present in all places; universal

ulterior – *adj.* – buried; concealed

uncanny – *adj.* – of a strange nature; weird

unequivocal – *adj.* – clear; definite

unique – *adj.* – without equal; incomparable

unruly – *adj.* – not submitting to discipline; disobedient

unwonted – *adj.* – not ordinary; unusual

urbane – *adj.* – cultured; suave

usurpation – *n.* – act of taking something for oneself; seizure

usury – *n.* – the act of lending money at illegal rates of interest

utopia – *n.* – imaginary land with perfect social and political systems

vacuous – *adj.* – containing nothing; empty

vagabond – *n.* – wanderer; one without a fixed place

vagrant – 1. *n.* – homeless person; 2. *adj.* – rambling; wandering; transient

valance – *n.* – short drapery hanging over the window frame

valor – *n.* – bravery

vantage – *n.* – position giving an advantage

vaunted – *adj.* – boasted of

velocity – *n.* – speed

vendetta – *n.* – feud

venue – *n.* – location

veracious – *adj.* – conforming to fact; accurate

verbatim – *adj.* – employing the same words as another; literal

versatile – *adj.* – having many uses; multifaceted

vertigo – *n.* – dizziness

vex – *v.* – to trouble the nerves; to annoy

vindicate – *v.* – to free from charge; to clear

vivacious – *adj.* – animated; gay

vogue – *n.* – modern fashion

voluble – *adj.* – fluent

waft – *v.* – to move gently by wind or breeze

waive – *v.* – to give up possession or right

wanton – *adj.* – unruly; excessive

warrant – *v.* – to justify; to authorize

wheedle – *v.* – to try to persuade; to coax

whet – *v.* – to sharpen

wrath – *n.* – violent or unrestrained anger; fury

wry – *adj.* – mocking; cynical

xenophobia – *n.* – fear of foreigners

yoke – *n.* – harness; collar; bond

yore – *n.* – former period of time

zephyr – *n.* – a gentle wind; breeze

II. KNOWING YOUR WORD PARTS

While taking the PSAT, you will have nothing but your own knowledge to rely on when you come into contact with unfamiliar words. Even though we have provided you with the 600 most commonly tested PSAT words, there is a very good chance that you will come across words that you still do not know. Therefore, you will need to review our list of the most common prefixes, roots, and suffixes in order to be prepared.

Learn the meanings of the prefixes, roots, and suffixes in the same way that you learned the vocabulary words and their meanings. Be sure to use index cards for the items you don't know or find unusual. Look over the examples given and then try to think of your own. Testing yourself in this way will allow you to see if you really do know the meaning of each item. Knowledge of prefixes, roots, and suffixes is essential to a strong vocabulary and, therefore, to a high score on the verbal PSAT.

PREFIXES

Prefix	Meaning	Example
ab –, a –, abs –	away, without, from	absent – away, not present apathy – without interest abstain – to keep from doing; to refrain
ad –	to, toward	adjacent – next to address – to direct towards
ante –	before	antecedent – going before in time anterior – occurring before
anti –	against	antidote – remedy to act against an evil antibiotic – substance that fights against bacteria
be –	over, thoroughly	bemoan – to mourn over belabor – to exert much labor upon
bi –	two	bisect – to divide biennial – happening every two years

Prefix	Meaning	Example
cata –, cat –, cath –	down	catacombs – underground passageways catalogue – descriptive list catheter – tubular medical device
circum –	around	circumscribe – to draw a circle around circumspect – watchful on all sides
com –	with	combine – to join together communication – to have dealings with
contra –	against	contrary – opposed contrast – to stand in opposition
de –	down, from	decline – to bend downward decontrol – to release from government control
di –	two	dichotomy – divided in two diarchy – system of government with two authorities
dis –, di–	apart, away	discern – to distinguish as separate dismiss – to send away digress – to turn aside
epi –, ep –, eph –	upon, among	epidemic – happening among many people epicycle – circle whose center moves round in the circumference of a greater circle epaulet – decoration worn to ornament or protect the shoulder ephedra – any of a large genus of desert shrubs
ex –, e –	from, out	exceed – to go beyond the limit emit – to send forth
extra –	outside, beyond	extraordinary – beyond or out of the common method extrasensory – beyond the senses

Prefix	Meaning	Example
hyper –	beyond, over	hyperactive – over the normal activity level hypercritic – one who is critical beyond measure
hypo –	beneath, lower	hypodermic – parts beneath the skin hypocrisy – to be under a pretense of goodness
in –, il –, im –, ir –	not	inactive – not active illogical – not logical imperfect – not perfect irreversible – not reversible
in –, il –, im –, ir –	in, on, into	instill – to put in slowly illation – action of bringing in impose – to lay on irrupt – to break in
inter –	among, between	intercom – to exchange conversations between people interlude – performance given between parts in a play
intra –	within	intravenous – within a vein intramural – within a single college or its students
meta –	beyond, over, along with	metamorphosis – change over in form or nature metatarsus – part of foot beyond the flat of the foot
mis –	badly, wrongly	misconstrue – to interpret wrongly misappropriate – to use wrongly
mono –	one	monogamy – to be married to one person at a time monotone – a single, unvaried tone
multi –	many	multiple – of many parts multitude – a great number
non –	no, not	nonsense – lack of sense nonentity – not existing

Prefix	Meaning	Example
ob –	against	obscene – offensive to modesty obstruct – to hinder the passage of
para –, par –	beside	parallel – continuously at equal distance apart parenthesis – sentence inserted within a passage
per –	through	persevere – to maintain an effort permeate – to pass through
poly –	many	polygon – a plane figure with many sides or angles polytheism – belief in the existence of many gods
post –	after	posterior – coming after postpone – to put off until a future time
pre –	before	premature – ready before the proper time premonition – a previous warning
pro –	in favor of, forward	prolific – bringing forth offspring project – to throw or cast forward
re –	back, against	reimburse – to pay back retract – to draw back
semi –	half	semicircle – half a circle semiannual – half-yearly
sub –	under	subdue – to bring under one's power submarine – to travel under the surface of the sea
super –	above	supersonic – above the speed of sound superior – higher in place or position
tele –, tel –	across	telecast – to transmit a television signal across a distance telepathy – communication between mind and mind at a distance

Prefix	Meaning	Example
trans –	across	transpose – to change the position of two things
		transmit – to send from one person, place, or thing to another
ultra –	beyond	ultraviolet – beyond the limit of visibility
		ultramarine – beyond the sea
un –	not	undeclared – not declared
		unbelievable – not believable
uni –	one	unity – state of oneness
		unison – sounding together
with –	away, against	withhold – to hold back
		withdraw – to take away

☞ Drill: Prefixes

DIRECTIONS: Provide a definition for each prefix.

1. pro– _____

2. com– _____

3. epi– _____

4. ob– _____

5. ad– _____

DIRECTIONS: Identify the prefix in each word.

6. efface _____

7. hypothetical _____

8. permeate _____

9. contrast _____

10. inevitable _____

ROOTS

Root	Meaning	Example
act, ag	do, act, drive	activate – to make active agile – having quick motion
alt	high	altitude – height alto – highest male singing voice
alter, altr	other, change	alternative – choice between two things altruism – living for the good of others
am, ami	love, friend	amiable – worthy of affection amity – friendship
anim	mind, spirit	animated – spirited animosity – violent hatred
annu, enni	year	annual – every year centennial – every hundred years
aqua	water	aquarium – tank for water animals and plants aquamarine – semiprecious stone of sea-green color
arch	first, ruler	archenemy – chief enemy archetype – original pattern from which things are copied
aud, audit	hear	audible – capable of being heard audience – assembly of hearers audition – the power or act of hearing
auto	self	automatic – self-acting autobiography – story about a person's life written by that person
bell	war	belligerent – a party taking part in a war bellicose – war-like
ben, bene	good	benign – kindly disposition beneficial – advantageous

Root	Meaning	Example
bio	life	biotic – relating to life biology – the science of life
brev	short	abbreviate – to make shorter brevity – shortness
cad, cas	fall	cadence – fall in voice casualty – loss caused by death, injury or illness
capit, cap	head	captain – the head or chief decapitate – to cut off the head
cede, ceed, cess	to go, to yield	recede – to move or fall back proceed – to move onward recessive – tending to go back
cent	hundred	century – hundred years centipede – insect with a hundred legs
chron	time	chronology – science dealing with historical dates chronicle – register of events in order of time
cide, cis	to kill, to cut	homicide – one who kills incision – a cut
clam, claim	to shout	acclaim – receive with applause proclamation – announce publicly
cogn	to know	recognize – to know again cognition – awareness
corp	body	incorporate – to combine into one body corpse – dead body
cred	to trust, to believe	incredible – unbelievable credulous – too prone to believe
cur, curr, curs	to run	current – flowing body of air or water excursion – short trip
dem	people	democracy – government formed for the people epidemic – affecting all people

Root	Meaning	Example
dic, dict	to say	dictate – to read aloud for another to transcribe verdict – decision of a jury
doc, doct	to teach	docile – easily instructed indoctrinate – to instruct
domin	to rule	dominate – to rule dominion – territory of rule
duc, duct	to lead	conduct – act of guiding induce – to overcome by persuasion
eu	well, good	eulogy – speech or writing in praise euphony – pleasantness or smoothness of sound
fac, fact, fect, fic	to do, to make	facilitate – to make easier factory – location of production confect – to put together fiction – something invented or imagined
fer	to bear, to carry	transfer – to move from one place to another refer – to direct to
fin	end, limit	infinity – unlimited finite – limited in quantity
flect, flex	to bend	flexible – easily bent reflect – to throw back
fort	luck	fortunate – lucky fortuitous – happening by chance
fort	strong	fortify – to strengthen fortress – stronghold
frag, fract	break	fragile – easily broken fracture – to break
fug	flee	fugitive – fleeing refugee – one who flees to a place of safety

Root	Meaning	Example
gen	class, race	engender – to breed generic – of a general nature in regard to all members
grad, gress	to go, to step	regress – to go back graduate – to divide into regular steps
graph	writing	telegraph – message sent by telegraph autograph – person's own handwriting or signature
ject	to throw	projectile – capable of being thrown reject – to throw away
leg	law	legitimate – lawful legal – defined by law
leg, lig, lect	to choose, gather, read	illegible – incapable of being read ligature – something that binds election – the act of choosing
liber	free	liberal – favoring freedom of ideals liberty – freedom from restraint
log	study, speech	archaeology – study of human antiquities prologue – address spoken before a performance
luc, lum	light	translucent – slightly transparent illuminate – to light up
magn	large, great	magnify – to make larger magnificent – great
mal, male	bad, wrong	malfunction – to operate incorrectly malevolent – evil
mar	sea	marine – pertaining to the sea submarine – below the surface of the sea
mater, matr	mother	maternal – motherly matriarchy – a social system in which descent is traced through females

Root	Meaning	Example
mit, miss	to send	transmit – to send from one person, place, or thing to another mission – the act of sending
morph	shape	metamorphosis – a changing in shape anthropomorphic – having a human shape
mut	change	mutable – subject to change mutate – to change
nat	born	innate – inborn native – a person born in a place
neg	deny	negative – expressing denial renege – to deny
nom	name	nominate – to put forward a name nomenclature – process of naming
nov	new	novel – new renovate – to make as good as new
omni	all	omnipotent – all powerful omnipresent – all present
oper	to work	operate – to work on something cooperate – to work with others
pass, path	to feel	pathetic – affecting the tender emotions passionate – moved by strong emotion
pater, patr	father	paternal – fatherly patriarchy – a social system in which descent is traced through males
ped, pod	foot	pedestrian – one who travels on foot podiatrist – foot doctor
pel, puls	to drive, to push	impel – to drive forward compulsion – irresistible force
phil	love	philharmonic – loving harmony or music philanthropist – one who loves and seeks to do good for others

Root	Meaning	Example
port	carry	export – to carry out of the country portable – able to be carried
psych	mind	psychology – study of the mind psychiatrist – specialist in mental disorders
quer, ques, quir, quis	to ask	querist – one who inquires inquire – to ask about question – that which is asked inquisitive – inclined to ask questions
rid, ris	to laugh	ridiculous – laughable derision – ridicule
rupt	to break	interrupt – to break in upon erupt – to break through
sci	to know	science – systematic knowledge of physical or natural phenomena conscious – having inward knowledge
scrib, script	to write	transcribe – to write over again script – text of words
sent, sens	to feel, to think	sentimental – feelings of great emotion sensitive – easily affected by changes
sequ, secut	to follow	sequence – connected series consecutive – following one another in unbroken order
solv, solu, solut	to loosen	dissolve – to break up absolute – without restraint
spect	to look at	spectator – one who watches inspect – to look at closely
spir	to breathe	inspire – to breathe in respiration – process of breathing
string, strict	to bind	stringent – binding strongly restrict – to restrain within bounds

146

Root	Meaning	Example
stru, struct	to build	strut – a structural piece designed to resist pressure construct – to build
tang, ting, tact, tig	to touch	tangent – touching, but not intersecting patting – to touch lightly contact – touching contiguous – to touch along a boundary
ten, tent, tain	to hold	tenure – holding of office contain – to hold
term	to end	terminate – to end terminal – having an end
terr	earth	terrain – tract of land terrestrial – existing on earth
therm	heat	thermal – pertaining to heat thermometer – instrument for measuring temperature
tort, tors	to twist	contortionist – one who twists violently torsion – act of turning or twisting
tract	to pull, to draw	attract – to draw toward distract – to draw away
vac	empty	vacant – empty evacuate – to empty out
ven, vent	to come	prevent – to stop from coming intervene – to come between
ver	true	verify – to prove to be true veracious – truthful
verb	word	verbose – use of excess words verbatim – word for word
vid, vis	to see	video – televised or taped image vision – act of seeing external objects

Root	Meaning	Example
vinc, vict, vang	to conquer	invincible – unconquerable victory – defeat of enemy vanguard – troops moving at the head of an army
viv, vit	life	vital – necessary to life vivacious – lively
voc	to call	vocation – a summons to a course of action vocal – uttered by voice
vol	to wish, to will	involuntary – outside the control of will volition – the act of willing or choosing

☞ Drill: Roots

DIRECTIONS: Provide a definition for each root.

1. cede _____

2. fact _____

3. path _____

4. ject _____

5. ver _____

DIRECTIONS: Identify the root in each word.

6. acclaim _____

7. verbatim _____

8. benefactor _____

9. relegate _____

10. tension _____

SUFFIXES

Suffix	Meaning	Example
–able, –ble	capable of	believable – capable of being believed legible – capable of being read
–acious, –icious, *–ous*	full of	vivacious – full of life delicious – full of pleasurable smell or taste wondrous – full of wonder
–ant, –ent	full of	eloquent – full of eloquence expectant – full of expectation
–ary	connected with	honorary – for the sake of honor disciplinary – relating to a field of study
–ate	to make	ventilate – to make public consecrate – to dedicate
–fy	to make	magnify – to make larger testify – to make witness
–ile	pertaining to, capable of	docile – capable of being managed easily infantile – pertaining to infancy
–ism	belief, condition	Mormonism – belief in the teachings of the Book of Mormon idiotism – utterly foolish conduct
–ist	doer	artist – one who creates art pianist – one who plays the piano
–ose	full of	verbose – full of words grandiose – striking, imposing
–osis	condition	neurosis – nervous condition psychosis – psychological condition
–tude	state	magnitude – state of greatness multitude – state of quantity

☞ Drill: Suffixes

DIRECTIONS: Provide a definition for each suffix.

1. –ant, –ent _____

2. –tude _____

3. –ile _____

4. –fy _____

5. –ary _____

DIRECTIONS: Identify the suffix in each word.

6. audacious _____

7. expedient _____

8. gullible _____

9. grandiose _____

10. antagonism _____

VERBAL DRILLS

ANSWER KEY

Drill: Group 1

1.	(J)	5.	(H)	9.	(F)	13.	(A)
2.	(G)	6.	(B)	10.	(E)	14.	(E)
3.	(A)	7.	(I)	11.	(D)	15.	(B)
4.	(C)	8.	(D)	12.	(C)		

Drill: Group 2

1.	(D)	5.	(A)	9.	(B)	13.	(B)
2.	(G)	6.	(J)	10.	(H)	14.	(E)
3.	(I)	7.	(E)	11.	(D)	15.	(C)
4.	(F)	8.	(C)	12.	(A)		

Drill: Group 3

1.	(E)	5.	(I)	9.	(F)	13.	(E)
2.	(H)	6.	(B)	10.	(D)	14.	(D)
3.	(J)	7.	(C)	11.	(C)	15.	(B)
4.	(A)	8.	(G)	12.	(A)		

Drill: Group 4

1.	(D)	5.	(J)	9.	(H)	13.	(B)
2.	(E)	6.	(B)	10.	(G)	14.	(C)
3.	(A)	7.	(C)	11.	(D)	15.	(E)
4.	(I)	8.	(F)	12.	(A)		

Drill: Group 5

1.	(H)	5.	(J)	9.	(D)	13.	(A)
2.	(F)	6.	(C)	10.	(G)	14.	(E)
3.	(A)	7.	(I)	11.	(B)	15.	(C)
4.	(B)	8.	(E)	12.	(D)		

Drill: Group 6

1.	(G)	5.	(C)	9.	(F)	13.	(A)
2.	(A)	6.	(B)	10.	(H)	14.	(C)
3.	(E)	7.	(D)	11.	(D)	15.	(B)
4.	(J)	8.	(I)	12.	(E)		

Drill: Group 7

1.	(F)	5.	(H)	9.	(D)	13.	(D)
2.	(E)	6.	(I)	10.	(J)	14.	(C)
3.	(A)	7.	(C)	11.	(B)	15.	(A)
4.	(B)	8.	(G)	12.	(E)		

Drill: Group 8

1.	(D)	5.	(B)	9.	(F)	13.	(A)
2.	(A)	6.	(C)	10.	(J)	14.	(E)
3.	(H)	7.	(E)	11.	(C)	15.	(D)
4.	(G)	8.	(I)	12.	(B)		

Drill: Group 9

1.	(D)	5.	(J)	9.	(C)	13.	(B)
2.	(I)	6.	(E)	10.	(H)	14.	(E)
3.	(G)	7.	(B)	11.	(A)	15.	(C)
4.	(A)	8.	(F)	12.	(D)		

Drill: Group 10

1.	(H)	5.	(J)	9.	(D)	13.	(A)
2.	(I)	6.	(B)	10.	(G)	14.	(C)
3.	(E)	7.	(F)	11.	(B)	15.	(E)
4.	(A)	8.	(C)	12.	(D)		

Drill: Group 11

1.	(F)	5.	(B)	9.	(E)	13.	(E)
2.	(I)	6.	(J)	10.	(G)	14.	(A)
3.	(A)	7.	(C)	11.	(C)	15.	(D)
4.	(H)	8.	(D)	12.	(B)		

Drill: Group 12

1.	(J)	5.	(C)	9.	(F)	13.	(D)
2.	(A)	6.	(H)	10.	(E)	14.	(A)
3.	(B)	7.	(D)	11.	(E)	15.	(B)
4.	(I)	8.	(G)	12.	(C)		

Drill: Prefixes

1. forward
2. with
3. upon, among
4. against
5. to, toward
6. ef–
7. hypo–
8. per–
9. con–
10. in–

Drill: Roots

1. to go, to yield
2. to do, to make
3. to feel
4. to throw
5. true
6. claim
7. verb
8. ben(e)
9. leg
10. ten

Drill: Suffixes

1. full of
2. state
3. pertaining to, capable of
4. to make
5. connected with
6. (a)cious
7. ent
8. ible
9. ose
10. ism

PSAT/ NMSQT

CHAPTER 4

Attacking Sentence Completion Questions

Chapter 4

ATTACKING SENTENCE COMPLETION QUESTIONS

Regardless of the verbal PSAT section in which one is working, all problem-solving techniques should be divided into two main categories: skills and strategies. This chapter will present skills and strategies that are effective in helping the test-taker successfully answer Sentence Completions. These techniques include the recognition of a context clue, a knowledge of the levels of difficulty in a Sentence Completion section, the application of deductive reasoning, and familiarity with the logical structure of sentence completions. You will encounter 17 Sentence Completion questions on the PSAT/NMSQT.

Success on the verbal PSAT begins with one fundamental insight: the underlying intent is to test your vocabulary. No matter what section you are working in, you will be expected to demonstrate a command of a wide array of vocabulary words drawn from a treasury of Greek and Latin roots and prefixes. Devote as much time as possible to strengthening your vocabulary, especially by studying the prefixes and roots of Greek- and Latin-derived words. The Vocabulary Enhancer section of the Basic Verbal Skills Review should be studied thoroughly.

ABOUT THE DIRECTIONS

The directions for Sentence Completion questions are relatively straightforward.

DIRECTIONS: Each sentence below has one or two blanks, each blank indicating that something has been omitted. Beneath the sentence are five lettered words or sets of words. Choose the word or set of words that BEST fits the meaning of the sentence as a whole.

Example:

Although the critics found the book _____, many of the readers found it rather _____.

(A) obnoxious ... perfect

(D) comical ... persuasive

(B) spectacular ... interesting

(E) popular ... rare

(C) boring ... intriguing

(A) (B) ● (D) (E)

ABOUT THE QUESTIONS

You will encounter two main types of questions in the Sentence Completion section of the PSAT. In addition, the questions will appear in varying difficulties which we will call Level I (easy), Level II (average), and Level III (difficult). The following explains the structure of the questions.

Question Type 1: One-Word Completions

One-Word Completions will require you to fill in one blank. The one-word completion can appear as a Level I, II, or III question depending on the difficulty of the vocabulary included.

Question Type 2: Two-Word Completions

Two-Word Completions will require you to fill in two blanks. As with the one-word completion, this type may be a Level I, II, or III question. This will depend not only on the difficulty of the vocabulary, but also on the relationship between the words and between the words and the sentence.

The remainder of this review will provide explicit details on what you will encounter when dealing with Sentence Completion questions, in addition to strategies for correctly completing these sentences.

➤ POINTS TO REMEMBER

- Like other verbal sections of the test, Sentence Completions can be divided into three basic levels of difficulty, and, as a general rule, PSAT verbal exercises *increase* in difficulty as they progress through a section.

- Level I exercises allow you to rely on your instincts and common sense. You should not be obsessed with analysis or second-guessing in Level I problems.

- In Level II questions, the PSAT often presents words that appear easy at first glance but that may have secondary meanings. Be wary of blindly following your gut reactions and common sense.

- All PSAT word problems contain "magnet words," answer choices that look good but are designed to draw the student away from the correct answer. Magnet words can effectively mislead you in Level III questions. Always watch for them. Remember that Level III questions are intentionally designed to work against your common sense and natural inclinations.

- Deductive reasoning is a tool that will be of constant assistance to you as you work through PSAT word problems. To deduce means to derive a truth (or answer) through a reasoning process.

- Sentence Completion questions are puzzles, and they are put together with a certain amount of predictability. One such predictable characteristic is the *structure* of a PSAT word exercise. Since there are always five possible answers from which to choose, you must learn to see which answers are easy to eliminate first. Use the process of elimination.

- Most PSAT word problems are designed around a "three-two" structure. This means that there are three easier answers to eliminate before you have to make the final decision between the remaining two.

- Use word roots, prefixes, and suffixes to find the meanings of words you do not know.

ANSWERING SENTENCE COMPLETION QUESTIONS

Follow these steps as you attempt to answer each question.

| STEP 1 | Identifying context clues is one of the most successful ways for students to locate correct answers in Sentence Completions. Practicing constantly in this area will help you strengthen one of your main strategies in this type of word problem. The sentence completion below is an example of a Level I question.

Pamela played her championship chess game _____ , avoiding all traps and making no mistakes.

(A) hurriedly   (D) imaginatively

(B) flawlessly   (E) aggressively

(C) prodigally

The phrase "avoiding all traps and making no mistakes" is your context clue. Notice that the phrase both follows *and* modifies the word in question. Since you know that Sentence Completions are exercises seeking to test your vocabulary knowledge, attack these problems accordingly. For example, ask yourself what word means "avoiding all traps and making no mistakes." In so doing, you discover the answer flawlessly (B), which means perfectly or without mistakes. If Pamela played hurriedly (A), she might well make mistakes. Difficult words are seldom the answer in easier questions; therefore, prodigally (C) stands out as a suspicious word. This could be a magnet word. However, before you eliminate it, ask yourself whether you know its meaning. If so, does it surpass flawlessly (B) in defining the context clue, "making no mistakes"? It does not. Imaginatively (D) is a tempting answer, since one might associate a perfect game of chess as one played imaginatively; however, there is no connection between the imagination and the absence of mistakes. Aggressively (E) playing a game may, in fact, cause you to make mistakes.

Here is an example of a Level II Sentence Completion. Try to determine the context clue.

Although most people believe the boomerang is the product of a
_____ design, that belief is deceptive; in fact, the boomerang is a
_____ example of the laws of aerodynamics.

(A) foreign . . . modern   (D) primitive . . . sophisticated

(B) symbolic . . . complex   (E) faulty . . . invalid

(C) practical . . . scientific

The most important context clue in this sentence is the opening word "although," which indicates that some kind of antonym relationship is present in the sentence. It tells us there is a reversal in meaning. Therefore, be on the lookout for words which will form an opposite relationship. The phrase "that belief is deceptive" makes certain the idea that there will be an opposite meaning between the missing words. Primitive . . . sophisticated (D) is the best answer, since the two are exact opposites. "Primitive" means crude and elementary, whereas "sophisticated" means refined and advanced. Foreign . . . modern (A) and symbolic . . . complex (B) have no real opposite relationship. Also, "complex" is a magnet word that sounds right in the context of scientific laws, but "symbolic" is not its counterpart.

Practical . . . scientific (C) and faulty . . . invalid (E) are rejectable because they are generally synonymous pairs of relationships.

The following is an example of a Level III question:

The weekly program on public radio is the most _____ means of educating the public about pollution.

(A) proficient   (D) capable

(B) effusive   (E) competent

(C) effectual

The context clue in this sentence is "means of educating the public about pollution." Effectual (C) is the correct answer. Effectual means having the power to produce the exact effect or result. Proficient (A) is not correct as it implies competency above the average—radio programs are not described in this manner. Effusive (B) does not fit the sense of the sentence. Both capable (D) and competent (E) are incorrect because they refer to people, not things.

| STEP 2 | Since the verbal PSAT is fundamentally a vocabulary test, it must resort to principles and techniques necessary for testing your vocabulary. Therefore, certain dynamics like antonyms (word opposites) and synonyms (word similarities) become very useful in setting up a question or word problem. This idea can be taken one step further. |

Another type of technique that utilizes the tension of opposites and the concurrence of similarities is *word values.* Word values begin with the recognition that most pivotal words in a PSAT word problem can be assigned a positive or negative value. Marking a "+" or "–" next to choices may help you eliminate inappropriate choices. In turn, you will be able to more quickly identify possible correct answers.

Dealing with Positive Value Words

Positive value words are usually easy to recognize. They usually convey a meaning which can be equated with gain, advantage, liveliness, intelligence, virtue, and positive emotions, conditions, or actions.

The ability to recognize positive and negative word values, however, will not bring you very far if you do not understand how to apply it to your advantage in Sentence Completions. Below you will find examples of how to do this, first with a study of positive value Sentence Completions, then with a study of negative value Sentence Completions. The following is an example of a Level I question.

An expert skateboarder, Tom is truly _____ ; he smoothly blends timing with balance.

(A) coordinated   (D) supportive

(B) erudite   (E) casual

(C) a novice

As you know, the context clue is the clause after the word in question, which acts as a modifier. Naturally, anyone who "smoothly blends" is creating a *positive* situation. Look for the positive answer.

An expert skateboarder, Tom is truly __+__ ; *he smoothly blends timing with balance.*

+(A) coordinated   +(D) supportive

+(B) erudite   –(E) casual

–(C) a novice

Coordinated (A), a positive value word that means ordering two or more things, fits the sentence perfectly. Erudite (B) is positive, but it is too difficult to be a Level I answer. A novice (C) in this context is negative. Supportive (D) and casual (E) don't fulfill the definition of the context clue, and casual is negative, implying a lack of attention. Notice that eliminating negatives *immediately reduces the number of options from which you have to choose.* This raises the odds of selecting the correct answer. (One of the analytic skills you should develop for the PSAT is being able to see the hidden vocabulary question in any exercise.)

A Level II question may appear as follows:

Despite their supposedly primitive lifestyle, Australian aborigines developed the boomerang, a _____ and _____ hunting tool that maximizes gain with minimum effort.

(A) ponderous . . . expensive   (D) sophisticated . . . efficient

(B) clean . . . dynamic   (E) useful . . . attractive

(C) dangerous . . . formidable

In this case, the context clues (in italics) begin and end the sentence.

Despite their supposedly primitive lifestyle, Australian aborigines developed the boomerang, a __+__ and __+__ hunting *tool that maximizes gain with minimum effort.*

–(A) ponderous . . . expensive   +(D) sophisticated . . . efficient

+(B) clean . . . dynamic   +(E) useful . . . attractive

–(C) dangerous . . . formidable

The first context clue (*despite*) helps you determine that this exercise
entails an antonym relationship with the word primitive, which means
simple or crude. The second context clue offers a definition of the missing
words. Since the meaning of primitive in this context is a negative word
value, you can be fairly confident that the answer will be a pair of positive
word values. Sophisticated . . . efficient (D) is positive *and* it satisfies the
definition of the latter context clue. This is the best answer. Ponderous . . .
expensive (A) is not correct. Clean . . . dynamic (B) is positive, but does
not meet the definition of the latter context clue. Dangerous . . . formidable (C) is negative. Useful . . . attractive (E) is positive, but it does not
work with the latter context clue.

Here is a Level III example.

When a physician describes an illness to a colleague, he must speak
an _____ language, using professional terms and concepts understood mostly by members of his profession.

(A) extrinsic   (D) esoteric

(B) inordinate   (E) abbreviated

(C) ambulatory

Looking at this question, we can see an important context clue. This
appears in italics below.

When a physician describes an illness to a colleague, he must speak
an __+__ language, *using professional terms and concepts understood mostly by members of his profession.*

+(A) extrinsic   +(D) esoteric

–(B) inordinate   –(E) abbreviated

+(C) ambulatory

This clue gives us a definition of the missing word. Begin by eliminating the two obvious negatives, inordinate (B) and abbreviated (E). This
leaves us with three positives. Since this is a Level III exercise, at first you
may be intimidated by the level of vocabulary. In the section on etymol-

ogy you will be given insights into how to handle difficult word problems. For now, note that esoteric (D) is the best answer, since it is an adjective that means *inside* or *part of a group*. Ambulatory (C) is positive, but it is a trap. It seems like an easy association with the world of medicine. In Level III there are *no* easy word associations. Extrinsic (A) is positive, but it means *outside of*, which would not satisfy the logic of the sentence.

Dealing with Negative Value Words

Here are examples of how to work with negative value Sentence Completion problems. The first example is Level I.

Although Steve loves to socialize, his fellow students find him _____ and strive to _____ his company.

(A) generous . . . enjoy   (D) sinister . . . delay

(B) boring . . . evade   (E) weak . . . limit

(C) altruistic . . . accept

The context clue (in italics) tells us that a reversal is being set up between what Steve thinks and what his fellow students think.

Although Steve loves to socialize, his fellow students find him __–__ and strive to __–__ his company.

+(A) generous . . . enjoy   –(D) sinister . . . delay

–(B) boring . . . evade   –(E) weak . . . limit

+(C) altruistic . . . accept

Boring . . . evade (B) is the best answer. The words appearing in Level 1 questions are not overly difficult, and they satisfy the logic of the sentence. Generous . . . enjoy (A) is positive. Altruistic . . . accept (C) is not only positive but contains a very difficult word (altruistic), and it would be unlikely that this would be a Level I answer. The same is true of sinister . . . delay (D), even though it is negative. Weak . . . limit (E) does not make sense in the context of the sentence.

This next example is Level II.

Because they reject _____ , conscientious objectors are given jobs in community work as a substitute for participation in the armed services.

(A) labor   (D) dictatorships

(B) belligerence   (E) poverty

(C) peace

Essentially, this example is a synonym exercise. The description of conscientious objectors (in italics) acts as a strong context clue. Conscientious objectors avoid ("reject") militancy.

Because they reject ___–___ , conscientious objectors *are given jobs in community work as a substitute for participation in the armed services.*

+(A) labor

–(B) belligerence

+(C) peace

–(D) dictatorships

–(E) poverty

Since we are looking for a negative word value (something to do with militancy), labor (A) is incorrect since it is positive. Belligerence (B) fits perfectly, as this is a negative value word having to do with war. Not only is peace (C) a positive value word, it is hardly something to be rejected by conscientious objectors. Dictatorships (D), although a negative word value, has no logical place in the context of this sentence. The same is true of poverty (E).

Here is a Level III example:

Dictators understand well how to centralize power, and that is why they combine a(n) _____ political process with military _____.

(A) foreign . . . victory

(B) electoral . . . escalation

(C) agrarian . . . strategies

(D) domestic . . . decreases

(E) totalitarian . . . coercion

Totalitarian . . . coercion (E) is the best answer. These are difficult words, and both have to do with techniques useful in the centralizing of power by a dictator. *Totalitarian* means centralized, and *coercion* means force.

Dictators understand well how to *centralize power,* and that is why they combine a(n) ___–___ political process with military ___–___.

+(A) foreign . . . victory

+(B) electoral . . . escalation

+(C) agrarian . . . strategies

+(D) domestic . . . decreases

–(E) totalitarian . . . coercion

Foreign . . . victory (A) are not only easy words, they do not appear to be strictly negative. Remember that easy word answers should be suspect in Level III. Agrarian . . . strategies (C) is positive. Domestic . . . decreases (D) is a positive combination. Since you are searching for two negatives, this answer is incorrect. There will be more about this in the next section.

Dealing with Mixed Value Words

In examples with two-word answers so far, you have searched for answers composed with identical word values, such as negative/negative and positive/positive. However, every PSAT Sentence Completion section will have exercises in which two-word answers are found in combinations. Below you will find examples of how to work with these. Here is a Level I example:

Despite a healthy and growing environmental _____ in America, there are many people who prefer to remain _____ .

(A)   awareness . . . ignorant   (D)   crisis . . . unencumbered

(B)   movement . . . enlightened   (E)   industry . . . satisfied

(C)   bankruptcy . . . wealthy

The context clue *despite* sets up the predictable antonym warning. In this case, the sentence seems to call for a positive and then a negative value word answer.

Despite a healthy and growing environmental ___+___ in America, there are many people who prefer to remain ___–___ .

+/–(A)   awareness . . . ignorant

+/+(B)   movement . . . enlightened

–/+(C)   bankruptcy . . . wealthy

–/+(D)   crisis . . . unencumbered

+/+(E)   industry . . . satisfied

Awareness . . . ignorant (A) is the best answer. These are logical antonyms, and they fit the meaning of the sentence. Notice that the order of the missing words is positive, *then* negative. This should help you eliminate (C) and (D) immediately, as they are a reversal of the correct order. Furthermore, industry . . . satisfied (E) and movement . . . enlightened (B) are both identical values, and so are eliminated. Practice these techniques until you confidently can recognize word values *and* the order in which they appear in a sentence.

Here is a Level II example:

Prone to creating characters of _____ quality, novelist Ed Abbey cannot be accused of writing _____ stories.

(A)   measly . . . drab   (D)   sinister . . . complete

(B)   romantic . . . imaginative   (E)   two-dimensional . . . flat

(C)   mythic . . . mundane

The best answer is mythic . . . mundane (C). Measly . . . drab (A) does not make sense when you consider the context clue *cannot,* which suggests the possibility of antonyms. The same is true for sinister . . . complete (D), romantic . . . imaginative (B), and two-dimensional . . . flat (E).

Prone to creating characters of ___+___ quality, novelist Ed Abbey *cannot* be accused of writing ___–___ stories.

–/–(A)   measly . . . drab

+/+(B)   romantic . . . imaginative

+/–(C)   mythic . . . mundane

–/+(D)   sinister . . . complete

–/–(E)   two-dimensional . . . flat

Notice that the value combinations help you determine where to search for the correct answer.

Here is a Level III example:

Reminding his students that planning ahead would protect them from _____ , Mr. McKenna proved to be a principal who understood the virtues of _____ .

(A)   exigency . . . foresight

(B)   grades . . . examinations

(C)   poverty . . . promotion

(D)   deprivation . . . abstinence

(E)   turbulence . . . amelioration

The best answer is exigency . . . foresight (A). The first context clue tells us that we are looking for a negative value word. The second context clue tells us the missing word is most likely positive. Furthermore, exigency . . . foresight is a well-suited antonym combination. Exigencies are emergencies, and foresight helps to lessen their severity, if not their occurrence.

Reminding his students that planning ahead would *protect them* from ___–___ , Mr. McKenna proved to be a principal who understood the *virtues* of ___+___ .

–/+(A)   exigency . . . foresight

0/0(B)   grades . . . examinations

–/+(C)   poverty . . . promotion

–/–(D) deprivation . . . abstinence

–/+(E) turbulence . . . amelioration

Grades . . . examinations (B) are a trap, since they imply school matters. Furthermore, they are neutrals. There will be more on this below. Poverty . . . promotion (C) is an easy word answer and should be immediately suspect, especially if there are no difficult words in the sentence completion itself. Also, this answer does not satisfy the logic of the sentence. Turbulence . . . amelioration (E) is a negative/positive combination, but it does not make sense in this sentence. Even if you are forced to guess between this answer and exigency . . . foresight (A), you have narrowed the field to two. These are excellent odds for success.

Dealing with Neutral Value Words

There is another category of word values that will help you determine the correct answer in a Sentence Completion problem. These are neutral word values. Neutral words are words that convey neither loss nor gain, advantage nor disadvantage, etc. Consider the example above, once again:

Reminding his students that planning ahead would *protect them* from
___–___ , Mr. McKenna proved to be a principal who understood the
virtues of ___+___ .

–/+(A) exigency . . . foresight

0/0(B) grades . . . examinations

–/+(C) poverty . . . promotion

–/–(D) deprivation . . . abstinence

–/+(E) turbulence . . . amelioration

Notice that grades . . . examinations (B) is rated as neutral. In fact, in this case, both words are considered of neutral value. This is because neither word conveys a usable value. Grades in and of themselves are not valued until a number is assigned. Examinations are not significant until a passing or failing value is implied or applied.

Neutral word values are significant because they are *never* the correct answer. Therefore, when you identify a neutral word or combination of words, you may eliminate that choice from your selection. You may eliminate a double-word answer even if only one of the words is obviously neutral.

Neutral words are rare, and you should be careful to measure their value before you make a choice. Here is another example from an exercise seen previously (Note: The answer choices have been altered.):

> *Dictators* understand well how *to centralize power,* and that is why they combine a(n) ___—___ political process with military ___—___.
>
> 0/+(A)   foreign . . . victory
>
> 0/+(B)   electoral . . . escalation
>
> 0/+(C)   agrarian . . . strategies
>
> 0/0(D)   current . . . jobs
>
> –/–(E)   totalitarian . . . coercion

Here, current . . . jobs (D) is an obvious neutral word combination, conveying no positive or negative values. You may eliminate this choice immediately. There is no fixed list of words that may be considered neutral. Rather, you should determine *from the context* of a word problem whether you believe a word or word combination is of a neutral value. This ability will come with practice and a larger vocabulary. As before, the correct answer remains totalitarian . . . coercion (E).

STEP 3	Another way to determine the correct answer is by using etymology. Etymology is the study of the anatomy of words. The most important components of etymology on the PSAT are prefixes and roots. PSAT vocabulary is derived almost exclusively from the etymology of Greek and Latin word origins, and that is where you should concentrate your study. In this section, you will learn how to apply your knowledge of prefixes and roots to Sentence Completion problems.

Etymological skills will work well in conjunction with other techniques you have learned, including positive/negative word values. Furthermore, the technique of "scrolling" will help you understand how to expand your knowledge of etymology.

Scrolling is a process whereby you "scroll" through a list of known related words, roots, or prefixes to help you discover the meaning of a word. As an example, consider the common PSAT word *apathy*. The prefix of apathy is *a*. This means *without*. To scroll this prefix, think of any other words that may begin with this prefix, such as *a*moral, *a*typical, *a*symmetrical. In each case, the meaning of the word is preceded by the meaning *without*.

At this point, you know that *apathy* means without something. Now try to scroll the root, *path,* which comes from the Greek word *pathos*. Words like pathetic, sympathy, antipathy, and empathy may come to mind. These words all have to do with feeling or sensing. In fact, that is what *pathos* means: *feeling*. So apathy means *without feeling*.

With this process you can often determine the fundamental meaning of a word or part of a word, and this may give you enough evidence with which to choose a correct answer. Consider the following familiar Level I example:

An expert skateboarder, Tom is truly __+__ ; he smoothly blends timing with balance.

+(A) coordinated   +(D) supportive

+(B) erudite   −(E) casual

−(C) a novice

As you should remember, the correct answer is coordinated (A). The prefix of this word is *co,* meaning together, and the root is *order.* Something that is "ordered together" fits the context clue perfectly. Combining that with the knowledge that you are looking for a positive value word certifies coordinated (A) as the correct answer.

Here is a Level II example:

Because they reject __−__ , conscientious objectors *are given jobs in community work as a substitute for participation in the armed services.*

+(A) labor   −(D) dictatorships

−(B) belligerence   −(E) poverty

+(C) peace

From working with this example previously, you know that the correct answer is belligerence (B). The root of this word is *bellum*, Latin for war. Belligerence is an inclination toward war. Other words that may be scrolled from this are bellicose, belligerent, and antebellum, all of which have to do with war. Study your roots and prefixes well. A casual knowledge is not good enough. Another root, *bellis,* might be confused with *bellum. Bellis* means beauty. Is it logical that a conscientious objector would reject beauty? Know when to use which root and prefix. This ability will come with study and practice.

Here is a Level III example:

When a physician describes an illness to a colleague, he must speak an __+__ language, *using professional terms and concepts understood mostly by members of his profession.*

+(A) extrinsic   +(D) esoteric

−(B) inordinate   −(E) abbreviated

+(C) ambulatory

Recalling this example, you will remember that the context clue defines the missing word as one meaning language that involves a special group of people, i.e., "inside information." The correct answer is esoteric (D). *Eso* is a prefix that means *inside*. The prefix of extrinsic (A) is *ex*, which means *out*, the opposite of the meaning you seek. Inordinate (B) means *not ordered*. In this case, the prefix *in* means *not*. This is Level III, so beware of easy assumptions! The root of ambulatory (C) is *ambulare*, which means *to walk*. Abbreviated (E) breaks down to *ab*, meaning *to*; and *brevis*, Latin for brief or short.

In many Level III words you may not be able to scroll or break down a word completely. However, often, as in the example above, a partial knowledge of the etymology may be enough to find the correct answer.

Now, take what you have learned and apply it to the questions appearing in the following drill. If you are unsure of an answer, refer back to the review material for help.

☞ Drill: Sentence Completions

> **DIRECTIONS**: Each sentence below has one or two blanks, each blank indicating that something has been omitted. Beneath the sentence are five lettered words or sets of words. Choose the word or set of words that BEST fits the meaning of the sentence as a whole.
>
> **EXAMPLE**:
>
> Although the critics found the book _____, many of the readers found it rather _____.
>
> (A) obnoxious . . . perfect   (D) comical . . . persuasive
>
> (B) spectacular . . . interesting   (E) popular . . . rare
>
> (C) boring . . . intriguing   (A) (B) ● (D) (E)

1.   The problems of the homeless were so desperate that he felt a need to help _____ them.

    (A) increase   (B) ameliorate

(C) authenticate   (D) collaborate

(E) justify

2. The activities of the business manager were so obviously unethical that the board had no choice but to _____ him.

(A) censure   (B) commend

(C) consecrate   (D) censor

(E) reiterate

3. _____ people often are taken in by _____ salespeople.

(A) Suave . . . futile   (D) Erratic . . . passive

(B) Benevolent . . . inept   (E) Pious . . . obstinate

(C) Gullible . . . larcenous

4. The speaker _____ the work of environmentalists as ineffective.

(A) dissented   (D) conceded

(B) savored   (E) tantalized

(C) disparaged

5. Her exceptionally well-written first novel was happily reviewed by the critics with _____ .

(A) ennui   (D) acclaim

(B) pessimism   (E) chagrin

(C) remorse

6. That commentator never has anything good to say; every remark is _____ .

(A) inept   (D) bombastic

(B) frivolous   (E) caustic

(C) aberrant

7. The principal's plan to gain students' and parents' cooperation by forming small work groups has worked well; it is both creative and _____ .

(A) sagacious   (D) erroneous

(B) ignoble   (E) conventional

(C) dissonant

8. My boss is so arrogant that we're surprised when he _____ to speak to us in the cafeteria.

(A) forbears   (D) delays

(B) declines   (E) deigns

(C) abhors

9. Scientists and environmentalists are very concerned about the _____ of the ozone layer.

(A) depletion   (D) defamation

(B) dissonance   (E) enhancement

(C) conglomeration

10. Resolving racist attitudes seems to happen most successfully in communities where different ethnic groups _____ around issues of justice.

(A) educe   (D) coalesce

(B) collapse   (E) diverge

(C) dissolve

11. One obstacle to solving the mass transit problem is a _____ of funds to build and repair systems.

(A) euphony   (D) dearth

(B) profusion   (E) vindication

(C) periphery

12. Terrorists, who are usually _____ , seldom can be dealt with _____ .

(A) rabid . . . timorously   (D) blasphemous . . . tersely

(B) unruly . . . fairly   (E) hedonistic . . . honestly

(C) zealots . . . rationally

13. The candidate argued that it was _____ to _____ democracy and yet not vote.

    (A) malicious . . . denounce   (D) inarticulate . . . defend

    (B) lucrative . . . allocate   (E) hypocritical . . . advocate

    (C) commendable . . . delineate

14. Of all the boring speeches I have ever heard, last night's address had to be the most _____ yet!

    (A) arrogant   (D) fervent

    (B) insipid   (E) indolent

    (C) effervescent

15. Malcolm X was a _____ of Martin Luther King, Jr., yet he had a _____ different view of integration.

    (A) disciple . . . reciprocally

    (B) codependent . . . uniquely

    (C) contemporary . . . radically

    (D) fanatic . . . futilely

    (E) biographer . . . unrealistically

16. In order to pass the hearing test, you have to be able to _____ high pitch tones from low pitch tones.

    (A) surmise   (D) document

    (B) define   (E) vindicate

    (C) discriminate

17. The committee _____ carefully before making the final report; nevertheless, a minority report _____ its conclusions.

    (A) deliberated . . . refuted   (D) gloated . . . implemented

    (B) analyzed . . . abased   (E) argued . . . accepted

    (C) discerned . . . emulated

..., _____ behavior will bring rewards.

languid   (D) disruptive

(B) rhetorical   (E) exemplary

(C) questionable

19. Colonial Americans, who had little extra money or leisure time, built simple and _____ homes.

    (A) baroque   (D) prodigious

    (B) unpretentious   (E) disreputable

    (C) grandiose

20. Communist countries today are trying to _____ the ineffective economic policies of the past.

    (A) ignore   (D) condone

    (B) rectify   (E) provoke

    (C) reiterate

21. Albert Einstein is the _____ of a genius.

    (A) rebuttal   (D) mentor

    (B) digression   (E) epitome

    (C) antithesis

22. He was tempted to cheat but did not want to _____ his morals.

    (A) obscure   (D) concede

    (B) refute   (E) succumb

    (C) compromise

23. Religious services have spiritual significance for those who are _____.

    (A) fastidious   (D) pious

    (B) pessimistic   (E) phlegmatic

    (C) pragmatic

24. Her _____ remarks seemed innocent enough, but in reality they were _____ .

    (A) caustic . . . fallacious   (D) innocuous . . . malicious

    (B) acrid . . . insipid   (E) ebullient . . . frivolous

    (C) magnanimous . . . affable

25. The legend of Beowulf is a famous Norse _____ .

    (A) saga   (D) utopia

    (B) reverie   (E) satire

    (C) soliloquy

26. An effective way to prevent the spread of infectious disease is to _____ the sick person.

    (A) alleviate   (D) salvage

    (B) efface   (E) absolve

    (C) quarantine

27. In international business and politics, English is virtually a _____ language.

    (A) mundane   (D) palpable

    (B) finite   (E) universal

    (C) dead

28. Spring break is a welcome _____ from _____ school work.

    (A) dichotomy . . . garbled   (D) liaison . . . difficult

    (B) quandary . . . lax   (E) zenith . . . phenomenal

    (C) respite . . . arduous

29. If you can't find an original form, just prepare a reasonable _____ .

    (A) paradigm   (D) aberration

    (B) facsimile   (E) equivocation

    (C) facade

...rous donation provided the _____ needed to raise the en-
...1.

(...) catalyst   (D) ideology

(B) alacrity   (E) plethora

(C) duress

31. The protestors got a better response to their requests when they
    _____ their anger.

(A) invoked   (D) tempered

(B) appeased   (E) censured

(C) condoned

32. Carelessly dumping chemicals has created many _____ waste sites.

(A) choleric   (D) toxic

(B) utopian   (E) vaunted

(C) torpid

33. The investment counselor had a _____ reputation for purchasing
    companies and then stripping them of all the assets.

(A) potent   (D) notorious

(B) commendable   (E) pervasive

(C) subtle

34. Staying active is important for people of all ages, so that neither the
    brain nor the muscles _____ .

(A) expand   (D) vacillate

(B) atrophy   (E) condescend

(C) endure

35. When a student consistently does not turn in homework, the teacher
    often _____ that the student is _____ .

(A) implies . . . zealous   (D) assures . . . taciturn

(B) concludes . . . ambitious   (E) infers . . . indolent

(C) assumes . . . depraved

36. Looking through the photo album brought warm feelings of _____ .

   (A) remorse   (D) ambiguity

   (B) nostalgia   (E) deference

   (C) complacence

37. There is a marked _____ between the salaries of skilled and unskilled workers.

   (A) disparity   (D) calamity

   (B) increase   (E) amorphousness

   (C) cohesion

38. Although the chairperson seemed to be neutral in her support of the plan, they suspected she had _____ motives.

   (A) satirical   (D) guileless

   (B) palpable   (E) ulterior

   (C) occult

39. They were elated to learn that the salary increases were _____ to the beginning of the year.

   (A) reciprocal   (D) germane

   (B) recessive   (E) subsidiary

   (C) retroactive

40. Scientists debate whether it is possible to even _____ exactly how life begins.

   (A) fathom   (D) rebut

   (B) juxtapose   (E) suppress

   (C) gloat

NTENCE COMPLETIONS

ANSWER KEY

Drill: Sentence Completions

1.	(B)	11.	(D)	21.	(E)	31.	(D)
2.	(A)	12.	(C)	22.	(C)	32.	(D)
3.	(C)	13.	(E)	23.	(D)	33.	(D)
4.	(C)	14.	(B)	24.	(D)	34.	(B)
5.	(D)	15.	(C)	25.	(A)	35.	(E)
6.	(E)	16.	(C)	26.	(C)	36.	(B)
7.	(A)	17.	(A)	27.	(E)	37.	(A)
8.	(E)	18.	(E)	28.	(C)	38.	(E)
9.	(A)	19.	(B)	29.	(B)	39.	(C)
10.	(D)	20.	(B)	30.	(A)	40.	(A)

PSAT/ NMSQT

CHAPTER 5

Attacking Analogy Questions

Chapter 5

ATTACKING ANALOGY QUESTIONS

Analogies are an important part of the Verbal Review for the PSAT. An analogy is simply a comparison between items that are basically different, but that also have some striking similarities. Because of these similarities, analogous terms may share a common bond or relationship that is the key to the analogy.

Actually, an analogy is the verbal equivalent of a proportion in mathematics. In math, recall that the colon between a pair of numbers shows that the numbers are a ratio, as, for example, "the odds are 4 to 1." The proportion then sets one ratio equal to a second ratio (for example, the relationship 4 to 1 is the same as the relationship 8 to 2). In a verbal comparison, a colon separates two words to be compared. We read "Word A is to Word B." In a PSAT Analogy, a double colon between two such comparisons means that the relationship Word A to Word B is the same as the relationship Word C to Word D.

The PSAT will have 13 analogies for you to complete. The beginning items are usually simple, but later items become progressively more difficult. For each item, your task is to compare a given or sample pair of capitalized words with five other pairs, and then pick the pair that best matches the relationship between the words in the sample.

It is important that you do not feel discouraged if you cannot complete the first or second analogy on the test. The way to proceed on the Analogies section of the PSAT is to try to work each item in the order in which it is presented. If you are stumped by an item, mark it and leave it; then go on to the next one. At the very end of the section, return to any items you could not complete earlier. Often, you will find that you *can* complete analogies that stopped you earlier. This is because success breeds confidence, which breeds further success. If you have successfully solved several questions, you can sometimes reach back and find solutions that eluded you before.

The key to completing analogies is to identify the pattern, and to do so in a timely fashion. As you know, you are expected to spend a limited amount of time working each section of the PSAT. This is because one purpose of the test is to assess your ability to do college-level work. The test makers have already set the standards for accuracy and speed, and they have incorporated these standards into the PSAT items. In the verbal sections, you will have 60 minutes to answer 60 items. So, if you can complete each analogy in approximately a minute, you will be able to finish the Analogy section.

This review for analogies assumes that you have an adequate vocabulary; it therefore does not employ any special word-building exercises. However, that does not mean that you can ignore vocabulary. Reading, of course, develops vocabulary. A Vocabulary Enhancer is also included in the Basic Verbal Skills Review. You are urged to study that section to improve the verbal skills you will need in college and for the verbal section of the PSAT.

ABOUT THE DIRECTIONS

As with all sections of the PSAT, it is important that you know the directions before the day of the test. Therefore, you will not waste valuable time while taking the actual test.

The directions will appear similar to the following:

DIRECTIONS: Each question below consists of a related pair of words or phrases, followed by five lettered pairs of words or phrases. Select the lettered pair that best expresses a relationship similar to that expressed in the original pair.

Example:

SMILE : MOUTH ::

(A) wink : eye   (D) tan : skin

(B) teeth : face   (E) food : gums

(C) voice : speech   ● Ⓑ Ⓒ Ⓓ Ⓔ

ABOUT THE QUESTIONS

The following is an overview of the different types of questions you will encounter on the PSAT, along with strategies for solving them quickly and accurately.

Question Type 1: Part-to-Whole

One frequent pattern is a part of an item or concept to the whole idea or concept. Examples are:

SONG : REPERTORY   CHAPTER : BOOK

If we assume that a singer has a repertory of songs, we see that a "song" is a part of a whole "repertory." A "chapter" is also a part of a whole "book." So, the pattern is Part-to-Whole, and the option to look for will have the same pattern.

This pattern can also be reversed, as indicated below:

BANK : VAULT   ZOO : CAGE

Now the pattern is Whole-to-Part. For example, if we assume that a "bank" is the whole building or organization, then a "vault" is a smaller part of it. Also, in the organization we call a "zoo," a "cage" is a part of this whole.

Question Type 2: Cause-and-Effect

Another frequent pattern is the relationship of the Cause to its Effect. Look at these examples:

BACTERIA : DISEASE   SUN : HEAT

In the first example, "bacteria" are the cause of the result "disease." In the second example, "sun" is the cause of the result "heat." In each case so far, you will look for a pattern with nouns.

The reverse pattern is Result to Cause. Examples are:

FOOD : AGRICULTURE   LAUGHTER : JOKE

Here, "food" is the result of "agriculture," which causes it to be produced. And "laughter" is the result that follows (or *should* follow) a "joke."

Question Type 3: User-to-Tool

These are examples of a third pattern, the relationship of the User-to-Tool:

DENTIST : DRILL   GARDENER : RAKE

A "dentist" uses a "drill" as a tool, and a "gardener" uses a "rake" as a tool.

The reversal of this pattern is Tool-to-User. For example:

COMPUTER : PROGRAMMER   HAMMER : CARPENTER

The "computer" is the tool, and the "programmer" is the user. The "hammer" is the tool, and the "carpenter" is the user.

A variation of this pattern might be the Instrument-to-Application, or Tool-to-Application, and its reversal. For example:

COMPUTER : WRITING   TROWEL : GARDENING

Examples of the reverse are:

OVEN : BAKING   PIANO : CONCERT

In these examples, too, the words are nouns.

Question Type 4: Group-to-Member

A fourth common pattern is the Group-to-Member. Examples are:

PRIDE : LION   SENATE : SENATOR

A "pride" is the group to which a "lion" belongs. The "Senate" is the group to which a senator belongs.

The reversal then is Member-to-Group. For example:

WOLF : PACK   WITCH : COVEN

The "wolf" is a member of a group called a "pack." And a "witch" is a member of a group called a "coven."

There are other variations of this basic pattern, such as Members-to-Group and the reverse.

Question Type 5: Trait-to-Example

Another pattern is a Trait or Characteristic to an Example of this Trait or Characteristic. For example:

DISHONESTY : LIE   BRILLIANCE : DIAMOND

Note that "dishonesty" is a character trait, and one example of this trait is a "lie." Also, "brilliance" is a physical trait and "diamond" is an example. Reversals of this pattern are common as well.

A variation of this pattern is a Greater Degree of a Characteristic to the Characteristic itself. For example:

INGENIOUS : INTELLIGENT   BRAZEN : EXTRAVERTED

In these examples, "ingenious" is a greater degree of the trait "intelligent," and "brazen" is a greater degree of the trait "extraverted." Note, too, that all four words here are adjectives.

One variation of the pattern is Lesser Degree of a Trait to the Trait itself. Another variation might be a Trait to an Opposite Trait, as here:

VALOR : COWARDICE   COURAGEOUS : PUSILLANIMOUS

The words in the first example are nouns; in the second example they are adjectives.

At times, you may not know the exact meanings of all the words. In that case, you will have to make some educated guesses. For example, you probably know words that bear resemblance to "valor" and "cowardice," such as "valiant" and "coward." So, "valor" must be a trait resembling courage, whereas "cowardice" is the opposite trait. And don't give up on the second example because of "pusillanimous." You already know what "courageous" means. If you did not know what "pusillanimous" meant, you will know what it means from now on: it means "cowardly," or the trait opposite to "courageous." However, on a test, you will know that you are looking for an adjective either opposite in meaning to "courageous" or having the same meaning. That narrows your options considerably. If you should see the option "brave : fearful," you can be reasonably sure that it is the correct option.

Question Type 6: Object-to-Material

The pattern of Object-to-Material creates an analogy between an object and the material from which it is made. This type of question is quite common, as is its reversal. For example:

SKIRT : GABARDINE   or   COTTON : SHIRT

The "skirt" is the object made of the material "gabardine," and "cotton" is the material of which the object "shirt" is made.

Question Type 7: Word-to-Definition, Synonym, or Antonym

These patterns are heavily dependent on their dictionary meanings. Examples include:

Word-Definition	*Word-Synonym*	*Word-Antonym*
SEGREGATE : SEPARATE	VACUOUS : EMPTY	DESOLATE : JOYOUS

In the first example, the word "segregate" means "separate'—it is both a definition and a synonym. Next, a synonym and definition for the word "vacuous" is "empty." Finally, a word opposite in meaning to "desolate" is the word "joyous."

Question Type 8: Symbol-to-Institution

These are examples of the pattern Symbol-to-Institution:

FLAG : GOVERNMENT   CROWN : MONARCHY

In the first case, "flag" is a symbol of the institution "government"; "crown" is the symbol of "monarchy."

These are the most commonly occurring patterns. However, many other types may appear including Plural-to-Singular, Creator-to-Creation, Male-to-Female, or Broad-Category-to-Narrow-Category (for example, FISH : SALMON).

➤ POINTS TO REMEMBER

- You will gain one point for each correct answer, and one-fourth of a point will be subtracted for each incorrect answer. Random guessing will not help you. However, if you can eliminate one choice, then you probably *should* guess. And you probably can eliminate at least one option by noting that one word or both are not in the same grammatical form as the words in the sample. By eliminating even one choice, you can make your decision from among the remaining four choices. This means you have a one in four chance of success. And since the penalty is only one-fourth of one point, you have an even chance of success.

- If you do not know the meanings, try to recall in what context you have heard the words used. This might provide some clues. However, keep in mind that you are looking for a match with the same relationship as the capitalized sample pair. You are *not* looking for a pair that matches in meaning.

- Check that the parts of speech used in both pairs of the analogy are consistent. INAUGURATE : PRESIDENT :: CORONATION : KING would not be correct because "inaugurate" is a verb and "coronation" is a noun. The two words are not the same part of speech.

- Sometimes, two options exhibit the same pattern and have the same grammatical form. This means they are the same part of speech, and they are the same in number—that is, both are singular or both are plural. In this case, you can eliminate them both, because they cannot both be right. One of the other options must be right—one that refines the pattern.

- Often, the correct option is of the same class, type, or species as the pair in the example. But this isn't ALWAYS true. For example, in the analogy PUPPY : DOG :: SAPLING : TREE, the first pair of words refers to an animal, whereas the second pair refers to a plant. However, the link between the words in both pairs is the same: the "immature subject" to the "mature subject."

- Sometimes, two options have a pattern that is the same as the sample except that one option shows the pattern in reverse. For example, assume that the sample exhibits the pattern Part-to-Whole. One choice shows this pattern, and another shows Whole-to-Part. In that case, one of these two options is probably right. The one that is right, of course, is presented in the same order as in the sample.

ANSWERING ANALOGY QUESTIONS

The recommended strategy for completing an analogy is to examine the two sample words; then, from the meanings of these words, trace the pattern or relationship between them. It is also helpful to identify the grammatical form of the words. Once you can identify the pattern and form, you can forget the meanings and search the five options for the same pattern.

You will not be looking for a match of dictionary meanings, although you will certainly need to use the dictionary meanings as clues. The match you want is the option whose members resemble one another in the same way the words of the sample pair are related. For example, if the relationship between the same pair is "part-to-whole," you will look for the option showing "part-to-whole." If the link between the same pair is "cause-to-effect," then the matching option must also be "cause-to-effect."

There are four basic steps to answering any analogy question:

| STEP 1 | Identify the meanings of both words in the sample. |

| STEP 2 | From the meanings, identify the pattern of the sample. Also identify the part of speech and the number (singular or plural) of each word. |

| STEP 3 | Ignoring the meanings of the words in the sample, now look over the options. Use the meanings of the words in each option ONLY to identify its pattern. Eliminate any options that do not match the pattern in every way, including the order of presentation and grammatical form. |

| STEP 4 | If one option remains, it is the exact match. If two options remain, examine them to see what is different about them. Compare these differences with the sample. Eliminate the option that does not match the sample perfectly. |

For example, suppose the original pair is AUTOMOBILE : BRAKE; an "automobile" is a whole and the "brake" is a part. The options are:

(A) doer : thinker

(B) man : conscience

(C) horse : ride

(D) carburetor : choke

(E) society : detergent

We can eliminate (A), since the two words have opposite meanings, and also (C), since "horse" is the doer and "ride" is what is done. We can also eliminate (E), since "society" is a whole, or producer, and "detergent" is a soap—what is produced by society.

Two options remain: (B) and (D). In (D), a "carburetor" is the part of an automobile that supplies the fuel, and "choke" is a part that restricts the amount of fuel flowing to the engine. Since these are two separate parts, we can eliminate (D). What is left is (B), the perfect match, since "conscience" is a part of the whole "man." Besides, a conscience restrains a man just as the brake restrains an automobile.

Always look for options to eliminate. However, occasionally you can save a lot of time if you just happen to note the perfect match from the start. In that case, though, you might also quickly review the other options, just to be sure your hunch was correct. For example:

CLOCK : SECOND ::

(A)   ruler : millimeter

(D)   product : shelf life

(B)   sundial : shadow

(E)   quart : capacity

(C)   arc: ellipse

Right from the start, option (A) looks right. The pattern seems to be an instrument and one of its measures, and option (A) fits nicely. A cursory look at the other options shows that no other option would be even tempting to choose.

Not all the analogies are so simple. In the previous example, suppose the original pair and all options except for option (B) remained the same. Then assume that option (B) is replaced by "scale : pounds." The pattern again is an instrument and one of its measures. Now we must choose between two options:

(A)   ruler : millimeter

(B)   scale : pounds

What is different about them? A ruler is calibrated in centimeters first and then millimeters. A scale is calibrated in pounds and then ounces. There's the difference: a millimeter is the smaller measure, but a pound is the larger measure. How is a clock calibrated? By minutes and then seconds. Obviously, the matching option should show the smaller measure—option (A).

Let's try an example in which you may need to refine the pattern you first identify. For example, suppose the original pair is SHELL : WALNUT. The five options are:

(A)   coating : candy

(D)   loaf : bread

(B)   peel : banana

(E)   root : tree

(C)   icing : cake

Our first assumption seems obvious here: Part-to-Whole. Looking more closely, we see this pattern won't work because it fits all the options except (D), loaf : bread. So, we need a more specific pattern. One possibility is "Covering-to-What-is-Covered." A "shell" covers a "walnut." Now we can eliminate (E), since the root doesn't cover the tree, and also (C), since icing doesn't cover the bottom of the cake. That leaves options (A) coating : candy and (B) peel : banana. So, what is different about a coating for a candy and the peel of a banana? The difference is that coating on candy is edible, but peel on a banana is not. Since the shell of a walnut is not edible, we can eliminate (A). This means that (B) is the exact match.

Completing the following drill questions will help you learn to apply the information you have just studied. When you complete the drill, make sure to check your answer. Refer back to the review material if you are unsure of an answer. Keep in mind that speed is important. Try to correctly answer each question in a minute or less.

☞ Drill: Analogies

DIRECTIONS: Each question below consists of a related pair of words or phrases, followed by five lettered pairs of words or phrases. Select the lettered pair that best expresses a relationship similar to that expressed in the original pair.

Example:

SMILE : MOUTH ::

(A) wink : eye

(B) teeth : face

(C) voice : speech

(D) tan : skin

(E) food : gums

● Ⓑ Ⓒ Ⓓ Ⓔ

1. BLUEPRINT : BUILDING ::

   (A) letter : alphabet

   (B) chapter : segment

   (C) score : music

   (D) clothes : closet

   (E) preface : novel

2. FINGER : KNUCKLE ::

   (A) eye : eyelid

   (B) ankle : knee

   (C) arm : elbow

   (D) hand : palm

   (E) jaw : tooth

3. RIDDLE : ENIGMA ::

   (A) string : labyrinth

   (B) ancient : sphinx

   (C) matador : bull

   (D) maze : labyrinth

   (E) alternative : dilemma

4. ENVY : GREEN ::

    (A) depressed : yellow   (D) cadaverous : ashen

    (B) red : henna   (E) fright : chalk

    (C) rage : red

5. OX : PLOW ::

    (A) teacher : prodigy   (D) horse : carriage

    (B) Shetland : pony   (E) mule : automobile

    (C) hen : egg

6. MOTORIST : ROAD SIGN ::

    (A) telegraph operator : Morse code

    (B) English : pronunciation

    (C) vocabulary : alphabet

    (D) bicyclist : roadblock

    (E) reader : pronunciation

7. WALL : MASON ::

    (A) cement : bricklayer   (D) picture : painter

    (B) magic : magician   (E) cure : doctor

    (C) friendship : stranger

8. TERSE : TURGID ::

    (A) cow : pig   (D) slim : obese

    (B) tremendous : prodigious   (E) mountain : sea

    (C) state : nation

9. BOOK : COVER ::

    (A) window : door   (D) spelling : grammar

    (B) write : compose   (E) body : skin

    (C) ink : crayon

10. SUNSET : SUNRISE ::
    (A) coming : going   (D) despair : hope
    (B) spring : autumn   (E) evening : morning
    (C) ten : five

11. TALON : HAWK ::
    (A) fang : snake   (D) tail : monkey
    (B) horn : bull   (E) shell : tortoise
    (C) claw : tiger

12. REHEARSAL : PLAY ::
    (A) draft : essay   (D) recital : concert
    (B) manual : process   (E) journal : news
    (C) applause : performance

13. GOSSIP : HAMLET ::
    (A) village : reputation   (D) chapter : book
    (B) truth : story   (E) rumor : newspaper
    (C) press : nation

14. LOOM : DISASTER ::
    (A) impend : catastrophe   (D) question : puzzle
    (B) howl : storm   (E) imminent : eminent
    (C) hurt : penalty

15. BULB : TULIP ::
    (A) pistil : stamen   (D) rose : thorn
    (B) root : grass   (E) acorn : oak
    (C) tree : leaf

16. PROBLEM : SOLUTION ::
    (A) crossword puzzle : design

(B) suitcase : handle

(C) frame: window

(D) password : entry

(E) door : key

17. VACILLATE : CHANGE ::

(A) vacate : rent

(B) index : chart

(C) trend : graph

(D) fluctuate : move

(E) endure : stamina

18. BEACH : LIFEGUARD ::

(A) fish : fisherman

(B) forest : ranger

(C) doctor : hospital

(D) mountain : climber

(E) restaurant : supplier

19. ECOLOGIST : ENVIRONMENT ::

(A) psychologist : plants

(B) botanist : animals

(C) geologist : earth

(D) ventriloquist : dummy

(E) cartographer : people

20. IMPROMPTU : MEMORIZED ::

(A) spontaneous : calculated

(B) read : recited

(C) glib : forced

(D) unrehearsed : extemporaneous

(E) tacit : verbose

21. HALCYON : MARTIAL ::

(A) moon : Mars

(B) military song : militant

(C) peaceful : warlike

(D) soothed : worried

(E) belligerent : fighting

22. TEAM : COACH ::

(A) corporal : squad

(B) army : general

(C) team : member   (D) club : advisor

(E) club : president

23. HYPOCHONDRIAC : HEALTH ::

(A) addict : drugs   (D) narcotic : sickness

(B) miser : money   (E) weakness : strength

(C) glutton : food

24. GOLD : ORE ::

(A) dear : cheap   (D) coal : miner

(B) iron : steel   (E) intelligence : astuteness

(C) pearls : oysters

25. EXUBERANT : DOWNCAST ::

(A) exultant : lavish   (D) eager : overzealous

(B) parsimonious : abundant (E) effusive : melancholy

(C) congregation : dispersal

26. MAY : MONTH ::

(A) year : decade   (D) day : hour

(B) Thursday : day   (E) Friday : week

(C) second : minute

27. PASSED : ELATION ::

(A) poem : intellectual   (D) success : emotion

(B) failed : dejection   (E) approved : disapproval

(C) rejected : angry

28. LARIAT : COWBOY ::

(A) medicine : patient   (D) lawyer : client

(B) scalpel : surgeon   (E) spice : gourmet

(C) manuscript : author

29. SALUTATORIAN : VALEDICTORIAN ::

   (A) crisis : climax

   (B) beginning : end

   (C) runner-up : best

   (D) prologue : play

   (E) incipient : terminal

30. GOURMET : CAVIAR ::

   (A) plebeian : patrician

   (B) clairvoyant : seance

   (C) connoisseur : masterpiece

   (D) critic : edition

   (E) million : wine

31. STAR : GALAXY ::

   (A) kennel : dog

   (B) atom : molecule

   (C) sea : fish

   (D) regiment : soldier

   (E) shelf : hook

32. MOVEMENT : SYMPHONY ::

   (A) act : play

   (B) notes : staff

   (C) melody : harmony

   (D) key : piano

   (E) harmony : counterpoint

33. LAUGH : JOKE ::

   (A) moral : story

   (B) pain : headache

   (C) film : negative

   (D) painting : sketch

   (E) caboose : train

34. RELIGION : RITUAL ::

   (A) society : etiquette

   (B) protocol : diplomacy

   (C) wisdom : education

   (D) science : truth

   (E) rules : game

35. EARTH : AXIS ::

   (A) wheel : hub

   (B) earth : sun

(C) state : nation   (D) orbit : firmament

(E) mountain : sea

36. PHILOLOGIST : LANGUAGE ::

   (A) ornithologist : birds   (D) etymologist : insects

   (B) botanist : animals   (E) pediatrician : feet

   (C) biologist : cells

37. AGNOSTIC : ATHEIST ::

   (A) orthodox : heterodox   (D) doubt : definition

   (B) heretic : pagan   (E) vague : defiant

   (C) unbeliever : iconoclast

38. SPECTACLES : VISION ::

   (A) statement : contention   (D) hay : horse

   (B) airplane : locomotion   (E) hero : worship

   (C) canoe : paddle

39. WATER : SPONGE ::

   (A) desert : dry   (D) margin : hole

   (B) pen : pencil   (E) wet : drink

   (C) ink : blotter

40. PRESCIENCE : ORACLE ::

   (A) blunderbuss : soldier

   (B) unimpressiveness : gnome

   (C) priest : deity

   (D) omniscience : seer

   (E) highness : prince

ANALOGIES

ANSWER KEY

Drill: Analogies

1.	(C)	11.	(C)	21.	(C)	31.	(B)
2.	(C)	12.	(A)	22.	(D)	32.	(A)
3.	(D)	13.	(C)	23.	(B)	33.	(B)
4.	(C)	14.	(A)	24.	(C)	34.	(A)
5.	(D)	15.	(E)	25.	(E)	35.	(A)
6.	(E)	16.	(E)	26.	(B)	36.	(A)
7.	(D)	17.	(D)	27.	(B)	37.	(D)
8.	(D)	18.	(B)	28.	(B)	38.	(B)
9.	(E)	19.	(C)	29.	(C)	39.	(C)
10.	(E)	20.	(A)	30.	(C)	40.	(D)

PSAT/ NMSQT

CHAPTER 6

Attacking Critical Reading Questions

Chapter 6

ATTACKING CRITICAL READING QUESTIONS

The Critical Reading sections of the PSAT are indeed critical, for they make up 50 percent of the entire verbal section content. In all, you will encounter 30 Critical Reading questions. "Why," you must wonder, "would this much importance be attached to reading?" The reason is simple. Your ability to read at a strong pace while grasping a solid understanding of the material is a key factor in your high school performance and your potential college success. But "critical" can be taken in another sense, for the PSAT will ask you to be a reading critic. You'll need not only to be able to summarize the material but analyze it, make judgments about it, and make educated guesses about what the writer implies and infers. Even your ability to understand vocabulary in context will come under scrutiny. "Can I," you ask yourself, "meet the challenge?" *Yes,* and preparation is the means!

CRITICAL READING PASSAGES AND QUESTIONS

Within the PSAT verbal section you will be given four Critical Reading passages, two of 400-500 words, one of 550-700 words, and two reading selections of 700-850 words combined, which are referred to as a double passage. The double passage will be composed of two separate works which you will be asked to compare or contrast. The reading content of the passages will cover:

- the humanities (philosophy, the fine arts)
- the social sciences (psychology, archaeology, anthropology, economics, political science, sociology, history)
- the natural sciences (biology, geology, astronomy, chemistry, physics)
- narration (fiction, nonfiction)

Following each passage are about 5-13 questions, depending on the length of the passage. These questions are of four types:

1. Synthesis/Analysis

2. Evaluation

3. Vocabulary-in-Context

4. Interpretation

Through this review, you'll learn not only how to identify these types of questions, but how to successfully attack each one. Familiarity with the test format, combined with solid reading strategies, will prove invaluable in answering the questions quickly and accurately.

ABOUT THE DIRECTIONS

Make sure to study and learn the directions to save yourself time during the actual test. You should simply skim them when beginning the section. The directions will read much like the following.

> **DIRECTIONS**: Read each passage and answer the questions that follow. Each question will be based on the information stated or implied in the passage or its introduction.

A variation of these directions will be presented as follows for the double passage.

> **DIRECTIONS**: Read the passages and answer the questions that follow. Each question will be based on the information stated or implied in the selections or their introductions, and may be based on the relationship between the passages.

ABOUT THE PASSAGES

You may encounter any of a number of passage types in the Critical Reading section. These passages may consist of straight text, dialogue and text, or narration. A passage may appear by itself or as part of a pair in a double passage. A brief introduction will be provided for each passage to set the scene for the text being presented.

To familiarize yourself with the types of passages you will encounter, review the examples which follow. Remember that two passages will be

400-500 words, one will be 550-700 words, and that the two passages in the double passage will consist of 700-850 words combined. The content of the passages will include the humanities, social sciences, natural sciences, and also narrative text.

A **humanities passage** may discuss such topics as philosophy, the fine arts, and language. The following is an example of such a passage. It falls into the 550- to 700-word range.

> *Throughout his pursuit of knowledge and enlightenment, the philosopher Socrates made many enemies among the Greek citizens. The following passage is an account of the trial resulting from their accusations.*

1   The great philosopher Socrates was put on trial in Athens in 400 B.C. on charges of corrupting the youth and of impiety. As recorded in Plato's dialogue *The Apology,* Socrates began his defense by saying he was going to "speak plainly and honestly," unlike the eloquent sophists the Athenian
5   jury was accustomed to hearing. His appeal to unadorned language offended the jurors, who were expecting to be entertained.

Socrates identified the two sets of accusers that he had to face: the past and the present. The former had filled the jurors' heads with lies about him when they were young, and was considered by Socrates to be
10 the most dangerous. The accusers from the past could not be cross-examined, and they had already influenced the jurors when they were both naive and impressionable. This offended the jury because it called into question their ability to be objective and render a fair judgment.

The philosopher addressed the charges himself, and dismissed them
15 as mere covers for the deeper attack on his philosophical activity. That activity, which involved questioning others until they revealed contradictions in their beliefs, had given rise to Socrates' motto, "The unexamined life is not worth living," and the "Socratic Method," which is still employed in many law schools today. This critical questioning of leading
20 Athenians had made Socrates very unpopular with those in power and, he insisted, was what led to his trial. This challenge to the legitimacy of the legal system itself further alienated his judges.

Socrates tried to explain that his philosophical life came about by accident. He had been content to be a humble stone mason until the day
25 that a friend informed him that the Oracle of Delphi had said that "Socrates is the wisest man in Greece." Socrates had been so surprised by this statement, and so sure of its inaccuracy, that he set about disproving it by talking to the reputed wise men of Athens and showing how much more knowledge they possessed. Unfortunately, as he told the jury, those

30 citizens reputed to be wise (politicians, businessmen, artists) turned out to
be ignorant, either by knowing absolutely nothing, or by having limited
knowledge in their fields of expertise and assuming knowledge of everything else. Of these, Socrates had to admit, "I am wiser, because although
all of us have little knowledge, I am aware of my ignorance, while they are
35 not." But this practice of revealing prominent citizens' ignorance and arrogance did not earn Socrates their affection, especially when the bright
young men of Athens began following him around and delighting in the
disgracing of their elders. Hence, in his view, the formal charges of "corrupting the youth" and "impiety" were a pretext to retaliate for the deeper
40 offense of challenging the pretensions of the establishment.

Although Socrates viewed the whole trial as a sham, he cleverly
refuted the charges by using the same method of questioning that got him
in trouble in the first place. Against the charges of corrupting the youth,
Socrates asked his chief accuser, Meletus, if any wanted to arm himself, to
45 which Meletus answered, "no." Then, Socrates asked if one's associates
had an effect on one: Good people for good, and evil people for evil, to
which Meletus answered, "yes." Next, Socrates asked if corrupting one's
companions makes them better or worse, to which Meletus responded,
"worse." Finally Socrates set the trap by asking Meletus if Socrates had
50 corrupted the youth intentionally or unintentionally. Meletus, wanting to
make the charges as bad as possible, answered, "intentionally." Socrates
showed the contradictory nature of the charge, since by intentionally corrupting his companions he made them worse, thereby bringing harm on
himself. He also refuted the second charge of impiety in the same manner,
55 by showing that its two components (teaching about strange gods and
atheism) were inconsistent.

Although Socrates had logically refuted the charges against him, the
Athenian jury found him guilty, and Meletus proposed the death penalty.
The defendant Socrates was allowed to propose an alternative penalty and
60 Socrates proposed a state pension, so he could continue his philosophical
activity to the benefit of Athens. He stated that this is what he deserved.
The Athenian jury, furious over his presumption, voted the death penalty
and, thus, one of the great philosophers of the Western heritage was ex-
ecuted.

The **social science passage** may discuss such topics as psychology,
archaeology, anthropology, economics, political science, sociology, and
history. The following is an example of such a passage. It falls into the
400- to 550-word range.

Not only does music have the ability to entertain and enthrall, but it also has the capacity to heal. The following passage illustrates the recent indoctrination of music therapy.

1   Music's power to affect moods and stir emotions has been well known for as long as music has existed. Stories about the music of ancient Greece tell of the healing powers of Greek music. Leopold Mozart, the father of Wolfgang, wrote that if the Greeks' music could heal the sick,
5   then our music should be able to bring the dead back to life. Unfortunately, today's music cannot do quite that much.

    The healing power of music, taken for granted by ancient man and by many primitive societies, is only recently becoming accepted by medical professionals as a new way of healing the emotionally ill.
10   Using musical activities involving patients, the music therapist seeks to restore mental and physical health. Music therapists usually work with emotionally disturbed patients as part of a team of therapists and doctors. Music therapists work together with physicians, psychiatrists, psychologists, physical therapists, nurses, teachers, recreation leaders, and families
15   of patients.

    The rehabilitation that a music therapist gives to patients can be in the form of listening, performing, taking lessons on an instrument, or even composing. A therapist may help a patient regain lost coordination by teaching the patient how to play an instrument. Speech defects can some-
20   times be helped by singing activities. Some patients need the social awareness of group activities, but others may need individual attention to build self-confidence. The music therapist must learn what kinds of activities are best for each patient.

    In addition to working with patients, the music therapist has to attend
25   meetings with other therapists and doctors that work with the same patients to discuss progress and plan new activities. Written reports to doctors about patients' responses to treatment are another facet of the music therapist's work.

    Hospitals, schools, retirement homes, and community agencies and
30   clinics are some of the sites where music therapists work. Some music therapists work in private studies with patients that are sent to them by medical doctors, psychologists, and psychiatrists. Music therapy can be done in studios, recreation rooms, hospital wards, or classrooms depending on the type of activity and needs of the patients.
35   Qualified music therapists have followed a four-year course with a major emphasis in music plus courses in biological science, anthropology, sociology, psychology, and music therapy. General studies in English, history, speech, and government complete the requirements for a Bachelor of Music Therapy. After college training, a music therapist must partici-

40 pate in a six-month training internship under the guidance of a registered music therapist.

Students who have completed college courses and have demonstrated their ability during the six-month internship can become registered music therapists by applying to the National Association for Music Therapy, Inc.
45 New methods and techniques of music therapy are always being developed, so the trained therapist must continue to study new articles, books, and reports throughout his/her career.

The **natural science passage** may discuss such topics as biology, geology, astronomy, chemistry, and physics. The following is an example of such a passage. It falls into the 550- to 700- word range.

The following article was written by a physical chemist and recounts the conflict between volcanic matter in the atmosphere and airplane windows. It was published in a scientific periodical in 1989.

(Reprinted by permission of *American Heritage Magazine*, a division of Forbes Inc., © Forbes Inc., 1989.)

1   Several years ago the airlines discovered a new kind of problem—a window problem. The acrylic windows on some of their 747s were getting hazy and dirty-looking. Suspicious travelers thought the airlines might have stopped cleaning them, but the windows were not dirty; they were
5 inexplicably deteriorating within as little as 390 hours of flight time, even though they were supposed to last for five to ten years. Boeing looked into it.

At first the company thought the culprit might be one well known in modern technology, the component supplier who changes materials with-
10 out telling the customer. Boeing quickly learned this was not the case, so there followed an extensive investigation that eventually brought in the Air Transport Association, geologists, and specialists in upper-atmosphere chemistry, and the explanation turned out to be not nearly so mundane. Indeed, it began to look like a grand reenactment of an ancient Aztec
15 myth: the struggle between the eagle and the serpent, which is depicted on the Mexican flag.

The serpent in this case is an angry Mexican volcano, El Chichon. Like its reptilian counterpart, it knows how to spit venom at the eyes of its adversary. In March and April of 1982 the volcano, in an unusual eruption
20 pattern, ejected millions of tons of sulfur-rich material directly into the stratosphere. In less than a year, a stratospheric cloud had blanketed the entire Northern Hemisphere. Soon the photochemistry of the upper atmosphere converted much of the sulfur into tiny droplets of concentrated sulfuric acid.

25   The eagle in the story is the 747, poking occasionally into the lower part of the stratosphere in hundreds of passenger flights daily. Its two hundred windows are made from an acrylic polymer, which makes beautifully clear, strong windows but was never intended to withstand attack by strong acids.

30   The stratosphere is very different from our familiar troposphere environment. Down here the air is humid, with a lot of vertical convection to carry things up and down; the stratosphere is bone-dry, home to the continent-striding jet stream, with unceasing horizontal winds at an average of 120 miles per hour. A mist of acid droplets accumulated gradually near the
35   lower edge of the stratosphere, settling there at a thickness of about a mile a year, was able to wait for planes to come along.

As for sulfuric acid, most people know only the relatively benign liquid in a car battery: 80 percent water and 20 percent acid. The stratosphere dehydrated the sulfuric acid into a persistent, corrosive mist 75
40   percent pure acid, an extremely aggressive liquid. Every time the 747 poked into the stratosphere—on almost every long flight—acid droplets struck the windows and began to react with their outer surface, causing it to swell. This built up stresses between the softened outer layer and the underlying material. Finally, parallel hairline cracks developed, creating
45   the hazy appearance. The hazing was sped up by the mechanical stresses always present in the windows of a pressurized cabin.

The airlines suffered through more than a year of window replacements before the acid cloud finally dissipated. Ultimately the drops reached the lower edge of the stratosphere, were carried away into the
50   lower atmosphere, and finally came down in the rain. In the meantime, more resistant window materials and coatings were developed. (As for the man-made sulfur dioxide that causes acid rain, it never gets concentrated enough to attack the window material. El Chichon was unusual in its ejection of sulfur directly into the stratosphere, and the 747 is unusual in
55   its frequent entrance into the stratosphere.)

As for the designers of those windows, it is hard to avoid the conclusion that a perfectly adequate engineering design was defeated by bad luck. After all, this was the only time since the invention of the airplane that there were acid droplets of this concentration in the upper atmosphere.
60   But reliability engineers, an eminently rational breed, are very uncomfortable when asked to talk about luck. In principle it should be possible to anticipate events, and the failure to do so somehow seems like a professional failure. The cosmos of the engineer has no room for poltergeists, demons, or other mystic elements. But might it accommodate the inexo-
65   rable scenario of an ancient Aztec myth?

A **narrative passage dealing with fictional material** may be in the form of dialogue between characters, or one character speaking to the reader. The following is an example of the latter. It falls into the 700- to 850-word range.

In this passage, the narrator discovers that he has been transported to King Arthur's court in the year A.D. 528

1   The moment I got a chance I slipped aside privately and touched an ancient common-looking man on the shoulder and said, in an insinuating, confidential way—

"Friend, do me a kindness. Do you belong to the asylum, or are you
5 just here on a visit or something like that?"

He looked me over stupidly, and said—

"Marry, fair sir, me seemeth—"

"That will do," I said; "I reckon you are a patient."

I moved away, cogitating, and at the same time keeping an eye out
10 for any chance passenger in his right mind that might come along and give me some light. I judged I had found one, presently; so I drew him aside and said in his ear—

"If I could see the head keeper a minute—only just a minute—"

"Prithee do not let me."
15   "Let you *what?*"

"Hinder me, then, if the word please thee better." Then he went on to say he was an under-cook and could not stop to gossip, though he would like it another time; for it would comfort his very liver to know where I got my clothes. As he started away he pointed and said yonder was one
20 who was idle enough for my purpose, and was seeking me besides, no doubt. This was an airy slim boy in shrimp-colored tights that made him look like a forked carrot; the rest of his gear was blue silk and dainty laces and ruffles; and he had long yellow curls, and wore a plumed pink satin cap tilted complacently over his ear. By his look, he was good-natured; by
25 his gait, he was satisfied with himself. He was pretty enough to frame. He arrived, looked me over with a smiling and impudent curiosity; said he had come for me, and informed me that he was a page.

"Go 'long," I said; "you ain't more than a paragraph."

It was pretty severe, but I was nettled. However, it never phazed him;
30 he didn't appear to know he was hurt. He began to talk and laugh, in happy, thoughtless, boyish fashion, as we walked along, and made himself old friends with me at once; asked me all sorts of questions about myself and about my clothes, but never waited for an answer—always chattered straight ahead, as if he didn't know he had asked a question and wasn't
35 expecting any reply, until at last he happened to mention that he was born

in the beginning of the year 513.

It made the cold chills creep over me! I stopped, and said, a little faintly:

"Maybe I didn't hear you just right. Say it again—and say it slow.
40 What year was it?"

"513."

"513! You don't look it! Come, my boy, I am a stranger and friend-less: be honest and honorable with me. Are you in your right mind?"

He said he was.

45   "Are these other people in their right minds?"

He said they were.

"And this isn't an asylum? I mean, it isn't a place where they cure crazy people?"

He said it wasn't.

50   "Well, then," I said, "either I am a lunatic, or something just as awful has happened. Now tell me, honest and true, where am I?"

"In King Arthur's Court."

I waited a minute, to let that idea shudder its way home, and then said:

55   "And according to your notions, what year is it now?"

"528—nineteenth of June."

I felt a mournful sinking at the heart, and muttered: "I shall never see my friends again—never, never again. They will not be born for more than thirteen hundred years yet."

60   I seemed to believe the boy, I didn't know why. *Something* in me seemed to believe him—my consciousness, as you may say; but my reason didn't. My reason straightway began to clamor; that was natural. I didn't know how to go about satisfying it, because I knew that the testimony of men wouldn't serve—my reason would say they were lunatics, and throw
65 out their evidence. But all of a sudden I stumbled on the very thing, just by luck. I knew that the only total eclipse of the sun in the first half of the sixth century occurred on the 21st of June, A. D. 528, o. s., and began at 3 minutes after 12 noon. I also knew that no total eclipse of the sun was due in what to *me* was the present year—*i.e.*, 1879. So, if I could keep my
70 anxiety and curiosity from eating the heart out of me for forty-eight hours, I should then find out for certain whether this boy was telling me the truth or not.

A narrative passage dealing with nonfiction material may appear in the form of a speech or any such discourse in which one person speaks to a group of people or to the reader. The following two selections are ex-amples of nonfiction narratives. Together, they are also an example of a double passage, in which the subject matter in the selections can be either compared or contrasted. As you will recall, the two selections will total 700 to 850.

The following passages are excerpts from two different Presidential Inaugural Addresses. Passage 1 comes from President John F. Kennedy's Inaugural Address, given on January 20, 1961. Passage 2 was given by President Franklin D. Roosevelt on March 4, 1933.

Passage 1

1   Let every nation know, whether it wishes us well or ill, that we shall pay any price, bear any burden, meet any hardship, support any friend, oppose any foe to assure the survival and the success of liberty.

     This much we pledge—and more.

5   To those old allies whose cultural and spiritual origins we share, we pledge the loyalty of faithful friends. United, there is little we cannot do in a host of co-operative ventures. Divided, there is little we can do, for we dare not meet a powerful challenge at odds and split asunder.

     To those new states whom we welcome to the ranks of the free, we
10 pledge our word that one form of colonial control shall not have passed away merely to be replaced by a far more iron tyranny. We shall not always expect to find them supporting our view. But we shall always hope to find them strongly supporting their own freedom, and to remember that, in the past, those who foolishly sought power by riding the back of the
15 tiger ended up inside.

     To those peoples in the huts and villages of half the globe struggling to break the bonds of mass misery, we pledge our best efforts to help them help themselves, for whatever period is required, not because the Communists may be doing it, not because we seek their votes, but because it is
20 right. If a free society cannot help the many who are poor, it cannot save the few who are rich.

Passage 2

     This is pre-eminently the time to speak the truth, the whole truth, frankly and boldly. Nor need we shrink from honestly facing conditions in our country today. This great nation will endure as it has endured, will
25 revive, and will prosper.

     So first of all let me assert my firm belief that the only thing we have to fear is fear itself—nameless, unreasoning, unjustified terror, which paralyzes needed efforts to convert retreat into advance.

     In every dark hour of our national life a leadership of frankness and
30 vigor has met with that understanding and support of the people them-

selves which is essential to victory. I am convinced that you will again give that support to leadership in these critical days.

In such a spirit on my part and yours we face our common difficulties. They concern, thank God, only material things. Values have shrunken
35 to fantastic levels; taxes have risen; our ability to pay has fallen; government of all kinds is faced by serious curtailment of income; the means of exchange are frozen in the currents of trade; the withered leaves of industrial enterprise lie on every side; farmers find no markets for their produce; the savings of many years in thousands of families are gone.

40 More important, a host of unemployed citizens face the grim problem of existence, and an equally great number toil with little return. Only a foolish optimist can deny the dark realities of the moment.

Yet our distress comes from no failure of substance. We are stricken by no plague of locusts. Compared with the perils which our forefathers
45 conquered because they believed and were not afraid, we have still much to be thankful for. Nature still offers her bounty, and human efforts have multiplied it. Plenty is at our doorstep, but a generous use of it languishes in the very sight of the supply.

Primarily, this is because the rulers of the exchange of mankind's
50 goods have failed through their own stubbornness and their own incompetence, have admitted their failure and abdicated. Practices of the unscrupulous money-changers stand indicted in the court of public opinion, rejected by the hearts and minds of men.

ABOUT THE QUESTIONS

As previously mentioned, there are four major question types which appear in the Critical Reading section. The following explains what these questions will cover.

Question Type 1: Synthesis/Analysis

Synthesis/analysis questions deal with the structure of the passage and how one part relates to another part or to the text as a whole. These questions may ask you to look at passage details and from them, point out general themes or concepts. They might ask you to trace problems, causes, effects, and solutions or to understand the points of an argument or persuasive passage. They might ask you to compare or contrast different aspects of the passage. Synthesis/analysis questions may also involve inferences, asking you to decide what the details of the passage imply about the author's general tone or attitude. Key terms in synthesis/analysis questions are example, difference, general, compare, contrast, cause, effect, and result.

Question Type 2: Evaluation

Evaluation questions involve judgments about the worth of the essay as a whole. You may be asked to consider concepts the author assumes rather than factually proves and to judge whether or not the author presents a logically consistent case. Does he/she prove the points through generalization, citing an authority, use of example, implication, personal experience, or factual data? You'll need to be able to distinguish the supportive bases for the argumentative theme. Almost as a book reviewer, you'll also be asked to pinpoint the author's writing techniques. What is the style, the tone? Who is the intended audience? How might the author's points relate to information outside the essay, itself? Key terms you'll often see in evaluation questions and answer choices are generalization, implication, and support.

Question Type 3: Vocabulary-in-Context

Vocabulary-in-context questions occur in several formats. You'll be given easy words with challenging choices or the reverse. You'll need to know multiple meanings of words. You'll encounter difficult words and difficult choices. In some cases, your knowledge of prefixes-roots-suffixes will gain you clear advantage. In addition, connotations will be the means of deciding, in some cases, which answer is the best. Of course, how the term works in the textual context is the key to the issue.

Question Type 4: Interpretation

Interpretation questions ask you to decide on a valid explanation or clarification of the author's points. Based on the text, you'll be asked to distinguish probable motivations and effects or actions not stated outright in the essay. Furthermore, you'll need to be familiar with clichés, euphemisms, catch phrases, colloquialisms, metaphors, and similes, and be able to explain them in straightforward language. Interpretation question stems usually have a word or phrase enclosed in quotation marks.

Keep in mind that being able to categorize accurately is not of prime importance. What is important, however, is that you are familiar with all the types of information you will be asked and that you have a set of basic strategies to use when answering questions. The remainder of this review will give you these skills.

➤ POINTS TO REMEMBER

- Do not spend too much time answering any one question.

- Vocabulary plays a large part in successful critical reading. As a long-term approach to improving your ability and therefore your test scores, read as much as you can of any type of material. Your speed, comprehension, and vocabulary will grow.

- Be an engaged reader. Don't let your mind wander. Focus through annotation and key terms.

- Time is an important factor on the PSAT. Therefore, the rate at which you are reading is very important. If you are concerned that you may be reading too slow, try to compete with yourself. For example, if you are reading at 120 words per minute, try to improve your speed to 250 words per minute (without decreasing your understanding). Remember that improving reading speed is not a means in itself. Improved comprehension with fewer regressions must accompany this speed increase. Make sure to read, read, read. The more you read, the more you will sharpen your skills.

ANSWERING CRITICAL READING QUESTIONS

You should follow these steps as you begin each critical reading passage. They will act as a guide when answering the questions.

| STEP 1 | Before you address the critical reading, answer all analogies and sentence completions within the given verbal section. You can answer more questions per minute in these short sections than in the reading, and since all answers are credited equally, you'll get the most for your time here.

Now, find the Critical Reading passage(s). If more than one passage appears, give each a brief overview. Attack the easiest and most interesting passages first. Critical Reading passages are not automatically presented in the order of least-to-most difficult. The difficulty or ease of a reading selection is an individual matter, determined by the reader's own specific interests and past experience, so what you might consider easy, someone else might consider hard, and *vice-versa*. Again, time is an issue, so you need to begin with something you can quickly understand in order to get to the questions, where the pay-off lies.

| STEP 2 | First, read the question stems following the passage, making sure to block out the answer choices with your free hand. (You don't want to be misled by incorrect choices.) |

In question stems, underline key words, phrases, and dates. For example:

1. In line 27, "<u>stand</u>" means:

2. From <u>1776</u> <u>to</u> <u>1812</u>, <u>King</u> <u>George</u> did:

3. <u>Lincoln</u> was <u>similar</u> to <u>Pericles</u> in that:

The act of underlining takes little time and will force you to focus first on the main ideas in the questions, then in the essays.

You will notice that questions often note a line number for reference. Place a small mark by the appropriate lines in the essay itself to remind yourself to read those parts very carefully. You'll still have to refer to these lines upon answering the questions, but you'll be able to find them quickly.

| STEP 3 | If the passage is not divided into paragraphs, read the first 10 lines. If the passage is divided into manageable paragraphs, read the first paragraph. Make sure to read at a moderate pace, as fast skimming will not be sufficient for comprehension, while slow, forced reading will take too much time and yield too little understanding of the overall passage. |

In the margin of your test booklet, using two or three words, note the main point of the paragraph/section. Don't labor long over the exact wording. Underline key terms, phrases, or ideas when you notice them. If a sentence is particularly difficult, don't spend too much time trying to figure it out. Bracket it, though, for easy reference in the remote instance that it might serve as the basis for a question.

You should proceed through each paragraph/section in a similar manner. Don't read the whole passage with the intention of going back and filling in the main points. Read carefully and consistently, annotating and underlining to keep your mind on the context.

Upon finishing the entire passage, quickly review your notes in the margin. They should give you main ideas and passage structure (chronological, cause and effect, process, comparison-contrast). Ask yourself what the author's attitude is toward his/her subject. What might you infer from the selection? What might the author say next? Some of these questions may appear, and you'll be immediately prepared to answer.

STEP 4 | Start with the first question and work through to the last question. The order in which the questions are presented follows the order of the passage, so going for the "easy" questions first rather than answering the questions consecutively will cost you valuable time in searching and backtracking.

Be sure to block the answer choices for each question before you read the question, itself. Again, you don't want to be misled.

If a line number is mentioned, quickly re-read that section. In addition, circle your own answer to the question *before* viewing the choices. Then, carefully examine each answer choice, eliminating those which are obviously incorrect. If you find a close match to your own answer, don't assume that it is the best answer, as an even better one may be among the last choices. Remember, in the PSAT, only one answer is correct, and it is the *best* one, not simply one that will work.

Once you've proceeded through all the choices, eliminating incorrect answers as you go, choose from among those remaining. If the choice is not clear, reread the question stem and the referenced passage lines to seek tone or content you might have missed. If the answer now is not readily obvious and you have reduced your choices by eliminating at least one, then simply choose one of the remaining and proceed to the next question. Place a small mark in your test booklet to remind you, should you have time at the end of this test section, to review the question and seek a more accurate answer.

Now, let's go back to our natural sciences passage. Read the passage, and then answer the questions which follow using the skills gained through this review.

The following article was written by a physical chemist and recounts the conflict between volcanic matter in the atmosphere and airplane windows. It was published in a scientific periodical in 1989.

(Reprinted by permission of *American Heritage Magazine*, a division of Forbes Inc., © Forbes Inc., 1989.)

1   Several years ago the airlines discovered a new kind of problem—a window problem. The acrylic windows on some of their 747s were getting hazy and dirty-looking. Suspicious travelers thought the airlines might have stopped cleaning them, but the windows were not dirty; they were
5   inexplicably deteriorating within as little as 390 hours of flight time, even though they were supposed to last for five to ten years. Boeing looked into it.

At first the company thought the culprit might be one well known in

modern technology, the component supplier who changes materials with-
10 out telling the customer. Boeing quickly learned this was not the case, so
there followed an extensive investigation that eventually brought in the
Air Transport Association, geologists, and specialists in upper-atmosphere
chemistry, and the explanation turned out to be not nearly so mundane.
Indeed, it began to look like a grand reenactment of an ancient Aztec
15 myth: the struggle between the eagle and the serpent, which is depicted on
the Mexican flag.

The serpent in this case is an angry Mexican volcano, El Chichon.
Like its reptilian counterpart, it knows how to spit venom at the eyes of its
adversary. In March and April of 1982 the volcano, in an unusual eruption
20 pattern, ejected millions of tons of sulfur-rich material directly into the
stratosphere. In less than a year, a stratospheric cloud had blanketed the
entire Northern Hemisphere. Soon the photochemistry of the upper atmosphere converted much of the sulfur into tiny droplets of concentrated
sulfuric acid.

25 The eagle in the story is the 747, poking occasionally into the lower
part of the stratosphere in hundreds of passenger flights daily. Its two
hundred windows are made from an acrylic polymer, which makes beautifully clear, strong windows but was never intended to withstand attack by
strong acids.

30 The stratosphere is very different from our familiar troposphere environment. Down here the air is humid, with a lot of vertical convection to
carry things up and down; the stratosphere is bone-dry, home to the continent-striding jet stream, with unceasing horizontal winds at an average of
120 miles per hour. A mist of acid droplets accumulated gradually near the
35 lower edge of the stratosphere, settling there at a thickness of about a mile
a year, was able to wait for planes to come along.

As for sulfuric acid, most people know only the relatively benign
liquid in a car battery: 80 percent water and 20 percent acid. The stratosphere dehydrated the sulfuric acid into a persistent, corrosive mist 75
40 percent pure acid, an extremely aggressive liquid. Every time the 747
poked into the stratosphere—on almost every long flight—acid droplets
struck the windows and began to react with their outer surface, causing it
to swell. This built up stresses between the softened outer layer and the
underlying material. Finally, parallel hairline cracks developed, creating
45 the hazy appearance. The hazing was sped up by the mechanical stresses
always present in the windows of a pressurized cabin.

The airlines suffered through more than a year of window replacements before the acid cloud finally dissipated. Ultimately the drops
reached the lower edge of the stratosphere, were carried away into the
50 lower atmosphere, and finally came down in the rain. In the meantime,

more resistant window materials and coatings were developed. (As for the man-made sulfur dioxide that causes acid rain, it never gets concentrated enough to attack the window material. El Chichon was unusual in its ejection of sulfur directly into the stratosphere, and the 747 is unusual in
55 its frequent entrance into the stratosphere.)

As for the designers of those windows, it is hard to avoid the conclusion that a perfectly adequate engineering design was defeated by bad luck. After all, this was the only time since the invention of the airplane that there were acid droplets of this concentration in the upper atmosphere.
60 But reliability engineers, an eminently rational breed, are very uncomfortable when asked to talk about luck. In principle it should be possible to anticipate events, and the failure to do so somehow seems like a professional failure. The cosmos of the engineer has no room for poltergeists, demons, or other mystic elements. But might it accommodate the inexo-
65 rable scenario of an ancient Aztec myth?

1. Initially the hazy windows were thought by the company to be a result of

    (A) small particles of volcanic glass abrading their surfaces.

    (B) substandard window material substituted by the parts supplier.

    (C) ineffectual cleaning products used by the maintenance crew.

    (D) a build-up of the man-made sulfur dioxide that also causes acid rain.

    (E) the humidity.

2. When first seeking a reason for the abraded windows, both the passengers and Boeing management exhibited attitudes of

    (A) disbelief.   (D) pacifism.

    (B) optimism.   (E) disregard.

    (C) cynicism.

3. In line 13, "mundane" means

    (A) simple.   (D) ordinary.

    (B) complicated.   (E) important.

    (C) far-reaching.

4. In what ways is El Chichon like the serpent on the Mexican flag, knowing how to "spit venom at the eyes of its adversary" (lines 18-19)?

    (A) It seeks to poison its adversary with its bite.

    (B) It carefully plans its attack on an awaited intruder.

    (C) It ejects tons of destructive sulfuric acid to damage jet windows.

    (D) It angrily blankets the Northern Hemisphere with sulfuric acid.

    (E) It protects itself with the acid rain it produces.

5. The term "photochemistry" in line 22 refers to a chemical change caused by

    (A) the proximity of the sun.

    (B) the drop in temperature at stratospheric altitudes.

    (C) the jet stream's "unceasing horizontal winds."

    (D) the vertical convection of the troposphere.

    (E) the amount of sulfur present in the atmosphere.

6. Unlike the troposphere, the stratosphere

    (A) is extremely humid as it is home to the jet stream.

    (B) contains primarily vertical convections to cause air particles to rise and fall rapidly.

    (C) is approximately one mile thick.

    (D) contains powerful horizontal winds resulting in an excessively dry atmosphere.

    (E) contains very little wind activity.

7. In line 40, "aggressive" means

    (A) exasperating.   (D) assertive.

    (B) enterprising.   (E) surprising.

    (C) prone to attack.

8. As the eagle triumphed over the serpent in the Mexican flag,

   (A) El Chichon triumphed over the plane, as the 747s had to change their flight altitudes.

   (B) the newly designed window material deflected the damaging acid droplets.

   (C) the 747 was able to fly unchallenged by acid droplets a year later as they drifted away to the lower atmosphere.

   (D) the reliability engineers are now prepared for any run of "bad luck" which may approach their aircraft.

   (E) the component supplier of the windows changed materials without telling the customers.

9. The reliability engineers are described as people who

   (A) are uncomfortable considering natural disasters.

   (B) believe that all events are predictable through scientific methodology.

   (C) accept luck as an inevitable and unpredictable part of life.

   (D) easily accept their failure to predict and protect against nature's surprises.

   (E) are extremely irrational and are comfortable speaking about luck.

The questions following the passage which you just read are typical of those in the Critical Reading section. After carefully reading the passage, you can begin to answer these questions. Let's look again at the questions.

1. Initially the hazy windows were thought by the company to be a result of

   (A) small particles of volcanic glass abrading their surfaces.

   (B) substandard window material substituted by the parts supplier.

   (C) ineffectual cleaning products used by the maintenance crew.

   (D) a build-up of the man-made sulfur dioxide that also causes acid rain.

   (E) the humidity.

As you read the question stem, blocking the answer choices, you'll note the key term "result" which should alert you to the question category *synthesis/analysis.* Argument structure is the focus here. Ask yourself what part of the argument is being questioned: cause, problem, result, or solution. Careful reading of the stem and perhaps mental rewording to "_____ caused hazy windows" reveals cause is the issue. Once you're clear on the stem, proceed to the choices.

The word "initially" clues you in to the fact that the correct answer should be the first cause considered. Answer choice (B) is the correct response, as "substandard window material" was the *company's* first (initial) culprit, as explained in the first sentence of the second paragraph. They had no hint of (A) a volcanic eruption's ability to cause such damage. In addition, they were not concerned, as were the *passengers,* that (C) the windows were not properly cleaned. Answer (D) is not correct since scientists had yet to consider testing the atmosphere. Along the same lines, answer choice (E) is incorrect.

2.   When first seeking a reason for the abraded windows, both the passengers and Boeing management exhibited attitudes of

   (A) disbelief.   (D) pacifism.

   (B) optimism.   (E) disregard.

   (C) cynicism.

As you read the stem before viewing the choices, you'll know you're being asked to judge or *evaluate* the tone of a passage. The tone is not stated outright, so you'll need to rely on your perception as you re-read that section, if necessary. Remember, questions follow the order of the passage, so you know to look after the initial company reaction to the windows, but not far after, as many more questions are to follow. Now, formulate your own word for the attitude of the passengers and employees. "Skepticism" or "criticism" work well. If you can't come up with a term, at least note if the tone is negative or positive. In this case, negative is clearly indicated as the passengers are distrustful of the maintenance crew and the company mistrusts the window supplier. Proceed to each choice, seeking the closest match to your term and/or eliminating words with positive connotations.

Choice (C) is correct because "cynicism" best describes the skepticism and distrust with which the passengers view the cleaning company and the parts suppliers. Choice (A) is not correct because both Boeing and the passengers believed the windows were hazy, they just didn't know why. Choice (B) is not correct because people were somewhat agitated that the windows were hazy—certainly not "optimistic." Choice (D), "pacifism," has a rather positive connotation, which the tone of the section does not. Choice (E) is incorrect because the people involved took notice of the situation and did not disregard it. In addition to the ability to discern tone, of course, your vocabulary knowledge is being tested. "Cynicism," should you be unsure of the term, can be viewed in its root, "cynic," which may trigger you to remember that it is negative, and therefore, appropriate in tone.

3. In line 13, "mundane" means

    (A) simple.   (D) ordinary.

    (B) complicated.   (E) important.

    (C) far-reaching.

This question obviously tests *vocabulary-in-context.* Your strategy here should be quickly to view line 13 to confirm usage, block answer choices while devising your own synonym for "mundane," perhaps "common," and then viewing each choice separately, looking for the closest match. Although you might not be familiar with "mundane," the choices are all relatively simple terms. Look for contextual clues in the passage if you can't define the term outright. While the "component supplies" explanation is "mundane," the Aztec myth is not. Perhaps, you could then look for an opposite of mythical; "real" or "down-to-earth" comes to mind.

Choice (D), "ordinary," fits best as it is clearly the opposite of the extraordinary Aztec myth of the serpent and the eagle, which is not as common as a supplier switching materials. Choice (A), "simple," works contextually, but not as an accurate synonym for the word "mundane"; it does not deal with "mundane's" "down-to-earth" definition. Choice (B), "complicated," is inaccurate because the parts switch is anything but complicated. Choice (C), "far-reaching," is not better as it would apply to the myth rather than the common, everyday action of switching parts. Choice (E), "important," does not work either, because the explanation was an integral part of solving the problem. Had you eliminated (B), (C), and (E) due to contextual inappropriateness, you were left with "ordinary" and "simple." A quick re-reading of the section, then, should clarify the better choice. But, if the re-reading did not clarify the better choice, your strategy would be to choose one answer, place a small mark in the booklet, and proceed to the next question. If time is left at the end of the test, you can then review your answer choice.

4. In what ways is El Chichon like the serpent on the Mexican flag, knowing how to "spit venom at the eyes of its adversary" (lines 18-19)?

    (A) It seeks to poison its adversary with its bite.

    (B) It carefully plans its attack on an awaited intruder.

    (C) It ejects tons of destructive sulfuric acid to damage jet windows.

    (D) It angrily blankets the Northern Hemisphere with sulfuric acid.

    (E) It protects itself with the acid rain it produces.

As you view the question, note the word "like" indicates a comparison is being made. The quoted simile forms the comparative basis of the question, and you must *interpret* that phrase with respect to the actual process. You must carefully seek to duplicate the tenor of the terms, coming close to the spitting action in which a harmful substance is expelled in the direction of an object similar to the eyes of an opponent. Look for key words when comparing images. "Spit," "venom," "eyes," and "adversary" are these keys.

In choice (C), the verb that is most similar to the serpent's "spitting" venom is the sulfuric acid "ejected" from the Mexican volcano, El Chichon. Also, the jet windows most closely resemble the "eyes of the adversary" that are struck by El Chichon. Being a volcano, El Chichon is certainly incapable of injecting poison into an adversary, as in choice (A), or planning an attack on an intruder, as in choice (B). In choice (D), although the volcano does indeed "blanket the Northern Hemisphere" with sulfuric acid, this image does not coincide with the "spitting" image of the serpent. Finally, in choice (E), although a volcano can indirectly cause acid rain, it cannot produce acid rain on its own and then spew it out into the atmosphere.

5. The term "photochemistry" in line 22 refers to a chemical change caused by

    (A) the proximity of the sun.

    (B) the drop in temperature at stratospheric altitudes.

    (C) the jet stream's "unceasing horizontal winds."

    (D) the vertical convection of the troposphere.

    (E) the amount of sulfur present in the atmosphere.

Even if you are unfamiliar with the term "photochemistry," you probably know its root or its prefix. Clearly, this question fits in the *vocabulary-in-context* mode. Your first step may be a quick reference to line 22. If you don't know the term, context may provide you a clue. The conversion of sulfur-rich *upper* atmosphere into droplets may help. If context does not yield information, look at the term "photochemistry," itself. "Photo" has to do with light or sun, as in photosynthesis. Chemistry deals with substance composition and change. Knowing these two parts can take you a long way toward a correct answer.

Answer choice (A) is the correct response, as the light of the sun closely compares with the prefix "photo." Although choice (B), "the drop in temperature," might lead you to associate the droplet formation with condensation, light is not a factor here, nor is it in choice (C), "the jet stream's winds"; choice (D), "the vertical convection"; or choice (E), "the amount of sulfur present."

6.   Unlike the troposphere, the stratosphere

   (A) is extremely humid as it is home to the jet stream.

   (B) contains primarily vertical convections to cause air particles to rise and fall rapidly.

   (C) is approximately one mile thick.

   (D) contains powerful horizontal winds resulting in an excessively dry atmosphere.

   (E) contains very little wind activity.

"Unlike" should immediately alert you to a *synthesis/analysis* question asking you to contrast specific parts of the text. Your margin notes should take you right to the section contrasting the atmospheres. Quickly scan it before considering the answers. Usually you won't remember this broad type of comparison from your first passage reading. Don't spend much time, though, on the scan before beginning to answer, as time is still a factor.

This question is tricky because all the answer choices contain key elements/ phrases in the passage, but again, a quick, careful scan will yield results. Answer (D) proves best as the "horizontal winds" dry the air of the stratosphere. Choices (A), (B), (C), and (E) are all characteristic of the troposphere, while only the acid droplets accumulate at the rate of one mile per year within the much larger stratosphere. As you answer such questions, remember to eliminate incorrect choices as you go; don't be misled by what seems familiar, yet isn't accurate—read all the answer choices.

7. In line 40, "aggressive" means

(A) exasperating.   (D) assertive.

(B) enterprising.   (E) surprising.

(C) prone to attack.

Another *vocabulary-in-context* surfaces here; yet, this time, the word is probably familiar to you. Again, before forming a synonym, quickly refer to the line number, aware that perhaps a secondary meaning is appropriate as the term already is a familiar one. Upon reading the line, you'll note "persistent" and "corrosive," both strong terms, the latter being quite negative in its destruction. Now, form an appropriate synonym for aggressive, one that has a negative connotation. "Hostile" might come to mind. You are ready at this point to view all choices for a match.

Using your vocabulary knowledge, you can answer this question. "Hostile" most closely resembles choice (C), "prone to attack," and is therefore the correct response. Choice (A), "exasperating," or irritating, is too weak a term, while choice (B), "enterprising," and (D), "assertive," are too positive. Choice (E), "surprising," is not a synonym for "aggressive."

8. As the eagle triumphed over the serpent in the Mexican flag,

(A) El Chichon triumphed over the plane, as the 747s had to change their flight altitudes.

(B) the newly designed window material deflected the damaging acid droplets.

(C) the 747 was able to fly unchallenged by acid droplets a year later as they drifted away to the lower atmosphere.

(D) the reliability engineers are now prepared for any run of "bad luck" which may approach their aircraft.

(E) the component supplier of the windows changed materials without telling the customer.

This question asks you to compare the eagle's triumph over the serpent to another part of the text. "As" often signals comparative relationships, so you are forewarned of the *synthesis/analysis* question. You are also dealing again with a simile, so, of course, the question can also be categorized as *interpretation.* The eagle-serpent issue is a major theme in the text. You are being asked, as you will soon discover in the answer choices, what this general theme is. Look at the stem keys: eagle, triumphed, and serpent. Ask yourself to what each corresponds. You'll arrive at the eagle and the 747, some sort of victory, and the volcano or its sulfur. Now that you've formed that corresponding image in your own mind, you're ready to view the choices.

Choice (C) is the correct choice because we know the statement "the 747 was able to fly unchallenged . . . " to be true. Not only do the remaining choices fail to reflect the eagle-triumphs-over-serpent image, but choice (A) is inaccurate because the 747 did not "change its flight altitudes." In choice (B), the windows did not deflect "the damaging acid droplets." Furthermore, in choice (D), "the reliability engineers" cannot be correct because they cannot possibly predict the future, and therefore, cannot anticipate what could go wrong in the future. Finally, we know that in (E) the window materials were never changed.

9. The reliability engineers are typified as people who

   (A) are uncomfortable considering natural disasters.

   (B) believe that all events are predictable through scientific methodology.

   (C) accept luck as an inevitable and unpredictable part of life.

   (D) easily accept their failure to predict and protect against nature's surprises.

   (E) are extremely irrational and are comfortable speaking about luck.

When the question involves such terms as type, kind, example, or typified, be aware of possible *synthesis/analysis* or *interpretation* issues. Here the question deals with implications: what the author means but doesn't state outright. Types can also lead you to situations which ask you to make an unstated generalization based on specifically stated details. In fact, this question could even be categorized as *evaluation* because specific detail to generalization is a type of argument/essay structure. In any case, before viewing the answer choices, ask yourself what general traits the reliability engineers portray. You may need to check back in the text for typical characteristics. You'll find the engineers to be rational unbelievers in luck. These key characteristics will help you to make a step toward a correct answer.

Choice (B) is the correct answer because the passage specifically states that the reliability engineers "are very uncomfortable when asked to talk about luck" and believe "it should be possible to anticipate events" scientifically. The engineers might be uncomfortable, as in choice (A), but this is not a main concern in the passage. Choice (C) is obviously incorrect, because the engineers do not believe in luck at all, and choice (D) is not correct because "professional failure" is certainly unacceptable to these scientists. There is no indication in the passage that (E) the scientists are "irrational and are comfortable speaking about luck."

The following drill should be used to test what you have just learned. Read the passages and answer the questions. If you are unsure of an answer, refer back to the review for help.

☞ Drill: Critical Reading

DIRECTIONS: Read each passage and answer the questions that follow. Each question will be based on the information stated or implied in the passage or its introduction.

In this excerpt from Dickens's Oliver Twist, *we read the early account of Oliver's birth and the beginning of his impoverished life.*

1   Although I am not disposed to maintain that the being born in a workhouse, is in itself the most fortunate and enviable circumstance that can possibly befall a human being, I do mean to say that in this particular instance, it was the best thing for Oliver Twist that could by possibility

5   have occurred. The fact is, that there was considerable difficulty in inducing Oliver to take upon himself the office of respiration,—a troublesome practice, but one which custom has rendered necessary to our easy existence; and for some time he lay gasping on a little flock mattress, rather unequally poised between this world and the next: the balance being de-

10 cidedly in favour of the latter. Now, if, during this brief period, Oliver had been surrounded by careful grandmothers, anxious aunts, experienced nurses, and doctors of profound wisdom, he would most inevitably and indubitably have been killed in no time. There being nobody by, however, but a pauper old woman, who was rendered rather misty by an unwonted

15 allowance of beer; and a parish surgeon who did such matters by contract; Oliver and Nature fought out the point between them. The result was, that, after a few struggles, Oliver breathed, sneezed, and proceeded to advertise to the inmates of the workhouse the fact of a new burden having been imposed upon the parish, by setting up as loud a cry as could reasonably

20 have been expected from a male infant who had not been possessed of that
very useful appendage, a voice, for a much longer space of time than three
minutes and a quarter. . . .

For the next eight or ten months, Oliver was the victim of a systematic course of treachery and deception. He was brought up by hand. The
25 hungry and destitute situation of the infant orphan was duly reported by
the workhouse authorities to the parish authorities. The parish authorities
inquired with dignity of the workhouse authorities, whether there was no
female then domiciled in 'the house' who was in a situation to impart to
Oliver Twist, the consolation and nourishment of which he stood in need.
30 The workhouse authorities replied with humility, that there was not. Upon
this, the parish authorities magnanimously and humanely resolved, that
Oliver should be 'farmed,' or, in other words, that he should be des-
patched to a branchworkhouse some three miles off, where twenty or
thirty other juvenile offenders against the poor-laws, rolled about the floor
35 all day, without the inconvenience of too much food or too much clothing,
under the parental superintendence of an elderly female, who received the
culprits at and for the consideration of sevenpence-halfpenny per small
head per week. Sevenpence-halfpenny's worth per week is a good round
diet for a child; a great deal may be got for sevenpence-halfpenny: quite
40 enough to overload its stomach, and make it uncomfortable. The elderly
female was a woman of wisdom and experience; she knew what was good
for children; and she had a very accurate perception of what was good for
herself. So, she appropriated the greater part of the weekly stipend to her
own use, and consigned the rising parochial generation to even a shorter
45 allowance than was originally provided for them. Thereby finding in the
lowest depth a deeper still; and proving herself a very great experimental
philosopher.

Everybody knows the story of another experimental philosopher, who
had a great theory about a horse being able to live without eating, and who
50 demonstrated it so well, that he got his own horse down to a straw a day,
and would most unquestionably have rendered him a very spirited and
rampacious animal on nothing at all, if he had not died, just four-and-
twenty hours before he was to have had his first comfortable bait of air.
Unfortunately for the experimental philosophy of the female to whose
55 protecting care Oliver Twist was delivered over, a similar result usually
attended the operation of *her* system . . .

It cannot be expected that this system of farming would produce any
very extraordinary or luxuriant crop. Oliver Twist's ninth birth-day found
him a pale thin child, somewhat diminutive in stature, and decidedly small
60 in circumference. But nature or inheritance had implanted a good sturdy
spirit in Oliver's breast. It had had plenty of room to expand, thanks to the

spare diet of the establishment; and perhaps to this circumstance may be attributed his having any ninth birth-day at all.

1. After Oliver was born, he had an immediate problem with his

    (A) heart rate.   (D) hearing.

    (B) breathing.   (E) memory.

    (C) vision.

2. What are the two worlds that Oliver stands "unequally poised be-tween" in lines 8-10?

    (A) Poverty and riches

    (B) Infancy and childhood

    (C) Childhood and adolescence

    (D) Love and hatred

    (E) Life and death

3. What does the author imply about "careful grandmothers, anxious aunts, experienced nurses, and doctors of profound wisdom" in lines 11-12?

    (A) They can help nurse sick children back to health.

    (B) They are necessary for every being's survival.

    (C) They are the pride of the human race.

    (D) They tend to adversely affect the early years of children.

    (E) Their involvement in Oliver's birth would have had no outcome on his survival.

4. What is the outcome of Oliver's bout with Nature?

    (A) He is unable to overcome Nature's fierceness.

    (B) He loses, but gains some dignity from his will to fight.

    (C) It initially appears that Oliver has won, but moments later he cries out in crushing defeat.

    (D) Oliver cries out with the breath of life in his lungs.

    (E) There is no way of knowing who won the struggle.

5. What is the "systematic course of treachery and deception" that Oliver falls victim to in the early months of his life?

   (A) He is thrown out into the streets.

   (B) His inheritance is stolen by caretakers of the workhouse.

   (C) He is relocated by the uncaring authorities of the workhouse and the parish.

   (D) The records of his birth are either lost or destroyed.

   (E) He is publicly humiliated by the parish authorities.

6. What is meant when the residents of the branch-workhouse are referred to by the phrase "juvenile offenders against the poor-laws" (line 34)?

   (A) They are children who have learned to steal early in life.

   (B) They are adolescents who work on probation.

   (C) They are infants who have no money to support them.

   (D) They are infants whose parents were law offenders.

   (E) They are adults who have continuously broken the law.

7. What is the author's tone when he writes that the elderly caretaker "knew what was good for children" (lines 41-42)?

   (A) Sarcastic   (D) Astonished

   (B) Complimentary   (E) Outraged

   (C) Impressed

8. What does the author imply when he further writes that the elderly caretaker "had a very accurate perception of what was good for herself" (lines 42-43)?

   (A) She knew how to keep herself groomed and clean.

   (B) She knew how to revenge herself on her enemies.

   (C) She had a sense of confidence that inspired others.

   (D) She really had no idea how to take care of herself.

   (E) She knew how to selfishly benefit herself despite the cost to others.

9. Why is the elderly caretaker considered "a very great experimental philosopher" (lines 46–47)?

    (A) She was scientifically weaning the children off of food trying to create stronger humans.

    (B) She experimented with the survival of the children in her care.

    (C) She thought children were the key to a meaningful life.

    (D) She made sure that the children received adequate training in philosophy.

    (E) She often engaged in parochial and philosophical discussions.

10. In line 53, "bait" most nearly means

    (A) worms.   (D) a trap.

    (B) a hook.   (E) a meal.

    (C) a breeze.

11. To what does the author attribute Oliver's survival to his ninth year?

    (A) A strong, healthy diet

    (B) Money from an anonymous donor

    (C) Sheer luck

    (D) His diminutive stature

    (E) His sturdy spirit

12. Based upon the passage, what is the author's overall attitude concerning the city where Oliver lives?

    (A) It is the best of all possible worlds.

    (B) It should be the prototype for future cities.

    (C) It is a dark place filled with greedy, selfish people.

    (D) Although impoverished, most of its citizens are kind.

    (E) It is a flawed place, but many good things often happen there.

The following passage analyzes the legal and political philosophy of John Marshall, a chief justice of the Supreme Court in the nineteenth century.

1   As chief justice of the Supreme Court from 1801 until his death in 1835, John Marshall was a staunch nationalist and upholder of property rights. He was not, however, as the folklore of American politics would have it, the lonely and embattled Federalist defending these values against
5   the hostile forces of Jeffersonian democracy. On the contrary, Marshall's opinions dealing with federalism, property rights, and national economic development were consistent with the policies of the Republican Party in its mercantilist phase from 1815 to 1828. Never an extreme Federalist, Marshall opposed his party's reactionary wing in the crisis of 1798-1800.
10 Like almost all Americans of his day, Marshall was a Lockean republican who valued property not as an economic end in itself, but rather as the foundation of civil liberty and a free society. Property was the source both of individual happiness and social stability and progress.

Marshall evinced strong centralizing tendencies in his theory of fed-
15 eralism and completely rejected the compact theory of the Union ex- pressed in the Virginia and Kentucky Resolutions. Yet his outlook was compatible with the Unionism that formed the basis of the post-1815 American System of the Republican Party. Not that Marshall shared the democratic sensibilities of the Republicans; like his fellow Federalists, he
20 tended to distrust the common people and saw in legislative majori- tarianism a force that was potentially hostile to constitutionalism and the rule of law. But aversion to democracy was not the hallmark of Marshall's constitutional jurisprudence. Its central features rather were a commitment to federal authority versus states' rights and a socially productive and
25 economically dynamic conception of property rights. Marshall's support of these principles placed him near the mainstream of American politics in the years between the War of 1812 and the conquest of Jacksonian De- mocracy.

In the long run, the most important decisions of the Marshall Court
30 were those upholding the authority of the federal government against the states. *Marbury v. Madison* provided a jurisprudential basis for this under- taking, but the practical significance of judicial review in the Marshall era concerned the state legislatures rather than Congress. The most serious challenge to national authority resulted from state attempts to administer
35 their judicial systems independent of the Supreme Court's appellate super- visions as directed by the Judiciary Act of 1789. In successfully resisting this challenge, the Marshall Court not only averted a practical disruption of the federal system, but it also evolved doctrines of national supremacy which helped preserve the Union during the Civil War.

13. The primary purpose of this passage is to

    (A) describe Marshall's political jurisprudence.

    (B) discuss the importance of centralization to the preservation of the Union.

    (C) criticize Marshall for being disloyal to his party.

    (D) examine the role of the Supreme Court in national politics.

    (E) chronicle Marshall's tenure on the Supreme Court.

14. According to the author, Marshall viewed property as

    (A) an investment.

    (B) irrelevant to constitutional liberties.

    (C) the basis of a stable society.

    (D) inherent to the upper class.

    (E) an important centralizing incentive.

15. In line 15, the "compact theory" was most likely a theory

    (A) supporting states' rights.

    (B) of the extreme Federalists.

    (C) of the Marshall Court's approach to the Civil War.

    (D) supporting centralization.

    (E) advocating jurisprudential activism.

16. According to the author, Marshall's attitude toward mass democratic politics can best be described as

    (A) hostile.   (D) nurturing.

    (B) supportive.   (E) distrustful.

    (C) indifferent.

17. In line 22, the word "aversion" means

    (A) loathing.   (D) forbidding.

    (B) acceptance.   (E) misdirection.

    (C) fondness.

18. The author argues the Marshall Court

    (A) failed to achieve its centralizing policies.

    (B) failed to achieve its decentralizing policies.

    (C) helped to bring on the Civil War.

    (D) supported federalism via judicial review.

    (E) had its greatest impact on Congress.

19. According to the author, Marshall's politics were

    (A) extremist.   (D) moderate.

    (B) right-wing.   (E) majoritarian.

    (C) democratic.

In this passage, the author discusses the properties and uses of selenium cells, which convert sunlight to energy, creating solar power.

1   The physical phenomenon responsible for converting light to electricity—the photovoltaic effect—was first observed in 1839 by the renowned French physicist, Edmund Becquerel. Becquerel noted that a voltage appeared when one of two identical electrodes in a weak conducting solution
5 was illuminated. The PV effect was first studied in solids, such as selenium, in the 1870s. In the 1880s, selenium photovoltaic cells were built that exhibited 1%-2% efficiency in converting light to electricity. Selenium converts light in the visible part of the sun's spectrum; for this reason, it was quickly adopted by the then merging field of photography
10 for photometric (light-measuring) devices. Even today, the light-sensitive cells on cameras used for adjusting shutter speed to match illumination are made of selenium.
     Selenium cells have never become practical as energy converters because their cost is too high relative to the tiny amount of power they
15 produce (at 1% efficiency). Meanwhile, work on the physics of PV phenomena has expanded. In the 1920s and 1930s, quantum mechanics laid the theoretical foundation for our present understanding of PV. A major step forward in solar-cell technology came in the 1940s and early 1950s when a new method (called the Czochralski method) was developed for
20 producing highly pure crystalline silicon. In 1954, work at Bell Telephone Laboratories resulted in a silicon photovoltaic cell with a 4% efficiency. Bell Labs soon bettered this to a 6% and then 11% efficiency, heralding an entirely new era of power-producing cells.
     A few schemes were tried in the 1950s to use silicon PV cells com-

25 mercially. Most were for cells in regions geographically isolated from electric utility lines. But an unexpected boom in PV technology came from a different quarter. In 1958, the U.S. Vanguard space satellite used a small (less than one-watt) array of cells to power its radio. The cells worked so well that space scientists soon realized the PV could be an effective power
30 source for many space missions. Technology development of the solar cell has been a part of the space program ever since.

Today, photovoltaic systems are capable of transforming one kilowatt of solar energy falling on one square meter into about a hundred watts of electricity. One hundred watts can power most household appliances: a
35 television, a stereo, an electric typewriter, or a lamp. In fact, standard solar cells covering the sun-facing roof space of a typical home can provide about 8,500-kilowatt-hours of electricity annually, which is about the average household's yearly electric consumption. By comparison, a modern, 200-ton electric-arc steel furnace, demanding 50,000 kilowatts of electric-
40 ity, would require about a square kilometer of land for a PV power supply.

Certain factors make capturing solar energy difficult. Besides the sun's low illuminating power per square meter, sunlight is intermittent, affected by time of day, climate, pollution, and season. Power sources based on photovoltaics require either back-up from other sources or stor-
45 age for times when the sun is obscured.

In addition, the cost of a photovoltaic system is far from negligible (electricity from PV systems in 1980 cost about 20 times more than that from conventional fossil-fuel-powered systems).

Thus, solar energy for photovoltaic conversion into electricity is
50 abundant, inexhaustible, and clean; yet, it also requires special techniques to gather enough of it effectively.

20. To the author, Edmund Becquerel's research was

   (A) unimportant.

   (B) of some significance.

   (C) not recognized in its time.

   (D) weak.

   (E) an important breakthrough.

21. In the first paragraph, it can be concluded that the photovoltaic effect is the result of

   (A) two identical negative electrodes.

   (B) one weak solution and two negative electrodes.

(C) two positive electrodes of different qualities.

(D) positive electrodes interacting in a weak environment.

(E) one negative electrode and one weak solution.

22. The author establishes that selenium was used for photometric devices because

(A) selenium was the first solid to be observed to have the PV effect.

(B) selenium is inexpensive.

(C) selenium converts the visible part of the sun's spectrum.

(D) selenium can adjust shutter speeds on cameras.

(E) selenium is abundant.

23. Which of the following can be concluded from the passage?

(A) Solar energy is still limited by problems of technological efficiency.

(B) Solar energy is the most efficient source of heat for most families.

(C) Solar energy represents the PV effect in its most complicated form.

(D) Solar energy is 20 percent cheaper than fossil-fuel-powered systems.

(E) Solar energy is 40 percent more expensive than fossil-fuel-powered systems.

24. In line 22, the word "heralding" most nearly means

(A) celebrating.   (D) anticipating.

(B) observing.   (E) introducing.

(C) commemorating.

25. According to the passage, commercially used PV cells have powered

(A) car radios.   (D) electric utility lines.

(B) space satellite radios.   (E) space stations.

(C) telephones.

26. Through the information in lines 32-34, it can be inferred that two kilowatts of solar energy transformed by a PV system equal

    (A) 200 watts of electricity.

    (B) 100 watts of electricity.

    (C) no electricity.

    (D) two square meters.

    (E) 2,000 watts of electricity.

27. Sunlight is difficult to procure for transformation into solar energy. Which of the following statements most accurately supports this belief derived from the passage?

    (A) Sunlight is erratic and subject to variables.

    (B) Sunlight is steady but never available.

    (C) Sunlight is not visible because of pollution.

    (D) Sunlight would have to be artificially produced.

    (E) Sunlight is never erratic.

28. The author's concluding paragraph would be best supported with additional information regarding

    (A) specific benefits of solar energy for photovoltaic conversion into electricity.

    (B) the negative effects of solar energy for photovoltaic conversion into electricity.

    (C) the negative effects of photovoltaic conversion.

    (D) why solar energy is clean.

    (E) why solar energy is abundant.

> **DIRECTIONS**: Read the passages and answer the questions that follow. Each question will be based on the information stated or implied in the selections or their introductions, and may be based on the relationship between the passages.

In Passage 1, the author writes a general summary about the nature of comedy. In Passage 2, the author sums up the essentials of tragedy.

Passage 1

1   The primary aim of comedy is to amuse us with a happy ending, although comedies can vary according to the attitudes they project, which can be broadly identified as either high or low, terms having nothing to do with an evaluation of the play's merit. Generally, the amusement found in
5   comedy comes from an eventual victory over threats or ill fortune. Much of the dialogue and plot development might be laughable, yet a play need not be funny to be comic. In fact, some critics in the Renaissance era thought that the highest form of comedy should elicit no laughter at all from its audience. A comedy that forced its audience into laughter failed
10   in the highest comic endeavor, whose purpose was to amuse as subtly as possible. Note that Shakespeare's comedies themselves were often under attack for their appeal to laughter.

   Farce is low comedy intended to make us laugh by means of a series of exaggerated, unlikely situations that depend less on plot and character
15   than on gross absurdities, sight gags, and coarse dialogue. The "higher" a comedy goes, the more natural the characters seem and the less boisterous their behavior. The plots become more sustained, and the dialogue shows more weighty thought. As with all dramas, comedies are about things that go wrong. Accordingly, comedies create deviations from accepted nor-
20   malcy, presenting problems which we might or might not see as harmless. If these problems make us judgmental about the involved characters and events, the play takes on the features of satire, a rather high comic form implying that humanity and human institutions are in need of reform. If the action triggers our sympathy for the characters, we feel even less
25   protected from the incongruities as the play tilts more in the direction of tragicomedy. In other words, the action determines a figurative distance between the audience and the play. Such factors as characters' personalities and the plot's predictability influence this distance. The farther away we sit, the more protected we feel and usually the funnier the play be-
30   comes. Closer proximity to believability in the script draws us nearer to the conflict, making us feel more involved in the action and less safe in its presence.

Passage 2

The term "tragedy" when used to define a play has historically meant something very precise, not simply a drama which ends with unfortunate
35 consequences. This definition originated with Aristotle, who insisted that the play be an imitation of complex actions which should arouse an emotional response combining fear and pity. Aristotle believed that only a certain kind of plot could generate such a powerful reaction. Comedy shows us a progression from adversity to prosperity. Tragedy must show
40 the reverse; moreover, this progression must be experienced by a certain kind of character, says Aristotle, someone whom we can designate as the tragic hero. This central figure must be basically good and noble: "good" because we will not be aroused to fear and pity over the misfortunes of a villain, and "noble" both by social position and moral stature because the
45 fall to misfortune would not otherwise be great enough for tragic impact. These virtues do not make the tragic hero perfect, however, for he must also possess hamartia—a tragic flaw—the weakness which leads him to make an error in judgment which initiates the reversal in his fortunes, causing his death or the death of others or both. These dire consequences
50 become the hero's catastrophe. The most common tragic flaw is hubris; an excessive pride that adversely influences the protagonist's judgment.

Often the catastrophic consequences involve an entire nation because the tragic hero's social rank carries great responsibilities. Witnessing these events produces the emotional reaction Aristotle believed the audience
55 should experience, the catharsis. Although tragedy must arouse our pity for the tragic hero as he endures his catastrophe and must frighten us as we witness the consequences of a flawed behavior which anyone could exhibit, there must also be a purgation, "a cleansing," of these emotions which should leave the audience feeling not depressed but relieved and
60 almost elated. The assumption is that while the tragic hero endures a crushing reversal, somehow he is not thoroughly defeated as he gains new stature through suffering and the knowledge that comes with suffering. Classical tragedy insists that the universe is ordered. If truth or universal law is ignored, the results are devastating, causing the audience to react
65 emotionally; simultaneously, the tragic results prove the existence of truth, thereby reassuring our faith that existence is sensible.

29. In Passage 1, the term "laughable" (line 6) suggests that on occasion comic dialogue and plot development can be

    (A) senselessly ridiculous.

    (B) foolishly stupid.

(C) amusingly droll.

(D) theoretically depressing.

(E) critically unsavory.

30. The author of Passage 1 makes an example of Shakespeare (lines 11-12) in order to

    (A) make the playwright look much poorer in our eyes.

    (B) emphasize that he wrote the highest form of comedy.

    (C) degrade higher forms of comedy.

    (D) suggest the foolishness of Renaissance critics.

    (E) show that even great authors do not always use high comedy.

31. The protagonist in a play discovers he has won the lottery, only to misplace the winning ticket. According to the author's definition, this situation would be an example of which type of comedy?

    (A) Satire   (D) Sarcasm

    (B) Farce   (E) Slapstick

    (C) Tragicomedy

32. In line 26, the phrase "figurative distance" suggests

    (A) the distance between the seats in the theater and the stage.

    (B) the lengths the comedy will go to elicit laughter.

    (C) the years separating the composition of the play and the time of its performance.

    (D) the degree to which an audience relates to the play's action.

    (E) that the play's subject matter is too high for the audience to grasp.

33. What is the author trying to espouse in lines 28-32?

    (A) He warns us not to get too involved with the action of the drama.

    (B) He wants the audience to immerse itself in the world of the drama.

    (C) He wants us to feel safe in the presence of the drama.

(D) He wants us to be critical of the drama's integrity.

(E) He feels that we should not enjoy the drama overly much.

34. In Passage 2, the author introduces Aristotle as a leading source for the definition of tragedy. He does this

    (A) to emphasize how outdated the tragedy is for the modern audience.

    (B) because Greek philosophy is the only way to truly understand the world of the theater.

    (C) because Aristotle was one of Greece's greatest actors.

    (D) because Aristotle instituted the definition of tragedy still used widely today.

    (E) in order to prove that Aristotle's sense of tragedy was based on false conclusions.

35. In line 42, "noble" most nearly means

    (A) of high degree and superior virtue.

    (B) of great wealth and self-esteem.

    (C) of quick wit and high intelligence.

    (D) of manly courage and great strength.

    (E) of handsome features and social charm.

36. Which of the following is an example of *harmatia* (line 47)?

    (A) Courtesy to the lower class

    (B) The ability to communicate freely with others

    (C) A refusal to acknowledge the power of the gods

    (D) A weak, miserly peasant

    (E) A desire to do penance for one's crimes

37. Which of the following best summarizes the idea of *catharsis* explained in lines 52-55?

    (A) All of the tragic consequences are reversed at the last moment; the hero is rescued from certain doom and is allowed to live happily for the rest of his life.

(B) The audience gains a perverse pleasure from watching another's suffering.

(C) The play's action ends immediately, unresolved, and the audience is left in a state of blissful confusion.

(D) When the play ends, the audience is happy to escape the drudgery of the tragedy's depressing conclusion.

(E) The audience lifts itself from a state of fear and pity for the tragic hero to a sense of renewal and absolution for the hero's endurance of great suffering.

38. The authors of both passages make an attempt to

(A) ridicule their subject matter.

(B) outline the general terms and guidelines of a particular aspect of drama.

(C) thrill their readers with sensational information.

(D) draw upon Shakespeare as an authority to back up their work.

(E) persuade their readers to study only one or the other type of drama (i.e., comedy or tragedy).

39. Which of the following best describes the differences between the structure of both passages?

(A) Passage 1 is concerned primarily with the Renaissance era. Passage 2 is concerned primarily with Classical Greece.

(B) Passage 1 is concerned with dividing its subject into subcategories. Passage 2 is concerned with extracting its subject's individual elements.

(C) Passage 1 makes fun of its subject matter. Passage 2 treats its subject matter very solemnly.

(D) Passage 1 draws upon a series of plays that serve as examples. Passage 2 draws upon no outside sources.

(E) Passage 1 introduces special vocabulary to illuminate the subject matter; Passage 2 fails to do this.

40. What assumption do both passages seem to draw upon?

(A) Tragedy is a higher form of drama than comedy.

(B) Tragedy is on the decline in modern society; comedy, however, is on the rise.

(C) *Catharsis* is an integral part of both comedy and tragedy.

(D) An audience's role in the performance of either comedy or tragedy is a vital one.

(E) The tragicomedy is a form that is considered greater than drama that is merely comic or tragic.

CRITICAL READING

ANSWER KEY

Drill: Critical Reading

1.	(B)	11.	(E)	21.	(D)	31.	(C)
2.	(E)	12.	(C)	22.	(C)	32.	(D)
3.	(D)	13.	(A)	23.	(A)	33.	(B)
4.	(D)	14.	(C)	24.	(E)	34.	(D)
5.	(C)	15.	(A)	25.	(B)	35.	(A)
6.	(C)	16.	(E)	26.	(A)	36.	(C)
7.	(A)	17.	(A)	27.	(A)	37.	(E)
8.	(E)	18.	(D)	28.	(A)	38.	(B)
9.	(B)	19.	(D)	29.	(C)	39.	(B)
10.	(E)	20.	(E)	30.	(E)	40.	(D)

PSAT/ NMSQT

CHAPTER 7

Basic Math Skills Review

Chapter 7

BASIC MATH SKILLS REVIEW

    I. ARITHMETIC

    II. ALGEBRA

   III. GEOMETRY

   IV. WORD PROBLEMS

Are you ready to tackle the math sections of the PSAT? Well, the chances are that you will be, but only after some reviewing of basic concepts in arithmetic, algebra, and geometry. The more familiar you are with these fundamental principles, the better you will do on the math sections of the PSAT. Our math review represents the various mathematical topics that will appear on the PSAT. You will not find any calculus, trigonometry, or even imaginary numbers in our math review. Why? Because these concepts are not tested on the math sections of the PSAT. The mathematical concepts presented on the PSAT are ones with which you are already familiar and simply need to review in order to score well.

Along with a knowledge of these topics, how quickly and accurately you can answer the math questions will have an effect upon your success. Therefore, memorize the directions in order to save time and decrease your chances of making careless mistakes. Then, complete the practice drills that are provided for you in our review. Even if you are sure you know your fundamental math concepts, the drills will help to warm you up so that you can go into the math sections of the PSAT with quick, sharp math skills.

REFERENCE TABLE

SYMBOLS AND THEIR MEANINGS

$=$	is equal to	$\leq$	is less than or equal to
$\neq$	is unequal to	$\geq$	is greater than or equal to
$<$	is less than	$\parallel$	is parallel to
$>$	is greater than	$\perp$	is perpendicular to

FORMULAS

DESCRIPTION	FORMULA
Area (A) of a:	
square	$A = s^2$; where s = side
rectangle	$A = lw$; where l = length, w = width
parallelogram	$A = bh$; where b = base, h = height
triangle	$A = \frac{1}{2}bh$; where b = base, h = height
circle	$A = \pi r^2$; where π = 3.14, r = radius
Perimeter (P) of a:	
square	$P = 4s$; where s = side
rectangle	$P = 2l + 2w$; where l = length, w = width
triangle	$P = a + b + c$; where a, b, and c are the sides
circumference (C) of a circle	$C = \pi d$; where π = 3.14, d = diameter = $2r$
Volume (V) of a:	
cube	$V = s^3$; where s = side
rectangular container	$V = lwh$; where l = length, w = width, h = height
Pythagorean Theorem	$c^2 = a^2 + b^2$; where c = hypotenuse, a and b are legs of a right triangle
Distance (d):	
between two points in a plane	$d = \sqrt{(x_2 - x_1)^2 + (y_2 - y_1)^2}$ where (x_1, y_1) and (x_2, y_2) are two points in a plane
as a function of rate and time	$d = rt$; where r = rate, t = time
Mean	$\text{mean} = \dfrac{x_1 + x_2 + \ldots + x_n}{n}$ where the x's are the values for which a mean is desired, and n = number of values in the series
Median	median = the point in an ordered set of numbers at which half of the numbers are above and half of the numbers are below this value
Simple Interest (i)	$i = prt$; where p = principal, r = rate, t = time
Total Cost (c)	$c = nr$; where n = number of units, r = cost per unit

I. ARITHMETIC

INTEGERS AND REAL NUMBERS

Most of the numbers used in algebra belong to a set called the **real numbers** or **reals**. This set can be represented graphically by the real number line.

Given the number line below, we arbitrarily fix a point and label it with the number 0. In a similar manner, we can label any point on the line with one of the real numbers, depending on its position relative to 0. Numbers to the right of 0 are positive, while those to the left are negative. Value increases from left to right, so that if *a* is to the right of *b*, it is said to be greater than *b*.

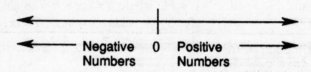

If we now divide the number line into equal segments, we can label the points on this line with real numbers. For example, the point 2 lengths to the left of 0 is -2, while the point 3 lengths to the right of 0 is $+3$ (the $+$ sign is usually assumed, so $+3$ is written simply as 3). The number line now looks like this:

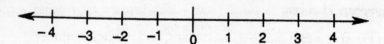

These boundary points represent the subset of the reals known as the **integers**. The set of integers is made up of both the positive and negative whole numbers:

$$\{\dots, -4, -3, -2, -1, 0, 1, 2, 3, 4, \dots\}.$$

Some subsets of integers are:

Natural Numbers or Positive Numbers—the set of integers starting with 1 and increasing:

$$N = \{1, 2, 3, 4, \dots\}.$$

Whole Numbers—the set of integers starting with 0 and increasing:

$$W = \{0, 1, 2, 3, \dots\}.$$

Negative Numbers—the set of integers starting with -1 and decreasing:

$$Z = \{-1, -2, -3, \ldots\}.$$

Prime Numbers—the set of positive integers greater than 1 that are divisible only by 1 and themselves:

$$\{2, 3, 5, 7, 11, \ldots\}.$$

Even Integers—the set of integers divisible by 2:

$$\{\ldots, -4, -2, 0, 2, 4, 6, \ldots\}.$$

Odd Integers—the set of integers not divisible by 2:

$$\{\ldots, -3, -1, 1, 3, 5, 7, \ldots\}.$$

Consecutive Integers—the set of integers that differ by 1:

$$\{n, n+1, n+2, \ldots\} \ (n = \text{an integer}).$$

PROBLEM

Classify each of the following numbers into as many different sets as possible. Example: real, integer ...

(1) 0   (3) $\sqrt{6}$ (5) $\dfrac{2}{3}$

(2) 9   (4) $\dfrac{1}{2}$ (6) 1.5

SOLUTION

(1) 0 is a real number, an integer, and a whole number.

(2) 9 is a real number, an odd number, and a natural number.

(3) $\sqrt{6}$ is a real number.

(4) $\dfrac{1}{2}$ is a real number.

(5) $\dfrac{2}{3}$ is a real number.

(6) 1.5 is a real number and a decimal.

ABSOLUTE VALUE

The **absolute value** of a number is represented by two vertical lines around the number, and is equal to the given number, regardless of sign.

The absolute value of a real number A is defined as follows:

$$|A| = \begin{cases} A \text{ if } A \geq 0 \\ -A \text{ if } A < 0 \end{cases}$$

EXAMPLES

$$|5| = 5, |-8| = -(-8) = 8$$

Absolute values follow the given rules:

(A) $\quad |-A| = |A|$

(B) $\quad |A| \geq 0$, equality holding only if $A = 0$

(C) $\quad \left|\dfrac{A}{B}\right| = \dfrac{|A|}{|B|}, \quad B \neq 0$

(D) $\quad |AB| = |A| \times |B|$

(E) $\quad |A|^2 = A^2$

Absolute value can also be expressed on the real number line as the distance of the point represented by the real number from the point labeled 0.

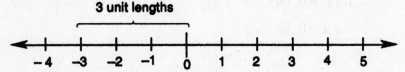

So $|-3| = 3$ because -3 is 3 units to the left of 0.

PROBLEM

Classify each of the following statements as true or false. If it is false, explain why.

(1) $\quad |-120| > 1$ (4) $\quad |12 - 3| = 12 - 3$

(2) $\quad |4 - 12| = |4| - |12|$ (5) $\quad |-12a| = 12|a|$

(3) $\quad |4 - 9| = 9 - 4$

SOLUTION

(1)   True

(2)   False, $|4 - 12| = |4| - |12|$

$$|-8| = 4 - 12$$

$$8 \neq -8$$

In general, $|a + b| \neq |a| + |b|$

(3) True

(4) True

(5) True

PROBLEM

Find the absolute value for each of the following:

(1) 0   (3) $-\pi$

(2) 4   (4) a, where a is a real number

SOLUTION

(1) $|0| = 0$

(2) $|4| = 4$

(3) $|-\pi| = \pi$

(4) for $a > 0, |a| = a$

for $a = 0, |a| = 0$

for $a < 0, |a| = a$

i.e., $|a| = \begin{cases} a \text{ if } a > 0 \\ 0 \text{ if } a = 0 \\ -a \text{ if } a < 0 \end{cases}$

POSITIVE AND NEGATIVE NUMBERS

A) **To add two numbers with like signs,** add their absolute values and write the sum with the common sign. So,

$6 + 2 = 8, (-6) + (-2) = -8$

B) **To add two numbers with unlike signs,** find the difference between their absolute values, and write the result with the sign of the number with the greater absolute value. So,

$(-4) + 6 = 2, 15 + (-19) = -4$

C) **To subtract a number b from another number a,** change the sign of b and add to a. Examples:

$10 - (3) = 10 + (-3) = 7$ (1)

$$2 - (-6) = 2 + 6 = 8 \tag{2}$$

$$(-5) - (-2) = -5 + 2 = -3 \tag{3}$$

D) **To multiply (or divide) two numbers having like signs,** multiply (or divide) their absolute values and write the result with a positive sign. Examples:

$$(5)(3) = 15 \tag{1}$$

$$(-6) \div (-3) = 2 \tag{2}$$

E) **To multiply (or divide) two numbers having unlike signs,** multiply (or divide) their absolute values and write the result with a negative sign. Examples:

$$(-2)(8) = -16 \tag{1}$$

$$9 \div (-3) = -3 \tag{2}$$

According to the law of signs for real numbers, the square of a positive or negative number is always positive. This means that it is impossible to take the square root of a negative number in the real number system.

PROBLEM

Calculate the value of each of the following expressions:

(1) $||2 - 5| + 6 - 14|$ (2) $|-5| \times 4 + \dfrac{|-12|}{4}$

SOLUTION

Before solving this problem, one must use the rules for the **order of operations.** Always work within the parentheses or with absolute values first while keeping in mind that multiplication and division are carried out before addition and subtraction.

(1) $||-3| + 6 - 14| = |3 + 6 - 14|$

$$= |9 - 14|$$

$$= |-5|$$

$$= 5$$

(2) $(5 \times 4) + \dfrac{12}{4} = 20 + 3$

$$= 23$$

ODD AND EVEN NUMBERS

When dealing with odd and even numbers keep in mind the following:

Adding:

> even + even = even
>
> odd + odd = even
>
> even + odd = odd

Multiplying:

> even × even = even
>
> even × odd = even
>
> odd × odd = odd

☞ Drill: Integers and Real Numbers

Addition

1. Simplify $4 + (-7) + 2 + (-5)$.

    (A) -6　　(B) -4　　(C) 0　　(D) 6　　(E) 18

2. Simplify $144 + (-317) + 213$.

    (A) -357　(B) -40　(C) 40　　(D) 357　　(E) 674

3. Simplify $|4 + (-3)| + |-2|$.

    (A) -2　　(B) -1　　(C) 1　　(D) 3　　(E) 9

4. What integer makes the equation $-13 + 12 + 7 + ? = 10$ a true statement?

    (A) -22　(B) -10　(C) 4　　(D) 6　　(E) 10

5. Simplify $4 + 17 + (-29) + 13 + (-22) + (-3)$.

    (A) -44　(B) -20　(C) 23　　(D) 34　　(E) 78

Subtraction

6. Simplify $319 - 428$.

(A) -111 (B) -109 (C) -99 (D) 109 (E) 747

7. Simplify $91,203 - 37,904 + 1,073$.

(A) $54,372$ (B) $64,701$ (C) $128,034$ (D) $129,107$ (E) $130,180$

8. Simplify $| 43 - 62 | - | - 17 - 3 |$.

(A) -39 (B) -19 (C) -1 (D) 1 (E) 39

9. Simplify $-(-4 - 7) + (-2)$.

(A) -22 (B) -13 (C) -9 (D) 7 (E) 9

10. In the St. Elias Mountains, Mt. Logan rises from 1,292 meters above sea level to 7,243 meters above sea level. How tall is Mt. Logan?

(A) $4,009$ m   (B) $5,951$ m   (C) $5,699$ m   (D) $6,464$ m   (E) $7,885$ m

Multiplication

11. Simplify $(-3) \times (-18) \times (-1)$.

(A) -108 (B) -54 (C) -48 (D) 48 (E) 54

12. Simplify $| -42 | \times | 7 |$.

(A) -294 (B) -49 (C) -35 (D) 284 (E) 294

13. Simplify $(-6) \times 5 \times (-10) \times (-4) \times 0 \times 2$.

(A) $-2,400$ (B) -240 (C) 0 (D) 280 (E) $2,700$

14. Simplify $-| -6 \times 8 |$.

(A) -48 (B) -42 (C) 2 (D) 42 (E) 48

15. A city in Georgia had a record low temperature of $-3°$F one winter. During the same year, a city in Michigan experienced a record low that was nine times the record low set in Georgia. What was the record low in Michigan that year?

(A) $-31°$F   (B) $-27°$F   (C) $-21°$F   (D) $-12°$F   (E) $-6°$F

Division

16. Simplify $(-24) \div 8$.

(A) -4 (B) -3 (C) -2 (D) 3 (E) 4

17. Simplify $(-180) \div (-12)$.

(A) -30 (B) -15 (C) 1.5 (D) 15 (E) 216

18. Simplify $|-76| \div |-4|$.

(A) -21 (B) -19 (C) 13 (D) 19 (E) 21.5

19. Simplify $|216 \div (-6)|$.

(A) -36 (B) -12 (C) 36 (D) 38 (E) 43

20. At the end of the year, a small firm has $2,996 in its account for bonuses. If the entire amount is equally divided among the 14 employees, how much does each one receive?

(A) $107   (B) $114   (C) $170   (D) $210   (E) $214

Order of Operations

21. Simplify $\dfrac{4+8\times2}{5-1}$

(A) 4 (B) 5 (C) 6 (D) 8 (E) 12

22. $96 \div 3 \div 4 \div 2 =$

(A) 65 (B) 64 (C) 16 (D) 8 (E) 4

23. $3 + 4 \times 2 - 6 \div 3 =$

(A) -1 (B) $\dfrac{5}{3}$ (C) $\dfrac{8}{3}$ (D) 9 (E) 12

24. $[(4+8) \times 3] \div 9 =$

(A) 4 (B) 8 (C) 12 (D) 24 (E) 36

25. $18 + 3 \times 4 \div 3 =$

(A) 3 (B) 5 (C) 10 (D) 22 (E) 28

26. $(29 - 17 + 4) \div 4 + |-2| =$

(A) $2^2/_3$ (B) 4   (C) $4^2/_3$ (D) 6   (E) 15

27. $(-3) \times 5 - 20 \div 4 =$

(A) -75 (B) -20 (C) -10 (D) $-8^3/_4$ (E) 20

28. $\dfrac{11 \times 2 + 2}{16 - 2 \times 2} =$

(A) $\dfrac{11}{16}$ (B) 1   (C) 2   (D) $3^2/_3$ (E) 4

29. $|-8 - 4| \div 3 \times 6 + (-4) =$

(A) 20   (B) 26   (C) 32   (D) 62   (E) 212

30. $32 \div 2 + 4 - 15 \div 3 =$

(A) 0   (B) 7   (C) 15   (D) 23   (E) 63

FRACTIONS

The fraction, *a/b*, where the **numerator** is *a* and the **denominator** is *b*, implies that *a* is being divided by *b*. The denominator of a fraction can never be zero since a number divided by zero is not defined. If the numerator is greater than the denominator, the fraction is called an **improper fraction**. A **mixed number** is the sum of a whole number and a fraction, i.e.,

$$4\frac{3}{8} = 4 + \frac{3}{8}.$$

OPERATIONS WITH FRACTIONS

A) **To change a mixed number to an improper fraction**, simply multiply the whole number by the denominator of the fraction and add the numerator. This product becomes the numerator of the result and the denominator remains the same, e.g.,

$$5\frac{2}{3} = \frac{(5 \times 3) + 2}{3} = \frac{15 + 2}{3} = \frac{17}{3}$$

To change an improper fraction to a mixed number, simply divide the numerator by the denominator. The remainder becomes the numerator of the fractional part of the mixed number, and the denominator remains the same, e.g.,

$$\frac{35}{4} = 35 \div 4 = 8\frac{3}{4}$$

To check your work, change your result back to an improper fraction to see if it matches the original fraction.

B) **To find the sum of fractions having a common denominator**, simply add together the numerators of the given fractions and put this sum over the common denominator.

$$\frac{11}{3} + \frac{5}{3} = \frac{11+5}{3} = \frac{16}{3}$$

Similarly for subtraction,

$$\frac{11}{3} - \frac{5}{3} = \frac{11-5}{3} = \frac{6}{3} = 2$$

C) **To find the sum of two fractions having different denominators**, it is necessary to find the **lowest common denominator (LCD)** of the different denominators using a process called **factoring**.

To **factor** a number means to find two numbers that when multiplied together have a product equal to the original number. These two numbers are then said to be **factors** of the original number; e.g., the factors of 6 are

(1) 1 and 6 since $1 \times 6 = 6$.

(2) 2 and 3 since $2 \times 3 = 6$.

Every number is the product of itself and 1. A **prime factor** is a number that does not have any factors besides itself and 1. This is important when finding the LCD of two fractions having different denominators.

To find the LCD of $^{11}/_6$ and $^5/_{16}$, we must first find the prime factors of each of the two denominators.

$$6 = 2 \times 3$$

$$16 = 2 \times 2 \times 2 \times 2$$

$$LCD = 2 \times 2 \times 2 \times 2 \times 3 = 48$$

Note that we do not need to repeat the 2 that appears in both the factors of 6 and 16.

Once we have determined the LCD of the denominators, each of the fractions must be converted into equivalent fractions having the LCD as a denominator.

Rewrite $^{11}/_6$ and $^5/_{16}$ to have 48 as their denominators.

$$6 \times ? = 48 \qquad\qquad 16 \times ? = 48$$

$$6 \times 8 = 48 \qquad\qquad 16 \times 3 = 48$$

If the numerator and denominator of each fraction is multiplied (or divided) by the same number, the value of the fraction will not change. This is because a fraction b/b, b being any number, is equal to the multiplicative identity, 1.

Therefore,

$$\frac{11}{6} \times \frac{8}{8} = \frac{88}{48} \qquad \frac{5}{16} \times \frac{3}{3} = \frac{15}{48}$$

We may now find

$$\frac{11}{6} + \frac{5}{16} = \frac{88}{48} + \frac{15}{48} = \frac{103}{48}$$

Similarly for subtraction,

$$\frac{11}{6} - \frac{5}{16} = \frac{88}{48} - \frac{15}{48} = \frac{73}{48}$$

D) **To find the product of two or more fractions,** simply multiply the numerators of the given fractions to find the numerator of the product and multiply the denominators of the given fractions to find the denominator of the product, e.g.,

$$\frac{2}{3} \times \frac{1}{5} \times \frac{4}{7} = \frac{2 \times 1 \times 4}{3 \times 5 \times 7} = \frac{8}{105}$$

E) **To find the quotient of two fractions,** simply invert (or flip-over) the divisor and multiply; e.g.,

$$\frac{8}{9} \div \frac{1}{3} = \frac{8}{9} \times \frac{3}{1} = \frac{24}{9} = \frac{8}{3}$$

F) **To simplify a fraction** is to convert it into a form in which the numerator and denominator have no common factor other than 1; e.g.,

$$\frac{12}{18} = \frac{12 \div 6}{18 \div 6} = \frac{2}{3}$$

G) A **complex fraction** is a fraction whose numerator and/or denominator is made up of fractions. To simplify the fraction, find the LCD of all the fractions. Multiply both the numerator and denominator by this number and simplify.

PROBLEM

If $a = 4$ and $b = 7$, find the value of $\dfrac{a + \frac{a}{b}}{a - \frac{a}{b}}$.

SOLUTION

By substitution,

$$\frac{a + \frac{a}{b}}{a - \frac{a}{b}} = \frac{4 + \frac{4}{7}}{4 - \frac{4}{7}}$$

In order to combine the terms, we must find the LCD of 1 and 7. Since both are prime factors, the LCD $= 1 \times 7 = 7$.

Multiplying both the numerator and denominator by 7, we get

$$\frac{7\left(4 + \frac{4}{7}\right)}{7\left(4 - \frac{4}{7}\right)} = \frac{28 + 4}{28 - 4} = \frac{32}{24}$$

By dividing both the numerator and denominator by 8, $^{32}/_{24}$ can be reduced to $^4/_3$.

☞ Drill: Fractions

Changing an Improper Fraction to a Mixed Number

DIRECTIONS: Write each improper fraction as a mixed number in simplest form.

1. $\dfrac{50}{4}$

(A) $10\frac{1}{4}$ (B) $11\frac{1}{2}$ (C) $12\frac{1}{4}$ (D) $12\frac{1}{2}$ (E) 25

2. $\dfrac{17}{5}$

(A) $3\frac{2}{5}$ (B) $3\frac{3}{5}$ (C) $3\frac{4}{5}$ (D) $4\frac{1}{5}$ (E) $4\frac{2}{5}$

3. $\dfrac{42}{3}$

(A) $10\dfrac{2}{3}$ (B) 12 (C) $13\dfrac{1}{3}$ (D) 14 (E) $21\dfrac{1}{3}$

4. $\dfrac{85}{6}$

(A) $9\dfrac{1}{6}$ (B) $10\dfrac{5}{6}$ (C) $11\dfrac{1}{2}$ (D) 12 (E) $14\dfrac{1}{6}$

5. $\dfrac{151}{7}$

(A) $19\dfrac{6}{7}$ (B) $20\dfrac{1}{7}$ (C) $21\dfrac{4}{7}$ (D) $31\dfrac{2}{7}$ (E) $31\dfrac{4}{7}$

Changing a Mixed Number to an Improper Fraction

DIRECTIONS: Change each mixed number to an improper fraction in simplest form.

6. $2\dfrac{3}{5}$

(A) $\dfrac{4}{5}$ (B) $\dfrac{6}{5}$ (C) $\dfrac{11}{5}$ (D) $\dfrac{13}{5}$ (E) $\dfrac{17}{5}$

7. $4\dfrac{3}{4}$

(A) $\dfrac{7}{4}$ (B) $\dfrac{13}{4}$ (C) $\dfrac{16}{3}$ (D) $\dfrac{19}{4}$ (E) $\dfrac{21}{4}$

8. $6\dfrac{7}{6}$

(A) $\dfrac{13}{6}$ (B) $\dfrac{43}{6}$ (C) $\dfrac{19}{36}$ (D) $\dfrac{42}{36}$ (E) $\dfrac{48}{6}$

9. $12\dfrac{3}{7}$

(A) $\dfrac{87}{7}$ (B) $\dfrac{164}{14}$ (C) $\dfrac{34}{3}$ (D) $\dfrac{187}{21}$ (E) $\dfrac{252}{7}$

10. $21\dfrac{1}{2}$

(A) $\dfrac{11}{2}$ (B) $\dfrac{22}{2}$ (C) $\dfrac{24}{2}$ (D) $\dfrac{42}{2}$ (E) $\dfrac{43}{2}$

Adding Fractions with the Same Denominator

DIRECTIONS: Add and write the answer in simplest form.

11. $\dfrac{5}{12}+\dfrac{3}{12}=$

(A) $\dfrac{5}{24}$ (B) $\dfrac{1}{3}$ (C) $\dfrac{8}{12}$ (D) $\dfrac{2}{3}$ (E) $1\dfrac{1}{3}$

12. $\dfrac{5}{8}+\dfrac{7}{8}+\dfrac{3}{8}=$

(A) $\dfrac{15}{24}$ (B) $\dfrac{3}{4}$ (C) $\dfrac{5}{6}$ (D) $\dfrac{7}{8}$ (E) $1\dfrac{7}{8}$

13. $131\dfrac{2}{15}+28\dfrac{3}{15}=$

(A) $159\dfrac{1}{6}$ (B) $159\dfrac{1}{5}$ (C) $159\dfrac{1}{3}$ (D) $159\dfrac{1}{2}$ (E) $159\dfrac{3}{5}$

14. $3\dfrac{5}{18}+2\dfrac{1}{18}+8\dfrac{7}{18}=$

(A) $13\dfrac{13}{18}$ (B) $13\dfrac{3}{4}$ (C) $13\dfrac{7}{9}$ (D) $14\dfrac{1}{6}$ (E) $14\dfrac{2}{9}$

15. $17\dfrac{9}{20}+4\dfrac{3}{20}+8\dfrac{11}{20}=$

(A) $29\dfrac{23}{60}$ (B) $29\dfrac{23}{20}$ (C) $30\dfrac{3}{20}$ (D) $30\dfrac{1}{5}$ (E) $30\dfrac{3}{5}$

Subtracting Fractions with the Same Denominator

DIRECTIONS: Subtract and write the answer in simplest form.

16. $4\dfrac{7}{8} - 3\dfrac{1}{8} =$

(A) $1\dfrac{1}{4}$ (B) $1\dfrac{3}{4}$ (C) $1\dfrac{12}{16}$ (D) $1\dfrac{7}{8}$ (E) 2

17. $132\dfrac{5}{12} - 37\dfrac{3}{12} =$

(A) $94\dfrac{1}{6}$ (B) $95\dfrac{1}{12}$ (C) $95\dfrac{1}{6}$ (D) $105\dfrac{1}{6}$ (E) $169\dfrac{2}{3}$

18. $19\dfrac{1}{3} - 2\dfrac{2}{3} =$

(A) $16\dfrac{2}{3}$ (B) $16\dfrac{5}{6}$ (C) $17\dfrac{1}{3}$ (D) $17\dfrac{2}{3}$ (E) $17\dfrac{5}{6}$

19. $\dfrac{8}{21} - \dfrac{5}{21} =$

(A) $\dfrac{1}{21}$ (B) $\dfrac{1}{7}$ (C) $\dfrac{3}{21}$ (D) $\dfrac{2}{7}$ (E) $\dfrac{3}{7}$

20. $82\dfrac{7}{10} - 38\dfrac{9}{10} =$

(A) $43\dfrac{4}{5}$ (B) $44\dfrac{1}{5}$ (C) $44\dfrac{2}{5}$ (D) $45\dfrac{1}{5}$ (E) $45\dfrac{2}{10}$

Finding the LCD

DIRECTIONS: Find the lowest common denominator of each group of fractions.

21. $\dfrac{2}{3}, \dfrac{5}{9},$ and $\dfrac{1}{6}$

(A) 9 (B) 18 (C) 27 (D) 54 (E) 162

22. $\dfrac{1}{2}, \dfrac{5}{6},$ and $\dfrac{3}{4}$

(A) 2 (B) 4 (C) 6 (D) 12 (E) 48

23. $\dfrac{7}{16}$, $\dfrac{5}{6}$, and $\dfrac{2}{3}$

(A) 3   (B) 6   (C) 12   (D) 24   (E) 48

24. $\dfrac{8}{15}$, $\dfrac{2}{5}$, and $\dfrac{12}{25}$

(A) 5   (B) 15   (C) 25   (D) 75   (E) 375

25. $\dfrac{2}{3}$, $\dfrac{1}{5}$, and $\dfrac{5}{6}$

(A) 15   (B) 30   (C) 48   (D) 90   (E) 120

26. $\dfrac{1}{3}$, $\dfrac{9}{42}$, and $\dfrac{4}{21}$

(A) 21   (B) 42   (C) 126   (D) 378   (E) 4,000

27. $\dfrac{4}{9}$, $\dfrac{2}{5}$, and $\dfrac{1}{3}$

(A) 15   (B) 17   (C) 27   (D) 45   (E) 135

28. $\dfrac{7}{12}$, $\dfrac{11}{36}$, and $\dfrac{1}{9}$

(A) 12   (B) 36   (C) 108   (D) 324   (E) 432

29. $\dfrac{3}{7}$, $\dfrac{5}{21}$, and $\dfrac{2}{3}$

(A) 21   (B) 42   (C) 31   (D) 63   (E) 441

30. $\dfrac{13}{16}$, $\dfrac{5}{8}$, and $\dfrac{1}{4}$

(A) 4   (B) 8   (C) 16   (D) 32   (E) 64

Adding Fractions with Different Denominators

DIRECTIONS: Add and write the answer in simplest form.

31. $\dfrac{1}{3} + \dfrac{5}{12} =$

(A) $\dfrac{2}{5}$ (B) $\dfrac{1}{2}$ (C) $\dfrac{9}{12}$ (D) $\dfrac{3}{4}$ (E) $1\dfrac{1}{3}$

32. $3\dfrac{5}{9} + 2\dfrac{1}{3} =$

(A) $5\dfrac{1}{2}$ (B) $5\dfrac{2}{3}$ (C) $5\dfrac{8}{9}$ (D) $6\dfrac{1}{9}$ (E) $6\dfrac{2}{3}$

33. $12\dfrac{9}{16} + 17\dfrac{3}{4} + 8\dfrac{1}{8} =$

(A) $37\dfrac{7}{16}$ (B) $38\dfrac{7}{16}$ (C) $38\dfrac{1}{2}$ (D) $38\dfrac{2}{3}$ (E) $39\dfrac{3}{16}$

34. $28\dfrac{4}{5} + 11\dfrac{16}{25} =$

(A) $39\dfrac{2}{3}$ (B) $39\dfrac{4}{5}$ (C) $40\dfrac{9}{25}$ (D) $40\dfrac{2}{5}$ (E) $40\dfrac{11}{25}$

35. $2\dfrac{1}{8} + 1\dfrac{3}{16} + \dfrac{5}{12} =$

(A) $3\dfrac{35}{48}$ (B) $3\dfrac{3}{4}$ (C) $3\dfrac{19}{24}$ (D) $3\dfrac{13}{16}$ (E) $4\dfrac{1}{12}$

Subtracting Fractions with Different Denominators

DIRECTIONS: Subtract and write the answer in simplest form.

36. $8\dfrac{9}{12} - 2\dfrac{2}{3} =$

(A) $6\dfrac{1}{12}$ (B) $6\dfrac{1}{6}$ (C) $6\dfrac{1}{3}$ (D) $6\dfrac{7}{12}$ (E) $6\dfrac{2}{3}$

37. $185\frac{11}{15} - 107\frac{2}{5} =$

(A) $77\frac{2}{15}$ (B) $78\frac{1}{5}$ (C) $78\frac{3}{10}$ (D) $78\frac{1}{3}$ (E) $78\frac{9}{15}$

38. $34\frac{2}{3} - 16\frac{5}{6} =$

(A) 16   (B) $16\frac{1}{3}$ (C) $17\frac{1}{2}$ (D) 17   (E) $17\frac{5}{6}$

39. $3\frac{11}{48} - 2\frac{3}{16} =$

(A) $\frac{47}{48}$ (B) $1\frac{1}{48}$ (C) $1\frac{1}{24}$ (D) $1\frac{8}{48}$ (E) $1\frac{7}{24}$

40. $81\frac{4}{21} - 31\frac{1}{3} =$

(A) $47\frac{3}{7}$ (B) $49\frac{6}{7}$ (C) $49\frac{1}{6}$ (D) $49\frac{5}{7}$ (E) $49\frac{13}{21}$

Multiplying Fractions

<u>DIRECTIONS</u>: Multiply and reduce the answer.

41. $\frac{2}{3} \times \frac{4}{5} =$

(A) $\frac{6}{8}$ (B) $\frac{3}{4}$ (C) $\frac{8}{15}$ (D) $\frac{10}{12}$ (E) $\frac{6}{5}$

42. $\frac{7}{10} \times \frac{4}{21} =$

(A) $\frac{2}{15}$ (B) $\frac{11}{31}$ (C) $\frac{28}{210}$ (D) $\frac{1}{6}$ (E) $\frac{4}{15}$

43. $5\frac{1}{3} \times \frac{3}{8} =$

(A) $\frac{4}{11}$ (B) 2   (C) $\frac{8}{5}$ (D) $5\frac{1}{8}$ (E) $5\frac{17}{24}$

44. $6\dfrac{1}{2} \times 3 =$

(A) $9\dfrac{1}{2}$ (B) $18\dfrac{1}{2}$ (C) $19\dfrac{1}{2}$ (D) 20 (E) $12\dfrac{1}{2}$

45. $3\dfrac{1}{4} \times 2\dfrac{1}{3} =$

(A) $5\dfrac{7}{12}$ (B) $6\dfrac{2}{7}$ (C) $6\dfrac{5}{7}$ (D) $7\dfrac{7}{12}$ (E) $7\dfrac{11}{12}$

Dividing Fractions

DIRECTIONS: Divide and reduce the answer.

46. $\dfrac{3}{16} \div \dfrac{3}{4} =$

(A) $\dfrac{9}{64}$ (B) $\dfrac{1}{4}$ (C) $\dfrac{6}{16}$ (D) $\dfrac{9}{16}$ (E) $\dfrac{3}{4}$

47. $\dfrac{4}{9} \div \dfrac{2}{3} =$

(A) $\dfrac{1}{3}$ (B) $\dfrac{1}{2}$ (C) $\dfrac{2}{3}$ (D) $\dfrac{7}{11}$ (E) $\dfrac{8}{9}$

48. $5\dfrac{1}{4} \div \dfrac{7}{10} =$

(A) $2\dfrac{4}{7}$ (B) $3\dfrac{27}{40}$ (C) $5\dfrac{19}{20}$ (D) $7\dfrac{1}{2}$ (E) $8\dfrac{1}{4}$

49. $4\dfrac{2}{3} \div \dfrac{7}{9} =$

(A) $2\dfrac{24}{27}$ (B) $3\dfrac{2}{9}$ (C) $4\dfrac{14}{27}$ (D) $5\dfrac{12}{27}$ (E) 6

50. $3\dfrac{2}{5} \div 1\dfrac{7}{10} =$

(A) 2 (B) $3\dfrac{4}{7}$ (C) $4\dfrac{7}{25}$ (D) $5\dfrac{1}{10}$ (E) $5\dfrac{2}{7}$

DECIMALS

When we divide the denominator of a fraction into its numerator, the result is a **decimal**. The decimal is based upon a fraction with a denominator of 10, 100, 1,000, ... and is written with a **decimal point**. Whole numbers are placed to the left of the decimal point where the first place to the left is the units place; the second to the left is the tens; the third to the left is the hundreds, etc. The fractions are placed on the right where the first place to the right is the tenths; the second to the right is the hundredths, etc.

EXAMPLES

$$12 \frac{3}{10} = 12.3 \qquad 4 \frac{17}{100} = 4.17 \qquad \frac{3}{100} = .03$$

Since a **rational number** is of the form a/b, $b \neq 0$, then all rational numbers can be expressed as decimals by dividing b into a. The result is either a **terminating decimal**, meaning that b divides a with a remainder of 0 after a certain point; or **repeating decimal**, meaning that b continues to divide a so that the decimal has a repeating pattern of integers.

EXAMPLES

(A) $\dfrac{1}{2} = .5$

(B) $\dfrac{1}{3} = .333...$

(C) $\dfrac{11}{16} = .6875$

(D) $\dfrac{2}{7} = .285714285714...$

(A) and (C) are terminating decimals; (B) and (D) are repeating decimals. This explanation allows us to define **irrational numbers** as numbers whose decimal form is non-terminating and non-repeating, e.g.,

$$\sqrt{2} = 1.414...$$
$$\sqrt{3} = 1.732...$$

PROBLEM

Express $-\dfrac{10}{20}$ as a decimal.

SOLUTION

$$-\frac{10}{20} = -\frac{50}{100} = -.5$$

PROBLEM

> Write $\frac{2}{7}$ as a repeating decimal.

SOLUTION

To write a fraction as a repeating decimal divide the numerator by the denominator until a pattern of repeated digits appears.

$$2 \div 7 = .285714285714...$$

Identify the entire portion of the decimal which is repeated. The repeating decimal can then be written in the shortened form:

$$\frac{2}{7} = .\overline{285714}$$

OPERATIONS WITH DECIMALS

A) **To add numbers containing decimals,** write the numbers in a column making sure the decimal points are lined up, one beneath the other. Add the numbers as usual, placing the decimal point in the sum so that it is still in line with the others. It is important not to mix the digits in the tenths place with the digits in the hundredths place, and so on.

EXAMPLES

$$2.558 + 6.391 \qquad\qquad 57.51 + 6.2$$

$$
\begin{array}{r}
2.558 \\
+\ 6.391 \\
\hline
8.949
\end{array}
\qquad\qquad
\begin{array}{r}
57.51 \\
+\ \ \ 6.20 \\
\hline
63.71
\end{array}
$$

Similarly with subtraction,

$$78.54 - 21.33 \qquad\qquad 7.11 - 4.2$$

$$
\begin{array}{r}
78.54 \\
-\ 21.33 \\
\hline
57.21
\end{array}
\qquad\qquad
\begin{array}{r}
7.11 \\
-\ 4.20 \\
\hline
2.91
\end{array}
$$

Note that if two numbers differ according to the number of digits to the right of the decimal point, zeros must be added.

.63 – .214   15.224 – 3.6891

$$\begin{array}{r} .630 \\ -.214 \\ \hline .416 \end{array} \qquad \begin{array}{r} 15.2240 \\ -\ 3.6891 \\ \hline 11.5349 \end{array}$$

B) **To multiply numbers with decimals,** simply multiply as usual. Then, to figure out the number of decimal places that belong in the product, find the total number of decimal places in the numbers being multiplied.

EXAMPLES

$$\begin{array}{r} 6.555 \ \text{(3 decimal places)} \\ \times\quad 4.5 \ \text{(1 decimal place)} \\ \hline 32775 \\ 26220 \\ \hline 294975 \end{array} \qquad \begin{array}{r} 5.32 \ \text{(2 decimal places)} \\ \times\quad .04 \ \text{(2 decimal places)} \\ \hline 2128 \\ 000 \\ \hline 2128 \end{array}$$

    29.4975 (4 decimal places)   .2128 (4 decimal places)

C) **To divide numbers with decimals,** you must first make the divisor a whole number by moving the decimal point the appropriate number of places to the right. The decimal point of the dividend should also be moved the same number of places. Place a decimal point in the quotient, directly in line with the decimal point in the dividend.

EXAMPLES

12.92 ÷ 3.4   40.376 ÷ 7.21

$$\begin{array}{r} 3.8 \\ 3.4.\overline{)12.9.2} \\ -102 \\ \hline 272 \\ -272 \\ \hline 0 \end{array} \qquad \begin{array}{r} 5.6 \\ 7.21.\overline{)40.37.6} \\ -3605 \\ \hline 4326 \\ -4326 \\ \hline 0 \end{array}$$

If the question asks you to find the correct answer to two decimal places, simply divide until you have three decimal places and then round off. If the third decimal place is a 5 or larger, the number in the second decimal place is increased by 1. If the third decimal place is less than 5, that number is simply dropped.

PROBLEM

Find the answer to the following to two decimal places:

(1)   44.3 ÷ 3   (2)   56.99 ÷ 6

SOLUTION

(1)   14.766
     3)44.300
      −3
      14
     −12
      23
     −21
      20
     −18
      20
     −18
       2

(2)   9.498
     6)56.990
      −54
      29
     −24
      59
     −54
      50
     −48
       2

14.766 can be rounded off to 14.77

9.498 can be rounded off to 9.50

D)   When comparing two numbers with decimals to see which is the larger, first look at the tenths place. The larger digit in this place represents the larger number. If the two digits are the same, however, take a look at the digits in the hundredths place, and so on.

EXAMPLES

.518 and .216

5 is larger than 2, therefore .518 is larger than .216

.723 and .726

6 is larger than 3, therefore .726 is larger than .723

☞ Drill: Decimals

Addition

DIRECTIONS: Solve the following equations.

1.   1.032 + 0.987 + 3.07 =

(A) 4.089   (B) 5.089   (C) 5.189   (D) 6.189   (E) 13.972

2. 132.03 + 97.1483 =

(A) 98.4686   (B) 110.3513   (C) 209.1783

(D) 229.1486   (E) 229.1783

3. 7.1 + 0.62 + 4.03827 + 5.183 =

(A) 0.2315127   (B) 16.45433   (C) 16.94127

(D) 18.561   (E) 40.4543

4. 8 + 17.43 + 9.2 =

(A) 34.63   (B) 34.86   (C) 35.63   (D) 176.63   (E) 189.43

5. 1,036.173 + 289.04 =

(A) 382.6573   (B) 392.6573   (C) 1,065.077

(D) 1,325.213   (E) 3,926.573

Subtraction

DIRECTIONS: Solve the following equations.

6. 3.972 − 2.04 =

(A) 1.932   (B) 1.942   (C) 1.976   (D) 2.013   (E) 2.113

7. 16.047 − 13.06 =

(A) 2.887   (B) 2.987   (C) 3.041   (D) 3.141   (E) 4.741

8. 87.4 − 56.27 =

(A) 30.27   (B) 30.67   (C) 31.1   (D) 31.13   (E) 31.27

9. 1,046.8 − 639.14 =

(A) 303.84   (B) 313.74   (C) 407.66   (D) 489.74   (E) 535.54

10. 10,000 − 842.91 =

(A) 157.09   (B) 942.91   (C) 5,236.09

(D) 9,057.91   (E) 9,157.09

Multiplication

DIRECTIONS: Solve the following equations.

11. $1.03 \times 2.6 =$

(A) 2.18   (B) 2.678   (C) 2.78   (D) 3.38   (E) 3.63

12. $93 \times 4.2 =$

(A) 39.06   (B) 97.2   (C) 223.2   (D) 390.6   (E) 3,906

13. $0.04 \times 0.23 =$

(A) 0.0092   (B) 0.092   (C) 0.27   (D) 0.87   (E) 0.920

14. $0.0186 \times 0.03 =$

(A) 0.000348 (B) 0.000558 (C) 0.0548   (D) 0.0848   (E) 0.558

15. $51.2 \times 0.17 =$

(A) 5.29   (B) 8.534   (C) 8.704   (D) 36.352   (E) 36.991

Division

DIRECTIONS: Solve the following equations.

16. $123.39 \div 3 =$

(A) 31.12   (B) 41.13   (C) 401.13   (D) 411.3   (E) 4,113

17. $1,428.6 \div 6 =$

(A) 0.2381   (B) 2.381   (C) 23.81   (D) 238.1   (E) 2,381

18. $25.2 \div 0.3 =$

(A) 0.84   (B) 8.04   (C) 8.4   (D) 84   (E) 840

19. $14.95 \div 6.5 =$

(A) 2.3   (B) 20.3   (C) 23   (D) 230   (E) 2,300

20. $46.33 \div 1.13 =$

(A) 0.41   (B) 4.1   (C) 41   (D) 410   (E) 4,100

Comparing

<u>DIRECTIONS</u>: Solve the following equations.

21. Which is the **largest** number in this set—{0.8, 0.823, 0.089, 0.807, 0.852}?

(A) 0.8   (B) 0.823   (C) 0.089   (D) 0.807   (E) 0.852

22. Which is the **smallest** number in this set—{32.98, 32.099, 32.047, 32.5, 32.304}?

(A) 32.98   (B) 32.099   (C) 32.047   (D) 32.5   (E) 32.304

23. In which set below are the numbers arranged correctly from smallest to largest?

(A) {0.98, 0.9, 0.993}   (B) {0.113, 0.3, 0.31}

(C) {7.04, 7.26, 7.2}   (D) {0.006, 0.061, 0.06}

(E) {12.84, 12.801, 12.6}

24. In which set below are the numbers arranged correctly from largest to smallest?

(A) {1.018, 1.63, 1.368}   (B) {4.219, 4.29, 4.9}

(C) {0.62, 0.6043, 0.643}   (D) {16.34, 16.304, 16.3}

(E) {12.98, 12.601, 12.86}

25. Which is the **largest** number in this set—{0.87, 0.89, 0.889, 0.8, 0.987}?

(A) 0.87   (B) 0.89   (C) 0.889   (D) 0.8   (E) 0.987

Changing a Fraction to a Decimal

<u>DIRECTIONS</u>: Solve the following equations.

26. What is $\frac{1}{4}$ written as a decimal?

(A) 1.4   (B) 0.14   (C) 0.2   (D) 0.25   (E) 0.3

27. What is $\frac{3}{5}$ written as a decimal?

(A) 0.3   (B) 0.35   (C) 0.6   (D) 0.65   (E) 0.8

28. What is $\dfrac{7}{20}$ written as a decimal?

(A) 0.35   (B) 0.4   (C) 0.72   (D) 0.75   (E) 0.9

29. What is $\dfrac{2}{3}$ written as a decimal?

(A) 0.23   (B) 0.33   (C) 0.5   (D) 0.6   (E) $0.\overline{6}$

30. What is $\dfrac{11}{25}$ written as a decimal?

(A) 0.1125   (B) 0.25   (C) 0.4   (D) 0.44   (E) 0.5

PERCENTAGES

A **percent** is a way of expressing the relationship between part and whole, where whole is defined as 100%. A percent can be defined by a fraction with a denominator of 100. Decimals can also represent a percent. For instance,

$$56\% = 0.56 = \dfrac{56}{100}$$

PROBLEM

Compute the value of

(1) 90% of 400   (3) 50% of 500

(2) 180% of 400   (4) 200% of 4

SOLUTION

The symbol % means per hundred, therefore $5\% = {}^{5}/_{100}$

(1) 90% of 400 = 90 ÷ 100 × 400 = 90 × 4 = 360

(2) 180% of 400 = 180 ÷ 100 × 400 = 180 × 4 = 720

(3) 50% of 500 = 50 ÷ 100 × 500 = 50 × 5 = 250

(4) 200% of 4 = 200 ÷ 100 × 4 = 2 × 4 = 8

PROBLEM

What percent of

(1) 100 is 99.5   (2) 200 is 4

SOLUTION

(1) $99.5 = x \times 100$

$99.5 = 100x$

$.995 = x;$ but this is the value of x per hundred. Therefore,

$99.5\% = x$

(2) $4 = x \times 200$

$4 = 200x$

$.02 = x.$ Again this must be changed to percent, so

$2\% = x$

EQUIVALENT FORMS OF A NUMBER

Some problems may call for converting numbers into an equivalent or simplified form in order to make the solution more convenient.

A)   Converting a fraction to a decimal:

$$\frac{1}{2} = 0.50$$

Divide the numerator by the denominator:

```
     .50
2) 1.00
    -10
     00
```

B)   Converting a number to a percent:

$0.50 = 50\%$

Multiply by 100:

$0.50 = (0.50 \times 100)\% = 50\%$

C)   Converting a percent to a decimal:

$30\% = 0.30$

Divide by 100:

$30\% = 30 \div 100 = 0.30$

D)   Converting a decimal to a fraction:

$$0.500 = \frac{1}{2}$$

Convert .500 to $^{500}/_{1000}$ and then simplify the fraction by dividing the numerator and denominator by common factors:

$$\frac{\cancel{2}\times\cancel{2}\times\cancel{5}\times\cancel{5}\times\cancel{5}}{\cancel{2}\times\cancel{2}\times 2\times\cancel{5}\times\cancel{5}\times\cancel{5}}$$

and then cancel out the common numbers to get $^1/_2$.

PROBLEM

Express

(1) 1.65 as a percent   (2) 0.7 as a fraction

(3) $-\dfrac{10}{20}$ as a decimal   (4) $\dfrac{4}{2}$ as an integer

SOLUTION

(1) $1.65 \times 100 = 165\%$

(2) $0.7 = \dfrac{7}{10}$

(3) $-\dfrac{10}{20} = -0.5$

(4) $\dfrac{4}{2} = 2$

☞ Drill: Percentages

Finding Percents

DIRECTIONS: Solve to find the correct percentages.

1. Find 3% of 80.

(A) 0.24   (B) 2.4   (C) 24   (D) 240   (E) 2,400

2. Find 50% of 182.

(A) 9   (B) 90   (C) 91   (D) 910   (E) 9,100

3. Find 83% of 166.

(A) 0.137   (B) 1.377   (C) 13.778   (D) 137   (E) 137.78

4. Find 125% of 400.

(A) 425   (B) 500   (C) 525   (D) 600   (E) 825

5. Find 300% of 4.

(A) 12   (B) 120   (C) 1,200   (D) 12,000   (E) 120,000

6. Forty-eight percent of the 1,200 students at Central High are males. How many male students are there at Central High?

(A) 57   (B) 576   (C) 580   (D) 600   (E) 648

7. For 35% of the last 40 days, there has been measurable rainfall. How many days out of the last 40 days have had measurable rainfall?

(A) 14   (B) 20   (C) 25   (D) 35   (E) 40

8. Of every 1,000 people who take a certain medicine, 0.2% develop severe side effects. How many people out of every 1,000 who take the medicine develop the side effects?

(A) 0.2   (B) 2   (C) 20   (D) 22   (E) 200

9. Of 220 applicants for a job, 75% were offered an initial interview. How many people were offered an initial interview?

(A) 75   (B) 110   (C) 120   (D) 155   (E) 165

10. Find 0.05% of 4,000.

(A) 0.05   (B) 0.5   (C) 2   (D) 20   (E) 400

Changing Percents to Fractions

DIRECTIONS: Solve to find the correct fractions.

11. What is 25% written as a fraction?

(A) $\dfrac{1}{25}$ (B) $\dfrac{1}{5}$ (C) $\dfrac{1}{4}$ (D) $\dfrac{1}{3}$ (E) $\dfrac{1}{2}$

12. What is $33\dfrac{1}{3}$% written as a fraction?

(A) $\dfrac{1}{4}$ (B) $\dfrac{1}{3}$ (C) $\dfrac{1}{2}$ (D) $\dfrac{2}{3}$ (E) $\dfrac{5}{9}$

13. What is 200% written as a fraction?

(A) $\dfrac{1}{2}$　　(B) $\dfrac{2}{1}$　　(C) $\dfrac{20}{1}$　　(D) $\dfrac{200}{1}$　　(E) $\dfrac{2,000}{1}$

14. What is 84% written as a fraction?

(A) $\dfrac{1}{84}$　　(B) $\dfrac{4}{8}$　　(C) $\dfrac{17}{25}$　　(D) $\dfrac{21}{25}$　　(E) $\dfrac{44}{50}$

15. What is 2% written as a fraction?

(A) $\dfrac{1}{50}$　　(B) $\dfrac{1}{25}$　　(C) $\dfrac{1}{10}$　　(D) $\dfrac{1}{4}$　　(E) $\dfrac{1}{2}$

Changing Fractions to Percents

DIRECTIONS: Solve to find the following percentages.

16. What is $\dfrac{2}{3}$ written as a percent?

(A) 23%　　(B) 32%　　(C) $33\dfrac{1}{3}$%　　(D) $57\dfrac{1}{3}$%　　(E) $66\dfrac{2}{3}$%

17. What is $\dfrac{3}{5}$ written as a percent?

(A) 30%　　(B) 35%　　(C) 53%　　(D) 60%　　(E) 65%

18. What is $\dfrac{17}{20}$ written as a percent?

(A) 17%　　(B) 70%　　(C) 75%　　(D) 80%　　(E) 85%

19. What is $\dfrac{45}{50}$ written as a percent?

(A) 45%　　(B) 50%　　(C) 90%　　(D) 95%　　(E) 97%

20. What is $1\dfrac{1}{4}$ written as a percent?

(A) 114%　　(B) 120%　　(C) 125%　　(D) 127%　　(E) 133%

Changing Percents to Decimals

DIRECTIONS: Convert the percentages to decimals.

21. What is 42% written as a decimal?

(A) 0.42   (B) 4.2   (C) 42   (D) 420   (E) 422

22. What is 0.3% written as a decimal?

(A) 0.0003   (B) 0.003   (C) 0.03   (D) 0.3   (E) 3

23. What is 8% written as a decimal?

(A) 0.0008   (B) 0.008   (C) 0.08   (D) 0.80   (E) 8

24. What is 175% written as a decimal?

(A) 0.175   (B) 1.75   (C) 17.5   (D) 175   (E) 17,500

25. What is 34% written as a decimal?

(A) 0.00034   (B) 0.0034   (C) 0.034   (D) 0.34   (E) 3.4

Changing Decimals to Percents

DIRECTIONS: Convert the following decimals to percents.

26. What is 0.43 written as a percent?

(A) 0.0043%   (B) 0.043%   (C) 4.3%   (D) 43%   (E) 430%

27. What is 1 written as a percent?

(A) 1%   (B) 10%   (C) 100%   (D) 111%   (E) 150%

28. What is 0.08 written as a percent?

(A) 0.08%   (B) 8%   (C) 8.8%   (D) 80%   (E) 800%

29. What is 3.4 written as a percent?

(A) 0.0034%   (B) 3.4%   (C) 34%   (D) 304%   (E) 340%

30. What is 0.645 written as a percent?

(A) 64.5%   (B) 65%   (C) 69%   (D) 70%   (E) 645%

RADICALS

The **square root** of a number is a number that when multiplied by itself results in the original number. Thus, the square root of 81 is 9 since $9 \times 9 = 81$. However, -9 is also a root of 81 since $(-9)(-9) = 81$. Every positive number will have two roots. The principal root is the positive one. Zero has only one square root, while negative numbers do not have real numbers as their roots.

A **radical sign** indicates that the root of a number or expression will be taken. The **radicand** is the number of which the root will be taken. The **index** tells how many times the root needs to be multiplied by itself to equal the radicand, e.g.,

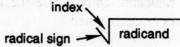

(1) $\sqrt[3]{64}$;

> 3 is the index and 64 is the radicand. Since $4 \times 4 \times 4 = 64$, then $\sqrt[3]{64} = 4$.

(2) $\sqrt[5]{32}$;

> 5 is the index and 32 is the radicand. Since $2 \times 2 \times 2 \times 2 \times 2 = 32$, then $\sqrt[5]{32} = 2$.

OPERATIONS WITH RADICALS

A) **To multiply two or more radicals**, we utilize the law that states,

$$\sqrt{a} \times \sqrt{b} = \sqrt{ab}.$$

Simply multiply the whole numbers as usual. Then, multiply the radicands and put the product under the radical sign and simplify, e.g.,

> (1) $\sqrt{12} \times \sqrt{5} = \sqrt{60} = 2\sqrt{15}$
>
> (2) $3\sqrt{2} \times 4\sqrt{8} = 12\sqrt{16} = 48$
>
> (3) $2\sqrt{10} \times 6\sqrt{5} = 12\sqrt{50} = 60\sqrt{2}$

B) **To divide radicals**, simplify both the numerator and the denominator. By multiplying the radical in the denominator by itself, you can make the denominator a rational number. The numerator, however, must also be multiplied by this radical so that the value of the expression does not change. You must choose as many factors as necessary to rationalize the denominator, e.g.,

(1) $\dfrac{\sqrt{128}}{\sqrt{2}} = \dfrac{\sqrt{64} \times \sqrt{2}}{\sqrt{2}} = \dfrac{8\sqrt{2}}{\sqrt{2}} = 8$

(2) $\dfrac{\sqrt{10}}{\sqrt{3}} = \dfrac{\sqrt{10} \times \sqrt{3}}{\sqrt{3} \times \sqrt{3}} = \dfrac{\sqrt{30}}{3}$

(3) $\dfrac{\sqrt{8}}{2\sqrt{3}} = \dfrac{\sqrt{8} \times \sqrt{3}}{2\sqrt{3} \times \sqrt{3}} = \dfrac{\sqrt{24}}{2 \times 3} = \dfrac{2\sqrt{6}}{6} = \dfrac{\sqrt{6}}{3}$

C) **To add two or more radicals**, the radicals must have the same index and the same radicand. Only where the radicals are simplified can these similarities be determined.

EXAMPLES

(1) $6\sqrt{2} + 2\sqrt{2} = (6+2)\sqrt{2} = 8\sqrt{2}$

(2) $\sqrt{27} + 5\sqrt{3} = \sqrt{9}\sqrt{3} + 5\sqrt{3} = 3\sqrt{3} + 5\sqrt{3} = 8\sqrt{3}$

(3) $7\sqrt{3} + 8\sqrt{2} + 5\sqrt{3} = 12\sqrt{3} + 8\sqrt{2}$

Similarly, to subtract,

(1) $12\sqrt{3} - 7\sqrt{3} = (12-7)\sqrt{3} = 5\sqrt{3}$

(2) $\sqrt{80} - \sqrt{20} = \sqrt{16}\sqrt{5} - \sqrt{4}\sqrt{5} = 4\sqrt{5} - 2\sqrt{5} = 2\sqrt{5}$

(3) $\sqrt{50} - \sqrt{3} = 5\sqrt{2} - \sqrt{3}$

☞ Drill: Radicals

Multiplication

DIRECTIONS: Multiply and simplify each answer.

1. $\sqrt{6} \times \sqrt{5} =$

(A) $\sqrt{11}$ (B) $\sqrt{30}$ (C) $2\sqrt{5}$ (D) $3\sqrt{10}$ (E) $2\sqrt{3}$

2. $\sqrt{3} \times \sqrt{12} =$

(A) 3 (B) $\sqrt{15}$ (C) $\sqrt{36}$ (D) 6 (E) 8

3. $\sqrt{7} \times \sqrt{7} =$

(A) 7   (B) 49   (C) $\sqrt{14}$ (D) $2\sqrt{7}$ (E) $2\sqrt{14}$

4. $3\sqrt{5} \times 2\sqrt{5} =$

(A) $5\sqrt{5}$ (B) 25   (C) 30   (D) $5\sqrt{25}$ (E) $6\sqrt{5}$

5. $4\sqrt{6} \times \sqrt{2} =$

(A) $4\sqrt{8}$ (B) $8\sqrt{2}$ (C) $5\sqrt{8}$ (D) $4\sqrt{12}$ (E) $8\sqrt{3}$

Division

DIRECTIONS: Divide and simplify the answer.

6. $\sqrt{10} \div \sqrt{2} =$

(A) $\sqrt{8}$ (B) $2\sqrt{2}$ (C) $\sqrt{5}$ (D) $2\sqrt{5}$ (E) $2\sqrt{3}$

7. $\sqrt{30} \div \sqrt{15} =$

(A) $\sqrt{2}$ (B) $\sqrt{45}$ (C) $3\sqrt{5}$ (D) $\sqrt{15}$ (E) $5\sqrt{3}$

8. $\sqrt{100} \div \sqrt{25} =$

(A) $\sqrt{4}$ (B) $5\sqrt{5}$ (C) $5\sqrt{3}$ (D) 2   (E) 4

9. $\sqrt{48} \div \sqrt{8} =$

(A) $4\sqrt{3}$ (B) $3\sqrt{2}$ (C) $\sqrt{6}$ (D) 6   (E) 12

10. $3\sqrt{12} \div \sqrt{3} =$

(A) $3\sqrt{15}$ (B) 6   (C) 9   (D) 12   (E) $3\sqrt{36}$

Addition

DIRECTIONS: Simplify each radical and add.

11. $\sqrt{7} + 3\sqrt{7} =$

(A) $3\sqrt{7}$ (B) $4\sqrt{7}$ (C) $3\sqrt{14}$ (D) $4\sqrt{14}$ (E) $3\sqrt{21}$

12. $\sqrt{5} + 6\sqrt{5} + 3\sqrt{5} =$

(A) $9\sqrt{5}$ (B) $9\sqrt{15}$ (C) $5\sqrt{10}$ (D) $10\sqrt{5}$ (E) $18\sqrt{15}$

13. $3\sqrt{32} + 2\sqrt{2} =$

(A) $5\sqrt{2}$ (B) $\sqrt{34}$ (C) $14\sqrt{2}$ (D) $5\sqrt{34}$ (E) $6\sqrt{64}$

14. $6\sqrt{15} + 8\sqrt{15} + 16\sqrt{15} =$

(A) $15\sqrt{30}$ (B) $30\sqrt{45}$ (C) $30\sqrt{30}$ (D) $15\sqrt{45}$ (E) $30\sqrt{15}$

15. $6\sqrt{5} + 2\sqrt{45} =$

(A) $12\sqrt{5}$ (B) $8\sqrt{50}$ (C) $40\sqrt{2}$ (D) $12\sqrt{50}$ (E) $8\sqrt{5}$

Subtraction

DIRECTIONS: Simplify each radical and subtract.

16. $8\sqrt{5} - 6\sqrt{5} =$

(A) $2\sqrt{5}$ (B) $3\sqrt{5}$ (C) $4\sqrt{5}$ (D) $14\sqrt{5}$ (E) $48\sqrt{5}$

17. $16\sqrt{33} - 5\sqrt{33} =$

(A) $3\sqrt{33}$ (B) $33\sqrt{11}$ (C) $11\sqrt{33}$ (D) $11\sqrt{0}$ (E) $\sqrt{33}$

18. $14\sqrt{2} - 19\sqrt{2} =$

(A) $5\sqrt{2}$ (B) $-5\sqrt{2}$ (C) $-33\sqrt{2}$ (D) $33\sqrt{2}$ (E) $-4\sqrt{2}$

19. $10\sqrt{2} - 3\sqrt{8} =$

(A) $6\sqrt{6}$ (B) $-2\sqrt{2}$ (C) $7\sqrt{6}$ (D) $4\sqrt{2}$ (E) $-6\sqrt{6}$

20. $4\sqrt{3} - 2\sqrt{12} =$

(A) $-2\sqrt{9}$ (B) $-6\sqrt{15}$ (C) 0 (D) $6\sqrt{15}$ (E) $2\sqrt{12}$

EXPONENTS

When a number is multiplied by itself a specific number of times, it is said to be **raised to a power**. The way this is written is $a^n = b$ where a is the number or **base**, n is the **exponent** or **power** that indicates the number of times the base is to be multiplied by itself, and b is the product of this multiplication.

In the expression 3^2, 3 is the base and 2 is the exponent. This means that 3 is multiplied by itself 2 times and the product is 9.

An exponent can be either positive or negative. A negative exponent implies a fraction such that if n is a negative integer

$$a^{-n} = \frac{1}{a^n}, \ a \neq 0. \ \text{So, } 2^{-4} = \frac{1}{2^4} = \frac{1}{16}.$$

An exponent that is 0 gives a result of 1, assuming that the base is not equal to 0.

$$a^0 = 1, \ a \neq 0.$$

An exponent can also be a fraction. If m and n are positive integers,

$$a^{\frac{m}{n}} = \sqrt[n]{a^m}$$

The numerator remains the exponent of a, but the denominator tells what root to take. For example,

(1) $4^{\frac{3}{2}} = \sqrt[2]{4^3} = \sqrt{64} = 8$ (2) $3^{\frac{4}{2}} = \sqrt[2]{3^4} = \sqrt{81} = 9$

If a fractional exponent were negative, the same operation would take place, but the result would be a fraction. For example,

(1) $27^{-\frac{3}{2}} = \frac{1}{27^{2/3}} = \frac{1}{\sqrt[3]{27^2}} = \frac{1}{\sqrt[3]{729}} = \frac{1}{9}$

PROBLEM

Simplify the following expressions:

(1) -3^{-2} (3) $\dfrac{-3}{4^{-1}}$

(2) $(-3)^{-2}$

SOLUTION

(1) Here the exponent applies only to 3. Since

$$x^{-y} = \frac{1}{x^y}, \quad -3^{-2} = -(3)^{-2} = -\left(\frac{1}{3^2}\right) = -\frac{1}{9}$$

(2) In this case the exponent applies to the negative base. Thus,

$$(-3)^{-2} = \frac{1}{(-3)^2} = \frac{1}{(-3)(-3)} = \frac{1}{9}$$

(3) $\dfrac{-3}{4^{-1}} = \dfrac{-3}{\left(\dfrac{1}{4}\right)^1} = \dfrac{-3}{\dfrac{1}{4^1}} = \dfrac{-3}{\dfrac{1}{4}}$

Division by a fraction is equivalent to multiplication by that fraction's reciprocal, thus

$$\frac{-3}{\dfrac{1}{4}} = -3 \times \frac{4}{1} = -12 \quad \text{and} \quad \frac{-3}{4^{-1}} = -12$$

General Laws of Exponents

A) $a^p a^q = a^{p+q}$

$$4^2 4^3 = 4^{2+3} = 1{,}024$$

B) $(a^p)^q = a^{pq}$

$$(2^3)^2 = 2^6 = 64$$

C) $\dfrac{a^p}{a^q} = a^{p-q}$

$$\frac{3^6}{3^2} = 3^4 = 81$$

D) $(ab)^p = a^p b^p$

$$(3 \times 2)^2 = 3^2 \times 2^2 = (9)(4) = 36$$

E) $\left(\dfrac{a}{b}\right)^p = \dfrac{a^p}{b^p}, \quad b \neq 0$

$$\left(\frac{4}{5}\right)^2 = \frac{4^2}{5^2} = \frac{16}{25}$$

☞ Drill: Exponents

Multiplication

DIRECTIONS: Simplify.

1. $4^6 \times 4^2 =$

(A) 4^4 (B) 4^8 (C) 4^{12} (D) 16^8 (E) 16^{12}

2. $2^2 \times 2^5 \times 2^3 =$

(A) 2^{10} (B) 4^{10} (C) 8^{10} (D) 2^{30} (E) 8^{30}

3. $6^6 \times 6^2 \times 6^4 =$

(A) 18^8 (B) 18^{12} (C) 6^{12} (D) 6^{48} (E) 18^{48}

4. $a^4 b^2 \times a^3 b =$

(A) ab (B) $2a^7 b^2$ (C) $2a^{12}b$ (D) $a^7 b^3$ (E) $a^7 b^2$

5. $m^8 n^3 \times m^2 n \times m^4 n^2 =$

(A) $3m^{16}n^6$ (B) $m^{14}n^6$ (C) $3m^{17}n^5$ (D) $3m^{14}n^5$ (E) m^2

Division

DIRECTIONS: Simplify.

6. $6^5 \div 6^3 =$

(A) 0   (B) 1   (C) 6   (D) 12   (E) 36

7. $11^8 \div 11^5 =$

(A) 1^3 (B) 11^3 (C) 11^{13} (D) 11^{40} (E) 88^5

8. $x^{10}y^8 \div x^7 y^3 =$

(A) $x^2 y^5$ (B) $x^3 y^4$ (C) $x^3 y^5$ (D) $x^2 y^4$ (E) $x^5 y^3$

9. $a^{14} \div a^9 =$

(A) 1^5 (B) a^5 (C) $2a^5$ (D) a^{23} (E) $2a^{23}$

10. $c^{17}d^{12}e^4 \div c^{12}d^8 e =$

(A) $c^4 d^5 e^3$ (B) $c^4 d^4 e^3$ (C) $c^5 d^8 e^4$ (D) $c^5 d^4 e^3$ (E) $c^5 d^4 e^4$

Power to a Power

DIRECTIONS: Simplify.

11. $(3^6)^2 =$

(A) 3^4 (B) 3^8 (C) 3^{12} (D) 9^6 (E) 9^8

12. $(4^3)^5 =$

(A) 4^2 (B) 2^{15} (C) 4^8 (D) 20^3 (E) 4^{15}

13. $(a^4b^3)^2 =$

(A) $(ab)^9$ (B) a^8b^6 (C) $(ab)^{24}$ (D) a^6b^5 (E) $2a^4b^3$

14. $(r^3p^6)^3 =$

(A) r^9p^{18} (B) $(rp)^{12}$ (C) r^6p^9 (D) $3r^3p^6$ (E) $3r^9p^{18}$

15. $(m^6n^5q^3)^2 =$

(A) $2m^6n^5q^3$ (B) m^4n^3q (C) $m^8n^7q^5$

(D) $m^{12}n^{10}q^6$ (E) $2m^{12}n^{10}q^6$

MEAN, MEDIAN, MODE

MEAN

The mean is the arithmetic average. It is the sum of the variables divided by the total number of variables. For example, the mean of 4, 3, and 8 is

$$\frac{4+3+8}{3} = \frac{15}{3} = 5$$

PROBLEM

Find the mean salary for four company employees who make $5/hr., $8/hr., $12/hr., and $15/hr.

SOLUTION

The mean salary is the average.

$$\frac{\$5+\$8+\$12+\$15}{4} = \frac{\$40}{4} = \$10/hr$$

PROBLEM

> Find the mean length of five fish with lengths of 7.5 in., 7.75 in., 8.5 in., 8.5 in., 8.25 in.

SOLUTION

The mean length is the average length.

$$\frac{7.5+7.75+8.5+8.5+8.25}{5}=\frac{40.5}{5}=8.1 \text{ in}$$

MEDIAN

The median is the middle value in a set when there is an odd number of values. There is an equal number of values larger and smaller than the median. When the set is an even number of values, the average of the two middle values is the median. For example:

The median of (2, 3, 5, 8, 9) is 5.

The median of (2, 3, 5, 9, 10, 11) is $\frac{5+9}{2}=7$.

MODE

The mode is the most frequently occurring value in the set of values. For example, the mode of 4, 5, 8, 3, 8, 2 would be 8, since it occurs twice while the other values occur only once.

PROBLEM

> For this series of observations find the mean, median and mode.
>
> 500, 600, 800, 800, 900, 900, 900, 900, 900, 1,000, 1,100

SOLUTION

The mean is the value obtained by adding all the measurements and dividing by the number of measurements.

$$\frac{500+600+800+800+900+900+900+900+900+1,000+1,100}{11}$$

$$=\frac{9,300}{11}=845.45.$$

The median is the value appearing in the middle. We have 11 values, so here the sixth, 900, is the median.

The mode is the value that appears most frequently. That is also 900, which has five appearances.

All three of these numbers are measures of central tendency. They describe the "middle" or "center" of the data.

PROBLEM

Nine rats run through a maze. The time each rat took to traverse the maze is recorded and these times (in minutes) are listed below.

1 min, 2.5 min, 3 min, 1.5 min, 2 min, 1.25 min, 1 min, .9 min, 30 min

Which of the three measures of central tendency would be the most appropriate in this case?

SOLUTION

We will calculate the three measures of central tendency and then compare them to determine which would be the most appropriate in describing these data.

The mean is the sum of the values listed divided by the number of values. In this case

$$\frac{1+2.5+3+1.5+2+1.25+1+.9+30}{9} = \frac{43.15}{9} = 4.79.$$

The median is the "middle number" in an array of the values from the lowest to the highest.

0.9, 1.0, 1.0, 1.25, 1.5, 2.0, 2.5, 3.0, 30.0

The median is the fifth value in this ordered array or 1.5. There are four values larger than 1.5 and four values smaller than 1.5.

The mode is the most frequently occurring value in the sample. In this data set the mode is 1.0.

mean = 4.79

median = 1.5

mode = 1.0

The mean is not appropriate here. Only one rat took more than 4.79 minutes to run the maze and this rat took 30 minutes. We see that the mean has been distorted by this one large value.

The median or mode seems to describe this data set better and would be more appropriate to use.

☞ Drill: Averages

Mean

DIRECTIONS: Find the mean of each set of numbers.

1. 18, 25, and 32

    (A) 3   (B) 25   (C) 50   (D) 75   (E) 150

2. $\dfrac{4}{9}, \dfrac{2}{3},$ and $\dfrac{5}{6}$

    (A) $\dfrac{11}{18}$ (B) $\dfrac{35}{54}$ (C) $\dfrac{41}{54}$ (D) $\dfrac{35}{18}$ (E) $\dfrac{54}{18}$

3. 97, 102, 116, and 137

    (A) 40   (B) 102   (C) 109   (D) 113   (E) 116

4. 12, 15, 18, 24, and 31

    (A) 18   (B) 19.3   (C) 20   (D) 25   (E) 100

5. 7, 4, 6, 3, 11, and 14

    (A) 5   (B) 6.5   (C) 7   (D) 7.5   (E) 8

Median

DIRECTIONS: Find the median value of each set of numbers.

6. 3, 8, and 6

    (A) 3   (B) 6   (C) 8   (D) 17   (E) 20

7. 19, 15, 21, 27, and 12

    (A) 19   (B) 15   (C) 21   (D) 27   (E) 94

8. $1\dfrac{2}{3}, 1\dfrac{7}{8}, 1\dfrac{3}{4},$ and $1\dfrac{5}{6}$

(A) $1\frac{30}{48}$ (B) $1\frac{2}{3}$ (C) $1\frac{3}{4}$ (D) $1\frac{19}{24}$ (E) $1\frac{21}{24}$

9. 29, 18, 21, and 35

(A) 29   (B) 18   (C) 21   (D) 35   (E) 25

10. 8, 15, 7, 12, 31, 3, and 28

(A) 7   (B) 11.6   (C) 12   (D) 14.9   (E) 104

Mode

DIRECTIONS: Find the mode(s) of each set of numbers.

11. 1, 3, 7, 4, 3, and 8

(A) 1   (B) 3   (C) 7   (D) 4   (E) None

12. 12, 19, 25, and 42

(A) 12   (B) 19   (C) 25   (D) 42   (E) None

13. 16, 14, 12, 16, 30, and 28

(A) 6   (B) 14   (C) 16   (D) $19.\overline{3}$ (E) None

14. 4, 3, 9, 2, 4, 5, and 2

(A) 3 and 9   (B) 5 and 9   (C) 4 and 5   (D) 2 and 4   (E) None

15. 87, 42, 111, 116, 39, 111, 140, 116, 97, and 111

(A) 111   (B) 116   (C) 39   (D) 140   (E) None

ARITHMETIC DRILLS

ANSWER KEY

Drill: Integers and Real Numbers

1.	(A)	9.	(E)	17.	(D)	25.	(D)
2.	(C)	10.	(B)	18.	(D)	26.	(D)
3.	(D)	11.	(B)	19.	(C)	27.	(B)
4.	(C)	12.	(E)	20.	(E)	28.	(C)
5.	(B)	13.	(C)	21.	(B)	29.	(A)
6.	(B)	14.	(A)	22.	(E)	30.	(C)
7.	(A)	15.	(B)	23.	(D)		
8.	(C)	16.	(B)	24.	(A)		

Drill: Fractions

1.	(D)	14.	(A)	27.	(D)	40.	(B)
2.	(A)	15.	(C)	28.	(B)	41.	(C)
3.	(D)	16.	(B)	29.	(A)	42.	(A)
4.	(E)	17.	(C)	30.	(C)	43.	(B)
5.	(C)	18.	(A)	31.	(D)	44.	(C)
6.	(D)	19.	(B)	32.	(C)	45.	(D)
7.	(D)	20.	(A)	33.	(B)	46.	(B)
8.	(B)	21.	(B)	34.	(E)	47.	(C)
9.	(A)	22.	(D)	35.	(A)	48.	(D)
10.	(E)	23.	(E)	36.	(A)	49.	(E)
11.	(D)	24.	(D)	37.	(D)	50.	(A)
12.	(E)	25.	(B)	38.	(E)		
13.	(C)	26.	(B)	39.	(C)		

Drill: Decimals

1.	(B)	9.	(C)	17.	(D)	25.	(E)
2.	(E)	10.	(E)	18.	(D)	26.	(D)
3.	(C)	11.	(B)	19.	(A)	27.	(C)
4.	(A)	12.	(D)	20.	(C)	28.	(A)
5.	(D)	13.	(A)	21.	(E)	29.	(E)
6.	(A)	14.	(B)	22.	(C)	30.	(D)
7.	(B)	15.	(C)	23.	(B)		
8.	(D)	16.	(B)	24.	(D)		

Drill: Percentages

1.	(B)	9.	(E)	17.	(D)	25.	(D)
2.	(C)	10.	(C)	18.	(E)	26.	(D)
3.	(E)	11.	(C)	19.	(C)	27.	(C)
4.	(B)	12.	(B)	20.	(C)	28.	(B)
5.	(A)	13.	(B)	21.	(A)	29.	(E)
6.	(B)	14.	(D)	22.	(B)	30.	(A)
7.	(A)	15.	(A)	23.	(C)		
8.	(B)	16.	(E)	24.	(B)		

Drill: Radicals

1.	(B)	6.	(C)	11.	(B)	16.	(A)
2.	(D)	7.	(A)	12.	(D)	17.	(C)
3.	(A)	8.	(D)	13.	(C)	18.	(B)
4.	(C)	9.	(C)	14.	(E)	19.	(D)
5.	(E)	10.	(B)	15.	(A)	20.	(C)

Drill: Exponents

1.	(B)	9.	(B)
2.	(A)	10.	(D)
3.	(C)	11.	(C)
4.	(D)	12.	(E)
5.	(B)	13.	(B)
6.	(E)	14.	(A)
7.	(B)	15.	(D)
8.	(C)		

Drill: Averages

1.	(B)	9.	(E)
2.	(B)	10.	(C)
3.	(D)	11.	(B)
4.	(C)	12.	(E)
5.	(D)	13.	(C)
6.	(B)	14.	(D)
7.	(A)	15.	(A)
8.	(D)		

II. ALGEBRA

In algebra, letters or variables are used to represent numbers. A **variable** is defined as a placeholder, which can take on any of several values at a given time. A **constant**, on the other hand, is a symbol which takes on only one value at a given time. A **term** is a constant, a variable, or a combination of constants and variables. For example: 7.76, $3x$, xyz, $5z/_x$, $(0.99)x^2$ are terms. If a term is a combination of constants and variables, the constant part of the term is referred to as the **coefficient** of the variable. If a variable is written without a coefficient, the coefficient is assumed to be 1.

EXAMPLES

$3x^2$
coefficient: 3
variable: x

y^3
coefficient: 1
variable: y

An **expression** is a collection of one or more terms. If the number of terms is greater than 1, the expression is said to be the sum of the terms.

EXAMPLES

$$9, 9xy, 6x + \frac{x}{3}, 8yz - 2x$$

An algebraic expression consisting of only one term is called a **monomial**; of two terms is called a **binomial**; of three terms is called a **trinomial**. In general, an algebraic expression consisting of two or more terms is called a **polynomial**.

OPERATIONS WITH POLYNOMIALS

A) **Addition of polynomials** is achieved by combining like terms, terms which differ only in their numerical coefficients, e.g.,

$$P(x) = (x^2 - 3x + 5) + (4x^2 + 6x - 3)$$

Note that the parentheses are used to distinguish the polynomials.

By using the commutative and associative laws, we can rewrite $P(x)$ as:

$$P(x) = (x^2 + 4x^2) + (6x - 3x) + (5 - 3)$$

Using the distributive law, $ab + ac = a(b + c)$, yields:

$(1 + 4)x^2 + (6 - 3)x + (5 - 3)$

$= 5x^2 + 3x + 2$

B) **Subtraction of two polynomials** is achieved by first changing the sign of all terms in the expression which are being subtracted and then adding this result to the other expression, e.g.,

$(5x^2 + 4y^2 + 3z^2) - (4xy + 7y^2 - 3z^2 + 1)$

$= 5x^2 + 4y^2 + 3z^2 - 4xy - 7y^2 + 3z^2 - 1$

$= 5x^2 + (4y^2 - 7y^2) + (3z^2 + 3z^2) - 4xy - 1$

$= 5x^2 + (-3y^2) + 6z^2 - 4xy - 1$

C) **Multiplication of two or more polynomials** is achieved by using the laws of exponents, the rules of signs, and the commutative and associative laws of multiplication. Begin by multiplying the coefficients and then multiply the variables according to the laws of exponents, e.g.,

$(y^2)\ (5)\ (6y^2)\ (yz)\ (2z^2)$

$= (1)\ (5)\ (6)\ (1)\ (2)\ (y^2)\ (y^2)\ (yz)\ (z^2)$

$= 60[(y^2)\ (y^2)\ (y)]\ [(z)\ (z^2)]$

$= 60(y^5)\ (z^3)$

$= 60y^5z^3$

D) **Multiplication of a polynomial by a monomial** is achieved by multiplying each term of the polynomial by the monomial and combining the results, e.g.,

$(4x^2 + 3y)\ (6xz^2)$

$= (4x^2)\ (6xz^2) + (3y)\ (6xz^2)$

$= 24x^3z^2 + 18xyz^2$

E) **Multiplication of a polynomial by a polynomial** is achieved by multiplying each of the terms of one polynomial by each of the terms of the other polynomial and combining the result, e.g.,

$(5y + z + 1)\ (y^2 + 2y)$

$[(5y)\ (y^2) + (5y)\ (2y)] + [(z)\ (y^2) + (z)\ (2y)] + [(1)\ (y^2) + (1)\ (2y)]$

$$= (5y^3 + 10y^2) + (y^2z + 2yz) + (y^2 + 2y)$$

$$= (5y^3) + (10y^2 + y^2) + (y^2z) + (2yz) + (2y)$$

$$= 5y^3 + 11y^2 + y^2z + 2yz + 2y$$

F) **Division of a monomial by a monomial** is achieved by first dividing the constant coefficients and the variable factors separately, and then multiplying these quotients, e.g.,

$$6xyz^2 \div 2y^2z$$

$$= \left(\frac{6}{2}\right)\left(\frac{x}{1}\right)\left(\frac{y}{y^2}\right)\left(\frac{z^2}{z}\right)$$

$$= 3xy^{-1}z$$

$$= \frac{3xz}{y}$$

G) **Division of a polynomial by a polynomial** is achieved by following the given procedure, called long division.

Step 1: The terms of both the polynomials are arranged in order of ascending or descending powers of one variable.

Step 2: The first term of the dividend is divided by the first term of the divisor which gives the first term of the quotient.

Step 3: This first term of the quotient is multiplied by the entire divisor and the result is subtracted from the dividend.

Step 4: Using the remainder obtained from Step 3 as the new dividend, Steps 2 and 3 are repeated until the remainder is zero or the degree of the remainder is less than the degree of the divisor.

Step 5: The result is written as follows:

$$\frac{dividend}{divisor} = quotient + \frac{remainder}{divisor}$$

divisor $\neq 0$

e.g., $(2x^2 + x + 6) \div (x + 1)$

$$
\begin{array}{r}
2x - 1 \\
(x+1)\overline{\smash{\big)}\, 2x^2 + x + 6} \\
\underline{-(2x^2 + 2x)} \\
-x + 6 \\
\underline{-(-x-1)} \\
7
\end{array}
$$

The result is $(2x^2 + x + 6) \div (x + 1) = 2x - 1 + \dfrac{7}{x+1}$

☞ Drill: Operations with Polynomials

Addition

DIRECTIONS: Add the following polynomials.

1. $9a^2b + 3c + 2a^2b + 5c =$

(A) $19a^2bc$ (B) $11a^2b + 8c$ (C) $11a^4b^2 + 8c^2$

(D) $19a^4b^2c^2$ (E) $12a^2b + 8c^2$

2. $14m^2n^3 + 6m^2n^3 + 3m^2n^3 =$

(A) $20m^2n^3$ (B) $23m^6n^9$ (C) $23m^2n^3$

(D) $32m^6n^9$ (E) $23m^8n^{27}$

3. $3x + 2y + 16x + 3z + 6y =$

(A) $19x + 8y$ (B) $19x + 11yz$ (C) $19x + 8y + 3z$

(D) $11xy + 19xz$ (E) $30xyz$

4. $(4d^2 + 7e^3 + 12f) + (3d^2 + 6e^3 + 2f) =$

(A) $23d^2e^3f$ (B) $33d^2e^2f$ (C) $33d^4e^6f^2$

(D) $7d^2 + 13e^3 + 14f$ (E) $23d^2 + 11e^3f$

5. $3ac^2 + 2b^2c + 7ac^2 + 2ac^2 + b^2c =$

(A) $12ac^2 + 3b^2c$ (B) $14ab^2c^2$ (C) $11ac^2 + 4ab^2c$

(D) $15ab^2c^2$ (E) $15a^2b^4c^4$

Subtraction

DIRECTIONS: Subtract the following polynomials.

6. $14m^2n - 6m^2n =$

(A) $20m^2n$ (B) $8m^2n$ (C) $8m$ (D) 8 (E) $8m^4n^2$

7. $3x^3y^2 - 4xz - 6x^3y^2 =$

(A) $-7x^2y^2z$ (B) $3x^3y^2 - 10x^4y^2z$ (C) $-3x^3y^2 - 4xz$

(D) $-x^2y^2z - 6x^3y^2$ (E) $-7xyz$

8. $9g^2 + 6h - 2g^2 - 5h =$

(A) $15g^2h - 7g^2h$ (B) $7g^4h^2$ (C) $11g^2 + 7h$

(D) $11g^2 - 7h^2$ (E) $7g^2 + h$

9. $7b^3 - 4c^2 - 6b^3 + 3c^2 =$

(A) $b^3 - c^2$ (B) $-11b^2 - 3c^2$ (C) $13b^3 - c$

(D) $7b - c$ (E) 0

10. $11q^2r - 4q^2r - 8q^2r =$

(A) $22q^2r$ (B) q^2r (C) $-2q^2r$

(D) $-q^2r$ (E) $2q^2r$

Multiplication

<u>DIRECTIONS</u>: Multiply the following polynomials.

11. $5p^2t \times 3p^2t =$

(A) $15p^2t$ (B) $15p^4t$ (C) $15p^4t^2$

(D) $8p^2t$ (E) $8p^4t^2$

12. $(2r + s)\,14r =$

(A) $28rs$ (B) $28r^2 + 14sr$ (C) $16r^2 + 14rs$

(D) $28r + 14sr$ (E) $17r^2s$

13. $(4m + p)(3m - 2p) =$

(A) $12m^2 + 5mp + 2p^2$ (B) $12m^2 - 2mp + 2p^2$ (C) $7m - p$

(D) $12m - 2p$ (E) $12m^2 - 5mp - 2p^2$

14. $(2a + b)(3a^2 + ab + b^2) =$

(A) $6a^3 + 5a^2b + 3ab^2 + b^3$ (B) $5a^3 + 3ab + b^3$

(C) $6a^3 + 2a^2b + 2ab^2$ (D) $3a^2 + 2a + ab + b + b^2$

(E) $6a^3 + 3a^2b + 5ab^2 + b^3$

15. $(6t^2 + 2t + 1)\, 3t =$

(A) $9t^2 + 5t + 3$ (B) $18t^2 + 6t + 3$ (C) $9t^3 + 6t^2 + 3t$

(D) $18t^3 + 6t^2 + 3t$ (E) $12t^3 + 6t^2 + 3t$

Division

DIRECTIONS: Divide the following polynomials.

16. $(x^2 + x - 6) \div (x - 2) =$

(A) $x - 3$ (B) $x + 2$ (C) $x + 3$ (D) $x - 2$ (E) $2x + 2$

17. $24b^4c^3 \div 6b^2c =$

(A) $3b^2c^2$ (B) $4b^4c^3$ (C) $4b^3c^2$ (D) $4b^2c^2$ (E) $3b^4c^3$

18. $(3p^2 + pq - 2q^2) \div (p + q) =$

(A) $3p + 2q$ (B) $2q - 3p$ (C) $3p - q$

(D) $2q + 3p$ (E) $3p - 2q$

19. $(y^3 - 2y^2 - y + 2) \div (y - 2) =$

(A) $(y - 1)^2$ (B) $y^2 - 1$ (C) $(y + 2)(y - 1)$

(D) $(y + 1)^2$ (E) $(y + 1)(y - 2)$

20. $(m^2 + m - 14) \div (m + 4) =$

(A) $m - 2$ (B) $m - 3 + \dfrac{-2}{m + 4}$ (C) $m - 3 + \dfrac{4}{m + 4}$

(D) $m - 3$ (E) $m - 2 + \dfrac{-3}{m + 4}$

FACTORING ALGEBRAIC EXPRESSIONS

To factor a polynomial completely is to find the prime factors of the polynomial with respect to a specified set of numbers.

The following concepts are important while factoring or simplifying expressions.

A) The factors of an algebraic expression consist of two or more algebraic expressions which, when multiplied together, produce the given algebraic expression.

B) A **prime factor** is a polynomial with no factors other than itself and 1. The **least common multiple (LCM)** for a set of numbers is the smallest quantity divisible by every number of the set. For algebraic expressions the least common numerical coefficients for each of the given expressions will be a factor.

C) The **greatest common factor (GCF)** for a set of numbers is the largest factor that is common to all members of the set.

D) For algebraic expressions, the greatest common factor is the polynomial of highest degree and the largest numerical coefficient which is a factor of all the given expressions.

Some important formulas, useful for the factoring of polynomials, are listed below.

$$a(c + d) = ac + ad$$

$$(a + b)(a - b) = a^2 - b^2$$

$$(a + b)(a + b) = (a + b)^2 = a^2 + 2ab + b^2$$

$$(a - b)(a - b) = (a - b)^2 = a^2 - 2ab + b^2$$

$$(x + a)(x + b) = x^2 + (a + b)x + ab$$

$$(ax + b)(cx + d) = acx^2 + (ad + bc)x + bd$$

$$(a + b)(c + d) = ac + bc + ad + bd$$

$$(a + b)(a + b)(a + b) = (a + b)^3 = a^3 + 3a^2b + 3ab^2 + b^3$$

$$(a - b)(a - b)(a - b) = (a - b)^3 = a^3 - 3a^2b + 3ab^2 - b^3$$

$$(a - b)(a^2 + ab + b^2) = a^3 - b^3$$

$$(a + b)(a^2 - ab + b^2) = a^3 + b^3$$

$$(a + b + c)^2 = a^2 + b^2 + c^2 + 2ab + 2ac + 2bc$$

$$(a - b)(a^3 + a^2b + ab^2 + b^3) = a^4 - b^4$$

$$(a - b)(a^4 + a^3b + a^2b^2 + ab^3 + b^4) = a^5 - b^5$$

$$(a - b)(a^5 + a^4b + a^3b^2 + a^2b^3 + ab^4 + b^5) = a^6 - b^6$$

$$(a - b)(a^{n-1} + a^{n-2}b + a^{n-3}b^2 + \ldots + ab^{n-2} + b^{n-1}) = a^n - b^n$$

where n is any positive integer (1, 2, 3, 4, ...).

$$(a + b) (a^{n-1} - a^{n-2}b + a^{n-3}b^2 - \ldots - ab^{n-2} + b^{n-1}) = a^n + b^n$$

where n is any positive odd integer $(1, 3, 5, 7, \ldots)$.

The procedure for factoring an algebraic expression completely is as follows:

Step 1: First find the greatest common factor if there is any. Then examine each factor remaining for greatest common factors.

Step 2: Continue factoring the factors obtained in Step 1 until all factors other than monomial factors are prime.

EXAMPLE

Factoring $4 - 16x^2$,

$$4 - 16x^2 = 4(1 - 4x^2) = 4(1 + 2x)(1 - 2x)$$

PROBLEM

Express each of the following as a single term.

(1) $3x^2 + 2x^2 - 4x^2$ (2) $5axy^2 - 7axy^2 - 3xy^2$

SOLUTION

(1)   Factor x^2 in the expression.

$$3x^2 + 2x^2 - 4x^2 = (3 + 2 - 4)x^2 = 1x^2 = x^2$$

(2)   Factor xy^2 in the expression and then factor a.

$$5axy^2 - 7axy^2 - 3xy^2 = (5a - 7a - 3)xy^2$$
$$= [(5 - 7)a - 3]xy^2$$
$$= (-2a - 3)xy^2$$

PROBLEM

Simplify $\dfrac{\frac{1}{x-1} - \frac{1}{x-2}}{\frac{1}{x-2} - \frac{1}{x-3}}$.

SOLUTION

Simplify the expression in the numerator by using the addition rule:

$$\frac{a}{b} + \frac{c}{d} = \frac{ad + bc}{bd}$$

Notice bd is the Least Common Denominator, LCD. We obtain

$$\frac{x-2-(x-1)}{(x-1)(x-2)} = \frac{-1}{(x-1)(x-2)}$$

in the numerator.

Repeat this procedure for the expression in the denominator:

$$\frac{x-3-(x-2)}{(x-2)(x-3)} = \frac{-1}{(x-2)(x-3)}$$

We now have

$$\frac{\frac{-1}{(x-1)(x-2)}}{\frac{-1}{(x-2)(x-3)}},$$

which is simplified by inverting the fraction in the denominator and multiplying it by the numerator and cancelling like terms

$$\frac{-1}{(x-1)(x-2)} \times \frac{(x-2)(x-3)}{-1} = \frac{x-3}{x-1}.$$

☞ Drill: Simplifying Algebraic Expressions

<u>DIRECTIONS</u>: Simplify the following expressions.

1. $16b^2 - 25z^2 =$

(A) $(4b - 5z)^2$ (B) $(4b + 5z)^2$ (C) $(4b - 5z)(4b + 5z)$

(D) $(16b - 25z)^2$ (E) $(5z - 4b)(5z + 4b)$

2. $x^2 - 2x - 8 =$

(A) $(x - 4)^2$ (B) $(x - 6)(x - 2)$ (C) $(x + 4)(x - 2)$

(D) $(x - 4)(x + 2)$ (E) $(x - 4)(x - 2)$

3. $2c^2 + 5cd - 3d^2 =$

(A) $(c - 3d)(c + 2d)$ (B) $(2c - d)(c + 3d)$ (C) $(c - d)(2c + 3d)$

(D) $(2c + d)(c + 3d)$ (E) Not possible.

4. $4t^3 - 20t =$

(A) $4t(t^2 - 5)$ (B) $4t^2(t - 20)$ (C) $4t(t + 4)(t - 5)$

(D) $2t(2t^2 - 10)$ (E) Not possible.

5. $x^2 + xy - 2y^2 =$

(A) $(x - 2y)(x + y)$ (B) $(x - 2y)(x - y)$ (C) $(x + 2y)(x + y)$

(D) $(x + 2y)(x - y)$ (E) Not possible.

6. $5b^2 + 17bd + 6d^2 =$

(A) $(5b + d)(b + 6d)$ (B) $(5b + 2d)(b + 3d)$ (C) $(5b - 2d)(b - 3d)$

(D) $(5b - 2d)(b + 3d)$ (E) Not possible.

7. $x^2 + x + 1 =$

(A) $(x + 1)^2$ (B) $(x + 2)(x - 1)$ (C) $(x - 2)(x + 1)$

(D) $(x + 1)(x - 1)$ (E) Not possible.

8. $3z^3 + 6z^2 =$

(A) $3(z^3 + 2z^2)$ (B) $3z^2(z + 2)$ (C) $3z(z^2 + 2z)$

(D) $z^2(3z + 6)$ (E) $3z^2(1 + 2z)$

9. $m^2p^2 + mpq - 6q^2 =$

(A) $(mp - 2q)(mp + 3q)$ (B) $mp(mp - 2q)(mp + 3q)$

(C) $mpq(1 - 6q)$ (D) $(mp + 2q)(mp + 3q)$

(E) Not possible.

10. $2h^3 + 2h^2t - 4ht^2 =$

(A) $2(h^3 - t)(h + t)$ (B) $2h(h - 2t)^2$ (C) $4h(ht - t^2)$

(D) $2h(h + t) - 4ht^2$ (E) $2h(h + 2t)(h - t)$

EQUATIONS

An **equation** is defined as a statement that two separate expressions are equal.

A **solution** to an equation containing a single variable is a number that makes the equation true when it is substituted for the variable. For example, in the equation $3x = 18$, 6 is the solution since $3(6) = 18$. Depending on the equation, there can be more than one solution. Equations with the same solutions are said to be **equivalent equations**. An equation without a solution is said to have a solution set that is the **empty** or **null** set and is represented by ϕ.

Replacing an expression within an equation by an equivalent expression will result in a new equation with solutions equivalent to the original equation. Suppose we are given the equation

$$3x + y + x + 2y = 15.$$

By combining like terms we get

$$3x + y + x + 2y = 4x + 3y.$$

Since these two expressions are equivalent, we can substitute the simpler form into the equation to get

$$4x + 3y = 15$$

Performing the same operation to both sides of an equation by the same expression will result in a new equation that is equivalent to the original equation.

A) **Addition or subtraction**

$$y + 6 = 10$$

We can add (-6) to both sides

$$y + 6 + (-6) = 10 + (-6)$$

to get $y + 0 = 10 - 6 \rightarrow y = 4$

B) **Multiplication or division**

$$3x = 6$$

$$\frac{3x}{3} = \frac{6}{3}$$

$$x = 2$$

$3x = 6$ is equivalent to $x = 2$.

C) **Raising to a power**

$$a = x^2 y$$

$$a^2 = (x^2 y)^2$$

$$a^2 = x^4 y^2$$

This can be applied to negative and fractional powers as well, e.g.,

$$x^2 = 3y^4$$

If we raise both sides to the -2 power, we get

$$(x^2)^{-2} = (3y^4)^{-2}$$
$$\frac{1}{(x^2)^2} = \frac{1}{(3y^4)^2}$$
$$\frac{1}{x^4} = \frac{1}{9y^8}$$

If we raise both sides to the $^1/_2$ power, which is the same as taking the square root, we get

$$(x^2)^{1/2} = (3y^4)^{1/2}$$
$$x = \pm\sqrt{3}y^2$$

D) The **reciprocal** of both sides of an equation are equivalent to the original equation. Note: The reciprocal of zero is undefined.

$$\frac{2x+y}{z} = \frac{5}{2} \qquad \frac{z}{2x+y} = \frac{2}{5}$$

PROBLEM

Solve for x, justifying each step.

$$3x - 8 = 7x + 8$$

SOLUTION

$$3x - 8 = 7x + 8$$

Add 8 to both sides: $\qquad\qquad 3x - 8 + 8 = 7x + 8 + 8$

Additive inverse property: $\qquad\qquad 3x + 0 = 7x + 16$

Additive identity property: $\qquad\qquad 3x = 7x + 16$

Add $(-7x)$ to both sides: $\qquad\qquad 3x - 7x = 7x + 16 - 7x$

Commute: $\qquad\qquad -4x = 7x - 7x + 16$

Additive inverse property: $\qquad\qquad -4x = 0 + 16$

Additive identity property: $\qquad\qquad -4x = 16$

Divide both sides by -4: $\qquad\qquad x = {}^{16}/_{-4}$

$$x = -4$$

Check: Replacing x with -4 in the original equation:

$$3x - 8 = 7x + 8$$
$$3(-4) - 8 = 7(-4) + 8$$
$$-12 - 8 = -28 + 8$$
$$-20 = -20$$

LINEAR EQUATIONS

A linear equation with one unknown is one that can be put into the form $ax + b = 0$, where a and b are constants, $a \neq 0$.

To solve a linear equation means to transform it in the form $x = -b/a$.

A) If the equation has unknowns on both sides of the equality, it is convenient to put similar terms on the same sides. Refer to the following example.

$$4x + 3 = 2x + 9$$
$$4x + 3 - 2x = 2x + 9 - 2x$$
$$(4x - 2x) + 3 = (2x - 2x) + 9$$
$$2x + 3 = 0 + 9$$
$$2x + 3 - 3 = 0 + 9 - 3$$
$$2x = 6$$
$$\frac{2x}{2} = \frac{6}{2}$$
$$x = 3$$

B) If the equation appears in fractional form, it is necessary to transform it, using cross-multiplication, and then repeating the same procedure as in A), we obtain:

$$\frac{3x + 4}{3} \diagup\hspace{-1.2em}\diagdown \frac{7x + 2}{5}$$

By using cross-multiplication we would obtain:

$$3(7x + 2) = 5(3x + 4).$$

This is equivalent to:

$$21x + 6 = 15x + 20,$$

which can be solved as in A).

$$21x + 6 = 15x + 20$$
$$21x - 15x + 6 = 15x - 15x + 20$$

$$6x + 6 - 6 = 20 - 6$$

$$6x = 14$$

$$x = \frac{14}{6}$$

$$x = \frac{7}{3}$$

C) If there are radicals in the equation, it is necessary to square both sides and then apply A).

$$\sqrt{3x+1} = 5$$

$$(\sqrt{3x+1})^2 = 5^2$$

$$3x + 1 = 25$$

$$3x + 1 - 1 = 25 - 1$$

$$3x = 24$$

$$x = \frac{24}{3}$$

$$x = 8$$

PROBLEM

Solve the equation $2(x + 3) = (3x + 5) - (x - 5)$.

SOLUTION

We transform the given equation to an equivalent equation in which we can easily recognize the solution set.

$$2(x + 3) = 3x + 5 - (x - 5)$$

Distribute: $2x + 6 = 3x + 5 - x + 5$

Combine terms: $2x + 6 = 2x + 10$

Subtract $2x$ from both sides: $6 = 10$

Since $6 = 10$ is not a true statement, there is no real number x which will make the original equation true. The equation is inconsistent and the solution set is ϕ, the empty set.

PROBLEM

Solve the equation $2(^2/_3\, y + 5) + 2(y + 5) = 130$.

SOLUTION

The procedure for solving this equation is as follows:

Distribute:
$$\frac{4}{3}y + 10 + 2y + 10 = 130$$

Combine like terms:
$$\frac{4}{3}y + 2y + 20 = 130$$

Subtract 20 from both sides:
$$\frac{4}{3}y + 2y = 110$$

Convert $2y$ into a fraction with denominator 3:
$$\frac{4}{3}y + \frac{6}{3}y = 110$$

Combine like terms:
$$\frac{10}{3}y = 110$$

Divide by $^{10}/_3$:
$$y = 110 \times \frac{3}{10} = 33$$

Check: Replace y with 33 in the original equation.

$$2(\frac{2}{3}(33) + 5) + 2(33 + 5) = 130$$

$$2(22 + 5) + 2(38) = 130$$

$$2(27) + 76 = 130$$

$$54 + 76 = 130$$

$$130 = 130$$

Therefore, the solution to the given equation is $y = 33$.

☞ Drill: Linear Equations

DIRECTIONS: Solve for x.

1. $4x - 2 = 10$

(A) -1 (B) 2   (C) 3   (D) 4   (E) 6

2. $7z + 1 - z = 2z - 7$

(A) -2 (B) 0   (C) 1   (D) 2   (E) 3

3. $\frac{1}{3}b + 3 = \frac{1}{2}b$

(A) $\frac{1}{2}$ (B) 2   (C) $3\frac{3}{5}$ (D) 6   (E) 18

4. $0.4p + 1 = 0.7p - 2$

(A) 0.1   (B) 2   (C) 5   (D) 10   (E) 12

5. $4(3x + 2) - 11 = 3(3x - 2)$

(A) – 3   (B) – 1   (C) 2   (D) 3   (E) 7

TWO LINEAR EQUATIONS

Equations of the form $ax + by = c$, where a, b, c are constants and a, b $\neq 0$ are called **linear equations** with two unknown variables.

There are several ways to solve systems of linear equations with two variables.

Method 1: **Addition or subtraction**—if necessary, multiply the equations by numbers that will make the coefficients of one unknown in the resulting equations numerically equal. If the signs of equal coefficients are the same, subtract the equation, otherwise add.

The result is one equation with one unknown; we solve it and substitute the value into the other equations to find the unknown that we first eliminated.

Method 2: **Substitution**—find the value of one unknown in terms of the other. Substitute this value in the other equation and solve.

Method 3: **Graph**—graph both equations. The point of intersection of the drawn lines is a simultaneous solution for the equations and its coordinates correspond to the answer that would be found analytically.

If the lines are parallel they have no simultaneous solution.

Dependent equations are equations that represent the same line; therefore, every point on the line of a dependent equation represents a solution. Since there is an infinite number of points on a line there is an infinite number of simultaneous solutions, for example,

$$\begin{cases} 2x + y = 8 \\ 4x + 2y = 16 \end{cases}$$

The equations on the previous page are dependent. Since they represent the same line, all points that satisfy either of the equations are solutions of the system.

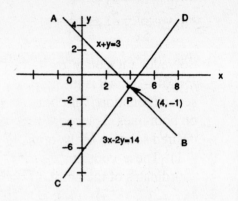

A system of linear equations is consistent if there is only one solution for the system.

A system of linear equations is inconsistent if it does not have any solutions.

EXAMPLE

Find the point of intersection of the graphs of the equations as shown in the previous figure.

$$x + y = 3$$

$$3x - 2y = 14$$

To solve these linear equations, solve for y in terms of x. The equations will be in the form $y = mx + b$, where m is the slope and b is the intercept on the y-axis.

$$x + y = 3$$

Subtract x from both sides: $y = 3 - x$

Subtract $3x$ from both sides: $3x - 2y = 14$

Divide by -2: $-2y = 14 - 3x$

$$y = -7 + \frac{3}{2}x$$

The graphs of the linear functions, $y = 3 - x$ and $y = 7 + {}^3/_2 x$ can be determined by plotting only two points. For example, for $y = 3 - x$, let $x = 0$, then $y = 3$. Let $x = 1$, then $y = 2$. The two points on this first line are $(0, 3)$ and $(1, 2)$. For $y = -7 + {}^3/_2 x$, let $x = 0$, then $y = -7$. Let $x = 1$, then $y = -5^1/_2$. The two points on this second line are $(0, -7)$ and $(1, -5^1/_2)$.

To find the point of intersection P of

$$x + y = 3 \quad \text{and} \quad 3x - 2y = 14,$$

solve them algebraically. Multiply the first equation by 2. Add these two equations to eliminate the variable y.

$$2x + 2y = 6$$
$$\underline{3x - 2y = 14}$$
$$5x \qquad = 20$$

Solve for x to obtain $x = 4$. Substitute this into $y = 3 - x$ to get $y = 3 - 4 = -1$. P is $(4, -1)$. AB is the graph of the first equation, and CD is the graph of the second equation. The point of intersection P of the two graphs is the only point on both lines. The coordinates of P satisfy both equations and represent the desired solution of the problem. From the graph, P seems to be the point $(4, -1)$. These coordinates satisfy both equations, and hence are the exact coordinates of the point of intersection of the two lines.

To show that $(4, -1)$ satisfies both equations, substitute this point into both equations.

$$x + y = 3 \qquad\qquad 3x - 2y = 14$$
$$4 + (-1) = 3 \qquad\qquad 3(4) - 2(-1) = 14$$
$$4 - 1 = 3 \qquad\qquad 12 + 2 = 14$$
$$3 = 3 \qquad\qquad 14 = 14$$

EXAMPLE

Solve the equations $2x + 3y = 6$ and $4x + 6y = 7$ simultaneously.

We have 2 equations and 2 unknowns,

$$2x + 3y = 6 \quad (1)$$

and

$$4x + 6y = 7 \quad (2)$$

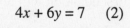

There are several methods to solve this problem. We have chosen to multiply each equation by a different number so that when the two equations are added, one of the variables drops out. Thus,

Multiply equation (1) by 2: $\qquad 4x + 6y = 12 \qquad\qquad\qquad (3)$

Multiply equation (2) by -1: $\qquad \underline{-4x - 6y = -7} \qquad\qquad\qquad (4)$

Add equations (3) and (4): $\qquad\qquad 0 = 5$

We obtain a peculiar result!

Actually, what we have shown in this case is that if there were a simultaneous solution to the given equations, then 0 would equal 5. But the conclusion is impossible; therefore there can be no simultaneous solution to these two equations, hence no point satisfying both.

The straight lines which are the graphs of these equations must be parallel if they never intersect, but not identical, which can be seen from the graph of these equations (see the accompanying diagram).

EXAMPLE

Solve the equations $2x + 3y = 6$ and $y = -(2x/3) + 2$ simultaneously.

We have 2 equations and 2 unknowns.

$$2x + 3y = 6 \qquad (1)$$

and

$$y = -\left(\frac{2x}{3}\right) + 2 \qquad (2)$$

There are several methods of solution for this problem. Since equation (2) already gives us an expression for y, we use the method of substitution. Substitute: $-(2x/3) + 2$ for y in the first equation:

$$2x + 3(-\frac{2x}{3} + 2) = 6$$

Distribute: $\qquad\qquad 2x - 2x + 6 = 6$

$$6 = 6$$

Apparently we have gotten nowhere! The result $6 = 6$ is true, but indicates no solution. Actually, our work shows that no matter what real number x is, if y is determined by the second equation, then the first equation will always be satisfied.

The reason for this peculiarity may be seen if we take a closer look at the equation $y = -(2x/3) + 2$. It is equivalent to $3y = -2x + 6$, or $2x + 3y = 6$.

In other words, the two equations are equivalent. Any pair of values of x and y which satisfies one satisfies the other.

It is hardly necessary to verify that in this case the graphs of the given equations are identical lines, and that there are an infinite number of simultaneous solutions of these equations.

A system of three linear equations in three unknowns is solved by eliminating one unknown from any two of the three equations and solving them. After finding two unknowns substitute them in any of the equations to find the third unknown.

PROBLEM

Solve the system

$$2x + 3y - 4z = -8 \qquad (1)$$

$$x + y - 2z = -5 \qquad (2)$$

$$7x - 2y + 5z = 4 \qquad (3)$$

SOLUTION

We cannot eliminate any variable from two pairs of equations by a single multiplication. However, both x and z may be eliminated from equations 1 and 2 by multiplying equation (2) by -2. Then

$$2x + 3y - 4z = -8 \qquad (1)$$

$$-2x - 2y + 4z = 10 \qquad (4)$$

By addition, we have $y = 2$. Although we may now eliminate either x or z from another pair of equations, we can more conveniently substitute $y = 2$ in equations (2) and (3) to get two equations in two variables. Thus, making the substitution $y = 2$ in equations (2) and (3), we have

$$x - 2z = -7 \qquad (5)$$

$$7x + 5z = 8 \qquad (6)$$

Multiply equation (5) by 5 and multiply (6) by 2. Then add the two new equations. Then $x = -1$. Substitute x in either equation (5) or (6) to find z.

The solution of the system is $x = -1$, $y = 2$, and $z = 3$. Check by substitution.

A system of equations, as shown below, that has all constant terms b_1, b_2, ..., b_n equal to zero is said to be a homogeneous system.

$$\begin{cases} a_{11}x_1 + a_{12}x_2 + \ldots + a_{1n}x_m = b_1 \\ a_{21}x_1 + a_{22}x_2 + \ldots + a_{2n}x_m = b_2 \\ \vdots \qquad \vdots \qquad \qquad \vdots \qquad \vdots \\ a_{n1}x_1 + a_{n2}x_2 + \ldots + a_{nn}x_m = b_n \end{cases}$$

A homogeneous system (one in which each variable can be replaced by a constant and the constant can be factored out) always has at least one solution which is called the trivial solution that is $x_1 = 0, x_2 = 0, \ldots, x_m = 0$.

For any given homogeneous system of equations, in which the number of variables is greater than or equal to the number of equations, there are non-trivial solutions.

Two systems of linear equations are said to be equivalent if and only if they have the same solution set.

PROBLEM

Solve for x and y.

$$x + 2y = 8 \tag{1}$$

$$3x + 4y = 20 \tag{2}$$

SOLUTION

Solve equation (1) for x in terms of y: $\qquad x = 8 - 2y \quad$ (3)

Substitute $(8 - 2y)$ for x in (2): $\qquad 3(8 - 2y) + 4y = 20 \qquad$ (4)

Solve (4) for y as follows:

Distribute: $\qquad 24 - 6y + 4y = 20$

Combine like terms and then subtract 24 from both sides:

$$24 - 2y = 20$$

$$24 - 24 - 2y = 20 - 24$$

$$-2y = -4$$

Divide both sides by -2: $\qquad\qquad\qquad\qquad\qquad y = 2$

Substitute 2 for y in equation (1): $\qquad x + 2(2) = 8$

$$x = 4$$

Thus, our solution is $x = 4, y = 2$.

Check: Substitute $x = 4, y = 2$ in equations (1) and (2):

$$4 + 2(2) = 8$$

$$8 = 8$$

$$3(4) + 4(2) = 20$$

$$20 = 20$$

PROBLEM

Solve algebraically.

$$4x + 2y = -1 \tag{1}$$
$$5x - 3y = 7 \tag{2}$$

SOLUTION

We arbitrarily choose to eliminate x first.

Multiply (1) by 5: $\qquad 20x + 10y = -5 \tag{3}$

Multiply (2) by 4: $\qquad 20x - 12y = 28 \tag{4}$

Subtract (3) from (4): $\qquad 22y = -33 \tag{5}$

Divide (5) by 22: $\qquad y = \dfrac{33}{22} = -\dfrac{3}{2},$

To find x, substitute $y = -{}^3\!/_2$ in either of the original equations. If we use equation (1), we obtain $4x + 2(-{}^3\!/_2) = -1$, $4x - 3 = -1$, $4x = 2$, $x = {}^1\!/_2$.

The solution $({}^1\!/_2, -{}^3\!/_2)$ should be checked in both equations of the given system.

Replacing $({}^1\!/_2, -{}^3\!/_2)$ in equation (1):

$$4x + 2y = -1$$
$$4\left(\frac{1}{2}\right) + 2\left(-\frac{3}{2}\right) = -1$$
$$\frac{4}{2} - 3 = -1$$
$$2 - 3 = -1$$
$$-1 = -1$$

Replacing $({}^1\!/_2, -{}^3\!/_2)$ in equation (2):

$$5x - 3y = 7$$
$$5\left(\frac{1}{2}\right) - 3\left(-\frac{3}{2}\right) = 7$$
$$\frac{5}{2} + \frac{9}{2} = 7$$

$$\frac{14}{2} = 7$$

$$7 = 7$$

(Instead of eliminating x from the two given equations, we could have eliminated y by multiplying equation (1) by 3, multiplying equation (2) by 2, and then adding the two derived equations.)

☞ Drill: Two Linear Equations

DIRECTIONS: Find the solution set for each pair of equations.

1. $3x + 4y = -2$
    $x - 6y = -8$

(A) $(2, -1)$ (B) $(1, -2)$ (C) $(-2, -1)$

(D) $(1, 2)$ (E) $(-2, 1)$

2. $2x + y = -10$
    $-2x - 4y = 4$

(A) $(6, -2)$ (B) $(-6, 2)$ (C) $(-2, 6)$

(D) $(2, 6)$ (E) $(-6, -2)$

3. $6x + 5y = -4$
    $3x - 3y = 9$

(A) $(1, -2)$ (B) $(1, 2)$ (C) $(2, -1)$

(D) $(-2, 1)$ (E) $(-1, 2)$

4. $4x + 3y = 9$
    $2x - 2y = 8$

(A) $(-3, 1)$ (B) $(1, -3)$ (C) $(3, 1)$

(D) $(3, -1)$ (E) $(-1, 3)$

5. $x + y = 7$
    $x = y - 3$

(A) $(5, 2)$ (B) $(-5, 2)$ (C) $(2, 5)$

(D) $(-2, 5)$ (E) $(2, -5)$

6. $5x + 6y = 4$
   $3x - 2y = 1$

(A) $(3, 6)$ (B) $\left(\dfrac{1}{2}, \dfrac{1}{4}\right)$ (C) $(-3, 6)$

(D) $(2, 4)$ (E) $\left(\dfrac{1}{3}, \dfrac{3}{2}\right)$

7. $x - 2y = 7$
   $x + y = -2$

(A) $(-2, 7)$ (B) $(3, -1)$ (C) $(-7, 2)$

(D) $(1, -3)$ (E) $(1, -2)$

8. $4x + 3y = 3$
   $-2x + 6y = 3$

(A) $\left(\dfrac{1}{2}, \dfrac{2}{3}\right)$ (B) $(-0.3, 0.6)$ (C) $\left(\dfrac{2}{3}, -1\right)$

(D) $(-0.2, 0.5)$ (E) $(0.3, 0.6)$

9. $4x - 2y = -14$
   $8x + y = 7$

(A) $(0, 7)$ (B) $(2, -7)$ (C) $(7, 0)$

(D) $(-7, 2)$ (E) $(0, 2)$

10. $6x - 3y = 1$
    $-9x + 5y = -1$

(A) $(1, -1)$ (B) $\left(\dfrac{2}{3}, 1\right)$ (C) $\left(1, \dfrac{2}{3}\right)$

(D) $(-1, 1)$ (E) $\left(\dfrac{2}{3}, -1\right)$

QUADRATIC EQUATIONS

A second degree equation in x of the type $ax^2 + bx + c = 0, a \neq 0, a, b$ and c are real numbers, is called a **quadratic equation**.

To solve a quadratic equation is to find values of x which satisfy $ax^2 + bx + c = 0$. These values of x are called **solutions**, or **roots**, of the equation.

A quadratic equation has a maximum of two roots. Methods of solving quadratic equations:

A) **Direct solution**: Given $x^2 - 9 = 0$.

We can solve directly by isolating the variable x.

$$x^2 = 9$$

$$x = \pm 3$$

B) **Factoring**: Given a quadratic equation $ax^2 + bx + c = 0$, a, b, $c \neq 0$, to factor means to express it as the product $a(x - r_1)(x - r_2) = 0$, where r_1 and r_2 are the two roots.

Some helpful hints to remember are

a) $r_1 + r_2 = -\dfrac{b}{a}$.

b) $r_1 r_2 = \dfrac{c}{a}$.

Given $x^2 - 5x + 4 = 0$.

Since

$$r_1 + r_2 = -\frac{b}{a} = -\frac{(-5)}{1} = 5,$$

the possible solutions are $(3, 2)$, $(4, 1)$, and $(5, 0)$. Also

$$r_1 r_2 = \frac{c}{a} = \frac{4}{1} = 4;$$

this equation is satisfied only by the second pair, so $r_1 = 4$, $r_2 = 1$, and the factored form is $(x - 4)(x - 1) = 0$.

If the coefficient of x^2 is not 1, it is necessary to divide the equation by this coefficient and then factor.

Given $2x^2 - 12x + 16 = 0$.

Dividing by 2, we obtain

$$x^2 - 6x + 8 = 0.$$

Since

$$r_1 + r_2 = -\frac{b}{a} = 6,$$

the possible solutions are (6, 0), (5, 1), (4, 2), and (3, 3). Also $r_1 r_2 = 8$, so the only possible answer is (4, 2) and the expression $x^2 - 6x + 8 = 0$ can be factored as $(x - 4)(x - 2)$.

C) **Completing the Squares**: If it is difficult to factor the quadratic equation using the previous method, we can complete the squares.

Given $x^2 - 12x + 8 = 0$.

We know that the two roots added up should be 12 because

$$r_1 + r_2 = -\frac{b}{a} = \frac{-(-12)}{1} = 12.$$

The possible roots are (12, 0), (11, 1), (10, 2), (9, 3), (8, 4), (7, 5), and (6, 6).

But none of these satisfy $r_1 r_2 = 8$, so we cannot use (B).

To complete the square, it is necessary to isolate the constant term,

$$x^2 - 12x = -8.$$

Then take $1/2$ coefficient of x, square it and add to both sides.

$$x^2 - 12x + \left(\frac{-12}{2}\right)^2 = -8 + \left(\frac{-12}{2}\right)^2$$

$$x^2 - 12x + 36 = -8 + 36 = 28$$

Now we can use the previous method to factor the left side.

$$r_1 + r_2 = 12, \ r_1 r_2 = 36$$

is satisfied by the pair (6, 6), so we have

$$(x - 6)^2 = 28.$$

Now extract the root of both sides and solve for x.

$$(x - 6) = \pm \sqrt{28} = \pm 2\sqrt{7}$$
$$x = \pm 2\sqrt{7} + 6$$

So the roots are

$$x = 2\sqrt{7} + 6, \ x = -2\sqrt{7} + 6.$$

PROBLEM

> Solve the equation $x^2 + 8x + 15 = 0$.

SOLUTION

Since

$$(x + a)(x + b) = x^2 + bx + ax + ab$$

$$= x^2 + (a + b)x + ab,$$

we may factor the given equation,

$$0 = x^2 + 8x + 15,$$

replacing $a + b$ by 8 and ab by 15. Thus,

$$a + b = 8, \quad \text{and} \quad ab = 15.$$

We want the two numbers a and b whose sum is 8 and whose product is 15. We check all pairs of numbers whose product is 15.

(a) $1 \times 15 = 15$; thus, $a = 1$, $b = 15$, and $ab = 15$.

$1 + 15 = 16$; therefore, we reject these values because $a + b \neq 8$.

(b) $3 \times 5 = 15$; thus, $a = 3$, $b = 5$, and $ab = 15$.

$3 + 5 = 8$; therefore, $a + b = 8$, and we accept these values.

Hence, $x^2 + 8x + 15 = 0$ is equivalent to

$$0 = x^2 + (3 + 5)x + 3 \times 5 = (x + 3)(x + 5)$$

Hence, $x + 5 = 0$ or $x + 3 = 0$

since the product of these two numbers is zero, one of the numbers must be zero. Hence, $x = -5$, or $x = -3$, and the solution set is $x = \{-5, -3\}$.

The student should note that $x = -5$ or $x = -3$. We are certainly not making the statement that $x = -5$ and $x = -3$. Also, the student should check that both these numbers do actually satisfy the given equations and hence are solutions.

Check: Replacing x by (-5) in the original equation:

$$x^2 + 8x + 15 = 0$$

$$(-5)^2 + 8(-5) + 15 = 0$$

$$25 - 40 + 15 = 0$$

$$-15 + 15 = 0$$

$$0 = 0$$

Replacing x by (-3) in the original equation:

$$x^2 + 8x + 15 = 0$$

$$(-3)^2 + 8(-3) + 15 = 0$$

$$9 - 24 + 15 = 0$$

$$-15 + 15 = 0$$

$$0 = 0$$

PROBLEM

Solve the following equations by factoring.

(1) $2x^2 + 3x = 0$ (2) $y^2 - 2y - 3 = y - 3$

(3) $z^2 - 2z - 3 = 0$ (4) $2m^2 - 11m - 6 = 0$

SOLUTION

(1) $2x^2 + 3x = 0$. Factor out the common factor of x from the left side of the given equation.

$$x(2x + 3) = 0$$

Whenever a product $ab = 0$, where a and b are any two numbers, either $a = 0$ or $b = 0$. Then, either

$$x = 0 \quad \text{or} \quad 2x + 3 = 0$$

$$2x = -3$$

$$x = -\frac{3}{2}$$

Hence, the solution set to the original equation $2x^2 + 3x = 0$ is: $\{-3/2, 0\}$.

(2) $y^2 - 2y - 3 = y - 3$. Subtract $(y - 3)$ from both sides of the given equation :

$$y^2 - 2y - 3 - (y - 3) = y - 3 - (y - 3)$$

$$y^2 - 2y - 3 - y + 3 = y - 3 - y + 3$$

$$y^2 - 2y - \cancel{3} - y + \cancel{3} = \cancel{y} - \cancel{3} - \cancel{y} + \cancel{3}$$

$$y^2 - 3y = 0$$

Factor out a common factor of y from the left side of this equation:

$$y(y - 3) = 0$$

Thus, $y = 0$ or $y - 3 = 0$, $y = 3$.

Therefore, the solution set to the original equation $y^2 - 2y - 3 = y - 3$ is $\{0, 3\}$.

(3) $z^2 - 2z - 3 = 0$. Factor the original equation into a product of two polynomials.

$$z^2 - 2z - 3 = (z - 3)(z + 1) = 0$$

Hence,

$$(z - 3)(z + 1) = 0; \text{ and } z - 3 = 0 \quad \text{or } z + 1 = 0$$

$$z = 3 \qquad\qquad z = -1$$

Therefore, the solution set to the original equation $z^2 - 2z - 3 = 0$ is $\{-1, 3\}$.

(4) $2m^2 - 11m - 6 = 0$. Factor the original equation into a product of two polynomials.

$$2m^2 - 11m - 6 = (2m + 1)(m - 6) = 0$$

Thus,

$$2m + 1 = 0 \quad \text{or} \quad m - 6 = 0$$

$$2m = -1 \qquad\qquad m = 6$$

$$m = -\frac{1}{2}$$

Therefore, the solution set to the original equation $2m^2 - 11m - 6 = 0$ is $\{-\frac{1}{2}, 6\}$.

☞ Drill: Quadratic Equations

DIRECTIONS: Solve for all values of x.

1. $x^2 - 2x - 8 = 0$

(A) 4 and -2 (B) 4 and 8   (C) 4

(D) -2 and 8   (E) -2

2. $x^2 + 2x - 3 = 0$

(A) -3 and 2   (B) 2 and 1   (C) 3 and 1

(D) -3 and 1   (E) -3

3. $x^2 - 7x = -10$

(A) -3 and 5   (B) 2 and 5   (C) 2

(D) -2 and -5 (E) 5

4. $x^2 - 8x + 16 = 0$

(A) 8 and 2   (B) 1 and 16   (C) 4

(D) -2 and 4   (E) 4 and -4

5. $3x^2 + 3x = 6$

(A) 3 and -6 (B) 2 and 3   (C) -3 and 2

(D) 1 and -3 (E) 1 and -2

6. $x^2 + 7x = 0$

(A) 7   (B) 0 and -7 (C) -7

(D) 0 and 7   (E) 0

7. $x^2 - 25 = 0$

(A) 5   (B) 5 and -5 (C) 15 and 10

(D) -5 and 10   (E) -5

8. $2x^2 + 4x = 16$

(A) 2 and -2 (B) 8 and -2 (C) 4 and 8

(D) 2 and -4 (E) 2 and 4

9. $6x^2 - x - 2 = 0$

(A) 2 and 3   (B) $\dfrac{1}{2}$ and $\dfrac{1}{3}$ (C) $-\dfrac{1}{2}$ and $\dfrac{2}{3}$

(D) $\dfrac{2}{3}$ and 3   (E) 2 and $-\dfrac{1}{3}$

10. $12x^2 + 5x = 3$

(A) $\dfrac{1}{3}$ and $-\dfrac{1}{4}$
(B) 4 and -3
(C) 4 and $\dfrac{1}{6}$

(D) $\dfrac{1}{3}$ and -4
(E) $-\dfrac{3}{4}$ and $\dfrac{1}{3}$

ABSOLUTE VALUE EQUATIONS

The absolute value of a, $|a|$, is defined as

$|a| = a$ when $a > 0$,

$|a| = -a$ when $a < 0$,

$|a| = 0$ when $a = 0$.

When the definition of absolute value is applied to an equation, the quantity within the absolute value symbol is considered to have two values. This value can be either positive or negative before the absolute value is taken. As a result, each absolute value equation actually contains two separate equations.

When evaluating equations containing absolute values, proceed as follows:

EXAMPLE

$|5 - 3x| = 7$ is valid if either

$$5 - 3x = 7 \qquad \text{or} \qquad 5 - 3x = -7$$

$$-3x = 2 \qquad\qquad\qquad -3x = -12$$

$$x = -\frac{2}{3} \qquad\qquad\qquad x = 4$$

The solution set is therefore $x = (-^2/_3, 4)$.

Remember, the absolute value of a number cannot be negative. So, for the equation $|5x + 4| = -3$, there would be no solution.

EXAMPLE

Solve for x in $|2x - 6| = |4 - 5x|$.

There are four possibilities here. $2x - 6$ and $4 - 5x$ can be either positive or negative. Therefore,

$$2x - 6 = 4 - 5x \qquad\qquad\qquad\qquad (1)$$

$$-(2x-6) = 4 - 5x \qquad (2)$$

$$2x - 6 = -(4 - 5x) \qquad (3)$$

$$-(2x-6) = -(4 - 5x) \qquad (4)$$

Equations (2) and (3) result in the same solution, as do equations (1) and (4). Therefore, it is necessary to solve only for equations (1) and (2). This gives

$$2x - 6 = 4 - 5x \qquad \text{or} \qquad -(2x-6) = 4 - 5x$$

$$7x = 10 \qquad\qquad\qquad -2x + 6 = 4 - 5x$$

$$x = \frac{10}{7} \qquad\qquad\qquad x = -\frac{2}{3}$$

The solution set is $(^{10}/_7, -^2/_3)$.

☞ Drill: Absolute Value Equations

DIRECTIONS: Find the appropriate solutions.

1. $|4x - 2| = 6$

(A) -2 and -1 (B) -1 and 2   (C) 2

(D) $\dfrac{1}{2}$ and -2 (E) No solution

2. $\left|3 - \dfrac{1}{2}y\right| = -7$

(A) -8 and 20   (B) 8 and -20 (C) 2 and -5

(D) 4 and -2 (E) No solution

3. $2|x + 7| = 12$

(A) -13 and -1 (B) -6 and 6   (C) -1 and 13

(D) 6 and -13 (E) No solution

4. $|5x| - 7 = 3$

(A) 2 and 4   (B) $\dfrac{4}{5}$ and 3   (C) -2 and 2

(D) 2   (E) No solution

5. $\left| \dfrac{3}{4}m \right| = 9$

(A) 24 and -16 (B) $\dfrac{4}{27}$ and $-\dfrac{4}{3}$ (C) $\dfrac{4}{3}$ and 12

(D) -12 and 12   (E) No solution

INEQUALITIES

An inequality is a statement where the value of one quantity or expression is greater than (>), less than (<), greater than or equal to (≥), less than or equal to (≤), or not equal to (≠) that of another.

EXAMPLE

$5 > 4$

The expression above means that the value of 5 is greater than the value of 4.

A **conditional inequality** is an inequality whose validity depends on the values of the variables in the sentence. That is, certain values of the variables will make the sentence true, and others will make it false.

$3 - y > 3 + y$

is a conditional inequality for the set of real numbers, since it is true for any replacement less than zero and false for all others.

$x + 5 > x + 2$

is an **absolute inequality** for the set of real numbers, meaning that for any real value x, the expression on the left is greater than the expression on the right.

$5y < 2y + y$

is inconsistent for the set of non-negative real numbers. For any y greater than 0 the sentence is always false. A sentence is inconsistent if it is always false when its variables assume allowable values.

The solution of a given inequality in one variable x consists of all values of x for which the inequality is true.

The graph of an inequality in one variable is represented by either a ray or a line segment on the real number line.

The endpoint is not a solution if the variable is strictly less than or greater than a particular value.

EXAMPLE

$x > 2$

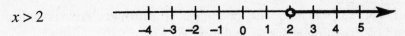

2 is not a solution and should be represented as shown.

The endpoint is a solution if the variable is either (1) less than or equal to or (2) greater than or equal to, a particular value.

EXAMPLE

$5 > x \geq 2$

In this case 2 is the solution and should be represented as shown.

PROPERTIES OF INEQUALITIES

If x and y are real numbers, then one and only one of the following statements is true.

$x > y$, $x = y$, or $x < y$.

This is the order property of real numbers.

If a, b, and c are real numbers, the following are true:

A)   If $a < b$ and $b < c$ then $a < c$.

B)   If $a > b$ and $b > c$ then $a > c$.

This is the transitive property of inequalities.

If a, b, and c are real numbers and $a > b$, then $a + c > b + c$ and $a - c > b - c$. This is the **addition property of inequality**.

Two inequalities are said to have the same **sense** if their signs of inequality point in the same direction.

The sense of an inequality remains the same if both sides are multiplied or divided by the same positive real number.

EXAMPLE

$4 > 3$
If we multiply both sides by 5, we will obtain

$4 \times 5 > 3 \times 5$

$20 > 15$

The sense of the inequality does not change.

The sense of an inequality becomes opposite if each side is multiplied or divided by the same negative real number.

EXAMPLE

$4 > 3$

If we multiply both sides by -5, we would obtain

$4 \times -5 < 3 \times -5$

$-20 < -15$

The sense of the inequality becomes opposite.

If $a > b$ and a, b, and n are positive real numbers, then

$a^n > b^n$ and $a^{-n} < b^{-n}$

If $x > y$ and $q > p$, then $x + q > y + p$.

If $x > y > 0$ and $q > p > 0$, then $xq > yp$.

Inequalities that have the same solution set are called **equivalent inequalities**.

PROBLEM

Solve the inequality $2x + 5 > 9$.

SOLUTION

Add -5 to both sides: $\quad\quad\quad\quad\quad 2x + 5 + (-5) > 9 + (-5)$

Additive inverse property: $\quad\quad\quad 2x + 0 > 9 + (-5)$

Additive identity property: $\quad\quad\quad 2x > 9 + (-5)$

Combine terms: $\quad\quad\quad\quad\quad\quad\quad 2x > 4$

Multiply both sides by $\dfrac{1}{2}$: $\quad\quad\quad \dfrac{1}{2}(2x) > \dfrac{1}{2} \times 4$

$x > 2$

The solution set is

$X = \{x \mid 2x + 5 > 9\}$

$= \{x \mid x > 2\}$

(that is all x, such that x is greater than 2).

PROBLEM

Solve the inequality $4x + 3 < 6x + 8$.

SOLUTION

In order to solve the inequality $4x + 3 < 6x + 8$, we must find all values of x which make it true. Thus, we wish to obtain x alone on one side of the inequality.

Add -3 to both sides:

$$\begin{array}{r} 4x + 3 < 6x\ +8 \\ \underline{-3 \qquad\quad -3} \\ 4x < 6x + 5 \end{array}$$

Add $-6x$ to both sides:

$$\begin{array}{r} 4x\ <\ \ 6x + 5 \\ \underline{-6x\quad -6x} \\ -2x\ <\ \ \ 5 \end{array}$$

In order to obtain x alone we must divide both sides by (-2). Recall that dividing an inequality by a negative number reverses the inequality sign, hence

$$\frac{-2x}{-2} > \frac{5}{-2}$$

Cancelling $^{-2}/_{-2}$ we obtain, $x > -\,^{5}/_{2}$.

Thus, our solution is $\{x : x > -\,^{5}/_{2}\}$ (the set of all x such that x is greater than $-\,^{5}/_{2}$).

☞ Drill: Inequalities

DIRECTIONS: Find the solution set for each inequality.

1. $3m + 2 < 7$

(A) $m \geq \dfrac{5}{3}$ (B) $m \leq 2$ (C) $m < 2$

(D) $m > 2$ (E) $m < \dfrac{5}{3}$

2. $\dfrac{1}{2}x - 3 \leq 1$

(A) $-4 \leq x \leq 8$ (B) $x \geq -8$ (C) $x \leq 8$

(D) $2 \leq x \leq 8$ (E) $x \geq 8$

3. $-3p + 1 \geq 16$

(A) $p \geq -5$ (B) $p \geq \dfrac{-17}{3}$ (C) $p \leq \dfrac{-17}{3}$

(D) $p \leq -5$ (E) $p \geq 5$

4. $-6 < \dfrac{2}{3}r + 6 \leq 2$

(A) $-6 < r \leq -3$ (B) $-18 < r \leq -6$ (C) $r \geq -6$

(D) $-2 < r \leq -\dfrac{4}{3}$ (E) $r \leq -6$

5. $0 < 2 - y < 6$

(A) $-4 < y < 2$ (B) $-4 < y < 0$ (C) $-4 < y < -2$

(D) $-2 < y < 4$ (E) $0 < y < 4$

RATIOS AND PROPORTIONS

The ratio of two numbers x and y written $x : y$ is the fraction x/y where $y \neq 0$. A ratio compares x to y by dividing one by the other. Therefore, in order to compare ratios, simply compare the fractions.

A proportion is an equality of two ratios. The laws of proportion are listed below.

If $\dfrac{a}{b} = \dfrac{c}{d}$, then

(A) $ad = bc$

(B) $\dfrac{b}{a} = \dfrac{d}{c}$

(C) $\dfrac{a}{c} = \dfrac{b}{d}$

(D) $\dfrac{a+b}{b} = \dfrac{c+d}{d}$

(E) $\dfrac{a-b}{b} = \dfrac{c-d}{d}$

Given a proportion $a : b = c : d$, then a and d are called extremes, b and c are called the means, and d is called the fourth proportion to a, b, and c.

PROBLEM

Solve the proportion $\dfrac{x+1}{4} = \dfrac{15}{12}$.

SOLUTION

Cross-multiply to determine x; that is, multiply the numerator of the first fraction by the denominator of the second, and equate this to the product of the numerator of the second and the denominator of the first.

$$(x + 1)\, 12 = 4 \times 15$$

$$12x + 12 = 60$$

$$x = 4$$

PROBLEM

Find the ratios of $x : y : z$ from the equations

$$7x = 4y + 8z, \quad 3z = 12x + 11y.$$

SOLUTION

By transposition we have

$$7x - 4y - 8z = 0$$

$$12x + 11y - 3z = 0$$

To obtain the ratio of $x : y$, we convert the given system into an equation in terms of just x and y. We may eliminate z as follows: Multiply each term of the first equation by 3 and each term of the second equation by 8 (because they are both z variables which we wish to eliminate), and then subtract the second equation from the first. We thus obtain

$$21x - 12y - 24z = 0$$
$$\underline{-(96x + 88y - 24z = 0)}$$
$$-75x \quad\quad -100y = 0$$

Dividing each term of the last equation by 25, we obtain

$$-3x - 4y = 0$$

or, $-3x = 4y$

Dividing both sides of this equation by 4 and by -3, we have the proportion

$$\frac{x}{4} = \frac{y}{-3}.$$

We are now interested in obtaining the ratio of $y : z$. To do this we convert the given system of equations into an equation in terms of just y and z, by eliminating x as follows: Multiply each term of the first equation by 12, and each term of the second equation by 7, and then subtract the second equation from the first. We thus obtain

$$84x - 48y - 96z = 0$$
$$\underline{-(84x + 77y - 21z = 0)}$$
$$-125y - 75z = 0$$

Dividing each term of the last equation by 25, we obtain

$$-5y - 3z = 0$$

or, $-3z = 5y$

Dividing both sides of this equation by 5 and by -3, we have the proportion

$$\frac{z}{5} = \frac{y}{-3}.$$

From this result and our previous result we obtain

$$\frac{x}{4} = \frac{y}{-3} = \frac{z}{5}$$

as the desired ratios.

☞ Drill: Ratios and Proportions

DIRECTIONS: Find the appropriate solutions.

1. Solve for n: $\dfrac{4}{n} = \dfrac{8}{5}$.

   (A) 10   (B) 8   (C) 6   (D) 2.5   (E) 2

2. Solve for n: $\dfrac{2}{3} = \dfrac{n}{72}$.

   (A) 12   (B) 48   (C) 64   (D) 56   (E) 24

3. Solve for n: $n : 12 = 3 : 4$.

   (A) 8   (B) 1   (C) 9   (D) 4   (E) 10

4. Four out of every five students at West High take a mathematics course. If the enrollment at West is 785, how many students take mathematics?

   (A) 628   (B) 157   (C) 705   (D) 655   (E) 247

5. At a factory, three out of every 1,000 parts produced are defective. In a day, the factory can produce 25,000 parts. How many of these parts would be defective?

   (A) 7   (B) 75   (C) 750   (D) 7,500   (E) 75,000

6. A summer league softball team won 28 out of the 32 games they played. What is the ratio of games won to games played?

   (A) 4 : 5   (B) 3 : 4   (C) 7 : 8   (D) 2 : 3   (E) 1 : 8

7. A class of 24 students contains 16 males. What is the ratio of females to males?

   (A) 1 : 2   (B) 2 : 1   (C) 2 : 3   (D) 3 : 1   (E) 3 : 2

8. A family has a monthly income of $1,250, but they spend $450 a month on rent. What is the ratio of the amount of income to the amount paid for rent?

   (A) 16 : 25   (B) 25 : 9   (C) 25 : 16   (D) 9 : 25   (E) 36 : 100

9. A student attends classes 7.5 hours a day and works a part-time job for 3.5 hours a day. She knows she must get 7 hours of sleep a night. Write the ratio of the number of free hours in this student's day to the total number of hours in a day.

(A) 1 : 3   (B) 4 : 3   (C) 8 : 24   (D) 1 : 4   (E) 5 : 12

10. In a survey by mail, 30 out of 750 questionnaires were returned. Write the ratio of questionnaires returned to questionnaires mailed (write in simplest form).

(A) 30 : 750   (B) 24 : 25   (C) 3 : 75   (D) 1 : 4   (E) 1 : 25

ALGEBRA DRILLS

ANSWER KEY

Drill: Operations with Polynomials

1.	(B)	6.	(B)	11.	(C)	16.	(C)
2.	(C)	7.	(C)	12.	(B)	17.	(D)
3.	(C)	8.	(E)	13.	(E)	18.	(E)
4.	(D)	9.	(A)	14.	(A)	19.	(B)
5.	(A)	10.	(D)	15.	(D)	20.	(B)

Drill: Simplifying Algebraic Expressions

1.	(C)	6.	(B)
2.	(D)	7.	(E)
3.	(B)	8.	(B)
4.	(A)	9.	(A)
5.	(D)	10.	(E)

Drill: Linear Equations

1.	(C)
2.	(A)
3.	(E)
4.	(D)
5.	(B)

Drill: Two Linear Equations

1.	(E)	6.	(B)
2.	(B)	7.	(D)
3.	(A)	8.	(E)
4.	(D)	9.	(A)
5.	(C)	10.	(B)

Drill: Quadratic Equations

1.	(A)	6.	(B)
2.	(D)	7.	(B)
3.	(B)	8.	(D)
4.	(C)	9.	(C)
5.	(E)	10.	(E)

Drill: Absolute Value Equations

1.	(B)	4.	(C)
2.	(E)	5.	(D)
3.	(A)		

Drill: Inequalities

1.	(E)	4.	(B)
2.	(C)	5.	(A)
3.	(D)		

Drill: Ratios and Proportions

1.	(D)	4.	(A)	7.	(A)	10.	(E)
2.	(B)	5.	(B)	8.	(B)		
3.	(C)	6.	(C)	9.	(D)		

III. GEOMETRY

POINTS, LINES, AND ANGLES

Geometry is built upon a series of undefined terms. These terms are those which we accept as known in order to define other undefined terms.

A) **Point**: Although we represent points on paper with small dots, a point has no size, thickness, or width.

B) **Line**: A line is a series of adjacent points which extends indefinitely. A line can be either curved or straight; however, unless otherwise stated, the term "line" refers to a straight line.

C) **Plane**: A plane is a collection of points lying on a flat surface, which extends indefinitely in all directions.

If A and B are two points on a line, then the **line segment** $\overline{AB}$ is the set of points on that line between A and B and including A and B, which are endpoints. The line segment is referred to as $\overline{AB}$.

A **ray** is a series of points that lie to one side of a single endpoint.

PROBLEM

How many lines can be found that contain (a) one given point (b) two given points (c) three given points?

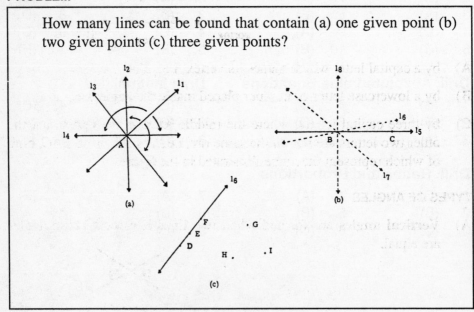

SOLUTION

(a)   *Given one point A*, there are an infinite number of distinct lines that contain the given point. To see this, consider line l_1 passing through point *A*. By rotating l_1 around *A* like the hands of a clock, we obtain different lines l_2, l_3, etc. Since we can rotate l_1 in infinitely many ways, there are infinitely many lines containing *A*.

(b)   *Given two distinct points B and C*, there is one and only one straight line passing through both. To see this, consider all the lines containing point *B*: l_5, l_6, l_7, and l_8. Only l_5 contains both points *B* and *C*. Thus, there is only one line containing both points *B* and *C*. Since there is always at least one line containing two distinct points and never more than one, the line passing through the two points is said to be determined by the two points.

(c)   *Given three distinct points*, there may be one line or none. If a line exists that contains the three points, such as *D*, *E*, and *F*, then the points are said to be **colinear**. If no such line exists (as in the case of points *G*, *H*, and *I*) then the points are said to be **noncolinear**.

INTERSECTION LINES AND ANGLES

An **angle** is a collection of points which is the union of two rays having the same endpoint. An angle such as the one illustrated below can be referred to in any of the following ways:

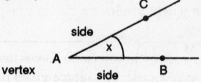

A)   by a capital letter which names its vertex, i.e., $\angle A$;

B)   by a lowercase letter or number placed inside the angle, i.e., $\angle x$;

C)   by three capital letters, where the middle letter is the vertex and the other two letters are not on the same ray, i.e., $\angle CAB$ or $\angle BAC$, both of which represent the angle illustrated in the figure.

TYPES OF ANGLES

A)   **Vertical angles** are formed when two lines intersect. These angles are equal.

$$\angle a = \angle b$$

B) **Adjacent angles** are two angles with a common vertex and a common side, but no common interior points. In the following figure, $\angle DAC$ and $\angle BAC$ are adjacent angles. $\angle DAB$ and $\angle BAC$ are not.

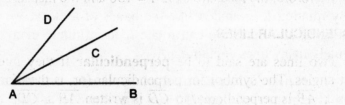

C) A **right angle** is an angle whose measure is 90°.

D) An **acute angle** is an angle whose measure is larger than 0°, but less than 90°.

E) An **obtuse angle** is an angle whose measure is larger than 90° but less than 180°.

F) A **straight angle** is an angle whose measure is 180°. Such an angle is, in fact, a straight line.

G) A **reflex angle** is an angle whose measure is greater than 180° but less than 360°.

H) **Complementary angles** are two angles whose measures total 90°.

I) **Supplementary angles** are two angles whose measures total 180°.

J) **Congruent angles** are angles of equal measure.

PROBLEM

In the figure, we are given $\overline{AB}$ and triangle ABC. We are told that the measure of $\angle 1$ is five times the measure of $\angle 2$. Determine the measures of $\angle 1$ and $\angle 2$.

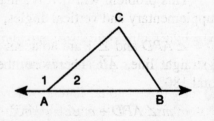

SOLUTION

Since $\angle 1$ and $\angle 2$ are adjacent angles whose non-common sides lie on a straight line, they are, by definition, supplementary. As supplements, their measures must total 180°.

If we let x = the measure of $\angle 2$, then $5x$ = the measure of $\angle 1$.

To determine the respective angle measures, set $x + 5x = 180$ and solve for x. $6x = 180$. Therefore, $x = 30$ and $5x = 150$.

Therefore, the measure of $\angle 1 = 150$ and the measure of $\angle 2 = 30$.

PERPENDICULAR LINES

Two lines are said to be **perpendicular** if they intersect and form right angles. The symbol for perpendicular (or, is therefore perpendicular to) is $\perp$; $\overline{AB}$ is perpendicular to $\overline{CD}$ is written $\overline{AB} \perp \overline{CD}$.

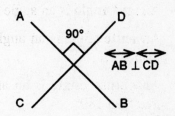

PROBLEM

We are given straight lines $\overline{AB}$ and $\overline{CD}$ intersecting at point P. $\overline{PR} \perp \overline{AB}$ and the measure of $\angle APD$ is 170°. Find the measures of $\angle 1$, $\angle 2$, $\angle 3$, and $\angle 4$.

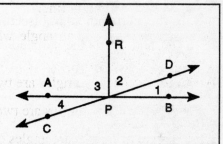

SOLUTION

This problem will involve making use of several of the properties of supplementary and vertical angles, as well as perpendicular lines.

$\angle APD$ and $\angle 1$ are adjacent angles whose non-common sides lie on a straight line, $\overline{AB}$. Therefore, they are supplements and their measures total 180°.

$$m \angle APD + m \angle 1 = 180°.$$

We know $m \angle APD = 170°$. Therefore, by substitution, $170° + m \angle 1 = 180°$. This implies $m \angle 1 = 10°$.

$\angle 1$ and $\angle 4$ are vertical angles because they are formed by the intersection of two straight lines, $\overline{CD}$ and $\overline{AB}$, and their sides form two pairs of opposite rays. As vertical angles, they are, by theorem, of equal measure. Since $m \angle 1 = 10°$, then $m \angle 4 = 10°$.

Since $\overline{PR} \perp \overline{AB}$, at their intersection the angles formed must be right angles. Therefore, $\angle 3$ is a right angle and its measure is 90°. $m \angle 3 = 90°$.

The figure shows us that $\angle APD$ is composed of $\angle 3$ and $\angle 2$. Since the measure of the whole must be equal to the sum of the measures of its parts, $m \angle APD = m \angle 3 + m \angle 2$. We know the $m \angle APD = 170°$ and $m \angle 3 = 90°$, therefore, by substitution, we can solve for $m \angle 2$, our last unknown.

$$170° = 90° + m \angle 2$$

$$80° = m \angle 2$$

Therefore, $m \angle 1 = 10°$, $m \angle 2 = 80°$,

$m \angle 3 = 90°$, $m \angle 4 = 10°$.

PROBLEM

In the accompanying figure $\overline{SM}$ is the perpendicular bisector of $\overline{QR}$, and $\overline{SN}$ is the perpendicular bisector of $\overline{QP}$. Prove that $SR = SP$.

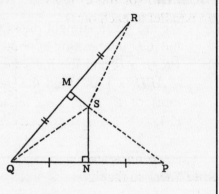

SOLUTION

Every point on the perpendicular bisector of a segment is equidistant from the endpoints of the segment.

Since point S is on the perpendicular bisector of $\overline{QR}$,

$SR = SQ$ (1)

Also, since point S is on the perpendicular bisector of $\overline{QP}$,

$SQ = SP$ (2)

By the transitive property (quantities equal to the same quantity are equal), we have

$SR = SP$.   (3)

PARALLEL LINES

Two lines are called **parallel lines** if, and only if, they are in the same plane (coplanar) and do not intersect. The symbol for parallel, or is parallel to, is ∥; $\overline{AB}$ is parallel to $\overline{CD}$ is written $\overline{AB} \parallel \overline{CD}$.

The distance between two parallel lines is the length of the perpendicular segment from any point on one line to the other line.

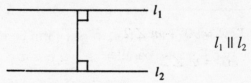

$l_1 \parallel l_2$

Given a line l and a point P not on line l, there is one and only one line through point P that is parallel to line l.

Two coplanar lines are either intersecting lines or parallel lines.

If two (or more) lines are perpendicular to the same line, then they are parallel to each other.

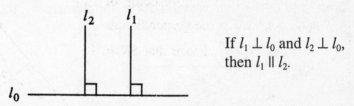

If $l_1 \perp l_0$ and $l_2 \perp l_0$, then $l_1 \parallel l_2$.

If two lines are cut by a transversal (a line intersecting two or more other lines) so that alternate interior angles are equal, the lines are parallel.

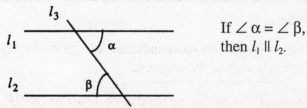

If $\angle \alpha = \angle \beta$, then $l_1 \parallel l_2$.

If two lines are parallel to the same line, then they are parallel to each other.

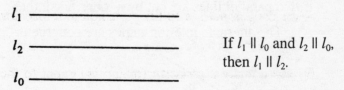

If $l_1 \parallel l_0$ and $l_2 \parallel l_0$, then $l_1 \parallel l_2$.

If a line is perpendicular to one of two parallel lines, then it is perpendicular to the other line, too.

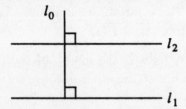

If $l_1 \parallel l_2$ and $l_1 \perp l_0$, then $l_0 \perp l_2$.

If two lines being cut by a transversal form congruent corresponding angles, then the two lines are parallel.

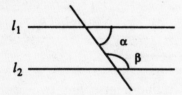

If $\angle \alpha = \angle \beta$, then $l_1 \parallel l_2$.

If two lines being cut by a transversal form interior angles on the same side of the transversal that are supplementary, then the two lines are parallel.

If $m \angle \alpha + m \angle \beta = 180°$, then $l_1 \parallel l_2$.

If a line is parallel to one of two parallel lines, it is also parallel to the other line.

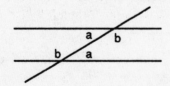

If $l_1 \parallel l_2$ and $l_0 \parallel l_1$, then $l_0 \parallel l_2$.

If two parallel lines are cut by a transversal, then:

A) The alternate interior angles are congruent.

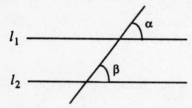

B) The corresponding angles are congruent.

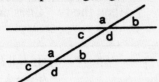

C) The consecutive interior angles are supplementary.

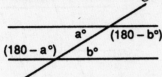

D) The alternate exterior angles are congruent.

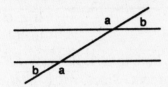

PROBLEM

Given: $\angle 2$ is supplementary to $\angle 3$.

Prove: $l_1 \parallel l_2$.

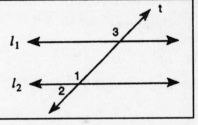

SOLUTION

Given two lines intercepted by a transversal, if a pair of corresponding angles are congruent, then the two lines are parallel. In this problem, we will show that since $\angle 1$ and $\angle 2$ are supplementary and $\angle 2$ and $\angle 3$ are supplementary, $\angle 1$ and $\angle 3$ are congruent. Since corresponding angles $\angle 1$ and $\angle 3$ are congruent, it follows $l_1 \parallel l_2$.

Statement	Reason
1. $\angle 2$ is supplementary to $\angle 3$.	1. Given.
2. $\angle 1$ is supplementary to $\angle 2$.	2. Two angles that form a linear pair are supplementary.
3. $\angle 1 \cong \angle 3$.	3. Angles supplementary to the same angle are congruent.
4. $l_1 \parallel l_2$.	4. Given two lines intercepted by a transversal, if a pair of corre-

sponding angles are congruent, then the two lines are parallel.

PROBLEM

If line $\overline{AB}$ is parallel to line $\overline{CD}$ and line $\overline{EF}$ is parallel to line $\overline{GH}$, prove that $m \angle 1 = m \angle 2$.

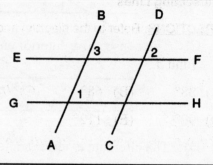

SOLUTION

To show $\angle 1 \cong \angle 2$, we relate both to $\angle 3$. Because $\overline{EF} \parallel \overline{GH}$, corresponding angles 1 and 3 are congruent. Since $\overline{AB} \parallel \overline{CD}$, corresponding angles 3 and 2 are congruent. Because both $\angle 1$ and $\angle 2$ are congruent to the same angle, it follows that $\angle 1 \cong \angle 2$.

Statement	Reason
1. $\overline{EF} \parallel \overline{GH}$	1. Given.
2. $m \angle 1 = m \angle 3$	2. If two parallel lines are cut by a transversal, corresponding angles are of equal measure.
3. $\overline{AB} \parallel \overline{CD}$	3. Given.
4. $m \angle 2 = m \angle 3$	4. If two parallel lines are cut by a transversal, corresponding angles are equal in measure.
5. $m \angle 1 = m \angle 2$	5. If two quantities are equal to the same quantity, they are equal to each other.

☞ Drill: Lines and Angles

Intersecting Lines

DIRECTIONS: Refer to the diagram and find the appropriate solution.

1. Find a.

(A) 38° (B) 68° (C) 78°

(D) 90° (E) 112°

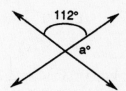

2. Find c.

(A) 32° (B) 48° (C) 58°

(D) 82° (E) 148°

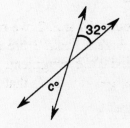

3. Determine x.

(A) 21° (B) 23° (C) 51°

(D) 102° (E) 153°

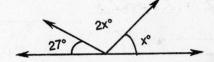

4. Find x.

(A) 8 (B) 11.75 (C) 21

(D) 23 (E) 32

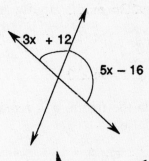

5. Find z.

(A) 29° (B) 54° (C) 61°

(D) 88° (E) 92°

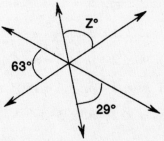

Perpendicular Lines

DIRECTIONS: Refer to the diagram and find the appropriate solution.

6. $\overrightarrow{BA} \perp \overrightarrow{BC}$ and $m \angle DBC = 53°$.
    Find $m \angle ABD$.

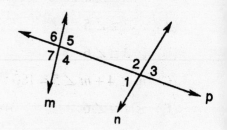

(A) 27°   (B) 33°   (C) 37°

(D) 53°   (E) 90°

7. $m \angle 1 = 90°$. Find $m \angle 2$.

(A) 80°   (B) 90°   (C) 100°

(D) 135°   (E) 180°

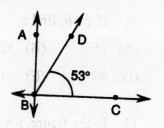

8. If $n \perp p$, which of the following
    statements is true?

(A) $\angle 1 \cong \angle 2$

(B) $\angle 4 \cong \angle 5$

(C) $m \angle 4 + m \angle 5 > m \angle 1 + m \angle 2$

(D) $m \angle 3 > m \angle 2$

(E) $m \angle 4 = 90°$

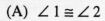

9. $\overline{CD} \perp \overline{EF}$. If $m \angle 1 = 2x$, $m \angle 2 = 30°$,
    and $m \angle 3 = x$, find x.

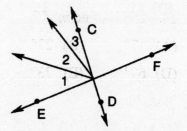

(A) 5°   (B) 10°   (C) 12°

(D) 20°   (E) 25°

10. In the figure, $p \perp t$ and $q \perp t$, which of the following statements is
    false?

(A) $\angle 1 \cong \angle 4$

(B) $\angle 2 \cong \angle 3$

(C) $m \angle 2 + m \angle 3 = m \angle 4 + m \angle 6$

(D) $m \angle 5 + m \angle 6 = 180°$

(E) $m \angle 2 > m \angle 5$

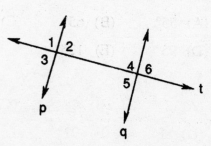

Parallel Lines

DIRECTIONS: Refer to the diagram and find the appropriate solution.

11. If $a \parallel b$, find z.

(A) 26°   (B) 32°   (C) 64°

(D) 86°   (E) 116°

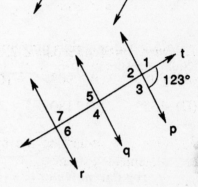

12. In the figure, $p \parallel q \parallel r$. Find $m \angle 7$.

(A) 27°   (B) 33°   (C) 47°

(D) 57°   (E) 64°

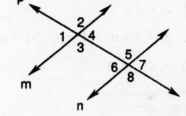

13. If $m \parallel n$, which of the following statements is not necessarily true?

(A) $\angle 2 \cong \angle 5$

(B) $\angle 3 \cong \angle 6$

(C) $m \angle 4 + m \angle 5 = 180°$

(D) $\angle 1 \cong \angle 6$

(E) $m \angle 7 + m \angle 3 = 180°$

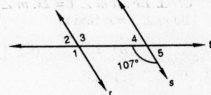

14. If $r \parallel s$, find $m \angle 2$.

(A) 17°   (B) 27°   (C) 43°

(D) 67°   (E) 73°

15. If $a \parallel b$ and $c \parallel d$, find $m \angle 5$.

(A) 55°   (B) 65°   (C) 75°

(D) 95°   (E) 125°

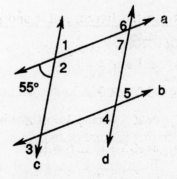

POLYGONS (CONVEX)

A **polygon** is a figure with the same number of sides as angles.

An **equilateral polygon** is a polygon all of whose sides are of equal measure.

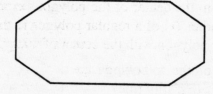

An **equiangular polygon** is a polygon all of whose angles are of equal measure.

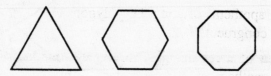

A **regular polygon** is a polygon that is both equilateral and equiangular.

PROBLEM

Each interior angle of a regular polygon contains 120°. How many sides does the polygon have?

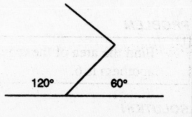

120°   60°

SOLUTION

At each vertex of a polygon, the exterior angle is supplementary to the interior angle, as shown in the diagram.

Since we are told that the interior angles measure 120°, we can deduce that the exterior angle measures 60°.

Each exterior angle of a regular polygon of n sides measure $360°/n$ degrees. We know that each exterior angle measures 60°, and, therefore, by setting $360°/_n$ equal to 60°, we can determine the number of sides in the polygon. The calculation is as follows:

$$\frac{360°}{n} = 60°$$

$$60°n = 360°$$

$$n = 6$$

Therefore, the regular polygon, with interior angles of 120°, has six sides and is called a hexagon.

The area of a regular polygon can be determined by using the **apothem** and **radius** of the polygon. The apothem (*a*) of a regular polygon is the segment from the center of the polygon perpendicular to a side of the polygon. The radius (*r*) of a regular polygon is the segment joining any vertex of a regular polygon with the center of that polygon.

(1) All radii of a regular polygon are congruent.

(2) The radius of a regular polygon is congruent to a side.

(3) All apothems of a regular polygon are congruent.

The **area** of a regular polygon equals one-half the product of the length of the apothem and the perimeter.

$$\text{Area} = \frac{1}{2}\, a \times p$$

PROBLEM

Find the area of the regular pentagon whose radius is 8 and whose apothem is 6.

SOLUTION

If the radius is 8, the length of a side is also 8. Therefore, the perimeter of the polygon is 40.

$$A = \frac{1}{2}\, a \times p$$

$$A = \frac{1}{2}\, (6)\,(40)$$

$$A = 120$$

PROBLEM

Find the area of a regular hexagon if one side has length 6.

SOLUTION

Since the length of a side equals 6, the radius also equals 6 and the perimeter equals 36. The base of the right triangle, formed by the radius and apothem, is half the length of a side, or 3. You can find the length of the apothem by using what is known as the Pythagorean Theorem (discussed further in the next section).

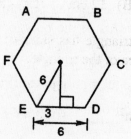

$$a^2 + b^2 = c^2$$

$$a^2 + (3)^2 = (6)^2$$

$$a^2 = 36 - 9$$

$$a^2 = 27$$

$$a = 3\sqrt{3}$$

The apothem equals $3\sqrt{3}$. Therefore, the area of the hexagon

$$= \frac{1}{2} a \times p$$

$$= \frac{1}{2} (3\sqrt{3})(36)$$

$$= 54\sqrt{3}$$

☞ Drill: Regular Polygons

Angle Measures

<u>DIRECTIONS</u>: Find the appropriate solution.

1. Find the measure of an interior angle of a regular pentagon.

(A) 55°   (B) 72°   (C) 90°   (D) 108°   (E) 540°

2. Find the measure of an exterior angle of a regular octagon.

(A) 40°   (B) 45°   (C) 135°   (D) 540°   (E) 1,080°

3. Find the sum of the measures of the exterior angles of a regular triangle.

(A) 90°   (B) 115°   (C) 180°   (D) 250°   (E) 360°

Area(s) and Perimeter(s)

DIRECTIONS: Find the appropriate solution.

4. Find the area of a square with a perimeter of 12 cm.

(A) 9 cm²   (B) 12 cm²   (C) 48 cm²   (D) 96 cm²   (E) 144 cm²

5. A regular triangle has sides of 24 mm. If the apothem is $4\sqrt{3}$ mm, find the area of the triangle.

(A) 72 mm²   (B) $96\sqrt{3}$ mm²   (C) 144 mm²

(D) $144\sqrt{3}$ mm²   (E) 576 mm²

6. Find the area of a regular hexagon with sides of 4 cm.

(A) $12\sqrt{3}$ cm²   (B) 24 cm²   (C) $24\sqrt{3}$ cm²

(D) 48 cm²   (E) $48\sqrt{3}$ cm²

7. Find the area of a regular decagon with sides of length 6 cm and an apothem of length 9.2 cm.

(A) 55.2 cm²   (B) 60 cm²   (C) 138 cm²

(D) 138.3 cm²   (E) 276 cm²

8. The perimeter of a regular heptagon (7-gon) is 36.4 cm. Find the length of each side.

(A) 4.8 cm   (B) 5.2 cm   (C) 6.7 cm   (D) 7 cm   (E) 10.4 cm

9. The apothem of a regular quadrilateral is 4 in. Find the perimeter.

(A) 12 in.   (B) 16 in.   (C) 24 in.   (D) 32 in.   (E) 64 in.

10. A regular triangle has a perimeter of 18 cm; a regular pentagon has a perimeter of 30 cm; a regular hexagon has a perimeter of 33 cm. Which figure (or figures) have sides with the longest measure?

(A) Regular triangle

(B) Regular triangle and regular pentagon

(C) Regular pentagon

(D) Regular pentagon and regular hexagon

(E) Regular hexagon

TRIANGLES

A closed three-sided geometric figure is called a **triangle**. The points of the intersection of the sides of a triangle are called the **vertices** of the triangle.

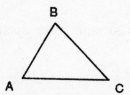

The **perimeter** of a triangle is the sum of the measures of the sides of the triangle.

A triangle with no equal sides is called a **scalene** triangle.

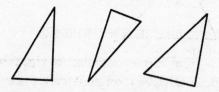

A triangle having at least two equal sides is called an **isosceles** triangle. The third side is called the **base** of the triangle.

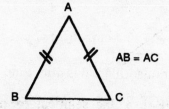

A side of a triangle is a line segment whose endpoints are the vertices of two angles of the triangle.

An **interior angle** of a triangle is an angle formed by two sides and includes the third side within its collection of points.

An **equilateral triangle** is a triangle having three equal sides. $\overline{AB} = \overline{AC} = \overline{BC}$.

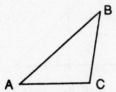

AB = AC = BC

The sum of the measures of the interior angles of a triangle is 180°.

A triangle with one obtuse angle greater than 90° is called an **obtuse triangle**.

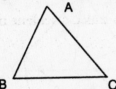

An **acute triangle** is a triangle with three acute angles (less than 90°).

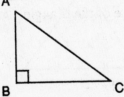

A triangle with a right angle is called a **right triangle**. The side opposite the right angle in a right triangle is called the hypotenuse of the right triangle. The other two sides are called arms or legs of the right triangle.

An **altitude** of a triangle is a line segment from a vertex of the triangle perpendicular to the opposite side.

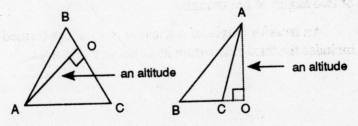

an altitude

an altitude

A line segment connecting a vertex of a triangle and the midpoint of the opposite side is called a **median** of the triangle.

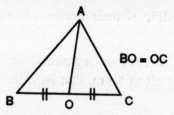

$$BO = OC$$

A line that bisects and is perpendicular to a side of a triangle is called a **perpendicular bisector** of that side.

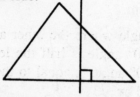

An **angle bisector** of a triangle is a line that bisects an angle and extends to the opposite side of the triangle.

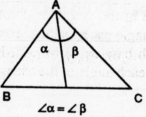

$$\angle \alpha = \angle \beta$$

The line segment that joins the midpoints of two sides of a triangle is called a **midline** of the triangle.

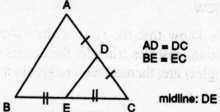

$$AD = DC$$
$$BE = EC$$

midline: DE

An **exterior angle** of a triangle is an angle formed outside a triangle by one side of the triangle and the extension of an adjacent side.

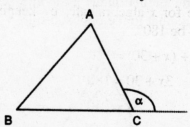

A triangle whose three interior angles have equal measure (60° each) is said to be **equiangular**.

Two triangles are **similar** if their corresponding sides are proportional.

Three or more lines (or rays or segments) are concurrent if there exists one point common to all of them, that is, if they all intersect at the same point.

In a right triangle, the square of the hypotenuse is equal to the sum of the squares of the other two sides. This is commonly known as the Pythagorean Theorem.

In a right triangle where the other angles measure 30° and 60°, the side opposite the 30° angle is half the length of the hypotenuse and the side opposite the 60° angle is equal to the length of the side opposite the 30° angle multiplied by $\sqrt{3}$.

PROBLEM

The measure of the vertex angle of an isosceles triangle exceeds the measurement of each base angle by 30°. Find the value of each angle of the triangle.

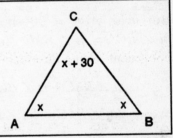

SOLUTION

We know that the sum of the values of the angles of a triangle is 180°. In an isosceles triangle, the angles opposite the congruent sides (the base angles) are, themselves, congruent and of equal value.

Therefore,

(1) Let x = the measure of each base angle.

(2) Then $x + 30$ = the measure of the vertex angle.

We can solve for x algebraically by keeping in mind the sum of all the measures will be 180°.

$$x + x + (x + 30) = 180$$
$$3x + 30 = 180$$
$$3x = 150$$
$$x = 50$$

Therefore, the base angles each measure 50°, and the vertex angle measures 80°.

PROBLEM

Prove that the base angles of an isosceles right triangle measure 45° each.

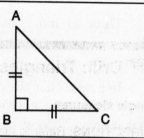

SOLUTION

As drawn in the figure, $\triangle ABC$ is an isosceles right triangle with base angles BAC and BCA. The sum of the measures of the angles of any triangle is 180°. For $\triangle ABC$, this means

$$m \angle BAC + m \angle BCA + m \angle ABC = 180° \qquad (1)$$

But $m \angle ABC = 90°$ because ABC is a right triangle. Furthermore, $m \angle BCA = m \angle BAC$, since the base angles of an isosceles triangle are congruent. Using these facts in equation (1)

$$m \angle BAC + m \angle BCA + 90° = 180°$$

or $\qquad 2m \angle BAC = 2m \angle BCA = 90°$

or $\qquad m \angle BAC = m \angle BCA = 45°.$

Therefore, the base angles of an isosceles right triangle measure 45° each.

The area of a triangle is given by the formula $A = \frac{1}{2}bh$, where b is the length of a base, which can be any side of the triangle, and h is the corresponding height of the triangle, which is the perpendicular line segment that is drawn from the vertex opposite the base to the base itself.

$$A = \frac{1}{2} bh$$

$$A = \frac{1}{2} (10)(3)$$

$$A = 15$$

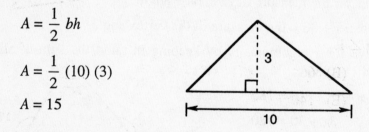

The area of a right triangle is found by taking $\frac{1}{2}$ the product of the lengths of its two arms.

$A = \dfrac{1}{2}\,(5)\,(12)$

$A = 30$

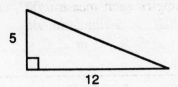

5

12

☞ Drill: Triangles

Angle Measures

<u>DIRECTIONS</u>: Refer to the diagram and find the appropriate solution.

1.　In $\triangle PQR$, $\angle Q$ is a right angle. Find $m \angle R$.

(A)　27°　　　(B)　33°　　　(C)　54°

(D)　67°　　　(E)　157°

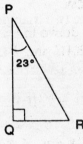

2.　$\triangle MNO$ is isosceles. If the vertex angle, $\angle N$, has a measure of 96°, find the measure of $\angle M$.

(A)　21°　　　(B)　42°　　　(C)　64°

(D)　84°　　　(E)　96°

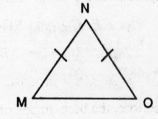

3.　Find x.

(A)　15°　　　(B)　25°　　　(C)　30°

(D)　45°　　　(E)　90°

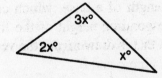

4.　Find $m \angle 1$.

(A)　40°　　　(B)　66°　　　(C)　74°

(D)　114°　　　(E)　140°

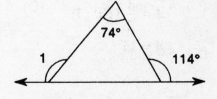

5. $\triangle ABC$ is a right triangle with a right angle at B. $\triangle BDC$ is a right triangle with right angle $\angle BDC$. If $m \angle C = 36°$. Find $m \angle A$.

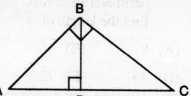

(A) 18°   (B) 36°   (C) 54°

(D) 72°   (E) 180°

Similar Triangles

DIRECTIONS: Refer to the diagram and find the appropriate solution.

6. The two triangles shown are similar. Find b.

(A) $2\dfrac{2}{3}$ (B) 3   (C) 4

(D) 16   (E) 24

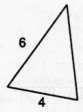

7. The two triangles shown are similar. Find $m \angle 1$.

(A) 48°   (B) 53°   (C) 74°

(D) 127°   (E) 180°

8. The two triangles shown are similar. Find a and b.

(A) 5 and 10   (B) 4 and 8

(C) $4\dfrac{2}{3}$ and $7\dfrac{1}{3}$ (D) 5 and 8

(E) $5\dfrac{1}{3}$ and 8

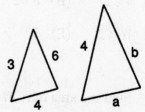

9. The perimeter of △ *LXR* is 45 and the perimeter of △ *ABC* is 27. If $\overline{LX}$ = 15, find the length of $\overline{AB}$.

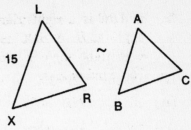

(A) 9   (B) 15   (C) 27

(D) 45   (E) 72

10. Find *b*.

(A) 9   (B) 15   (C) 20

(D) 45   (E) 60

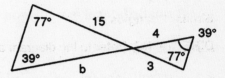

Area

DIRECTIONS: Refer to the diagram and find the appropriate solution.

11. Find the area of △ *MNO*.

(A) 22   (B) 49   (C) 56

(D) 84   (E) 112

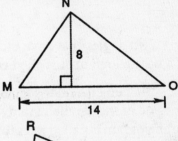

12. Find the area of △ *PQR*.

(A) 31.5   (B) 38.5   (C) 53

(D) 77   (E) 82.5

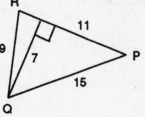

13. Find the area of △ *STU*.

(A) $4\sqrt{2}$ (B) $8\sqrt{2}$ (C) $12\sqrt{2}$

(D) $16\sqrt{2}$ (E) $32\sqrt{2}$

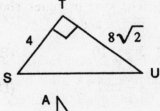

14. Find the area of △ *ABC*.

(A) 54 cm²   (B) 81 cm²   (C) 108 cm²

(D) 135 cm²   (E) 180 cm²

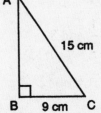

15. Find the area of △ *XYZ*.

(A) 20 cm²   (B) 50 cm²   (C) 50√2 cm²

(D) 100 cm²   (E) 200 cm²

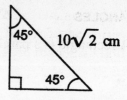

QUADRILATERALS

A **quadrilateral** is a polygon with four sides.

PARALLELOGRAMS

A **parallelogram** is a quadrilateral whose opposite sides are parallel.

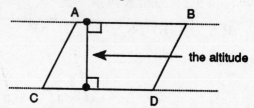

Two angles that have their vertices at the endpoints of the same side of a parallelogram are called **consecutive angles**.

The perpendicular segment connecting any point of a line containing one side of the parallelogram to the line containing the opposite side of the parallelogram is called the **altitude** of the parallelogram.

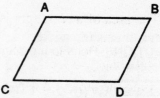

A diagonal of a polygon is a line segment joining any two non-consecutive vertices.

The area of a parallelogram is given by the formula $A = bh$, where b is the base and h is the height drawn perpendicular to that base. Note that the height equals the altitude of the parallelogram.

$A = bh$

$A = (10)(3)$

$A = 30$

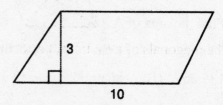

RECTANGLES

A rectangle is a parallelogram with right angles.

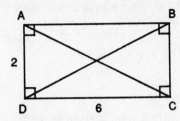

The diagonals of a rectangle are equal.

If the diagonals of a parallelogram are equal, the parallelogram is a rectangle.

If a quadrilateral has four right angles, then it is a rectangle.

The area of a rectangle is given by the formula $A = lw$, where l is the length and w is the width.

$A = lw$

$A = (3)(10)$

$A = 30$

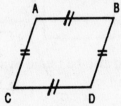

RHOMBI

A rhombus is a parallelogram which has two adjacent sides that are equal.

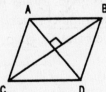

All sides of a rhombus are equal.

The diagonals of a rhombus are perpendicular to each other.

The diagonals of a rhombus bisect the angles of the rhombus.

If the diagonals of a parallelogram are perpendicular, the parallelogram is a rhombus.

If a quadrilateral has four equal sides, then it is a rhombus.

A parallelogram is a rhombus if either diagonal of the parallelogram bisects the angles of the vertices it joins.

SQUARES

A square is a rhombus with a right angle.

A square is an equilateral quadrilateral.

A square has all the properties of parallelograms and rectangles.

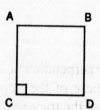

A rhombus is a square if one of its interior angles is a right angle.

In a square, the measure of either diagonal can be calculated by multiplying the length of any side by the square root of 2.

The area of a square is given by the formula $A = s^2$, where s is the side of the square. Since all sides of a square are equal, it does not matter which side is used.

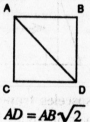

$$AD = AB\sqrt{2}$$

$A = s^2$

$A = 6^2$

$A = 36$

6

The area of a square can also be found by taking $\frac{1}{2}$ the product of the length of the diagonal squared.

$$A = \frac{1}{2}d^2$$

$$A = \frac{1}{2}(8)^2$$

$$A = 32$$

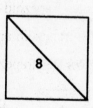

8

TRAPEZOIDS

A **trapezoid** is a quadrilateral with two and only two sides parallel. The parallel sides of a trapezoid are called **bases**.

The **median** of a trapezoid is the line joining the midpoints of the non-parallel sides.

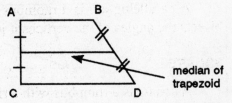

median of trapezoid

The perpendicular segment connecting any point in the line containing one base of the trapezoid to the line containing the other base is the **altitude** of the trapezoid.

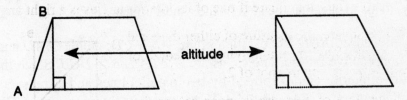

altitude

An **isosceles trapezoid** is a trapezoid whose non-parallel sides are equal. A pair of angles including only one of the parallel sides is called **a pair of base angles**.

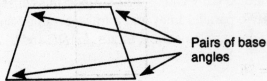

Pairs of base angles

The median of a trapezoid is parallel to the bases and equal to one-half their sum.

The base angles of an isosceles trapezoid are equal.

The diagonals of an isosceles trapezoid are equal.

The opposite angles of an isosceles trapezoid are supplementary.

The area of a trapezoid is equal to one-half the product of the length of its altitude and the sum of its bases.

$$A = \frac{1}{2}h(b + b')$$

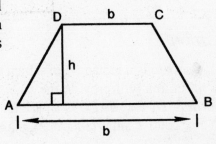

PROBLEM

Prove that all pairs of consecutive angles of a parallelogram are supplementary.

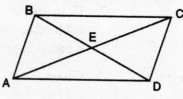

SOLUTION

We must prove that the pairs of angles ∠ BAD and ∠ ADC, ∠ ADC and ∠ DCB, ∠ DCB and ∠ CBA, and ∠ CBA and ∠ BAD are supplementary. (This means that the sum of their measures is 180°.)

Because ABCD is a parallelogram, $\overline{AB} \parallel \overline{CD}$. Angles BAD and ADC are consecutive interior angles, as are ∠ CBA and ∠ DCB. Since the consecutive interior angles formed by two parallel lines and a transversal are supplementary, ∠ BAD and ∠ ADC are supplementary, as are ∠ CBA and ∠ DCB.

Similarly, $\overline{AD} \parallel \overline{BC}$. Angles ADC and DCB are consecutive interior angles, as are ∠ CBA and ∠ BAD. Since the consecutive interior angles formed by two parallel lines and a transversal are supplementary, ∠ CBA and ∠ BAD are supplementary, as are ∠ ADC and ∠ DCB.

PROBLEM

In the accompanying figure, Δ ABC is given to be an isosceles right triangle with ∠ ABC a right angle and $\overline{AB} \cong \overline{BC}$. Line segment $\overline{BD}$, which bisects $\overline{CA}$, is extended to E, so that $\overline{BD} \cong \overline{DE}$. Prove BAEC is a square.

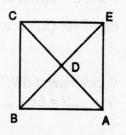

SOLUTION

A square is a rectangle in which two consecutive sides are congruent. This definition will provide the framework for the proof in this problem. We will prove that BAEC is a parallelogram that is specifically a rectangle with consecutive sides congruent, namely a square.

Statement	Reason
1. $\overline{BD} \cong \overline{DE}$ and $\overline{AD} \cong \overline{DC}$.	1. Given ($\overline{BD}$ bisects $\overline{CA}$).
2. $BAEC$ is a parallelogram.	2. If diagonals of a quadrilateral bisect each other, then the quadrilateral is a parallelogram.
3. $\angle ABC$ is a right angle.	3. Given.
4. $BAEC$ is a rectangle.	4. A parallelogram, one of whose angles is a right angle, is a rectangle.
5. $\overline{AB} \cong \overline{BC}$.	5. Given.
6. $BAEC$ is a square.	6. If a rectangle has two congruent consecutive sides, then the rectangle is a square.

☞ Drill: Quadrilaterals

Parallelograms, Rectangles, Rhombi, Squares, Trapezoids

DIRECTIONS: Refer to the diagram and find the appropriate solution.

1. In parallelogram $WXYZ$, $\overline{WX} = 14$, $\overline{WZ} = 6$, $\overline{ZY} = 3x + 5$, and $\overline{XY} = 2y - 4$. Find x and y.

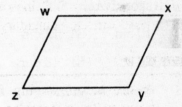

(A) 3 and 5 (B) 4 and 5 (C) 4 and 6

(D) 6 and 10 (E) 6 and 14

2. Quadrilateral $ABCD$ is a parallelogram. If $m \angle B = 6x + 2$ and $m \angle D = 98$, find x.

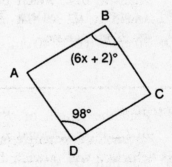

(A) 12 (B) 16 (C) $16\frac{2}{3}$

(D) 18 (E) 20

3. Find the area of parallelogram *STUV*.

(A) 56   (B) 90   (C) 108

(D) 162   (E) 180

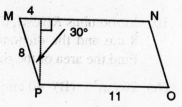

4. Find the area of parallelogram *MNOP*.

(A) 19   (B) 32   (C) $32\sqrt{3}$

(D) 44   (E) $44\sqrt{3}$

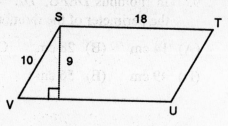

5. If the perimeter of rectangle *PQRS* is 40, find *x*.

(A) 31   (B) 38   (C) 2

(D) 44   (E) 121

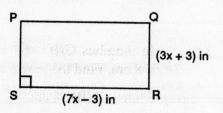

6. In rectangle *ABCD*, $\overline{AD}$ = 6 cm and $\overline{DC}$ = 8 cm. Find the length of the diagonal $\overline{AC}$.

(A) 10 cm   (B) 12 cm   (C) 20 cm

(D) 28 cm   (E) 48 cm

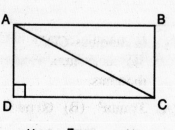

7. Find the area of rectangle *UVXY*.

(A) 17 cm²   (B) 34 cm²   (C) 35 cm²

(D) 70 cm²   (E) 140 cm²

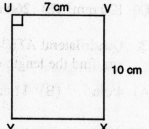

8. Find the length of $\overline{BO}$ in rectangle *BCDE* if the diagonal $\overline{EC}$ is 17 mm.

(A) 6.55 mm (B) 8 mm   (C) 8.5 mm

(D) 17 mm   (E) 34 mm

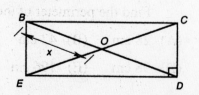

9. In rhombus *DEFG*, $\overline{DE}$ = 7 cm. Find the perimeter of the rhombus.

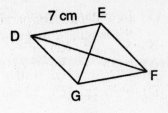

(A) 14 cm   (B) 28 cm   (C) 42 cm

(D) 49 cm   (E) 56 cm

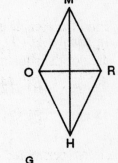

10. In rhombus *RHOM*, the diagonal $\overline{RO}$ is 8 cm and the diagonal $\overline{HM}$ is 12 cm. Find the area of the rhombus.

(A) 20 cm²   (B) 40 cm²   (C) 48 cm²

(D) 68 cm²   (E) 96 cm²

11. In rhombus *GHIJ*, $\overline{GI}$ = 6 cm and $\overline{HJ}$ = 8 cm. Find the length of $\overline{GH}$.

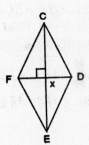

(A) 3 cm   (B) 4 cm   (C) 5 cm

(D) $4\sqrt{3}$ cm (E) 14 cm

12. In rhombus *CDEF*, $\overline{CD}$ is 13 mm and $\overline{DX}$ is 5 mm. Find the area of the rhombus.

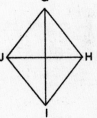

(A) 31 mm² (B) 60 mm² (C) 78 mm²

(D) 120 mm² (E) 260 mm²

13. Quadrilateral *ATUV* is a square. If the perimeter of the square is 44 cm, find the length of $\overline{AT}$.

(A) 4 cm   (B) 11 cm   (C) 22 cm   (D) 30 cm   (E) 40 cm

14. The area of square *XYZW* is 196 cm². Find the perimeter of the square.

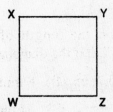

(A) 28 cm   (B) 42 cm   (C) 56 cm

(D) 98 cm   (E) 196 cm

15. In square *MNOP*, $\overline{MN}$ is 6 cm. Find the length of diagonal $\overline{MO}$.

(A) 6 cm   (B) $6\sqrt{2}$ cm (C) $6\sqrt{3}$ cm

(D) $6\sqrt{6}$ cm (E) 12 cm

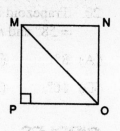

16. In square *ABCD*, $\overline{AB}$ = 3 cm. Find the area of the square.

(A) 9 cm² (B) 12 cm² (C) 15 cm²

(D) 18 cm² (E) 21 cm²

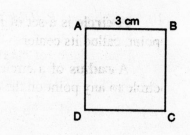

17. Find the area of trapezoid *RSTU*.

(A) 80 cm² (B) 87.5 cm² (C) 140 cm²

(D) 147 cm² (E) 175 cm²

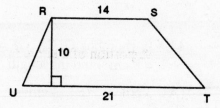

18. *ABCD* is an isosceles trapezoid. Find the perimeter.

(A) 21 cm   (B) 27 cm   (C) 30 cm

(D) 50 cm   (E) 54 cm

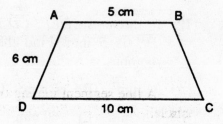

19. Find the area of trapezoid *MNOP*.

(A) $(17 + 3\sqrt{3})$ mm²

(B) $\dfrac{33}{2}$ mm²

(C) $\dfrac{33\sqrt{3}}{2}$ mm²

(D) 33 mm²

(E) $33\sqrt{3}$ mm²

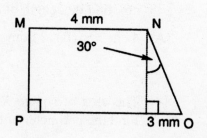

20. Trapezoid *XYZW* is isosceles. If $m \angle W$ = 58° and $m \angle Z = (4x - 6)$, find $x°$.

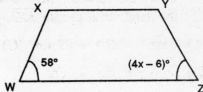

(A) 8°   (B) 12°   (C) 13°

(D) 16°   (E) 58°

CIRCLES

A **circle** is a set of points in the same plane equidistant from a fixed point, called its center.

A **radius** of a circle is a line segment drawn from the center of the circle to any point on the circle.

A portion of a circle is called an **arc** of the circle.

A line that intersects a circle in two points is called a **secant.**

A line segment joining two points on a circle is called a **chord** of the circle.

A chord that passes through the center of the circle is called a **diameter** of the circle.

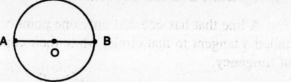

The line passing through the centers of two (or more) circles is called the **line of centers**.

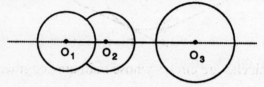

An angle whose vertex is on the circle and whose sides are chords of the circle is called an **inscribed angle**.

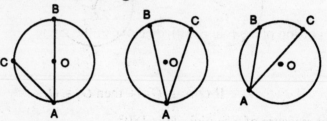

An angle whose vertex is at the center of a circle and whose sides are radii is called a **central angle.**

The measure of a minor arc is the measure of the central angle that intercepts that arc.

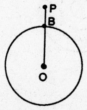

$$m \overset{\frown}{AB} = \alpha = m \angle AOB$$

The distance from a point P to a given circle is the distance from that point to the point where the circle intersects with a line segment with endpoints at the center of the circle and point P.

The distance of point P to the diagrammed circle with center O is the line segment $\overline{PB}$ of line segment $\overline{PO}$.

A line that has one and only one point of intersection with a circle is called a tangent to that circle, while their common point is called a **point of tangency**.

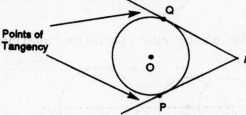

Congruent circles are circles whose radii are congruent.

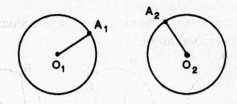

If $O_1A_1 \cong O_2A_2$, then $O_1 \cong O_2$.

The measure of a semicircle is $180°$.

A **circumscribed circle** is a circle passing through all the vertices of a polygon.

Circles that have the same center and unequal radii are called **concentric circles**.

PROBLEM

A and B are points on circle Q such
that △ AQB is equilateral. If the length
of side $\overline{AB} = 12$, find the length of arc
AB.

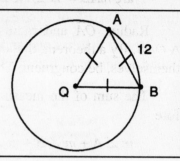

SOLUTION

To find the arc length of arc AB, we must find the measure of the
central angle ∠ AQB and the measure of the radius $\overline{QA}$. ∠ AQB is an
interior angle of the equilateral triangle △ AQB. Therefore,

$$m \angle AQB = 60°.$$

Similarly, in the equilateral △ AQB,

$$\overline{AQ} = \overline{AB} = \overline{QB} = 12.$$

Given the radius, r, and the central angle, n, the arc length is given by

$$\frac{n}{360} \times 2\pi r.$$

Therefore, by substitution,

$$\angle AQB = \frac{60}{360} \times 2\pi \times 12 = \frac{1}{6} \times 2\pi \times 12 = 4\pi.$$

Therefore, the length of arc $AB = 4\pi$.

PROBLEM

In circle O, the measure of arc AB is
80°. Find the measure of ∠ A.

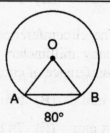

SOLUTION

The accompanying figure shows that arc AB is intercepted by central
angle AOB. By definition, we know that the measure of the central angle is
the measure of its intercepted arc. In this case,

arc $mAB = m \angle AOB = 80°$.

Radius $\overline{OA}$ and radius $\overline{OB}$ are congruent and form two sides of $\triangle OAB$. By a theorem, the angles opposite these two congruent sides must, themselves, be congruent. Therefore, $m \angle A = m \angle B$.

The sum of the measures of the angles of a triangle is 180°. Therefore,

$$m \angle A + m \angle B + m \angle AOB = 180°.$$

Since $m \angle A = m \angle B$, we can write

$$m \angle A + m \angle A + 80° = 180°$$

or $\quad 2m \angle A = 100°$

or $\quad m \angle A = 50°$.

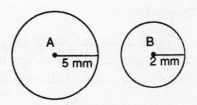

Therefore, the measure of $\angle A$ is 50°.

☞ Drill: Circles

Circumference, Area, Concentric Circles

DIRECTIONS: Determine the accurate measure.

1. Find the circumference of circle A if its radius is 3 mm.

(A) 3π mm (B) 6π mm (C) 9π mm (D) 12π mm (E) 15π mm

2. The circumference of circle H is 20π cm. Find the length of the radius.

(A) 10 cm (B) 20 cm (C) 10π cm (D) 15π cm (E) 20π cm

3. The circumference of circle A is how many millimeters larger than the circumference of circle B?

(A) 3 mm (B) 6 mm (C) 3π mm

(D) 6π mm (E) 7π mm

4. If the diameter of circle X is 9 cm and if $\pi = 3.14$, find the circumference of the circle to the nearest tenth.

(A) 9 cm (B) 14.1 cm (C) 21.1 cm (D) 24.6 cm (E) 28.3 cm

5. Find the area of circle I.

    (A) 22 mm²   (B) 121 mm²

    (C) 121π mm²   (D) 132 mm²

    (E) 132π mm²

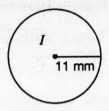

6. The diameter of circle Z is 27 mm. Find the area of the circle.

    (A) 91.125 mm²   (B) 182.25 mm²   (C) 191.5π mm²

    (D) 182.25π mm²   (E) 729 mm²

7. The area of circle B is 225π cm². Find the length of the diameter of the circle.

    (A) 15 cm   (B) 20 cm   (C) 30 cm   (D) 20π cm   (E) 25π cm

8. The area of circle X is 144π mm² while the area of circle Y is 81π mm². Write the ratio of the radius of circle X to that of circle Y.

    (A) 3 : 4   (B) 4 : 3   (C) 9 : 12   (D) 27 : 12   (E) 18 : 24

9. The circumference of circle M is 18π cm. Find the area of the circle.

    (A) 18π cm² (B) 81 cm²   (C) 36 cm²   (D) 36π cm² (E) 81π cm²

10. In two concentric circles, the smaller circle has a radius of 3 mm while the larger circle has a radius of 5 mm. Find the area of the shaded region.

    (A) 2π mm²   (B) 8π mm²

    (C) 13π mm²   (D) 16π mm²

    (E) 26π mm²

11. The radius of the smaller of two concentric circles is 5 cm while the radius of the larger circle is 7 cm. Determine the area of the shaded region.

    (A) 7π cm²   (B) 24π cm²

    (C) 25π cm²   (D) 36π cm²

    (E) 49π cm²

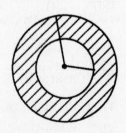

12. Find the measure of arc *MN* if *m* ∠ *MON* = 62°.

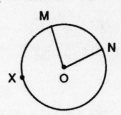

(A) 16°   (B) 32°   (C) 59°

(D) 62°   (E) 124°

13. Find the measure of arc *AXC*.

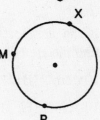

(A) 150°   (B) 160°   (C) 180°

(D) 270°   (E) 360°

14. If arc *MXP* = 236°, find the measure of arc *MP*.

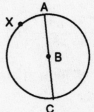

(A) 62°   (B) 124°   (C) 236°

(D) 270°   (E) 360°

15. In circle *S*, major arc *PQR* has a measure of 298°. Find the measure of the central angle ∠ *PSR*.

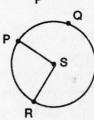

(A) 62°   (B) 124°   (C) 149°

(D) 298°   (E) 360°

16. . Find the measure of arc *XY* in circle *W*.

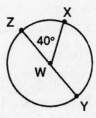

(A) 40°   (B) 120°   (C) 140°

(D) 180°   (E) 220°

17. Find the area of the sector shown.

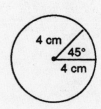

(A) 4 cm^2 (B) 2π cm^2 (C) 16 cm^2

(D) 8π cm^2 (E) 16π cm^2

18. Find the area of the shaded region.

(A) 10   (B) 5π   (C) 25

(D) 20π   (E) 25π

19. Find the area of the shaded sector shown.

(A) $\dfrac{9\pi\ \text{mm}^2}{4}$ (B) $\dfrac{9\pi\ \text{mm}^2}{2}$ (C) 18 mm²

(D) 6π mm²   (E) 9π mm²

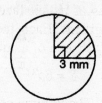

20. If the area of the square is 100 cm², find the area of the shaded sector.

(A) 10π cm²   (B) 25 cm²   (C) 25π cm²

(D) 100 cm²   (E) 100π cm²

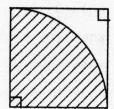

SOLIDS

Solid geometry is the study of figures which consist of points not all in the same plane.

RECTANGULAR SOLIDS

A solid with lateral faces and bases that are rectangles is called a **rectangular solid**.

The surface area of a rectangular solid is the sum of the areas of all the faces.

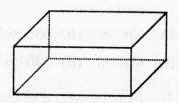

The volume of a rectangular solid is equal to the product of its length, width, and height.

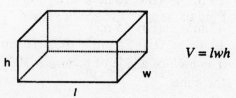

$$V = lwh$$

PROBLEM

What are the dimensions of a solid cube whose surface area is numerically equal to its volume?

SOLUTION

The surface area of a cube of edge length a is equal to the sum of the areas of its six faces. Since a cube is a regular polygon, all six faces are congruent. Each face of a cube is a square of edge length a. Hence, the surface area of a cube of edge length a is

$S = 6a^2$.

The volume of a cube of edge length a is

$V = a^3$.

We require that $A = V$, or that

$6a^2 = a^3 \quad$ or $\quad a = 6$

Hence, if a cube has edge length 6, its surface area will be numerically equal to its volume.

☞ Drill: Solids

Area and Volume

DIRECTIONS: Refer to the diagram and find the appropriate solution.

1. Find the surface area of the rectangular prism shown.

    (A) 138 cm² (B) 336 cm² (C) 381 cm²

    (D) 426 cm² (E) 540 cm²

    12 cm

    9 cm

    5 cm

2. Find the volume of the rectangular storage tank shown.

    (A) 24 m³ (B) 36 m³ (C) 38 m³

    (D) 42 m³ (E) 45 m³

    1.5 m

    4 m

    6 m

3. The area of a side of a cube is 100 cm². Find the length of an edge of the cube.

    (A) 4 cm (B) 5 cm (C) 10 cm (D) 12 cm (E) 15 cm

COORDINATE GEOMETRY

Coordinate geometry refers to the study of geometric figures using algebraic principles.

The graph shown is called the Cartesian coordinate plane. The graph consists of a pair of perpendicular lines called **coordinate axes**. The **vertical axis** is the y-axis and the **horizontal axis** is the x-axis. The point of intersection of these two axes is called the **origin**; it is the zero point of both axes. Furthermore, points to the right of the origin on the x-axis and above the origin on the y-axis represent positive real numbers. Points to the left of the origin on the x-axis or below the origin on the y-axis represent negative real numbers.

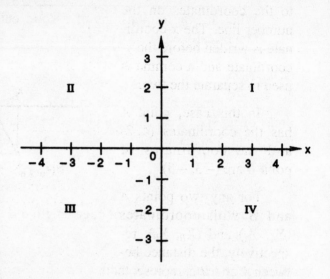

The four regions cut off by the coordinate axes are, in counterclockwise direction from the top right, called the first, second, third, and fourth quadrant, respectively. The first quadrant contains all points with two positive coordinates.

In the graph shown, two points are identified by the ordered pair, (x, y) of numbers. The x-coordinate is the first number and the y-coordinate is the second number.

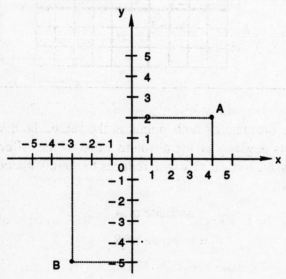

To plot a point on the graph when given the coordinates, draw perpendicular lines from the number-line coordinates to the point where the two lines intersect.

To find the coordinates of a given point on the graph, draw perpendicular lines from the point to the coordinates on the number line. The x-coordinate is written before the y-coordinate and a comma is used to separate the two.

In this case, point A has the coordinates $(4, 2)$ and the coordinates of point B are $(-3, -5)$.

For any two points A and B with coordinates (X_A, Y_A) and (X_B, Y_B), respectively, the distance between A and B is represented by:

$$AB = \sqrt{(X_A - X_B)^2 + (Y_A - Y_B)^2}$$

This is commonly known as the distance formula.

PROBLEM

Find the distance between the point $A(1, 3)$ and $B(5, 3)$.

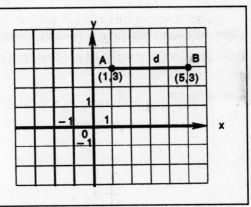

SOLUTION

In this case, where the ordinate of both points is the same, the distance between the two points is given by the absolute value of the difference between the two abscissas. In fact, this case reduces to merely counting boxes as the figure shows.

Let, x_1 = abscissa of A y_1 = ordinate of A

           x_2 = abscissa of B y_2 = ordinate of B

           d = the distance

Therefore, $d = |x_1 - x_2|$. By substitution, $d = |1 - 5| = |-4| = 4$. This answer can also be obtained by applying the general formula for distance between any two points.

$$d = \sqrt{(x_1 - x_2)^2 + (y_1 - y_2)^2}$$

By substitution,

$$
\begin{aligned}
d &= \sqrt{(1-5)^2 + (3-3)^2} \\
&= \sqrt{(-4)^2 + (0)^2} \\
&= \sqrt{16} \\
&= 4
\end{aligned}
$$

The distance is 4.

To find the midpoint of a segment between the two given endpoints, use the formula

$$MP = \left(\frac{x_1 + x_2}{2}, \frac{y_1 + y_2}{2} \right)$$

where x_1 and y_1 are the coordinates of one point; x_2 and y_2 are the coordinates of the other point.

☞ Drill: Coordinate Geometry

Coordinates

DIRECTIONS: Refer to the diagram and find the appropriate solution.

1. Which point shown has the co-ordinates $(-3, 2)$?

   (A) A   (B) B   (C) C

   (D) D   (E) E

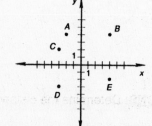

2. Name the coordinates of point A.

   (A) $(4, 3)$ (B) $(3, -4)$ (C) $(3, 4)$

   (D) $(-4, 3)$ (E) $(4, -3)$

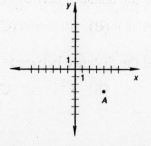

3. Which point shown has the coordinates (2.5, – 1)?

(A) M   (B) N   (C) P

(D) Q   (E) R

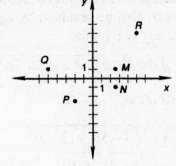

4. The correct x-coordinate for point H is what number?

(A) 3   (B) 4   (C) – 3

(D) – 4   (E) – 5

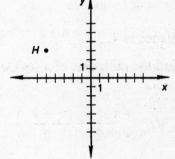

5. The correct y-coordinate for point R is what number?

(A) –7   (B) 2   (C) – 2

(D) 7   (E) 8

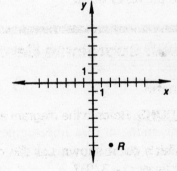

Distance

DIRECTIONS: Determine the distance or value as appropriate.

6. Find the distance between (4, – 7) and (– 2, – 7).

(A) 4   (B) 6   (C) 7   (D) 14   (E) 15

7. Find the distance between (3, 8) and (5, 11).

(A) 2   (B) 3   (C) $\sqrt{13}$ (D) $\sqrt{15}$ (E) $3\sqrt{3}$

8. How far from the origin is the point $(3, 4)$?

(A) 3   (B) 4   (C) 5   (D) $5\sqrt{3}$ (E) $4\sqrt{5}$

9. Find the distance between the point $(-4, 2)$ and $(3, -5)$.

(A) 3   (B) $3\sqrt{3}$ (C) 7   (D) $7\sqrt{2}$ (E) $7\sqrt{3}$

10. The distance between points A and B is 10 units. If A has coordinates $(4, -6)$ and B has coordinates $(-2, y)$, determine the value of y.

(A) -6 (B) -2 (C) 0   (D) 1   (E) 2

Midpoints and Endpoints

DIRECTIONS: Determine the coordinates or value as appropriate.

11. Find the midpoint between the points $(-2, 6)$ and $(4, 8)$.

(A) $(3, 7)$ (B) $(1, 7)$ (C) $(3, 1)$ (D) $(1, 1)$ (E) $(-3, 7)$

12. Find the coordinates of the midpoint between the points $(-5, 7)$ and $(3, -1)$.

(A) $(-4, 4)$ (B) $(3, -1)$ (C) $(1, -3)$ (D) $(-1, 3)$ (E) $(4, -4)$

13. The y-coordinate of the midpoint of segment $\overline{AB}$ if A has coordinates $(-3, 7)$ and B has coordinates $(-3, -2)$ is what value?

(A) $\dfrac{5}{2}$ (B) 3   (C) $\dfrac{7}{2}$ (D) 5   (E) $\dfrac{15}{2}$

14. One endpoint of a line segment is $(5, -3)$. The midpoint is $(-1, 6)$. What is the other endpoint?

(A) $(7, 3)$ (B) $(2, 1.5)$ (C) $(-7, 15)$

(D) $(-2, 1.5)$ (E) $(-7, 12)$

15. The point $(-2, 6)$ is the midpoint for which of the following pair of points?

(A) $(1, 4)$ and $(-3, 8)$ (B) $(-1, -3)$ and $(5, 9)$

(C) $(1, 4)$ and $(5, 9)$ (D) $(-1, 4)$ and $(3, -8)$

(E) $(1, 3)$ and $(-5, 9)$

GEOMETRY DRILLS

ANSWER KEY

Drill: Lines and Angles

1.	(B)	5.	(D)	9.	(D)	13.	(B)
2.	(A)	6.	(C)	10.	(E)	14.	(E)
3.	(C)	7.	(B)	11.	(C)	15.	(A)
4.	(D)	8.	(A)	12.	(D)		

Drill: Regular Polygons

1.	(D)	4.	(A)	7.	(E)	10.	(B)
2.	(B)	5.	(D)	8.	(B)		
3.	(E)	6.	(C)	9.	(D)		

Drill: Triangles

1.	(D)	5.	(C)	9.	(A)	13.	(D)
2.	(B)	6.	(A)	10.	(C)	14.	(A)
3.	(C)	7.	(B)	11.	(C)	15.	(B)
4.	(E)	8.	(E)	12.	(B)		

Drill: Quadrilaterals

1.	(A)	6.	(A)	11.	(C)	16.	(A)
2.	(B)	7.	(D)	12.	(D)	17.	(E)
3.	(D)	8.	(C)	13.	(B)	18.	(B)
4.	(E)	9.	(B)	14.	(C)	19.	(C)
5.	(C)	10.	(C)	15.	(B)	20.	(D)

Drill: Circles

1.	(B)	6.	(D)	11.	(B)	16.	(C)
2.	(A)	7.	(C)	12.	(D)	17.	(B)
3.	(D)	8.	(B)	13.	(C)	18.	(D)
4.	(E)	9.	(E)	14.	(B)	19.	(A)
5.	(C)	10.	(D)	15.	(A)	20.	(C)

Drill: Solids

1. (D)   2. (B)   3. (C)

Drill: Coordinate Geometry

1.	(C)	5.	(A)	9.	(D)	13.	(A)
2.	(E)	6.	(B)	10.	(E)	14.	(C)
3.	(B)	7.	(C)	11.	(B)	15.	(E)
4.	(E)	8.	(C)	12.	(D)		

IV. WORD PROBLEMS

One of the main problems students have in mathematics involves solving word problems. The secret to solving these problems is being able to convert words into numbers and variables in the form of an algebraic equation.

The easiest way to approach a word problem is to read the question and ask yourself what you are trying to find. This unknown quantity can be represented by a variable.

Next, determine how the variable relates to the other quantities in the problem. More than likely, these quantities can be explained in terms of the original variable. If not, a separate variable may have to be used to represent a quantity.

Using these variables and the relationships determined among them, an equation can be written. Solve for a particular variable and then plug this number in for each relationship that involves this variable in order to find any unknown quantities.

Lastly, re-read the problem to be sure that you have answered the questions correctly and fully.

ALGEBRAIC

The following illustrates how to formulate an equation and solve the problem.

EXAMPLE

Find two consecutive odd integers whose sum is 36.

Let x = the first odd integer

Let $x + 2$ = the second odd integer

The sum of the two numbers is 36. Therefore,

$$x + (x + 2) = 36$$

Simplifying,

$$2x + 2 = 36$$

$$2x + 2 + (-2) = 36 + (-2)$$

$$2x = 34$$

$$x = 17$$

Plugging 17 in for x, we find the second odd integer $= (x + 2) = (17 + 2) = 19$. Therefore, we find that the two consecutive odd integers whose sum is 36 are 17 and 19, respectively.

☞ Drill: Algebraic

Algebraic Word Problems

DIRECTIONS: Solve the following word problems algebraically.

1.   The sum of two numbers is 41. One number is one less than twice the other. Find the larger of the two numbers.

(A) 13   (B) 14   (C) 21   (D) 27   (E) 41

2.   The sum of two consecutive integers is 111. Three times the larger integer less two times the smaller integer is 58. Find the value of the smaller integer.

(A) 55   (B) 56   (C) 58   (D) 111   (E) 112

3.   The difference between two integers is 12. The sum of the two integers is 2. Find both integers.

(A) 7 and 5   (B) 7 and – 5   (C) – 7 and 5

(D) 2 and 12   (E) – 2 and 12

RATE

One of the formulas you will use for rate problems will be

Rate × Time = Distance

PROBLEM

If a plane travels five hours from New York to California at a speed of 600 miles per hour, how many miles does the plane travel?

SOLUTION

Using the formula rate × time = distance, multiply 600 mph × 5 hours

= 3,000 miles.

The average rate at which an object travels can be solved by dividing the total distance traveled by the total amount of time.

PROBLEM

> On a 40-mile bicycle trip, Cathy rode half the distance at 20 mph and the other half at 10 mph. What was Cathy's average speed on the bike trip?

SOLUTION

First you need to break down the problem. On half of the trip which would be 20 miles, Cathy rode 20 mph. Using the rate formula,

$$\frac{\text{distance}}{\text{rate}} = \text{time},$$

you would compute,

$$\frac{20 \text{ miles}}{20 \text{ miles per hour}} = 1 \text{ hour}$$

to travel the first 20 miles. During the second 20 miles, Cathy traveled at 10 miles per hour, which would be

$$\frac{20 \text{ miles}}{10 \text{ miles per hour}} = 2 \text{ hours}$$

Thus, the average speed Cathy traveled would be $^{40}/_3 = 13.3$ miles per hour.

In solving for some rate problems you can use cross multiplication involving ratios to solve for x.

PROBLEM

> If 2 pairs of shoes cost $52, then what is the cost of 10 pairs of shoes at this rate?

SOLUTION

$$\frac{2}{52} = \frac{10}{x}, \; 2x = 52 \times 10, \; x = \frac{520}{2}, \; x = \$260$$

☞ **Drill: Rate**

Rate Word Problems

<u>DIRECTIONS</u>: Solve to find the rate.

1. Two towns are 420 miles apart. A car leaves the first town traveling toward the second town at 55 mph. At the same time, a second car leaves the other town and heads toward the first town at 65 mph. How long will it take for the two cars to meet?

(A) 2 hr   (B) 3 hr   (C) 3.5 hr   (D) 4 hr   (E) 4.25 hr

2. A camper leaves the campsite walking due east at a rate of 3.5 mph. Another camper leaves the campsite at the same time but travels due west. In two hours the two campers will be 15 miles apart. What is the walking rate of the second camper?

(A) 2.5 mph   (B) 3 mph   (C) 3.25 mph

(D) 3.5 mph   (E) 4 mph

3. A bicycle racer covers a 75 mile training route to prepare for an upcoming race. If the racer could increase his speed by 5 mph, he could complete the same course in $3/4$ of the time. Find his average rate of speed.

(A) 15 mph   (B) 15.5 mph   (C) 16 mph

(D) 18 mph   (E) 20 mph

WORK

In work problems, one of the basic formulas is

$$\frac{1}{x} + \frac{1}{y} = \frac{1}{z}$$

where x and y represent the number of hours it takes two objects or people to complete the work and z is the total number of hours when both are working together.

PROBLEM

Otis can seal and stamp 400 envelopes in 2 hours while Elizabeth seals and stamps 400 envelopes in 1 hour. In how many hours can Otis and Elizabeth, working together, complete a 400-piece mailing at these rates?

SOLUTION

$$\frac{1}{2} + \frac{1}{1} = \frac{1}{z}$$

$$\frac{1}{2} + \frac{2}{2} = \frac{3}{2}$$

$$\frac{3}{2} = \frac{1}{z}$$

$$3z = 2$$

$z = \frac{2}{3}$ of an hour or 40 minutes. Working together, Otis and Elizabeth can seal and stamp 400 envelopes in 40 minutes.

☞ Drill: Work

Work Word Problems

<u>DIRECTIONS</u>: Solve to find amount of work.

1. It takes Marty 3 hours to type the address labels for his club's newsletter. It only takes Pat $2^1/_4$ hours to type the same amount of labels. How long would it take them working together to complete the address labels?

(A) $\frac{7}{9}$ hr

(B) $1\frac{2}{7}$ hr

(C) $1\frac{4}{5}$ hour

(D) $2\frac{5}{8}$ hr

(E) $5\frac{1}{4}$ hr

2. It takes Troy 3 hours to mow his family's large lawn. With his little brother's help, he can finish the job in only 2 hours. How long would it take the little brother to mow the entire lawn alone?

(A) 4 hr   (B) 5 hr   (C) 5.5 hr   (D) 6 hr   (E) 6.75 hr

3. A tank can be filled by one inlet pipe in 15 minutes. It takes an outlet pipe 75 minutes to drain the tank. If the outlet pipe is left open by accident, how long would it take to fill the tank?

(A) 15.5 min   (B) 15.9 min   (C) 16.8 min

(D) 18.75 min   (E) 19.3 min

MIXTURE

Mixture problems present the combination of different products and ask you to solve for different parts of the mixture.

PROBLEM

A chemist has an 18% solution and a 45% solution of a disinfectant. How many ounces of each should be used to make 12 ounces of a 36% solution?

SOLUTION

Let x = Number of ounces from the 18% solution, and

y = Number of ounces from the 45% solution.

$$x + y = 12 \tag{1}$$

$$.18x + .45y = .36(12) \tag{2}$$

Note that .18 of the first solution is pure disinfectant and that .45 of the second solution is pure disinfectant. When the proper quantities are drawn from each mixture the result is 12 ounces of mixture which is .36 pure disinfectant.

The second equation cannot be solved with two unknowns. Therefore, write one variable in terms of the other and plug it into the second equation.

$$x = 12 - y \tag{1}$$

$$.18(12 - y) + .45y = .36(12) \tag{2}$$

Simplifying,

$$2.16 - .18y + .45y = 4.32$$

$$.27y = 4.32 - 2.16$$

$$.27y = 2.16$$

$$y = 8$$

Plugging in for y in the first equation,

$$x + 8 = 12$$

$$x = 4$$

Therefore, 4 ounces of the first and 8 ounces of the second solution should be used.

PROBLEM

Clark pays $2.00 per pound for 3 pounds of peanut butter chocolates and then decides to buy 2 pounds of chocolate covered raisins at $2.50 per pound. If Clark mixes both together, what is the cost per pound of the mixture?

SOLUTION

The total mixture is 5 pounds and the total value of the chocolates is

$$3(\$2.00) + 2(\$2.50) = \$11.00$$

The price per pound of the chocolates is

$$\frac{\$11.00}{5 \text{ pounds}} = \$2.20.$$

☞ Drill: Mixture

Mixture Word Problems

DIRECTIONS: Find the appropriate solution.

1. How many liters of a 20% alcohol solution must be added to 80 liters of a 50% alcohol solution to form a 45% solution?

(A) 4   (B) 8   (C) 16   (D) 20   (E) 32

2. How many kilograms of water must be evaporated from 50 kg of a 10% salt solution to obtain a 15% salt solution?

(A) 15   (B) 15.75   (C) 16   (D) $16.\overline{66}$ (E) 16.75

3. How many pounds of coffee A at $3.00 a pound should be mixed with 2.5 pounds of coffee B at $4.20 a pound to form a mixture selling for $3.75 a pound?

(A) 1   (B) 1.5   (C) 1.75   (D) 2   (E) 2.25

INTEREST

If the problem calls for computing simple interest, the interest is computed on the principal alone. If the problem involves compounded interest, then the interest on the principal is taken into account in addition to the interest earned before.

PROBLEM

How much interest will Jerry pay on his loan of $400 for 60 days at 6% per year?

SOLUTION

Use the formula:

Interest = Principal × Rate × Time ($I = P \times R \times T$).

$$\$400 \times 6\%/\text{year} \times 60 \text{ days} = \$400 \times .06 \times \frac{60}{365}$$

$$= \$400 \times 0.00986 = \$3.94$$

Jerry will pay $4.00.

PROBLEM

Mr. Smith wishes to find out how much interest he will receive on $300 if the rate is 3% compounded annually for three years.

SOLUTION

Compound interest is interest computed on both the principal and the interest it has previously earned. The interest is added to the principal at the end of every year. The interest on the first year is found by multiplying the rate by the principal. Hence, the interest for the first year is

$$3\% \times \$300 = .03 \times \$300 = \$9.00.$$

The principal for the second year is now $309, the old principal ($300) plus the interest ($9). The interest for the second year is found by multiplying the rate by the new principal. Hence, the interest for the second year is

$$3\% \times \$309 = .03 \times \$309 = \$9.27.$$

The principal now becomes $309 + $9.27 = $318.27.

The interest for the third year is found using this new principal. It is

$$3\% \times \$318.27 = .03 \times \$318.27 = \$9.55.$$

At the end of the third year his principal is $318.27 + $9.55 = 327.82. To find how much interest was earned, we subtract his starting principal ($300) from his ending principal ($327.82), to obtain

$$\$327.82 - \$300.00 = \$27.82.$$

☞ Drill: Interest

Interest Word Problems

DIRECTIONS: Determine the amount of money invested or possible amount earned as appropriate.

1. A man invests $3,000, part in a 12-month certificate of deposit paying 8% and the rest in municipal bonds that pay 7% a year. If the yearly return from both investments is $220, how much was invested in bonds?

   (A) $80   (B) $140   (C) $220   (D) $1,000   (E) $2,000

2. A sum of money was invested at 11% a year. Four times that amount was invested at 7.5%. How much was invested at 11% if the total annual return was $1,025?

   (A) $112.75   (B) $1,025   (C) $2,500

   (D) $3,400   (E) $10,000

3. One bank pays 6.5% a year simple interest on a savings account while a credit union pays 7.2% a year. If you had $1,500 to invest for three years, how much more would you earn by putting the money in the credit union?

   (A) $10.50   (B) $31.50   (C) $97.50   (D) $108   (E) $1,500

DISCOUNT

If the discount problem asks to find the final price after the discount, first multiply the original price by the percent of discount. Then subtract this result from the original price.

If the problem asks to find the original price when only the percent of discount and the discounted price are given, simply subtract the percent of discount from 100% and divide this percent into the sale price. This will give you the original price.

PROBLEM

> A popular bookstore gives a 10% discount to students. What does a student actually pay for a book costing $24.00?

SOLUTION

10% of $24 is $2.40 and hence the student pays

$24 – $2.40 = $21.60.

PROBLEM

> Eugene paid $100 for a business suit. The suit's price included a 25% discount. What was the original price of the suit?

SOLUTION

Let x represent the original price of the suit and take the complement of .25 (discount price) which is .75.

$.75x = 100 or $x = 133.34$.

So, the original price of the suit is $133.34.

☞ Drill: Discount

Discount Word Problems

<u>DIRECTIONS</u>: Find cost, price, or discount as appropriate.

1. A man bought a coat marked 20% off for $156. How much had the coat cost originally?

(A) $136   (B) $156   (C) $175   (D) $195   (E) $205

2. A woman saved $225 on the new sofa which was on sale for 30% off. What was the original price of the sofa?

(A) $25   (B) $200   (C) $225   (D) $525   (E) $750

3. At an office supply store, customers are given a discount if they pay in cash. If a customer is given a discount of $9.66 on a total order of $276, what is the percent of discount?

(A) 2%   (B) 3.5%   (C) 4.5%   (D) 9.66%   (E) 276%

PROFIT

The formula used for the profit problems is

Profit = Revenue − Cost

or   Profit = Selling Price − Expenses.

PROBLEM

Four high school and college friends started a business of remodeling and selling old automobiles during the summer. For this purpose they paid $600 to rent an empty barn for the summer. They obtained the cars from a dealer for $250 each, and it takes an average of $410 in materials to remodel each car. How many automobiles must the students sell at $1,440 each to obtain a gross profit of $7,000?

SOLUTION

Total Revenues − Total Cost = Gross Profit

Revenue − [Variable Cost + Fixed Cost] = Gross Profit

Let a = number of cars

Revenue = $1,440a$

Variable Cost = ($250 + 410)a$

Fixed Cost = $600

The desired gross profit is $7,000.

Using the equation for the gross profit,

$$1,440a - [660a + 600] = 7,000$$
$$1,440a - 660a - 600 = 7,000$$
$$780a = 7,000 + 600$$
$$780a = 7,600$$
$$a = 9.74$$

or to the nearest car, $a = 10$.

PROBLEM

A glass vase sells for $25.00. The net profit is 7%, and the operating expenses are 39%. Find the gross profit on the vase.

SOLUTION

The gross profit is equal to the net profit plus the operating expenses. The net profit is 7% of the selling cost; thus, it is equal to

$$7\% \times \$25.00 = .07 \times \$25 = \$1.75.$$

The operating expenses are 39% of the selling price, thus equal to

$$39\% \times \$25 = .39 \times \$25 = \$9.75.$$

$$
\begin{array}{rl}
\$1.75 & \text{net profit} \\
+ \ \$9.75 & \text{operating expenses} \\
\hline
\$11.50 & \text{gross profit}
\end{array}
$$

☞ Drill: Profit

Profit Word Problems

<u>DIRECTIONS</u>: Determine profit or stock value as appropriate.

1. An item cost a store owner $50. She marked it up 40% and advertised it at that price. How much profit did she make if she later sold it at 15% off the advertised price?

(A) $7.50   (B) $9.50   (C) $10.50   (D) $39.50   (E) $50

2. An antique dealer makes a profit of 115% on the sale of an oak desk. If the desk cost her $200, how much profit did she make on the sale?

(A) $230   (B) $315   (C) $430   (D) $445   (E) $475

3. As a graduation gift, a young man was given 100 shares of stock worth $27.50 apiece. Within a year the price of the stock had risen by 8%. How much more were the stocks worth at the end of the first year than when they were given to the young man?

(A) $110   (B) $220   (C) $1,220   (D) $2,750   (E) $2,970

SETS

A **set** is any collection of well defined objects called elements.

A set which contains only a finite number of elements is called a **finite set**; a set which contains an infinite number of elements is called an **infinite set**. Often the sets are designated by listing their elements. For example:

{*a, b, c, d*} is the set which contains elements *a, b, c,* and *d*.

The set of positive integers is {1, 2, 3, 4, ...}.

Venn diagrams can represent sets. These diagrams are circles which help to visualize the relationship between members or objects of a set.

PROBLEM

> In a certain Broadway show audition, it was asked of 30 performers if they knew how to either sing or dance, or both. If 20 auditioners said they could dance and 14 said they could sing, how many could sing and dance?

SOLUTION

Divide the 30 people into 3 sets: those who dance, those who sing, and those who dance and sing. S is the number of people who both sing and dance. So $20 - S$ represents the number of people who dance and $14 - S$ represents the number of people who sing.

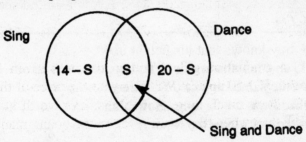

The equation for this problem is as follows:

$$(20 - S) + S + (14 - S) = 30$$
$$20 + 14 - 30 = S$$
$$34 - 30 = S$$
$$4 = S$$

So, 4 people in the audition both sing and dance.

☞ Drill: Sets

Set Word Problems

__DIRECTIONS__: Determine the appropriate set.

1. In a small school there are 147 sophomores. Of this number, 96 take both Biology and Technology I. Eighty-three take both Chemistry and Technology I. How many students are taking Technology I?

(A) 32   (B) 51   (C) 64   (D) 83   (E) 96

2. In a survey of 100 people, 73 owned only stocks. Six of the people invested in both stocks and bonds. How many people owned bonds only?

(A) 6   (B) 21   (C) 73   (D) 94   (E) 100

3. On a field trip, the teachers counted the orders for a snack and sent the information in with a few people. The orders were for 77 colas only and 39 fries only. If there were 133 orders, how many were for colas and fries?

(A) 17   (B) 56   (C) 77   (D) 95   (E) 150

GEOMETRY

PROBLEM

A boy knows that his height is 6 ft. and his shadow is 4 ft. long. At the same time of day, a tree's shadow is 24 ft. long. How high is the tree? (See the figure.)

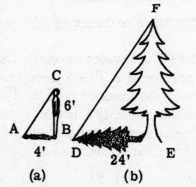

(a)   (b)

SOLUTION

Show that $\triangle ABC \approx \triangle DEF$, and then set up a proportion between the known sides $\overline{AB}$ and $\overline{DE}$, and the sides $\overline{BC}$ and $\overline{EF}$.

First, assume that both the boy and the tree are $\perp$ to the earth. Then, $\overline{BC} \perp \overline{BA}$ and $\overline{EF} \perp \overline{ED}$. Hence,

$$\angle ABC \cong \angle DEF.$$

Since it is the same time of day, the rays of light from the sun are incident on both the tree and the boy at the same angle, relative to the earth's surface. Therefore,

$$\angle BAC \cong \angle EDF.$$

We have shown, so far, that two pairs of corresponding angles are congruent. Since the sum of the angles of any triangle is 180°, the third pair of corresponding angles is congruent (i.e., $\angle ACB \cong \angle DFE$). By the Angle-Angle-Angle Theorem

$$\angle ABC \approx \angle DEF.$$

By definition of similarity,

$$\frac{\overline{FE}}{\overline{CB}} = \frac{\overline{ED}}{\overline{BA}}$$

$\overline{CB} = 6'$, $\overline{ED} = 24'$, and $\overline{BA} = 4'$. Therefore,

$$FE = (6')\left(\frac{24'}{4'}\right) = 36'.$$

☞ Drill: Geometry

Geometry Word Problems

DIRECTIONS: Find the appropriate measurements.

1. $\triangle PQR$ is a scalene triangle. The measure of $\angle P$ is 8 more than twice the measure of $\angle R$. The measure of $\angle Q$ is two less than three times the measure of $\angle R$. Determine the measure of $\angle Q$.

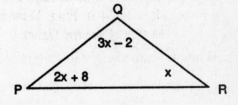

(A) 29°   (B) 53°   (C) 60°

(D) 85°   (E) 174°

2. Angle A and angle B are supplementary. The measure of angle B is 5 more than four times the measure of angle A. Find the measure of angle B.

(A) 35°   (B) 125°   (C) 140°   (D) 145°   (E) 155°

3. Triangle RUS is isosceles with base $\overline{SU}$. Each leg is 3 less than 5 times the length of the base. If the perimeter of the triangle is 60 cm, find the length of a leg.

(A) 6 cm   (B) 12 cm   (C) 27 cm   (D) 30 cm   (E) 33 cm

MEASUREMENT

When measurement problems are presented in either metric or English units which involve conversion of units, the appropriate data will be given in the problem.

PROBLEM

The Eiffel Tower is 984 feet high. Express this height in meters, in kilometers, in centimeters, and in millimeters.

SOLUTION

A meter is equivalent to 39.370 inches. In this problem, the height of the tower in feet must be converted to inches and then the inches can be converted to meters. There are 12 inches in 1 foot. Therefore, feet can be converted to inches by using the factor 12 inches/1 foot.

984 feet × 12in/1 ft = 118 × 10^2 inches.

Once the height is found in inches, this can be converted to meters by the factor 1 meter/39.370 inches.

11,808 in × 1 m/39.370 inches = 300 m.

Therefore, the height in meters is 300 m.

There are 1,000 meters in one kilometer. Meters can be converted to kilometers by using the factor 1 km/1,000 m.

300 m × 1 km/1,000 m = .300 km.

As such, there are .300 kilometers in 300 m.

There are 100 centimeters in 1 meter, thus meters can be converted to centimeters by multiplying by the factor 100 cm/1 m.

$$300 \text{ m} \times 100 \text{ cm/1 m} = 300 \times 10^2 \text{ cm}.$$

There are 30,000 centimeters in 300 m.

There are 1,000 millimeters in 1 meter; therefore, meters can be converted to millimeters by the factor 1,000 mm/1 m.

$$300 \text{ m} \times 1,000 \text{ mm/1 m} = 300 \times 10^3 \text{ mm}.$$

There are 300,000 millimeters in 300 meters.

PROBLEM

> The unaided eye can perceive objects which have a diameter of 0.1 mm. What is the diameter in inches?

SOLUTION

From a standard table of conversion factors, one can find that 1 inch = 2.54 cm. Thus, cm can be converted to inches by multiplying by 1 inch/2.54 cm. Here, one is given the diameter in mm, which is .1 cm. Millimeters are converted to cm by multiplying the number of mm by .1 cm/1 mm. Solving for cm, you obtain

$$0.1 \text{ mm} \times .1 \text{ cm/1 mm} = .01 \text{ cm}.$$

Solving for inches:

$$0.01 \text{ cm} \times \frac{1 \text{ inch}}{2.54 \text{ cm}} = 3.94 = 10^{-3} \text{ inches}.$$

☞ Drill: Measurement

Measurement Word Problems

DIRECTIONS: Determine the appropriate solution from the information provided.

1. A brick walkway measuring 3 feet by 11 feet is to be built. The bricks measure 4 inches by 6 inches. How many bricks will it take to complete the walkway?

(A) 132   (B) 198   (C) 330   (D) 1,927   (E) 4,752

2. A wall to be papered is three times as long as it is wide. The total area to be covered is 192 ft^2. Wallpaper comes in rolls that are 2 feet wide by 8 feet long. How many rolls will it take to cover the wall?

(A) 8   (B) 12   (C) 16   (D) 24   (E) 32

3. A bottle of medicine containing 2 kg is to be poured into smaller containers that hold 8 grams each. How many of these smaller containers can be filled from the 2 kg bottle?

(A) 0.5   (B) 1   (C) 5   (D) 50   (E) 250

DATA INTERPRETATION

Some of the problems test ability to apply information given in graphs and tables.

PROBLEM

In which year was the least number of bushels of wheat produced? (See figure below)

SOLUTION

By inspection of the graph, we find that the shortest bar representing wheat production is the one representing the wheat production for 1976. Thus, the least number of bushels of wheat was produced in 1976.

Number of bushels (to the nearest 5 bushels) of wheat and corn produced by farm RQS from 1975 – 1985

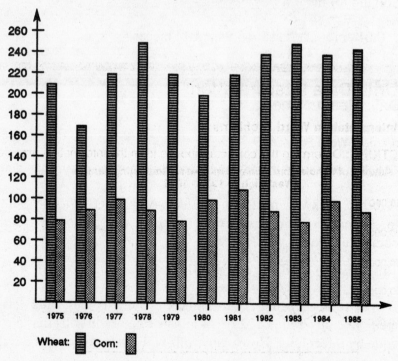

Wheat: ▤ Corn: ▦

PROBLEM

What was the ratio of wheat production in 1985 to that of 1975?

SOLUTION

From the graph representing wheat production, the number of bushels of wheat produced in 1975 is equal to 210 bushels. This number can be found by locating the bar on the graph representing wheat production in 1975 and then drawing a horizontal line from the top of that bar to the vertical axis. The point where this horizontal line meets the vertical axis represents the number of bushels of wheat produced in 1975. This number on the vertical axis is 210. Similarly, the graph indicates that the number of bushels of wheat produced in 1985 is equal to 245 bushels.

Thus, the ratio of wheat production in 1985 to that of 1975 is 245 to 210, which can be written as $^{245}/_{210}$. Simplifying this ratio to its simplest form yields

$$\frac{245}{210} = \frac{5 \times 7 \times 7}{2 \times 3 \times 5 \times 7}$$

$$= \frac{7}{2 \times 3}$$

$$= \frac{7}{6} \text{ or } 7{:}6$$

☞ **Drill: Data Interpretation**

Date Interpretation Word Problems

<u>**DIRECTIONS:**</u> Determine the correct response from the information provided.

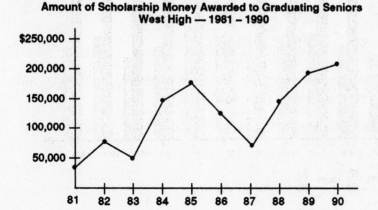

Amount of Scholarship Money Awarded to Graduating Seniors
West High — 1981 – 1990

1. What was the approximate amount of scholarship money awarded in 1985?

(A) $150,000   (B) $155,000   (C) $165,000

(D) $175,000   (E) $190,000

2. By how much did the scholarship money increase between 1987 and 1988?

(A) $25,000   (B) $30,000   (C) $50,000

(D) $55,000   (E) $75,000

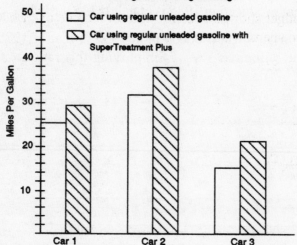

3. By how much did the mileage increase for Car 2 when the new product was used?

(A) 5 mpg   (B) 6 mpg   (C) 7 mpg   (D) 10 mpg   (E) 12 mpg

4. Which car's mileage increased the most in this test?

(A) Car 1   (B) Car 2   (C) Car 3

(D) Cars 1 and 2   (E) Cars 2 and 3

5. According to the bar graph, if your car averages 25 mpg, what mileage might you expect with the new product?

(A) 21 mpg   (B) 30 mpg   (C) 31 mpg   (D) 35 mpg   (E) 37 mpg

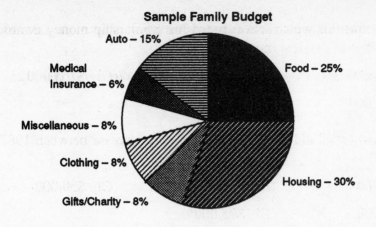

Sample Family Budget

Auto – 15%

Medical Insurance – 6%

Miscellaneous – 8%

Clothing – 8%

Gifts/Charity – 8%

Food – 25%

Housing – 30%

6. Using the budget shown, a family with an income of $1,500 a month would plan to spend what amount on housing?

(A) $300   (B) $375   (C) $450   (D) $490   (E) $520

7. In this sample family budget, how does the amount spent on an automobile compare to the amount spent on housing?

(A) $\frac{1}{3}$ (B) $\frac{1}{2}$ (C) $\frac{2}{3}$ (D) $1\frac{1}{2}$ (E) 2

8. A family with a monthly income of $1,240 spends $125 a month on clothing. By what amount do they exceed the sample budget?

(A) $1.00   (B) $5.20   (C) $10.00   (D) $25.80   (E) $31.75

CALORIE CHART — BREADS

Bread	Amount	Calories
French Bread	2 oz	140
Bran Bread	1 oz	95
Whole Wheat Bread	1 oz	115
Oatmeal Bread	0.5 oz	55
Raisin Bread	1 oz	125

9. One dieter eats two ounces of French bread. A second dieter eats two ounces of bran bread. The second dieter has consumed how many more calories than the first dieter?

(A) 40   (B) 45   (C) 50   (D) 55   (E) 65

10. One ounce of whole wheat bread has how many more calories than an ounce of oatmeal bread?

(A) 5   (B) 15   (C) 60   (D) 75   (E) 125

WORD PROBLEM DRILLS

ANSWER KEY

Drill: Algebraic

1.	(D)	2.	(A)	3.	(B)

Drill: Rate

1.	(C)	2.	(E)	3.	(A)

Drill: Work

1.	(B)	2.	(D)	3.	(D)

Drill: Mixture

1.	(C)	2.	(D)	3.	(B)

Drill: Interest

1.	(E)	2.	(C)	3.	(B)

Drill: Discount

1.	(D)	2.	(E)	3.	(B)

Drill: Profit

1.	(B)	2.	(A)	3.	(B)

Drill: Sets

1.	(A)	2.	(B)	3.	(A)

Drill: Geometry

1.	(D)	2.	(D)	3.	(C)

Drill: Measurement

1.	(B)	2.	(B)	3.	(E)

Drill: Data Interpretation

1.	(D)	4.	(E)	7.	(B)	10.	(A)
2.	(E)	5.	(B)	8.	(D)		
3.	(B)	6.	(C)	9.	(C)		

PSAT/
NMSQT

CHAPTER 8

Attacking Regular
Math Questions

Chapter 8

ATTACKING REGULAR MATH QUESTIONS

The Regular Math questions of the PSAT are designed to test your ability to solve problems involving arithmetic, algebra, and geometry. A few of the problems may be similar to those found in a math textbook and will require nothing more than the use of basic rules and formulas. Most of the problems, however, will require more than that. Regular Math questions will ask you to think creatively and apply basic skills to solve problems.

All Regular Math questions are in a multiple-choice format with five possible responses. There are a number of advantages and disadvantages associated with multiple-choice math tests. Learning what some of these advantages and disadvantages are can help you improve your test performance.

The greatest disadvantage of a multiple-choice math test is that every question presents you with four wrong answers. These wrong answers are not randomly chosen numbers—they are the answers that students are most likely to get if they make certain mistakes. They also tend to be answers that "look right" to someone who does not know how to solve the problem. Thus, on a particular problem, you may be relieved to find "your" answer among the answer choices, only to discover later that you fell into a common error trap. Wrong answer choices can also distract or confuse you when you are attempting to solve a problem correctly, causing you to question your answer even though it is right.

The greatest *advantage* of a multiple-choice math test is that the *right* answer is also presented to you. This means that you may be able to spot the right answer even if you do not understand a problem completely or do not have time to finish it. It means that you may be able to pick the right answer by guessing intelligently. It also means that you may be saved from getting a problem wrong when the answer you obtain is not among the answer choices—and you have to go back and work the problem again.

Keep in mind, also, that the use of a calculator is permitted during the test. Do not be tempted, however, to use this as a crutch. Some problems can actually be solved more quickly without a calculator, and you still have to work through the problem to know what numbers to punch. No calculator in the world can solve a problem for you.

ABOUT THE DIRECTIONS

The directions found at the beginning of each Regular Math section are simple—solve each problem, then mark the best of five answer choices on your answer sheet. Following these instructions, however, is important information that you should understand thoroughly before you attempt to take a test. This information includes definitions of standard symbols and formulas that you may need in order to solve Regular Math problems. The formulas are given so that you don't have to memorize them—however, in order to benefit from this information, you need to know what is and what is not included. Otherwise, you may waste time looking for a formula that is not listed, or you may fail to look for a formula that is listed. The formulas given to you at the beginning of a Regular Math section include:

- The number of degrees in a straight line
- Area and circumference of a circle; number of degrees in a circle
- Area of a triangle; Pythagorean Theorem for a right triangle; sum of angle measures of a triangle

Following the formulas and definitions of symbols is a very important statement about the diagrams, or figures, that may accompany Regular Math questions. This statement tells you that, unless stated otherwise in a specific question, figures are drawn to scale.

ABOUT THE QUESTIONS

Most Regular Math questions on the PSAT fall into one of three categories: arithmetic, algebra, and geometry. In the following three sections, we will review the kinds of questions you will encounter on the actual test.

ARITHMETIC QUESTIONS

Most arithmetic questions on the PSAT fall into one of the following four question types. For each question type, an example and solution will be given, highlighting strategies and techniques for completing the problems as quickly as possible.

Question Type 1: Evaluating Expressions

Arithmetic questions on the PSAT often ask you to find the value of an arithmetic expression or to find the value of a missing term in an expression. The temptation when you see one of these expressions is to calculate its value—a process that is time-consuming and can easily lead to an error. A better way to approach an arithmetic expression is to use your knowledge of properties of numbers to spot shortcuts.

PROBLEM

$7(8 + 4) - (3 \times 12) =$

(A) 24   (D) 144

(B) 48   (E) 3,024

(C) 110

SOLUTION

Before you jump into multiplication, look at the numbers inside the first parentheses. This is the sum $(8 + 4) = 12$, which makes the entire expression equal to $7(12) - (3 \times 12)$. The distributive property tells you that $a(b + c) = ab + ac$ and $a(b - c) = ab - ac$. The expression $7(12) - (3 \times 12)$ can be made to fit the second formula, with a equal to 12 and 7 and 3 equal to b and c, respectively. Thus, $7(12) - (3 \times 12)$ becomes $12(7 - 3)$, and the answer is simply 12×4, or 48.

Question Type 2: Undefined Symbols

Most PSAT math sections include problems that involve undefined symbols. In some problems, these symbols define a value by asking you to perform several arithmetic operations. For example, the symbol $\boxed{x}$ may tell you to square some number x then subtract 3: $\boxed{x} = x^2 - 3$. In other problems, a symbol may represent a missing numeral, such as $10 - \Delta = 7$. By looking at the arithmetic, you can see that Δ must equal 3.

PROBLEM

Let $[n] = n^2 + 1$ for all numbers n. Which of the following is equal to the product of [2] and [3]?

(A) [6]

(D) [9]

(B) [7]

(E) [11]

(C) [8]

SOLUTION

The newly defined symbol is [ ]. To find the values for [2] and [3], plug them into the formula $[n] = n^2 + 1$:

$[2] = 2^2 + 1 = 4 + 1 = 5$

$[3] = 3^2 + 1 = 9 + 1 = 10$

Since, [2] = 5, and [3] = 10, we can compute the product: $5 \times 10 = 50$.

Now look at the answers. You will see that the answers are given in terms of [ ]. Once again, you must plug them into the formula $[n] = n^2 + 1$. If we plug each answer choice into the equation, we get:

$[6] = 6^2 + 1 = 36 + 1 = 37$

$[7] = 7^2 + 1 = 49 + 1 = 50$

$[8] = 8^2 + 1 = 64 + 1 = 65$

$[9] = 9^2 + 1 = 81 + 1 = 82$

$[11] = 11^2 + 1 = 121 + 1 = 122$

Question Type 3: Averages

Some PSAT math problems ask you to simply compute the average of a given set of values. More challenging problems ask you to apply the definition of *average*. You will recall that the average of a given set of values is equal to the sum of the values divided by the number of values in the set.

PROBLEM

> The average of 10 numbers is 53. What is the sum of the numbers?
>
> (A) 106   (D) 530
>
> (B) 350   (E) 615
>
> (C) 363

SOLUTION

You can solve this problem using the formula:

$$\text{Average} = \frac{\text{sum of values}}{\text{number of values}}$$

In this question,

$$53 = \frac{\text{sum of values}}{10}$$

Therefore, the sum of the numbers is 530:

$$10 \times 53 = \text{sum of values}$$

$$530 = \text{sum of values}$$

PROBLEM

> The average of three numbers is 16. If one of the numbers is 5, what is the sum of the other two?
>
> (A) 11   (D) 38
>
> (B) 24   (E) 43
>
> (C) 27

SOLUTION

In this problem, if we plug in the numbers we know we get

$$16 = \frac{a+b+c}{3}$$

This can be converted to

$$3 \times 16 = a + b + c,$$

which means that

$$48 = a + b + c.$$

If $a = 5$, we can solve:

$$48 = 5 + b + c, \text{ or } 48 - 5 = b + c,$$

and finally $43 = b + c$. Therefore, the sum of the other two numbers is 43 which is choice (E). Notice that choice (A) is waiting for the person who fails to work the formula and simply subtracts 5 from 16.

Question Type 4: Data Interpretation

Data interpretation problems usually require two basic steps. First, you have to read a chart or graph in order to obtain certain information. Then you have to apply or manipulate the information in order to obtain an answer.

PROBLEM

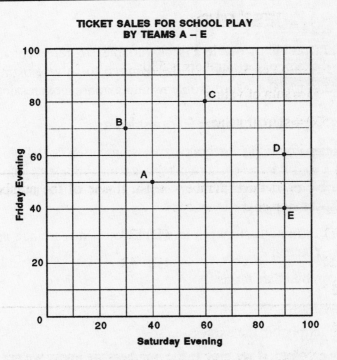

Which team sold the greatest number of tickets for Friday evening and Saturday evening combined?

(A) Team A

(D) Team D

(B) Team B

(E) Team E

(C) Team C

SOLUTION

Glancing over the data, you see that the number of tickets sold for Friday evening is represented vertically, while the number of tickets sold for Saturday evening is represented horizontally. Points placed on the grid represent each team's ticket sales for the two evenings.

Read the graph to determine the number of tickets sold by each team for Friday evening and Saturday evening.

Add each pair of numbers to find the total number of tickets sold by each team for both evenings.

Compare the totals to see which team sold the most tickets.

The answer is (D), since team D sold 60 tickets for Friday evening and 90 tickets for Saturday evening for a highest total of 150.

ALGEBRA QUESTIONS

Algebra problems use letters or variables to represent numbers. In these types of problems, you will be required to solve existing algebraic expressions or translate word problems into algebraic expressions.

Question Type 1: Algebraic Expressions

Problems involving algebraic expressions often contain hidden shortcuts. You can find these shortcuts by asking yourself, "How can this expression be rearranged?" Often rearrangement will cause an answer to appear almost magically.

There are three basic ways in which you can rearrange an algebraic expression. You can

1. combine like terms

2. factor the expression

3. multiply out the expression

PROBLEM

If $x = \frac{1}{2}$, which of the following equals $x^2 - x + \frac{1}{4}$?

(A) $-\frac{1}{2}$ (D) $\frac{1}{2}$

(B) 0   (E) 1

(C) $\frac{1}{4}$

SOLUTION

You can find the answer by substituting $x = \frac{1}{2}$ into the given expression, but there is an easier way. Look at $x^2 - x + \frac{1}{4}$. Remembering the strategy tip, this expression is equal to the trinomial square $(x - \frac{1}{2})^2$. Now you can see at a glance that since you are told that

$$x = \frac{1}{2},\ (x - \frac{1}{2})^2$$

must equal 0. Thus, the answer is (B).

Question Type 2: Word Problems

Among the most common types of word problems found on the PSAT are age problems, mixture problems, distance problems, and percent problems. You can find detailed explanations of these and other problem types in the Basic Math Skills Review. There is a strategy, however, that can help you to solve all types of word problems—learning to recognize "keywords."

Keywords are words or phrases that can be translated directly into a mathematical symbol, expression, or operation. As you know, you usually cannot solve a word problem without writing some kind of equation. Learning to spot keywords will enable you to write the equations you need more easily.

Listed below are some of the most common keywords. As you practice solving word problems, you will probably find others.

Keyword	Mathematical Equivalent
is	equals
sum	add
plus	add
more than, older than	add
difference	subtract
less than, younger than	subtract
twice, double	multiply by 2
half as many	divided by 2
increase by 3	add 3
decrease by 3	subtract 3

PROBLEM

Adam has 50 more than twice the number of "frequent flier" miles that Erica has. If Adam has 200 frequent flier miles, how many does Erica have?

(A) 25

(B) 60

(C) 75

(D) 100

(E) 250

SOLUTION

The keywords in this problem are "more" and "twice." If you let $a =$ the number of frequent flier miles that Adam has and $e =$ the number of frequent flier miles that Erica has, you can write: $a = 50 + 2e$. Since $a = 200$, the solution becomes: $200 = 50 + 2e$. Therefore, $200 - 50 = 2e$, or $150 = 2e$, and $^{150}/_2 = e$ or $75 = e$, which is choice (C).

GEOMETRY QUESTIONS

PSAT geometry questions require you to find the area or missing sides of figures given certain information. These problems require you to use "if . . . then" reasoning or to draw figures based on given information.

Question Type 1: "If . . . Then" Reasoning

You will not have to work with geometric proofs on the PSAT, but the logic used in proofs can help you enormously when it comes to solving PSAT geometry problems. This type of logic is often referred to as "If . . . then" reasoning. In "if . . . then" reasoning, you say to yourself, "If A is true, then B must be true." By using "if . . . then" reasoning, you can draw conclusions based on the rules and definitions that you know. For example, you might say, "If ABC is a triangle, then the sum of its angles must equal 180°."

PROBLEM

If triangle *QRS* is an equilateral triangle, what is the value of $a + b$? (See figure on following page.)

(A) 60°

(B) 80°

(C) 85°

(D) 100°

(E) 120°

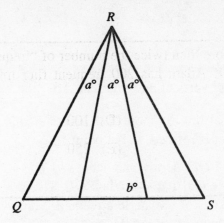

SOLUTION

You can obtain the information that you need to solve this problem by using a series of "if ... then" statements: "If *QRS* is an equilateral triangle, then each angle must equal 60°." "If angle *R* = 60°, then *a* must equal 20°." "If *a* = 20°, then *b* must equal half of (180° – 20°) or 80°." "If *a* = 20° and *b* = 80°, then *a* + *b* – 100°." Therefore, answer (D) is correct.

Question Type 2: Drawing Diagrams

Among the most difficult geometry problems on the PSAT are those that describe a geometric situation without providing a diagram. For these problems, you must learn to draw your own diagram based on the information that is given. The best way to do this is step-by-step, using each piece of information that the problem provides. As you draw, you should always remember to:

1. label all points, angles, and line segments according to the information provided.

2. indicate parallel or perpendicular lines.

3. write in any measures that you are given.

PROBLEM

If vertical line segment $\overline{AB}$ is perpendicular to line segment $\overline{CD}$ at point *O* and if ray *OE* bisects angle *BOD*, what is the value of angle *AOE*?

(A) 45°

(D) 135°

(B) 90°

(E) 180°

(C) 120°

SOLUTION

Draw as follows:

Draw and label vertical line segment $\overline{AB}$.

Draw and label line segment $\overline{CD}$ perpendicular to $\overline{AB}$. Label the right angle that is formed. Label point O.

Locate angle BOD. Draw and label ray OE so that it bisects, or cuts into two equal parts, angle BOD. Use equal marks to show that the two parts of the angle are equal. Since you are bisecting a right angle, you can write in the measure 45°.

Your diagram should resemble that shown below. Now you can evaluate your drawing to answer the question. Angle AOE is equal to 90° + 45°, or 135°. The answer is (D).

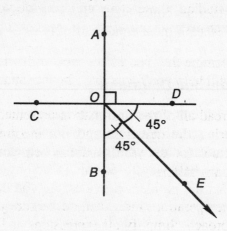

➤ POINTS TO REMEMBER

- Certain patterns of factoring appear so often on the PSAT that you should learn to spot them in every possible form. These include: difference of squares, where $x^2 - y^2 = (x + y)(x - y)$; and trinomial squares, where $(x + y)^2 = x^2 + 2xy + y^2$ or $(x - y)^2 = x^2 - 2xy + y^2$.

- When solving data interpretation problems, you should take a moment to look at the graph or chart in order to see how it is set up and what types of information are displayed. You should not, however, waste time reading or analyzing the data until you read the question(s) and find out what is being asked.

- If you are dealing with a geometry question that refers to a figure and the question does not provide the figure, draw the figure. This will help you visualize the problem. In addition, if a figure is provided, note whether or not it is drawn to size.

- Do not use your calculator for simple mathematic calculations. Using your calculator for such purposes may waste more time than it saves.

- Be sure to review the reference information. It provides some common formulas that may prove valuable when you are answering the questions.

ANSWERING REGULAR MATH QUESTIONS

The following steps should be used to help guide you through answering Regular Math questions. Combined with the review material which you have just studied, these steps will provide you with the tools necessary to correctly answer the questions you will encounter.

| STEP 1 | Try to determine the type of question with which you are dealing. This will help you focus in on how to attack the question. |

| STEP 2 | Carefully read all of the information presented. Make sure you are answering the question, and not incorrectly reading the question. Look for key words that can help you determine what the question is asking. |

| STEP 3 | Perform the operations indicated, but be sure you are taking the easiest approach. Simplify all expressions and equations before performing your calculations. Draw your own figures if a question refers to them, but does not provide them. |

| STEP 4 | Try to work backwards from the answer choices if you are having difficulty determining an answer. |

| STEP 5 | If you are still having difficulty determining an answer, use the process of elimination. If you can eliminate at least two choices, you will greatly increase your chances of correctly answering the question. Eliminating three choices means that you have a fifty-fifty chance of correctly answering the question if you guess. |

| STEP 6 | Once you have chosen an answer, fill in the oval which corresponds to the question and answer which you have chosen. |

Beware of stray lines on your answer sheet, as they may cause your answers to be scored incorrectly.

Now, use the information you have just learned to answer the following drill questions. Doing so will help reinforce the material learned, and will better prepare you for the actual test.

☞ Drill: Regular Math

DIRECTIONS: Choose the best answer choice and fill in the corresponding oval on the answer sheet.

1.   If $8 - (7 - 6 - 5) = 8 - 7 - (x - 5)$, what is the value of x?

   (A) -6 (D) 4

   (B) -16 (E) 6

   (C) -18

2.   The average (arithmetic mean) volume of 4 containers is 40 liters. If 3 of these containers each has a volume of 35 liters, what is the volume in liters of the fourth container?

   (A) 40   (D) 105

   (B) 50   (E) 160

   (C) 55

3.   2 ◊ 5
        ×   7
      ‾‾‾‾‾‾‾‾‾
      1,8 ⊕ 5

   In the correctly computed multiplication problem above, if ◊ and ⊕ are different digits, then ◊ =

   (A) 2.   (D) 4.

   (B) 6.   (E) 7.

   (C) 5.

4. If for any number *n*, [*n*] is defined as the least whole number that is greater than or equal to *n*, then [– 3.7] + 14 =

    (A) 10.3
    (D) 10
    (B) 17.7
    (E) 11
    (C) 18

5. How many tenths of a kilometer will a cyclist travel in 1 minute if she cycles at a rate of 30 km/hour?

    (A) 0.5
    (D) 5
    (B) 1
    (E) $\dfrac{1}{30}$
    (C) 2

6. If $\overline{DE}$ is parallel to $\overline{ST}$ and triangle *RST* is an isoceles triangle, then ∠ *E* is

    (A) 50°.
    (B) 40°.
    (C) 70°.
    (D) 90°.
    (E) 75°.

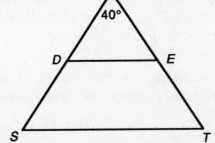

7. If 20 students share the cost equally of a gift for Coach Brown, what percent of the total cost do 5 of the students share?

    (A) 5%
    (D) 40%
    (B) 10%
    (E) 50%
    (C) 25%

8. If *n* ÷ 5 = 150 ÷ 25, then *n* =

    (A) 5.
    (D) 30.
    (B) 6.
    (E) 125.
    (C) 25.

9. If the average (arithmetic mean) of -9 and s is -9, then $s =$

    (A) -9 (D) -18

    (B) 0   (E) -4.5

    (C) 9

10. If $x \lozenge y = (x-3)y$, then $8 \lozenge 3 + 5 \lozenge 2 =$

    (A) 34.   (D) -5.

    (B) 50.   (E) 19.

    (C) 0.

11. If $22 \times 3 \times R = 6$, the $R =$

    (A) $\dfrac{1}{9}$.   (D) 11.

    (B) $\dfrac{1}{11}$.   (E) 9.

    (C) $\dfrac{1}{8}$.

12. What is the total area, in square meters, of two adjacent square garden plots with sides 4 meters and 1 meter, respectively?

    (A) 1   (D) 17

    (B) 4   (E) 20

    (C) 16

13. If line m is parallel to line n as shown, then $\angle b =$

    (A) 30°.

    (B) 45°.

    (C) 55°.

    (D) 60°.

    (E) 120°.

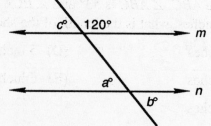

14. If $6m/9 = 4$, then $18m =$

    (A) 6.   (D) 72.

    (B) 24.   (E) 108.

    (C) 36.

15. During a local high school track meet, all three contestants earn points. Olivia earns 12 times more points than Barbara, and Diane earns 8 times more points than Barbara. What is the ratio of Diane's points to Olivia's points?

    (A) 96 : 1   (D) 2 : 3

    (B) 8 : 1   (E) 1 : 8

    (C) 3 : 2

16. If $x^2 - z^2 = 130$, and $x - z = 10$, then $x + z =$

    (A) 10.   (D) 30.

    (B) 13.   (E) 120.

    (C) 36.

17. In the figure shown here, what does x equal?

    (A) 80

    (B) 90

    (C) 100

    (D) 110

    (E) 120

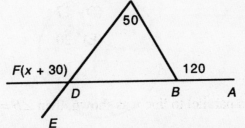

18. In triangle ABC, $\angle ABC$ is 53° and $\angle BCA$ is 37°, $\overline{BC} = 5$ inches and $\overline{AC} = 4$ inches, what is the length of the shortest side?

    (A) 2 inches   (D) 5 inches

    (B) 3 inches   (E) 6 inches

    (C) 4 inches

19. If 22 is the average of n, n, n, 15, and 35, then $n =$

    (A) 16.   (D) 50.

    (B) 18.   (E) 110.

    (C) 20.

20. If $7x + 18 = 16x$, then $x =$

    (A) -2.   (D) 2.

    (B) $\dfrac{18}{23}$.   (E) 36.

    (C) $\dfrac{23}{18}$.

21. A circular piece of turquoise with radius 5 inches is inscribed in a square piece of tile. What is the area in square inches of the tile?

    (A) 25   (D) 10

    (B) 78.5   (E) 100

    (C) 50

22. If the area of the shaded region is 24π, then the radius of circle O is

    (A) 4.

    (B) 16.

    (C) $2\sqrt{6}$.

    (D) $4\sqrt{2}$.

    (E) $2\sqrt{2}$.

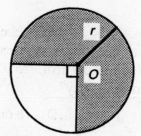

23. If, in the triangle shown here, $\overline{AS} < \overline{ST}$ which of the following cannot be the value of t?

    (A) 20

    (B) 36

    (C) 65

    (D) 71

    (E) 80

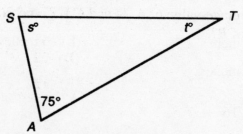

24. If $R \# S = \dfrac{R+2}{S}$, then $(4 \# 3) \# k =$

   (A) $\dfrac{5}{4}$.

   (B) 2.

   (C) $\dfrac{2}{k}$.

   (D) $\dfrac{4}{k}$.

   (E) $4k$.

25. If $48x - 6y = 1$, then $16x - 2y =$

   (A) -3.

   (B) 0.

   (C) $\dfrac{1}{3}$.

   (D) $\dfrac{1}{2}$.

   (E) 1.

26. Sam is 5 years older than Marcia, and Marcia is 6 years older than Jack. How many years older than Jack is Sam?

   (A) 11

   (B) 9

   (C) 7

   (D) 6

   (E) 2

27. A cat ate $^1\!/_2$ of the food in its dish in the morning, and 2 ounces of food in the afternoon. The cat's owner came home to find $^2\!/_5$ of the original amount of food in the dish. How many ounces of food were in the dish at the start of the day?

   (A) 4 ounces

   (B) 5 ounces

   (C) 8 ounces

   (D) 16 ounces

   (E) 20 ounces

28. The average value of A, B, and C is 8, and $2(A + C) = 24$. What is the value of B?

   (A) 0

   (B) 3

   (C) -16

   (D) 32

   (E) 12

29. If S is the sum of the positive integers from 1 to n, inclusive, then the average (arithmetic mean), k, of these integers can be represented by the formula

    (A) $S \times n$.

    (B) $\dfrac{S}{n}$.

    (C) $\dfrac{k}{n}$.

    (D) $S + n$.

    (E) $n + 1$.

30. If $3a + 4a = 14$, and $b + 6b = 20$, then $7(a + b) =$

    (A) 21.

    (B) 28.

    (C) 34.

    (D) 40.

    (E) 42.

31. The perimeter of an equilateral triangle is 18. What is the altitude of the triangle?

    (A) 3

    (B) 6

    (C) 9

    (D) $\sqrt{3}$

    (E) $3\sqrt{3}$

32. A truck driver covered 450 miles during a 9-hour period, stopped for one hour, then drove 90 miles in 2 hours. What was the driver's average rate, in miles per hour, for the total distance traveled?

    (A) 45

    (B) 49

    (C) 50

    (D) 54

    (E) 60

33. If $x + y = 7$ and $x - y = 3$, then $x^2 - y^2 =$

    (A) 4.

    (B) 10.

    (C) 16.

    (D) 21.

    (E) 40.

34. If $a \times b = 6a \,\square\, 5b$, then $(6 \,\square\, 5) \times (3 \,\square\, 2) =$

    (A) 1.   (D) 0.

    (B) 180.   (E) 14.

    (C) 66.

35. If $m < n < 0$, which expression must be < 0?

    (A) The product of m and n

    (B) The square of the product of m and n

    (C) The sum of m and n

    (D) The result of subtracting m from n

    (E) The quotient of dividing n by m

36. In the figure shown, if $\overline{BD}$ is the bisector of angle ABC, and angle ABD is one-fourth the size of angle XYZ, what is the size of angle ABC?

    (A) 21°

    (B) 28°

    (C) 42°

    (D) 63°

    (E) 168°

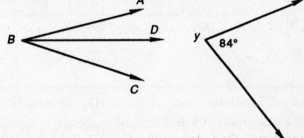

37. A cube of volume 8 cubic centimeters is placed directly next to a cube of volume 125 cubic centimeters. What is the perpendicular distance in centimeters from the top of the larger cube to the top of the smaller cube?

    (A) 7   (D) 2

    (B) 5   (E) 0

    (C) 3

38. If Company A's November income is $1 million less than the average income of July and September, what will the November income be?

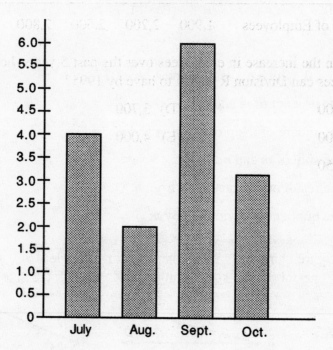

Income for Company A
July–October 1992
(in millions of dollars)

(A) $2 million

(D) $5 million

(B) $3 million

(E) $10 million

(C) $4 million

39. If $21 - (a - b) = 2(b + 9)$, and $a = 8$, what is the value of b?

(A) 31

(D) $-\dfrac{5}{3}$

(B) 13

(E) -5

(C) 4

40. **EMPLOYEES IN DIVISION R OF CORPORATION S**

Year	1989	1990	1991	1992	1993
Number of Employees	1,900	2,200	2,500	2,800	3,100

Based on the increase in employees over the past 5 years, how many employees can Division R expect to have by 1995?

(A) 3,100

(B) 3,400

(C) 3,550

(D) 3,700

(E) 4,000

REGULAR MATH

ANSWER KEY

Drill: Regular Math

1.	(A)	11.	(B)	21.	(E)	31.	(E)
2.	(C)	12.	(D)	22.	(D)	32.	(A)
3.	(B)	13.	(D)	23.	(E)	33.	(D)
4.	(E)	14.	(E)	24.	(D)	34.	(A)
5.	(A)	15.	(D)	25.	(C)	35.	(C)
6.	(C)	16.	(B)	26.	(A)	36.	(C)
7.	(C)	17.	(A)	27.	(E)	37.	(C)
8.	(D)	18.	(B)	28.	(E)	38.	(C)
9.	(A)	19.	(C)	29.	(B)	39.	(E)
10.	(E)	20.	(D)	30.	(C)	40.	(D)

PSAT/ NMSQT

CHAPTER 9

Attacking Quantitative Comparison Questions

Chapter 9

ATTACKING QUANTITATIVE COMPARISON QUESTIONS

In the Quantitative Comparison section of the PSAT you are asked to compare two quantities. Since you only have to compare quantities, the questions in this section usually take less time to solve than regular multiple-choice questions.

The two quantities are always presented in two columns, Column A and Column B.

Column A	**Column B**
2^3	2^2

Your job is to determine which quantity, if either, is greater. The directions tell you that there are four possible answer choices:

- If the quantity in Column A is greater than the quantity in Column B, the correct choice is (A).

- If the quantity in Column B is greater than the quantity in Column A, the correct choice is (B).

- If the two quantities are equal, the correct choice is (C).

- If the relationship cannot be determined, the correct choice is (D).

What would the correct choice be for the problem above? Since the quantity in Column A is equal to 8 and the quantity in Column B is equal to 4, and $8 > 4$, the correct choice is (A).

ABOUT THE DIRECTIONS

Now that you have seen some of the directions, let's go over the rest of them. It's important to become familiar with the directions before the test so you don't waste time reading them during the test. You will also see the same reference information that appeared before the regular multiple-choice problems. Become familiar with this material before you take the PSAT. If you have to refer to any part of this page during the test, you are taking away valuable time needed to solve the problems.

Each of the following questions consist of two quantities, one in Column A and one in Column B. You are to compare the two quantities and on the answer sheet blacken space

(A) if the quantity in Column A is greater;

(B) if the quantity in Column B is greater;

(C) if the two quantities are equal;

(D) if the relationship cannot be determined from the information given.

NOTES:

1. In certain questions, information concerning one or both of the quantities to be compared is centered above the two columns.

2. In a given question, a symbol that appears in both columns represents the same thing in Column A as it does in Column B.

3. Letters such as x, n, and k stand for real numbers.

EXAMPLES:

	Column A	Column B	Answer
E1:	$3 + 4$	3×4	Ⓐ ● Ⓒ Ⓓ Ⓔ

	Column A	Column B	Answer
E2:	x	150	Ⓐ Ⓑ ● Ⓓ Ⓔ

ABOUT THE QUESTIONS

The following section will take you through the different types of Quantitative Comparison questions that you will encounter on the PSAT. Five main types exist and will be described here.

Question Type 1: Calculations

This type of question will ask you to perform addition, subtraction, multiplication, or division. The question may ask you to perform one or more of these operations in order to compare the quantities in columns A and B.

PROBLEM

<u>Column A</u>	<u>Column B</u>
$(13 + 44)(37 - 40)$	$(13 - 44)(37 - 40)$

SOLUTION

You could do the addition and subtraction in each column, but if you use your number knowledge, you can get the right answer in a matter of seconds! Try working with just signs. Remember that a smaller number minus a larger number yields a negative result so the answers to all the subtractions are negative. You'll get:

$$(+)(-) \qquad \text{and} \qquad (-)(-)$$

which becomes

$$(-) \qquad \text{and} \qquad (+)$$

The correct choice is (B).

Question Type 2: Conversions

This type of question may require you to convert the quantities given by asking you to find a percentage of a number, find a fraction of a number, find the area if given length and width, etc., in order to compare the quantities in columns A and B.

PROBLEM

<u>Column A</u>	<u>Column B</u>
60% of $\dfrac{3}{4}$	75% of $\dfrac{3}{5}$

SOLUTION

Change the way the quantities look; change the percents to fractions. You'll get:

$$\left(\frac{3}{5}\right)\left(\frac{3}{4}\right) \qquad\qquad \left(\frac{3}{4}\right)\left(\frac{3}{5}\right)$$

You can now *compare parts*. The correct choice is (C).

Question Type 3: Exponents and Roots

This type of question will ask you to determine a number's value, and then may ask you to use the value to perform an indicated operation in order to compare the quantities in columns A and B.

PROBLEM

Column A	Column B
$\sqrt{.81}$	$\sqrt[3]{.81}$

SOLUTION:

In this problem, $\sqrt{.81}$ is easy to find—it's 0.9. The problem is finding $\sqrt[3]{.81}$. There is no procedure to find $\sqrt[3]{.81}$ except estimating and multiplying. Since you are really concerned with seeing how $\sqrt[3]{.81}$ compares to 0.9 and not finding out exactly what it is, try 0.9 as an estimate. That means you have to cube 0.9. 0.9^3 is .729. Since .729 is less than .81, the $\sqrt[3]{.81}$ must be greater than 0.9. The correct choice is (B).

Question Type 4: Variables

This type of question will present you with variables of unknown quantities. You will be provided with additional information which must be applied in order to compare the quantities in columns A and B.

PROBLEM

Column A	Column B
$y^* = y(y + 1)$ if y is even	
$y^* = y(y - 1)$ if y is odd	
7*	6*

SOLUTION

Change the way the quantities look by applying the rules that appear between the two columns:

$$7* = (7)(7-1) \qquad\qquad 6* = 6(6+1)$$

$$7* = (7)(6) \qquad\qquad\qquad 6* = (6)(7)$$

The factors are identical in the two columns. The correct choice is (C).

Question Type 5: Figures

This type of question will include a figure. You will be asked to use the figure provided to compare the quantities in columns A and B. The figures may or may not be drawn to scale.

PROBLEM

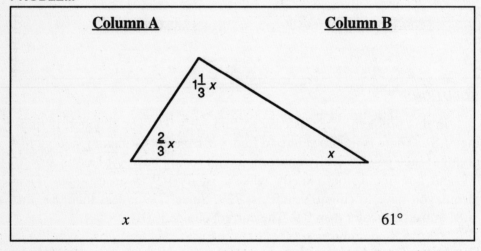

SOLUTION

The sum of the three angles of a triangle equals 180°. Therefore, we can add together the angles in the triangle above and set them equal to 180° to solve for x.

$$1\frac{1}{3}x + \frac{2}{3}x + x = 180$$

If we multiply this equation by three, we can eliminate the fractions.

$$3\,(1\frac{1}{3}x + \frac{2}{3}x + x = 180)$$

$$4x + 2x + 3x = 540$$

Simplifying the equation, we obtain

$9x = 540$

$x = 60$

Therefore, the correct choice is (B), since 60° is less than 61°.

As you attempt to answer Quantitative Comparison questions, it is not completely necessary that you be able to classify each question. However, you should be familiar with how to handle each question type. The remainder of this review will teach you how to answer the questions.

➤ POINTS TO REMEMBER

- Save time by becoming familiar with the reference information and the directions before the test. As you go through the practice problems at the end of this section, mark your answers on the grid—that will help you learn the directions before the test.

- Always examine *both columns and* the information in the *center,* if there is any, *before* you begin to work. By doing this, you won't overlook any information and you will be able to decide upon the appropriate strategy to use.

- If a problem seems to involve a lot of calculations, there is probably a faster way to do it. The numbers that are used in the problems are not selected to make you do a lot of calculations; they are selected so that if you are aware of certain mathematical relationships or properties, you can do the problems relatively quickly.

- Since you only have to compare quantities, don't work out the problems completely once you have enough information to make the comparison.

- Keep your work neat and in the appropriate columns so it will be easier to make comparisons.

- Be suspicious of problems with obvious answers if they occur toward the end of the section. The problems at the end of the section are always the more difficult ones. If the answer seems obvious, you have probably overlooked something important.

- If you have to guess, remember if a problem contains only numbers in both columns, the answer cannot be (D). If a problem contains only numbers, you can get an exact value for the quantities in each column and a comparison can be made.

ANSWERING QUANTITATIVE COMPARISON QUESTIONS

As you go through Quantitative Comparison questions, some seem to require a lot of calculations. On the other hand, there are some questions for which the answer seems immediately obvious. Often neither is the case. Excessive calculations can often be avoided and questions for which the answer seems obvious are often tricky.

The following steps will help guide you through answering Quantitative Comparison questions. These steps will cover strategies for every situation that you may encounter. Therefore, you may not need to go through every step for every question.

| STEP 1 | When you are presented with an addition or multiplication problem, you can often avoid these calculations just by comparing individual quantities. |

PROBLEM

Column A	Column B
$\dfrac{1}{3} + \dfrac{1}{6} + \dfrac{1}{12}$	$\dfrac{1}{4} + \dfrac{1}{8} + \dfrac{1}{16}$

SOLUTION

Both columns contains an addition problem. Don't bother to add! Compare the fractions in each column:

	Column A		Column B
	$\dfrac{1}{3}$	$>$	$\dfrac{1}{4}$
	$\dfrac{1}{6}$	$>$	$\dfrac{1}{8}$
and	$\dfrac{1}{12}$	$>$	$\dfrac{1}{16}$

For each fraction in Column B, there is a greater fraction in Column A. Therefore, the sum in Column A must be greater than the sum in Column B. The correct choice is (A).

PROBLEM

Column A	Column B
The area of a rectangle with a base of 3 and a height of 4	The area of a circle with a radius of 2

SOLUTION

You have to compare the area of a rectangle to the area of a circle. Your two columns will look like:

Area of rectangle	Area of circle
(3) (4)	$\pi 2^2 = 4\pi$

Both columns contain a multiplication problem with positive numbers. Don't multiply! Compare the factors in each column:

	3	<	π
and	4	=	4

The factors in Column B are greater than or equal to the factors in Column A so the product in Column B (the area of the circle) must be greater than the product in Column A (the area of the rectangle). The correct choice is (B).

STEP 2 | Sometimes you are faced with problems in which comparing parts seems to apply but you can't compare the quantities the way they are presented in the problem. If you change the way the quantities look, you may be able to compare parts.

PROBLEM

Column A	Column B
20% of 368	$\dfrac{1}{4}$ of 368

SOLUTION

Both columns contain multiplication of positive quantities:

(20%) (368)	$\left(\dfrac{1}{4}\right)$ (368)

This means that you can compare individual quantities to avoid multiplication. Both columns contain 368 but Column A contains a percent and Column B contains a fraction. You can either change the percent to a fraction or the fraction to a percent.

If you change 20% to a fraction, the columns will look like:

$$\left(\frac{1}{5}\right)(368) \qquad\qquad \left(\frac{1}{4}\right)(368).$$

Now you can compare quantities:

$$\frac{1}{5} < \frac{1}{4}$$

$$368 = 368$$

or

If you change $1/4$ to a percent, the columns will look like:

$$(20\%)(368) \qquad\qquad (25\%)(368)$$

Now you can compare quantities in the two columns:

$$20\% < 25\%$$

$$368 = 368$$

Using either approach, the product in Column B is greater than the product in Column A. The correct choice is (B).

PROBLEM

Column A	Column B
The area of a rectangle with length of 2.5 feet and width of 2 feet	The area of a rectangle with length of 27 inches and width of 23 inches

SOLUTION

Since you multiply length by width to find the area of a rectangle, both columns contain multiplication of positive quantities:

$$(2.5)(2) \qquad\qquad (27)(23)$$

If you write the problem this way and forget about the units, you have:

$$2.5 < 27$$

$$2 < 23$$

The product in Column B seems to be greater than the product in Column A. But this is wrong! Column A contains feet and Column B contains inches. Make sure you change feet to inches or inches to feet before you make the comparisons!

Let's change the feet to inches and see what happens. 2.5 feet equals 30 inches and 2 feet equals 24 inches. Now all the quantities are in inches so you can make the comparisons. Your two columns look like:

(30) (24)   (27) (23).

Now compare:

$$30 > 27$$

$$24 > 23$$

The product in Column A is greater than the product in Column B. The correct choice is (A).

PROBLEM

Column A	Column B
The number of ounces in 2 pints	The number of pints in in 2 gallons

SOLUTION

In this problem you must make sure to convert to the units specified in each column.

1 pint = 16 ounces   1 gallon = 8 pints

2 pints = 32 ounces   2 gallons = 16 pints

There are more *ounces* in 2 pints (Column A) than there are *pints* in 2 gallons (Column B). The correct choice is (A).

PROBLEM

Column A	Column B
(4.37) (125)	(437) (1.25)

SOLUTION

Each column contains a multiplication problem with positive numbers but comparing parts doesn't work since:

Column A		Column B
4.37	<	437
but 125	>	1.25

Even if you switch the numbers around, it still won't help:

125	<	437
but 4.37	>	1.25

You may think that you are forced to multiply, but you don't have to if you notice that all the digits are the same. The only differences between the quantities in the two columns are where the decimal points are. You can move the decimal points to try to get some or all of the numbers to look the same and then make the comparisons. When you move the decimal points, you are really multiplying or dividing by powers of 10 and what you do in one column must be done in the other column.

You can move the decimal point in 4.37 to the right 2 places in Column A (you're really multiplying by 100). You must then move the decimal point in Column B two places to the right.

Column A	Column B
(4.37) (125)	(437) (1.25)

becomes

(437) (125)	(437) (125)

Now you have identical factors in both columns. The correct choice is (C).

PROBLEM

Column A	Column B
$\dfrac{(14)\,(15)}{(35)\,(8)}$	1

SOLUTION

Sometimes changing the way quantities look won't help you compare parts, but it will make the arithmetic a lot easier!

Column A contains multiplication and division of positive numbers. Factor and reduce and you will make the problem a lot easier to solve.

When you factor,

Column A	Column B
$\dfrac{(14)\,(15)}{(35)\,(8)}$	1

becomes

$\dfrac{(2)\,(7)\,(3)\,(5)}{(7)\,(5)\,(2)\,(4)}$	1

When you reduce, you get:

$\dfrac{3}{4}$	1

The quantity in Column B is greater than the quantity in Column A so the correct choice is (B).

STEP 3	Make sure to look at the numbers presented. Numbers have important properties that can be used to save time. There are many properties that will be useful to know for the PSAT. We'll highlight two here.

PROBLEM

Column A	Column B
$(17)\,(15)\,(13)$	$(18)\,(16)\,(14)\,(0)$

SOLUTION

You may be tempted to compare factors in this problem, but you don't have to if you remember to look at both columns before you do any work. Notice that 0 is a factor in Column B. The quantity in Column B is equal to 0 since 0 times any number is 0. The quantity in Column A is greater than 0 since all the factors are positive. The correct choice is (A).

PROBLEM

Column A	Column B
$(2)^5 + (-2)^5$	$(3)^5 + (-3)^5$

SOLUTION

When you first look at this problem, you probably want to compare parts. To do that, you might think that you have to find the values of each part, but you don't! Getting the values involves a lot of multiplication so there must be a faster way and there is. Analyze the numbers in each column:

$(2)^5$ = some positive number $(3)^5$ = some positive number
$(-2)^5$ = the same as $(2)^5$ but $(-3)^5$ = the same as $(3)^5$ but
     with a negative sign   with a negative sign

The two numbers in each column are the same but opposite in sign. What does that mean when you add the two numbers in each column? The sum in each column is 0? The quantities in the two columns are equal. The correct choice is (C).

PROBLEM

Column A	Column B
$\dfrac{(-1)^7 + (-1)^9}{(-1)^4 + (-1)^6}$	1

SOLUTION

When -1 is raised to an odd power, the result is -1. When -1 is raised to an even power, the result is $+1$. Using that information, you get the following:

$\dfrac{(-1) + (-1)}{(+1) + (+1)}$	1
$\dfrac{-2}{+2}$	1
-1	1

The correct choice is (B).

STEP 4 | Try substituting values for the variables, in particular $0, 1, -1$, and fractions between 0 and -1. Sometimes you can use values that appear in the problem. To get a better understanding of how this will help you solve problems, let's look at a few.

PROBLEM

Column A	Column B
x is positive	
2^x	2^3

SOLUTION

In order to compare the two quantities, you have to know the value of *x*. According to the information centered above the two columns, *x* can be any positive number. You could try different values for *x*, but where do you begin? Column B gives you a starting point. What happens if *x* = 3? The quantities in the two columns would be equal. Now that you have tried one value for *x* and established that the two quantities can be equal, try another value to see if you can make one quantity greater than the other. What if *x* > 3? Then the quantity in Column A would be greater than the quantity in Column B (you shouldn't have to do the arithmetic!). By making these two comparisons, you have determined that:

the quantity in Column A = the quantity in Column B

or

the quantity in Column A > the quantity in Column B

The correct choice is (D).

(It's unnecessary to check values for *x* < 3 since you have already determined that (D) is the correct choice.)

PROBLEM

Column A	Column B
The average of *a*, *b*, and *c* is 10.	
$a > b > c$	
$a - b$	$b - c$

SOLUTION

Try some values for *a*, *b*, and *c*. The choice of numbers is up to you, but keep it simple. If you have 3 numbers with an average of 10, then their sum is 30. This may help you choose numbers.

You could start with a = 11, b = 10, and c = 9. Then you would have:

$$a - b = 11 - 10 = 1 \quad \text{and} \quad b - c = 10 - 9 = 1$$

The quantities in the two columns can be equal. But can there be some other relationship? Try some more numbers.

What if $a = 12$, $b = 11$, and $c = 7$? Then you would have:

$$a - b = 12 - 11 = 1 \qquad \text{and} \qquad b - c = 11 - 7 = 4$$

In this case, the quantity in Column B is greater than the quantity in Column A.

You have determined that:

> the quantity is Column A = the quantity in Column B

or

> the quantity in Column A < the quantity in Column B

The correct choice is (D).

PROBLEM

Column A	Column B
x is positive	
$x \neq 1$	
x	x^2

SOLUTION

Once again you have to try different values for *x*. Keep the arithmetic as simple as possible.

If $x = 2$, then you get:

2	4

If $x = 3$, then you get:

3	9

The answer seems obvious, doesn't it! Column B > Column A.

But if you try $x = {}^1/_2$, you get:

$\dfrac{1}{2}$	$\dfrac{1}{4}$

Column A > Column B!

Depending upon the value selected for *x*, the quantity in Column A can be greater or less than the quantity in Column B. The correct choice is (D).

PROBLEM

Column A	Column B
A pound of apples costs 89 cents.	
A pound of pears costs 99 cents.	
The number of apples in a pound	The number of pears in a pound

SOLUTION

Although a pound of pears costs more than a pound of apples, that does not mean that there are more pears than apples in a pound. There is no way to know how many pears or apples make up a pound. The correct choice is (D).

PROBLEM

Column A	Column B
A rectangle has an area of 8.	
The perimeter of the rectangle	12

SOLUTION

The centered information tells you the area of the rectangle. Since the area is 8, the length could be 4, and the width would be 2. If these are the measurements, then the perimeter would equal 12. But could the length and width have other values? What if the length is 8 and the width is 1? The area would still be 8 but the perimeter would be 18. We have found one set of values which make the quantities in Column A and Column B equal (4 and 2) and another set which make the quantities not equal (8 and 1). The correct choice is (D).

STEP 5 Estimation is useful when the numbers in the problem are close to any number that is easy to work with like $1/2$ or 1, or when an approximation will do.

PROBLEM

Column A	Column B
$\frac{3}{8}+\frac{3}{7}$	1

SOLUTION

In this problem, you have to compare the sum of two fractions, with different denominators, to 1. One way to do this is to change both fractions so that they have a common denominator and then do the arithmetic. A faster way is to estimate values. In Column A, $3/8$ is close to $1/2$, but a little less. $3/7$ is also close to $1/2$, but a little less. Since both numbers are each a little less than $1/2$, their sum must be less than 1, the quantity in Column B. The correct choice is (B).

PROBLEM

Column A	Column B
(16.8) (.51)	(8.4) (.99)

SOLUTION

Each column contains a multiplication problem with positive numbers but comparing parts doesn't work since:

Column A		Column B
16.8	>	8.4
but .51	<	.99

Even if you switch the numbers around, it still won't help:

Column A		Column B
16.8	>	.99
but .51	<	8.4

You may think that you are forced to multiply, but you don't have to if you notice that .51 is a little more than .5 and .99 is a little less than 1. Using these estimates will help you work out the problem without doing all the multiplication in the original problem! (You may find it faster to use $1/2$ instead of .5 to multiply 16.8 by.)

Using these estimated values in the columns, you get:

Column A	Column B
$(16.8) \left(\dfrac{1}{2} \right)$	(8.4) (1)

which becomes

8.4	8.4

But *remember that you are using estimated values!* The real value in Column A is a little more than 8.4 since you really had to multiply 16.8 by .51. The real value in Column B is a little less than 8.4 since you really had to multiply 8.4 by .99. The correct choice is (A).

| STEP 6 | If figures are not drawn to scale or do not look accurate, do not use them to help you solve the problem. These types of figures can throw you off and cause you to select the wrong answer.

PROBLEM

Column A	Column B
Line ℓ1 is parallel to line ℓ2.	
Line ℓ2 is parallel to line ℓ3.	
The distance between ℓ1 and ℓ2	The distance between ℓ2 and ℓ3

SOLUTION

This problem involves parallel lines but there is no figure. Draw a figure that fits the description in the problem, and then try to draw another figure that also fits the description but shows a different relationship. Below are two acceptable figures for this problem. Note that if you draw only one figure, you will get an incorrect answer.

In this first figure, the lines are evenly spaced so the distance between lines ℓ1 and ℓ2 is the same as the distance between lines ℓ2 and ℓ3. If this is the only figure you draw, you would choose (C) as your answer.

ℓ1
_____

ℓ2
_____

ℓ3
_____

In this second figure, the distance between lines ℓ1 and ℓ2 is greater than the distance between lines ℓ2 and ℓ3. If this is the only figure you draw, you would choose (B) as your answer.

ℓ1
_____

ℓ2
_____

ℓ3
_____

But if you draw both figures, you will choose the correct answer. The correct choice is (D).

The following questions should be completed to further reinforce what you have just learned. After you have completed all of the questions, check your answers against the answer key. Make sure to refer back to the review for help.

☞ Drill: Quantitative Comparisons

Each of the following questions consist of two quantities, one in Column A and one in Column B. You are to compare the two quantities and on the answer sheet blacken space

(A) if the quantity in Column A is greater;

(B) if the quantity in Column B is greater;

(C) if the two quantities are equal;

(D) if the relationship cannot be determined from the information given.

NOTES:

1. In certain questions, information concerning one or both of the quantities to be compared is centered above the two columns.

2. In a given question, a symbol that appears in both columns represents the same thing in Column A as it does in Column B.

3. Letters such as x, n, and k stand for real numbers.

EXAMPLES:

	Column A	Column B	Answer
E1:	$3 + 4$	3×4	Ⓐ ● Ⓒ Ⓓ Ⓔ

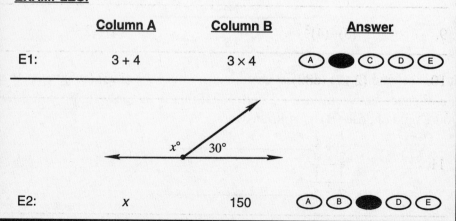

	Column A	Column B	Answer
E2:	x	150	Ⓐ Ⓑ ● Ⓓ Ⓔ

	Column A	**Column B**
1.	The average of 560, 374, and 241	The average of 560, 364, and 251

$$a > b > c > d$$

	Column A	**Column B**
2.	$a + c$	$b + d$
3.	The number of months in 7 years	The number of days in 12 weeks
4.	$\left(\dfrac{1}{4}\right)\left(\dfrac{3}{5}\right)\left(\dfrac{9}{8}\right)$	$\left(\dfrac{4}{3}\right)\left(\dfrac{1}{3}\right)\left(\dfrac{10}{7}\right)$
5.	(5) (7) (9) (11)	(8) (10) (4) (6)
6.	The distance a car travels in 30 minutes at 60 mph	The distance a car travels in 2 hours at 30 mph
7.	(1.75) (24)	(175) (2.4)
8.	$\dfrac{(14)\,(21)}{(49)\,(6)}$	1
9.	$(3)^2\,(4)^3$	$(\pi)^2\,(2)^6$
10.	(2.17) (682)	(196) (6.7)
11.	$\dfrac{\dfrac{1}{2} + \dfrac{1}{4}}{\dfrac{1}{3} + \dfrac{1}{5}}$	1

	__Column A__	__Column B__
12.	$\dfrac{(78-94)}{(35-41)}$	$\dfrac{(175-123)}{(134-167)}$
13.	$\dfrac{(5)\,(0)}{(19)\,(3)\,(21)}$	$(-3)^7 + (9)\,(3)^5$
14.	$\dfrac{(-2)^4\,(-5)^3}{(-3)^2}$	$\dfrac{(174-356)}{(97-132)}$
15.	$-\dfrac{7}{8}$	$-\dfrac{8}{7}$

$$\frac{x}{y} = 7$$

16.	x	y

There are 40 students in Class A.
There are 30 students in Class B.
There are more boys in each class than girls.

17.	The number of boys in Class A	The number of boys in Class B

$$a > b,\ c > d,\ c \neq 0,\ d \neq 0$$

18.	$\dfrac{a}{c}$	$\dfrac{b}{d}$

$$|X| > 1$$

19.	X^3	X^2

Column A	**Column B**

$$XY = 1, X > 0$$

	Column A	**Column B**
20.	X	Y
21.	$\dfrac{9}{10} \times \dfrac{12}{13}$	$\dfrac{5}{9} \times \dfrac{6}{11}$
22.	$\sqrt{37} + \sqrt{27}$	$\sqrt{37 + 27}$
23.	$\sqrt{\dfrac{7}{3} \times \dfrac{1}{5} \times \dfrac{11}{5}}$	$\sqrt{\dfrac{5 \times 2}{6}}$
24.	$\dfrac{1}{\sqrt{2}} + \dfrac{1}{\sqrt{3}}$	$\dfrac{1}{\sqrt{6}}$
25.	$(6.9)(8.9)$	$\sqrt{(50)(82)}$

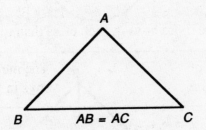

Note: Figure not drawn to scale.

26.	$\angle A$	$\angle B$

<u>Column A</u>	<u>Column B</u>

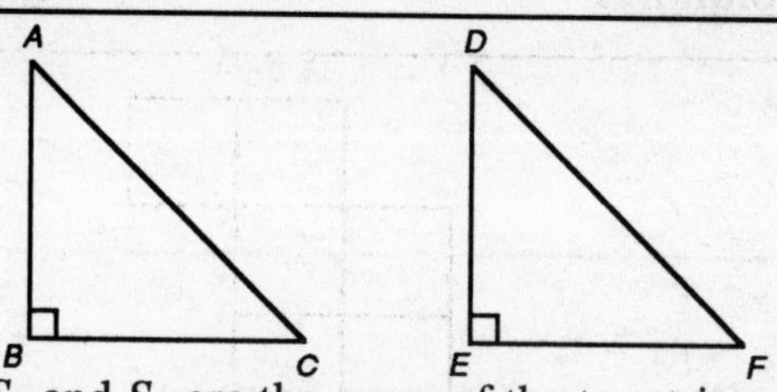

Note: S_1 and S_2 are the areas of the two triangles.

$S_1 = S_2$

27.	AC	DF

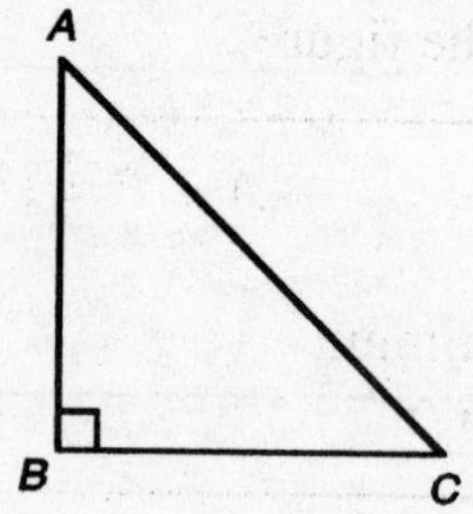

28.	$\angle A$	$\angle C$

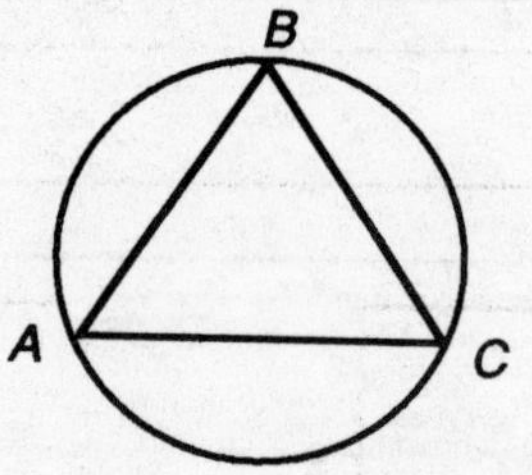

29.	AB	AC

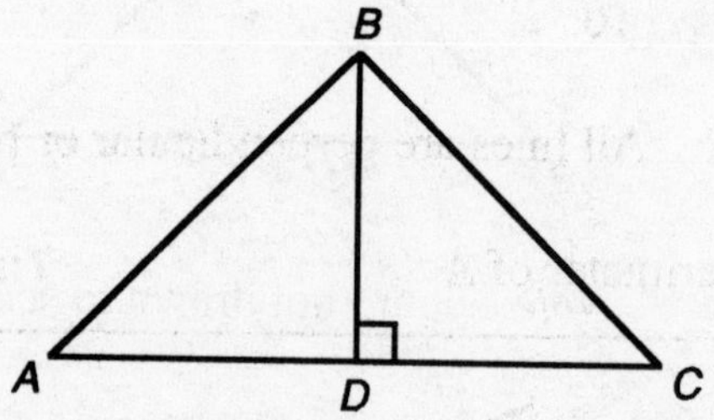

$AB = BC$

30.	AD	DC

Column A	Column B

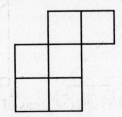

6 congruent squares
The area of the figure is 150.

31. The perimeter of the figure   65

$$A + B = 18$$

32. What is the maximum   70
     value of *AB*?

$$x = (.03 \div \frac{3}{.5})$$

33.   *x*   .0025

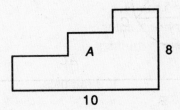 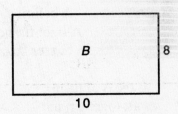

All lines are perpendicular or parallel.

34.   The perimeter of *A*   The perimeter of *B*

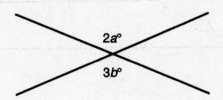

35.   *a*   *b*

Column A	Column B

$$N > 0$$

	Column A	Column B
36.	N^{10}	N^{12}

It takes a motorist 1 minute and 40 seconds to go 1 mile.

37.	The motorist's speed in m.p.h.	35 m.p.h.

$$N = \frac{7}{12}$$

38.	Find the value of $\dfrac{N^{12}}{N^{10}}$.	$\dfrac{1}{2}$

39.	Find the average of all numbers ending in 8 between 200 and 310.	250

A bell rings every 5 minutes.
A light flashes every 6 minutes.
A buzzer buzzes every 8 minutes.

40.	If the 3 of them start together, in how many minutes will the 3 happen again together?	110 minutes

QUANTITATIVE COMPARISONS

ANSWER KEY

Drill: Quantitative Comparisons

1. (C)	11. (A)	21. (A)	31. (B)
2. (A)	12. (A)	22. (A)	32. (A)
3. (C)	13. (C)	23. (A)	33. (A)
4. (B)	14. (B)	24. (A)	34. (C)
5. (A)	15. (A)	25. (B)	35. (A)
6. (B)	16. (D)	26. (D)	36. (D)
7. (B)	17. (D)	27. (D)	37. (A)
8. (C)	18. (D)	28. (D)	38. (B)
9. (B)	19. (D)	29. (D)	39. (A)
10. (A)	20. (D)	30. (C)	40. (A)

PSAT/ NMSQT

CHAPTER 10

Attacking Student-Produced Response Questions

Chapter 10

ATTACKING STUDENT-PRODUCED RESPONSE QUESTIONS

The Student-Produced Response format of the PSAT is designed to give the student a certain amount of flexibility in answering questions. In this section the student must calculate the answer to a given question and then enter the solution into a grid. The grid is constructed so that a solution can be given in either decimal or fraction form. Either form is acceptable unless otherwise stated.

The problems in the Student-Produced Response section try to reflect situations arising in the real world. Here calculations will involve objects occurring in everyday life. There is also an emphasis on problems involving data interpretation. In keeping with this emphasis, students will be allowed the use of a calculator during the exam.

Through this review, you will learn how to successfully attack Student-Produced Response questions. Familiarity with the test format combined with solid math strategies will prove invaluable in answering the questions quickly and accurately.

ABOUT THE DIRECTIONS

Each Student-Produced Response question will require you to solve the problem and enter your answer in a grid. There are specific rules you will need to know for entering your solution. If you enter your answer in an incorrect form, you will not receive credit, even if you originally solved the problem correctly. Therefore, you should carefully study the following rules now, so you don't have to waste valuable time during the actual test:

DIRECTIONS: Each of the following questions requires you to solve the problem and enter your answer in the ovals in the special grid:

Answer: $\frac{5}{12}$

Write answers here

Answer: 3.5

Answer: 525
Either position is correct

Fraction line

Decimal line

Grid in answer

- You may begin filling in your answer in any column, space permitting. Columns not needed should be left blank.

- Answers may be entered in either decimal or fraction form. For example, $^3/_{12}$ or .25 are equally acceptable.

- A mixed number, such as $4^1/_2$, must be entered either as 4.5 or $^9/_2$. If you entered 41/2, the machine would interpret your answer as $^{41}/_2$, not $4^1/_2$.

- There may be some instances where there is more than one correct answer to a problem. Should this be the case, grid only one answer.

- Be very careful when filling in ovals. Do not fill in more than one oval in any column, and make sure to completely darken the ovals.

- It is suggested that you fill in your answer in the boxes above each column. Although you will not be graded incorrectly if you do not write in your answer, it will help you fill in the corresponding ovals.

- If your answer is a decimal, grid the most accurate value possible. For example, if you need to grid a repeating decimal such as 0.6666, enter the answer as .666 or .667. A less accurate value, such as .66 or .67, is not acceptable.

- A negative answer cannot appear for any question.

SAMPLE QUESTION

How many pounds of apples can be bought with $5.00 if apples cost $.40 a pound?

SOLUTION

Converting dollars to cents we obtain the equation

$$x = 500 \div 40$$

$$x = 12.5$$

The solution to this problem would be gridded as

ABOUT THE QUESTIONS

Within the PSAT Student-Produced Response section you will be given 8 questions. You will have 30 minutes to answer these questions in addition to 12 Quantitative Comparison questions. This means you will be required to answer 20 questions in 25 minutes. Therefore, you should work quickly.

The Student-Produced Response questions will come from the areas of arithmetic, algebra, and geometry. There is an emphasis on word problems and on data interpretation, which usually involves reading tables to answer questions. Many of the geometry questions will refer to diagrams or will ask you to create a figure from information given in the question.

The following will detail the different types of questions you should expect to encounter on the Student-Produced Response section.

ARITHMETIC QUESTIONS

These arithmetic questions test your ability to perform standard manipulations and simplifications of arithmetic expressions. For some questions, there is more than one approach. There are six kinds of arithmetic questions you may encounter in the Student-Produced Response section. For each type of question, we will show how to solve the problem and grid your answer.

Question Type 1: Properties of a Whole Number *N*

This problem tests your ability to find a whole number with a given set of properties. You will be given a list of properties of a whole number and asked to find that number.

PROBLEM

The properties of a whole number *N* are

(A) *N* is a perfect square.

(B) *N* is divisible by 2.

(C) *N* is divisible by 3.

Grid in the second smallest whole number with the above properties.

SOLUTION

Try to first obtain the smallest number with the above properties. The smallest number with properties (B) and (C) is 6. Since property (A) says the number must be a perfect square, the smallest number with properties (A), (B), and (C) is 36.

$6^2 = 36$ is the smallest whole number with the above properties. The second smallest whole number (the solution) is

$2^2 6^2 = 144.$

The correct answer entered into the grid is

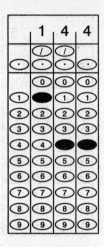

Question Type 2: Simplifying Fractions

This type of question requires you to simplify fractional expressions and grid the answer in the format specified. By canceling out terms common to both the numerator and denominator, we can simplify complex fractional expressions.

PROBLEM

Change $\dfrac{1}{2} \times \dfrac{3}{7} \times \dfrac{2}{8} \times \dfrac{14}{10} \times \dfrac{1}{3}$ to decimal form.

SOLUTION

The point here is to cancel out terms common to both the numerator and denominator. Once the fraction is brought down to lowest terms, the result is entered into the grid as a decimal.

After cancellation we are left with the fraction $^1/_{40}$. Equivalently,

$$\frac{1}{40} = \frac{1}{10} \times \frac{1}{4} = \frac{1}{10}(.25) = .025$$

Hence, in our grid we enter

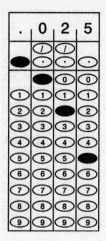

Note: If "decimal" was not specified, any correct version of the answer could be entered into the grid.

Question Type 3: Prime Numbers of a Particular Form

Here, you will be asked to find a prime number with certain characteristics. Remember—a prime number is a number that can only be divided by itself and 1.

PROBLEM

Find a prime number of the form $7k + 1 < 50$.

SOLUTION

This is simply a counting problem. The key is to list all the numbers of the form $7k + 1$ starting with $k = 0$. The first one that is prime is the solution to the problem.

The whole numbers of the form $7k + 1$ which are less than 50 are 1, 8, 15, 22, 29, 36, and 43. Of these, 29 and 43 are prime numbers. The possible solutions are 29 and 43.

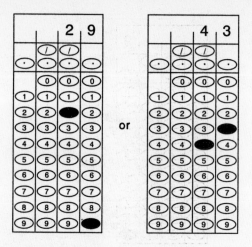

Question Type 4: Order of Operations

The following question type tests your knowledge of the arithmetic order of operations. Always work within the parentheses or with absolute values first, while keeping in mind that multiplication and division are carried out before addition and subtraction.

PROBLEM

Find a solution to the equation $x \div 3 \times 4 \div 2 = 6$.

SOLUTION

The key here is to recall the order of precedence for arithmetic operations. After simplifying the expression one can solve for x.

Since multiplication and division have the same level of precedence, we simplify the equation from left to right to obtain

$$\frac{x}{3} \times 4 \div 2 = 6$$

$$\frac{4x}{3} \div 2 = 6$$

$$\frac{2x}{3} = 6$$

$$x = 9$$

As 9 solves the above problem, our entry in the grid is

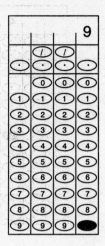

Question Type 5: Solving for Ratios

This type of question tests your ability to manipulate ratios given a set of constraints.

PROBLEM

Let A, B, C, and D be positive integers. Assume that the ratio of A to B is equal to the ratio of C to D. Find a possible value for A if the product of $BC = 24$ and D is odd.

SOLUTION

The quickest way to find a solution is to list the possible factorizations of 24:

1×24

2×12

3×8

4×6

Since $AD = BC = 24$ and D is odd, the only possible solution is $A = 8$ (corresponding to $D = 3$).

In the following grid we enter

Question Type 6: Simplifying Arithmetic Expressions

Here you will be given an arithmetic problem that is easier to solve if you transform it into a basic algebra problem. This strategy saves valuable time by cutting down on the number and complexity of computations involved.

PROBLEM

Simplify $1-\left(\dfrac{1}{2}+\dfrac{1}{4}+\dfrac{1}{8}+\dfrac{1}{16}+\dfrac{1}{32}+\dfrac{1}{64}\right)$.

SOLUTION

This problem can be done one of two ways. The "brute force" approach would be to get a common denominator and simplify. An approach involving less computation is given below.

$$\text{Set } S = 1-\left(\frac{1}{2}+\frac{1}{4}+\frac{1}{8}+\frac{1}{16}+\frac{1}{32}+\frac{1}{64}\right)$$

Multiplying this equation by 2 we obtain

$$2S = 2-\left(1+\frac{1}{2}+\frac{1}{4}+\frac{1}{8}+\frac{1}{16}+\frac{1}{32}\right)$$

$$2S = 1-\left(\frac{1}{2}+\frac{1}{4}+\frac{1}{8}+\frac{1}{16}+\frac{1}{32}\right)$$

$$2S = 1-\left(\frac{1}{2}+\frac{1}{4}+\frac{1}{8}+\frac{1}{16}+\frac{1}{32}+\frac{1}{64}\right)+\frac{1}{64}$$

$$2S = S + \frac{1}{64}$$

$$S = \frac{1}{64}$$

We enter into the grid

ALGEBRA QUESTIONS

Within the Student-Produced Response section, you will also encounter algebra questions which will test your ability to solve algebraic expressions in the setting of word problems. You may encounter the following six types of algebra questions during the PSAT. As in the previous section, we provide methods for approaching each type of problem.

Question Type 1: Solving a System of Linear Equations

This is a standard question which will ask you to find the solution to a system of two linear equations with two unknowns.

PROBLEM

Consider the system of simultaneous equations given by

$y - 2 = x - 4$

$y + 3 = 6 - x$

Solve for the quantity $6y + 3$.

SOLUTION

This problem can be solved by taking the first equation given and solving for x. This would yield

$x = y + 2.$

Next, we plug this value for x into the second equation, giving us

$y + 3 = 6 - (y + 2).$

Solve this equation for y and we get

$y = {}^1\!/_2.$

We are asked to solve for $6y + 3$, so we can plug our value for y in and get

$6({}^1\!/_2) + 3 = 6.$

Our answer is 6 and gridded correctly it is

Question Type 2: Word Problems Involving Age

When dealing with this type of question, you will be asked to solve for the age of a particular person. The question may require you to determine how much older one person is, how much younger one person is, or the specific age of the person.

PROBLEM

Tim is 2 years older than Jane and Joe is 4 years younger than Jane. If the sum of the ages of Jane, Joe, and Tim is 28, how old is Joe?

SOLUTION

Define Jane's age to be the variable x and work from there.

Let

Jane's age $= x$

Tim's age $= x + 2$

Joe's age $= x - 4$

Summing up the ages we get

$$x + x + 2 + x - 4 = 28$$

$$3x - 2 = 28$$

$$3x = 30$$

$$x = 10$$

Joe's age $= 10 - 4 = 6$.

Hence, we enter into the grid

Question Type 3: Word Problems Involving Money

Word problems involving money will test your ability to translate the information given into an algebraic statement. You will also be required to solve your algebraic statement.

PROBLEM

After receiving his weekly paycheck on Friday, a man buys a television for $100, a suit for $200, and a radio for $50. If the total money he spent amounts to 40% of his paycheck, what is his weekly salary?

SOLUTION

Simply set up an equation involving the man's expenditures and the percentage of his paycheck that he used to buy them.

Let the amount of the man's paycheck equal x. We then have the equation

$$40\%x = 100 + 200 + 50$$

$$0.4x = 350$$

$$x = \$875$$

In the grid we enter

Question Type 4: Systems of Non-Linear Equations

This type of question will test your ability to perform the correct algebraic operations for a given set of equations in order to find the desired quantity.

PROBLEM

> Consider the system of equations
>
> $$x^2 + y^2 = 8$$
>
> $$xy = 4$$
>
> Solve for the quantity $3x + 3y$.

SOLUTION

Solve for the quantity $x + y$ and not for x or y individually.

First, multiply the equation $xy = 4$ by 2 to get $2xy = 8$. Adding this to $x^2 + y^2 = 8$ we obtain

$$x^2 + 2xy + y^2 = 16$$

$$(x + y)^2 = 16$$

$$x + y = 4$$

or
$$x + y = -4$$

Hence, $3x + 3y = 12$ or $3x + 3y = -12$. We enter 12 for a solution since -12 cannot be entered into the grid.

Question Type 5: Word Problems Involving Hourly Wage

When dealing with this type of question, you will be required to form an algebraic expression from the information based on a person's wages. You will then solve the expression to determine the person's wages (i.e., hourly, daily, annually, etc.).

PROBLEM

Jim works 25 hours a week earning $10 an hour. Sally works 50 hours a week earning y dollars an hour. If their combined income every two weeks is $2,000, find the amount of money Sally makes an hour.

SOLUTION

Be careful. The combined income is given over a two-week period.

Simply set up an equation involving income. We obtain

$$2[(25)(10) + (50)(y)] = 2,000$$

$$[(25)(10) + (50)(y)] = 1,000$$

$$250 + 50y = 1,000$$

$$50y = 750$$

$$y = \$15 \text{ an hour}$$

We enter in the grid

Question Type 6: Word Problems Involving Consecutive Integers

In this type of question, you will need to set up an equation involving consecutive integers based on the product of the integers, which is given.

PROBLEM

Consider two positive consecutive odd integers such that their product is 143. Find their sum.

SOLUTION

Be careful. Notice x and y are consecutive odd integers.

Let

1st odd integer $= x$

2nd odd integer $= x + 2$.

We get

$$x(x + 2) = 143$$

$$x^2 + 2x - 143 = 0$$

$$(x - 11)(x + 13) = 0$$

Hence

$$x = 11$$

and

$$x = -13.$$

From the above we obtain the solution sets $\{11, 13\}$ and $\{-13, -11\}$ whose sums are 24 and -24, respectively. Since the problem specifies that the integers are positive, we enter 24.

GEOMETRY QUESTIONS

In this section, we will explain how to solve questions which test your ability to find the area of various geometric figures. There are six types of questions you may encounter.

Question Type 1: Area of an Inscribed Triangle

This question asks you to find the area of a triangle which is inscribed in a square. By knowing certain properties of both triangles and squares, we can deduce the necessary information.

PROBLEM

Consider the triangle inscribed in the square.

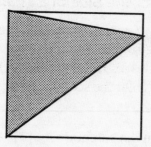

If the area of the square is 36, find the area of the triangle.

SOLUTION

Find the height of the triangle.

Let x be the length of the square. Since the four sides of a square are equal, and the area of a square is the length of a side squared, $x^2 = 36$. Therefore, $x = 6$.

The area of a triangle is given by

$$\frac{1}{2} \text{ (base) (height)}.$$

Here x is both the base and height of the triangle. The area of the triangle is

$$\frac{1}{2} (6) (6) = 18.$$

This is how the answer would be gridded.

Question Type 2: Length of the Side of a Triangle

For this type of question, one must find the length of a right triangle given information about the other sides. The key here is to apply the Pythagorean Theorem, which states that the square of the hypotenuse of a right triangle is equal to the sum of the squares of the other two sides.

PROBLEM

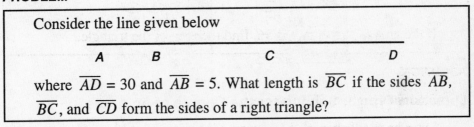

Consider the line given below

where $\overline{AD}$ = 30 and $\overline{AB}$ = 5. What length is $\overline{BC}$ if the sides $\overline{AB}$, $\overline{BC}$, and $\overline{CD}$ form the sides of a right triangle?

SOLUTION

Draw a diagram and fill in the known information.

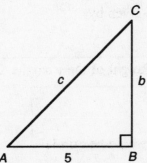

Next, apply the Pythagorean Theorem ($a^2 + b^2 = c^2$), filling in the known variables. Here, we are solving for BC (b in our equation). We know that a

= 5, and since $AD = 30$ and $AB = 5$, $BD = 25$. Filling in these values, we obtain this equation:

$$5^2 + x^2 = (25 - x)^2$$

$$25 + x^2 = 625 - 50x + x^2$$

$$50x = 600$$

$$x = 12$$

This is one possible solution. If we had chosen $x = CD$ and $25 - x = BC$, one obtains $BC = 13$, which is another possible solution. The possible grid entries are shown here.

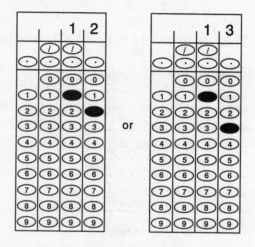

Question Type 3: Solving for the Degree of an Angle

Here you will be given a figure with certain information provided. You will need to deduce the measure of an angle based both on this information, as well as other geometric principles. The easiest way to do this is by setting up an algebraic expression.

PROBLEM

Find the angle y in the diagram below.

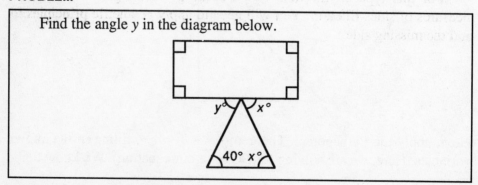

SOLUTION

Use the fact that the sum of the angles on the bottom side of the box is 180°.

Let z be the angle at the top of the triangle. Since we know the sum of the angles of a triangle is 180°,

$$z = 180 - (x + 40).$$

Summing all the angles at the bottom of the square, we get

$$y + [180 - (x + 40)] + x = 180$$

$$y + 140 - x + x = 180$$

$$y + 140 = 180$$

$$y = 40$$

In the grid we enter

Question Type 4: Solving for the Length of a Side

For this type of question, you will be given a figure with certain measures of sides filled in. You will need to apply geometric principles to find the missing side.

PROBLEM

Consider the figure below.

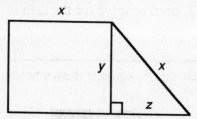

In the figure let x and y be whole numbers where $xy = 65$. Also assume the area of the whole figure is 95 square inches. Find z.

SOLUTION

The key point here is that x and y are whole numbers. Using the figure we only have a finite number of possibilities for z.

The equation for the area of the above figure is

$$xy + yz = 95.$$

Substituting $xy = 65$ into the above equation we get

$$yz = 30.$$

Using the fact that $xy = 65$ we know y can be either 1, 5, or 13. As $y = 13$ does not yield a factorization for $yz = 30$, y is either 1 or 5. If $y = 1$ this implies $x = 65$ and $z = 60$ which contradicts the Pythagorean Theorem (i.e., $1^2 + 60^2 = 13^2$). If $y = 5$ this implies $x = 13$ and $z = 12$ which satisfies $y^2 + z^2 = x^2$; hence, the solution is $y = 5$.

In our grid we enter

Question Type 5: Solving for the Area of a Region

Here, you will be given a figure with a shaded region. Given certain information, you will need to solve for the area of that region.

PROBLEM

Consider the concentric squares drawn below.

Assume that the side of the larger square is length 1. Also assume that the smaller square's perimeter is equal to the diameter of the larger square. Find the area of the shaded region.

SOLUTION

The key here is to find the length of the side for the smaller square.

By the Pythagorean Theorem the diameter of the square is

$$d^2 = 1^2 + 1^2$$

which yields $d = \sqrt{2}$. Similarly, the smaller square's perimeter is $\sqrt{2}$; hence, the smaller square's side

$$= \frac{\sqrt{2}}{4}.$$

Calculating the area for the shaded region we get

$$A = A_{large} - A_{small}$$

$$A = 1 - \left(\frac{\sqrt{2}}{4}\right)^2$$

$$A = 1 - \frac{2}{16}$$

$$A = \frac{7}{8}$$

In the grid we enter

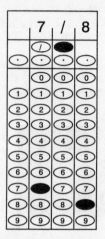

Question Type 6: Solve for a Sum of Lengths

The question here involves solving for a sum of lengths in the figure given knowledge pertaining to its area.

PROBLEM

Consider the figure below.

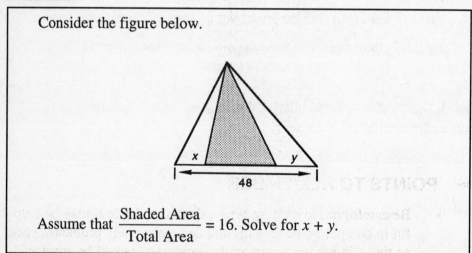

Assume that $\dfrac{\text{Shaded Area}}{\text{Total Area}} = 16$. Solve for $x + y$.

SOLUTION

Solve for $x + y$ and not for x or y individually. Denote by b the base of the smaller triangle. Then

$$48 - b = x + y.$$

From the information given

$$\frac{\frac{1}{2}48h}{\frac{1}{2}bh} = 16$$

$$\frac{1}{2}48h = 16\left(\frac{1}{2}bh\right)$$

$$24 = 8b$$

$$3 = b$$

This yields

$$x + y = 48 - 3 = 45.$$

We enter in the grid

> ## POINTS TO REMEMBER

- Be careful not to overuse your calculator. While it may be helpful in computing large sums and decimals, many problems, such as those involving common denominators, would be more efficiently solved without one.

- Immediately plug the values of all specific information into your equation.

- To visualize exactly what the question is asking and what information you need to find, draw a sketch of the problem.

- Even though you may think you have the equation worked out, make sure your result is actually answering the question. For example, although you may solve an equation for a specific variable, this may not be the final answer. You may have to use this answer to find another quantity.

- Make sure to work in only one unit, and convert if more than one is presented in the problem. For example, if a problem gives numbers in decimals and fractions, convert one in terms of the other and then work out the problem.

- Eliminate all dollar and percent signs when gridding your answers.

ANSWERING STUDENT-PRODUCED RESPONSE QUESTIONS

When answering Student-Produced Response questions, you should follow these steps.

| STEP 1 | Identify the type of question with which you are presented (i.e., arithmetic, algebra, or geometry). |

| STEP 2 | Once you have determined if the question deals with arithmetic, algebra, or geometry, further classify the question. Then, try to determine what type of arithmetic (or algebra or geometry) question is being presented. |

| STEP 3 | Solve the question using the techniques explained in this review. Make sure your answer can be gridded. |

| STEP 4 | Grid your answer in the question's corresponding answer grid. Make sure you are filling in the correct grid. Keep in mind that it is not mandatory to begin gridding your answer on any particular side of the grid. Fill in the ovals as completely as possible, and beware of stray lines—stray lines may cause your answer to be marked incorrect. |

The drill questions which follow should be completed to help reinforce the material which you have just studied. Be sure to refer back to the review if you need help answering the questions.

☞ Drill: Student-Produced Response Questions

(An answer sheet appears at the end of this book.)

DIRECTIONS: Each of the following questions requires you to solve the problem and enter your answer in the ovals in the special grid:

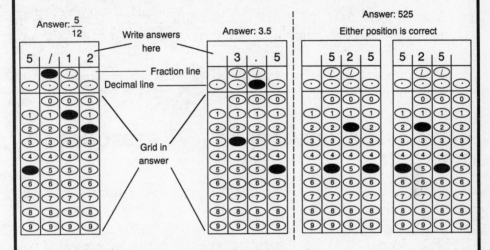

• You may begin filling in your answer in any column, space permitting. Columns not needed should be left blank.

• Answers may be entered in either decimal or fraction form. For example, $3/12$ or .25 are equally acceptable.

• A mixed number, such as $4^1/_2$, must be entered either as 4.5 or $9/_2$. If you entered 41/2, the machine would interpret your answer as $41/_2$, not $4^1/_2$.

• There may be some instances where there is more than one correct answer to a problem. Should this be the case, grid only one answer.

• Be very careful when filling in ovals. Do not fill in more than one oval in any column, and make sure to completely darken the ovals.

• It is suggested that you fill in your answer in the boxes above each column. Although you will not be graded incorrectly if you do not write in your answer, it will help you fill in the corresponding ovals.

• If your answer is a decimal, grid the most accurate value possible. For example, if you need to grid a repeating decimal such as 0.6666, enter the answer as .666 or .667. A less accurate value, such as .66 or .67, is not acceptable.

• A negative answer cannot appear for any question.

1. At the end of the month, a woman pays $714 in rent. If the rent constitutes 21% of her monthly income, what is her hourly wage given the fact that she works 34 hours per week?

2. Find the largest integer which is less than 100 and divisible by 3 and 7.

3. The radius of the smaller of two concentric circles is 5 cm while the radius of the larger circle is 7 cm. Determine the area of the shaded region.

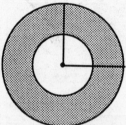

4. $\dfrac{1}{6}+\dfrac{2}{3}+\dfrac{1}{6}-\dfrac{1}{3}+1-\dfrac{3}{4}-\dfrac{1}{4}=$

5. The sum of the squares of two consecutive integers is 41. What is the sum of their cubes?

6. Find x.

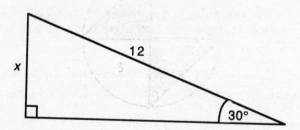

7. $|-8-4|\div 3\times 6+(-4)=$

8. A class of 24 students contains 16 males. What is the ratio of females to males?

9. At an office supply store, customers are given a discount if they pay in cash. If a customer is given a discount of $9.66 on a total order of $276, what is the percent of discount?

10. Let $\overline{RO}$ = 16, $\overline{HM}$ = 30. Find the perimeter of rhombus *HOMR*.

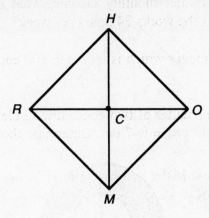

11. Solve for *x*.
$$x + 2y = 8$$
$$3x + 4y = 20$$

12. Six years ago, Henry's mother was nine times as old as Henry. Now she is only three times as old as Henry. How old is Henry now?

13. Find a prime number less than 40 which is of the form $5k + 1$.

14. Find the area of the shaded triangles.

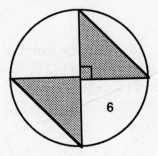

15. $\dfrac{7}{10} \times \dfrac{4}{21} \times \dfrac{25}{36} =$

16. Find the solution for *x* in the pair of equations.
$$x + y = 7$$
$$x = y - 3$$

17. Given the square *RHOM*, find the length of the diagonal $\overline{RO}$.

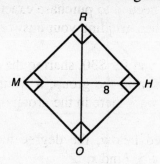

18. Δ*MNO* is isosceles. If the vertex angle, ∠ *N*, has a measure of 96°, find the measure of ∠ *M*.

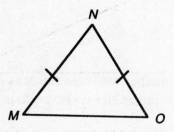

19. Simplify $\dfrac{\dfrac{1}{2} + \dfrac{1}{3}}{\dfrac{1}{6}}$.

20. In the diagram shown, *ABC* is an isosceles triangle. Sides $\overline{AC}$ and $\overline{BC}$ are extended through *C* to *E* and *D* to form triangle *CDE*. What is the sum of the measures of angles *D* and *E*?

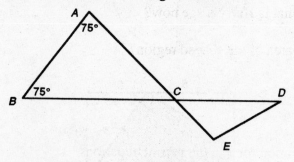

21.

Number of Muffins	Total Price
1	$0.55
Box of 4	$2.10
Box of 8	$4.00

According to the information in the table above, what would be the *least* amount of money needed to purchase exactly 19 muffins? (Disregard the dollar sign when gridding your answer.)

22. Several people rented a van for $30, sharing the cost equally. If there had been one more person in the group, it would have cost each $1 less. How many people were there in the group originally?

23. For the triangle pictured below, the degree measures of the three angles are x, $3x$, and $3x + 5$. Find x.

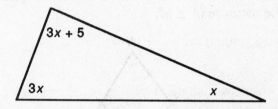

24. $\triangle PQR$ is a scalene triangle. The measure of $\angle P$ is 8 more than twice the measure of $\angle R$. The measure of $\angle Q$ is two less than three times the measure of $\angle R$. Determine the measure of $\angle Q$.

25. A mother is now 24 years older than her daughter. In 4 years, the mother will be 3 times as old as the daughter. What is the present age of the daughter?

26. John is 4 times as old as Harry. In six years John will be twice as old as Harry. What is Harry's age now?

27. What is the area of the shaded region?

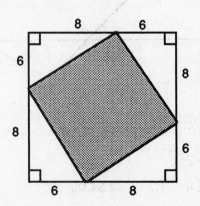

28. In an apartment building there are 9 apartments having terraces for every 16 apartments. If the apartment building has a total of 144 apartments, how many apartments have terraces?

29. Solve the equation $2x^2 - 5x + 3 = 0$.

30. Find the length of a side of an equilateral triangle whose area is $4\sqrt{3}$.

31. Solve $\dfrac{3}{x-1} + \dfrac{1}{x-2} = \dfrac{5}{(x-1)(x-2)}$.

32. Solve the proportion $\dfrac{x+1}{4} = \dfrac{15}{12}$.

33. In an isosceles triangle, the length of each of the congruent sides is 10 and the length of the base is 12. Find the length of the altitude drawn to the base.

34. The following are three students' scores on Mr. Page's Music Fundamentals midterm. The given score is the number of correct answers out of 55 total questions.

    Liz   48

    Jay   45

    Carl   25

    What is the *average* percentage of questions correct for the three students?

35. Reserved seat tickets to a football game are $6 more than general admission tickets. Mr. Jones finds that he can buy general admission tickets for his whole family of five for only $3 more than the cost of reserved seat tickets for himself and Mrs. Jones. How much do the general admission tickets cost?

36. The sum of three numbers is 96. The ratio of the first to the second is $1 : 2$, and the ratio of the second to the third is $2 : 3$. What is the third number?

37. What is the smallest even integer n for which $(.5)^n$ is less than .01?

38. The mean (average) of the numbers 50, 60, 65, 75, x, and y is 65. What is the mean of x and y?

39. The ages of the students enrolled at XYZ University are given in the following table:

Age	Number of students
18	750
19	1,600
20	1,200
21	450

What percent of students are 19 and 20 years old?

40. Find the larger side of a rectangle whose area is 24 and whose perimeter is 22.

STUDENT-PRODUCED RESPONSE

ANSWER KEY

1. 2 5

2. 8 4

3. 7 5 . 4

4. 2 / 3

5. 1 8 9

6. 6

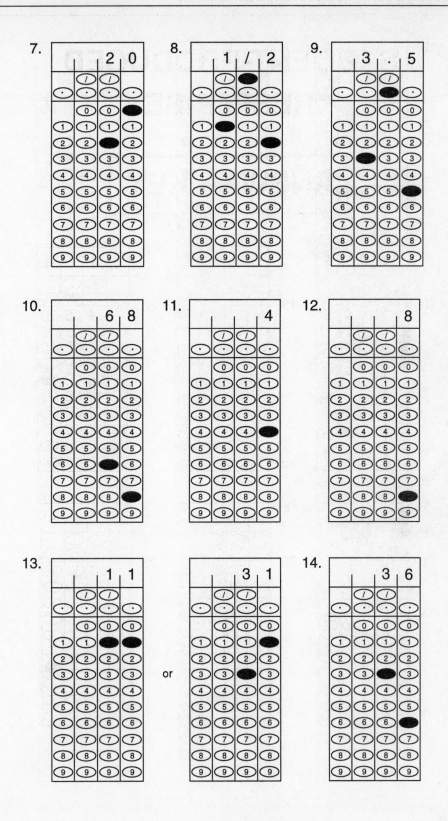

7. 2 0

8. 1 / 2

9. 3 . 5

10. 6 8

11. 4

12. 8

13. 1 1   or   3 1

14. 3 6

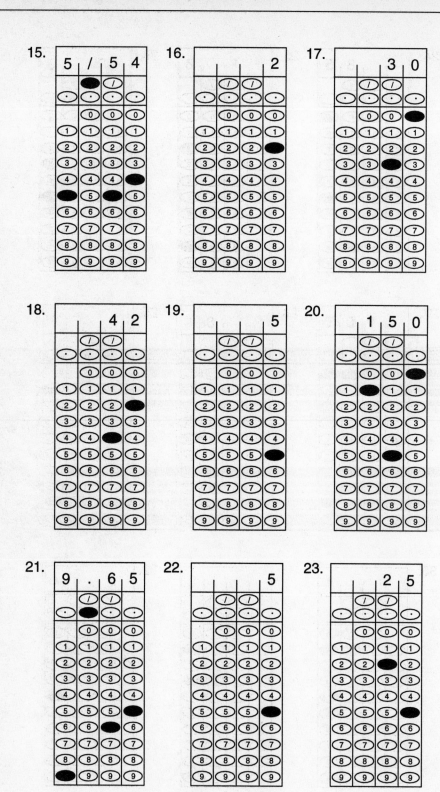

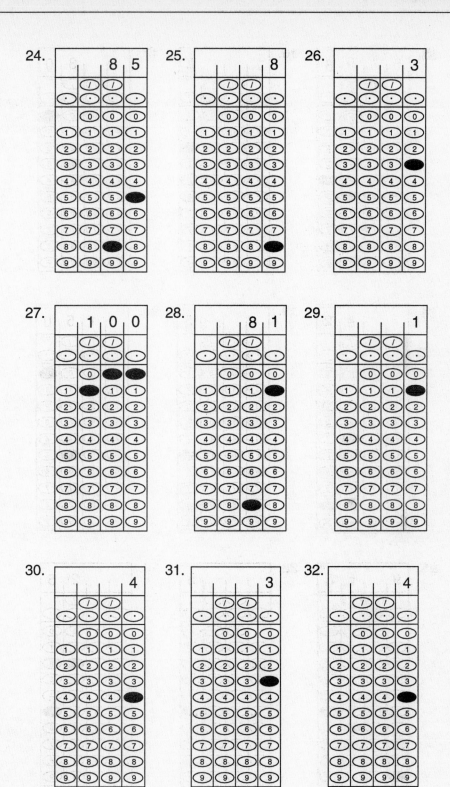

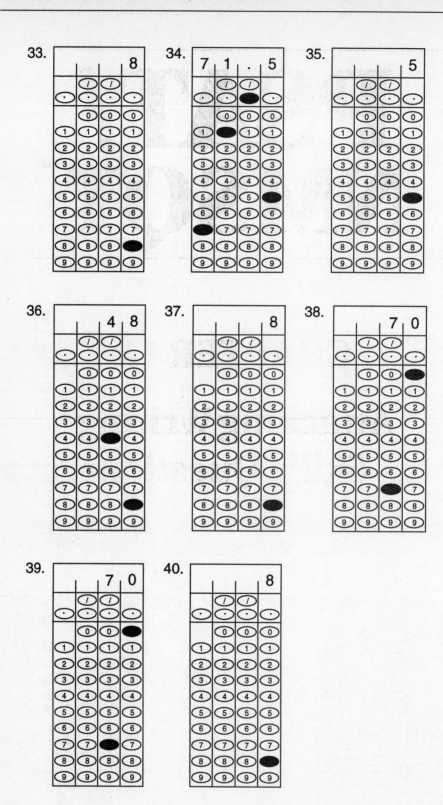

PSAT/ NMSQT

CHAPTER 11

Attacking Writing Skills Questions

Chapter 11

ATTACKING WRITING SKILLS QUESTIONS

ABOUT THE DIRECTIONS

Familiarize yourself with the following sets of directions before taking the PSAT so that you do not waste valuable test time reading the directions on exam day. As there are three different types of questions in the writing skills section, there are three sets of directions.

These instructions are for the nineteen Error Identification questions:

DIRECTIONS: Each of the following sentences may contain an error in diction, usage, idiom, or grammar. Some sentences are correct. Some sentences contain one error. No sentence contains more than one error.

If there is an error, it will appear in one of the underlined portions labeled A, B, C, or D. If there is no error, choose the portion labeled E. If there is an error, select the letter of the portion that must be changed in order to correct the sentence.

EXAMPLE:

He drove <u>slowly</u> and <u>cautiously</u> in order to <u>hopefully</u> avoid having an
          A   **B**   **C**
<u>accident</u>. <u>No error</u>.
   D   **E**

These instructions are for the fourteen Sentence Improvement questions:

DIRECTIONS: In each of the following sentences, some portion of the sentence is underlined. Under each sentence are five choices. The first choice has the same wording as the original. The other four choices are reworded. Sometimes the first choice containing the original wording is the best; sometimes one of the other choices is the best. Choose the letter of the best choice. Your choice should produce a sentence which is not ambiguous or awkward and which is correct, clear, and precise.

This is a test of correct and effective English expression. Keep in mind the standards of English usage, punctuation, grammar, word choice, and construction.

EXAMPLE:

When you listen to opera, <u>a person may not appreciate it.</u>

(A)   a person may not appreciate it.

(B)   it may not be appreciated by a person.

(C)   which may not be appreciated by one.

(D)   you may not appreciate it.

(E)   appreciating it may be a problem for you.

These instructions are for the six Paragraph Improvement questions:

DIRECTIONS: The following passages are considered early draft efforts of a student. Some sentences need to be rewritten to make the ideas clearer and more precise.

Read each passage carefully and answer the questions that follow. Some of the questions are about particular sentences or parts of sentences and ask you to make decisions about sentence structure, diction, and usage. Some of the questions refer to the entire essay or parts of the essay and ask you to make decisions about organization, development, appropriateness of language, audience, and logic. Choose the answer that most effectively makes the intended meaning clear and follows the requirements of standard written English. After you have chosen your answer, fill in the corresponding oval on your answer sheet.

EXAMPLE:

(1) On the one hand, I think television is bad, But it also does some good things for all of us. (2) For instance, my little sister thought she wanted to be a policemen until she saw police shows on television.

Which of the following is the best revision of the underlined portion of sentence 1 below?

On the one hand, I think television <u>is bad, But it also</u> does some good thing for all of us.

(A)   is bad; But it also

(B)   is bad. but is also

(C)   is bad, and it also

(D)   is bad, but it also

(E)   is bad because it also

ABOUT THE QUESTIONS

There are three different types of questions on the PSAT Writing Skills section. This chapter will give you examples of each kind of question, along with strategies for solving them quickly.

Question Type 1: Identifying Sentence Errors

These sentences will test your knowledge of word use, syntax, meaning, and grammar. The correct answers will follow the rules of standard written English. For each sentence in which you find an error, choose the one underlined part that must be changed to make the sentence correct and fill in the appropriate space on your answer sheet.

Be sure to read the sentence exactly as it is written:

Some people fail to realize that a twice-yearly dental cleaning
   A   **B**

and exam are a relatively painless way to avoid more serious
      C   **D**

complications later. No error.
               E

If you determine that the sentence contains an error, proceed as follows:

| Step 1 | Identify the incorrect part of the sentence. The incorrect part of the sentence is "a twice-yearly dental cleaning and exam are." |

| Step 2 | Substitute the underlined answer that employs the correct usage. |

The word "are" is underlined; if it was changed to "is" the sentence would be correct.

| Step 3 | Re-read the sentence with your own usage substituted for the underlined part. |

Some people fail to realize that a twice-yearly dental cleaning and exam is a relatively painless way to avoid more serious complications later.

If you cannot find an error in the sentence, look for common errors first, such as subject-verb agreement and verb tense errors. Do not waste time looking for errors that are not there, since choice (E)—"No error" is sometimes the correct answer.

Question Type 2: Improving Sentences

These questions test your ability to make appropriate revisions in accordance with the rules of standard written English. In the following sentences some part of the sentence, or all of the sentence, is underlined. Below each sentence you will find five ways of phrasing the underlined part. Choose the answer that most effectively expresses the meaning of the original sentence. The correct sentence should be clear and neither awkward nor ambiguous. Choice (A) is always exactly the same as the underlined part. Choose (A) if you think the original sentence needs no revision.

Read the sentence carefully:

Intelligence is determined contrary to public opinion not by the size of the brain but by the number and complexity of dendrites in the brain.

(A) Intelligence is determined contrary to public opinion by not

(B) Intelligence is contrary to public opinion and determined not by

(C) Contrary to public opinion, intelligence is determined not by

(D) Not by popular opinion is intelligence determined but by

(E) Contrary to public opinion, intelligence determines not by

---

If you determine that the sentence contains an error, proceed as follows:

Step 1 Eliminate choice (A) since it restates exactly what is underlined in the sentence.

Step 2 Eliminate the obviously incorrect choices.

(B) ELIMINATE — changes the meaning of the sentence

(C) Maybe

(D) Maybe

(E) ELIMINATE — awkward and unclear

| Step 3 | Choose between the most likely answers.

(C) is clearer than (D). (C) directly links the phrase "Intelligence is determined not by" with the part of the sentence that logically follows this statement.

If you cannot find an error in the sentence, look over the answer choices and compare what is changed to the original sentence. If the original sentence seems best, choose answer choice (A), which is an exact restatement of the original sentence.

Question Type 3: Improving Paragraphs

The passage below is the first draft of an essay written by a student. Following the essay are three questions based on the essay. The questions concern revisions that will make the essay clearer, more concise, and error-free.

The following essay was written by a student in response to an essay question about how his/her use of language differs from proper English when speaking with a friend.

(1) The language I would use in talking to a friend would certainly differ from standard English. (2) In talking with a friend I would be prone to phrases drawn from popular culture that we are both aware of. (3) I would know that by employing certain phrases that my friends and I were members of a peer group, and thus friends.

(4) In talking with friends I would be more prone to use certain words and phrases, such as "hey," "like," and "you know," in ways that are both unconventional and grammatically incorrect. (5) This informal use of language implies the casualness and familiarity that I feel when among my friends.

(6) I would pepper my vocabulary with words that have no set meaning on their own, such as "like." (7) "Like" functions as an intensifier; "He was, like, so dumb," would imply that the person of whom I was speaking was quite stupid. (8) My friends would easily understand what I was saying.

1. Which of the following revisions most clearly states the meaning of sentence 3?

    (A) As it is now

    (B) I would know, by employing certain phrases, that my friends and I shared similar interests.

    (C) My friends and I would be peers by employing certain phrases that show we are friends.

    (D) I would know that my friends and I had things in common by our similar uses of language.

    (E) I would know, that by employing certain phrases and words, that my friends and I shared common interests and were, because of this knowledge, peers.

This type of question is very similar to the sentence correction questions. If you feel that the sentence is not in need of revision choose answer choice (A). If you determine that the sentence would benefit from revision, proceed as follows:

| Step 1 | Eliminate choice (A) since it makes no revision. |

| Step 2 | Eliminate the obviously incorrect choices. Choice (D) says something completely different that the idea implied by the original sentence, while (E) is a verbose and repetitive run-on sentence. |

| Step 3 | Choose between the most likely answers. Choice (B) is clearer than (C) and (B) better expresses the thought that sentence (3) attempts to convey. |

2. Which sentence would best follow sentence 8?

    (A) And that is all that matters.

    (B) Furthermore, my friends and I would employ many more non-standard usages.

    (C) The language I would use in talking to a friend would certainly be different from standard English.

    (D) My friends and I have our own way of speaking.

    (E) My use of language among friends would be casual, informal and idiosyncratic, reflecting these same qualities in our relationships.

This type of question tests your ability to write a good concluding sentence. Proceed as follows:

Step 1 | Eliminate the obviously incorrect answer choices. (B) is not a concluding sentence, since it introduces a new idea. (C) merely restates the opening sentence.

Step 2 | Eliminate the answers that fail to both organize and summarize the main idea of the essay.

Choice (A) does neither. Choice (D) restates one idea from the essay. Choice (E) both summarizes and organizes the main idea of the essay. (E) is the correct answer.

3. How could the author make paragraph 1 stronger?

    (A) By using concrete examples, as in the second and third paragraph.

    (B) By combining sentences (2) and (3).

    (C) By focusing on the meaning of "standard English."

    (D) By switching the order of paragraph 1 and paragraph 2.

    (E) By clearly stating a thesis in the paragraph.

This type of question deals with the essay as a whole. There are no simple steps to answering questions such as these; you must read the entire essay and then carefully, yet quickly, evaluate each answer choice. Answer choice (A) makes sense, since the opening paragraph lacks the concrete examples that help to strengthen the second and third paragraphs. (B) would serve no useful purpose; (C) is unnecessary; (D) would harm the essay, since the opening paragraph states the main idea of the essay. (E) is a poor choice because the opening paragraph already clearly states a thesis.

PSAT/ NMSQT

CHAPTER 12

English Language Skills Review

Chapter 12

ENGLISH LANGUAGE SKILLS REVIEW

The requirements for informal spoken English are much more relaxed than the rigid rules for "standard written English." While slang, colloquialisms, and other informal expressions are acceptable and sometimes very appropriate in casual speech, they are inappropriate in academic and business writing. More often than not, writers, especially student writers, do not make a distinction between the two: they use the same words, grammar, and sentence structure from their everyday speech in their college papers, albeit unsuccessfully.

The PSAT Writing Skills section does not require you to know grammatical terms such as *gerund*, *subject complement*, or *dependent clause*, although general familiarity with such terms may be helpful to you in determining whether a sentence or part of a sentence is correct or incorrect. You should watch for errors in grammar, punctuation, sentence structure, and word choice. Remember: this is a test of written language skills; therefore, your responses should be based on what you know to be correct for written work, not what you know to be appropriate for a casual conversation. For instance, in informal speech, you might say "Who are you going to choose?" But in formal academic writing, you would write "Whom are you going to choose?" Your choices, then, should be dictated by requirements for *written*, not *conversational* English.

WORD CHOICE SKILLS

Connotative and Denotative Meanings

The denotative meaning of a word is its *literal* dictionary definition: what the word denotes or "means." The connotative meaning of a word is what the word connotes or "suggests"; it is a meaning apart from what the word literally means. A writer should choose a word based on the tone and context of the sentence; this ensures that a word bears the appropriate connotation while still conveying some exactness in denotation. For example, a gift might be described as "cheap," but the directness of this word has a negative connotation—something cheap is something of little or no value. The word "inexpensive" has a more positive connotation, though "cheap" is a synonym for "inexpensive." Questions of this type require you to make a decision regarding the appropriateness of words and phrases for the context of a sentence.

Wordiness and Conciseness

Effective writing is concise. Wordiness, on the other hand, decreases the clarity of expression by cluttering sentences with unnecessary words.

Wordiness questions test your ability to detect redundancies (unnecessary repetitions), circumlocution (failure to get to the point), and padding with loose synonyms. Wordiness questions require you to choose sentences that use as few words as possible to convey a message clearly, economically, and effectively.

Notice the difference in impact between the first and second sentences in the following pairs:

INCORRECT: The medical exam that he gave me was entirely complete.

CORRECT: The medical exam he gave me was complete.

INCORRECT: Larry asked his friend John, who was a good, old friend, if he would join him and go along with him to see the foreign film made in Japan.

CORRECT: Larry asked his good, old friend John if he would join him in seeing the Japanese film.

INCORRECT: I was absolutely, totally happy with the present that my parents gave to me at 7 a.m. on the morning of my birthday.

CORRECT: I was happy with the present my parents gave me on the morning of my birthday.

☞ Drill: Word Choice Skills

DIRECTIONS: Choose the correct option.

1. His <u>principal</u> reasons for resigning were his <u>principles</u> of right and wrong.

    (A) principal . . . principals   (C) principle . . . principles

    (B) principle . . . principals   (D) No change is necessary.

2. The book tells about Alzheimer's disease—how it <u>affects</u> the patient and what <u>effect</u> it has on the patient's family.

    (A) effects . . . affect   (C) effects . . . effects

    (B) affects . . . affect   (D) No change is necessary.

3. The <u>amount</u> of homeless children we can help depends on the <u>number</u> of available shelters.

    (A) number . . . number   (C) number . . . amount

    (B) amount . . . amount   (D) No change is necessary.

4. All students are <u>suppose to</u> pass the test before <u>achieving</u> upper-division status.

    (A) suppose to . . . acheiving

    (B) suppose to . . . being achieved

    (C) supposed to . . . achieving

    (D) No change is necessary.

5. The reason he <u>succeeded</u> is <u>because</u> he worked hard.

    (A) succeeded . . . that   (C) succede . . . because of

    (B) seceded . . . that   (D) No change is necessary.

DIRECTIONS: Select the sentence that clearly and effectively states the idea and has no structural errors.

6. (A) South of Richmond, the two roads converge together to form a single highway.

   (B) South of Richmond, the two roads converge together to form an interstate highway.

   (C) South of Richmond, the two roads converge to form an interstate highway.

   (D) South of Richmond, the two roads converge to form a single interstate highway.

7. (A) The student depended on his parents for financial support.

   (B) The student lacked the ways and means to pay for his room and board, so he depended on his parents for this kind of money and support.

   (C) The student lacked the ways and means or the wherewithal to support himself, so his parents provided him with the financial support he needed.

   (D) The student lacked the means to pay for his room and board, so he depended on his parents for financial support.

8. (A) Vincent van Gogh and Paul Gauguin were close personal friends and companions who enjoyed each other's company and frequently worked together on their artwork.

   (B) Vincent van Gogh and Paul Gauguin were friends who frequently painted together.

   (C) Vincent van Gogh was a close personal friend of Paul Gauguin's, and the two of them often worked together on their artwork because they enjoyed each other's company.

   (D) Vincent van Gogh, a close personal friend of Paul Gauguin's, often worked with him on their artwork.

9. (A) A college education often involves putting away childish thoughts, which are characteristic of youngsters, and concentrating on the future, which lies ahead.

(B) A college education involves putting away childish thoughts, which are characteristic of youngsters, and concentrating on the future.

(C) A college education involves putting away childish thoughts and concentrating on the future.

(D) A college education involves putting away childish thoughts and concentrating on the future which lies ahead.

10. (A) I had the occasion to visit an Oriental pagoda while I was a tourist on vacation and visiting in Kyoto, Japan.

(B) I visited a Japanese pagoda in Kyoto.

(C) I had occasion to visit a pagoda when I was vacationing in Kyoto, Japan.

(D) On my vacation, I visited a Japanese pagoda in Kyoto.

SENTENCE STRUCTURE SKILLS

Parallelism

Parallel structure is used to express matching ideas. It refers to the grammatical balance of a series of any of the following:

Phrases:

The squirrel ran *along the fence, up the tree,* and *into his burrow* with a mouthful of acorns.

Adjectives:

The job market is flooded with *very talented, highly motivated,* and *well-educated* young people.

Nouns:

You will need a *notebook, pencil,* and *dictionary* for the test.

Clauses:

The children were told to decide which toy they would keep and which toy they would give away.

Verbs:

The farmer *plowed*, *planted*, and *harvested* his corn in record time.

Verbals:

Reading, *writing*, and *calculating* are fundamental skills that all of us should possess.

Correlative conjunctions:

Either you will do your homework *or* you will fail.

Repetition of structural signals:

(such as articles, auxiliary verbs, prepositions, and conjunctions)

> INCORRECT: I have quit my job, enrolled in school, and am looking for a reliable babysitter.

> CORRECT: I *have quit* my job, *have enrolled* in school, and *am looking* for a reliable babysitter.

Note: Repetition of prepositions is considered formal and is not necessary.

> You can travel *by car, by plane, or by train*; it's all up to you.

OR

> You can travel *by car, plane, or train*; it's all up to you.

When a sentence contains items in a series, check for both punctuation and sentence balance. When you check for punctuation, make sure the commas are used correctly. When you check for parallelism, make sure that the conjunctions connect similar grammatical constructions, such as all adjectives or all clauses.

Misplaced and Dangling Modifiers

A misplaced modifier is one that is in the wrong place in the sentence. Misplaced modifiers come in all forms—words, phrases, and clauses. Sentences containing misplaced modifiers are often very comical: *Mom made me eat the spinach instead of my brother*. Misplaced modifiers, like the one in this sentence, are usually too far away from the word or words they modify. This sentence should read: *Mom made me, instead of my brother, eat the spinach.*

Modifiers like *only*, *nearly*, and *almost* should be placed next to the word they modify and not in front of some other word, especially a verb, that they are not intended to modify.

A modifier is misplaced if it appears to modify the wrong part of the sentence or if we cannot be certain what part of the sentence the writer intended it to modify. To correct a misplaced modifier, move the modifier next to the word it describes.

> INCORRECT: He served hamburgers to the guests on paper plates.

> CORRECT: He served hamburgers on paper plates to the guests.

Split infinitives also result in misplaced modifiers. Infinitives consist of the marker *to* plus the plain form of the verb. The two parts of the infinitive make up a grammatical unit that should not be split. Splitting an infinitive is placing an adverb between the *to* and the verb.

> INCORRECT: The weather service expects temperatures to not rise.

> CORRECT: The weather service expects temperatures not to rise.

Sometimes a split infinitive may be natural and preferable, though it may still bother some readers.

> EX: Several U.S. industries expect *to* more than *triple* their use of robots within the next decade.

A squinting modifier is one that may refer to either a preceding or a following word, leaving the reader uncertain about what it is intended to modify. Correct a squinting modifier by moving it next to the word it is intended to modify.

> INCORRECT: Snipers who often fired on the soldiers escaped capture.

> CORRECT: Snipers who fired on the soldiers often escaped capture.

> OR Snipers who fired on the soldiers escaped capture often.

A dangling modifier is a modifier or verb in search of a subject: the modifying phrase (usually an *-ing* word group, an *-ed* or *-en* word group, or a *to* + *a verb* word group—participle phrase or infinitive phrase respectively) either appears to modify the wrong word or has nothing to modify. It is literally dangling at the beginning or the end of a sentence. The sentences often look and sound correct: *To be a student government officer, your grades must be above average.* (However, the verbal modifier has nothing to describe. Who is *to be a student government officer*? Your grades?) Questions of this type require you to determine whether a modifier has a headword or whether it is dangling at the beginning or the end of the sentence.

To correct a dangling modifier, reword the sentence by either: 1) changing the modifying phrase to a clause with a subject, or 2) changing the subject of the sentence to the word that should be modified. The following are examples of a dangling gerund, a dangling infinitive, and a dangling participle:

INCORRECT: Shortly after leaving home, the accident occurred.

Who is <u>leaving home</u>, the accident?

CORRECT: Shortly after we left home, the accident occurred.

INCORRECT: To get up on time, a great effort was needed.

<u>To get up</u> needs a subject.

CORRECT: To get up on time, I made a great effort.

Fragments

A fragment is an incomplete construction which may or may not have a subject and a verb. Specifically, a fragment is a group of words pretending to be a sentence. Not all fragments appear as separate sentences, however. Often, fragments are separated by semicolons.

INCORRECT: Traffic was stalled for ten miles on the freeway. Because repairs were being made on potholes.

CORRECT: Traffic was stalled for ten miles on the freeway because repairs were being made on potholes.

INCORRECT: It was a funny story; one that I had never heard before.

CORRECT: It was a funny story, one that I had never heard before.

Run-on/Fused Sentences

A run-on/fused sentence is not necessarily a long sentence or a sentence that the reader considers too long; in fact, a run-on may be two short sentences: *Dry ice does not melt it evaporates.* A run-on results when the writer fuses or runs together two separate sentences without any correct mark of punctuation separating them.

INCORRECT: Knowing how to use a dictionary is no problem each dictionary has a section in the front of the book telling how to use it.

CORRECT: Knowing how to use a dictionary is no problem. Each dictionary has a section in the front of the book telling how to use it.

Even if one or both of the fused sentences contains internal punctuation, the sentence is still a run-on.

INCORRECT: Bob bought dress shoes, a suit, and a nice shirt he needed them for his sister's wedding.

CORRECT: Bob bought dress shoes, a suit, and a nice shirt. He needed them for his sister's wedding.

Comma Splices

A comma splice is the unjustifiable use of only a comma to combine what really is two separate sentences.

INCORRECT: One common error in writing is incorrect spelling, the other is the occasional use of faulty diction.

CORRECT: One common error in writing is incorrect spelling; the other is the occasional use of faulty diction.

Both run-on sentences and comma splices may be corrected in one of the following ways:

RUN-ON: Neal won the award he had the highest score.

COMMA SPLICE: Neal won the award, he had the highest score.

Separate the sentences with a period:

Neal won the award. He had the highest score.

Separate the sentences with a comma and a coordinating conjunction (*and, but, or, nor, for, yet, so*):

Neal won the award for he had the highest score.

Separate the sentences with a semicolon:

Neal won the award; he had the highest score.

Separate the sentences with a subordinating conjunction such as *although, because, since, if*:

Neal won the award because he had the highest score.

Subordination, Coordination, and Predication

Suppose, for the sake of clarity, you wanted to combine the information in these two sentences to create one statement:

I studied a foreign language. I found English quite easy.

How you decide to combine this information should be determined by the relationship you'd like to show between the two facts. *I studied a foreign language, and I found English quite easy* seems rather illogical. The **coordination** of the two ideas (connecting them with the coordinating conjunction *and*) is ineffective. Using **subordination** instead (connecting the sentences with a subordinating conjunction) clearly shows the degree of relative importance between the expressed ideas:

After I studied a foreign language, I found English quite easy.

When using a conjunction, be sure that the sentence parts you are joining are in agreement.

INCORRECT: She loved him dearly but not his dog.

CORRECT: She loved him dearly but she did not love his dog.

A common mistake that is made is to forget that each member of the pair must be followed by the same kind of construction.

INCORRECT: They complimented them both for their bravery and they thanked them for their kindness.

CORRECT: They both complimented them for their bravery and thanked them for their kindness.

While refers to time and should not be used as a substitute for *although*, *and*, or *but*.

INCORRECT: While I'm usually interested in Fellini movies, I'd rather not go tonight.

CORRECT: Although I'm usually interested in Fellini movies, I'd rather not go tonight.

Where refers to time and should not be used as a substitute for *that*.

INCORRECT: We read in the paper where they are making great strides in DNA research.

CORRECT: We read in the paper that they are making great strides in DNA research.

After words like reason and explanation, use *that*, not *because*.

INCORRECT: His explanation for his tardiness was because his alarm did not go off.

CORRECT: His explanation for his tardiness was that his alarm did not go off.

☞ **Drill: Sentence Structure Skills**

DIRECTIONS: Choose the sentence that expresses the thought most clearly and that has no error in structure.

1. (A) Many gases are invisible, odorless, and they have no taste.

    (B) Many gases are invisible, odorless, and have no taste.

    (C) Many gases are invisible, odorless, and tasteless.

2. (A) Everyone agreed that she had neither the voice or the skill to be a speaker.

    (B) Everyone agreed that she had neither the voice nor the skill to be a speaker.

    (C) Everyone agreed that she had either the voice nor the skill to be a speaker.

3. (A) The mayor will be remembered because he kept his campaign promises and because of his refusal to accept political favors.

    (B) The mayor will be remembered because he kept his campaign promises and because he refused to accept political favors.

    (C) The mayor will be remembered because of his refusal to accept political favors and he kept his campaign promises.

4. (A) While taking a shower, the doorbell rang.

    (B) While I was taking a shower, the doorbell rang.

    (C) While taking a shower, someone rang the doorbell.

5. (A) He swung the bat, while the runner stole second base.

    (B) The runner stole second base while he swung the bat.

    (C) While he was swinging the bat, the runner stole second base.

DIRECTIONS: Choose the correct option.

6. Nothing grows as well in Mississippi as <u>cotton. Cotton</u> being the state's principal crop.

    (A) cotton, cotton   (C) cotton cotton

    (B) cotton; cotton   (D) No change is necessary.

7. It was a heartwrenching <u>movie; one</u> that I had never seen before.

    (A) movie and   (C) movie. One

    (B) movie, one   (D) No change is necessary.

8. Traffic was stalled for three miles on the <u>bridge. Because</u> repairs were being made.

    (A) bridge because   (C) bridge, because

    (B) bridge; because   (D) No change is necessary.

9. The ability to write complete sentences comes with <u>practice writing</u> run-on sentences seems to occur naturally.

    (A) practice, writing   (C) practice and

    (B) practice. Writing   (D) No change is necessary.

10. Even though she had taken French classes, she could not understand native French <u>speakers they</u> all spoke too fast.

    (A) speakers, they   (C) speaking

    (B) speakers. They   (D) No change is necessary.

VERBS

Verb Forms

This section covers the principal parts of some irregular verbs including troublesome verbs like *lie* and *lay*. The use of regular verbs like *look* and *receive* poses no real problem to most writers since the past and past participle forms end in -*ed*; it is the irregular forms which pose the most serious problems—for example, *seen, written,* and *begun.*

Verb Tenses

Tense sequence indicates a logical time sequence.

Use present tense

in statements of universal truth:

I learned that the sun *is* ninety-million miles from the earth.

in statements about the contents of literature and other published works:

In this book, Sandy *becomes* a nun and *writes* a book on psychology.

Use past tense

in statements concerning writing or publication of a book:

He *wrote* his first book in 1949, and it *was published* in 1952.

Use present perfect tense

for an action that began in the past but continues into the future:

I *have lived* here all my life.

Use past perfect tense

for an earlier action that is mentioned in a later action:

Cindy ate the apple that she *had picked.*

(First she picked it, then she ate it.)

Use future perfect tense

for an action that will have been completed at a specific future time:

By May, I shall have graduated.

Use a present participle

for action that occurs at the same time as the verb:

Speeding down the interstate, I saw a cop's flashing lights.

Use a perfect participle

for action that occurred before the main verb:

Having read the directions, I started the test.

Use the subjunctive mood

to express a wish or state a condition contrary to fact:

> *If it were not raining*, we could have a picnic.

in *that* clauses after verbs like *request, recommend, suggest, ask, require*, and *insist*; and after such expressions as *it is important* and *it is necessary*:

> It is necessary that all papers *be* submitted on time.

Subject-Verb Agreement

Agreement is the grammatical correspondence between the subject and the verb of a sentence: *I do, we do, they do, he, she, it does*.

Every English verb has five forms, two of which are the bare form (plural) and the *-s* form (singular). Simply put, singular verb forms end in *-s;* plural forms do not.

Study these rules governing subject-verb agreement:

A verb must agree with its subject, not with any additive phrase in the sentence such as a prepositional or verbal phrase. Ignore such phrases.

> Your *copy* of the rules *is* on the desk.
>
> Ms. Craig's *record* of community service and outstanding teaching *qualifies* her for promotion.

In an inverted sentence beginning with a prepositional phrase, the verb still agrees with its subject.

> At the end of the summer *come* the best *sales*.
>
> Under the house *are* some old Mason *jars*.

Prepositional phrases beginning with compound prepositions such as *along with, together with, in addition to,* and *as well as* should be ignored, for they do not affect subject-verb agreement.

> *Gladys Knight*, as well as the Pips, *is* riding the midnight train to Georgia.

A verb must agree with its subject, not its subject complement.

> *Taxes are* a problem.
>
> A *problem is* taxes.
>
> His main *source* of pleasure *is* food and sleep.
>
> *Food and sleep are* his main source of pleasure.

When a sentence begins with an expletive such as *there, here,* or *it,* the verb agrees with the subject, not the expletive.

Surely, there *are* several *alumni* who would be interested in forming a group.

There *are* 50 *students* in my English class.

There *is* a horrifying *study* on child abuse in *Psychology Today.*

Indefinite pronouns such as *each, either, one, everyone, everybody,* and *everything* are singular.

Somebody in Detroit *loves* me.

Does either [one] of you have a pencil?

Neither of my brothers *has* a car.

Indefinite pronouns such as *several, few, both,* and *many* are plural.

Both of my sorority sisters *have* decided to live off campus.

Few seek the enlightenment of transcendental meditation.

Indefinite pronouns such as *all, some, most,* and *none* may be singular or plural depending on their referents.

Some of the food *is* cold.

Some of the vegetables *are* cold.

I can think of some retorts, but *none seem* appropriate.

None of the children *is* as sweet as Sally.

Fractions such as *one-half* and *one-third* may be singular or plural depending on the referent.

Half of the mail *has* been delivered.

Half of the letters *have* been read.

Subjects joined by *and* take a plural verb unless the subjects are considered one item or unit.

Jim and *Tammy were* televangelists.

Simon and Garfunkel is my favorite group.

In cases when the subjects are joined by *or, nor, either . . . or,* or *neither . . . nor,* the verb must agree with the subject closer to it.

Either the teacher or the *students are* responsible.

Neither the students nor the *teacher is* responsible.

Relative pronouns, such as *who, which,* or *that,* which refer to plural antecedents require plural verbs. However, when the relative pronoun refers to a singular subject, the pronoun takes a singular verb.

> She is one of the girls *who play basketball* on Friday nights.

> She is the only basketball player *who has* a broken leg.

Subjects preceded by *every, each,* and *many a* are singular.

> *Every* man, woman, and child *was* given a life preserver.

> *Each* undergraduate *is* required to pass a proficiency exam.

> *Many a* tear *has* to fall before one matures.

A collective noun, such as *audience, faculty, jury,* etc., requires a singular verb when the group is regarded as a whole, and a plural verb when the members of the group are regarded as individuals.

> The *jury has* made its decision.

> The *faculty are* preparing their grade rosters.

Subjects preceded by *the number of* or *the percentage of* are singular, while subjects preceded by *a number of* or *a percentage of* are plural.

> The *number of* vacationers in Florida *increases* every year.

> *A number of* vacationers *are* young couples.

Titles of books, companies, name brands, and groups are singular or plural depending on their meaning.

> *Great Expectations is* my favorite novel.

> The *Rolling Stones are* performing in the Super Dome.

Certain nouns of Latin and Greek origin have unusual singular and plural forms.

Singular	Plural
criterion	criteria
alumnus	alumni
datum	data
medium	media

> The *data are* available for inspection.

> The only *criterion* for membership *is* a high GPA.

Some nouns such as *deer, shrimp,* and *sheep* have the same spellings for both their singular and plural forms. In these cases, the meaning of the sentence will determine whether they are singular or plural.

> *Deer are* beautiful animals.

> The spotted *deer is* licking the sugar cube.

Some nouns like *scissors*, *jeans*, and *wages* have plural forms but no singular counterparts. These nouns almost always take plural verbs.

> The *scissors are* on the table.

> My new *jeans fit* me like a glove.

Words used as examples, not as grammatical parts of the sentence, require singular verbs.

> *Can't is* the contraction for "cannot."

> *Cats is* the plural form of "cat."

Mathematical expressions of subtraction and division require singular verbs, while expressions of addition and multiplication take either singular or plural verbs.

> Ten *divided* by two *equals* five.

> Five *times* two *equals* ten.

> OR   Five *times* two *equal* ten.

Nouns expressing time, distance, weight, and measurement are singular when they refer to a unit and plural when they refer to separate items.

> *Fifty yards is* a short distance.

> *Ten years have* passed since I finished college.

Expressions of quantity are usually plural.

> *Nine out of ten* dentists *recommend* that their patients floss.

Some nouns ending in *-ics,* such as *economics* and *ethics*, take singular verbs when they refer to principles or a field of study; however, when they refer to individual practices, they usually take plural verbs.

> *Ethics is* being taught in the spring.

> His unusual business *ethics are* what got him into trouble.

Some nouns like *measles*, *news*, and *calculus* appear to be plural but are actually singular in number. These nouns require singular verbs.

> *Measles is* a very contagious disease.

> *Calculus requires* great skill in algebra.

A verbal noun (infinitive or gerund) serving as a subject is treated as singular, even if the object of the verbal phrase is plural.

> *Hiding* your mistakes *does* not make them go away.

> *To run* five miles *is* my goal.

A noun phrase or clause acting as the subject of a sentence requires a singular verb.

> What I need is to be loved.

> Whether there is any connection between them is unknown.

Clauses beginning with *what* may be singular or plural depending on the meaning, that is, whether *what* means "the thing" or "the things."

> What I want for Christmas is a new motorcycle.

> What matters are Clinton's ideas.

A plural subject followed by a singular appositive requires a plural verb; similarly, a singular subject followed by a plural appositive requires a singular verb.

> When the girls throw a party, *they* each bring a *gift*.

> The *board*, all ten members, *is* meeting today.

☞ Drill: Verbs

DIRECTIONS: Choose the correct option.

1. If you <u>had been concerned</u> about Marilyn, you <u>would have went</u> to greater lengths to ensure her safety.

    (A) had been concern . . . would have gone

    (B) was concerned . . . would have gone

    (C) had been concerned . . . would have gone

    (D) No change is necessary.

2. Susan <u>laid</u> in bed too long and missed her class.

    (A) lays   (C) lied

    (B) lay   (D) No change is necessary.

3. The Great Wall of China <u>is</u> fifteen hundred miles long; it <u>was built</u> in the third century B.C.

   (A) was ... was built   (C) has been ... was built

   (B) is ... is built   (D) No change is necessary.

4. Joe stated that the class <u>began</u> at 10:30 a.m.

   (A) begins   (C) was beginning

   (B) had begun   (D) No change is necessary.

5. The ceiling of the Sistine Chapel <u>was</u> painted by Michelangelo; it <u>depicted</u> scenes from the Creation in the Old Testament.

   (A) was ... depicts   (C) has been ... depicting

   (B) is ... depicts   (D) No change is necessary.

6. After Christmas <u>comes</u> the best sales.

   (A) has come   (C) is coming

   (B) come   (D) No change is necessary.

7. The bakery's specialty <u>are</u> wedding cakes.

   (A) is   (C) be

   (B) were   (D) No change is necessary.

8. Every man, woman, and child <u>were given</u> a life preserver.

   (A) have been given   (C) was given

   (B) had gave   (D) No change is necessary.

9. Hiding your mistakes <u>don't</u> make them go away.

   (A) doesn't   (C) have not

   (B) do not   (D) No change is necessary.

10. The Board of Regents <u>has recommended</u> a tuition increase.

    (A) have recommended   (C) had recommended

    (B) has recommend   (D) No change is necessary.

PRONOUNS

Pronoun Case

Pronoun case questions test your knowledge of the use of nominative and objective case pronouns:

Nominative Case	Objective Case
I	me
he	him
she	her
we	us
they	them
who	whom

This review section answers the most frequently asked grammar questions: when to use *I* and when to use *me*; when to use *who* and when to use *whom*. Some writers avoid *whom* altogether, and instead of distinguishing between *I* and *me*, many writers incorrectly use *myself*.

Use the nominative case (subject pronouns)

for the subject of a sentence:

We students studied until early morning for the final.

Alan and *I* "burned the midnight oil," too.

for pronouns in apposition to the subject:

Only two students, Alex and *I*, were asked to report on the meeting.

for the predicate nominative/subject complement:

The actors nominated for the award were *she* and *I*.

for the subject of an elliptical clause:

Molly is more experienced than *he*.

for the subject of a subordinate clause:

Robert is the driver *who* reported the accident.

for the complement of an infinitive with no expressed subject:

I would not want to be *he*.

Use the objective case (object pronouns)

for the direct object of a sentence:

Mary invited *us* to her party.

for the object of a preposition:

The books that were torn belonged to *her*.

Just between you and *me*, I'm bored.

for the indirect object of a sentence:

Walter gave a birthday gift to *her*.

for the appositive of a direct object:

The committee elected two delegates, Barbara and *me*.

for the object of an infinitive:

The young boy wanted to help *us* paint the fence.

for the object of a gerund:

Enlisting *him* was surprisingly easy.

for the object of a past participle:

Having called the other students and *us*, the secretary went home for the day.

for a pronoun that precedes an infinitive (the subject of an infinitive):

The supervisor told *him* to work late.

for the complement of an infinitive with an expressed subject:

The fans thought the best player to be *him*.

for the object of an elliptical clause:

Bill tackled Joe harder than *me*.

for the object of a verb in apposition:

Charles invited two extra people, Carmen and *me*, to the party.

When a conjunction connects two pronouns or a pronoun and a noun, remove the "and" and the other pronoun or noun to determine what the correct pronoun form should be:

Mom gave ~~Tom and~~ myself a piece of cake.

Mom gave ~~Tom and~~ I a piece of cake

Mom gave ~~Tom and~~ me a piece of cake.

Removal of these words reveals what the correct pronoun should be:

Mom gave *me* a piece of cake.

The only pronouns that are acceptable after *between* and other prepositions are: *me, her, him, them,* and *whom.* When deciding between *who* and *whom,* try substituting *he* for *who* and *him* for *whom;* then follow these easy transformation steps:

1. Isolate the *who* clause or the *whom* clause:

   whom we can trust

2. Invert the word order, if necessary. Place the words in the clause in the natural order of an English sentence, subject followed by the verb:

   we can trust whom

3. Read the final form with the *he* or *him* inserted:

   We can trust ~~whom~~ him.

When a pronoun follows a comparative conjunction like *than* or *as,* complete the elliptical construction to help you determine which pronoun is correct.

EX: She has more credit hours than me [do].

She has more credit hours than I [do].

Pronoun-Antecedent Agreement

These kinds of questions test your knowledge of using an appropriate pronoun to agree with its antecedent in number (singular or plural form) and gender (masculine, feminine, or neuter). An antecedent is a noun or pronoun to which another noun or pronoun refers.

Here are the two basic rules for pronoun reference-antecedent agreement:

1. Every pronoun must have a conspicuous antecedent.

2. Every pronoun must agree with its antecedent in number, gender, and person.

When an antecedent is one of dual gender like *student, singer, artist, person, citizen,* etc., use *his* or *her.* Some careful writers change the antecedent to a plural noun to avoid using the sexist, singular masculine pronoun *his*:

INCORRECT: Everyone hopes that he will win the lottery.

CORRECT: Most people hope that they will win the lottery.

Ordinarily, the relative pronoun *who* is used to refer to people, *which* to refer to things and places, *where* to refer to places, and *that* to refer to places or things. The distinction between *that* and *which* is a grammatical distinction (see the section on Word Choice Skills).

Many writers prefer to use *that* to refer to collective nouns.

EX: A family *that* traces its lineage is usually proud of its roots.

Many writers, especially students, are not sure when to use the reflexive case pronoun and when to use the possessive case pronoun. The rules governing the usage of the reflexive case and the possessive case are quite simple.

Use the possessive case

before a noun in a sentence:

Our friend moved during the semester break.

My dog has fleas, but *her* dog doesn't.

before a gerund in a sentence:

Her running helps to relieve stress.

His driving terrified her.

as a noun in a sentence:

Mine was the last test graded that day.

to indicate possession:

Karen never allows anyone else to drive *her* car.

Brad thought the book was *his,* but it was someone else's.

Use the reflexive case

as a direct object to rename the subject:

I kicked *myself.*

as an indirect object to rename the subject:

Henry bought *himself* a tie.

as an object of a prepositional phrase:

> Tom and Lillie baked the pie for *themselves*.

as a predicate pronoun:

> She hasn't been *herself* lately.

Do not use the reflexive in place of the nominative pronoun:

INCORRECT: Both Randy and *myself* plan to go.

CORRECT: Both Randy and *I* plan to go.

INCORRECT: *Yourself* will take on the challenges of college.

CORRECT: *You* will take on the challenges of college.

INCORRECT: Either James or *yourself* will paint the mural.

CORRECT: Either James or *you* will paint the mural.

Watch out for careless use of the pronoun form:

INCORRECT: George *hisself* told me it was true.

CORRECT: George *himself* told me it was true.

INCORRECT: They washed the car *theirselves*.

CORRECT: They washed the car *themselves*.

Notice that reflexive pronouns are not set off by commas:

INCORRECT: Mary, *herself*, gave him the diploma.

CORRECT: Mary *herself* gave him the diploma.

INCORRECT: I will do it, *myself*.

CORRECT: I will do it *myself*.

Pronoun Reference

Pronoun reference questions require you to determine whether the antecedent is conspicuously written in the sentence or whether it is remote, implied, ambiguous, or vague, none of which results in clear writing. Make sure that every italicized pronoun has a conspicuous antecedent and that one pronoun substitutes only for another noun or pronoun, not for an idea or a sentence.

Pronoun reference problems occur

when a pronoun refers to either of two antecedents:

INCORRECT: Joanna told Jen that *she* was happy with her weight.

CORRECT: Joanna told Jen, "I'm happy with my weight."

when a pronoun refers to a remote antecedent:

INCORRECT: A strange car followed us closely, and *he* kept blinking his lights at us.

CORRECT: A strange car followed us closely, and its driver kept blinking his lights at us.

when *this*, *that*, and *which* refer to the general idea of the preceding clause or sentence rather than the preceding word:

INCORRECT: The students could not understand the pronoun reference handout, which annoyed them very much.

CORRECT: The students could not understand the pronoun reference handout, a fact which annoyed them very much.

OR The students were annoyed because they could not understand the pronoun reference handout.

when a pronoun refers to an unexpressed but implied noun:

INCORRECT: My husband wants me to knit a blanket, but I'm not interested in it.

CORRECT: My husband wants me to knit a blanket, but I'm not interested in knitting.

when *it* is used as something other than an expletive to postpone a subject:

INCORRECT: It says in today's paper that the newest shipment of cars from Detroit, Michigan, seems to include outright imitations of European models.

CORRECT: Today's paper says that the newest shipment of cars from Detroit, Michigan, seems to include outright imitations of European models.

INCORRECT: The football game was canceled because it was bad weather.

CORRECT: The football game was canceled because the weather was bad.

when *they* or *it* is used to refer to something or someone indefinitely, and there is no definite antecedent:

> INCORRECT: At the job placement office, they told me to stop wearing ripped jeans to my interviews.

> CORRECT: At the job placement office, I was told to stop wearing ripped jeans to my interviews.

when the pronoun does not agree with its antecedent in number, gender, or person:

> INCORRECT: Any graduate student, if they are interested, may attend the lecture.

> CORRECT: Any graduate student, if he or she is interested, may attend the lecture.

> OR All graduate students, if they are interested, may attend the lecture.

> INCORRECT: Many Americans are concerned that the overuse of slang and colloquialisms is corrupting the language.

> CORRECT: Many Americans are concerned that the overuse of slang and colloquialisms is corrupting their language.

> INCORRECT: The Board of Regents will not make a decision about tuition increase until their March meeting.

> CORRECT: The Board of Regents will not make a decision about tuition increase until its March meeting.

when a noun or pronoun has no expressed antecedent:

> INCORRECT: In the President's address to the union, he promised no more taxes.

> CORRECT: In his address to the union, the President promised no more taxes.

☞ Drill: Pronouns

DIRECTIONS: Choose the correct option.

1. My friend and <u>myself</u> bought tickets for *Cats*.

   (A) I

   (B) me

   (C) us

   (D) No change is necessary.

2. Alcohol and tobacco are harmful to <u>whomever</u> consumes them.

    (A) whom   (C) whoever

    (B) who   (D) No change is necessary.

3. Everyone is wondering <u>whom</u> her successor will be.

    (A) who   (C) who'll

    (B) whose   (D) No change is necessary.

4. Rosa Lee's parents discovered that it was <u>her who</u> wrecked the family car.

    (A) she who   (C) her whom

    (B) she whom   (D) No change is necessary.

5. A student <u>who</u> wishes to protest <u>his or her</u> grades must file a formal grievance in the Dean's office.

    (A) that . . . their   (C) whom . . . their

    (B) which . . . his   (D) No change is necessary.

6. One of the best things about working for this company is that <u>they pay</u> big bonuses.

    (A) it pays   (C) they paid

    (B) they always pay   (D) No change is necessary.

7. Every car owner should be sure that <u>their</u> automobile insurance is adequate.

    (A) your   (C) its

    (B) his or her   (D) No change is necessary.

8. My mother wants me to become a teacher, but I'm not interested in <u>it</u>.

    (A) this   (C) that

    (B) teaching   (D) No change is necessary.

9. Since I had not paid my electric bill, <u>they</u> sent me a delinquent notice.

    (A) the power company   (C) it

    (B) he   (D) No change is necessary.

10. Margaret seldom wrote to her sister when <u>she</u> was away at college.

    (A) who

    (B) her

    (C) her sister

    (D) No change is necessary.

ADJECTIVES AND ADVERBS

Correct Usage

Adjectives are words that modify nouns or pronouns by defining, describing, limiting, or qualifying those nouns or pronouns.

Adverbs are words that modify verbs, adjectives, or other adverbs and that express such ideas as time, place, manner, cause, and degree. Use adjectives as subject complements with linking verbs; use adverbs with action verbs.

EX: The old man's speech was *eloquent*.	ADJECTIVE
Mr. Brown speaks *eloquently*.	ADVERB
Please be *careful*.	ADJECTIVE
Please drive *carefully*.	ADVERB

Good or well

Good is an adjective; its use as an adverb is colloquial and nonstandard.

    INCORRECT: He plays *good*.

    CORRECT: He looks *good* to be an octogenarian.

                The quiche tastes very *good*.

Well may be either an adverb or an adjective. As an adjective, *well* means "in good health."

CORRECT: He plays *well*.	ADVERB
My mother is not *well*.	ADJECTIVE

Bad or badly

Bad is an adjective used after sense verbs such as *look, smell, taste, feel*, or *sound*, or after linking verbs (*is, am, are, was, were*).

    INCORRECT: I feel *badly* about the delay.

    CORRECT: I feel *bad* about the delay.

Badly is an adverb used after all other verbs.

    INCORRECT: It doesn't hurt very *bad.*

    CORRECT: It doesn't hurt very *badly.*

Real or really

Real is an adjective; its use as an adverb is colloquial and nonstandard. It means "genuine."

    INCORRECT: He writes *real* well.

    CORRECT: This is *real* leather.

Really is an adverb meaning "very."

    INCORRECT: This is *really* diamond.

    CORRECT: Have a *really* nice day.

EX:	This is *real* amethyst.	ADJECTIVE
	This is *really* difficult.	ADVERB
	This is a *real* crisis.	ADJECTIVE
	This is *really* important.	ADVERB

Sort of and kind of

Sort of and *kind of* are often misused in written English by writers who actually mean *rather* or *somewhat.*

    INCORRECT: Jan was *kind of* saddened by the results of the test.

    CORRECT: Jan was *somewhat* saddened by the results of the test.

Faulty Comparisons

Sentences containing a faulty comparison often sound correct because their problem is not one of grammar but of logic. Read these sentences closely to make sure that like things are being compared, that the comparisons are complete, and that the comparisons are logical.

When comparing two persons or things, use the comparative, not the superlative form, of an adjective or an adverb. Use the superlative form for comparison of more than two persons or things. Use *any, other,* or *else* when comparing one thing or person with a group of which it/he or she is a part.

Most one- and two-syllable words form their comparative and superlative degrees with *-er* and *-est* suffixes. Adjectives and adverbs of more than two syllables form their comparative and superlative degrees with the addition of *more* and *most*.

Positive	Comparative	Superlative
good	better	best
old	older	oldest
friendly	friendlier	friendliest
lonely	lonelier	loneliest
talented	more talented	most talented
beautiful	more beautiful	most beautiful

A double comparison occurs when the degree of the modifier is changed incorrectly by adding both *-er* and *more* or *-est* and *most* to the adjective or adverb.

INCORRECT: He is the *most nicest* brother.

CORRECT: He is the *nicest* brother.

INCORRECT: She is the *more meaner* of the sisters.

CORRECT: She is the *meaner* sister.

Illogical comparisons occur when there is an implied comparison between two things that are not actually being compared or that cannot be logically compared.

INCORRECT: The interest at a loan company is higher *than* a bank.

CORRECT: The interest at a loan company is higher *than* that *at* a bank.

OR The interest at a loan company is higher *than at* a bank.

Ambiguous comparisons occur when elliptical words (those omitted) create for the reader more than one interpretation of the sentence.

INCORRECT: I like Mary better than you. (than you *what?*)

CORRECT: I like Mary better than I like you.

OR I like Mary better than you do.

Incomplete comparisons occur when the basis of the comparison (the two categories being compared) is not explicitly stated.

INCORRECT: Skywriting is *more* spectacular.

CORRECT: Skywriting is *more* spectacular *than* billboard advertising.

Do not omit the words *other, any,* or *else* when comparing one thing or person with a group of which it/he or she is a part.

> INCORRECT: Joan writes better *than any* student in her class.

> CORRECT: Joan writes better *than any other* student in her class.

Do not omit the second *as* of *as . . . as* when making a point of equal or superior comparison.

> INCORRECT: The University of West Florida is *as large* or larger than the University of North Florida.

> CORRECT: The University of West Florida is *as large as* or larger than the University of Northern Florida.

Do not omit the first category of the comparison, even if the two categories are the same.

> INCORRECT: This is one of the best, if not the best, college in the country.

> CORRECT: This is one of the best colleges in the country, if not the best.

The problem with the incorrect sentence is that *one of the best* requires the plural word *colleges,* not *college.*

☞ Drill: Adjectives and Adverbs

DIRECTIONS: Choose the correct option.

1. Although the band performed <u>badly</u>, I feel <u>real bad</u> about missing the concert.

    (A) badly . . . real badly

    (B) bad . . . badly

    (C) badly . . . very bad

    (D) No change is necessary.

2. These reports are <u>relative simple</u> to prepare.

    (A) relatively simple

    (B) relative simply

    (C) relatively simply

    (D) No change is necessary.

3. He did <u>very well</u> on the test although his writing skills are not <u>good</u>.

    (A) real well . . . good

    (B) very good . . . good

    (C) good . . . great

    (D) No change is necessary.

4. Shake the medicine bottle <u>good</u> before you open it.

    (A) very good   (C) well

    (B) real good   (D) No change is necessary.

5. Though she speaks <u>fluently</u>, she writes <u>poorly</u> because she doesn't observe <u>closely</u> or think <u>clear</u>.

    (A) fluently, poorly, closely, clearly

    (B) fluent, poor, close, clear

    (C) fluently, poor, closely, clear

    (D) No change is necessary.

DIRECTIONS: Select the sentence that clearly and effectively states the idea and has no structural errors.

6. (A) Los Angeles is larger than any city in California.

    (B) Los Angeles is larger than all the cities in California.

    (C) Los Angeles is larger than any other city in California.

7. (A) Art history is as interesting as, if not more interesting than, music appreciation.

    (B) Art history is as interesting, if not more interesting than, music appreciation.

    (C) Art history is as interesting as, if not more interesting, music appreciation.

8. (A) The baseball team here is as good as any other university.

    (B) The baseball team here is as good as all the other universities.

    (C) The baseball team here is as good as any other university's.

9. (A) I like him better than you.

    (B) I like him better than I like you.

    (C) I like him better.

10. (A) You are the most stingiest person I know.

    (B) You are the most stingier person I know.

    (C) You are the stingiest person I know.

PUNCTUATION

Commas

Commas should be placed according to standard rules of punctuation for purpose, clarity, and effect. The proper use of commas is explained in the following rules and examples:

In a series:

When more than one adjective describes a noun, use a comma to separate and emphasize each adjective. The comma takes the place of the word *and* in the series.

> the long, dark passageway
>
> another confusing, sleepless night
>
> an elaborate, complex, brilliant plan
>
> the old, grey, crumpled hat

Some adjective-noun combinations are thought of as one word. In these cases, the adjective in front of the adjective-noun combination needs no comma. If you inserted *and* between the adjective-noun combination, it would not make sense.

> a stately oak tree
>
> an exceptional wine glass
>
> my worst report card
>
> a china dinner plate

The comma is also used to separate words, phrases, and whole ideas (clauses); it still takes the place of *and* when used this way.

> an apple, a pear, a fig, and a banana
>
> a handsome man, an elegant suit, and many admirers
>
> She lowered the shade, closed the curtain, turned off the light, and went to bed.

The only question that exists about the use of commas in a series is whether or not one should be used before the final item. It is standard usage to do so, although many newspapers and magazines have stopped using the final comma. Occasionally, the omission of the comma can be confusing.

INCORRECT: He got on his horse, tracked a rabbit and a deer and rode on to Canton.

We planned the trip with Mary and Harold, Susan, Dick and Joan, Gregory and Jean and Charles.

With a long introductory phrase:

Usually if a phrase of more than five or six words or a dependent clause precedes the subject at the beginning of a sentence, a comma is used to set it off.

After last night's fiasco at the disco, she couldn't bear the thought of looking at him again.

Whenever I try to talk about politics, my husband leaves the room.

Provided you have said nothing, they will never guess who you are.

It is not necessary to use a comma with a short sentence.

In January she will go to Switzerland.

After I rest I'll feel better.

During the day no one is home.

If an introductory phrase includes a verb form that is being used as another part of speech (a *verbal*), it must be followed by a comma.

INCORRECT: When eating Mary never looked up from her plate.

CORRECT: When eating, Mary never looked up from her plate.

INCORRECT: Because of her desire to follow her faith in James wavered.

CORRECT: Because of her desire to follow, her faith in James wavered.

INCORRECT: Having decided to leave Mary James wrote her a letter.

CORRECT: Having decided to leave Mary, James wrote her a letter.

To separate sentences with two main ideas:

To understand this use of the comma, you need to be able to recognize compound sentences. When a sentence contains more than two subjects and verbs (clauses), and the two clauses are joined by a conjunction (*and, but, or, nor, for, yet*), use a comma before the conjunction to show that another clause is coming.

I thought I knew the poem by heart, but he showed me three lines I had forgotten.

Are we really interested in helping the children, or are we more concerned with protecting our good names?

He is supposed to leave tomorrow, but he is not ready to go.

Jim knows you are disappointed, and he has known it for a long time.

If the two parts of the sentence are short and closely related, it is not necessary to use a comma.

He threw the ball and the dog ran after it.

Jane played the piano and Michael danced.

Be careful not to confuse a sentence that has a compound verb and a single subject with a compound sentence. If the subject is the same for both verbs, there is no need for a comma.

INCORRECT: Charles sent some flowers, and wrote a long letter explaining why he had not been able to attend.

CORRECT: Charles sent some flowers and wrote a long letter explaining why he had not been able to attend.

INCORRECT: Last Thursday we went to the concert with Julia, and afterwards dined at an old Italian restaurant.

CORRECT: Last Thursday we went to the concert with Julia and afterwards dined at an old Italian restaurant.

INCORRECT: For the third time, the teacher explained that the literacy level for high school students was much lower than it had been in previous years, and, this time, wrote the statistics on the board for everyone to see.

CORRECT: For the third time, the teacher explained that the literacy level for high school students was much lower than it had been in previous years and this time wrote the statistics on the board for everyone to see.

In general, words and phrases that stop the flow of the sentence or are unnecessary for the main idea are set off by commas.

Abbreviations after names:

Did you invite John Paul, Jr., and his sister?

Martha Harris, Ph.D., will be the speaker tonight.

Interjections (an exclamation without added grammatical connection):

Oh, I'm so glad to see you.

I tried so hard, alas, to do it.

Hey, let me out of here.

Direct address:

Roy, won't you open the door for the dog?

I can't understand, Mother, what you are trying to say.

May I ask, Mr. President, why you called us together?

Hey, lady, watch out for that car!

Tag questions:

I'm really hungry, aren't you?

Jerry looks like his father, doesn't he?

Geographical names and addresses:

The concert will be held in Chicago, Illinois, on August 12.

The letter was addressed to Ms. Marion Heartwell, 1881 Pine Lane, Palo Alto, California 95824.

(Note: No comma is needed before the zip code, because it is already clearly set off from the state name.)

Transitional words and phrases:

On the other hand, I hope he gets better.

In addition, the phone rang constantly this afternoon.

I'm, nevertheless, going to the beach on Sunday.

You'll find, therefore, that no one is more loyal than I am.

Parenthetical words and phrases:

You will become, I believe, a great stateswoman.

We know, of course, that this is the only thing to do.

In fact, I planted corn last summer.

The Mannes affair was, to put it mildly, a surprise.

Unusual word order:

The dress, new and crisp, hung in the closet.

Intently, she stared out the window.

With nonrestrictive elements:

Parts of a sentence that modify other parts are sometimes essential to the meaning of the sentence and sometimes not. When a modifying word or group of words is not vital to the meaning of the sentence, it is set off by commas. Since it does not restrict the meaning of the words it modifies, it is called "nonrestrictive." Modifiers that are essential to the meaning of the sentence are called "restrictive" and are not set off by commas.

ESSENTIAL: The woman *who wrote the story* is my sister.

NONESSENTIAL: My sister, *the woman who wrote the story*, has always loved to write.

ESSENTIAL: John Milton's famous poem *Paradise Lost* tells a remarkable story.

NONESSENTIAL: Dante's greatest work, *The Divine Comedy*, marked the beginning of the Renaissance.

ESSENTIAL: The cup *that is on the piano* is the one I want.

NONESSENTIAL: The cup, *which my brother gave me last year*, is on the piano.

ESSENTIAL: The people *who arrived late* were not seated.

NONESSENTIAL: George, *who arrived late*, was not seated.

To set off direct quotations:

Most direct quotes or quoted materials are set off from the rest of the sentence by commas.

"Please read your part more loudly," the director insisted.

"I won't know what to do," said Michael, "if you leave me."

The teacher said sternly, "I will not dismiss this class until I have silence."

Who was it who said "Do not ask for whom the bell tolls; it tolls for thee"?

Note: Commas always go inside the closing quotation mark, even if the comma is not part of the material being quoted.

Be careful not to set off indirect quotes or quotes that are used as subjects or complements.

"To be or not to be" is the famous beginning of a soliloquy in Shakespeare's *Hamlet*. (subject)

She said she would never come back. (indirect quote)

Back then my favorite poem was "Evangeline." (complement)

To set off contrasting elements:

Her intelligence, not her beauty, got her the job.

Your plan will take you a little further from, rather than closer to, your destination.

It was a reasonable, though not appealing, idea.

He wanted glory, but found happiness instead.

In dates:

Both forms of the date are acceptable.

She will arrive on April 6, 1998.

He left on 5 December 1980.

In January 1967, he handed in his resignation.

On October 22, 1992, Frank and Julie were married.

Usually, when a subordinate clause is at the end of a sentence, no comma is necessary preceding the clause. However, when a subordinate clause introduces a sentence, a comma should be used after the clause. Some common subordinating conjunctions are:

after	so that
although	though
as	till
as if	unless

because	until
before	when
even though	whenever
if	while
inasmuch as	since

Semicolons

Questions testing semicolon usage require you to be able to distinguish between the semicolon and the comma, and the semicolon and the colon. This review section covers the basic uses of the semicolon: to separate independent clauses not joined by a coordinating conjunction, to separate independent clauses separated by a conjunctive adverb, and to separate items in a series with internal commas. It is important to be consistent; if you use a semicolon between *any* of the items in the series, you must use semicolons to separate *all* of the items in the series.

Usually, a comma follows the conjunctive adverb. Note also that a period can be used to separate two sentences joined by a conjunctive adverb. Some common conjunctive adverbs are:

accordingly	nevertheless
besides	next
consequently	nonetheless
finally	now
furthermore	on the other hand
however	otherwise
indeed	perhaps
in fact	still
moreover	therefore

Then is also used as a conjunctive adverb, but it is not usually followed by a comma.

Use the semicolon

to separate independent clauses which are not joined by a coordinating conjunction:

> I understand how to use commas; the semicolon I have not yet mastered.

to separate two independent clauses connected by a conjunctive adverb:

> He took great care with his work; *therefore*, he was very successful.

to combine two independent clauses connected by a coordinating conjunction if either or both of the clauses contain other internal punctuation:

> Success in college, some maintain, requires intelligence, industry, and perseverance; *but* others, fewer in number, assert that only personality is important.

to separate items in a series when each item has internal punctuation:

> I bought an old, dilapidated chair; an antique table which was in beautiful condition; and a new, ugly, blue and white rug.

> Call our customer service line for assistance: Arizona, 1-800-555-6020; New Mexico, 1-800-555-5050; California, 1-800-555-3140; or Nevada, 1-800-555-3214.

Do not use the semicolon

to separate a dependent and an independent clause:

> INCORRECT: You should not make such statements; even though they are correct.

> CORRECT: You should not make such statements even though they are correct.

to separate an appositive phrase or clause from a sentence:

> INCORRECT: Her immediate aim in life is centered around two things; becoming an engineer and learning to fly an airplane.

> CORRECT: Her immediate aim in life is centered around two things: becoming an engineer and learning to fly an airplane.

to precede an explanation or summary of the first clause:

Note: Although the sentence below is punctuated correctly, the use of the semicolon provides a miscue, suggesting that the second clause is merely an extension, not an explanation, of the first clause. The colon provides a better clue.

> WEAK: The first week of camping was wonderful; we lived in cabins instead of tents.

> BETTER: The first week of camping was wonderful: we lived in cabins instead of tents.

to substitute for a comma:

INCORRECT: My roommate also likes sports; particularly football, basketball, and baseball.

CORRECT: My roommate also likes sports, particularly football, basketball, and baseball.

to set off other types of phrases or clauses from a sentence:

INCORRECT: Being of a cynical mind; I should ask for a recount of the
ballots.

CORRECT: Being of a cynical mind, I should ask for a recount of the
ballots.

INCORRECT: The next meeting of the club has been postponed two
weeks; inasmuch as both the president and vice-presi-
dent are out of town.

CORRECT: The next meeting of the club has been postponed two
weeks, inasmuch as both the president and vice-presi-
dent are out of town.

Note: The semicolon is not a terminal mark of punctuation; therefore, it should not be followed by a capital letter unless the first word in the second clause ordinarily requires capitalization.

Colons

While it is true that a colon is used to precede a list, one must also make sure that a complete sentence precedes the colon. The colon signals the reader that a list, explanation, or restatement of the preceding will follow. It is like an arrow, indicating that something is to follow. The difference between the colon and the semicolon and between the colon and the period is that the colon is an introductory mark, not a terminal mark. Look at the following examples:

The Constitution provides for a separation of powers among the three branches of government.

government. The period signals a new sentence.

government; The semicolon signals an interrelated sentence.

government, The comma signals a coordinating conjunction followed by another independent clause.

government: The colon signals a list.

The Constitution provides for a separation of powers among the three branches of *government*: executive, legislative, and judicial.

Ensuring that a complete sentence precedes a colon means following these rules:

Use the colon to introduce a list (one item may constitute a list):

I hate this one course: English.

Three plays by William Shakespeare will be presented in repertory this summer at the University of Michigan: *Hamlet, Macbeth,* and *Othello.*

To introduce a list preceded by *as follows* or *the following*:

The reasons he cited for his success are as follows: integrity, honesty, industry, and a pleasant disposition.

To separate two independent clauses, when the second clause is a restatement or explanation of the first:

All of my high school teachers said one thing in particular: college is going to be difficult.

To introduce a word or word group which is a restatement, explanation, or summary of the first sentence:

She asks for two things: a pen and a sheet of paper.

To introduce a formal appositive:

I am positive there is one appeal which you can't overlook: money.

To separate the introductory words from a quotation which follows, if the quotation is formal, long, or paragraphed separately:

The actor then stated: "I would rather be able to adequately play the part of Hamlet than to perform a miraculous operation, deliver a great lecture, or build a magnificent skyscraper."

The colon should only be used after statements that are grammatically complete.

Do *not* use a colon after a verb:

INCORRECT: My favorite holidays are: Christmas, New Year's, and Halloween.

CORRECT: My favorite holidays are Christmas, New Year's, and Halloween.

Do *not* use a colon after a preposition:

    INCORRECT: I enjoy different ethnic foods such as: Greek, Chinese, and Italian.

    CORRECT: I enjoy different ethnic foods such as Greek, Chinese, and Italian.

Do *not* use a colon interchangeably with the dash:

    INCORRECT: Mathematics, German, English: These gave me the greatest difficulty of all my studies.

    CORRECT: Mathematics, German, English—these gave me the greatest difficulty of all my studies.

Information preceding the colon should be a complete sentence regardless of the explanatory information following the clause.

Do *not* use the colon before the words *for example, namely, that is,* or *for instance* even though these words may be introducing a list.

    INCORRECT: We agreed to it: namely, to give him a surprise party.

    CORRECT: There are a number of well-known American women writers: for example, Nikki Giovanni, Phillis Wheatley, Emily Dickinson, and Maya Angelou.

Colon usage questions test your knowledge of the colon preceding a list, restatement, or explanation. These questions also require you to be able to distinguish between the colon and the period, the colon and the comma, and the colon and the semicolon.

Apostrophes

Apostrophe questions require you to know when an apostrophe has been used appropriately to make a noun possessive, not plural. Remember the following rules when considering how to show possession.

Add *'s* to singular nouns and indefinite pronouns:

    Tiffany's flowers

    a dog's bark

    everybody's computer

    at the owner's expense

    today's paper

Add *'s* to singular nouns ending in s, unless this distorts the pronunciation:

> Delores's paper
>
> the boss's pen
>
> Dr. Yots' class
>
> for righteousness' sake
>
> Dr. Evans's office OR Dr. Evans' office

Add *an apostrophe* to plural nouns ending in s or *es*:

> two cents' worth
>
> ladies' night
>
> thirteen years' experience
>
> two weeks' pay

Add *'s* to plural nouns not ending in s:

> men's room
>
> children's toys

Add *'s* to the last word in compound words or groups:

> brother-in-law's car
>
> someone else's paper

Add *'s* to the last name when indicating joint ownership:

> Joe and Edna's home
>
> Julie and Kathy's party
>
> women and children's clinic

Add *'s* to both names if you intend to show ownership by each person:

> Joe's and Edna's trucks
>
> Julie's and Kathy's pies
>
> Ted's and Jane's marriage vows

Possessive pronouns change their forms *without* the addition of an apostrophe:

> her, his, hers
>
> your, yours
>
> their, theirs
>
> it, its

Use the possessive form of a noun preceding a gerund:

> His driving annoys me.
>
> My bowling a strike irritated him.
>
> Do you mind our stopping by?
>
> We appreciate your coming.

Unless confusion will result, add *s* alone to form the plural of single or multiple letters or numerals used as words:

> TVs
>
> IRAs
>
> the three Rs
>
> the 1800s
>
> POWs

But:

> SOS's

Use *'s* when forming the plural of abbreviations with periods:

> R.N.'s

Quotation Marks and Italics

These kinds of questions test your knowledge of the proper use of quotation marks with other marks of punctuation, with titles, and with dialogue. These kinds of questions also test your knowledge of the correct use of italics and underlining with titles and words used as sample words (for example, *the word is is a common verb*).

The most common use of double quotation marks (") is to set off quoted words, phrases, and sentences.

> "If everybody minded their own business," said the Duchess in a hoarse growl, "the world would go round a great deal faster than it does."
>
> "Then you would say what you mean," the March Hare went on.
>
> "I do," Alice hastily replied: "at least—at least I mean what I say—that's the same thing, you know."
>
> —from Lewis Carroll's *Alice in Wonderland*

Single quotation marks are used to set off quoted material within a quote.

> "Shall I bring 'Rime of the Ancient Mariner' along with us?" she asked her brother.

Mrs. Green said, "The doctor told me, 'Go immediately to bed when you get home!'"

"If she said that to me," Katherine insisted, "I would tell her, 'I never intend to speak to you again! Goodbye, Susan!'"

When writing dialogue, begin a new paragraph each time the speaker changes.

"Do you know what time it is?" asked Jane.

"Can't you see I'm busy?" snapped Mary.

"It's easy to see that you're in a bad mood today!" replied Jane.

Use quotation marks to enclose words used as words (sometimes italics are used for this purpose).

"Judgment" has always been a difficult word for me to spell.

Do you know what "abstruse" means?

"Horse and buggy" and "bread and butter" can be used either as adjectives or as nouns.

If slang is used within more formal writing, the slang words or phrases should be set off with quotation marks.

Harrison's decision to leave the conference and to "stick his neck out" by flying to Jamaica was applauded by the rest of the conference attendees.

When words are meant to have an unusual or specific significance to the reader—for instance, irony or humor—they are sometimes placed in quotation marks.

For years, women were not allowed to buy real estate in order to "protect" them from unscrupulous dealers.

The "conversation" resulted in one black eye and a broken nose.

To set off titles of TV shows, poems, stories, and book chapters, use quotation marks. (Book, motion picture, newspaper, and magazine titles are underlined when handwritten and italicized when printed.)

The article "Moving South in the Southern Rain," by Jergen Smith in the *Southern News*, attracted the attention of our editor.

The assignment is "Childhood Development," Chapter 18 of *Human Behavior.*

My favorite essay by Montaigne is "On Silence."

"Happy Days" led the TV ratings for years, didn't it?

You will find Keats' "Ode on a Grecian Urn" in Chapter 3, "The Romantic Era," in Lastly's *Selections from Great English Poets.*

Errors to avoid:

Be sure to remember that quotation marks always come in pairs. Do not make the mistake of using only one set.

INCORRECT: "You'll never convince me to move to the city, said Thurman. I consider it an insane asylum."

CORRECT: "You'll never convince me to move to the city," said Thurman. "I consider it an insane asylum."

INCORRECT: "Idleness and pride tax with a heavier hand than kings and parliaments," Benjamin Franklin is supposed to have said. If we can get rid of the former, we may easily bear the latter."

CORRECT: "Idleness and pride tax with a heavier hand than kings and parliaments," Benjamin Franklin is supposed to have said. "If we can get rid of the former, we may easily bear the latter."

When a quote consists of several sentences, do not put the quotation marks at the beginning and end of each sentence; put them at the beginning and end of the entire quotation.

INCORRECT: "It was during his student days in Bonn that Beethoven fastened upon Schiller's poem." "The heady sense of liberation in the verses must have appealed to him." "They appealed to every German." —John Burke

CORRECT: "It was during his student days in Bonn that Beethoven fastened upon Schiller's poem. The heady sense of liberation in the verses must have appealed to him. They appealed to every German." —John Burke

Instead of setting off a long quote with quotation marks, if it is longer than five or six lines you may want to indent and single space it. If you do indent, do not use quotation marks.

In his *First Inaugural Address,* Abraham Lincoln appeals to the strife-torn American people:

We are not enemies, but friends. We must not be enemies. Though passion may have strained, it must not break, our bonds of affection. The mystic chords of memory, stretching from every battlefield and patriot grave to every living heart

and hearthstone all over this broad land, will yet swell the
chorus of the Union when again touched, as surely they will
be, by the better angels of our nature.

Be careful not to use quotation marks with indirect quotations.

INCORRECT: Mary wondered "if she would get over it."

CORRECT: Mary wondered if she would get over it.

INCORRECT: The nurse asked "how long it had been since we had
visited the doctor's office."

CORRECT: The nurse asked how long it had been since we had
visited the doctor's office.

When you quote several paragraphs, it is not sufficient to place quotation marks at the beginning and end of the entire quote. Place quotation
marks at the *beginning of each paragraph,* but only at the *end of the last
paragraph.* Here is an abbreviated quotation for an example:

"Here begins an odyssey through the world of classical mythology,
starting with the creation of the world . . .

"It is true that themes similar to the classical may be found in any
corpus of mythology . . . Even technology is not immune to the influence of Greece and Rome . . .

"We need hardly mention the extent to which painters and
sculptors . . . have used and adapted classical mythology to illus-
trate the past, to reveal the human body, to express romantic or
antiromantic ideals, or to symbolize any particular point of view."

Remember that commas and periods are *always* placed inside the
quotation marks even if they are not actually part of the quote.

INCORRECT: "Life always gets colder near the summit", Nietzsche is
purported to have said, "—the cold increases, responsibility grows".

CORRECT: "Life always gets colder near the summit," Nietzsche is
purported to have said, "—the cold increases, responsibility grows."

INCORRECT: "Get down here right away", John cried. "You'll miss the
sunset if you don't."

CORRECT: "Get down here right away," John cried. "You'll miss the
sunset if you don't."

INCORRECT: "If my dog could talk", Mary mused, "I'll bet he would say, 'Take me for a walk right this minute'".

CORRECT: "If my dog could talk," Mary mused, "I'll bet he would say, 'Take me for a walk right this minute'."

Other marks of punctuation, such as question marks, exclamation points, colons, and semicolons, go inside the quotation marks if they are part of the quoted material. If they are not part of the quotation, however, they go outside the quotation marks. Be careful to distinguish between the guidelines for the comma and period, which always go inside the quotation marks, and those for other marks of punctuation.

INCORRECT: "I'll always love you"! he exclaimed happily.

CORRECT: "I'll always love you!" he exclaimed happily.

INCORRECT: Did you hear her say, "He'll be there early?"

CORRECT: Did you hear her say, "He'll be there early"?

INCORRECT: She called down the stairs, "When are you going"?

CORRECT: She called down the stairs, "When are you going?"

INCORRECT: "Let me out"! he cried. "Don't you have any pity"?

CORRECT: "Let me out!" he cried. "Don't you have any pity?"

Remember to use only one mark of punctuation at the end of a sentence ending with a quotation mark.

INCORRECT: She thought out loud, "Will I ever finish this paper in time for that class?".

CORRECT: She thought out loud, "Will I ever finish this paper in time for that class?"

INCORRECT: "Not the same thing a bit!", said the Hatter. "Why, you might just as well say that 'I see what I eat' is the same thing as 'I eat what I see'!".

CORRECT: "Not the same thing a bit!" said the Hatter. "Why, you might just as well say that 'I see what I eat' is the same thing as 'I eat what I see'!"

☞ **Drill: Punctuation**

DIRECTIONS: Choose the correct option.

1. Indianola, <u>Mississippi, where B.B. King and my father grew up,</u> has a population of less than 50,000 people.

    (A) Mississippi where, B.B. King and my father grew up,

    (B) Mississippi where B.B. King and my father grew up,

    (C) Mississippi; where B.B. King and my father grew up,

    (D) No change is necessary.

2. John Steinbeck's best known novel *The Grapes of Wrath* is the story of the <u>Joads and Oklahoma family</u> who were driven from their dustbowl farm and forced to become migrant workers in California.

    (A) Joads, an Oklahoma family

    (B) Joads, an Oklahoma family,

    (C) Joads; an Oklahoma family

    (D) No change is necessary.

3. All students who are interested in student teaching next <u>semester, must submit an application to the Teacher Education Office.</u>

    (A) semester must submit an application to the Teacher Education Office.

    (B) semester, must submit an application, to the Teacher Education Office.

    (C) semester: must submit an application to the Teacher Education Office.

    (D) No change is necessary.

4. Whenever you travel by <u>car, or plane, you</u> must wear a seatbelt.

    (A) car or plane you   (C) car or plane, you

    (B) car, or plane you   (D) No change is necessary.

5. Wearing a seatbelt is not just a good <u>idea, it's</u> the law.

    (A) idea; it's   (C) idea. It's

    (B) idea it's   (D) No change is necessary.

6. Senators and representatives can be reelected <u>indefinitely; a</u> president can only serve two terms.

    (A) indefinitely but a   (C) indefinitely a

    (B) indefinitely, a   (D) No change is necessary.

7. Students must pay a penalty for overdue library <u>books, however, there</u> is a grace period.

    (A) books; however, there   (C) books: however, there

    (B) books however, there   (D) No change is necessary.

8. Among the states that seceded from the Union to join the Confederacy in 1860-1861 <u>were</u>: Mississippi, Florida, and Alabama.

    (A) were   (C) were.

    (B) were;   (D) No change is necessary.

9. The art exhibit displayed works by many famous <u>artists such as:</u> Dali, Picasso, and Michelangelo.

    (A) artists such as;   (C) artists. Such as

    (B) artists such as   (D) No change is necessary.

10. The National Shakespeare Company will perform <u>the following plays:</u> *Othello, Macbeth, Hamlet,* and *As You Like It.*

    (A) the following plays,   (C) the following plays

    (B) the following plays;   (D) No change is necessary.

ENGLISH LANGUAGE SKILLS

ANSWER KEY

Drill: Word Choice Skills

1.	(D)	4.	(C)	7.	(A)	10.	(B)
2.	(D)	5.	(A)	8.	(B)		
3.	(A)	6.	(C)	9.	(C)		

Drill: Sentence Structure Skills

1.	(C)	4.	(B)	7.	(B)	10.	(B)
2.	(B)	5.	(A)	8.	(A)		
3.	(B)	6.	(A)	9.	(B)		

Drill: Verbs

1.	(C)	4.	(A)	7.	(A)	10.	(D)
2.	(D)	5.	(A)	8.	(C)		
3.	(D)	6.	(B)	9.	(A)		

Drill: Pronouns

1.	(A)	4.	(A)	7.	(B)	10.	(C)
2.	(C)	5.	(D)	8.	(B)		
3.	(A)	6.	(A)	9.	(A)		

Drill: Adjectives and Adverbs

1.	(C)	4.	(C)	7.	(A)	10.	(C)
2.	(A)	5.	(A)	8.	(C)		
3.	(D)	6.	(C)	9.	(B)		

Drill: Punctuation

1. (D)	4. (C)	7. (A)	10. (D)
2. (A)	5. (A)	8. (A)	
3. (A)	6. (D)	9. (B)	

DETAILED EXPLANATIONS OF ANSWERS

Drill: Word Choice Skills

1. **(D)** Choice (D) is correct. No change is necessary. *Principal* as a noun means "head of a school." *Principle* is a noun meaning "axiom" or "rule of conduct."

2. **(D)** Choice (D) is correct. No change is necessary. *Affect* is a verb meaning "to influence" or "to change." *Effect* as a noun meaning "result."

3. **(A)** Choice (A) is correct. Use *amount* with noncountable, mass nouns (*amount* of food, help, money); use *number* with countable, plural nouns (*number* of children, classes, bills).

4. **(C)** Choice (C) is correct. *Supposed to* and *used to* should be spelled with a final *d*. *Achieving* follows the standard spelling rule—*i* before *e*.

5. **(A)** Choice (A) is correct. Use *that*, not *because*, to introduce clauses after the word *reason*. Choice (A) is also the only choice that contains the correct spelling of "succeeded."

6. **(C)** Choice (C) is correct. *Converge together* is redundant, and *single* is not needed to convey the meaning of *a highway*.

7. **(A)** Choice (A) is correct. It is economical and concise. The other choices contain unnecessary repetition.

8. **(B)** Choice (B) is correct. Choices (A) and (C) pad the sentences with loose synonyms that are redundant. Choice (D), although a short sentence, does not convey the meaning as clearly as choice (B).

9. **(C)** Choice (C) is correct. The other choices all contain unnecessary repetition.

10. **(B)** Choice (B) is correct. Choices (A) and (C) contain circumlocution; they fail to get to the point. Choice (D) does not express the meaning of the sentence as concisely as choice (B).

Drill: Sentence Structure Skills

1.   **(C)**   Choice (C) is correct. Each response contains items in a series. In choices (A) and (B), the word group after the conjunction is not an adjective like the first words in the series. Choice (C) contains three adjectives.

2.   **(B)**   Choice (B) is correct. Choices (A), (C), and (D) combine conjunctions incorrectly.

3.   **(B)**   Choice (B) is correct. Choices (A) and (C) appear to be parallel because the conjunction *and* connects two word groups that both begin with *because*, but the structure on both sides of the conjunction are very different. *Because he kept his campaign promises* is a clause; *because of his refusal to accept political favors* is a prepositional phrase. Choice (B) connects two dependent clauses.

4.   **(B)**   Choice (B) is correct. Choices (A) and (C) contain the elliptical clause *While . . . taking a shower*. It appears that the missing subject in the elliptical clause is the same as that in the independent clause—the *doorbell* in choice (A) and *someone* in choice (C), neither of which is a logical subject for the verbal *taking a shower*. Choice (B) removes the elliptical clause and provides the logical subject.

5.   **(A)**   Choice (A) is correct. Who swung the bat? Choices (B) and (C) both imply that it is the runner who swung the bat. Only choice (A) makes it clear that as *he* swung the bat, someone else (the *runner*) stole second base.

6.   **(A)**   Choice (A) is correct. The punctuation in the original sentence and in choice (B) creates a fragment. *Cotton being the state's principal crop* is not an independent thought because it lacks a complete verb—*being* is not a complete verb.

7.   **(B)**   Choice (B) is correct. The punctuation in the original sentence and in choice (A) creates a fragment. Both the semicolon and the period should be used to separate two independent clauses. The word group *one that I have never seen before* does not express a complete thought and therefore is not an independent clause.

8.   **(A)**   Choice (A) is correct. The dependent clause *because repairs were being made* in choices (B) and (C) is punctuated as if it were a sentence. The result is a fragment.

9.   **(B)**   Choice (B) is correct. Choices (A) and (C) do not separate the complete thoughts in the independent clauses with the correct punctuation.

10.   **(B)**   Choice (B) is correct. Choices (A) and (C) do not separate the independent clauses with the correct punctuation.

Drill: Verbs

1.   **(C)**   Choice (C) is correct. The past participle form of each verb is required because of the auxiliaries (helping verbs) *had been* (concerned) and *would have* (gone).

2.   **(D)**   Choice (D) is correct. The forms of the irregular verb meaning *to rest* are *lie (rest), lies (rests), lay (rested),* and *has lain (has rested).* The forms of the verb meaning *to put* are *lay (put), lays (puts), laying (putting), laid (put),* and *have laid (have put).*

3.   **(D)**   Choice (D) is correct. The present tense is used for universal truths and the past tense is used for historical truths.

4.   **(A)**   Choice (A) is correct. The present tense is used for customary happenings. Choice (B), *had begun,* is not a standard verb form. Choice (C), *was beginning,* indicates that 10:30 a.m. is not the regular class time.

5.   **(A)**   Choice (A) is correct. The past tense is used for historical statements, and the present tense is used for statements about works of art.

6.   **(B)**   Choice (B) is correct. The subject of the sentence is the plural noun *sales,* not the singular noun *Christmas,* which is the object of the prepositional phrase.

7.   **(A)**   Choice (A) is correct. The subject *specialty* is singular.

8.   **(C)**   Choice (C) is correct. Subjects preceded by *every* are considered singular and therefore require a singular verb form.

9.   **(A)**   Choice (A) is correct. The subject of the sentence is the gerund *hiding,* not the object of the gerund phrase *mistakes. Hiding* is singular; therefore, the singular verb form *does* should be used.

10. **(D)** Choice (D) is correct. Though the form of the subject *Board of Regents* is plural, it is singular in meaning.

Drill: Pronouns

1. **(A)** Choice (A) is correct. Do not use the reflexive pronoun *myself* as a substitute for I.

2. **(C)** Choice (C) is correct. In the clause *whoever consumes them*, *whoever* is the subject. *Whomever* is the objective case pronoun and should be used only as the object of a sentence, never as the subject.

3. **(A)** Choice (A) is correct. Use the nominative case pronoun *who* as the subject complement after the verb *is*.

4. **(A)** Choice (A) is correct. In this sentence use the nominative case/subject pronouns *she who* as the subject complement after the *be* verb *was*.

5. **(D)** Choice (D) is correct. *Student* is an indefinite, genderless noun that requires a singular personal pronoun. While *his* is a singular personal pronoun, a genderless noun includes both the masculine and feminine forms and requires *his or her* as the singular personal pronoun.

6. **(A)** Choice (A) is correct. The antecedent *company* is singular, requiring the singular pronoun *it*, not the plural *they*.

7. **(B)** Choice (B) is correct. Choice (A) contains a person shift: *Your* is a second person pronoun, and *his* and *her* are third person pronouns. The original sentence uses the third person plural pronoun *their* to refer to the singular antecedent *every car owner*. Choice (B) correctly provides the masculine and feminine forms *his or her* required by the indefinite, genderless *every car owner*.

8. **(B)** Choice (B) is correct. The implied antecedent is *teaching*. Choices (A) and (C) each contain a pronoun with no antecedent. Neither *it* nor *this* are suitable substitutions for *teacher*.

9. **(A)** Choice (A) is correct. The pronoun *they* in the original sentence has no conspicuous antecedent. Since the doer of the action is obviously unknown (and therefore genderless), choice (B), *he*, is not the correct choice.

10. **(C)** Choice (C) is correct. The original sentence is ambiguous: the pronoun *she* has two possible antecedents; we don't know whether it is Margaret or her sister who is away at college.

Drill: Adjectives and Adverbs

1. **(C)** Choice (C) is correct. *Bad* is an adjective; *badly* is an adverb. *Real* is an adjective meaning *genuine* (*a real problem, real leather*). To qualify an adverb of degree to express how bad, how excited, how boring, etc., choose *very*.

2. **(A)** Choice (A) is correct. Use an adverb as a qualifier for an adjective. *How simple? Relatively simple.*

3. **(D)** Choice (D) is correct. *Good* is an adjective; *well* is both an adjective and an adverb. As an adjective, *well* refers to health; it means "not ill."

4. **(C)** Choice (C) is correct. All the other choices use *good* incorrectly as an adverb. *Shake* is an action verb that requires an adverb, not an adjective.

5. **(A)** Choice (A) is correct. The action verbs *speaks, writes, observe,* and *think* each require adverbs as modifiers.

6. **(C)** Choice (C) is correct. The comparisons in choices (A) and (B) are illogical: these sentences suggest that Los Angeles is not in California because it *is larger than any city in California.*

7. **(A)** Choice (A) is correct. Do not omit the second *as* of the correlative pair *as . . . as* when making a point of equal or superior comparison, as in choice (B). Choice (C) omits *than* from "if not more interesting [than]".

8. **(C)** Choice (C) is correct. Choice (A) illogically compares *baseball team* to a *university*, and choice (B) illogically compares *baseball team* to *all the other universities*. Choice (C) logically compares the baseball team here to the one at any other university, as implied by the possessive ending on university—*university's.*

9. **(B)** Choice (B) is correct. Choices (A) and (C) are ambiguous;

because these sentences are too elliptical, the reader does not know where to place the missing information.

10.   **(C)**   Choice (C) is correct. Choice (A) is redundant; there is no need to use *most* with *stingiest*. Choice (B) incorrectly combines the comparative word *more* with the superlative form *stingiest*.

Drill: Punctuation

1.   **(D)**   Choice (D) is correct. Nonrestrictive clauses, like other nonrestrictive elements, should be set off from the rest of the sentence with commas.

2.   **(A)**   Choice (A) is correct. Use a comma to separate a nonrestrictive appositive from the word it modifies. "An Oklahoma family" is a nonrestrictive appositive.

3.   **(A)**   Choice (A) is correct. Do not use unnecessary commas to separate a subject and verb from their complement. Both choices (B) and (C) use superfluous punctuation.

4.   **(C)**   Choice (C) is correct. Do not separate two items in a compound with commas. The original sentence incorrectly separates "car or plane." Choice (A) omits the comma after the introductory clause.

5.   **(A)**   Choice (A) is correct. Use a semicolon to separate two independent clauses/sentences that are not joined by a coordinating conjunction, especially when the ideas in the sentences are interrelated.

6.   **(D)**   Choice (D) is correct. Use a semicolon to separate two sentences not joined by a coordinating conjunction.

7.   **(A)**   Choice (A) is correct. Use a semicolon to separate two sentences joined by a conjunctive adverb.

8.   **(A)**   Choice (A) is correct. Do not use a colon after a verb or a preposition. Remember that a complete sentence must precede a colon.

9.   **(B)**   Choice (B) is correct. Do not use a colon after a preposition, and do not use a colon to separate a preposition from its objects.

10.   **(D)**   Choice (D) is correct. Use a colon preceding a list that is introduced by words such as *the following* and *as follows*.

PSAT/ NMSQT

Practice Test 1

TEST 1

Section 1

(Answer sheets appear in the back of this book.)

TIME: 25 Minutes
26 Questions

For each question in this section, select the best answer from among the given choices and fill in the corresponding oval on the answer sheet.

DIRECTIONS: Each sentence below has one or two blanks, each blank indicating that something has been omitted. Beneath the sentence are five lettered words or sets of words. Choose the word or set of words that **BEST** fits the meaning of the sentence as a whole.

EXAMPLE:

Although the critics found the book _____, many of the readers found it rather _____.

(A) obnoxious . . . perfect   (D) comical . . . persuasive

(B) spectacular . . . interesting   (E) popular . . . rare

(C) boring . . . intriguing   Ⓐ Ⓑ ● Ⓓ Ⓔ

---

1. Frustrated by many _____, the scientist reluctantly _____ his experiment.

    (A) complications . . . terminated

    (B) dangers . . . extended

    (C) successes . . . finished

    (D) situations . . . submitted

    (E) liabilities . . . studied

2. During the Middle Ages, the majority of the population were _____ since working the land was an _____ occupation.

566

(A) nobles . . . enjoyable   (D) merchants . . . impersonal

(B) serfs . . . endless   (E) knights . . . inconsequential

(C) monks . . . everlasting

3. The speaker's monotonous delivery made his hour-long speech seem
    _____ and the audience became _____ waiting for the end.

(A) exciting . . . interested   (D) long . . . doubtful

(B) interminable . . . impatient (E) uninteresting . . . grumpy

(C) unbelievable . . . skeptical

4. Even though his published verses were _____, the poet received great
    acclaim for his work.

(A) grand   (D) inane

(B) impressive   (E) unlikely

(C) musical

5. Because the actor's temperament was so _____, directors often re-
    jected him for parts since no one could be sure how he would behave.

(A) confident   (D) overpowering

(B) mercurial   (E) inhibited

(C) pessimistic

6. Finishing a marathon can be a _____ task when leg cramps _____ the
    runner.

(A) Herculean . . . debilitate   (D) invigorating . . . slow

(B) hard . . . impel   (E) thrilling . . . sedate

(C) frustrating . . . spur

7. Scientists warn us that unless we _____ the poisons in the air, global
    warming could occur as the sun's rays _____ the atmosphere.

(A) collect . . . destroy   (D) aggravate . . . permeate

(B) combine . . . weaken   (E) curtail . . . penetrate

(C) restrict . . . expedite

DIRECTIONS: Each question below consists of a related pair of words or phrases, followed by five lettered pairs of words or phrases. Select the lettered pair that best expresses a relationship similar to that expressed in the original pair.

EXAMPLE:

SMILE : MOUTH ::

(A) wink : eye

(B) teeth : face

(C) voice : speech

(D) tan : skin

(E) food : gums

8. ESPIONAGE : SPY ::

   (A) treachery : traitor

   (B) books : novelist

   (C) money : banker

   (D) honesty : thief

   (E) navigation : captain

9. WATER : LIQUID ::

   (A) mineral : vitamin

   (B) balloon : gas

   (C) flower : bouquet

   (D) brass : metal

   (E) atom : bomb

10. FRAGRANT : SMELL ::

   (A) shrill : music

   (B) audible : sound

   (C) savory : taste

   (D) shadow : light

   (E) finger : touch

11. IMPOSTER : DECEIVE ::

   (A) idealist : values

   (B) glutton : overindulges

   (C) hypochondriac : illness

   (D) felon : remorse

   (E) exorcist : prays

12. DISPERSE : CROWD ::

    (A) dig : pile   (D) scatter : convene

    (B) study : genius   (E) broadcast : news

    (C) fertilize : garden

13. REFORMER : IMPROVEMENT ::

    (A) pathologist : disease   (D) pacifist : harmony

    (B) teacher : textbook   (E) messenger : deception

    (C) salesperson : commission

DIRECTIONS: Read each passage and answer the questions that follow. Each question will be based on the information stated or implied in the passage or its introduction.

Questions 14–18 are based on the following passage.

The following passage discusses the exclusion of Catholics from the Eighteenth Century Irish Parliament.

1   The condition of the Irish Parliament all through the eighteenth century is truly pitiable. Its existence as a legislative body is a huge sham, a ghastly simulacrum. The Parliament was one of the most eccentrically composed, most circumscribed, most corrupt legislative assemblies that
5 the ingenuity of man has ever devised. To begin with: no Catholic could sit in Parliament; no Catholic could even record his vote for a Protestant member. The Catholics were as absolutely unrepresented as if they did not exist; and yet they made up the vast majority of the population which the Irish Parliament tried to govern or misgovern, and by an amazing fiction
10 was supposed to represent. "The borough system," says Mr. Lecky, "which had been chiefly the work of the Stuarts—no less than 40 boroughs have been created by James I alone—had been developed to such an extent that out of the 300 members who composed the Parliament"—Mr. Lecky is, of course, speaking of the Lower House—"216 were returned
15 for boroughs or manors. Of these borough members 200 were elected by 100 individuals, and nearly 50 by 10. According to a secret report drawn up by the Irish Government for Pitt in 1784, Lord Shannon at that time returned no less than 16 members, the Ponsonby family 14, Lord Hillsborough nine, and the Duke of Leinster seven."
20   That borough system was the successful means of corrupting both Houses. James I had been earnestly remonstrated with for calling 40 bor-

oughs into existence at one blow, and we have it on authority of Hely Hutchinson that the king replied: "I have made 40 boroughs, suppose I had made 400—the more the merrier." A pleasant statesmanlike, truly Stuart
25 way of looking at all things, which was destined to prove fatal to the Stuarts and to nobler hearts and heads than theirs. Borough-owners who returned supple lieges to the Irish Parliament generally found their reward in a peerage. Thus, with a simplicity of corruption, the two Houses were undermined at once, for it is said that some half a hundred peers nomi-
30 nated no less than 123 members of the Lower House.

The Irish Parliament was like one of those buried cities dear to Irish legend which lie beneath the waters of some legend-haunted lake. The dark waters of corruption covered it; there came a moment when those waters fell away and revealed an ancient institution, defaced, indeed, but
35 still honourable and imposing; then the engulfing waves closed over it again, and it vanished—but not for ever.

14. The author describes the Irish Parliament all through the 1700s as being

   (A) different from that of the eighteenth century.

   (B) contrived for the benefit of the Catholic clergy.

   (C) corrupt in the Upper House only; the Lower House was circumspect.

   (D) a model of decency.

   (E) corrupt in many respects.

15. The main idea of the passage is to

   (A) point out a truly distinct and admirable system of government.

   (B) point out the sincerity and honesty of those who brought about the system.

   (C) stress again the model Irish Parliament, which many countries could use as a successful system of government.

   (D) bring to the surface the forgotten system with its many attributes.

   (E) raise the sham from the dark waters of the past.

16. The writer attributes corruption in the Parliament to

    (A) the Catholic religion.   (D) a two-house system.

    (B) Mr. Lecky.   (E) the borough system.

    (C) the legend-haunted lake.

17. The word "simulacrum" in line 3 can be best defined as

    (A) symmetry, or one side like that of the other.

    (B) a ghost or haunting.

    (C) a type of government of the 1700s.

    (D) a pretense.

    (E) a legislature or law-making body.

18. To give credence to his writings, the author

    (A) calls on the statements of Hely Hutchinson.

    (B) calls on subliminal persuasion.

    (C) gives all facts and figures; no opinions are given at all.

    (D) neglects to consult the voting records.

    (E) ignores the complicated method of corrupting both Houses.

Questions 19–26 are based on the following passage.

The following passage discusses the fertilization of flowers by the class of insects known as Lepidoptera, which includes butterflies and moths.

1   If the chief divisions of insects are to be arranged in the order of their importance as fertilizers of our native flowers, the first place must decidedly be given to bees,—while the Lepidoptera take only the second or third place, before or after the flies. But if, as here, we base our arrange-
5   ment on the degrees of adaptation to flowers, they undoubtedly take the first place, as the only order which throughout, and not only in certain of its families, is fitted for obtaining honey.
     In the perfect state, butterflies, so far as they take food at all, which is not the case in all species, restrict themselves almost entirely to honey;
10   and since they take no further thought for their young than to lay their eggs sufficiently concealed upon the food-plant, their mouth-parts have been quite free to adapt themselves to the easy winning of honey from the

most various flowers. This adaptation is attained by an astonishing development of the maxillary laminæ, with suppression of the greater part of
15 the rest of the mouth-organs. The upper lip and mandibles are aborted.
The laminæ of the maxillæ are transformed into two immensely long,
hollow, rounded filaments, provided with semicircular grooves on their
inner surfaces, and so forming a tube when placed in close apposition; in
the state of rest this tube is spirally coiled, and concealed between the
20 labial palps. The maxillary palps, which are not visible in my figure, and
also the labium, are usually more or less abortive. The whole mechanism
of the mouth, so complex and many-jointed in bees, is thus here reduced
to a long, thin, suctorial tube formed of two apposed grooves and capable
of being rolled up into small space, and of a protective covering for this
25 tube.

With this simple mechanism, Lepidoptera are able to probe the most
various flowers, whether flat or long and tubular, and to secure their
honey. Peculiar stiff, sharp-pointed appendages at the ends of the laminæ
enable them also to tear open delicate succulent tissues, and make use of
30 the sap in flowers which secrete no free honey. In a former work I have
sought to establish the pedigree of Lepidoptera, which has been foreshad-
owed by entomologists since last century: the subject has been much
more thoroughly discussed by my friend Dr. A. Speyer, by Mr. R.
MacLachlan, and by my brother Fritz Müller. Apart from tiny midges and
35 from those insects, especially beetles and bees, which occasionally or
habitually take up their quarters for the night in flowers, Lepidoptera
seem to be the only insects which do not confine their visits to flowers to
the daylight: a large number of their species have acquired the habit of
seeking their honey in the dusk of summer nights and evenings, free from
40 the competition of other insects. But in our climate, summer evenings on
which twilight-loving and nocturnal Lepidoptera fly abundantly are not
very numerous. Though the swift and violent movements of these species
may be due to the shortness of the period suitable for their flight, or to the
pursuit of bats, this peculiarity is of very great importance to the plants
45 they visit; for the more flowers will be visited in a given time, the less
time that is spent on each, and the shorter the time that is spent in the
flight from one to another. This explains how many flowers have adapted
themselves specially to nocturnal insects, both by their light colours, visible in the dusk, and by their time of opening, of secreting honey, or of
50 emitting their odour.

19. The author believes that the order of insects as fertilizers of native flowers in order of their importance is

    (A) flies, butterflies, bees.

    (B) butterflies, Lepidoptera, flies.

    (C) bees, butterflies, Lepidoptera.

    (D) Lepidoptera, then flies or bees.

    (E) bees, Lepidoptera, flies.

20. The only order(s) which is fitted for taking honey from flowers in all its family is the

    (A) bee.

    (B) bee and Lepidoptera.

    (C) Lepidoptera, butterflies, and bees.

    (D) flies, bees, Lepidoptera, and butterflies.

    (E) Lepidoptera.

21. The mouth of the butterfly can be best described as

    (A) simple.

    (B) a long, thin tube which extends in a stiff manner.

    (C) a long, thin tube which can be rolled up into a small space.

    (D) a long, thin tube which can be rolled up into a small space and an upper lip and mandibles which are short.

    (E) a pointed "stinger" for sucking up the pollen.

22. The Lepidoptera, at the time of this writing, had been studied by

    (A) Müller only, up to the time of this writing.

    (B) Müller and his brother.

    (C) the two Müllers, Speyer, and MacLachlan.

    (D) too many scientists to list.

    (E) no one since its work it inconsequential.

23. The main purpose of this passage is to

   (A) emphasize the importance of the mouth parts of the bee.

   (B) show the importance of the bee in fertilization of native flowers.

   (C) show that the butterfly is number one in fertilization of native flowers.

   (D) show the importance and development of the Lepidoptera.

   (E) show that the Lepidoptera seem to be the only insects which do not confine their visits to flowers to the daylight.

24. The writer speculates that there are few nocturnal Lepidoptera in our climate because of

   (A) the pursuit of collectors during nocturnal hours.

   (B) the shortness of the period suitable for their flight.

   (C) the swift movements of the Lepidoptera.

   (D) the violent movements of the Lepidoptera.

   (E) the lack of nocturnal flowers in our climate.

25. Nocturnal flowers to be visited by the Lepidoptera usually

   (A) are dark-colored.

   (B) are without odor.

   (C) open early in the day.

   (D) secrete their nectar early in the day.

   (E) are light-colored.

26. In line 21, "abortive" most nearly means

   (A) shortened.   (D) incompletely formed.

   (B) imperfect.   (E) obsolete.

   (C) mangled.

Section 2

TIME: 25 Minutes
20 Questions

DIRECTIONS: Solve each problem, using any available space on the page for scratch work. Then decide which answer choice is the best and fill in the corresponding oval on the answer sheet.

NOTES:

(1) The use of a calculator is permitted. All numbers used are real numbers.

(2) Figures that accompany problems in this test are intended to provide information useful in solving the problems. They are drawn as accurately as possible EXCEPT when it is stated in a specific problem that the figure is not drawn to scale. All figures lie in a plane unless otherwise indicated.

REFERENCE INFORMATION:

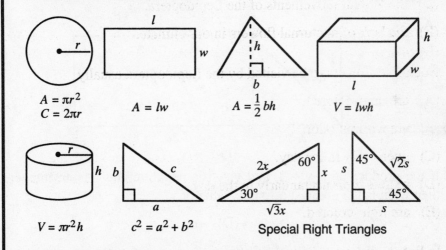

$$A = \pi r^2$$
$$C = 2\pi r$$

$$A = lw$$

$$A = \frac{1}{2}bh$$

$$V = lwh$$

$$V = \pi r^2 h$$

$$c^2 = a^2 + b^2$$

Special Right Triangles

The number of degrees of arc in a circle is 360.
The measure in degrees of a straight angle is 180.
The sum of the measures in degrees of the angles of a triangle is 180.

1. There were 70 students in a high school graduating class. Of the 70, 40 were members of the French club. Of the 40 members of the French club, $^2/_5$ were females. Of the remaining students who were not in the French club, $^1/_3$ were males. How many students in the graduating class were females?

(A) 16　　　　　　　　(D) 28

(B) 20　　　　　　　　(E) 36

(C) 24

2. One-third of what number is the same as 40 percent of 75?

(A) 10　　　　　　　　(D) 90

(B) 30　　　　　　　　(E) 100

(C) 60

3. In the figure shown, *ABCD* is a square and *DEFC* is a rectangle. What is the area of *DEFC*?

(A) 32

(B) 48

(C) 64

(D) 72

(E) 128

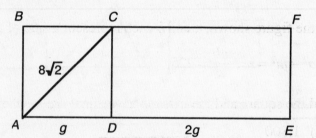

4. If the product of y, $y + 3$, and $y + 5$ is negative and y is an integer, then what is the greatest possible value of y?

(A) 2　　　　　　　　(D) –1

(B) 1　　　　　　　　(E) –2

(C) 0

5. Five different positive integers have an average (arithmetic mean) of 8. What is the largest that any of the integers could be?

(A) 20　　　　　　　　(D) 35

(B) 25　　　　　　　　(E) 40

(C) 30

6. A triangle with angles of 45, 45, and 90 degrees has an area of 64. What is the perimeter of the triangle?

(A) $8 + 8\sqrt{2}$

(D) $16 + 16\sqrt{2}$

(B) $8 + 16\sqrt{2}$

(E) $24\sqrt{2}$

(C) $16 + 8\sqrt{2}$

7. If

$$\frac{m}{g} = \frac{1}{y} \text{ and } \frac{m}{d} = \frac{1}{(y+1)},$$

which of the following correctly expresses the relationship between g and d?

(A) $g = d - 1$

(D) $g = d + m$

(B) $g = \dfrac{d}{m}$

(E) $g = d - m$

(C) $g = d + 1$

8. In the figure shown, a and b each represent a side of a square. If

$$o^2 - m^2 = n^2, \frac{ab}{4} = 225,$$

and the square and the triangle have equal areas, what does mn equal?

(A) 1,800

(B) 1,000

(C) 900

(D) 750

(E) 500

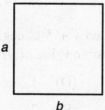
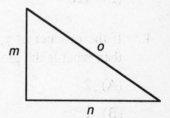

9. A middle grade oil is to be made by combining two different grades of oil. One grade costs $16 a barrel and the other costs $6 a barrel. If the new oil will cost $10 a barrel, how many barrels of the $16 oil will be needed to make 100 barrels of the blend?

(A) 40

(D) 55

(B) 45

(E) 60

(C) 50

10. From looking at the legend on her map, Cindy notices that one centimeter on the map represents 1,000 kilometers. If her destination is 4.8 centimeters away on the map, how many kilometers must she drive before she arrives at her destination?

    (A) 4,000.8

    (B) 4,008.0

    (C) 4,080.0

    (D) 4,800.0

    (E) 4,800.8

11. If angle $ABE = 30°$, and angle $ABD = 80°$, what does angle $DBC +$ angle $BCD = ?$

    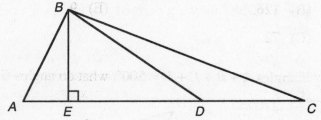

    (A) 40°

    (B) 50°

    (C) 60°

    (D) 75°

    (E) 90°

12. $\dfrac{2}{6} \times \dfrac{3}{9} \times \dfrac{4}{12} \times \dfrac{5}{15} \times \dfrac{6}{18} =$

    (A) $\dfrac{1}{3}$

    (B) $\dfrac{1}{9}$

    (C) $\dfrac{1}{27}$

    (D) $\dfrac{1}{81}$

    (E) $\dfrac{1}{243}$

13. A recipe requires 2 cups of cashews, 6 cups of whole wheat flour, and $\frac{1}{4}$ of a cup of sunflower seeds. The ratio of cashews to whole wheat flour to sunflower seeds could be accurately expressed as which of the following?

    (A) 2:6:4

    (B) 2:6:1

    (C) 8:6:4

    (D) 8:24:1

    (E) 12:24:1

14. John walks at a pace of 90 feet per minute while Debbie walks at a rate of 65 feet per minute. In a two-hour period, how many more feet will John walk than Debbie?

(A) 1,500

(D) 9,000

(B) 3,000

(E) 15,000

(C) 6,000

15. If $25a^4 - 36b^{18} = 72$, then $4(5a^2 - 6b^9)(5a^2 + 6b^9) =$

(A) 288.

(D) 36.

(B) 126.

(E) 9.

(C) 72.

16. If angles $A + B + C + D = 500°$, what do angles $G + H + I = ?$

(A) 270°

(B) 320°

(C) 360°

(D) 400°

(E) 540°

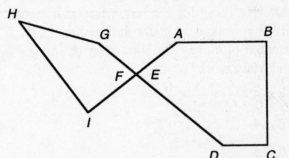

17. Change $4^5/_6$ to an improper fraction.

(A) $\dfrac{5}{24}$

(D) $\dfrac{30}{4}$

(B) $\dfrac{9}{6}$

(E) $\dfrac{120}{6}$

(C) $\dfrac{29}{6}$

18. The ratio of the angles of a triangle are x, $2x$, and $3x$. If one of the sides is m, the second is $m - n$, and the longest is $m + n$, what would be the value of n, expressed in terms of m?

(A) $2m$

(B) m

(C) $\dfrac{m}{2}$

(D) $\dfrac{m}{3}$

(E) $\dfrac{m}{4}$

19. If $AD \parallel CB$, $AD = CB$, $GM = {}^3/_4\ AD$, and $MY = {}^4/_5\ CE$, what is the ratio of the area of GMY to the area of $ABCD$?

(A) 7:8

(B) 5:8

(C) 1:2

(D) 3:5

(E) 3:10

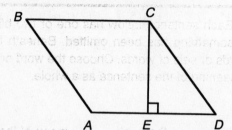
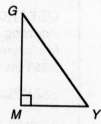

20. After working for g hours, Mary had earned \$75. On the same day, Rosina worked m hours and earned \$225. If they receive the same amount of money per hour of work and $g + m = 16$, how many hours did Mary work?

(A) 3

(B) 4

(C) 5

(D) 6

(E) 7

Section 3

TIME: 25 Minutes
26 Questions

For each question in this section, select the best answer from among the given choices and fill in the corresponding oval on the answer sheet.

DIRECTIONS: Each sentence below has one or two blanks, each blank indicating that something has been omitted. Beneath the sentence are five lettered words or sets of words. Choose the word or set of words that **BEST** fits the meaning of the sentence as a whole.

EXAMPLE:

Although the critics found the book _____, many of the readers found it rather _____.

(A) obnoxious . . . perfect

(B) spectacular . . . interesting

(C) boring . . . intriguing

(D) comical . . . persuasive

(E) popular . . . rare

(A) (B) ● (D) (E)

---

27. People who live in cities in high-rise buildings view country houses with cupolas and white picket fences as _____ and a throwback to another era.

    (A) aloof

    (B) capricious

    (C) redundant

    (D) ornate

    (E) quaint

28. They hated each other's friends. They liked different books and movies. She preferred outdoor sports; he enjoyed cooking and reading. They got a divorce because they were _____.

    (A) dispassionate

    (B) incompatible

    (C) arbitrary

    (D) meticulous

    (E) nostalgic

29. After many years of art school, Marcia could _____ an authentic painting from its copy.

(A) discern

(D) emulate

(B) condone

(E) rationalize

(C) laud

30. The hot summer sun and high humidity left the residents of the town feeling _____ and _____.

(A) unruly . . . urbane

(D) immune . . . articulate

(B) pallid . . . vulnerable

(E) depleted . . . contrite

(C) torpid . . . lethargic

31. Not wanting to miss the deadline for submission of his manuscript, the author hurried to _____ the conclusion of his last chapter.

(A) expand

(D) endorse

(B) execute

(E) extol

(C) exhaust

32. Some environmental groups are so _____ in their beliefs that they will face overwhelming forces to protect the environment.

(A) adamant

(D) fallacious

(B) deliberate

(E) pragmatic

(C) didactic

DIRECTIONS: Each question below consists of a related pair of words or phrases, followed by five lettered pairs of words or phrases. Select the lettered pair that best expresses a relationship similar to that expressed in the original pair.

EXAMPLE:

SMILE : MOUTH ::

(A) wink : eye

(D) tan : skin

(B) teeth : face

(E) food : gums

(C) voice : speech

● Ⓑ Ⓒ Ⓓ Ⓔ

33. DURABLE : PERMANENT ::

    (A) intelligent : persuasive   (D) rational : idea

    (B) innocent : difficult   (E) transient : changeable

    (C) tedious : dialogue

34. VEX : ANNOY ::

    (A) ignore : depress   (D) liberate : free

    (B) enjoy : please   (E) imitate : rescue

    (C) harass : entice

35. ANXIOUS : CAREFREE ::

    (A) error : fail   (D) sympathetic : hostile

    (B) design : plan   (E) alienate : enemies

    (C) believe : devotion

36. REBUTTAL : SPEECH ::

    (A) question : test   (D) tantrum : tears

    (B) apology : agreement   (E) lull : quiet

    (C) fight : provocation

37. EGOTISTIC : VAIN ::

    (A) compliant : colorful   (D) gentle : canny

    (B) gregarious : sociable   (E) deranged : witty

    (C) urbane : sincere

38. GLORIFY : DENIGRATE ::

    (A) burnish : statement   (D) revive : restore

    (B) approve : censure   (E) infer : guess

    (C) deviate : highway

39. ACQUIT : GUILT ::

   (A) divorce : marriage   (D) revise : manuscript

   (B) support : pain   (E) withdraw : worry

   (C) influence : cause

DIRECTIONS: Read the passage and answer the questions that follow. Each question will be based on the information stated or implied in the passage or its introduction.

Questions 40–43 are based on the following passage.

The following passage is excerpted from a book of the travels of Theodore F. Wolfe.

1   From the wilderness to the ocean the course of the lordly Hudson is replete with the enchantments of poetry, romance, and tradition. From the time of Juet's quaint narrative of its first exploration the river has been the scene of events which have been recounted in every form of literature,
5 while its legendary associations and its beauties of flood and shore have inspired many noble works of art. For the literary wayfarer the majestic stream has the added charm of intimate connection with the lives of gifted writers who have found homes as well as themes upon its banks, and have embalmed in their books its scenery and traditions.
10 Irving gave to it the devotion of a lifetime and, although the tales of Cooper invest its upper course with the glamour of romance, yet it is chiefly to the facile pen of Irving that the Hudson owes its opulence of poetical and sentimental associations; everywhere along the lower and middle reaches of the river—the portions traversed in this ramble—we
15 may find the impress of his genius and love.
    Opposite to the city of Irving's birth lies Hoboken, the sometime home of Bryant and Sands, which gave title to Fay's once popular romance, and a little way beyond is the spot, sung by the muse of Sands where, at the foot of the ledge by the riverside, the great writer of "The Federalist" fell
20 by the hand of Burr. Above this place tower the cliffs of the Weehawken...
    From the Manhattan shore at the foot of Eighty-third Street rises a rocky knoll where Poe often sat and looked upon the river's moving tides while he meditated his compositions; possibly "The Raven" was pondered here,
25 since there is some reason to believe it was written while the poet boarded with the Brennans in this neighborhood . . .
    Poe was once a cadet in the military school on the rock-bound promon-

tory of West Point in the heart of the Highlands, and upon the opposite
margin of the grand river-pass lies historic Constitution Island, long the
30 home of the sisters Warner. The picturesque island is largely composed of
steep and rude masses of rock, partially clothed by native trees, and it is
now connected with the eastern shore by reedy marshlands.

In Irving's early manhood Lindenwald was the country-seat of Judge
Van Ness—the author of "Aristides"—to whose ancestors Knickerbocker
35 avers we are indebted for the invention of buckwheat cakes. The judge,
who had been Burr's second in the fateful duel with Hamilton, was an
attached friend of Irving, and when he suffered the sorrow of his life in the
death of his fair fiancé, Matilda Hoffman, he was invited to retire for a
time to this spot, and during the months of his sojourn he sought forgetful-
40 ness of his grief in absorbing literary occupation. Here he revised and
complete the peerless "History of New York,"—in which he mentions his
host's family,—working upon it for some hours of each day in the same
chamber where Van Buren afterward died.

40. In line 9 the word "embalmed" means

   (A) decayed.

   (B) exaggerated, as in death.

   (C) written about in a boring, deadly manner.

   (D) perfumed, made fragrant, omitted the faults of.

   (E) preserved.

41. The writer's main objective in the writing of the passage is to

   (A) present a geographical description to the reader.

   (B) present both a geographical and a literary description of the area
   to the reader.

   (C) present both a geographical description and a historical description.

   (D) present a fictional narrative to the reader.

   (E) inform the reader of outstanding literary contributions.

42. The writer would attest that

   (A) the gift for writing comes from within.

(B) one can use an element of control to block out external elements and to be able to develop ideas for writing.

(C) Cooper was more influenced by the environment that other writers were influenced.

(D) Irving was more influenced by the environment that other writers were influenced.

(E) such a lovely site on the Hudson could not be the site of crime and violence.

43. The passage describes Constitution Island as

(A) far from the river's moving tides.

(B) beauties of flood and shore.

(C) in the heart of the Highlands.

(D) composed of rude masses of rock.

(E) opulent in poetical and sentimental associations.

DIRECTIONS: Read the passages and answer the questions that follow. Each question will be based on the information stated or implied in the selection or its introduction, and may be based on the relationship between the passages.

Questions 44–52 are based on the following passages.

The following passages, written at the turn of the century, present two views toward education. Passage 1 was written by Andrew Carnegie; Passage 2 was written by Alfred Fouillee.

Passage 1

1   We occasionally find traces even at this day of the old prejudice which existed against educating the masses of the people. I do not wonder that this should exist when I reflect upon what has hitherto passed for education. Men have wasted their precious years trying to extract education
5   from an ignorant past whose chief province is to teach us, not what to adopt, but what to avoid. Men have sent their sons to colleges to waste their energies upon obtaining a knowledge of such languages as Greek and Latin, which are of no more practical use to them than Choctaw. I have known few college graduates that knew Shakespeare or Milton. They
10 might be able to tell you all about Ulysses or Agamemnon or Hector, but

what are these compared to the characters that we find in our own classics? One service Robert Lowell has done, for which he should be
thanked—he has boldly said that in Shakespeare alone we have a greater
treasure than in all the classics of ancient time. They have been crammed
15 with the details of petty and insignificant skirmishes between savages, and
taught to exalt a band of ruffians into heroes; and we have called them
"educated." They have been "educated" as if they were destined for life
upon some other planet than this. They have in no sense received instruction. On the contrary, what they have obtained has served to imbue them
20 with false ideas and to give them a distaste for practical life. I do not
wonder that a prejudice has arisen and still exists against such education.
In my own experience I can say that I have known few young men intended for business who were not injured by a collegiate education. Had
they gone into active work during the years spent at college they would
25 have been better educated men in every true sense of that term. The fire
and energy have been stamped out of them, and how to so manage as to
live a life of idleness and not a life of usefulness has become the chief
question with them. But a new idea of education is now upon us.

We have begun to realize that a knowledge of chemistry, for instance, is
30 worth a knowledge of all the dead languages that ever were spoken upon
the earth; a knowledge of mechanics more useful than all the classical
learning that can be crammed into young men at college.

Passage 2

Is ignorance of Latin and the substitution of German and English exercises a sufficient guarantee of preparation for commerce, of the acquisition
35 of the genius of commerce and agriculture? "Oh! but we shall include
book-keeping in the program." What! is the unity of secondary instruction
to be sacrificed to book-keeping? Is your so-called general culture to be
subordinated to the requirements of an office or of a bank? If you are in
such a hurry to teach your children book-keeping—which can be learned
40 in a few weeks—let them have special lessons in keeping accounts or let
them have a complementary course at the lyceeum. Let us look a little
closer at the program at our present special instruction, which has a better
claim than "modern humanities" as a preparation for industrial, commercial, and agricultural life, and let us see in what it prepares for it. Classical
45 instruction contains all that is comprised in special instruction....As for
the programs of French instruction put forward, there is nearly as great a
medley of the different subjects as in the present classical programs. With
the exception of a few differences in detail in the proportion of the different sciences, the science subjects appear in the same order as in the classi-
50 cal course. The only essential difference is the substitution of a second

modern language for Latin. So we are saved by adding Goethe's "Faust" to Shakespeare's "Hamlet," instead of the "Aeneid"! And for this magnificent result secondary education is to be turned upside down, classical training to be disorganized, and to be asphyxiated by a rarefication of its
55 environment. Instead of all learning Latin and one modern language chosen by themselves, our children will learn a fundamental modern language and a complementary modern language.

What essential diversity of aptitudes will be thus satisfied [by the new program]? What minds are unsuited to Latin and English and suited to
60 German and English? I repeat that the whole system of modern humanities is a mass of contradictions—it is a general, special, a disinterested utilitarian system of instruction.

44. The main idea of Passage 1 is

   (A) to promote a classical education.

   (B) to promote the prejudice against educating the masses.

   (C) to renounce a study of mythology.

   (D) to suggest active work for young men, not a collegiate education.

   (E) to espouse the values of liberal arts.

45. The author of Passage 1 describes the college graduates of today as

   (A) having received valuable instruction.

   (B) having been bettered by collegiate life.

   (C) educated for life in our world.

   (D) ignorant of Shakespeare.

   (E) filled with fire and energy.

46. The main purpose of Passage 2 is to

   (A) renounce the modern humanities.

   (B) present the modern humanities as important general culture.

   (C) ridicule the traditional courses of study.

   (D) advocate the so-called "special education."

   (E) recommend the total reorganization of secondary education.

47. When the writer of Passage 2 states that "we are saved by adding Goethe's 'Faust' to Shakespeare's 'Hamlet,' instead of the 'Aeneid' " (lines 51-52), he is

    (A) using alliteration.

    (B) using a simile.

    (C) employing a tongue-in-cheek attitude.

    (D) using a stylistic device called denotation.

    (E) using an understatement.

48. The best meaning of being "asphyxiated by a rarefication of its environment" (lines 54-55) is

    (A) killed by purification.

    (B) destroying learning through vocational education.

    (C) a reference to Greek mythology where the cure killed.

    (D) being smothered by important concepts.

    (E) being choked with the amount of material to be learned.

49. The main point made by the writer of Passage 2 about "practical" courses like bookkeeping is

    (A) subordinate general culture to bookkeeping, a useful course of study.

    (B) that they should be provided by the schools and not at special lessons.

    (C) they are within the scope of the public schools and not the responsibility of the lyceeum.

    (D) that they can be taught at special classes; they are not to be a part of the school curriculum.

    (E) that they should be substituted for "dead" courses like Latin.

50. The writer of Passage 1, when questioned about classical education,

    (A) would criticize those who say negative things about classical education.

    (B) would show the recent research to back up his beliefs.

(C) would point out its inadequacies.

(D) would point out the quality of the structure which has survived for a long period of time.

(E) would show the humility of those who would dispense with the classics.

51. The writer's question as to which minds are insulted by Latin and English

(A) brings out the mistakes made in the past.

(B) indicates why the secondary education program had to be changed.

(C) shows what should be as opposed to what is.

(D) highlights the distinction between the ideal and what was.

(E) criticizes those who seek to change the curriculum.

52. The writer of Passage 2 would agree that modern humanities

(A) should not be employed by secondary education.

(B) includes important classical components, like Latin.

(C) prepares students for industrial, commercial, and agricultural life.

(D) has a superior science component which is evident when compared with the classical course of study.

(E) invokes past errors in order to advocate present improvements.

Section 4

TIME: 25 Minutes
         20 Questions

DIRECTIONS: Solve each problem, using any available space on the page for scratch work. Then decide which answer choice is the best and fill in the corresponding oval on the answer sheet.

NOTES:

(1) The use of a calculator is permitted. All numbers used are real numbers.

(2) Figures that accompany problems in this test are intended to provide information useful in solving the problems. They are drawn as accurately as possible EXCEPT when it is stated in a specific problem that the figure is not drawn to scale. All figures lie in a plane unless otherwise indicated.

REFERENCE INFORMATION:

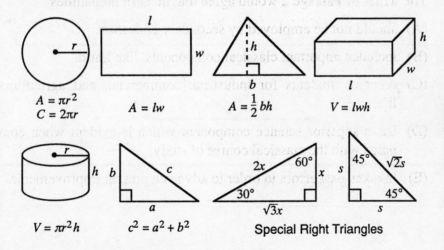

$A = \pi r^2$
$C = 2\pi r$

$A = lw$

$A = \frac{1}{2}bh$

$V = lwh$

$V = \pi r^2 h$

$c^2 = a^2 + b^2$

Special Right Triangles

The number of degrees of arc in a circle is 360.
The measure in degrees of a straight angle is 180.
The sum of the measures in degrees of the angles of a triangle is 180.

QUESTIONS 26–40 each consist of two quantities, one in Column A and one in Column B. You are to compare the two quantities and on the answer sheet blacken space

(A) if the quantity in Column A is greater;

(B) if the quantity in Column B is greater;

(C) if the two quantities are equal;

(D) if the relationship cannot be determined from the information given.

NOTES:

(1) In certain questions, information concerning one or both of the quantities to be compared is centered above the two columns.

(2) In a given question, a symbol that appears in both columns represents the same thing in Column A as it does in Column B.

(3) Letters such as x, n, and k stand for real numbers.

EXAMPLES:

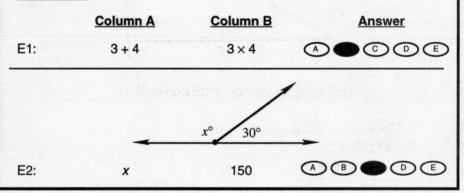

	Column A	**Column B**	**Answer**
E1:	$3 + 4$	3×4	Ⓐ ⬤ Ⓒ Ⓓ Ⓔ
E2:	x	150	Ⓐ Ⓑ ⬤ Ⓓ Ⓔ

Column A	**Column B**

$$x^2 - 4x - 7 = 0$$

	Column A	Column B
21.	$x^2 - 4x$	7

The volume of a cube is 27.

	Column A	Column B
22.	Total surface area of the cube	50

Column A	Column B

$$y = \sqrt{9} + \sqrt{16} - \sqrt{49}$$

23.	y	1

$$.2B + .8B = 1$$

24.	B	10

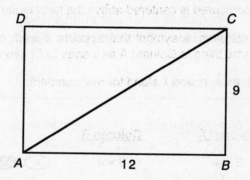

ABCD is a rectangle with diagonal *AC*.

25.	The ratio of the diagonal of the rectangle to its perimeter	$\dfrac{1}{2}$

$$8x = \frac{1}{3}$$

26.	$\dfrac{12x}{5}$	$\dfrac{1}{9}$

A fence post is placed every 12 feet in a straight line.

27.	The number of fence posts required to cover 144 feet in a straight line	12

Column A	Column B

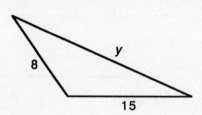

28. y 6

---

1 person in 1 day can build 1 desk.
2 people in 2 days can build x desks.

29. x 2

$N =$ the numerical difference between
$(5 \times 6 + 2)$ and $(5 + 6 \times 2)$.

30. 16 .... N

$$36, 18, 9, 4\frac{1}{2}, y$$

31. y .... $2\frac{1}{2}$

$$\frac{-1}{A} = 1$$

32. $-A$ .... A^2

DIRECTIONS: Questions 33–40 require you to solve the problem and enter your answer in the ovals in the special grid:

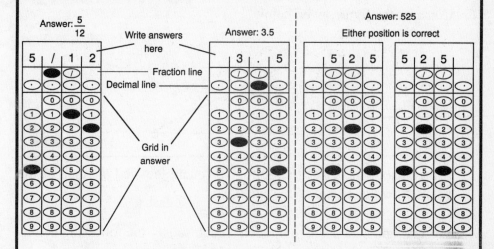

Answer: $\frac{5}{12}$

Write answers here

Fraction line

Decimal line

Grid in answer

Answer: 3.5

Answer: 525

Either position is correct

- You may begin filling in your answer in any column, space permitting. Columns not needed should be left blank.

- Answers may be entered in either decimal or fraction form. For example, $^3/_{12}$ or .25 are equally acceptable.

- A mixed number, such as $4^1/_2$, must be entered either as 4.5 or $^9/_2$. If you entered 41/2, the machine would interpret your answer as $^{41}/_2$, not $4^1/_2$.

- There may be some instances where there is more than one correct answer to a problem. Should this be the case, grid only one answer.

- Be very careful when filling in ovals. Do not fill in more than one oval in any column, and make sure to completely darken the ovals.

- It is suggested that you fill in your answer in the boxes above each column. Although you will not be graded incorrectly if you do not write in your answer, it will help you fill in the corresponding ovals.

- If your answer is a decimal, grid the most accurate value possible. For example, if you need to grid a repeating decimal such as $0.66\overline{6}$, enter the answer as .666 or .667. A less accurate value, such as .66 or .67, is not acceptable.

33. If $4^{n+4} = 64$, what is the value of 5^n?

34. Three numbers x, y, and z form a "triple" if $x + y + z = 1$. If A, B, and C form a triple where a) $C = 1$ and b) $3A + 2B + 2C = 5$, find $2A + B$.

35. Find a prime number less than 40 which is of the form $3K + 1$ and $5K + 2$, where $0 \leq k < 13$.

36. Consider the figure given below.

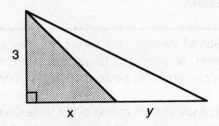

If the area of the shaded region is 15 square feet and the area of the whole figure is 27 square feet, find y.

37. Let x, y, and z be positive integers which satisfy the following conditions:

    a) $x < 10$

    b) $6y < 3x$

    c) $z < y$

    d) $z > 1$

Find a possible value for z which satisfies these conditions.

38. Consider the system of linear equations given below.

$$3x - y = 2$$
$$4x + y = 5$$

Find y.

39. Let $xyz = 24$ where x, y, and z are positive integers greater than or equal to 2. If x is a perfect square find a possible value for z.

40. Consider the triangle inset in the square below.

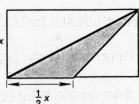

If $x = 2^3$ ft, find the area of the triangle.

Section 5

TIME: 30 Minutes
39 Questions

DIRECTIONS: Each of the following sentences may contain an error in diction, usage, idiom, or grammar. Some sentences are correct. Some sentences contain one error. No sentence contains more than one error.

If there is an error, it will appear in one of the underlined portions labeled A, B, C, or D. If there is no error, choose the portion labeled E. If there is an error, select the letter of the portion that must be changed in order to correct the sentence.

EXAMPLE:

He drove <u>slowly</u> and <u>cautiously</u> in order to <u>hopefully</u> avoid having an
      A   **B**   **C**

<u>accident</u>. <u>No error</u>.
  D   **E**

---

1. In 1877 Chief Joseph of the Nez Perces, <u>together with</u> 250 warriors
                                        A

    and 500 women and children, <u>were praised</u> by newspaper reporters
                                B

    for <u>bravery</u> during the 115-day fight <u>for</u> freedom. <u>No error</u>.
        C   **D**   **E**

2. The ideals <u>upon which</u> American society <u>is based</u> <u>are</u> primarily those
              A   **B**   **C**

    of Europe and not ones <u>derived from</u> the native Indian culture.
                           D

    <u>No error</u>.
      E

3. <u>An astute and powerful</u> woman, Frances Nadel <u>was</u> a beauty contest
           A   **B**

    winner before she <u>became</u> president of the company <u>upon the death</u>
                        C   **D**

    of her husband. <u>No error</u>.
                 E

4. Representative Wilson <u>pointed out</u>, however, that the legislature
                              A

   <u>had not finalized</u> the state budget and salary increases <u>had depended</u>
         B   **C**

   on decisions <u>to be made</u> in a special session. <u>No error</u>.
                     D   **E**

5. Now the <u>city</u> librarian, doing more than checking out books, must
              A

   help <u>to plan</u> puppet shows and movies for children, garage sales for
          B

   <u>used</u> books, and <u>arranging for</u> guest lecturers and exhibits for adults.
     C   **D**

   <u>No error</u>.
     E

6. In order <u>to completely understand</u> the psychological <u>effects</u> of the
                A   **B**

   Bubonic plague, <u>one must</u> realize that one-fourth to one-third of the
                       C

   population in an <u>affected</u> area died. <u>No error</u>.
                       D   **E**

7. Rural roads, <u>known</u> in the United States as farm to market roads,
                  A

   have always been a vital <u>link in</u> the economy of <u>more advanced</u>
                               B   **C**

   nations because transportation of goods to markets <u>is</u> essential.
                                                         D

   <u>No error</u>.
     E

8. <u>Many a</u> graduate <u>wishes</u> to return to college and <u>abide in</u> the pro-
     A   **B**   **C**

   tected environment of a university, particularly if <u>someone else</u> pays
                                                           D

   the bills. <u>No error</u>.
                E

9. <u>Confronted with</u> a choice of either <u>cleaning up</u> his room or <u>cleaning</u>
        A   **B**   **C**

    <u>out</u> the garage, the teenager became very <u>aggravated</u> with his parents.
                                                D

    <u>No error</u>.
      E

10. My brother and <u>I</u> dressed as <u>quickly</u> as we could, but we missed the
                   A   **B**

    school bus, <u>which</u> made <u>us</u> late for class today. <u>No error</u>.
            C   **D**   **E**

11. <u>Among</u> the activities <u>offered at</u> the local high school <u>through</u> the
      A   **B**   **C**

    community education program <u>are</u> singing in the couples' chorus,
                            D

    ballroom dancing, and Chinese cooking. <u>No error</u>.
                                 E

12. If you are <u>disappointed by</u> an <u>inexpensive</u> bicycle, then an option you
                A   **B**

    might consider is to work this summer and <u>save</u> your money for a
                                   C

    <u>more expensive</u> model. <u>No error</u>.
      D   **E**

13. Also being presented to the city council this morning <u>is</u> the mayor's
                                              A

    city budget for next year and plans <u>to renovate</u> the <u>existing</u> music
                                      B   **C**

    theater, so the session <u>will focus</u> on financial matters. <u>No error</u>.
                      D   **E**

14. Even a movement <u>so delicate</u> as a <u>fly's walking</u> triggers the Venus
                    A   **B**

    flytrap <u>to grow</u> extra cells on the outside of <u>its</u> hinge, immediately
           C   **D**

    closing the petals of the trap. <u>No error</u>.
                               E

15. Although <u>outwardly</u> Thomas Hardy seemed quite <u>the picture</u> of
          A   **B**

    <u>respectability</u> and contentment, his works, especially the prose,
    C

    <u>deals with</u> the theme of humans' inevitable suffering. <u>No error</u>.
    D   **E**

16. Though <u>unequal in</u> social standing, the everyday lives of ancient
         A

    Egyptian kings and commoners <u>alike</u> are visible in the pictures of
                              B   **C**

    <u>them</u> found <u>inside of</u> tombs and temples. <u>No error</u>.
    D   **D**   **E**

17. Sometimes considered <u>unsafe for</u> crops, land around river <u>deltas</u>
                      A   **B**

    <u>can be</u> excellent land for farming because periodic flooding deposits
    C

    silt rich <u>in</u> nutrients. <u>No error</u>.
          D   **E**

18. For years <u>people</u> concerned with the environment <u>have compiled</u> in-
          A   **B**

    formation which <u>show</u> many species are extinct and others <u>are either</u>
                   C   **D**

    endangered or bordering on becoming endangered. <u>No error</u>.
                                          E

19. Little is known about Shakespeare's boyhood or his early career as an

    actor and playwright, but he <u>appears to have been</u> a financial success
                                    A

    <u>because he bought</u> many properties, including <u>one of the finest</u> homes
          B   **C**

    in Stratford, the town he <u>was born in</u>. <u>No error</u>.
                        D   **E**

DIRECTIONS: In each of the following sentences, some portion of the sentence is underlined. Under each sentence are five choices. The first choice has the same wording as the original. The other four choices are reworded. Sometimes the first choice containing the original wording is the best; sometimes one of the other choices is the best. Choose the letter of the best choice. Your choice should produce a sentence which is not ambiguous or awkward and which is correct, clear, and precise.

This is a test of correct and effective English expression. Keep in mind the standards of English usage, punctuation, grammar, word choice, and construction.

EXAMPLE:

When you listen to opera, <u>a person may not appreciate it.</u>

(A) a person may not appreciate it.

(B) it may not be appreciated by a person.

(C) which may not be appreciated by one.

(D) you may not appreciate it.

(E) appreciating it may be a problem for you.

20. <u>Being that you bring home more money than I do</u>, it is only fitting you should pay proportionately more rent.

(A) Being that you bring home more money than I do

(B) Bringing home the more money of the two of us

(C) When more money is made by you than by me

(D) Because you bring home more money than I do

(E) If your bringing home more money than me

21. So tenacious is their grip on life, that sponge cells will regroup and form a new sponge even <u>when they are squeezed</u> through silk.

(A) when they are squeezed

(B) since they have been

(C) as they will be

(D) after they have been

(E) because they should be

22. <u>Seeing as how the plane is late</u>, wouldn't you prefer to wait for a while on the observation deck?

   (A) Seeing as how the plane is late

   (B) When the plane comes in

   (C) Since the plane is late

   (D) Being as the plane is late

   (E) While the plane is landing

23. Only with careful environmental planning can we protect the <u>world we live in</u>.

   (A) world we live in

   (B) world in which we live in

   (C) living in this world

   (D) world's living

   (E) world in which we live

24. In the last three years we have added more varieties of vegetables to our garden <u>than those you suggested in the beginning</u>.

   (A) than those you suggested in the beginning

   (B) than the ones we began with

   (C) beginning with your suggestion

   (D) than what you suggested to us

   (E) which you suggested in the beginning

25. As you know, I am not easily fooled by flattery, and while <u>nice words please you,</u> they don't get the job done.

   (A) nice words please you

   (B) nice words are pleasing

   (C) nice words please a person

(D) flattering words please people

(E) flattering words are pleasing to some

26. Some pieces of the puzzle, in spite of Jane's search, <u>are still missing and probably will never be found</u>.

(A) are still missing and probably will never be found

(B) is missing still but never found probably

(C) probably will be missing and never found

(D) are still probably missing and to never be found

(E) probably are missing and will not be found

27. Women live longer and have fewer illnesses than men, <u>which proves that women are the strongest sex</u>.

(A) which proves that women are the strongest sex.

(B) which proves that women are the stronger sex.

(C) facts which prove that women are the stronger sex.

(D) proving that women are the strongest sex.

(E) a proof that women are the stronger sex.

28. Eighteenth century architecture, with its columns and balanced lines, <u>was characteristic of those of previous times in Greece and Rome</u>.

(A) was characteristic of those of previous times in Greece and Rome

(B) is similar to characteristics of Greece and Rome

(C) is similar to Greek and Roman building styles

(D) is characteristic with earlier Greek and Roman architecture

(E) was similar to architecture of Greece and Rome

29. Plato, one of the famous Greek philosophers, won many wrestling prizes when he was a young man, thus <u>exemplifying the Greek ideal of balance between the necessity for physical activity and using one's mind</u>.

(A) exemplifying the Greek ideal of balance between the necessity for physical activity and using one's mind

(B) serving as an example of the Greek ideal of balance between physical and mental activities

(C) an example of balancing Greek mental and athletic games

(D) this as an example of the Greek's balance between mental physical pursuits

(E) shown to be exemplifying the balancing of two aspects of Greek life, the physical and the mental

30. Allied control of the Philippine Islands during World War II proved to be <u>another obstacle as the Japanese scattered resistance</u> until the end of the war.

(A) another obstacle as the Japanese scattered resistance

(B) difficult because of the Japanese giving resistance

(C) continuing scattered Japanese resistance as obstacles

(D) as another scattered obstacle due to Japanese resistance

(E) difficult because the Japanese gave scattered resistance

31. Flooding abated and the river waters receded as the <u>rainfall finally let up</u>.

(A) rainfall finally let up

(B) rain having let up

(C) letting up of the rainfall

(D) rainfall, when it finally let up

(E) raining finally letting up

32. Unless China slows its population growth to zero, that country <u>would still have</u> a problem feeding its people.

(A) would still have

(B) will have still had

(C) might have had still

(D) will still have

(E) would have still

33. In *The Music Man* Robert Preston portrays a fast-talking salesman who comes to a small town in Iowa <u>inadvertently falling in love with</u> the librarian.

(A) inadvertently falling in love with

(B) and inadvertently falls in love with

(C) afterwards he inadvertently falls in love with

(D) after falling inadvertently in love with

(E) when he inadvertently falls in love with

DIRECTIONS: The following passages are considered early draft efforts of a student. Some sentences need to be rewritten to make the ideas clearer and more precise.

Read each passage carefully and answer the questions that follow. Some of the questions are about particular sentences or parts of sentences and ask you to make decisions about sentence structure, diction, and usage. Some of the questions refer to the entire essay or parts of the essay and ask you to make decisions about organization, development, appropriateness of language, audience, and logic. Choose the answer that most effectively makes the intended meaning clear and follows the requirements of standard written English. After you have chosen your answer, fill in the corresponding oval on your answer sheet.

EXAMPLE:

(1) On the one hand, I think television is bad, But it also does some good things for all of us. (2) For instance, my little sister thought she wanted to be a policemen until she saw police shows on television.

Which of the following is the best revision of the underlined portion of sentence 1 below?

On the one hand, I think television <u>is bad, But it also</u> does some good thing for all of us.

(A) is bad; But it also

(B) is bad. but is also

(C) is bad, and it also

(D) is bad, but it also

(E) is bad because it also

Questions 34–39 are based on the following passage.

(1) In 1840 Dickens came up with the idea of using a raven as a character in his new novel, *Barnaby Rudge*. (2) Soon, the word got out among his friends and neighbors that the famous author was interested in ravens and wanted to know more about them. (3) When someone gave a raven as a pet, he was delighted. (4) The raven was named Grip by Dickens' children and became a successful member of the family. (5) Grip began to get his way around the household, and if he wanted something, he took it, and Grip would bite the children's ankles when he felt displeased. (6) The

raven in *Barnaby Rudge* is depicted as a trickster who slept "on horseback" in the stable and "has been known, by the mere superiority of his genius, to walk off unmolested with the dog's dinner." (7) So we get an idea of what life with Grip was like.

(8) Poe, however, was dissatisfied. (9) This was a comical presentation of the raven. (10) Poe felt that the large black bird should have a more prophetic use. (10) So, about a year after *Barnaby Rudge* was published, Poe began work on his poem, "The Raven." (11) Any schoolchild can quote the famous line, "Quoth the Raven, 'Nevermore,'" but almost no one knows about Grip. (12) What happened to Grip? (13) Well, when he died, the Dickens family had become so attached to him that they had him stuffed and displayed him in the parlor.

34. Which of the following is the best revision of the underlined portion of sentence 3 below?

    When <u>someone gave a raven as a pet, he was delighted</u>.

    (A) giving someone a raven as a pet, he was delighted.

    (B) someone gave Dickens a raven for a pet, the author was delighted.

    (C) someone delightedly gave a raven for a pet to Dickens.

    (D) someone gave Dickens a raven as a pet, the result was that the author was delighted with the gift.

    (E) receiving a raven as a pet, Dickens was delighted.

35. Which of the following is the best revision of the underlined portion of sentence 5 below?

    Grip began to get his way around the household, and <u>if he wanted something, he took it, and Grip would bite the children's ankles when he felt displeased</u>.

    (A) if he wanted something, he took it; if he felt displeased, he bit the children's ankles.

    (B) if wanting something, he would take, and if unhappy, he would bite.

    (C) when he wanted something, he would take it; being displeased, he would bite the children's ankles.

    (D) when taking something that he wanted, he would bite the children's ankles.

(E) if displeased and if wanting something, Grip would bite the children's ankles and he would take it.

36. In the context of the sentences preceding and following sentence 7, which of the following is the best revision of sentence 7?

    (A) So, you can get an idea of what life with Grip was like.

    (B) Therefore, the challenges of living with Grip must have been numerous and varied.

    (C) So, an idea of the life with Grip can be gotten.

    (D) So, life with Grip must have been entertaining.

    (E) These are some examples I have given of what life with Grip was like.

37. Which of the following is the best way to combine sentences 8, 9, and 10?

    (A) Having dissatisfaction with the comical presentation of the big black bird, Poe felt it should be more prophetic.

    (B) As a result of dissatisfaction, Poe felt the big black bird should be presented more prophetically than comically.

    (C) However, Poe felt the comical presentation was not as good as the prophetic one.

    (D) Poe, however, dissatisfied with the comical presentation of the big black bird, felt a more prophetic use would be better.

    (E) Poe, however, was dissatisfied with this comical presentation and felt that the large black bird should have a more prophetic use.

38. In relation to the passage as a whole, which of the following best describes the writer's intention in the first paragraph?

    (A) To provide background information

    (B) To provide a concrete example of a humorous episode

    (C) To arouse sympathy in the reader

    (D) To evaluate the effectiveness of the treatment of the subject

    (E) To contrast with treatment of the subject in the second paragraph

39. Which of the following is the best revision of the underlined portion of sentence 4 below?

    The raven was named Grip <u>by Dickens' children and became a successful member of the family</u>.

    (A) by the children and it became a successful member of his family.

    (B) by Dickens' children and was becoming a successful member of his family.

    (C) by Dickens' children and became a successful member of the family.

    (D) , Dickens' children named him that, and he became a successful member of the family.

    (E) by Dickens' children and the raven also became a successful member of his family.

TEST 1

ANSWER KEY

Section 1—Verbal

1.	(A)	9.	(D)	17.	(D)	25.	(E)
2.	(B)	10.	(C)	18.	(A)	26.	(D)
3.	(B)	11.	(B)	19.	(E)		
4.	(D)	12.	(D)	20.	(E)		
5.	(B)	13.	(D)	21.	(D)		
6.	(A)	14.	(E)	22.	(D)		
7.	(E)	15.	(E)	23.	(D)		
8.	(A)	16.	(E)	24.	(B)		

Section 2—Math

1.	(E)	8.	(A)	15.	(A)
2.	(D)	9.	(A)	16.	(B)
3.	(E)	10.	(D)	17.	(C)
4.	(D)	11.	(A)	18.	(E)
5.	(C)	12.	(E)	19.	(E)
6.	(D)	13.	(D)	20.	(B)
7.	(E)	14.	(B)		

Section 3—Verbal

27.	(E)	35.	(D)	43.	(D)	51.	(E)
28.	(B)	36.	(C)	44.	(D)	52.	(A)
29.	(A)	37.	(B)	45.	(D)		
30.	(C)	38.	(B)	46.	(A)		
31.	(B)	39.	(A)	47.	(C)		
32.	(A)	40.	(E)	48.	(A)		
33.	(E)	41.	(B)	49.	(D)		
34.	(D)	42.	(D)	50.	(C)		

Section 4—Math

21.	(C)	28.	(A)	35.	7 or 37
22.	(A)	29.	(A)	36.	8
23.	(B)	30.	(A)	37.	2 or 3
24.	(B)	31.	(B)	38.	1
25.	(B)	32.	(C)	39.	2 or 3
26.	(B)	33.	1/5 or .2	40.	16
27.	(A)	34.	3		

Section 5—Writing Skills

1.	(B)	11.	(E)	21.	(D)	31.	(A)
2.	(E)	12.	(A)	22.	(C)	32.	(D)
3.	(B)	13.	(A)	23.	(E)	33.	(B)
4.	(C)	14.	(A)	24.	(A)	34.	(B)
5.	(D)	15.	(D)	25.	(B)	35.	(A)
6.	(A)	16.	(D)	26.	(A)	36.	(D)
7.	(C)	17.	(E)	27.	(C)	37.	(E)
8.	(E)	18.	(C)	28.	(E)	38.	(A)
9.	(D)	19.	(D)	29.	(B)	39.	(C)
10.	(C)	20.	(D)	30.	(E)		

DETAILED EXPLANATIONS OF ANSWERS

Section 1 — Verbal

1. **(A)** The correct answer is (A) because the word "frustrated" indicates that some sort of problem was faced by the scientist. Because of this problem, the scientist had to do something that he or she wouldn't normally do: end or "terminate" the experiment. Choice (B) "dangers" is possible, but under few circumstances would an experiment be "extended" because of the dangers; nor, would a scientist "reluctantly" end a dangerous situation. Choice (C) is not correct because a scientist would not be frustrated by "successes." Choice (D) makes no sense semantically. Choice (E) is not correct because, although the scientist might be frustrated by many "liabilities" or limitations of the experiment, he would enthusiastically, not "reluctantly," want to "study" where he went wrong.

2. **(B)** Although some knowledge of history might be helpful in answering this question, it was the "serfs" who toiled in "endless" jobs. Therefore the correct answer is (B). The "nobles" (A) might have had a more "enjoyable" existence, but they did not do so by working the land. The "monks" (C), while praying for "everlasting" salvation, did not work the land either. "Merchants" (D) and "knights" (E) did not work the land. Nor did nobles, monks, merchants, or knights comprise the majority of the population. Serfs were more numerous.

3. **(B)** There are two clues in this sentence: "monotonous" and "hour-long" describing the "speech." Anyone who has sat through a monotonous, long speech would know that this situation would be never-ending or "interminable," and that you would be "impatient" for it to end. Therefore, choice (B) is the correct answer. Choice (A) is not correct because a monotone delivery would not be "exciting." Although an hour-long speech might be "unbelievable" (C), the audience would not be "skeptical" or disbelieving while waiting for the conclusion. An hour-long speech is "long" (D), and although the audience might be "doubtful" if it would ever end, this is not the best choice. An hour-long speech delivered in a monotone is undoubtedly "uninteresting" (E), but surely the audience would not be excited about the ending, just excited that it ended at all.

612

4.   **(D)**   The key words here are "even though," which will indicate that a contradiction is being set up. Therefore, the verses would not be those that would "receive great acclaim." Choice (D) "inane" (silly, absurd) is the best answer. Absurd verses would not normally receive great acclaim. Choice (A) "grand" and choice (B) "impressive" are wrong for the same reasons. Verses which were grand or impressive would be worthy of acclaim, and if these answers were chosen, it means that "even though" was not acknowledged properly by the test taker. Choice (C) "musical" is an adjective that describes the verses in a neutral way. We are looking for an adjective that is negative to show why the verses did not deserve "great acclaim." Choice (E) "unlikely" is a possibility, but not the best choice. "Unlikely" (improbable) is a negative way to describe a poem, but is not as strong or as satisfactory as "inane."

5.   **(B)**   The context of the sentence implies that the actor was rejected for parts because "no one could be sure how he would behave." The best answer is (B) "mercurial" (unpredictably changeable). (A) "confident" (self-assured) is an incorrect choice because it doesn't address the sense of change and wide mood swings that would cause the problems for directors. (C) is incorrect because "pessimistic" (an inclination to take the worst possible view) is an inappropriate choice for the context of the sentence. (D) "overpowering" (overcome by superior force) has no contextual meaning for the sentence. (E) "Inhibited" (restrained in expression or functioning), although a possible answer, is not appropriate to the sentence context of "no one could be sure how he would behave." An inhibited person does not necessarily exhibit change of temperament.

6.   **(A)**   The key word here is "marathon," which indicates that we are looking for a word that connotes a task requiring fortitude. The best answer would be "Herculean" (of extraordinary power). "Leg cramps" indicate that the second word means that the runner has problems. "Debilitate" (impair the health or strength of) would be the best choice because the cramps interfere with the runner's ability to participate in the marathon. This interference (the debilitation of leg cramps) would make running the marathon more difficult than normal (a Herculean task). (B) "hard" is a possibility, but not the best choice because it only connotes moderate difficulty as compared to "Herculean." In addition, "impel" (to urge or drive forward) is an incorrect choice because it means the opposite of what the sentence implies. (C) "frustrating" is a possibility, but "spur" (urge forward, incite) is contrary to the meaning of the sentence. (D) "invigorating" (give life and energy) and (E) "thrilling" are incorrect choices because both imply that leg cramps are a positive experience for the runner.

7.   **(E)**   Choice (E) "curtail" (limit) and "penetrate" (to enter into, permeate) is the best choice. When substituted into the sentence, this combination of words makes the most sense. Scientists warn us that unless we "limit" the poisons in the air, global warming could happen as the sun's rays "enter into" the atmosphere. Choice (A) is incorrect because scientists would not want to "collect" the poisons. This would not prevent "global warming." Choice (B) is wrong because although "weaken" is a possibility, "combine" is incorrect. "Combining" the poisons would not prevent global warming. (C) "restrict" (limit) is a possibility, however, "expedite" (carry out promptly) is wrong because the word makes no sense when inserted into the sentence. (D) "aggravate"makes no sense in the context of this sentence.

8.   **(A)**   The relationship between the given words can be stated as a SPY engages in ESPIONAGE (the practice of spying). The best answer is (A) because a TRAITOR engages in TREACHERY. Choice (B) is incorrect because stating that a NOVELIST engages in BOOKS is awkward. A BANKER does not engage in MONEY (C) and HONESTY and THIEF (D) does not fit the form of noun to noun. A CAPTAIN does not engage in NAVIGATION (E).

9.   **(D)**   The relationship between WATER and LIQUID can be phrased as one of a unit within a larger category. (D) best fits into this relationship because BRASS is a unit within the category of METAL. (A) is incorrect because this does not fit the format of unit and category. (B) is wrong because a BALLOON is filled with GAS. FLOWERS make up a BOUQUET but in order to fit the format, FLOWERS should be singular. (E) is also incorrect because ATOM is a type of BOMB.

10.   **(C)**   FRAGRANT refers to something that has a pleasant SMELL. The best answer would then be (C) because SAVORY refers to a pleasant TASTE. A SHRILL does not indicate a pleasant type of MUSIC (A). If something is AUDIBLE, it can be heard but it is not a pleasant SOUND (B). (D) is incorrect because SHADOW is created by LIGHT. (E) is also not correct because a FINGER is used to TOUCH.

11.   **(B)**   The relationship between the two words can best be described as a type of person and what they do; an IMPOSTER is one who DECEIVES. (B) is the correct response because a GLUTTON is one who OVERINDULGES. An IDEALIST may have certain VALUES (A) but this says nothing about what an idealist does. A HYPOCHONDRIAC has

imagined ILLNESS (C). REMORSE does not apply to a FELON (D) and is not necessarily a fitting description. An EXORCIST does not necessarily PRAY in their duties (E).

12. **(D)**   DISPERSE and CROWD can be best described as antonyms. (D) is the best choice because SCATTER is the opposite of CONVENE. (A) is incorrect because DIG is not the opposite of PILE. STUDY is not an antonym for GENIUS (B). FERTILIZE and GARDEN (C) are not opposites. NEWS is BROADCAST over the airwaves. The words are certainly related and not opposites (E).

13. **(D)**   A REFORMER tries to make IMPROVEMENT in the world or in other people's lives. The best choice is (D). A PACIFIST tries to make HARMONY in the world or in other people's lives. Choice (A) is wrong because a PATHOLOGIST tries to make DISEASE in the world or in other people's lives makes no sense. A PATHOLOGIST studies DISEASE. Choice (B) is incorrect because a TEACHER tries to make TEXTBOOK in the world or in other people's lives makes no sense. Choice (C) is not correct because a SALESPERSON tries to make COMMISSION in the world or in other people's lives makes no sense. Choice (E) is wrong because a MESSENGER does not try to make DECEPTION.

14. **(E)**   The author describes the Irish Parliament all through the 1700s as being corrupt in many respects. (E) is the best answer. Choice (A) cannot be chosen since the 1700s and the eighteenth century are the same time periods. The Parliament was not contrived for the benefit of the Catholic clergy; in fact, the Parliament worked against the Catholics, according to the author. (B) is not an appropriate answer. The passage implies corruption in both the Upper and the Lower Houses; (C) is an incorrect choice. The author in no way implies that the Irish Parliament was a model of decency; (D) should not be selected.

15. **(E)**   The main idea of the passage is to (E) raise the sham of the Irish Parliament from the dark waters of the past. The author in no way is trying to point out a truly distinct and admirable system of government. (A) should not be chosen. The author has little respect for the way that the Irish Parliament was "stacked"; he was not trying to point out the sincerity and honesty of those who brought about the system. (B) is not an appropriate choice. The author was not seeking to stress again the model Irish Parliament, which many countries could use as a successful system of

government (C) or to bring to the surface the forgotten system with its many attributes (D).

16. **(E)** The writer tries to attribute the corruption to the borough system (E). The Catholic religion did not develop the corruption so (A) should not be selected. Mr. Lecky (B) is only quoted in the passage and is not the source of the corruption nor is the legend-haunted lake (C). A two-house system does not necessarily result in corruption; (D) should not be chosen.

17. **(D)** The word "simulacrum" in line 3 can be best defined as (D) "a pretense." The test-taker who selected (A) "symmetry," or one side like that of the other, must have had the word "similar" in mind. "Simulacrum" has nothing to do with a ghost or haunting (B). As stated above the word means a pretense or a sham; it is not the name of a type of government (C) or a legislature or law-making body (D). Neither answer should be chosen.

18. **(A)** To give credence to his writings, the author calls on the statements of Hely Hutchinson. (A) is the best answer. The writer does not use subliminal persuasion; (B) should not be selected. The writer gives opinions as well as facts and figures; (C) should not be chosen. The author does consult the voting records so (D) cannot be chosen. The author does not ignore the complicated method of corrupting both Houses. (E) is not the best choice.

19. **(E)** The author believes that the order of insects as fertilizers of native flowers in order of their importance is bees, Lepidoptera, flies (E). The passage states that bees come first, and that the second place is either the Lepidoptera (butterflies) or the flies. Choice (A) is inappropriate because it does not place bees as the number one insect for fertilizing native flowers. Choice (B) is inappropriate because it omits bees and it lists both butterflies and Lepidoptera which are one and the same. Choice (C) is not the best choice because it, too, lists Lepidoptera and butterflies as two separate divisions; it is better than choice (B), however, since it does include bees. (D) is not the best choice because bees come first—not Lepidoptera.

20. **(E)** The only order which is fitted for taking honey from flowers in all its family is the Lepidoptera. This answer (E) is given in lines 5–7. Not all bees (A) are capable of doing this; this means that both choices (A) and (B) are inappropriate since they both include the bee. Since it has already

been established that Lepidoptera and butterflies are the same, we can disqualify choices (C) and (D) on that point alone. Choices (C) and (D) are also incorrect since they include bees also; choice (D) includes flies and bees (both of which are incorrect) and lists also Lepidoptera and butterflies which are one and the same. Again, the best answer is (E).

21. **(D)** The mouth of the butterfly can be best described as a long, thin, tube which can be rolled up into a small space and an upper lip and mandibles which are short (D). The mouth of the butterfly is definitely not simple (A). The long, thin tube on the butterfly does not extend in a stiff manner; (B) is not a good choice. Choice (C) is incomplete; the mouth does consist of a long, thin tube which can be rolled up into a small space, but it is more than that. Choice (E) is incorrect; the mouth cannot be accurately described as a pointed "stinger" for sucking up the pollen.

22. **(D)** The Lepidoptera, at the time of this writing, had been studied by too many scientists to list. (D) is the correct answer. Neither Müller only (A) nor Müller and his brother (B) are correct answers. Choice (C)— the two Müllers, Speyer, and MacLachlan—is an incomplete answer and should not be chosen. The study of the Lepidoptera is not inconsequential; choice (E) is false.

23. **(D)** The main purpose of this writing is to show the importance and development of the Lepidoptera. (D) is the best choice. The article is not just designed to emphasize the importance of the mouth parts of the bee. (A) is not the best choice. The article does show the importance of the bee in fertilization of native flowers, but that is not its primary purpose. (B) is not the best choice. The butterfly is NOT number one in fertilization of native flowers. Choice (C) is false and should not be chosen. Choice (E) is true; the Lepidoptera do seem to be the only insects which do not confine their visits to flowers to the daylight, but that is not the primary purpose of the article. (E) is not the best choice.

24. **(B)** The writer speculates that there are few nocturnal Lepidoptera in our climate because of the shortness of the period suitable for their flight. (B) is the best answer. The writer does not attribute the few nocturnal Lepidoptera to the pursuit of collectors during nocturnal hours. (A) is not the best choice. The Lepidoptera has swift movements (C) and violent movements (D) but this does not relate to the fact that there are few nocturnal Lepidoptera. There are nocturnal flowers in our climate so (E) is false. Choice (B) is clearly the best choice.

25. **(E)**   Nocturnal flowers to be visited by the Lepidoptera usually are light-colored. (E) is the best answer. If the flowers are dark-colored (A), they would be less visible. (A) is a poor choice. Odor helps attract nocturnal insects; choice (B) which states that they are without odor is incorrect and should not be chosen. If flowers open early in the day and close at night, then they cannot be visited by nocturnal Lepidoptera. (C) is not an acceptable answer. If the flowers secrete their nectar early in the day, they would not be attractive to nocturnal insects. (D) is not the best choice.

26. **(D)**   The context of the passage supports "incompletely formed" as the correct answer. The context clue is "which are not visible in my figure" indicates that the maxillary palps are not completely formed. Shortened (A), suggests that the maxillary palps were once complete, which is not supported by the material. Both imperfect (B) and mangled (C) suggest that the palps were damaged in some way. Obsolete (E) does not make sense; the author believes that Lepidoptera has adapted in a superior way.

1.   **(E)**   We know that $^2/_5$ of the French club were females. Thus, there were $^2/_5 \times 40 = 16$ females in the French club. Since there were a total of 70 students, there were 30 students who are not in the French club. Of these, $^1/_3$, or 10, were male. Therefore, there were 20 females not in the French club. By adding the 16 females in the French club to the 20 not in the club, we arrive at the answer: 36.

2.   **(D)**   If we take this problem one step at a time, it will cause no problems. First of all, the problem asks us to find a number such that $^1/_3$ of that number will be the same as 40% of 75.

The first computation is to find 40% of 75. We can do this by multiplying $.4 \times 75$, which equals 30. (40% = .4).

Now we are asked to find a number (x) such that $^1/_3$ of x would equal 30. To do this we can set up the following equation:

$$\frac{1}{3} \times x = 30$$

$$3 \times \frac{1}{3} \times x = 30 \times 3 \quad \text{multiply both sides of the equation by the}$$

coefficient of the variable

$$x = 90 \qquad \text{simplify}$$

3. **(E)**

angle ADC is a right angle	all angles of a square are right angles
ADC is a right triangle	a triangle with a right angle is a right triangle
$AD = DC$	all sides of a square are equal
angle DAC = angle ACD	if 2 sides of a triangle are equal, then the corresponding angles are equal
angle $DAC = 45$ = angle ACD	if 2 sides of a right triangle are equal, the 2 corresponding angles are equal and the triangle is a 45-45-90 right triangle

$$g = 8 = CD \qquad \text{in a 45-45-90 right triangle, each}$$
$$\text{leg} = {}^{1}/_{2} \times \text{hypotenuse} \times \sqrt{2}$$

$$\text{area of } DEFC = 64 \qquad \text{area of a rectangle} = l \times w \ (8 \times 8)$$

4.   **(D)**   With a problem such as this, it is easier to test the answer choices than to do the algebra.

Because we are asked to find the greatest possible integer, we will test the greatest answer choice first.

If $y = 2$, then all three expressions are positive, and the result of multiplying them is positive.

If $y = 1$, then all three expressions are positive, and the result of multiplying them is positive.

If $y = 0$, then one of the expressions equals 0, and the result of multiplying them is 0.

If $y = -1$, then one of the expressions (y) is negative and the other two expressions $(y + 3)$ and $(y + 5)$ are positive, and the result of multiplying them is negative.

Because -1 is greater than -2, (D) is the correct answer.

5.   **(C)**   Because an average is the sum of the numbers divided by the number of numbers, if five numbers have an average of 8, their sum must be $8 \times 5 = 40$.

We now must find the largest possible integer in the group, if the other four integers are different positive integers. To get the largest integer we must make the other integers as small as possible.

The four smallest different positive integers are 1, 2, 3, and 4. Thus we can set up the following equation:

$$1 + 2 + 3 + 4 + x = 40$$
$$10 + x = 40$$
$$x = 30$$

6.   **(D)**   A triangle with angles of 45, 45, 90 is an isosceles right triangle. The area of any triangle is equal to $^{1}/_{2}$ the base times its height, but in the case of the isosceles right triangle the two non-hypotenuse sides cannot only function as the base and height of the triangle, but they are

also equal to each other. Thus we can set up the following equation:

$$\text{Area} = \frac{1}{2} \text{ side} \times \text{side}$$

$$64 = \frac{1}{2} s \times s \qquad \text{substitute}$$

$$64 = \frac{1}{2} s^2 \qquad \text{simplify}$$

$$64 \times 2 = \frac{1}{2} \times 2 \times s^2 \qquad \text{equals} \times \text{equals are equal}$$

$$128 = s^2 \qquad \text{simplify}$$

$$\sqrt{128} = s \qquad \text{square roots of equals are equal}$$

$$\sqrt{2 \times 2 \times 2 \times 2 \times 2 \times 2 \times 2} = s \qquad \text{simplify}$$

$$2 \times 2 \times 2\sqrt{2} = s \qquad \text{manipulate of radicals}$$

$$8\sqrt{2} = s$$

If one leg of an isosceles right triangle is $8\sqrt{2}$, then the other leg of the triangle is also $8\sqrt{2}$. To find the hypotenuse of the triangle we can use the formula

the hypotenuse of a 45-45-90 right triangle $= s\sqrt{2}$ (where s is a side).

$$h = 8\sqrt{2} \times \sqrt{2}$$

$$h = 8\sqrt{4}$$

$$h = 8 \times 2$$

$$h = 16$$

Thus, the sides are 16, $8\sqrt{2}$, and $8\sqrt{2}$ and the perimeter is 16 + $16\sqrt{2}$.

7. **(E)**

$$\frac{m}{g} = \frac{1}{y}$$

$$g = my \qquad \text{cross-multiply}$$

$$\frac{m}{d} = \frac{1}{(y+1)}$$

$$d = m(y+1) \qquad \text{cross-multiply}$$

$$d = my + m \qquad \text{simplify}$$

$$g - d = my - (my + m) \qquad \text{equals minus equals are equal}$$

$$g - d = my - my - m \qquad \text{distribute the } -1$$

$$g - d = -m$$

$$g - d + d = -m + d \qquad \text{equals plus equals are equal}$$

$$g = d - m \qquad \text{simplify}$$

8. **(A)**

$$\frac{ab}{4} = 225 \qquad \text{given}$$

$$ab = 900 \qquad \text{cross-multiply}$$

Because a and b each represent a side of the square, their product is the area of the square. Thus, the area of the square = 900.

$$o^2 - m^2 = n^2 \qquad \text{given}$$

$$o^2 - m^2 + m^2 = m^2 + n^2 \qquad \text{equals plus equals are equal}$$

$$o^2 = m^2 + n^2 \qquad \text{simplify}$$

Because the triangle fits the Pythagorean Theorem, it must be a right triangle with o as the hypotenuse and m and n as the legs. Because the legs of a right triangle form a right angle, we know that

$$\text{area of triangle} = \frac{1}{2} m \times n.$$

Because the area of the triangle equal, the area of the square, we can substitute in the area of the square. Thus,

$$900 = \frac{1}{2} m \times n$$

$$900 \times 2 = 2 \times \frac{1}{2} m \times n \qquad \text{equals times equals are equal}$$

$$1{,}800 = mn$$

9. **(A)**   To do this problem we can rely on the formula

(Concentration 1 × Quantity 1) + (Concentration 2 + Quantity 2)

= Concentration 3 × (Quantity 1 + Quantity 2).

We will allow the first oil to be the $16 a barrel oil, the second to be the $6 oil, and the third to be the blend at $10 a barrel. If we assume the quantity of the first oil is x, then we can set up the following equation:

$$16x + 6(100 - x) = 10(x + 100 - x)$$

$$16x + 600 - 6x = 10 \times 100$$

$$10x + 600 - 600 = 1{,}000 - 600$$

$$10x = 400$$

$$\frac{10x}{10} = \frac{400}{10}$$

$$x = 40$$

Because x represents the number of barrels of $16 a barrel oil, the answer is (A).

10. **(D)**   To solve this problem, we can set up a single proportion.

$$\frac{1}{1{,}000} = \frac{4.8}{x}$$

$$x = 4.8 \times 1{,}000$$

$$x = 4{,}800$$

11. **(A)**

$BEA + EAB + ABE = 180$	angles of a triangle = 180°
$90 + EAB + 30 = 180$	substitute
$120 + EAB = 180$	simplify
$120 - 120 + EAB = 180 - 120$	equals minus equals are equal
$EAB = 60$	simplify
$ABD + BDA + DAB = 180$	angles of a triangle = 180°
$80 + BDA + 60 = 180$	simplify

$$140 + BDA = 180 \qquad \text{simplify}$$

$$140 - 140 + BDA = 180 - 140 \qquad \text{equals minus equals are equal}$$

$$BDA = 40 \qquad \text{simplify}$$

$$BDA + BDC = 180 \qquad \text{angles of a line add to } 180°$$

$$BDC + DBC + BCD = 180 \qquad \text{angles of a triangle add to } 180°$$

$$BDA + BDC = BDC + DBC + BCD$$

2 quantities equal to the same quantity are equal to each other

$$BDA + BDC - BDC = BDC - BDC + DBC + BCD$$

equals minus equals are equal

$$BDA = DBC + BCD \quad \text{simplify}$$

$$40 = DBC + BCD \quad \text{substitute}$$

Note: Angle *BDA* is known as an exterior angle of triangle *BDC*. And an exterior angle of a triangle is always equal to the sum of the two non-adjacent interior angles (in this case *CBD* and *BCD*).

12. **(E)** The key to doing this problem is to recognize that all the fractions equal $1/3$. Thus we have

$$\frac{1}{3} \times \frac{1}{3} \times \frac{1}{3} \times \frac{1}{3} \times \frac{1}{3} = \frac{1}{243}.$$

When you get a problem such as this, where it appears as though a great many computations are involved, you should realize that there is usually a way to simplify the problem. In your studies, try to avoid doing problems the long way, and work instead at finding the more efficient way to do the problem.

13. **(D)** Because all parts of all the answer choices are expressed as whole numbers, we must express all parts of the recipe as whole numbers. Cashews and whole wheat flour are already expressed as whole numbers so we can turn our attention to the sunflower seeds. The recipe given calls for $1/4$ of a cup of sunflower seeds.

To get from $1/4$ of a cup to a whole cup, we must multiply by 4:

$$\frac{1}{4} \times 4 = 1.$$

If, however, we multiply the amount of sunflower seeds by 4, we must multiply the amount of cashews and whole wheat flour by 4.

Cashews: 2 cups × 4 = 8 cups

Whole wheat flour: 6 cups × 4 = 24 cups

Thus, the ingredients could be expressed as 8:24:1.

14. **(B)**   Because John walks at 90 feet per minute and Debbie walks at 65 feet per minute, John travels 25 feet more per minute than Debbie.

90 − 65 = 25

25 feet per minute × 120 minutes (the number of minutes in 2 hours) yields 3,000 feet.

15. **(A)**   The key to this question is to recognize that $25a^4 - 36b^{18}$ can be factored into

$(5a^2 - 6b^9)(5a^2 + 6b^9)$.

Thus if $25a^4 - 36b^{18} = 72$, then

$4(5a^2 - 6b^9)(5a^2 + 6b^9)$

must be equal to 4×72, which equals 288.

16. **(B)**   To find the sum of the interior angles of a polygon, we can make use of the following formula: the sum of the interior angles of a polygon = $180 \times (n - 2)$, where n = the number of sides.

Because polygon *ABCDE* has 5 sides, it has 180 (5 − 2) or 180 × 3 or 540°. Thus,

$A + B + C + D + E = 540$ the whole equals the sum of its parts

$500 + E = 540$ substitute

$500 - 500 + E = 540 - 500$ equals minus equals are equal

$E = 40$ simplify

$F = 40$ vertical angles are equal

Because polygon *FGHI* has four sides, it equals 180 (4 − 2) = 180 (2) = 360°

$F + G + H + I = 360$ whole equals the sum of its parts

$$40 + G + H + I = 360 \qquad \text{substitute}$$

$$40 - 40 + G + H + I = 360 - 40 \qquad \text{equals minus equals are equal}$$

$$G + H + I = 320 \qquad \text{simplify}$$

17. **(C)** To change a mixed number to an improper fraction, multiply the whole number (4) by the denominator (6) of the fraction (4 times 6 is 24). Add the numerator (5) to the product (24). Write the sum (29) over the denominator of the fraction, $^{29}/_6$.

18. **(E)**

$$x + 2x + 3x = 180 \qquad \text{sum of the angles of the triangle equals } 180°$$

$$6x = 180 \qquad \text{simplify}$$

$$6x \div 6 = 180 \div 6 \qquad \text{equals divided by equals are equal}$$

$$x = 30$$

$$2x = 60$$

$$3x = 90 \qquad \text{Thus we have a 30°/60°/90° right triangle.}$$

Because we are told $m + n$ is the longest side (hypotenuse) of the triangle, we can set up the equation:

$$m^2 + (m - n)^2 = (m + n)^2$$

$$m^2 + m^2 - 2mn + n^2 = m^2 + 2mn + n^2$$
$$\text{square the polynomials}$$

$$m^2 - m^2 + m^2 - 2mn + n^2 - n^2 = m^2 - m^2 + 2mn + n^2 - n^2$$
$$\text{equals minus equals are equal}$$

$$m^2 - 2mn = 2mn \quad \text{simplify}$$

$$m^2 - 2mn + 2mn = 2mn + 2mn$$
$$\text{equal plus equals are equal}$$

$$m^2 = 4mn$$
$$\text{simplify}$$

$$m^2 \div 4m = 4mn \div 4m$$
$$\text{equals divided by equals are equal}$$

$$\frac{m}{4} = n \qquad \text{simplify}$$

19. **(E)**   If opposite sides of a quadrilateral are equal and parallel, the quadrilateral is a parallelogram. Thus, *ABCD* is a parallelogram.

If $GM = \frac{3}{4}$ of *AD*, then we can let $GM = 3$ and $AD = 4$. If $MY = \frac{4}{5}$ of *CE*, then we can let $MY = 4$ and $CE = 5$.

If $GM = 3$ and $MY = 4$, because *GMY* is a right triangle, its area would be $\frac{1}{2}(3 \times 4) = 6$.

Because *ABCD* is a parallelogram and *CE* is its altitude, its area would be $CE \times AD = 5 \times 4 = 20$.

Thus, the ratio of the area of *GMY* to *ABCD* would be $\frac{6}{20} = 3:10$.

20. **(B)**   The key to the problem is that they received the same amount of money per hour of work. Because Rosina earned $225 while Mary only earned $75, we know that Rosina worked longer than Mary did. Additionally, if we divide 225 by 75, we learn that Rosina worked 3 times as long as Mary did.

Thus, if *g* represents the amount of time Mary worked, then 3*g* would represent the amount of time Rosina worked. We can now set up an equation.

$$g + 3g = 16$$

$$4g = 16 \qquad \text{combine like terms}$$

$$4g \div 4 = 16 \div 4 \qquad \text{divide both sides by coefficient of the variable}$$

$$g = 4$$

Section 3 — Verbal

27. **(E)**   In this sentence there is a contrast between city living ("high-rises") and country living ("white picket fences and cupolas"). People usually view the city as "modern" and the country as old fashioned or "quaint"; therefore, (E) is the right answer. (A) is wrong because "aloof" (reserved) does not fit into the implied meaning of the sentence. (B) is also incorrect because "capricious" (changeable) would mean that country living is changeable as compared to city living, and that makes no sense. (C) "redundant" (repetitious) is wrong because the use of this word would make the sentence meaningless. The contrast between city and country living is not repetitious. The choice of (D) "ornate" (elaborate) is a possibility, because although cupolas are ornate, white picket fences are not. Cupolas and white picket fences may be considered more "quaint" than "ornate."

28. **(B)**   The best answer is (B) "incompatible" (disagreeing, disharmonious) because the sentence tells about two people who cannot agree on friends, books, movies, and sports. These people are definitely incompatible. Choice (A) "dispassionate" (lack of feeling, impartial) is a possible choice if the question only contained a sentence about two people getting a divorce. However, there are several sentences preceding that describe the situation where two people cannot agree. Choice (C) "arbitrary" (based on one's preference or whim) does not fit semantically. These people were not arbitrary about getting a divorce; they had reasons listed in several sentences in the question. Choice (D) "meticulous" (exacting, precise) is wrong because it is not a semantic equivalent of "not being able to agree," which was the context of this question. Choice (E) "nostalgic" (longing for the past; filled with bittersweet memories) is not semantically accurate. It does not fit into the implied meaning of the sentences.

29. **(A)**   "Discern" (distinguish one thing from another), choice (A), is the correct answer because we are looking for a verb that tells us that since Marcia is an art expert (many years of art school) she could distinguish an authentic painting from its copy. Choice (B) "condone" means "to forgive" and would make no sense if it was inserted as the verb in the sentence. "Laud" (praise), choice (C), is an incorrect verb substitution because "laud" is not a comparison word. You would "laud" something directly. Choice (D) "emulate" (follow the example of) makes no sense semantically. Choice (E) "rationalize" (to offer reasons for) is wrong,

because the word is commonly used as a way for people to account for something, not as a differentiating word.

30. **(C)**   The best answer here is "torpid" and "lethargic" (lazy, passive). The sentence sets up the conditions: "hot summer sun and high humidity." Certainly, anyone who has knowledge of what the effects of heat and humidity can do would choose two adjectives that described lazy, passive reactions. Choice (A) "unruly" (disobedient) and "urbane" (cultured, suave) is wrong because these words do not apply as adjectives for people who are faced with the kind of day described in the sentence. Choice (B) "pallid" (shallow, colorless) does not describe a feeling, and although people might be "vulnerable" (open to attack, unprotected) on a hot, humid day, this is not the correct answer because "pallid" is wrong. Choice (D) "immune" (protected, unthreatened by) is not semantically appropriate for the sentence; therefore, (D) is an incorrect choice. "Depleted" (to reduce, to empty) and "contrite" (regretful, sorrowful), choice (E), is incorrect because a hot summer day would not be considered sorrowful.

31. **(B)**   The contextual meaning of this sentence is that the author has to do something to the conclusion of his last chapter so that he doesn't miss his deadline. The next choice is (B) "execute" (carry to completion) because if he "executes" his last chapter, he won't miss his deadline. Choice (A) "expand" is incorrect because if he expands his chapter, he will be adding more information, and might miss the deadline. Choice (C) is incorrect because "exhaust" (tire, wear out) does not fit into the meaning of the sentence. Choice (D) "endorse" (support, approve of, recommend), when inserted into the sentence, makes the sentence meaningless. Choice (E) "extol" (praise) has no meaning in the sentence. Whether or not the author praised his last chapter would not help him meet his deadline.

32. **(A)**   The semantic implication of this sentence asks you to find an adjective that describes what type of belief would cause an environmental group to face "overwhelming forces." The best answer is (A) "adamant" (not yielding, firm), because only firm beliefs would stand up in the face of "overwhelming forces." Choice (B) "deliberate" (intentional) is a possibility, but not the best choice. Intentional beliefs are done with a purpose, but might back down in the face of adversity. Choice (C) "didactic" (instructive) is not correct because it is not semantically related to "overwhelming forces." Choice (D) "fallacious" (misleading) has no meaning

when inserted into the sentence. Choice (E) "pragmatic" (practical, matter-of-fact) beliefs would back down in the face of overwhelming forces as a matter of protection.

33. **(E)** The relationship between the given words can best be described as: If something is DURABLE (long-lasting), then it is PERMANENT. Choice (E) describes the same relationship: If something is TRANSIENT (SHORT-LIVED), THEN IT IS CHANGEABLE. Choice (A) is wrong because if something is INTELLIGENT, then it is PERSUASIVE is not an accurate statement. Choice (B) is wrong because if something is INNOCENT, then it is DIFFICULT makes no sense. Choice (C) is wrong because if something is TEDIOUS, then it is DIALOGUE is semantically inaccurate. Choice (D) is incorrect because if something is RATIONAL, then it is an IDEA is not accurate; an IDEA is not always RATIONAL.

34. **(D)** VEX and ANNOY are synonyms. If you VEX someone, you ANNOY them. If you LIBERATE someone, you FREE them (D). (A) is incorrect because if you IGNORE someone, you are not necessarily DEPRESSING them. ENJOY and PLEASE are not related in terms of usage (B). Choice (C) does not make sense because there is no clear relationship between HARASS and ENTICE. Choice (E) is incorrect for the same reason as choices (B) and (C); there is no apparent relationship between imitate and rescue.

35. **(D)** If you are ANXIOUS, then you are not CAREFREE. The two words are essentially opposite in meaning. Choice (D), SYMPATHETIC : HOSTILE, parallels the relationship in the original pair. ERROR : FAIL (A) is not a meaningful relationship. Choice (B) is incorrect because to say "if you DESIGN, you cannot PLAN" does not make sense. Choice (C), BELIEVE : DEVOTION is incorrect for the same reason. Choice (E), ALIENATE : ENEMIES, have a synonymous relationship. If you ALIENATE people, you are likely to have enemies.

36. **(C)** The best way of describing the relationship between the two given words is to say "A REBUTTAL comes after a SPEECH." The best match is (C) because a FIGHT comes after a PROVOCATION. Choice (A) is incorrect because a QUESTION does not come after a TEST. Choice (B) is incorrect because an APOLOGY does not necessarily follow an AGREEMENT. Choice (D) is in reverse order. A TANTRUM does not follow TEARS. LULL and QUIET (E) is incorrect because they are synonyms.

37. **(B)**   The original pair, EGOTISTIC and VAIN, are synonymous. An EGOTISTIC person is VAIN. The best choice is (B), GREGARIOUS : SOCIABLE. Choice (A) is incorrect because a COMPLIANT (yielding) person is not a COLORFUL person. Choices (C), (D), and (E) are also incorrect because there is not a synonymous relationship between any of the word pairs.

38. **(B)**   GLORIFY and DENIGRATE are antonyms, as are APPROVE and CENSURE (to find fault with). Choice (A) is incorrect because BUR-NISH (to make shiny) has no connection to STATEMENT. Choice (C), DEVIATE and HIGHWAY, also have no logical connection. REVIVE and RESTORE (D) is incorrect because the two words are synonymous, as are INFER and GUESS (E).

39. **(A)**   The relationship between ACQUIT and GUILT can be described as ACQUIT (to pronounce not guilty) means to be free from GUILT. The best choice is (A) because DIVORCE means to be free from MARRIAGE. Choice (B) is incorrect because if we say SUPPORT means to be free from PAIN, the sentence is illogical. Choice (C) is wrong because "INFLUENCE means to be free from CAUSE" has no meaning. Choice (D) is incorrect because, if the two words are used in the same kind of sentence relationship, there is no semantic meaning: REVISE means to be free from MANUSCRIPT. Choice (E) is wrong because saying WITHDRAW means to be free from WORRY, does not make sense.

40. **(E)**   In line 9 the word "embalmed" means preserved. (E) is the best answer. Embalming actually prevents decay; (A) is a poor choice. The word "embalmed" does not mean exaggerated; there is no hint given that the authors exaggerate in their writing. (B) should not be chosen. The writing of the authors mentioned is not referred to as boring (C) or that which omits the faults of (D); both answers should be avoided.

41. **(B)**   The writer's main objective in the writing of the passage is to present both a geographical and a literary description of the area to the reader. (B) is the best choice. The passage is not primarily geographical in nature; (A) is not accurate. Since the passage does not give a history of the area, choice (C)—to present both a geographical description and a histori-cal description—is inaccurate. The "ramble" is not fictional so (D) is not a good choice. The main purpose is not to inform the reader of outstanding literary contributions; some literary contributions are mentioned, but the geography must not be overlooked! (E) should not be chosen.

42. **(D)**   The writer would attest that Irving was more influenced by the environment than other writers were influenced. (D) is the best answer. The author of this passage has written—at length—on the influence of the environment on a writer. (A) should not be chosen. The writer does not talk about blocking out the environment; he talks about how it can influence the writer consciously and subconsciously; (B) should not be selected. It was Irving—not Cooper—who was more influenced by the environment than other writers were influenced. The author mentions the duel that was fought there; this murder shows that violence can occur even in this lonely spot. (Duels were, of course, legal at the time.)

43. **(D)**   The passage describes Constitution Island as composed of rude masses of rock. (D) is the best answer. (A) is not the best answer since the island is not far from water. (B) is a reference to the Hudson River. It should not be selected. The heart of the Highlands refers to West Point, not Constitution Island. (C) should not be used. (E) is a reference to the Hudson. (E) is not an appropriate answer.

44. **(D)**   The main idea of Passage 1 is (D). Carnegie suggests that active work (D) is superior to a college education. Carnegie does not promote a classical education. (A) should not be chosen. Carnegie does not promote the prejudice against educating the masses (B), but he does understand why it exists. (B) is not the correct answer. He does not advocate a study of mythology; (C) should not be chosen. Carnegie does not see the value of the liberal arts; (E) should not be chosen.

45. **(D)**   The author of Passage 1 describes the college graduates of today as ignorant of Shakespeare. (D) is the correct answer. The college graduates have NOT received valuable instruction in his opinion. (A) is not the best answer. He sees a college education as having hurt, not bettered, their life. (B) is not a good choice. Carnegie states that the students are NOT educated for life in our world. (C) is not the best choice. Graduates are NOT filled with fire and energy, according to Carnegie; that has been stamped out of them. (E) should not be chosen.

46. **(A)**   The main purpose of Passage 2 is to renounce the modern humanities. (A) should be chosen. The writer of Passage 2 does not view with pleasure the modern humanities. He believes the classical courses are most important. (B) should not be chosen since it states that the writer tries to present the modern humanities as important general culture. The writer of Passage 2 does not ridicule the traditional courses of study. The writer,

rather, seems to endorse the traditional courses. (C) is not the best answer. The writer does not advocate the new so-called "special education." (D) should not be chosen. The writer opposes the total reorganization of secondary education. (E) should not be chosen.

47. **(C)** When the writer of Passage 2 states that "we are saved by adding Goethe's 'Faust' to Shakespeare's 'Hamlet,' instead of the 'Aeneid,' he is employing a tongue-in-cheek attitude. (C) is the best answer. The author does not use alliteration. Alliteration (A) is a repetition of sounds. (A) should not be chosen. A simile (B) uses the words *like* or *as*; (B) is not the best choice. The writer does not use denotation—saying exactly what you mean. (D) should not be selected. The writer is not using an understatement. (E) is not a good choice.

48. **(A)** The best meaning of being "asphyxiated by a rarefication of its environment" in line 54 of Passage 2 is (A), killed by purification. In this case "purifying the schools" with the new curriculum, the writer feels, will kill education. The writer is fearful of destroying learning, but not through vocational education; he is fearful the academic curriculum will destroy learning. (B) is not the best choice. The reference is not to Greek mythology; (C) is not the best choice. The writer is fearful that important content is being left out; he is not fearful of being smothered by important concepts (D) or being choked with the amount of material to be learned (E).

49. **(D)** The main point made by the writer of Passage 2 about "practical" courses, like bookkeeping, is that they can be taught at special classes; they are not to be a part of the school curriculum. (D) is the best answer. The writer of Passage 1 would not advocate the subordination of general culture to bookkeeping; (A) should not be selected. The writer believes just the opposite of (B); he believes that the courses should be provided at special lessons—not by the schools. (B) should not be selected. The bookkeeping courses, in the mind of the writer of Passage 2, are NOT within the scope of the public schools; he believes they can be provided at special lessons. (C) should not be chosen. The writer does not believe that Latin should be given up for bookkeeping. (E) is an incorrect choice.

50. **(C)** The writer of Passage 1, when questioned about classical education, would point out its inadequacies. (C) is the best answer. Since the writer does not support classical education, he would not criticize those who say negative things about classical education. (A) should not be cho-

sen. Since no research was done, the writer could NOT show the recent research to back up his beliefs. (B) is not a good choice. The writer does not advocate classical education; he does not feel the structure is adequate; he would not point out the quality of the structure which has survived for a long period of time. (D) should not be selected. Those who would dispense with the system do not have humility; rather, they feel their system is best. (E) should not be chosen.

51. **(E)** The writer's question as to which minds are insulted by Latin and English criticizes those who seek to change the curriculum. (E) is the best choice. The writer advocates the classics; he thinks the past should be used as a model for education. He would not likely bring out the mistakes made in the past. (A) should not be chosen. The writer advocates the program of the past; he does not think it needs to be changed. He would not likely indicate why the secondary education program had to be changed. (B) is not the best choice. Since the classics are in effect and since the writer wants to keep what is, he would not show what should be as opposed to what is. He would advocate keeping what is. (C) should not be chosen. What was IS the ideal to the writer; he would NOT highlight the distinction between the ideal and what was. (D) should not be chosen.

52. **(A)** The writer of Passage 2 would agree that modern humanities should not be employed by secondary education. (A) is the best choice. The writer of Passage 2 does not think the modern humanities include the important classical components, like Latin. (B) should not be chosen. The writer claims that the classics contain "all that is comprised in special instruction" and does prepare students for industrial, commercial, and agriculture life. (C) should not be selected. The writer believes the science component of the modern humanities is basically like the science component in classical education; he would not agree that the modern humanities have a superior science component which is evident when compared with the classical course of study. The writer of Passage 2 does not advocate the present improvements; (E) is not a suitable choice.

Section 4 — Math

21. **(C)**   Add 7 to both sides:

$$x^2 - 4x = 7$$

22. **(A)**   Volume of a cube = edge³ $(V = e^3)$, $27 = e^3$

Take the cube root of both sides of the equation, $e = 3$.

The edge of the cube is 3.

A cube has 6 congruent faces; the area of 1 face is 3^2 or 9.

$$6(9) = 54$$

23. **(B)**   Simplify each square root:

$$y = \sqrt{9} + \sqrt{16} - \sqrt{49}$$

$$= 3 + 4 - 7 = 0$$

24. **(B)**

$$.2 + .8 \neq .10$$

$$.2 + .8 = 1.0$$

$$.2B + .8B = 1$$

$$1B = 1$$

$$B = 1$$

25. **(B)**   To find AC, use the Pythagorean Theorem $(a^2 + b^2 = c^2)$, where c is the hypotenuse.

$$9^2 + 12^2 = c^2$$

$$81 + 144 = c^2$$

$$225 = c^2$$

$$15 = c$$

The ratio of the diagonal to its perimeter is

$$\frac{15}{42} = \frac{5}{14}.$$

26. **(B)**

$$8x = \frac{1}{3}$$

$$24x = 1$$

$$x = \frac{1}{24}$$

Then

$$\frac{12x}{5} = \frac{12\left(\frac{1}{24}\right)}{5}$$

$$= \frac{\frac{1}{2}}{5} = \frac{1}{10}$$

27. **(A)** Remember that there is a fence post at the beginning *and* at the end. For example, 24 feet would need 3 posts, 36 feet would need 4 posts, 48 feet would need 5 posts, etc. There will be 1 extra fence post than you may have thought there were.

28. **(A)** Take any 2 sides of the triangle. Add these 2 numbers and subtract these 2 numbers. The 3rd side *must* fall between these 2 answers. For example, $15 + 8 = 23$ and $15 - 8 = 7$. Therefore, $7 < y < 23$. In any triangle, the sum of any 2 sides must be greater than the third side.

29. **(A)** Be careful! 2 is wrong. You are doubling the number of men and you are doubling the number of days, so the correct answer is 4.

30. **(A)** You must follow the order of operations. Parentheses, exponents, multiplication, and division as they appear from left to right, and lastly, addition and subtraction.

31. **(B)** Each number is $^1/_2$ the number before it, or divided by 2.

$$4\frac{1}{2} \times \frac{1}{2} = \frac{9}{2} \times \frac{1}{2}$$

$$= \frac{9}{4} = 2\frac{1}{4}$$

32. **(C)**

$$\frac{-1}{A} = 1$$

$$-1 = A$$

Remember that $-A = -1A$.

Therefore, $-A = 1$ and $A^2 = 1$.

33. The correct response is:

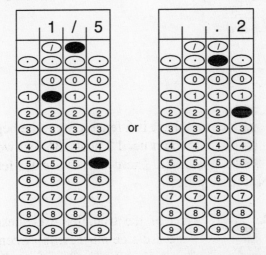

The equation $4^{n+4} = 64$ is equivalent to $2^{2n+8} = 2^6$. This yields $n = -1$; hence, $5^n = 1/5$ or 0.2.

34. The correct response is:

We have

$$3A + 2B + 2C = 5$$

and $\qquad A + B + C = 1.$

As $C = 1$ these equations become

$$3A + 2B + 2 = 5$$

and $\qquad A + B + 1 = 1.$

Subtracting the second equation from the first equation we get

$$2A + B + 1 = 4$$

hence $\qquad 2A + B = 3.$

35. The correct response is:

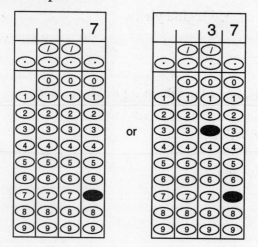

Primes of the form $3K + 1$ less than 40 are 7, 13, 19, 31, and 37. Primes of the form $5K + 2$ less than 40 are 2, 7, 17, and 37. The two possible solutions are 7 and 37.

36. The correct response is:

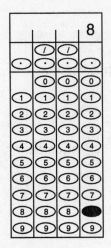

The area of the shaded region yields

$$\frac{1}{2}(3x) = 15,$$

yielding $x = 10$. The area of the whole figure is given by

$$\left(\frac{1}{2}\right)3\,(x+y) = 27.$$

Plugging in $x = 10$, we get

$$\left(\frac{1}{2}\right)3\,(10+y) = 27$$

$$10 + y = 18$$

$$y = 8$$

37. The correct response is:

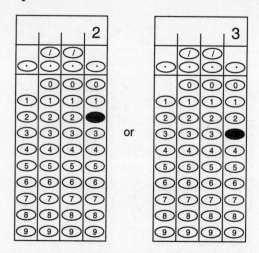

or

The largest possible value for x is 9; this will give rise to all the possible values for z. For $x = 9$ we have $6y < 3x = 27$; hence, $y = 1, 2, 3,$ or 4. For $y = 4$ we have $z < y = 4$; hence, the possible values for z are 1, 2, and 3. However, condition d states that $z > 1$. Therefore, the correct answers are 2 and 3.

38. The correct response is:

Adding the first equation to the second we obtain

$$7x = 7;$$

hence $\qquad x = 1.$

Plugging $x = 1$ into the second equation we have

$$4 + y = 5;$$

thus $\qquad y = 1.$

39. The correct response is:

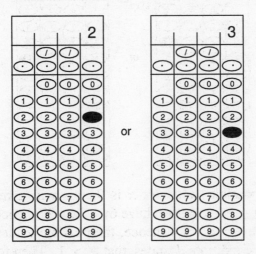 or

As $xyz = 24$ the only possible value for x (a perfect square) is 4; this implies $yz = 6$. The possible values are $z = 2$ or $z = 3$.

40. The correct response is:

As the area of a triangle is $\frac{1}{2}$ (base) (height), we get

$$\left(\frac{1}{2}\right)\left(\frac{x}{2}\right)(x)=\left(\frac{1}{2}\right)\left(\frac{2^3}{2}\right)(2^3)$$

$$=\frac{2^6}{2^2}=2^4=16\ \text{ft}^2$$

Section 5 — Writing Skills

1. **(B)** "Were praised" is a plural verb; since the subject is Chief Joseph, a singular proper noun, the verb should be "was praised." The intervening phrase of choice (A), "*together with* 250 warriors and 500 women and children," does not change the singular subject. Choice (C), "bravery," is the correct noun form, and choice (D), "for," is idiomatically correct in that phrase.

2. **(E)** Choice (A), "upon which," is a correct prepositional phrase. Choice (B), "is based," agrees with its subject, "society." In choice (C) "are" agrees with its subject, "ideals." "Derived from" in choice (D) is correct idiomatic usage.

3. **(B)** Two past actions are mentioned. The earlier of two past actions should be indicated by past perfect tense, so the answer is "had been." Choice (C) is correct. Choice (A) contains two adjectives as part of an appositive phrase modifying the subject, and choice (D), "upon the death," is idiomatically correct.

4. **(C)** Choice (C) should be "depend," not "had depended" because that use of past perfect would indicate prior past action. There is a series of events in this sentence: first, the legislature "had not finalized" the budget (B); then, Representative Wilson "pointed out" this failure (A). Choice (C), needs to be present tense as this situation still exists, and (D) is future action.

5. **(D)** In order to complete the parallelism, choice (D) should be "arrangements." Choice (A) is a noun used as an adjective. "To plan" (B) is an infinitive phrase followed by noun objects: "puppet shows and movies" and "garage sales." Choice (C), "used," is a participate modifying books.

6. **(A)** An infinitive, "to understand," should never be split by any adverbial modifier, "completely." Choice (B), "effects," is the noun form, and choice (D), "affected," is the adjective form. "One must," choice (C), is used in standard English.

7. **(C)** "More" is used to compare two things. Since the number of nations is not specified, "more" cannot be used in this sentence. Choice

(A), "known," modifies "roads"; choice (B) is idiomatically correct; choice (D), "is," agrees in number with its subject, "transportation."

8.   **(E)**   Choice (A), "many a," should always be followed by the singular verb, "wishes," of choice (B). Choice (C) is idiomatically correct. In "someone else," (D), "else" is needed to indicate a person other than the student would pay the bills.

9.   **(D)**   Choice (D) should read, "became very irritated." "To aggravate" means "to make worse"; "to irritate" means "to excite to impatience or anger." A situation is "aggravated" and becomes worse, but one does not become "aggravated" with people. Choices (A), (B), and (C) are correctly-used idioms.

10.   **(C)**   The reference in choice (C) is vague because it sounds as if the bus made the two students late. Choice (A) is a correct subject pronoun; choice (B) is the correct adverb form to modify "dressed"; choice (D) is a correct object pronoun.

11.   **(E)**   Choice (A), "among," indicates choice involving more than two things. The prepositions in (B) and (C) are correct. "Are," (D), is a plural verb, agreeing in number with the compound subject "singing...dancing...cooking."

12.   **(A)**   One is "disappointed by" a person or action but "disappointed in" what is not satisfactory. "Inexpensive," (B), is the adjective form. Parallel with "to work," choice (C), "save," had the word "to" omitted. Choice (D) compares the two models, one "inexpensive" and one "more expensive."

13.   **(A)**   The verb should be plural, "are," in order to agree with the compound subject, "budget...plans." Choice (B) begins an infinitive phrase which includes a participle, "existing," (C). Choice (D) is idiomatically correct.

14.   **(A)**   The expression should be phrased, "as delicate as." Choice (B) uses a possessive before a gerund; choice (C) is correctly used; and choice (D) is a possessive pronoun of neuter gender which is appropriate to use in referring to a plant.

15.   **(D)**   The verb "deal" must agree with the subject, "works," and not

a word in the intervening phrase. "Outwardly," choice (A), is an adverb modifying "seemed." Choices (B) and (C), "the picture of respectability," describe the subject; (D) is idiomatically correct.

16. **(D)** The word "of" in "inside of" is redundant and should not be used. Choice (A) is idiomatically correct and signals two classes of people once considered unequal in merit, and choice (B), "alike," is appropriate when comparing the two. Choice (C), "them," is correct pronoun usage.

17. **(E)** Choice (A), "unsafe for," is idiomatically correct; choice (B), "deltas," is a plural noun. Choice (C), "can be excellent," is grammatically correct. The preposition "in," choice (D), is correct.

18. **(C)** The verb in this subordinate clause is incorrect; the clause begins with, "which," and this word refers to "information." Therefore, the clause, in order to agree with antecedent, must read, "which shows." The verb "shows" should not be made to agree with "species" and "others." Choices (A), "people," and (B), "have compiled," agree in number. "Either" in choice (D) is correctly placed after the verb to show a choice of "endangered" or "becoming endangered."

19. **(D)** Do not end a sentence with a preposition; the phrase should read, "in which he was born." The verbs show proper time sequence in (A) and (B); choice (C) is correct pronoun usage and correct superlative degree of adjective.

20. **(D)** "Because" is the correct word to use in the cause and effect relationship in this sentence. Choice (A), "being that"; choice (E), "than me"; and choice (D), "the more" are not grammatically correct. Choice (C), "is made by you," is in the passive voice and not as direct as (D).

21. **(D)** "After they have been" completes the proper time sequence. Choice (A), "when"; choice (B), "have been"; and choice (C), "will be," are the wrong time sequences. Choice (E), "should be," is an idea not contained in the original sentence.

22. **(C)** "Since the plane is late" shows correct time sequence and good reasoning. Choice (A), "seeing as how," and choice (D), "being as," are poor wording. Choices (B), "when," and (E), "while," are the wrong time, logically, to be on the observation deck.

23. **(E)** Since a sentence should not end with a preposition, choices (A) and (B) are eliminated. Choices (C), "living in this world," and (D), "world's living," introduce new concepts.

24. **(A)** The construction, "than those," clarifies the fact that more vegetables have been added. Choice (C), "your suggestion"; choice (D), "than what"; and choice (E), "which," do not contain the idea of adding more varieties of vegetables. Choice (B) ends with a preposition.

25. **(B)** The voice must be consistent with "I", so (B) is the only possible correct answer. All other choices have a noun or pronoun that is not consistent with "I"; choice (A), "you"; choice (C), "a person"; choice (D), "people"; and choice (E), "some."

26. **(A)** The correct answer has two concepts—pieces are missing and pieces will probably never be found. Choice (B) has a singular verb, "is." Choice (C) indicates the pieces "probably will be" missing, which is not the problem. Choice (D) and choice (E) both indicate the pieces are "probably" missing, which is illogical because the pieces either are or are not missing.

27. **(C)** General reference should be avoided. The pronoun "which" does not have a clear reference in choices (A) or (B). In (C) "which" clearly refers to "facts." The reference "proving" in choice (D) is too general. In choice (E) "a proof" is an incorrect number to refer to the two strengths of women.

28. **(E)** Choice (E) is clear and concise and shows the correct comparison of architecture. The antecedent of "those" in choice (A) is not clear. Choice (B) is comparing "characteristics," not just architecture. Choice (C) is awkward, and choice (D) incorrectly uses an idiom, "characteristic with."

29. **(B)** Choice (B) is clear and direct. Choices (A) and (E) are too wordy. Choice (C) has the wrong concept, "balancing games." Choice (D) "this as an example" is poorly worded.

30. **(E)** An opposing force "gives" scattered resistance; therefore, choice (A) is incorrect. Choices (B), (C), and (D) are poorly worded and do not have the correct meaning.

31. **(A)** Choice (A) produces a complete sentence: "rainfall" is the subject and "let up" is the verb. None of the other choices produces a complete sentence.

32. **(D)** This choice uses the correct tense, "will have," showing action in the future. All the other verbs listed do not show correct future verb construction.

33. **(B)** The correct choice has a compound verb: "comes" and "falls in love." The salesman comes to town first, then he meets and falls in love with the librarian. Choice (A), with its misplaced participial phrase, sounds as if either the town or Iowa is in love with the librarian. Choice (C) would produce a run-on sentence. Choices (D) and (E) have unclear tense.

34. **(B)** Choice (B) clears up the pronoun usage problem, eliminating the ambiguous reference of "he"; it is clear that Dickens is delighted. Choice (A) does not clearly identify the antecedent of "he." Choice (C) incorrectly identified the "delighted" person as the giver, not Dickens. Choices (D) and (E) both create fragments.

35. **(A)** Choice (A) combines all the elements correctly and uses parallel structure, creating a balanced sentence. Choice (B) is not exactly parallel, and the many commas create confusion. Choice (C) does not have parallel verbs: "wanted" and "being." Choices (D) and (E) incorrectly combine the two ideas, making it seem as if the children are blocking Grip's action.

36. **(D)** Choice (D) keeps the formal tone of the essay and avoids passive voice. Choice (A) and choice (E) both break the formal tone and use another voice: "you" and "I." Choice (B) is perhaps too formal and not straightforward. Choice (C) uses the passive voice.

37. **(E)** Choice (E) smoothly combines both major ideas as a cause-and-effect sequence. Choice (A) is the next best choice, but it is not as smoothly worded in the first half; also, this choice eliminates the idea of "use" in the second half. Choice (B) does not clarify the source of Poe's dissatisfaction. Choice (C) does not clearly present the idea that the prophetic use was Poe's, not Dickens'. Choice (D) has too many interruptions.

38. **(A)**   Choice (A) is correct; the paragraph gives information on the origin of the bird. Although the paragraph gives one or two humorous incidents, choice (B) cannot be the main intention. Choice (C) is unlikely; the bird's biting is presented as more humorous than tragic. Choice (D) would be a more effective label for paragraph two. Choice (E) is partly correct, but the second paragraph returns to the Dickens' household.

39. **(C)**   Choice (C) clears up the confusion caused by the possessive pronoun "his," which in this sentence would incorrectly refer to "Dickens' children." "Their" would also be fine, but "the" is probably best, as it is clear from the context which family we are referring to. Choice (A) adds "it," which is unnecessary and redundant. Choice (B) replaces the past with the past progressive tense, which does not agree with the verb tense throughout the passage. Choice (D) replaces a neat prepositional phrase with an awkward clause. Choice (E) is repetitive; it is clear that "the raven" is still the subject of the sentence.

PSAT/ NMSQT

Practice Test 2

TEST 2

Section 1

(Answer sheets appear in the back of this book.)

TIME: 25 Minutes
26 Questions

For each question in this section, select the best answer from among the given choices and fill in the corresponding oval on the answer sheet.

DIRECTIONS: Each sentence below has one or two blanks, each blank indicating that something has been omitted. Beneath the sentence are five lettered words or sets of words. Choose the word or set of words that **BEST** fits the meaning of the sentence as a whole.

EXAMPLE:

Although the critics found the book _____, many of the readers found it rather _____.

(A) obnoxious . . . perfect

(B) spectacular . . . interesting

(C) boring . . . intriguing

(D) comical . . . persuasive

(E) popular . . . rare

(A) (B) ● (D) (E)

---

1. In the modern age, techniques of underwater photography have allowed scientists to _____ forms of life that previously could only have been imagined.

    (A) periscope

    (B) submarine

    (C) document

    (D) magnify

    (E) rancor

2. There are many small islands in the Mediterranean Sea that are _____ the mainland of Greece.

    (A) contingent upon

    (B) adjacent to

(C) dependent upon   (D) obstructed by

(E) neglected by

3. Lina's parents did not object to her going out with her friends after school; however, they wanted to be _____.

(A) consulted   (D) predicted

(B) insulted   (E) preordained

(C) isolated

4. The school orchestra needed a cymbal player, so the music teacher placed a notice in the school paper asking for someone to play in the _____ section.

(A) instrument   (D) percussion

(B) triangle   (E) brass

(C) harp

5. When working together on a project, people need to have a sense of _____.

(A) humor   (D) habituation

(B) cooperation   (E) affliction

(C) cooptation

6. Jennifer's mother contracted a carpenter to build more bookshelves in her room because the ones she had were filled to _____.

(A) perspective   (D) calamity

(B) triumvirate   (E) capacity

(C) tenacity

7. The girls on the basketball team thought the ball went out of bounds, but the referee did not _____ their shouts of protest.

(A) prohibit   (D) target

(B) acknowledge   (E) correct

(C) implement

---

8. PAMPHLET : TEXTBOOK ::

    (A) letter : noun   (D) aspect : panorama

    (B) window : door   (E) rhyme : poem

    (C) nation : language

9. BOAST : PRAISE ::

    (A) authorize : laws   (D) commend : ignore

    (B) fast : food   (E) atone : amend

    (C) detract : compliment

10. MALEVOLENT : EVIL ::

    (A) beneficient : good   (D) hurt : robust

    (B) prosperous : money (E) somnolent : clear

    (C) invincible : predictable

11. MISER : THRIFT ::

    (A) sadist : work   (D) hedonist : pleasure

    (B) villain : cheer   (E) glutton : food

    (C) pedestrian : defiance

12. INSIPID : SERIOUS ::

   (A) goal-directed : organized   (D) precarious : safe

   (B) precursor : forerunner   (E) silly : absurd

   (C) carefree : spurious

13. JUDGE : GAVEL ::

   (A) clerk : broom   (D) tennis : sport

   (B) carpenter : hammer   (E) barber : haircut

   (C) brief : lawyer

DIRECTIONS: Read each passage and answer the questions that follow. Each question will be based on the information stated or implied in the passage or its introduction.

Questions 14-18 are based on the following passage.

The following passage describes architecture in the American Colonies at the beginning of the eighteenth century.

1   Almost coincidental with the opening of the eighteenth century, Renaissance architecture finally reached the American Colonies. This "severely formal" adaptation of the classic Roman orders and design, born in Italy in the Fifteenth century, first appeared in England around 1570 and reached
5 its mature phase there 50 years later. The timelag of 130 years before it spread to the Colonies is a measure of the economic and social gap between the mother country and her offspring.

   Colonial Renaissance architecture, influenced directly by that of the late Stuart period in England, became known as the Georgian after the advent
10 of the Hanoverian dynasty. Its general features included a balanced design; the use of classic orders to embellish doorways and entrance facades; predominantly brick construction, laid in Flemish bond (although the wood-building tradition was so strong in New England that many of the finer Georgian mansions there were clapboarded); low-pitched roofs, fre-
15 quently hipped; sheathed and highly finished interiors; and such treatment of the entrance hall as to make it a room of major importance. After midcentury the Late Georgian style evolved, with such features as the projecting central pavilion, giant pilasters at the corners, small entrance portico, larger windowpanes, roofs pitched progressively lower,
20 balustraded roof decks, and dado interior decoration with wallpaper above paneling.

Although adapted from English antecedents, "Georgian architecture in America was singularly free from either the practice or the doctrine of exact imitation." Professional and amateur American architects, and the
25 humbler carpenter-builders who augmented the work of the few architects, all felt free to disregard their handbooks on occasion, "in accordance with necessity, invention, or taste."

In Charleston, South Carolina, the typical eighteenth-century dwelling was Georgian, but with a certain southern flavor. A disastrous fire in 1740
30 caused the assembly to specify nonflammable future construction. Charleston became a city of brick houses, faced with tinted stucco and covered with red tile roofs, unlike any other colonial metropolis. Many were "double houses" of typical Georgian design; others were of that peculiarly Charleston type called the "single house," standing "with its
35 shoulder to the street," only one room in width and having a long piazza on one side.

Not all eighteenth-century American architecture was Georgian, by any means. The cultural lag between England and the Colonies had its parallel within the Colonies. A progression from the seaboard to the frontier, or
40 from the top to bottom of the economic scale, would bring to view more humble dwellings—less durable, smaller, and of more antique design. Of these the best known was the log cabin, apparently introduced in New Sweden in the mid-seventeenth century, but reaching it present familiar role of a frontier home a century later through its popularity among the
45 Scotch-Irish frontiersmen.

14. Factors influencing the time-lag in the adoption of Renaissance architecture by the American Colonies

    (A) were primarily political, since Britain rigidly controlled Colonial tastes.

    (B) were neutralized in the case of Charleston, South Carolina, which immediately imported British architecture.

    (C) were both geographical and economic.

    (D) derived from resistance to the Stuart reign in England.

    (E) derived from a series of calamities, like the 1740 fire.

15. One of the singular qualities in the American architects is

    (A) their total fidelity to an already-established style.

    (B) their innovation of the Late Georgian style.

    (C) their complete devotion to the so-called "log cabin" format.

(D) their commitment to brick as a building material.

(E) their relative freedom in style from European rules.

16. The appearance of "clapboard" (line 14) in Georgian mansions is due to

(A) the dearth of lasting building materials in New England.

(B) the New England predilection for working in wood.

(C) the respect in New England for English antecedents.

(D) the need for nonflammable materials.

(E) the influence of Flemish models.

17. According to the article, Charleston represents

(A) a Georgian style of architecture unaffected by regional considerations.

(B) the typical Colonial metropolis of brick and stucco.

(C) a unique architectural city, blending the South with Georgian ideals.

(D) a city totally obliged to the single house concept.

(E) a city totally obliged to the double house concept.

18. The progression from the seaboard to the frontier

(A) reveals an unchanging architectural landscape.

(B) is analogous to the historical gap between England and the Colonies.

(C) shows the dominance of the eighteenth-century Georgian tradition.

(D) tends to reveal an increase in the affluence of the inhabitants.

(E) tends to introduce architectural forms for which there are no European precedents.

Questions 19-26 are based on the following passage.

The following passage is excerpted from the diary of Thomas Henry Huxley in Life and Letters of Thomas Henry Huxley.

1   It is not given to every medical student to make an anatomical discovery, even a small one. In this case Thomas Huxley the boy of 19, investigating things for himself, found a hitherto undiscovered membrance in the root of the human hair, which received the name of Huxley's layer.

5   Speculations, such as had filled his mind in early boyhood, still haunted his thoughts. In one of his letters from the *Ratlesnake*, he gives his account of how he was possessed in his student days by that problem which has beset so many a strong imagination, the problem of perpetual motion, and even sought an interview with Faraday, whom he left with the resolu-
10   tion to meet the great man some day on a more equal footing.

       To-day, ruminating over the manifold ins and outs of life in general, and my own in particular, it came into my head suddenly that I would write down my interview with Faraday—how many years ago? Aye, there's the rub, for I have completely forgotten. However, it must have
15   been in either my first or second winter session at Charing Cross, and it was before Christmas I feel sure.

       I remember how my long brooding perpetual motion scheme (which I had made more than one attempt to realize, but failed owing to insufficient mechanical dexterity) had been working upon me, depriving me of
20   rest even, and heating my brain with *chateaux d'Espagne* of endless variety. I remember, too, it was Sunday morning when I determined to put the questions, which neither my wits nor my hands would set at rest, into some hands for decision, and I determined to go before some tribunal from whence appeal should be absurd.

25   But to whom to go? I knew no one among the high priests of science, and going about with a scheme for perpetual motion was, I knew, for most people the same thing as courting ridicule among high and low. After all I fixed upon Faraday, possibly perhaps because I knew where he was to be found, but in part also because the cool logic of his works made
30   me hope that my poor scheme would be treated on some other principle than that of mere previous opinion one way or other. Besides, the known courtesy and affability of the man encouraged me. So I wrote a letter, drew a plan, enclosed the two in an envelope, and tremblingly betook myself on the following afternoon to the Royal Institution.

35   "Is Dr. Faraday here?" said I to the porter. "No, sir, he has just gone out." I felt relieved. "Be good enough to give him this letter," and I was out when a little man in a brown coat came in at the glass door. "Here is Dr. Faraday," said the man, and gave him my letter. He turned to me and

courteously inquired what I wished. "To submit to you that letter, sir, if
40 you are not occupied." "My time is always occupied, sir, but step this
way," and he led me into the museum or library, for I forget which it was,
only I know there was a glass case against which we leant. He read my
letter, did not think my plan would answer. Was I acquainted with mechanism, what we call the laws of motion? I saw all was up with my poor
45 scheme, so after trying a little to explain, in the course of which I certainly
failed in giving him a clear idea of what I would be at, I thanked him for
his attention, and went off as dissatisfied as ever. The sense of one part of
the conversation I well recollect. He said, "that were the perpetual motion
possible, it would have occurred spontaneously in nature, and would have
50 overpowered all other forces," or words to that effect. I did not see the
force of this, but did not feel competent enough to discuss the question.

However, all this exorcised my devil, and he has rarely come to trouble
me since. Some future day, perhaps, I may be able to call Faraday's
attention more decidedly . . . ."

19. The main purpose of the author's writing is to

    (A) describe his plans for a perpetual motion machine.

    (B) describe life in Charing Cross during the winter.

    (C) detail a meeting with Dr. Faraday and to speculate on future
          encounters with the learned man.

    (D) advance scientific knowledge of the Royal Institute.

    (E) present an abstract philosophical treatise.

20. The writer had not created the machine himself because

    (A) of his lack of mechanical dexterity.

    (B) of his desire to discuss the entire plan with Faraday first.

    (C) of his fear of ridicule.

    (D) inability to visit the Royal Institute.

    (E) lack of funds.

21. Faraday seemed to

    (A) suggest that the writer knew much of the laws of motion.

    (B) hint that nature would have already mastered perpetual motion if
          it were possible.

(C) suggest a lack of logic to the mind of the writer.

(D) be too busy to give audience to others at any time.

(E) get a clear idea of the writer's idea.

22. In line 52, "... all this exorcised my devil ..." means that

    (A) a haunting or supernatural being was at work.

    (B) the writer's desire to visit the Royal Institute had been satisfied.

    (C) the writer no longer was interested in ever seeing Faraday again.

    (D) the writer had permanently put science out of his life.

    (E) the writer no longer felt compelled to work on a perpetual motion machine at the present time.

23. The author's feeling after the interview is

    (A) indignation toward his treatment by Faraday.

    (B) dissatisfaction with Faraday's ability to communicate.

    (C) intense interest in visiting Faraday again with other schemes.

    (D) dissatisfaction with his ability to communicate well with Faraday.

    (E) pride in his ability to discuss science competently with an expert.

24. The author was least likely to choose Faraday for the interview because

    (A) Faraday had a reputation of being courteous.

    (B) fate had Faraday arriving when he delivered the letter.

    (C) Faraday was a noted scientist of the time.

    (D) Faraday was located conveniently to him.

    (E) he knew of Faraday's intemperate disposition.

25. The author's statement at the end of the passage would be best followed

    (A) by additional information on a perpetual motion machine created by a noted scientist.

    (B) by information on an interview with another noted scientist.

    (C) by information on a significant achievement by the writer.

    (D) by a personal letter written by Faraday to the writer.

    (E) by a relaxed conversation with the porter.

26. Faraday seemed to sense the power of

    (A) love.   (D) the author's scheme.

    (B) perpetual motion.   (E) logic.

    (C) the laws of science.

Section 2

TIME: 25 Minutes
20 Questions

DIRECTIONS: Solve each problem, using any available space on the page for scratch work. Then decide which answer choice is the best and fill in the corresponding oval on the answer sheet.

NOTES:

(1) The use of a calculator is permitted. All numbers used are real numbers.

(2) Figures that accompany problems in this test are intended to provide information useful in solving the problems. They are drawn as accurately as possible EXCEPT when it is stated in a specific problem that the figure is not drawn to scale. All figures lie in a plane unless otherwise indicated.

REFERENCE INFORMATION:

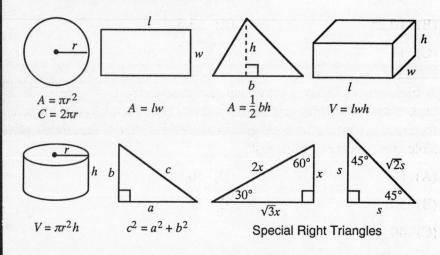

$A = \pi r^2$
$C = 2\pi r$

$A = lw$

$A = \frac{1}{2}bh$

$V = lwh$

$V = \pi r^2 h$

$c^2 = a^2 + b^2$

Special Right Triangles

The number of degrees of arc in a circle is 360.
The measure in degrees of a straight angle is 180.
The sum of the measures in degrees of the angles of a triangle is 180.

1. Grace is throwing a party for her friends and wishes to make a fruit punch of orange juice and pineapple juice. She has 24 ounces of orange juice and 72 ounces of pineapple juice. She would like the final punch to be 45 percent orange juice. If she is going to add x ounces of orange juice to what she already has, which of the following represents an equation she could solve to determine how may additional ounces of orange juice she must add?

   (A) $\dfrac{24}{72+x} = \dfrac{45}{100}$ (D) $\dfrac{24+x}{72+x} = \dfrac{45}{100}$

   (B) $\dfrac{24+x}{72} = \dfrac{45}{100}$ (E) $\dfrac{24+x}{96+x} = \dfrac{45}{100}$

   (C) $\dfrac{24+x}{96} = \dfrac{45}{100}$

2. The average (arithmetic mean) of nine consecutive integers is 16. What is the average of the four smallest of the integers?

   (A) 9   (D) 12.75

   (B) 10.25   (E) 13.5

   (C) 11

3. A high school biology class had 60 students in it. All the students took a test that was graded from 0 to 100. Precisely 40 students received grades equal to or greater than 75. What is the lowest possible class average for the test?

   (A) 60   (D) 30

   (B) 50   (E) 20

   (C) 40

4. At the beginning of the first week of a going out of business sale, the price of a complete bedroom set was x. At the close of each week the price of each item not yet sold was decreased by 20%. If no one bought the bedroom set, what would be its price, in terms of x, at the beginning of the fifth week?

   (A) $\dfrac{2x}{5}$ (B) $\dfrac{4x}{25}$

(C) $\dfrac{8x}{125}$ (D) $\dfrac{256x}{625}$

(E) $\dfrac{32x}{3,125}$

5. Set A: 10, 12, 14, 16
    Set B: 11, 13, 15, 17

    For all ordered pairs (a, b), a is a member of Set A and b is a member of Set B. How many different ordered pairs satisfy the expression $a + b < 27$?

    (A) 7 (D) 4

    (B) 6 (E) 3

    (C) 5

6. A major league baseball team is considering tearing down the present stadium and building a new stadium. In a survey of 10,000 people, 700 of them said they would support the idea of a new stadium and the rest would not. What percentage of the group surveyed does not support the idea of a new stadium?

    (A) 7% (D) 70%

    (B) 9.3% (E) 93%

    (C) 65%

7. In this problem, $a > b > c > d > e > f > g$ and a, b, c, d, e, f, and g represent consecutive integers. If $b + f = 0$, what does $ab = ?$

    (A) 0 (D) 6

    (B) 2 (E) 8

    (C) 4

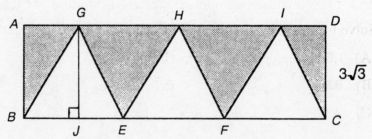

8. In the diagram on the previous page, *ABCD* is a rectangle, *GBE*, *HEF*, and *IFC* are equilateral triangles. What is the area of the shaded region?

   (A) $6\sqrt{3}$ (D) $36\sqrt{3}$

   (B) $18\sqrt{3}$ (E) $54\sqrt{3}$

   (C) $27\sqrt{3}$

9. A square has a side length of $^3/_4$. Find the difference between the perimeter and the area ignoring the dimensions associated with the numbers.

   (A) $3\dfrac{9}{16}$ (D) 2

   (B) $3\dfrac{3}{4}$ (E) $2\dfrac{7}{16}$

   (C) 3

10. $c = -6$ is *not* a solution for which of the following?

    (A) $\dfrac{1}{2}c + \dfrac{1}{3}c = -5$ (D) $c^2 + 6c = 0$

    (B) $c^2 + 5c - 6 = 0$ (E) $c^2 + 36 = 0$

    (C) $c^2 - 36 = 0$

11. If two positive integers are in the ratio of 5 : 3 and their difference is 12, find the larger number.

    (A) 24   (D) 32

    (B) 28   (E) 36

    (C) 30

12. Solve for *R*: $.004R + .04 = .4 + 4$.

    (A) 1,090   (D) .08

    (B) 109   (E) .012

    (C) .4

13. If $x \# y$ means $x^2 + \sqrt{y}$, then $4 \# 4 =$

    (A) 4.

    (B) 6.

    (C) 10.

    (D) 16.

    (E) 18.

14. $100 (.06 + .04) + 10 (.3 + .7) =$

    (A) 10

    (B) 20

    (C) .1

    (D) .01

    (E) .001

15. $.009 \times 10^{-2} =$

    (A) .09

    (B) .9

    (C) 9

    (D) .0009

    (E) .00009

16. Find $3^2/_3\%$ of 300.

    (A) 1,100

    (B) 110

    (C) 11

    (D) 1.1

    (E) .11

17. Simplify: $12 - 10 (12 - 10)^3$.

    (A) 16

    (B) −16

    (C) 12

    (D) −12

    (E) −68

18. If $^m/_9$ is between 3 and 4, then a possible value of m is which of the following?

    (A) 11

    (B) 15

    (C) 20

    (D) 24

    (E) 28

19. Which has the largest value?

    (A) $\sqrt{\dfrac{5}{8}}$

    (B) $\sqrt{\dfrac{7}{10}}$

    (C) $\sqrt{\dfrac{6}{13}}$

    (D) $\sqrt{\dfrac{4}{9}}$

    (E) $\dfrac{1}{2}$

20. If $2F = 3G$ and $5G = 7H$, find the ratio of $F : H$.

    (A) $21 : 10$

    (B) $2 : 7$

    (C) $7 : 2$

    (D) $3 : 7$

    (E) $7 : 3$

Section 3

TIME: 25 Minutes
26 Questions

For each question in this section, select the best answer from among the given choices and fill in the corresponding oval on the answer sheet.

DIRECTIONS: Each sentence below has one or two blanks, each blank indicating that something has been omitted. Beneath the sentence are five lettered words or sets of words. Choose the word or set of words that **BEST** fits the meaning of the sentence as a whole.

EXAMPLE:

Although the critics found the book _____, many of the readers found it rather _____.

(A) obnoxious . . . perfect   (D) comical . . . persuasive

(B) spectacular . . . interesting   (E) popular . . . rare

(C) boring . . . intriguing   (A) (B) ● (D) (E)

---

27. Jason called the store's customer service department about the defective stereo he had purchased, but he was told to contact the manufacturer because they could not assume _____ for the product's defect.

    (A) involvement   (D) concurrently

    (B) counteraction   (E) subjectivity

    (C) liability

28. Aristotle deplored many of the excesses in human behavior, and wrote about the need for _____ in life.

    (A) indulgence   (D) judiciousness

    (B) sacrifice   (E) subsistence

    (C) upheavals

29. The judge moved the trial to another location because the case was not under her _____.

    (A) jurisdiction   (D) deposition

    (B) territory   (E) litigation

    (C) jury

30. The detective had a(n) _____ about the murderer's identity because, as a(n) _____, he is proficient at reasoning carefully.

    (A) hunch . . . logician   (D) foreboding . . . idealist

    (B) inkling . . . mathematician   (E) tribulation . . . expert

    (C) premonition . . . sophist

31. In Greek mythology, Icarus flew too close to the sun, thereby _____ his wax-and-feather wings, _____ him to fall into the sea.

    (A) soldering . . . allowing   (D) melting . . . causing

    (B) rearranging . . . propelling   (E) aerating . . . directing

    (C) illuminating . . . enabling

32. Emily Dickinson's poems were all published _____, because they were not discovered until after her death.

    (A) secretly   (D) posthumously

    (B) appropriately   (E) inexplicably

    (C) preposterously

DIRECTIONS: Each question below consists of a related pair of words or phrases, followed by five lettered pairs of words or phrases. Select the lettered pair that best expresses a relationship similar to that expressed in the original pair.

EXAMPLE:

SMILE : MOUTH ::

(A) wink : eye   (D) tan : skin

(B) teeth : face   (E) food : gums

(C) voice : speech

---

33. DESK : FURNITURE ::

   (A) tennis : ball

   (B) milk : cow

   (C) heel : toe

   (D) chair : oak

   (E) penny : money

34. CEREBELLUM : BRAIN ::

   (A) foot : toe

   (B) lozenge : throat

   (C) fibula : wrist

   (D) bloom : flower

   (E) aorta : heart

35. SERENDIPITOUS : PLANNED ::

   (A) indefatigable : lazy

   (B) elegant : charming

   (C) cohesive : organized

   (D) cooperative : loyal

   (E) jumbled : disparate

36. PLAGIARIZE : STEAL::

   (A) crave : discrete

   (B) pollute : clean

   (C) originate : correct

   (D) act : masquerade

   (E) accessorize : decorate

37. RETARD : ADVANCE ::

   (A) garrulous : talkative

   (B) postpone : proceed

   (C) monitor : supervise

   (D) submit : yield

   (E) steal : burglar

38. POSTULATE : CLAIM ::

   (A) lionize : dethrone

   (B) offense : aggravate

   (C) ridicule : laugh

   (D) cavil : carp

   (E) challenge : swindle

39. ICHTHYOLOGIST : FISH ::

   (A) psychiatrist : insane   (D) cardiologist : lungs

   (B) botanist : plants   (E) anatomist : bones

   (C) podiatrist : children

DIRECTIONS: Read the passage and answer the questions that follow. Each question will be based on the information stated or implied in the passage or its introduction.

Questions 40-44 are based on the following passage.

The following passage is excerpted from a book of literary criticism analyzing the works of George Eliot and others from 1789-1877.

1   When we have passed in review the works of that great writer who calls herself George Eliot, and given for a time our use of sight to her portraitures of men and women, what form, as we move away, persists on the field of vision, and remains the chief centre of interest for the imagina-
5 tion? The form not of Tito, or Maggie, or Dinah, or Silas, but of one who, if not the real George Eliot, is that second self who writes her books, and lives and speaks through them. Such a second self of an author is perhaps more substantial than any mere human personality encumbered with the accidents of flesh and blood and daily living. It stands at some distance
10 from the primary self, and differs considerably from its fellow. It presents its person to us with fewer reserves; it is independent of local and temporary motives of speech or of silence; it knows no man after the flesh; it is more than an individual; it utters secrets, but secrets which all men of all ages are to catch; while, behind it, lurks well pleased the veritable histori-
15 cal self secure from impertinent observation and criticism. With this second self of George Eliot it is, not with the actual historical person, that we have to do. . . .

    [This] personal accent in the writing of George Eliot does not interfere with their dramatic truthfulness; it adds to the power with which they
20 grasp the heart and conscience of the reader. We cannot say with confidence of any of her creations that it is a projection of herself; the lines of their movement are not deflected by hidden powers of attraction or repulsion peculiar to the mind of the author; most noteworthy is her impartiality towards the several creatures of her imagination; she condemns but does
25 not hate; she is cold or indifferent to none; each lives his own life, good or bad; but the author is present in the midst of them, indicating, interpreting; and we discern in the moral laws, the operation of which presides over the action of each story, those abstractions from the common fund of truth

which the author has found most needful to her own deepest life. We feel
30 in reading these works that we are in the presence of a soul, and a soul
which has had a history.

At the same time the novels of George Eliot are not didactic treatises.
They are primarily works of art and George Eliot herself is artist as much
as she is teacher. Many good things in particular passages of her writings
35 are detachable; admirable sayings can be cleared from their surroundings,
and presented by themselves, knocked out clean as we knock out fossils
from a piece of limestone. But if we separate the moral soul of any complete work of hers from its artistic medium, if we murder to dissect, we
lose far more than we gain. When a work of art can be understood only by
40 enjoying it, the art is of a high kind.

40. The primary focus of the passage is on the

    (A) impressive number of portraitures of men and women created by
that great writer George Eliot.

    (B) lack of importance of the primary self of Eliot.

    (C) evident bias of Eliot toward each of her characters which is
"needful to her own deepest life."

    (D) writings of George Eliot which are considered by the writer to
be inferior since they can be understood only by enjoying them
and enjoyment is inferior to cognition.

    (E) projection of Eliot which appears in her creations.

41. The author describes George Eliot's writings primarily as

    (A) painful personal recollections.

    (B) compositions which must be kept intact at all cost.

    (C) didactic treatises.

    (D) a revelation of the historical person of George Eliot.

    (E) works of art with a moral soul.

42. In context, the reference to Eliot's works as being "not didactic treatises" (line 32) suggests that they are

    (A) moralistic compositions.

    (B) instructive writing.

    (C) dramatic revelations.

(D) social criticisms.

(E) pleasurable readings.

43. The passage indicates that the reader's correct response to Eliot's writing should be to

(A) analyze it completely.

(B) enjoy the writings given us by the artist and detach from them what we can.

(C) search for the glimpses of George Eliot's real self which are hidden there.

(D) dissect the works until we reach "the moral soul" which we should separate and savor.

(E) search for Eliot's feelings toward each character which is evident upon careful scrutiny.

44. Eliot's characters can best be described as

(A) projections of Eliot herself.

(B) impartial presentations.

(C) living their own lives without any presence of the author.

(D) didactic.

(E) incomplete portraitures.

DIRECTIONS: Read the passages and answer the questions that follow. Each question will be based on the information stated or implied in the selection or its introduction, and may be based on the relationship between the passages.

Questions 45-52 are based on the following passages.

The following passages discuss the philosophy of leadership.
Passage 1 examines the role of a university president, while
Passage 2 discusses the leadership style of a king.

Passage 1

1   Considering in retrospect the American university presidents under whom I have served and some others with whom I have had unofficial acquaintance, I feel that it is impossible to overestimate the services they

rendered in transforming some of our colleges from mediocre high schools
into great institutions of learning. For the performance of this gigantic task
centralization of power was necessary, and it is not surprising that often
administrative functions and the publicity incident to the provision of en-
dowments have taken precedence over preoccupation with what Lassere
has called the *importances philosophiques*. The administrative tail had
often to wag the education dog.

But the work of these great pioneers is done. Many of our universities
have already outgrown in magnitude the needs of the numerically small
percentage of truly educatable material in a stabilizing population. Serious
educators are beginning to realize that the country might be better served
by an improved high-school and a *Lycée*-like junior-college system leaving the universities to pursue their true functions with a minimum of rah-
rah boys and sorority sisters. The period before us will be one of intensifi-
cation and scholarly reorientation. But, in the transition, a crushing task
lies on the shoulders of the poor college president, for the corporations and
trustees from whom he receives his portfolio—largely composed of bank-
ers, merchants, and local Poo-Bahs—have rarely sensed the change in the
educational atmosphere, and expect of him the combined talents of the
director of a biscuit factory and those of a great intellectual leader.

Let us examine his predicament. The lay college of cardinals endows its
new pope with omnipotence, without being able to grant him at the same
time infallibility. Then what do they expect of him? He must supervise the
wise distribution of an income of anywhere from two hundred and fifty
thousand dollars to a million, or more. He must preside over the delibera-
tions of faculties, discussing educational problems, economics, history,
literature, languages, classics, mathematics, physics, chemistry, biology,
medicine, law, engineering, theology, philosophy, and so on. He has riv-
eted to his legs the academic balls and chains of business schools, schools
of education (to teach teachers teaching), schools of journalism, advertising academies, and similar vocational callings foisted upon universities by
well-meaning philanthropists. To these may be added, with the rising dignity of labor, graduate schools of taxidermy, plumbing, embalming, sales-
manship, and chiropody. These he must so fit into the academic picture
that they may do the least harm without breaking the deed of gift. He is
chairman of all committees and administrative boards, which he must
appoint with sagacity. He is court of last resort on all disciplinary measures of student body or faculty, and must get rid of old wood and take
responsibility for new appointments, becoming thereby involved with the
American Federation of Labor. He must preside at commencements,
alumni dinners, educational conventions, conclaves of a dozen varieties of
visiting firemen, and make at least one speech a week, with new stories

and profound and original educational theory; unless the occasion demands criticism—or prophecy—of domestic politics, European turpitude,
or the future of democracy. He must be ready at any time to don his
academic robes and by *his litteris . . . unanimi consensu et hoco poco*
50 *academico* perform medieval rites.

Passage 2

Meanwhile I had returned home and began working. When the King
appeared at the door of my castle he heard the hammers going, and ordered everyone to keep quiet. Everyone in the shop was hard at it and as a
result, not expecting the King, I was taken by surprise. He entered my hall,
55 and the first thing he saw was me myself, standing there working on a
great piece of silver, which I was using for the body of Jupiter. One man
was beating out the head and another the legs, and the noise was deafen-
ing. While I was working I had a little French lad of mine helping me: he
had annoyed me in some way or another and so I had given him a kick,
60 and, as luck had it, . . . I had sent him hurtling a good few yards. So as the
King came in the little lad clung to him to keep his balance.

His Majesty burst out laughing, while I stood there, dumbfounded. Then
the King began to ask me what I was doing, and wanted me to go on
working. He said that I would please him far more if I didn't exhaust
65 myself but instead hired as many men as I needed and made them do the
work, since he wanted me to safeguard my health so as to be able to serve
him longer. I replied that if I didn't work myself I would fall ill immediately, and besides this I wouldn't achieve the results I wanted to achieve
for him. Thinking I was saying this merely to sound impressive and not
70 because it was, in fact, the truth, the King made the Cardinal of Lorraine
repeat what he had said. I explained to the Cardinal the reasons for my
attitude so frankly and fully that he was thoroughly convinced and advised
the King to let me work little or much, just as I liked.

The King returned to the palace, highly satisfied with my work. He
75 overwhelmed me with favors and it would take too long to describe them
all. The very next day, at dinner, he sent for me. The Cardinal of Ferrara
was there dining with him. When I arrived the King was still on the
second course. I approached his Majesty and he began to talk to me at
once, saying that since he had such a beautiful bowl and jug from my hand
80 he wanted a fine salt-cellar to keep them company. He added that he
would like me to make a design for one, but that he wanted it in a hurry.

I answered: "Your Majesty will see a design much sooner than you ask,
because when I was making the bowl I thought that a salt-cellar should be
made to match: it's already done, and if you like I shall show it to you
85 without delay."

The King turned in great animation to the noblemen who were with him—the King of Navarre, the Cardinal of Lorraine, and the Cardinal of Ferrara—and said:

"He certainly knows how to win the love and friendship of everyone
90 who knows him."

Then he turned to me and said that he would be only too pleased to see the design I had made. I ran the errand very quickly, since I had only to cross the river, that is, the Seine; and I brought back with me a wax model I had already made in Rome at the request of the Cardinal of Ferrara.
95 When I was back in the King's presence I uncovered the model, and he said in astonishment:

"This is a hundred times more heavenly than I'd ever have thought: what a marvel the man is! He should never stop working."

45. The author of Passage 1 uses the statement "the administrative tail ... the education dog" (lines 9-10) to suggest that

    (A) administrative tasks can overshadow the more important task of educating college students.

    (B) administrative tasks should always take precedence over educating college students.

    (C) the number of students who are truly educatable is a small percentage of the actual number of students.

    (D) educating college students is not the role of a university president.

    (E) administrative tasks and the education of students cannot both be achieved in a university setting.

46. The discussion of "educatable material" and "rah-rah boys and sorority sisters" (lines 13-17) shows that the author feels that

    (A) colleges should completely do away with extracurricular activities.

    (B) education should be denied to all but the most scholarly students.

    (C) there should be separate learning institutions for those who want to pursue a serious education.

    (D) the American scholastic system should continue to function in the traditional manner.

(E) there is a lack of qualified instructors at the college level.

47. The phrase "old wood" (lines 41-42) most likely refers to

    (A) enemies of the president.

    (B) outdated faculty and administrators.

    (C) non-scholarly students.

    (D) discipline problems.

    (E) broken furniture.

48. The final paragraph of Passage 1 serves to

    (A) show that university presidents should have absolute authority.

    (B) show that the position of university president should be dissolved into various committees.

    (C) excuse any errors that a university president may make.

    (D) illustrate the magnitude of the responsibilities of a university president.

    (E) explain why there is a high turnover rate among university presidents.

49. The author of Passage 2 most likely considers the King's interest in table-settings to be

    (A) a very important issue that the King must confront.

    (B) an inconsequential detail that the King should not be so concerned with.

    (C) the result of the King's refined sensibilities.

    (D) a necessary ingredient in the running of an efficient kingdom.

    (E) a sign that the King is a wise, judicious leader.

50. The King's statement "He certainly . . . knows him" (lines 89-90) would probably be described by the author as

    (A) a deserved compliment.

    (B) a wise comment.

    (C) a brilliant observation.

(D) a comical overstatement.

(E) an important declaration.

51. The idea of the author of Passage 1 that the "centralization of power (is) necessary" (line 6) would most likely

(A) be in agreement with the philosophy of the author of Passage 2.

(B) not be a concern of the author of Passage 2.

(C) be contradicted by the author of Passage 2.

(D) justify the desires of the King in Passage 2.

(E) explain the social position of the narrator in Passage 2.

52. Both passages are primarily concerned with

(A) the role of leadership in today's society.

(B) the dangers of placing too much power in the hands of one person.

(C) the amount of involvement a leader should have in day-to-day decision making.

(D) the necessity that a leader be granted infallibility.

(E) the problem of class structure in a monarchical society.

Section 4

TIME: 25 Minutes
20 Questions

DIRECTIONS: Solve each problem, using any available space on the page for scratch work. Then decide which answer choice is the best and fill in the corresponding oval on the answer sheet.

NOTES:

(1) The use of a calculator is permitted. All numbers used are real numbers.

(2) Figures that accompany problems in this test are intended to provide information useful in solving the problems. They are drawn as accurately as possible EXCEPT when it is stated in a specific problem that the figure is not drawn to scale. All figures lie in a plane unless otherwise indicated.

REFERENCE INFORMATION:

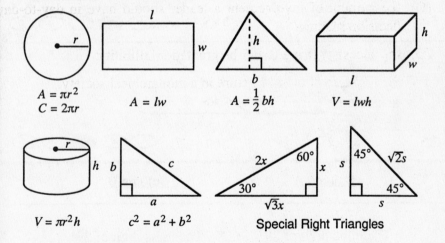

$$A = \pi r^2$$
$$C = 2\pi r$$

$$A = lw$$

$$A = \frac{1}{2}bh$$

$$V = lwh$$

$$V = \pi r^2 h$$

$$c^2 = a^2 + b^2$$

Special Right Triangles

The number of degrees of arc in a circle is 360.
The measure in degrees of a straight angle is 180.
The sum of the measures in degrees of the angles of a triangle is 180.

QUESTIONS 21–32 each consist of two quantities, one in Column A and one in Column B. You are to compare the two quantities and on the answer sheet blacken space

(A) if the quantity in Column A is greater;

(B) if the quantity in Column B is greater;

(C) if the two quantities are equal;

(D) if the relationship cannot be determined from the information given.

NOTES:

(1) In certain questions, information concerning one or both of the quantities to be compared is centered above the two columns.

(2) In a given question, a symbol that appears in both columns represents the same thing in Column A as it does in Column B.

(3) Letters such as x, n, and k stand for real numbers.

EXAMPLES:

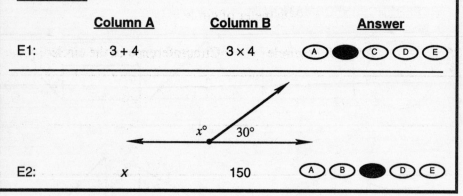

	Column A	Column B	Answer
E1:	$3 + 4$	3×4	Ⓐ ⬤ Ⓒ Ⓓ Ⓔ
E2:	x	150	Ⓐ Ⓑ ⬤ Ⓓ Ⓔ

Column A	Column B

21. | The units digit of 29^3 | The units digit of 29^4 |

A jar has 4 red jelly beans and 6 green jelly beans.

22. | The probability of picking a red jelly bean with one pick. | The probability of *not* picking a green jelly bean with one pick. |

23. | .5% of .5 | .10% of .10 |

	Column A	Column B
24.	$.39 \times 1{,}000$	$.039 \times 10{,}000$

A girl is waiting in line at the movie theater. She notices that she is 8th from the front of the line, and she is 12th from the end of the line.

25.	How many people are in the line, including her?	20

Diameter of circle = 1

	Column A	Column B
26.	Area of the circle	Circumference of the circle
27.	99×101	100^2
28.	$.5^2 - .4^2$	$.3^2$

$$A = 3$$
$$B = 4$$

	Column A	Column B
29.	$\dfrac{8A^4B^5}{2A^3B^5}$	$\dfrac{10A^5B^4}{2A^5B^3}$
30	$2^9 + 2^9$	2^{10}
31.	$(\sqrt{9} - 1)^3$	$(\sqrt{8})2$

Column A	Column B

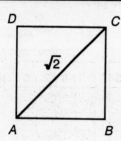

Square $ABCD$;

$AC = \sqrt{2}$

32. 4 times the area
of the square

The perimeter of
the square

DIRECTIONS: Questions 33–40 require you to solve the problem and enter your answer in the ovals in the special grid:

Answer: $\frac{5}{12}$

Write answers here

Answer: 3.5

Answer: 525
Either position is correct

Fraction line

Decimal line

Grid in answer

- You may begin filling in your answer in any column, space permitting. Columns not needed should be left blank.

- Answers may be entered in either decimal or fraction form. For example, $^3/_{12}$ or .25 are equally acceptable.

- A mixed number, such as $4^1/_2$, must be entered either as 4.5 or $^9/_2$. If you entered 41/2, the machine would interpret your answer as $^{41}/_2$, not $4^1/_2$.

- There may be some instances where there is more than one correct answer to a problem. Should this be the case, grid only one answer.

- Be very careful when filling in ovals. Do not fill in more than one oval in any column, and make sure to completely darken the ovals.

- It is suggested that you fill in your answer in the boxes above each column. Although you will not be graded incorrectly if you do not write in your answer, it will help you fill in the corresponding ovals.

- If your answer is a decimal, grid the most accurate value possible. For example, if you need to grid a repeating decimal such as $0.66\overline{6}$, enter the answer as .666 or .667. A less accurate value, such as .66 or .67, is not acceptable.

33. A crop duster reading a map learns that on the map she must treat a circular area of 9π sq. in. If 30 miles on the ground is represented by 1 inch on the map, the area in square miles that the crop duster must treat is _____ π?

34. Consider the half circle inscribed in the square below.

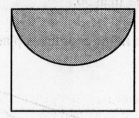

If the area of the half circle is $^{11}/_7$ square feet, find the area of the square. (Use the approximation $\pi = {}^{22}/_7$.)

35. Consider the square below.

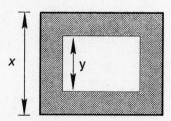

Let $x = 3$ meters and the area of the shaded region is 8 square meters. Find y.

36. The product of two consecutive even integers is 1,224. If both numbers are positive, find the smaller number.

37. Find the number(s) that satisfy x in the following:

(A) $50 < x < 60$

(B) The prime factorization of x involves primes less than 10.

38. Suppose $x^2 - y^2 = 1$ and $x = 3 + y$. Find the quantity $x + y + 6$.

39. Consider the triangle below.

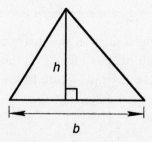

Given that the area is 100 square feet, find the quantity $b + h$ if both b and h are integers less than 30.

40. Consider the triangle in the coordinate plane below.

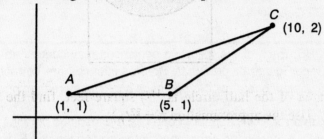

Find the area of the triangle.

Section 5

TIME: 30 Minutes
39 Questions

DIRECTIONS: Each of the following sentences may contain an error in diction, usage, idiom, or grammar. Some sentences are correct. Some sentences contain one error. No sentence contains more than one error.

If there is an error, it will appear in one of the underlined portions labeled A, B, C, or D. If there is no error, choose the portion labeled E. If there is an error, select the letter of the portion that must be changed in order to correct the sentence.

EXAMPLE:

He drove <u>slowly</u> and <u>cautiously</u> in order to <u>hopefully</u> avoid having an
      A   B   C

<u>accident</u>. <u>No error</u>.   
  D   E

---

1. *Huckleberry Finn*, by <u>general consensus agreement</u> Mark Twain's
                           A

   <u>greatest</u> work, is <u>supremely</u> the American <u>Classic</u>; it is also one of the
     B   C   D

   great books of the world. <u>No error</u>.
                     E

2. The U.S. <u>Constitution</u> <u>supposes</u> what the history of all governments
           A   B

   <u>demonstrate</u>, that the executive is the branch <u>most</u> interested in war
     C   D

   and most prone to it. <u>No error</u>.
                E

3. Mama, the <u>narrator</u> of Alice Walker's short story "Everyday Use,"
          A

   <u>speaks</u> fondly of her daughter upon her return home after a long
    B

   absence <u>like</u> Mama is <u>proud</u> of her. <u>No error</u>.
        C   D   E

4. <u>Nearly</u> one <u>hundred</u> years after the impoverished Vincent van Gogh
   A   **B**

   died, his paintings <u>had sold</u> for more than a <u>million dollars</u>. <u>No error</u>.
                C   **D**   **E**

5. Many athletes <u>recruited</u> for football by college coaches <u>expect</u> that
               A   **B**

   they will, <u>in fact</u>, receive an education when they <u>accept</u> a scholar-
           C   **D**

   ship. <u>No error</u>.
       E

6. <u>Hopefully</u>, by the end of the <u>Twentieth Century</u>, computer scientists
   A   **B**

   will invent machines with <u>enough</u> intelligence to work without break-
                         C

   ing down <u>continually</u>. <u>No error</u>.
             D   **E**

7. Studies <u>showing</u> that the earth includes a <u>vast series</u> of sedimentary
        A   **B**

   rocks, some with <u>embedded</u> fossils <u>that</u> prove the existence of ancient
                  C   **D**

   organisms. <u>No error</u>.
            E

8. When Martin Luther King, <u>Jr.</u>, wrote his famous letter from the Bir-
                   A

   mingham jail, he advocated neither evading <u>or</u> defying the law; <u>but</u>
                               B   **C**

   he accepted the idea that a penalty <u>results from</u> breaking a law, even
                            D

   an unjust one. <u>No error</u>.
               E

9. <u>The Eighteenth Century</u> philosopher Adam Smith <u>asserted</u> that a na-
         A   **B**

   tion <u>achieves</u> the best economic results when individuals work both
       C

   for their own interests and <u>to gain more goods</u>. <u>No error</u>.
                           D   **E**

10. According to Niccolò Machiavelli, wise rulers <u>cannot</u> and <u>should not</u>
                                                        A   **B**

    keep their word when such integrity would be to <u>their</u> disadvantage
                                                                          C

    and when the reasons for the promise no longer <u>exist</u>. <u>No error</u>.
                                                                             D   **E**

11. The Milky Way galaxy, which <u>comprises</u> millions of stars, has both
                                                        A

    <u>thin and congested</u> spots, but shines <u>their</u> <u>brightest</u> in the constella-
                B   **C**   **D**

    tion Sagittarius. <u>No error</u>.
                            E

12. <u>To learn</u> an ancient language <u>like</u> Latin or Greek is one way to dis-
         A   **B**

    cover the roots of Western Culture; studying Judeo-Christian reli-

    gious <u>beliefs</u> <u>is</u> another. <u>No error</u>.
            C   **D**   **E**

13. Many political conservatives <u>contribute</u> the problems of modern
                                        A

    American society to the twin evils of the New Deal and <u>secular</u>
                                                              B

    <u>humanism</u>, both <u>of which</u> <u>are</u> presumed to stem from Marxism. <u>No</u>
                            C   **D**

    <u>error</u>.
    E

14. <u>Having minimal exposure</u> to poetry when they <u>attended</u> school, most
                  A   **B**

    Americans <u>chose</u> to watch television or <u>to read</u> popular magazines for
                 C   **D**

    entertainment. <u>No error</u>.
                        E

15. What makes <u>we</u> humans <u>different from</u> other animals <u>can be defined</u>
                  A   **B**   **C**

    at least <u>partly</u> by our powerful and efficient intelligence. <u>No error</u>.
               D   **E**

16. When one contrasts the ideas of the Romantic William Wordsworth

    with those of Neoclassicist John Dryden, one finds that neither of the
    A   **B**   **C**
    poets differ as much as one would expect. No error.
         D   **E**

17. Carl Jung's hypothesis of the collective unconscious suggests that we
                                                          A
    inherit cultural-experimental memory in the form of mythological
               B
    archetype, which arise from repeated patterns of human behavior.
                  C   **D**
    No error.
    E

18. Bertrand Russell believed that a free person's liberation is effected by
                                          A   **B**
    a contemplation of Fate; one achieves emancipation through passion-
                       C
    ate pursuit of eternal things, not through the pursuit of private happi-
                                    D
    ness. No error.
          E

19. Latin American literature includes the works of Gabriel Garcia
    A   **B**
    Marquez, Pablo Neruda, and Jorge Luis Borges; each of these

    acclaimed artists has won their share of prizes. No error.
    C   **D**   **E**

DIRECTIONS: In each of the following sentences, some portion of the sentence is underlined. Under each sentence are five choices. The first choice has the same wording as the original. The other four choices are reworded. Sometimes the first choice containing the original wording is the best; sometimes one of the other choices is the best. Choose the letter of the best choice. Your choice should produce a sentence which is not ambiguous or awkward and which is correct, clear, and precise.

This is a test of correct and effective English expression. Keep in mind the standards of English usage, punctuation, grammar, word choice, and construction.

EXAMPLE:

When you listen to opera, <u>a person may not appreciate it.</u>

(A) a person may not appreciate it.

(B) it may not be appreciated by a person.

(C) which may not be appreciated by one.

(D) you may not appreciate it.

(E) appreciating it may be a problem for you.

---

20. Two-thirds of American 17-year-olds do not know that the Civil War <u>takes place</u> between 1850 and 1900.

   (A) takes place   (D) have taken place

   (B) took place   (E) is taking place

   (C) had taken place

21. Both professional and amateur ornithologists, <u>people that study birds</u>, recognize the Latin or scientific names of bird species.

   (A) people that study birds

   (B) people which study birds

   (C) the study of birds

   (D) people who study birds

   (E) in which people study birds

22. Many of the oil-producing states spent their huge surplus tax revenues during the oil boom of the 1970s and early 1980s <u>in spite of the fact that</u> oil production from new wells began to flood the world market as early as 1985.

    (A) in spite of the fact that

    (B) even in view of the fact that

    (C) however clearly it was known that

    (D) even though

    (E) when it was clear that

23. The president of the community college reported <u>as to the expectability of the tuition increase as well as the actual amount</u>.

    (A) as to the expectability of the tuition increase as well as the actual amount

    (B) that the tuition will likely increase by a specific amount

    (C) as to the expectability that tuition will increase by a specific amount

    (D) about the expected tuition increase of five percent.

    (E) regarding the expectation of a tuition increase expected to be five percent

24. Although Carmen developed an interest in classical music, <u>she did not read notes and had never played an instrument</u>.

    (A) she did not read notes and had never played an instrument

    (B) she does not read notes and has never played an instrument

    (C) it is without being able to read notes or having played an instrument

    (D) she did not read notes nor had she ever played them

    (E) it is without reading notes nor having played an instrument

25. Political candidates must campaign on issues and ideas that strike a chord within their constituency but <u>with their goal to sway</u> undecided voters to support their candidacy.

    (A) with their goal to sway

(B) need also to sway

(C) aiming at the same time to sway

(D) also trying to sway

(E) its goal should also be in swaying

26. The major reasons students give for failing courses in college <u>is that</u> <u>they have demanding professors and work at</u> full- or part-time jobs.

(A) is that they have demanding professors and work at

(B) are demanding professors and they work at

(C) is having demanding professors and having

(D) are demanding professors, in addition to working at

(E) are that they have demanding professors and that they have

27. <u>Having command of color, symbolism, as well as technique</u>, Georgia O'Keeffe is considered to be a great American painter.

(A) Having command of color, symbolism, as well as technique

(B) Having command of color, symbolism, and her technical ability

(C) Because of her command of color, symbolism, and technique

(D) With her command of color and symbolism and being technical

(E) By being in command of both color and symbolism and also technique

28. <u>Whether the ancient ancestors of American Indians actually migrated</u> <u>or did not</u> across a land bridge now covered by the Bering Strait remains uncertain, but that they could have has not been refuted by other theories.

(A) Whether the ancient ancestors of American Indians actually migrated or did not

(B) That the ancient ancestors of American Indians actually did migrate

(C) The actuality of whether the ancient ancestors of American Indians migrated

(D) Whether in actuality the ancient ancestors of American Indians migrated or not

(E) That the ancient ancestors of American Indians may actually have migrated

29. Caution in scientific experimentation can <u>sometimes be related more to integrity than to lack of knowledge</u>.

   (A) sometimes be related more to integrity than to lack of knowledge

   (B) sometimes be related more to integrity as well as lack of knowledge

   (C) often be related to integrity as to lack of knowledge

   (D) be related more to integrity rather than lack of knowledge

   (E) be related often to integrity, not only to lack of knowledge

30. Separated by their successful rebellion against England from any existing form of government, the citizens of the United States <u>have developed a unique constitutional political system</u>.

   (A) have developed a unique constitutional political system

   (B) had developed a very unique constitutional political system

   (C) had developed their constitutional political system uniquely

   (D) have developed their political system into a very unique constitutional one

   (E) have a unique political system, based on a constitution

31. <u>Returning to the ancestral home after 12 years, the house itself seemed much smaller to Joe</u> than it had been when he visited it as a child.

   (A) Returning to the ancestral home after 12 years, the house itself seemed much smaller to Joe

   (B) When Joe returned to the ancestral home after 12 years, he thought the house itself much smaller

   (C) Joe returned to the ancestral home after 12 years, and then he thought the house itself much smaller

    (D) After Joe returned to the ancestral home in 12 years, the house itself seemed much smaller

    (E) Having returned to the ancestral home after 12 years, it seemed a much smaller house to Joe

32. Historians say that the New River of North Carolina, Virginia, and West Virginia, <u>which is 2,700 feet above sea level and 2,000 feet above</u> the surrounding foothills, is the oldest river in the United States.

    (A) which is 2,700 feet above sea level and 2,000 feet above

    (B) with a height of 2,700 feet above sea level as well as 2,000 feet above that of

    (C) 2,700 feet higher than sea level and ascending 2,000 feet above

    (D) being 2,700 feet above sea level and 2,000 feet high measure from that of

    (E) located 2,700 feet high above sea level while measuring 2,000 feet above

33. <u>The age of 36 having been reached</u>, the Ukrainian-born Polish sailor Teodor Josef Konrad Korzeniowski changed his name to Joseph Conrad and began a new and successful career as a British novelist and short story writer.

    (A) The age of 36 having been reached

    (B) When having reached the age of 36

    (C) When he reached the age of 36

    (D) The age of 36 being reached

    (E) At 36, when he reached that age

DIRECTIONS: The following passages are considered early draft efforts of a student. Some sentences need to be rewritten to make the ideas clearer and more precise.

Read each passage carefully and answer the questions that follow. Some of the questions are about particular sentences or parts of sentences and ask you to make decisions about sentence structure, diction, and usage. Some of the questions refer to the entire essay or parts of the essay and ask you to make decisions about organization, development, appropriateness of language, audience, and logic. Choose the answer that most effectively makes the intended meaning clear and follows the requirements of standard written English. After you have chosen your answer, fill in the corresponding oval on your answer sheet.

EXAMPLE:

(1) On the one hand, I think television is bad, But it also does some good things for all of us. (2) For instance, my little sister thought she wanted to be a policemen until she saw police shows on television.

Which of the following is the best revision of the underlined portion of Sentence 1 below?

On the one hand, I think television is bad, But it also does some good things for all of us.

(A)   is bad; But it also

(B)   is bad. but is also

(C)   is bad, and it also

(D)   is bad, but it also

(E)   is bad because it also

Questions 34-39 are based on the following passage.

(1) The melt-water stream draining out along the floor of a glacier cave gives evidence of its origin. (2) It goes without saying that the origin of another kind of cave can be gotten from the pounding of sea waves at the mouth of a sea cave. (3) Solution caves, however, have always been a source of wonder to man. (4) How do these extensive, complex, and in some places beautifully decorated passageways develop?

(5) Solution caves are formed in limestone and similar rocks by the action of the water. (6) Think of them as part of a huge subterranean

plumbing system. (7) After a rain water seeps into cracks and pores of soil and rock and percolates beneath the land surface. (8) Eventually, some of the water reaches a zone of soil and rock where all the cracks are already filled with water. (9) The term <u>water table</u> refers to the upper surface of this saturated zone. (10) Calcite (calcium carbonate), the main mineral of limestone, is barely soluble in pure water. (11) Rainwater, however, absorbs some carbon dioxide as it passes through soil and decaying vegetation. (12) The water, combining chemically with the carbon dioxide, forms a weak carbonic acid solution which slowly dissolves calcite. (13) This acid slowly dissolves calcite, forms solution cavities, and excavates passageways. (14) This results in a solution cave.

(15) A second stage in cave development is when there is lowering of the water table. (16) During this stage, the solution cavities are stranded in the unsaturated zone where air can enter. (17) This leads to the deposition of calcite, which forms <u>dripstone</u> features, beautiful formations in strange shapes on the inside of caves.

34. Which of the following is the best revision of sentence 2 below?

   It goes without saying that the origin of another kind of cave can be gotten from the pounding of sea waves at the mouth of a sea cave.

   (A) It goes without saying that a sea cave can be formed by the pounding of waves at its mouth.

   (B) The pounding waves at the mouth of a sea cave offer evidence of the origin of this cave.

   (C) Evidence is offered of the origin of sea caves by the pounding of the waves.

   (D) In saying that another kind of cave can be formed by the pounding of waves at the entrance of sea caves.

   (E) It goes without saying that the pounding waves at the mouth of a sea cave offers evidence as to the origin of this kind of cave.

35. In the context of the sentences preceding and following sentence 6, which of the following is the best revision of sentence 6?

   (A) These caves can be considered part of a huge subterranean plumbing system.

   (B) You can think of these caves as part of a huge subterranean plumbing system.

(C) The formation of these caves can be thought of in terms of a huge subterranean plumbing system.

(D) If you think of it, these caves are similar to a huge subterranean plumbing system.

(E) When one visualizes the formation of these caves, one could compare them to part of a huge subterranean plumbing system.

36. Which of the following is the best way to combine sentences 13 and 14?

(A) This acid dissolving results in solution cavities, passageways, and caves.

(B) Solution caves are formed when this acid dissolves solution cavities and passageways.

(C) Slowly, this acid dissolves calcite, and the resulting effects are that cavities and passageways become caves.

(D) Excavating cavities, passageways, and caves, the acid slowly dissolves calcite.

(E) This acid slowly dissolves calcite, excavating cavities and passageways which eventually become solution caves.

37. In relation to the passage as a whole, which of the following best describes the writer's intention in paragraph 2?

(A) To provide an example

(B) To propose a solution to a problem

(C) To describe a location

(D) To examine opposing evidence

(E) To explain a process

38. Which of the following is the best revision of the underlined portion of sentence 15 below?

A second stage in cave development is when there is lowering of the water table.

(A) is because there is lowering of the water table

(B) is due to the water table going lower

(C) occurs after a lowering of the water table

(D) happens to be when the water table is lowered

(E) being when there is a lowering of the water table

39. Which of the following is the best punctuation of the underlined portion of sentence 7?

After a rain water seeps into cracks and pores of soil and rock and percolates beneath the land surface.

(A) After a rain, water seeps into

(B) After, a rain water seeps into

(C) After a rain: water seeps into

(D) After a rain-water seeps into

(E) Best as it is

TEST 2

ANSWER KEY

Section 1—Verbal

1.	(C)	9.	(E)	17.	(C)	25.	(C)
2.	(B)	10.	(A)	18.	(B)	26.	(C)
3.	(A)	11.	(D)	19.	(C)		
4.	(D)	12.	(D)	20.	(A)		
5.	(B)	13.	(B)	21.	(B)		
6.	(E)	14.	(C)	22.	(E)		
7.	(B)	15.	(E)	23.	(D)		
8.	(D)	16.	(B)	24.	(E)		

Section 2—Math

1.	(E)	8.	(C)	15.	(E)
2.	(E)	9.	(E)	16.	(C)
3.	(B)	10.	(E)	17.	(E)
4.	(D)	11.	(C)	18.	(E)
5.	(B)	12.	(A)	19.	(B)
6.	(E)	13.	(E)	20.	(A)
7.	(D)	14.	(B)		

Section 3—Verbal

27.	(C)	35.	(A)	43.	(B)	51.	(C)
28.	(D)	36.	(E)	44.	(B)	52.	(C)
29.	(A)	37.	(B)	45.	(A)		
30.	(A)	38.	(D)	46.	(C)		
31.	(D)	39.	(B)	47.	(B)		
32.	(D)	40.	(B)	48.	(D)		
33.	(E)	41.	(E)	49.	(B)		
34.	(E)	42.	(E)	50.	(D)		

Section 4—Math

21.	(A)	28.	(C)	35.	1
22.	(C)	29.	(B)	36.	34
23.	(A)	30.	(C)	37.	54 or 56
24.	(C)	31.	(C)	38.	19/3
25.	(B)	32.	(C)	39.	30
26.	(B)	33.	8100	40.	2
27.	(B)	34.	4		

Section 5—Writing Skills

1.	(A)	11.	(C)	21.	(D)	31.	(B)
2.	(C)	12.	(A)	22.	(D)	32.	(A)
3.	(C)	13.	(A)	23.	(B)	33.	(C)
4.	(C)	14.	(C)	24.	(A)	34.	(B)
5.	(B)	15.	(A)	25.	(B)	35.	(A)
6.	(A)	16.	(D)	26.	(E)	36.	(E)
7.	(A)	17.	(E)	27.	(C)	37.	(E)
8.	(B)	18.	(E)	28.	(B)	38.	(C)
9.	(D)	19.	(D)	29.	(A)	39.	(A)
10.	(E)	20.	(B)	30.	(A)		

DETAILED EXPLANATIONS OF ANSWERS

Section 1 — Verbal

1. **(C)**   The answer is "document" (C) because that means to provide evidence for something. A "periscope" (A) is a device for viewing objects. A "submarine" (B) is a kind of underwater ship that contains a periscope. Although it may be useful to "magnify" (D) forms of life which previously were unknown, that would not necessarily enhance our understanding of these forms of life. "Rancor" (E) is a noun meaning anger or bad feeling; the context of the sentence calls for a verb.

2. **(B)**   "Adjacent to" (B) means "next to" or "near" so this is the correct choice. Contingency (A) is established in terms of a relationship between two or more items and the sentence does not provide this sense in context of what is stated. While areas surrounding a mainland may well be "dependent upon" (C) the mainland, again, the sentence does not establish this as fact in this case. An obstruction (D) is a blockage, and this does not make sense in this sentence. Something in one geographic location does not block something in another—they are too far away to have this kind of relationship. For an area to be "neglected" by (E) another, a prior dependency relationship between them must be established, and again, the sentence does not provide this meaning.

3. **(A)**   "Consulted" (A) means asked for an opinion or advice and is the correct response. This fits best into the context of the sentence because Lina's parents probably want to know where she is going to be after school and believe they should be able to advise her as to where she spends her time. "Insulted" (B) is incorrect because it carries a negative connotation and no one would like to be put down because they wish to know of someone's schedule. "Isolated" (C) means to be left alone and does not make sense in the context of the sentence. "Predicted" (D) and "preordained" (E) are similar because they both imply something about the future. These terms apply to events, not people.

4.   **(D)**   "Percussion" (D) is the answer, because cymbals are part of the percussion section of an orchestra. A percussion player knows how to play all these instruments, including the cymbals. Although an orchestra is comprised of "instruments," (A) this is too vague a term to be the best answer here. While persons who can play "triangles" (B) might be able to also play cymbals, it is not necessarily true that they could. The "harp" (C) is another instrument, not related to cymbals. Cymbals are not part of the brass (E) section.

5.   **(B)**   The answer is (B) "cooperation," because it means the ability to work with others in a positive way, with goodwill. While a sense of "humor" (A) is desirable in life, it is not indicated within the context of the rest of the sentence. "Cooptation" (C) is a taking over. While this does happen among people, it is not indicated within the context of the sentence either, because the sentence describes people working together, not taking over. "Habituation" (D) is making something a habit, also not indicated by the rest of the sentence. An "affliction" (E) is an unfortunate condition, such as an illness.

6.   **(E)**   If something is filled to "capacity" (E), it is filled to the greatest extent that is possible. This fits in the context of this sentence, so it is the answer. "Perspective" (A) means a viewing angle. A triumvirate (B) is a group of three, so this makes no sense in the context of this sentence either. "Tenacity" (C) is the quality of being able to hold onto something; while bookshelves do hold books, this word is a quality that applies to people, not inanimate objects. While many people would agree that when one is out of bookshelf space, that is a "calamity" (D); however, the word does not apply to a bookshelf's physical dimensions ("filled to . . .").

7.   **(B)**   The cries of the girls were not "acknowledged" (B) by the official. To "prohibit" (A) is to forbid and while the referee may forbid shouts from the players, this is not the best answer. To "implement" (C) means to put something to use and the referee might have implemented their suggestion of calling the play out but he cannot implement their shouts. To "target" (D) is to pinpoint and this makes no sense in the context of the sentence. An official may "correct" (E) the girls because he felt differently about the call, but most referees will only pay attention to the coach and not the shouts from players. (B) is the best answer.

8.   **(D)**   The relationship between the given words can be described as: A PAMPHLET provides you with a small amount of information about a

topic and a TEXTBOOK gives you a lot of information about a topic. (D) is the best choice because the relationship between the words is similar: An ASPECT gives you a small view of a picture; a PANORAMA is a complete (or larger) view in every direction. (A) is an incorrect choice because "a LETTER is a small amount, but a NOUN is a large amount," makes no sense. A NOUN is a word which may contain many LETTERS, but the relationship is not as clear as in (D). (B) is incorrect because a WINDOW may or may not be part of a DOOR, and may not be considered a smaller aspect of the door. (C) is the wrong choice because a NATION is not a smaller amount than LANGUAGE. This is a meaningless statement. (E) is the wrong choice because a RHYME may sometimes be a small aspect of a POEM; however, not all POEMS have RHYME.

9. **(E)** The relationship between the given words can be indicated by the following sentence: If you BOAST, then you PRAISE yourself. (E) is the best choice because if you ATONE (make amends), then you AMEND (change for the better). A person who BOASTS always PRAISES. A person who ATONES always makes AMENDS. (A) is incorrect because if you AUTHORIZE (sanction), then you LAWS yourself, is a nonsense statement. (B) is wrong because "if you FAST yourself, then you FOOD," makes no sense. A person who FASTS does not eat FOOD. (C) "If you DETRACT (withdraw), then you COMPLIMENT," is an inaccurate relationship. If you DETRACT from something, then you would probably eliminate COMPLIMENTS. (D) is wrong because "if you COMMEND, then you IGNORE," makes no sense. If you COMMEND (praise) something, then you are ignoring it.

10. **(A)** Something that is MALEVOLENT is EVIL, or MALEVOLENT and EVIL are synonyms. (A) is the best choice. BENEFICIENT and GOOD are synonyms. Something that is BENEFICIENT is GOOD. (B) is incorrect because "something that is PROSPEROUS is MONEY" makes no sense. If you are PROSPEROUS, then you have MONEY. The words are not synonymous. (C) is wrong because "something that is INVINCIBLE (incapable of being conquered) is PREDICTABLE," makes no sense. (D) is incorrect because "something that is HURT is ROBUST," is an inaccurate statement. A ROBUST person is healthy which means that they would not be HURT. (E) is wrong because a SOMNOLENT (sleepy) person is CLEAR, makes no sense. The words are not related at all.

11. **(D)** The relationship expressed by the given words can be characterized by the following sentence: The best-known attribute of a MISER is

THRIFT. A MISER is characterized by THRIFT. (D) is the best choice because a HEDONIST is characterized by PLEASURE. (A) is incorrect because "a SADIST is characterized by WORK," is an inaccurate analogy. A SADIST is characterized by PAIN. (B) is wrong because "a VILLIAN is characterized by CHEER," is an erroneous fit. You would never associate a VILLIAN with the word CHEER, except perhaps in a negative way. (C) is incorrect because "a PEDESTRIAN is characterized by DEFIANCE," makes no sense, unless you specifically mention that the PEDESTRIAN is crossing against the light. (E) is wrong because a GLUTTON is not necessarily characterized by excessive consumption of FOOD. A GLUTTON can be characterized by anything excessive, and that may include food.

12. **(D)** The pattern is antonyms. The answer is PRECARIOUS:SAFE. Option (A) is incorrect, since GOAL-DIRECTED and ORGANIZED have similar meanings. Option (B) is incorrect, since PRECURSOR and FORERUNNER are synonyms. Option (C) is incorrect, since CAREFREE is not an antonym of SPURIOUS. Option (E) is incorrect, since SILLY and ABSURD are synonyms.

13. **(B)** The pattern is a worker and an object the worker typically uses. The answer is CARPENTER:HAMMER. Option (A) is not correct, since a CLERK doesn't typically use a BROOM. Option (C) is incorrect, even though a LAWYER uses a BRIEF, since the pattern is reversed here. Option (D) is incorrect, since TENNIS is just an example of a SPORT. Finally, option (E) is incorrect, since a BARBER gives a HAIRCUT.

14. **(C)** The text bears out the economic factor early (line 6); the geographic influence becomes obvious at line 37. (A) is a strong distractor, but line 23 has "America . . . free from . . . exact imitation." (D) is a misreading of line 9; material dealing with Charleston does not confirm (B) or (E).

15. **(E)** Line 23 bears out freedom of style, denying (A) (European/British tradition) and (C), since log cabins are not indigenous to the Eastern Coast. Line 14 denies that brick predominated all American architecture (D).

16. **(B)** Line 13 establishes the call to woodwork; wood is hardly "nonflammable" (D). (A) is unjustified by the text; (C) is a misreading of line 22. Clapboard is not a function of the Flemish (E); brick is.

17. **(C)** Charleston has "a certain southern flavor" (line 29) "unlike any other colonial metropolis" (line 32), denying (B) and (A) (since the South is a regional factor). Both (D) and (E) are invalidated by their respective generalizations.

18. **(B)** The geographic progression parallels the historic lag in architectural forms, denying (A). The frontier log cabin is Swedish (line 42), not Georgian (C). The cabin's relative simplicity does not bespeak affluence (D); and its Swedish influence denies (E).

19. **(C)** The main purpose of the author in writing is to detail a meeting with Dr. Faraday and to speculate on future encounters with the learned man. The author does not in detail describe his plans for a perpetual motion machine so (A) is not the best choice. The author does not spend a great deal of time describing life in Charing Cross during the winter so (B) is not the best choice. The author does little to advance scientific knowledge of the Royal Institute; (D) is not the best choice. The passage is not an abstract philosophical treatise; (E) is not the best choice.

20. **(A)** The writer had not created the machine himself because of his lack of mechanical dexterity; (A) is the answer of choice. His failure to produce the machine was not because of his desire to discuss the entire plan with Faraday first; it was a result of his "insufficient manual dexterity." (B) is not the best choice. The author did not fail to produce the machine just out of fear of ridicule. (C) should not be selected. The author could visit the Royal Institute so this was not the reason for his failure to produce the machine; (D) should not be chosen. The author makes no mention of a lack of funds prohibiting the production of his machine—just "insufficient manual dexterity." (E) should not be selected.

21. **(B)** Faraday seemed to hint that nature would have already mastered perpetual motion if it were possible. (B) is the best choice. The author did not seem to express himself very well during the interview with Faraday; it is unlikely that Faraday would suggest that the writer knew much of the laws of motion. (A) is not the best choice. The writing does not indicate that Faraday would suggest a lack of logic to the mind of the writer. (C) is not the best choice. Faraday did give audience to the writer so he was not too busy to give audience to others at any time. (D) is not the correct choice. The writer admits that he did not express himself very well so it is unlikely that Faraday was able to get a clear idea of the writer's idea. (E) should not be chosen.

22. **(E)**   In line 52 "... all this exorcised my devil ..." means that the writer no longer felt compelled to work on a perpetual motion machine at the present time. (E) is the best choice. "... exorcised my devil" has nothing to do with a haunting or supernatural being. (A) is not the best choice. The quotation did not relate to the writer's desire to visit the Royal Institute; (B) is not the best selection. Nothing in the writing suggests that the writer was no longer was interested in ever seeing Faraday again. (C) should not be chosen. The writer had definitely not put science permanently out of his life. (D) is not an appropriate choice.

23. **(D)**   The author's feeling after the interview is dissatisfaction with his ability to communicate well with Faraday. (D) is the best choice. The author is not indignant; (A) should not be selected. Faraday seemed to communicate well; it was the author who did not communicate well. (B) should not be chosen. The author does not express intense interest in visiting Faraday again with other schemes. (C) should not be chosen. The author did not feel he expressed himself very well, so (E) pride in his ability to discuss science competently with an expert should not be selected.

24. **(E)**   The author was least likely to choose Faraday for the interview because he knew of Faraday's intemperate disposition. In this case we are looking for a reason he would not interview with Faraday. There was nothing to suggest that Faraday was intemperate so (E) should be chosen. The other items—Faraday's reputation of being courteous (A), fate having Faraday arriving just as the letter was being delivered (B), the fact that Faraday was a noted scientist of the time (C), and the fact that Faraday was located conveniently to him (D)—would make the interview with Faraday easy to choose.

25. **(C)**   The author's statement at the end of the passage would be best followed by information on a significant achievement by the writer that could call Faraday's attention to him more decidedly. Information on a perpetual motion machine created by a noted scientist (A) would not fit well here. Neither would information on an interview with another noted scientist so (B) is not the best choice. Neither a personal letter written by Faraday to the writer (D) or a relaxed conversation with the porter (E) seems to follow logically. (C) is the best choice.

26. **(C)**   Faraday seemed to sense that the most powerful of all forces is that of the laws of science (C). No information is given regarding

Faraday's beliefs toward love (A) or logic (E). Faraday seemed not to place a lot of faith in perpetual motion (B) or the author's scheme (D) since he indicated that if such were possible "it would have occurred spontaneously in nature, and would have overpowered all other forces."

Section 2 — Math

1. **(E)**   Because Grace wants 45 percent of the solution to be orange juice, we can set up the following proportion.

$$\frac{\text{orange juice}}{\text{orange juice} + \text{pineapple juice}} = \frac{45}{100}$$

Before adding anything, we can substitute in the values she has.

$$\frac{24}{24+72} = \frac{45}{100}$$

To find out how much orange juice must be added, we add x to the top and bottom of the left-hand side of the equation. (x represents the amount of orange juice added to the mixture.) Thus,

$$\frac{24+x}{24+72+x} = \frac{45}{100}$$

(We added the x to the top and bottom of the fraction because adding orange juice not only increases the amount of orange juice, but it also increases the total amount of juice.)

Now we need only simplify.

$$\frac{24+x}{96+x} = \frac{45}{100}$$

2. **(E)**   Because the average of the nine is 16, their total must be

$$16 \times 9 = 144.$$

(Average = sum/number; therefore, sum = number $\times$ average.)

Thus, if $x=$ the smallest number, we can set up the equation.

$$x+x+1+x+2+x+3+x+4+x+5+x+6+x+7+x+8 = 144$$

$$9x + 36 = 144$$

$$9x + 36 - 36 = 144 - 36$$

$$\frac{9x}{9} = \frac{108}{9}$$

$$9x = 108$$

$$x = 12$$

If $x = 12$, the average of the four smallest numbers would be

$$\frac{12+13+14+15}{4} = \frac{54}{4} = 13.5$$

3. **(B)** An average is equal to the sum of the numbers divided by the number of numbers. In this case the number of numbers would be 60, the number of students who took the test.

The sum of the numbers would be the cumulative scores of all those who took the test. We were told to find the lowest average, and this would occur when the students scored the least number of points possible. We know that 40 of them had grades of at least 75 or better, so we assume they scored as few points as possible, which would be 75×40 or 3,000 points.

To find the lowest possible class average, we must assume that the remaining 20 students $(60 - 40)$ each scored the lowest he or she possibly could, which means each scored a 0.

Thus, the lowest possible sum of all the points scored by the class would be

$$(40 \times 75) + (20 \times 0) = 3,000 + 0 = 3,000.$$

Thus, the lowest number of points scored by the class would be 3,000. And the lowest average would be $3,000 \div 60 = 50$.

4. **(D)** Decreasing an amount by 20% is the same as taking 80% of that amount, which can be done by multiplying that amount by 80%. Because of the nature of this problem, we will convert 80% to a fraction which is $^{80}/_{100}$, which reduces to $^{4}/_{5}$.

Thus, to find the price at the beginning of the 2nd week we would have to take x and multiply it by $^{4}/_{5}$. And we would have to do the same for each successive week.

Beginning of:

1st week		2nd week		3rd week		4th week		5th week		
x	$\times$	$\dfrac{4}{5}$	$\times$	$\dfrac{4}{5}$	$\times$	$\dfrac{4}{5}$	$\times$	$\dfrac{4}{5}$	$=$	$\dfrac{256x}{625}$

5. **(B)** The following ordered pairs satisfy the expression $a + b < 27$:

$$10 + 15 < 27$$

$$10 + 13 < 27$$

$$10 + 11 < 27$$

$$12 + 13 < 27$$

$$12 + 11 < 27$$

$$14 + 11 < 27$$

Thus, there are six combinations.

6. **(E)** First we find the number of people who would not support the new stadium. To do this we subtract 700 from 10,000.

$$10,000 - 700 = 9,300$$

Now we must find out what percent 9,300 is of 10,000. To do this we set up the fraction 9,300/10,000, and then we convert that fraction to a percent by dividing the numerator by the denominator. $9,300 \div 10,000 = .93$, which is the same as 93%.

7. **(D)** If a, b, c, d, e, f, and g represent consecutive integers and a is the greatest of those integers and $b + f = 0$, then the values of the variables must be as follows:

g	f	e	d	c	b	a
-3	-2	-1	0	1	2	3

Thus, $ab = 3 \times 2 = 6$.

8. **(C)** The shaded area equals the area of the rectangle minus the sum of triangles GBE, HEF, and IFC. Because parallel lines (AD and BC) are everywhere equidistant, each of these triangles has the same height. Because equilateral triangles with equal heights are equal, these triangles are equal to one another. Thus, the shaded area equals

area of $ABCD - 3 \times$ area of GBE.

First we construct GJ, the altitude of triangle GBE. (See the following figure.)

$$GJ = 3\sqrt{3} \qquad \text{parallel lines are everywhere equidistant}$$

$$GEJ = 60° = BGE \qquad \text{all angles of an equilateral triangle are 60°}$$

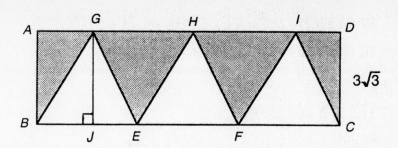

$JGE = 30°$ the altitude of an equilateral triangle bisects its angle

JGE is a 30–60–90 right triangle.

$$3\sqrt{3} = \frac{1}{2} \times GE \times \sqrt{3}$$ in a 30–60–90 right triangle, the side opposite the 60° angle = $\frac{1}{2}$ hypotenuse $\times \sqrt{3}$

$$3\sqrt{3} \div \sqrt{3} = \frac{1}{2} \times GE \times \sqrt{3} \div \sqrt{3}$$ equals divided by equals are equal

$$3 = \frac{1}{2}\,GE$$ simplification

$$3 \times 2 = \frac{1}{2}\,GE \times 2$$ equals times equals are equal

$$GE = 6$$ simplification

$$BE = 6$$ all sides of an equilateral triangle are equal

$$BE = 6 = EF = FC$$ corresponding sides of equal triangles are equal

$$BC = 18$$

$$ABCD = 18 \times 3\sqrt{3} = 54\sqrt{3}$$ area of a rectangle = length × width

$$\text{area of } GBE = \left(\frac{6^2}{4}\right)\sqrt{3}$$ area of equilateral triangle = $\left(\frac{s^2}{4}\right)\sqrt{3}$

$$\left(\frac{36}{4}\right)\sqrt{3} = 9\sqrt{3}$$ simplification

$$GBE + HEF + IFC = 9\sqrt{3} + 9\sqrt{3} + 9\sqrt{3} = 27\sqrt{3}$$

Thus, the shaded region $= 54\sqrt{3} - 27\sqrt{3} = 27\sqrt{3}$.

9. **(E)**

Area of square $= (^3/_4)^2 = {}^9/_{16}$

The perimeter of the square $= {}^3/_4 \times 4 = 3$

Their difference is $3 - {}^9/_{16} = 2^7/_{16}$

10. **(E)**   Substitute –6 in each of the choices.

Choice (A): $^1/_2 (-6) + {}^1/_3 (-6) = -5$

$(-3) + (-2) = -5$

Choice (B): $(-6)^2 + 5 (-6) - 6 = 0$

$36 + (-30) - 6 = 0$

$6 - 6 = 0$

Choice (C): $(-6)^2 - 36 = 0$

$36 - 36 = 0$

Choice (D): $(-6)^2 + 6(-6) = 0$

$36 + (-36) = 0$

Choice (E): $(-6)^2 + 36 \neq 0$

11. **(C)**   The two numbers are $5x$ and $3x$; their difference is 12.

$$5x - 3x = 12$$

$$2x = 12$$

$$x = 6$$

One number is $5(6) = 30$; the other is $3(6) = 18$.

12. **(A)**   Multiply each original term by 1,000.

$$4R + 40 = 400 + 4,000$$

$$4R + 40 = 4,400$$

$$4R = 4,360$$

$$R = 1,090$$

13. **(E)** According to the symbols

$$x \# y = x^2 + \sqrt{y},$$

square the first plus the square root of the second. So that, 4 # 4 means

$$4^2 + \sqrt{4} = 16 + 2 = 18.$$

14. **(B)**

$$100 \,(.06 + .04) + 10 \,(.3 + .7) = 100 \,(.10) + 10 \,(1.0)$$
$$= 10 + 10$$
$$= 20$$

15. **(E)** When a number is already in scientific notation, a negative exponent moves the decimal to the left that number of places.

−2 means 2 places to the left:

$$.009 \times 10^{-2} = .00009$$

16. **(C)** To eliminate a percent sign, put the number over 100.

$$3\frac{2}{3}\% = \frac{3\frac{2}{3}}{100}$$

$$= \frac{\frac{11}{3}}{100}$$

$$= \frac{11}{3} \div 100$$

$$= \frac{11}{3} \times \frac{1}{100}$$

$$= \frac{11}{300}$$

Now multiply $\frac{11}{300} \times 300 = 11$

17. **(E)** You must follow the order of operations. First, simplify what is in the parentheses.

$$12 - 10 \,(12 - 10)^3$$

$$12 - 10\,(2)^3$$

Then take care of the exponent.

$$12 - 10(8)$$

Multiply.

$$12 - 80 = -68$$

18. **(E)**   Try each of the choices. The only one that gives an answer between 3 and 4 is (E).

$$\frac{28}{9} = 3\frac{1}{9}$$

19. **(B)**   Square each answer, including $\frac{1}{2}$.

(A) $\sqrt{\dfrac{5}{8}}^2 = \dfrac{5}{8}$

(B) $\sqrt{\dfrac{7}{10}}^2 = \dfrac{7}{10}$

(C) $\sqrt{\dfrac{6}{13}}^2 = \dfrac{6}{13}$

(D) $\sqrt{\dfrac{4}{9}}^2 = \dfrac{4}{9}$

(E) $\left(\dfrac{1}{2}\right)^2 = \dfrac{1}{4}$

Compare these fractions by cross-multiplying. (B) is the largest.

20. **(A)**   Find a common denominator for 3 and 5 and multiply both sides of the equation.

$$2F = 3G$$

$$5G = 7H$$

$$\overline{}$$

$$10F = 15G$$

$$15G = 21H$$

$$\overline{}$$

Therefore, $10F = 21H$ (divide by H)

$$\frac{10F}{H} = 21 \text{ (divide by 10)}$$

$$\frac{F}{H} = \frac{21}{10}$$

Section 3 — Verbal

27. **(C)** "Liability" (C) is a willingness to claim responsibility for something. The store told Jason it was not liable, but rather the manufacturer was, so that is the answer. If the store responded to Jason's complaint at all, it was displaying "involvement" (A) in the matter, even though it was not to his satisfaction. A "counteraction" (B) is an action which is in opposition to another action (counter to it), so this word is irrelevant within the context of the sentence. "Concurrently" (D) is an adverb and the sentence calls for a noun; in addition, it means "at the same time," and that has no relevance for the sentence either. "Subjectivity" (E) is a personal point-of-view or feeling, which also is not relevant in this context.

28. **(D)** "Judiciousness" (D) is evenness or moderation, which Aristotle needed in human affairs. "Indulgence" (A) is carrying things to excess, which the sentence tells us Aristotle deplored (felt was wrong). While everyone must "sacrifice" some things in life to obtain others, it does not necessarily follow that not carrying things to excess implies sacrifice, which usually indicates something more severe and unpleasant than avoiding excesses. "Upheavals" (C) are similar to disruptions, which Aristotle would have felt were similar to excesses, and therefore, would have disliked. "Subsistence" (E) means survival, which has nothing to do with excesses, as stated in the first part of the sentence.

29. **(A)** The answer is "jurisdiction" (A) because that means legal authority for the administration of justice, and judges have specific locations in which they have such authority. "Territory" (B) is not a legal term a judge would use to describe a location; legal terms to describe places are more specific than words used in ordinary conversation. A "jury" (C) is not a place, but rather the people in court who deliver a verdict. A "deposition" (D) is also not a place (even though it sounds like "depository," which means a place where books are kept), but a procedure for making statements of allegation, or assigning responsibility for something by telling what happened. The word "litigation" (E) means a court case, and also does not describe location.

30. **(A)** If he has a "hunch" (A), he has a suspicion, and what a "logician" does is exercise careful reasoning, so this is the correct answer. An inkling (B) is a guess or hint, but why a "mathematician" would be good at careful reasoning, given relevant facts *in a case* (not a mathematics

problem) is not made clear in the sentence. A "premonition" (C) is a feeling of something about to happen, but something did already happen; a "sophist" is someone who uses superficial reasoning, so this makes no sense in context, either. A "foreboding" (D) is a misgiving or fear about the future, not about a person ("about the villain's identity"), and an "idealist" would not logically play a part in deducing that identity from the facts. "Tribulation" (E) is trouble, so that does not make sense, and the sentence does not say what kind of "expert" the detective was. If he was an expert in art history, how would that assist him in this case? A relationship between his area of expertise and the case is not made clear, so it cannot be assumed.

31. **(D)**   It stands to reason that such a flight would cause wax to "melt" (D), and the loss of his wings in this manner, then, would cause Icarus to fall into the sea. "Soldering" (A) is a process of making metals or materials stick together, but what the sentence describes would do the opposite. If Icarus is "allowed" to fall into the sea, the implication is that this is something Icarus wanted to do, which makes no sense. Similarly, Icarus's wings would not be "rearranged" (B) or put in different places by his flight near the sun, nor would such rearrangement "propel" (push) him into falling into the sea. While his flight might "illuminate" (C) or light up his wings, for similar reasons to the explanation for (A) above, there is no reason why Icarus would want to fall into the sea, which volition would be implied by use of the term "enabling," which has a similar meaning to "allowing." In addition, his flight would have no foreseeable influence on "aerating" (causing to be filled with air (E)) his wings, and "directing" is what people do, not inanimate objects or heavenly bodies; a direction is similar to a command.

32. **(D)**   "Posthumously" (D) is the answer because it means after someone's death. Although Dickinson kept her writing a secret, that does not necessarily imply that the publishing of her poetry, once it was found, also took place "secretly" (A). "Appropriately" (B) means according to generally accepted norms, and has little meaning in the context of this sentence. "Preposterously" (C) means, to some extent, the opposite of appropriately, so also has little meaning in the context of this sentence. "Inexplicably" (E) means without a good explanation. While it may be inexplicable to some people that no one knew of Dickinson's writing during her lifetime, that bears no relationship to the publishing of her poetry.

33. **(E)** The pattern is example and the class to which it belongs. The answer is PENNY:MONEY. Option (A) is incorrect, since TENNIS is the sport and BALL is a typical object used in that sport. Option (B) is incorrect, since MILK is the food a COW provides. Option (C) is incorrect, since HEEL and TOE are both parts of a foot. Option (D) is incorrect, since CHAIR is an object and OAK is the material from which it can be made.

34. **(E)** The pattern is part of a whole. The answer is AORTA:HEART. Option (A) is incorrect, since the whole (FOOT) and the part (TOE) are reversed. Option (B) is incorrect, since a LOZENGE is a kind of candy meant to relieve a sore THROAT. Option (C) is incorrect, since a FIBULA is a bone in the leg, not the WRIST. Finally, Option (D) is incorrect, since a BLOOM is a stage in the life of a FLOWER.

35. **(A)** The pattern is antonyms. The answer is INDEFATIG-ABLE:LAZY. Option (B) is incorrect, since ELEGANT and CHARMING are different but not opposite characteristics. Option (C) is incorrect, since COHESIVE and ORGANIZED have similar meanings. Option (D) is incorrect, since COOPERATIVE and LOYAL have different but not opposite meanings. Option (E) is incorrect, since JUMBLED and DISPARATE have similar meanings.

36. **(E)** The pattern is verbs with similar meanings, except that to PLAGIARIZE is a particular form of theft—to STEAL ideas. The answer is (E), ACCESSORIZE:DECORATE, since to ACCESSORIZE is a particular way to DECORATE. Option (A) is incorrect, since CRAVE is a verb and DISCRETE is an adjective; furthermore, their meanings are different. Option (D) is not correct. Although MASQUERADE is a particular way to ACT, their order is reversed. Option (B) is incorrect, since POL-LUTE and CLEAN are antonyms. Option (C) is incorrect, because ORIGINATE and CORRECT have different meanings.

37. **(B)** The pattern is verbs that are antonyms. The answer is POSTPONE:PROCEED. Option (A) is incorrect, since GARRULOUS and TALKATIVE are adjectives with similar meanings. Option (C) is incorrect, since MONITOR and SUPERVISE are verbs with similar meanings. Option (D) is incorrect, since SUBMIT and YIELD are also verbs with similar meanings. Option (E) is incorrect, since STEAL is what a BURGLAR does.

38. **(D)**   The pattern is two verbs with similar meaning. The answer is CAVIL:CARP. Option (A) is incorrect, since LIONIZE and DETHRONE are verbs having dissimilar meanings. Option (B) is incorrect, because OFFENSE is a noun and AGGRAVATE is a verb. Option (C) is incorrect, since RIDICULE is what one does to another—make fun of someone. To LAUGH is to respond to something funny. Option (E) is incorrect, since CHALLENGE and SWINDLE have different meanings.

39. **(B)**   The pattern is professional and what that professional studies. The answer is BOTANIST:PLANTS. Option (A) is incorrect, since the PSYCHIATRIST doesn't merely study the INSANE. Option (C) is incorrect, since a PODIATRIST studies feet, not CHILDREN. (A pediatrician studies children.) Option (D) is incorrect, since a CARDIOLOGIST studies the heart, not the LUNGS. Finally, an ANATOMIST studies the whole body, not just the BONES.

40. **(B)**   The primary focus of the passage is on the lack of importance of the primary self of Eliot. (B) is the correct answer. The passage does not indicate that there is an impressive number of portraitures of men and women created by that great writer George Eliot. (A) is not the best choice. The writer indicates that Eliot has impartiality toward her characters. Choice (C) states that the evident bias of Eliot toward each of her characters is "needful to her own deepest life." (C) is false and should not be chosen. The author states that "when a work of art can be understood only by enjoying it, the art is of a high kind." The writer does not consider the writings of George Eliot to be inferior. (D) is not an appropriate choice since it states that the works of Eliot are inferior; choice (D) indicates that her works can be understood only by enjoying them and enjoyment is inferior to cognition. (D) should not be chosen. The author states that we cannot say with any truthfulness that Eliot projects herself into any of her writings. (E) is false since it suggests that projection of Eliot appears in her creations.

41. **(E)**   The author refers to her writings primarily as works of art with a moral soul. (E) is the best choice. We cannot say with any confidence that Eliot's writings are a projection of herself. (A) should not be chosen since we do not know that they are painful personal recollections. The author indicates that many good things are detachable from Eliot's writings; they are not necessarily compositions which must be kept intact at all cost. (B) should not be chosen. The writer states emphatically that Eliot's works are not didactic treatises; (C) should not be chosen. The works are

described as the "second self of George Eliot." We do not know that Eliot projects herself into her writings. (D), then, should not be chosen.

42. **(E)** In context the reference to Eliot's works as being "not didactic treatises" (line 32) suggests that they are pleasurable readings (E). The word "didactic" suggests instruction, particularly moral instruction. This means that moralistic compositions (A) and instructive writing (B) must not be selected. Eliot's writings are not dramatic revelations (C) or social criticisms (D); neither choice should be chosen.

43. **(B)** The passage indicates that the reader's correct response to Eliot's writing should be to enjoy the writings given us by the artist and detach from them what we can. (B) is the correct answer. Eliot's works are not designed to be analyzed completely; (A) should not be chosen. We do not know that Eliot places herself in her writings; one should not, then, search for the glimpses of George Eliot's real self which are hidden there. The writer states that one should not separate the moral soul of any complete work of hers from its artistic medium; (C) should not be chosen. Since the author states that we should not dissect nor separate the moral soul from her work, (D) should not be chosen. Eliot is objective toward her characters; we cannot easily search for Eliot's feelings toward each character. Her true feelings are not evident upon careful scrutiny. (E) should not be chosen.

44. **(B)** Eliot's characters can best be described as impartial presentations. (B) is the best answer. We have no evidence that the characters are projections of Eliot herself. (A) is not the best choice. Eliot is said to condemn but not to hate; her characters do not live their own lives without any presence of the author; (C) is not the best choice. Eliot's writings are not instructive or didactic; (D) should not be chosen. Eliot's characters are complete since they live their own lives; "incomplete portraitures" (E) is not the best choice.

45. **(A)** The phrase "the tail wagging the dog" implies that cause and effect are reversed, since the dog should be wagging the tail. Since the author directly states that education is the main objective of a university, administrative tasks taking precedence over education can be seen as "the tail (administration) wagging the dog (education)." (B) is the opposite of this. (C) is mentioned elsewhere, but is not the point here. (D) is obviously false, while the ideas of (E) are set forth as goals that the author sets for university presidents.

46. **(C)** The author speaks of the true function of the university as a place for scholarly pursuits. He does not call for the doing away with extracurricular activities, nor of denying an education to anybody, he wishes for a less serious junior-college atmosphere for the less scholarly student, thus (A) and (B) are incorrect. (D) is in direct contrast with the author's feelings that the school system needs to be overhauled and (E) is never mentioned by the author.

47. **(B)** Within the same sentence the author states that the president "must . . . take responsibility for new appointments" (lines 41–42) after getting rid of outdated faculty and staff. (A) has no basis whatsoever. (C) is a concern elsewhere in the passage, but is irrelevant here. Likewise, (D) is a concern elsewhere, but not here, while (E) is an obviously incorrect literal interpretation of the metaphor.

48. **(D)** The final paragraph lists the various duties of a university president. (A) and (C) are tangential purposes at best, since the request for infallibility is not meant literally, knowable by the pope metaphor. (B) is in direct opposition to the author's belief that the centralization of power is necessary (lines 5–6). (E) is never mentioned by the author.

49. **(B)** The overall tone of Passage 2 suggests that the King is easily astonished and concerned mainly with his table-setting, while ignoring all other issues. Common sense invalidates (A), (D), and (E), since within the context of this passage a table-setting can have no importance in relation to the running of the Kingdom. While (C) may be true, it is not the main point of the passage.

50. **(D)** The author seems aware that a bowl, jug, and salt-cellar are not worthy of such a statement, thus (A) is incorrect. (B) and (C) are wrong, since nowhere does the passage refer to the King as a wise or brilliant man, while (E) is invalidated for the same reason as (A).

51. **(C)** The author of Passage 2 seems to think that the centralization of power leads only to attention being paid to trivial, personal desires, thus both (A) and (B) are incorrect. No attempt is made to explain the strange desires of the King so (D) is wrong, while the social position of the narrator is of only peripheral concern here (E).

52. **(C)** Both passages address this concern from different points of view. Passage 2 is not contemporary so (A) is wrong. Both (B) and (E) are concerns of only Passage 2, and (E) is only tangential.

21. **(A)**   Since we are only interested in the units place, in 29^3, multiply the 9 three times

$$9 \times 9 \times 9 = 729.$$

The units digit is 9. In 29^4, multiply the 9 four times

$$9 \times 9 \times 9 \times 9 = 6,561.$$

The units digit is 1.

22. **(C)**   The probability of an event is equal to the favorable ways divided by the total number of ways it can occur.

$$\text{Probability} = \frac{\text{Favorable}}{\text{Total Ways}}$$

To pick a red jelly bean, probability $= {}^4/_{10}$

To *not* pick a green jelly bean, you must pick a red jelly bean. Again, the probability is ${}^4/_{10.}$

23. **(A)**   To eliminate a percent sign, put what you have over 100.

$$.5\% \text{ of } .5 = \frac{.5}{100} \times \frac{.5}{1}$$

$$= \frac{.25}{100}$$

$$= .0025$$

$$.10\% \text{ of } .10 = \frac{.10}{100} \times \frac{.10}{1}$$

$$= \frac{.0100}{100}$$

$$= .0001$$

24. **(C)**   To multiply by 10, 100, 1,000, etc., move the decimal point to the right one place for each zero. For example:

$$.123 \times 10 = 1.23$$

$$.123 \times 100 = 12.3$$

$$.123 \times 1,000 = 123$$

So, $.39 \times 1,000 = 390$

$$.039 \times 10,000 = 390$$

The two columns are equivalent.

25. **(B)**   If you add 8 + 12, you will be counting yourself *twice,* so be sure to add and subtract 1.

$$(20 - 1 = 19)$$

Column (B), 20, is greater.

26. **(B)**   The radius is $^1/_2$.

$$A = \pi r^2 = \pi (^1/_2)^2 = {}^1/_4\pi.$$

$$C = 2\pi r = 2\pi(^1/_2) = \pi$$

27. **(B)**   The average of 2 different numbers squared will always be greater than the product of the original 2 numbers. Here, 100 is the average of 99 and 101.

$$99 \times 101 = 9,999$$

and $100^2 = 10,000$

28. **(C)**

$$.5^2 - .4^2 = .25 - .16$$

$$= .09$$

$$.3^2 = .09$$

29. **(B)**   Cancel out the equal expressions first.

$$\frac{8A^4B^5}{2A^3B^5} = 4A; \text{ since } A = 3, \text{ then } 4(3) = 12.$$

$$\frac{10A^5B^4}{2A^5B^3} = 5B; \text{ since } B = 4, \text{ then } 5(4) = 20.$$

30. **(C)**   Factor first.

$$2^9 + 2^9 = 2^9\,(1+1)$$
$$= 2^9\,(2)$$
$$= 2^{10}$$

31. **(C)**

$$(\sqrt{9} - 1)^3 = (3-1)^3$$
$$= (2)^3$$
$$= 8$$

$(\sqrt{8})^2 = 8$. Whenever you square a square root, you get the quantity under the square root. For example:

$$\left(\sqrt{\frac{2}{3}a^2b^3}\right)^2 = \frac{2}{3}a^2b^3$$

32. **(C)**   If the side of the square is x, then

$$x^2 + x^2 = (\sqrt{2})^2.$$
$$2x^2 = 2$$
$$x^2 = 1$$
$$x = 1$$

Area of a square $= s^2 = (1)^2 = 1$; so $4 \times 1 = 4$.

The perimeter of the square is also 4.

33. The correct response is:

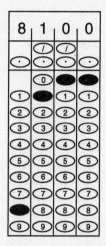

Given that we know the area on the map that the crop duster must treat (9π sq. in.), we can compute the radius of the circle required to form that area.

Area of a circle $= \pi r^2$

$$9\pi = \pi r^2$$

$$\frac{9\pi}{\pi} = \frac{\pi r^2}{\pi} \quad \text{equals divided by equals are equal}$$

$$9 = r^2 \qquad \text{simplify}$$

$$3 = r \qquad \text{the square roots of equals are equal}$$

Thus, the area of the radius on the map is 3 inches. Because one inch on the map equals 30 miles on the ground, we can set up a proportion to determine the radius of the circle on the ground.

$$\frac{30 \text{ (scaled miles on ground)}}{1 \text{ (scaled inches on map)}} = \frac{x \text{ (actual miles on ground)}}{3 \text{ (actual inches on map)}}$$

$$30 \times 3 = 1 \times x \qquad \text{Cross multiply.}$$

$$90 = x \qquad \text{Simplify.}$$

Thus, we see that the radius of the circle on the ground would be 90 miles. By using the formula for the area of a circle, we can compute the area of the circle on the ground.

Area of a circle $= \pi r^2$

$$\text{Area} = \pi \, 90^2$$

$$\text{Area} = 8,100\pi \text{ square miles}$$

34. The correct response is:

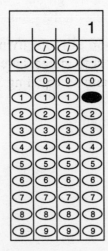

As the formula for a circle is given by πr^2, we have

$$\frac{1}{2}\left(\frac{22}{7}r^2\right) = \frac{11}{7};$$

thus $\qquad r^2 = 1$

which yields $\quad r = 1.$

As the length of the square is twice the radius, we obtain

$$A_{\text{square}} = 2^2 = 4 \text{ square feet.}$$

35. The correct response is:

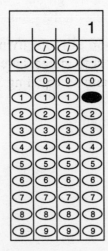

Since $x = 3$ meters the area of the larger square is

$A_{\text{large}} = 3^2 = 9$ square meters.

As the area of the shaded region is 8 square meters, the difference between the larger and smaller squares is 1 square meter. Since $y^2 = 1$ square meter, the solution is $y = 1$ meter.

36. The correct response is:

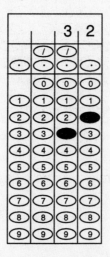

Let the 1st even integer $= x$ and the 2nd even integer $= x + 2$.

We know then that the product of the integers is given by

$$x(x + 2) = 1{,}224$$

$$x^2 + 2x - 1{,}224 = 0$$

Factoring, we obtain

$$(x - 34)\,(x + 36) = 0$$

which yields $x = 34$ and $x = -36$ as roots giving rise to solutions (34, 36) and (−36, −34). By hypothesis both integers are positive; hence, (34, 36) is the solution, with the smaller number equaling 34.

37. The correct response is:

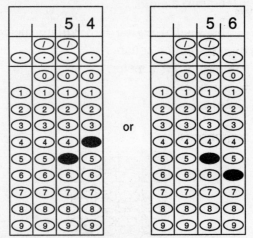

                                or

The possible answers are 54 and 56 since

$$54 = 2 \times 27 = 2 \times 3^3$$

and $56 = 8 \times 7 = 2^3 \times 7.$

All other x such that $50 < x < 60$ factorize with prime greater than 10.

38. The correct response is:

The equation $x^2 - y^2 =$ factors as

$$(x - y)(x + y) = 1.$$

Rearranging the second equation we get $x - y = 3$;

plugging this in we obtain

(3) $(x + y) = 1$,

i.e., $\qquad x + y = \dfrac{1}{3}.$

The desired quantity is

$$x + y + 6 = \frac{1}{3} + 6 = \frac{19}{3}.$$

39. The correct response is:

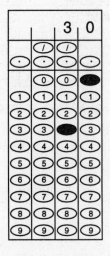

The area of the triangle is given by $\frac{1}{2}$ (base) (height); we have

$$\frac{1}{2} bh = 100$$

$$bh = 200$$

The only possibilities are ($b = 10$, $h = 20$) and ($b = 20$, $h = 10$); in both cases $b + h = 30$.

40. The correct response is:

The area of a triangle is given by $\frac{1}{2}$ (base) (height); here the base is 4 units (i.e., the difference in the x-coordinates of A and B) and the height is 1 unit (i.e., the difference in the y-coordinates of B and C). The area is given by $\frac{1}{2}$ (4) (1) = 2 square units.

Section 5 — Writing Skills

1. **(A)**   Choice (A) is obviously wordy, "consensus" meaning the same as "general agreement," so it is the best choice. None of the others has a usage error. Choice (B) is acceptable in that it implies a well-known fact that Twain wrote many other works. Choice (C) underscores the claim made in the whole sentence be establishing the book as the "best" American work. Finally, choice (D) is acceptable because of commas in other parts of the sentence. Choice (E) clearly does not apply.

2. **(C)**   This question has several potential errors. Choice (A) requires that you know to capitalize important historical documents, so it is correct. Choice (B) calls to question the attribution of human rationality to an inanimate object, but since the Constitution actually does have logical premises, we can correctly say that the document can posit the premise stated. Choice (D) is acceptable because the superlative is referenced within the sentence; one should know that the U.S. government has three branches. That leaves choices (C) and (E). Choice (C) is the verb in the clause beginning with the word "what"; it is plural, and therefore, incorrect because it does not agree with its subject "history," a singular noun. Do not be fooled by the intervening plural word "governments." Since choice (C) is the error, choice (E) would no longer be considered.

3. **(C)**   Even though people use "like" as a conjunction in conversation and public speaking, it is a preposition, and formal written English requires "as," "as if," or "as though" when what follows is a clause. No other choice is even suspect.

4. **(C)**   One could question the use of "nearly" (A), but it is correct. One might argue also that "million dollars" (D) should be written "$1 million," but choice (C) is so clearly an incorrect use of the past perfect tense that the other possibilities, remote at best, pale by comparison. The simple past tense ("sold"), the present progressive tense ("are selling"), or the present perfect progressive tense ("have been selling") could each be used correctly depending on the meaning intended.

5. **(B)**   This choice is not as obvious, but authorities agree that the use of "expect" to mean "suppose" or "believe" (the usage here) is either informal or colloquial, but again not formal written English. The next most likely choice, (E), would suggest that informal or colloquial usage is

appropriate. The third most likely choice, (D), brings to mind the distinction between "accept" and "except," a word pair often confused. However, "accept" is correct here.

6. **(A)** Regardless of its popular usage, "hopefully" is an adverb trying to be a clause ("it is hoped" or "I hope"). However, instances still exist that require a distinction between the two uses. To be clear, use "hopefully" when you mean "in a hopeful manner." ["He wished hopefully that she would accept his proposal of marriage."] Capitalizing "Twentieth Century" (B) is appropriate as it is here used as the specific historical period (like the "Middle Ages"). We would not capitalize the phrase if it were used simply to count, as in "The twentieth century from now will surely find enormous changes in the world." Choice (C), "enough," is correct as used. Choice (D) appears suspicious. "Continually" means recurrence at intervals over a period of time, so it is correctly used to imply that machines do break down often. It is incorrect to hyphenate a number-noun phrase like this one when it stands alone as a noun phrase.

7. **(A)** The two most suspicious choices are (A) and (D) because the item is a sentence fragment. No reasonable substitute for (D) would solve both the logic problem (incomplete thought) and the punctuation problem (comma splice if you omit "that"). Changing "showing" to "show" would, however, make the clause into a complete sentence with correct punctuation. Neither (B) or (C) provoke suspicion.

8. **(B)** Again, the two most questionable choices, (B) and (C), compete for our attention. The use of "but" makes sense because it shows contrast to the previous idea. ("Don't evade or defy the law, *but* if caught breaking a law, accept the penalty.") The use of "or," however, is clearly not parallel to the immediately preceding use of "neither." The proper phrase is "neither . . . nor" for negative alternate choices. Neither choice (A) nor choice (D) demands a second look.

9. **(D)** This choice involves parallel construction, or the lack of it. The word "both" introduces a pair of phrases, one a prepositional phrase ("for their own interests"), the other an infinitive phrase ("to gain more goods"). Aside from being inelegant, "to gain more goods" is also not the same structure and should be changed to "their own gain" to make the two phrases perfectly parallel. Choices (B) and (C) are not problematic. Choice (A) is another candidate because of the capitalization and the lack of a hyphen between "Eighteenth" and "Century." The capitalization is correct

and no hyphen is needed when the phrase becomes an adjective that has meaning as a single phrase, which the capitalization suggests, or if the first word forms a familiar pair with the following word and if there is no danger of confusion. [The sentence clearly does not mean that Smith is the eighteenth (small "e") philosopher, but *the* Eighteenth Century philosopher.]

10. **(E)** The other choices all fail to exhibit inappropriate usage. Choice (A), "cannot," is spelled as one word; choice (B), "should not," is parallel to "cannot" and adds meaning necessary to the thought. Choice (C) is a correct plural possessive pronoun, the antecedent of which is "rulers." Finally, choice (D) is a third-person plural verb agreeing with its subject, "reasons."

11. **(C)** "Milky Way galaxy" is the singular antecedent, for which the pronoun referent should be "its" (inanimate object). Do not be confused by the intervening words ("stars" and "spots"); it is the galaxy which shines in this sentence, not the stars or the spots. Choice (A) is the correct usage of "comprises." Choice (B) is an appropriate pair of adjectives with no apparent problem. Choice (D) is appropriate because the sentence has an internally supplied superlative sense; it does not need a "brightest of" phrase.

12. **(A)** Again, non-parallel structure is the key of this and many other test items. Because of the overwhelming importance of understanding balance in sentence structure, tests like this one emphasize parallel sentence structures. "To learn" clashes with "studying" in the parallel clause. You cannot choose "studying." "Learning" substituted for "To learn" would make the clauses parallel. Choice (B) is a correct use of "like" as a preposition (objects: "Latin," "Greek"). Choice (D) is correctly singular as the verb of the noun phrase "studying . . . beliefs." Nothing is incorrect about choice (C).

13. **(A)** This is a colloquial, nonstandard substitution for the correct word, "attribute." Choice (B) is correctly lowercase, not capitalized. Choice (C) is a correct, if a bit stiff, phrase. Choice (D) is a correct plural verb the subject of which is "both," also plural.

14. **(C)** This is an incorrect simple past verb tense. You have to spot the context clue "most Americans" "attended" school (B) in the past, which suggests they no longer do so now. They must then "choose" their

entertainment. Choice (A) is questionable, but the present participial phrase suggests coincidence with the time "most Americans" "attended school." It is, therefore, correct. Choice (D) is correctly an infinitive that is parallel to "to watch."

15. **(A)**   The two most questionable choices are (A) and (B). Choice (A) is incorrectly a subjective case pronoun when it should be objective (object of verb "makes," subject "What"). If you know the difference between "different from" (correctly used in this sentence) and "difference than" (correctly used only to introduce a clause), then choice (B) is no longer viable. Besides being a passive construction, choice (C) has no objectionable qualities; it is grammatically correct. So is choice (D) correctly an adverb that has meaning in context.

16. **(D)**   This is a case of subject-verb disagreement related to the definition of the word "neither" (subject) as singular. Its verb must also be singular, and "differ" is plural. Choice (A) correctly uses English idiom ("compare to"—"contrast with"). Choice (B) refers clearly to "ideas," its antecedent, and agrees with it (both plural). Choice (C) is a singular verb agreeing with its subject, "one."

17. **(E)**   Everything in the sentence is acceptable or correct usage, even though some of it may be a bit stuffy and pedantic, i.e., choice (B). You might question choice (A) in that instead of suggesting, perhaps asserting or stating would be more appropriate. Even though these terms clearly differ, there is nothing wrong with using "suggests" (correct subject-verb agreement with "hypothesis") because a hypothesis can suggest as well as theorize, assert, etc. Choice (C) correctly agrees with its subject "which" (plural, antecedent "archetypes"). Choice (D) might be considered redundant ("repeated" and "patterns"), but that is not apparent from the context.

18. **(E)**   You are likely to have chosen either (B) or (C) here. The affect/effect word pair often confuses students, and this instance is one in which "effected" is correctly used as a verb meaning "brought about" or "caused to happen." The question in choice (C) is whether or not to capitalize the word "Fate." When it refers to the collective term for the Greek concept of destiny (actually gods, the Fates), as it does here, it is appropriately capitalized. Choices (A) and (D) do not seem questionable.

19. **(D)**   Again, the problem here is pronoun-antecedent agreement. "Their" does not refer to the three writers collectively; its antecedent is

"each," which is always singular, not plural ("each one"). There is nothing wrong with choices (A), (B), and (C).

20. **(B)** This question of appropriate verb tense requires the simple past tense verb "took" because the Civil War happened in a finite time period in the past. The other choices all fail that test. The original and choice (E) are present tense, and do not logically fit the facts. Choice (D) is the present perfect tense, which suggests a continuous action from the past to the present. Choice (C) is the past perfect tense, which suggests a continuing action from one time in the past to another in the more recent past.

21. **(D)** We can eliminate fairly quickly choices (C) and (E) as either inappropriate or awkward appositives to "ornithology," instead of "ornithologists." Neither is (A) the best choice even though some may consider it acceptable. Likewise, choice (B) tends to be limited to nonrestrictive clauses, unlike this one. Choice (D) then correctly uses a "personal" relative pronoun.

22. **(D)** Choices (A), (D), and (E) are the best candidates because they are more concise than the other two choices. Each does express the same idea, but (E) does not as strongly indicate the contrast between the two clauses in the sentence as do choices (A) and (D). Choice (D) clearly makes its point in fewer words and is the better choice.

23. **(B)** The phrase "as to" often is overblown and unclear, so it is best to eliminate it when there are other choices. Likewise, "expectability" does not exactly roll of your tongue. That leaves choices (B) and (D). Choice (D) adds a definite figure, unwarranted by the original sentence. It also is duller than (B), which does change the wording for the better and also indicates that the "actual amount" is to be announced, rather than that it is already known.

24. **(A)** Choices (C) and (E) introduce unnecessary absolute phrases beginning with "it," which makes the sentences wordy. They can be eliminated immediately. Choice (D) has an illogical comparison suggesting notes = instrument, so it, too, is not the best choice. Between (A) and (B) the difference boils down to the present tense vs. the past tense. Choice (A) uses past tenses, which seem better in sequence to follow the past tense verb "developed."

25. **(B)** Choices (A), (C), and (D) can be disqualified quickly because they are not parallel to the structure of the main clause. Choice (E) is ungainly and introduces a vague pronoun "its" (unclear antecedent). Choice (B) reads well and has the virtue of brevity.

26. **(E)** The choices are easy to discern in this sentence. The original verb does not agree with its subject, nor is the structure parallel. The former reason also eliminates choice (C). Choice (B) does not have parallel structure (phrase and clause). Choice (D) does not logically agree with the subject ("reasons") since it names one ("demanding professors") but relegates the other reason to an afterthought. Choice (E) has both parallel structure and subject-verb agreement; it also names two reasons.

27. **(C)** The original suffers from inadequate causal relationship and non-parallel structure. Choices (D) and (E) are both unnecessarily wordy; (D) is still not parallel, and (E) is internally illogical ("both" with three things). Choice (B) switches its structure at the end. Although it is technically parallel, it is still awkward because of the addition of the possessive pronoun "her." Choice (C) solves both problems by clearly showing cause and by being parallel (three nouns in series).

28. **(B)** This sentence presents an incomplete comparison and a redundancy ("Whether"/"or did not"/"remains uncertain"). Choice (B) eliminates both problems clearly. Choice (C) tries to undo the damage, but it remains inelegant in syntax and leaves partial redundancy ("whether"/"remains uncertain"). Choice (D) is worse in both respects. Choice (E) clears up the syntax but leaves some redundancy ("may actually have"/"remains uncertain"). Choice (B) eliminates both problems clearly.

29. **(A)** The sentence as is reads well; it is perfectly balanced. Choice (B) introduces an incomplete comparison ("more" but no "than"). Choice (C) awkwardly uses "as to." Choices (D) and (E) make a scrambled mess by introducing illogical structures.

30. **(A)** "Unique" means just that; it should not have qualifiers like "very" or "nearly." That eliminates choices (B) and (D). Choice (C) changes the meaning by making the development unique, instead of the system. Choice (E) uses an inappropriate verb tense because the first of the sentence suggests the Revolutionary War period, definitely in the past.

31. **(B)** The original sentence (A) has a dangling modifier (participial

phrase); it remains that way in choice (E). The house cannot return to itself, nor can "it" (pronoun for house). Choice (D) seems to leave something out: "returned to . . . home in 12 years." Choice (C) solves the original problem but is unnecessarily wordy. Choice (B) properly solves the dangling modifier problem by subordinating the return in an adverbial clause.

32. **(A)** Choice (A) is the only response that makes sense. Each of the others introduces illogical comparisons or structures (non-parallel); (B), (D), and (E) are also verbose. Choice (C) is concise but not parallel.

33. **(C)** This sentence suggests causal relationships between the parts of the sentence that do not belong there. Choices (B) and (D) echo the original (A) in that regard. Choice (E) has garbled syntax. (C) shows clearly that the cause-effect relationship is, rather, a time relationship.

34. **(B)** Choice (B) is the most concise, least repetitive form of this sentence. Choices (A) and (E) contain the unnecessary phrase, "It goes without saying." Choice (C) leaves out the fact that waves are pounding at the mouth of a sea cave. Choice (D) is a fragment.

35. **(A)** Choice (A) is the best revision because it is precise and uses a voice consistent with the rest of the passage. Choice (B) and (C) both slip into the less formal "you." Choice (E) is too formal, using "one." Choice (C) is somewhat acceptable but uses the passive voice construction, "can be thought of."

36. **(E)** Choice (E) clearly shows the pattern of events, a sequence of cause-and-effect. Choice (A) contains the incorrect construction, "This acid dissolving"; it should be, "This acid's dissolving." Choice (B) neglects to extend clearly the process of cave formation to show that the passageways become caves. Choice (C) is somewhat acceptable, but it contains the awkward phrasing, "effects are that." Choice (D) reverses the cause with the effect, and so confuses the issues.

37. **(E)** The second paragraph explains the process (E) by which drip-stone features are formed in a cave. This process takes place in a location—caves—but description, choice (C), is not the main intent of the paragraph. Choices (A), (B), and (D) would be more suitable to persuasion.

38. **(C)**   Choice (C) is the most precise wording and uses an action verb, "occurs." Choices (A), (D), and (E) use two forms of the verb "to be" in the same sentence, thus producing a weaker construction. Choice (B) uses, "is due to," and so is a bit more awkward than choice (C).

39. **(A)**   Choice (A) sets the prepositional phrase apart from the main subject and verb ("water seeps"). Choice (B) makes it seem as though we are talking about "a rain water." In (C) and (D) both a colon and a hyphen are inappropriate. In (E), the sentence as it stands is ambiguous, especially because we use the phrase "rain water" in other contexts, and unless the prepositional phrase is set off by a comma, the sense is unclear.

PSAT/ NMSQT

Practice Test 3

TEST 3

Section 1

(Answer sheets appear in the back of this book.)

TIME: 25 Minutes
26 Questions

For each question in this section, select the best answer from among the given choices and fill in the corresponding oval on the answer sheet.

DIRECTIONS: Each sentence below has one or two blanks, each blank indicating that something has been omitted. Beneath the sentence are five lettered words or sets of words. Choose the word or set of words that **BEST** fits the meaning of the sentence as a whole.

EXAMPLE:

Although the critics found the book _____, many of the readers found it rather _____.

(A) obnoxious . . . perfect

(B) spectacular . . . interesting

(C) boring . . . intriguing

(D) comical . . . persuasive

(E) popular . . . rare

Ⓐ Ⓑ ● Ⓓ Ⓔ

---

1. When the teacher told us to include our sources used for the reports, he gave us instructions on how to compile a(n) _____ .

   (A) library

   (B) bibliography

   (C) index

   (D) abstract

   (E) depository

2. Whenever Bill and Mary go to dinner at the Browns' house, they remember to _____ the favor and _____ the Browns to dinner at their house.

   (A) extend . . . propel

   (B) reveal . . . restore

(C) return . . . invite   (D) classify . . . revolve

(E) represent . . . drive

3. The book sold out very quickly because it was advertised _____ on television.

   (A) primordially   (D) protectively

   (B) primarily   (E) pretentiously

   (C) previously

4. The committee's task was to research ways to protect the _____ while taking _____ factors into account.

   (A) household . . . paleontological

   (B) environment . . . economic

   (C) forest . . . geographic

   (D) farm . . . universal

   (E) nebula . . . galactic

5. Nobody in the small mountain village can predict when the shipments will _____ because of the _____ of the delivery schedule.

   (A) devolve . . . harrassment

   (B) cease . . . taxation

   (C) overlap . . . propitiousness

   (D) splatter . . . sparseness

   (E) arrive . . . randomness

6. Many animals travel in packs or groups because it gives them a feeling of _____ , which they would not have if they traveled alone.

   (A) comfort   (D) leeway

   (B) safety   (E) rapidity

   (C) adventure

7. There were many _____ to the invention of the airplane, but none were successful until the Wright brothers _____ their "flying machine."

   (A) successors . . . introduced

   (B) precedents . . . inaugurated

   (C) expirations . . . replaced

   (D) precursors . . . created

   (E) exigencies . . . destabilized

DIRECTIONS: Each question below consists of a related pair of words or phrases, followed by five lettered pairs of words or phrases. Select the lettered pair that best expresses a relationship similar to that expressed in the original pair.

EXAMPLE:

SMILE : MOUTH ::

(A) wink : eye   (D) tan : skin

(B) teeth : face   (E) food : gums

(C) voice : speech   ● Ⓑ Ⓒ Ⓓ Ⓔ

---

8. THERMOMETER : TEMPERATURE ::

   (A) odometer : distance   (D) hypothesis : proof

   (B) yardstick : space   (E) compass : fabric

   (C) barometer : rain

9. COMEDY : AMUSE ::

   (A) drama : save   (D) movie : praise

   (B) farce : enlighten   (E) play : thank

   (C) tragedy : sadden

10. INPUT : COMPUTER ::

    (A) fuel : engine   (D) data : production

    (B) uniform : soldier   (E) abode : dwelling

    (C) opportunity : experience

11. GARNISH : DECORATE ::

 (A) deface : mar   (D) chart : bridge

 (B) scrutinize : text   (E) extol : help

 (C) fix : furnish

12. SOOTHE : CALM ::

 (A) assess : propose   (D) energize : excite

 (B) defame : double   (E) moisten : destroy

 (C) outline : paper

13. BRAGGART : BOASTER ::

 (A) consumer : gullible   (D) liar : vigilant

 (B) politician : zealous   (E) charlatan : fraud

 (C) coward : hilarious

DIRECTIONS: Read each passage and answer the questions that follow. Each question will be based on the information stated or implied in the passage or its introduction.

Questions 14–18 are based on the following passage.

The following passage is excerpted from a book of letters and memories of the life of Charlotte Cushman.

1   In the old, historic part of Boston, close by the chime of bells given to the American colonists by King George, under the vigilant eye of the old cockerel, there stood, in 1816, a "rough cast" house. Here amid the summer heats, was born, of stern Puritan stock, a blue-eyed girl who after-
5 wards, single-handed, fought her way to an eminence where she stood a queen, her royal right unchallenged! Boston proudly boasts that her day and generation had not Charlotte Cushman's equal. In 1867 the old house was torn down, and in its place was built a handsome brick school-house. For five years it had no name; then—happy thought!—a member of the
10 school board proposed it should be called the "Cushman School," in honor of the celebrated actress. Some of the old conservatives were startled into a mild remonstrance. A public building named, forsooth, for a woman! What matter that it was a girls' school, and women only for teachers! Fortunately there was no mayor who must be flattered with an educational

15 namesake; so the vote was carried, and today a woman's name is graven in
letters of granite upon its facade. On the fifth of January, 1872, Miss
Cushman made a tour of the building, gracing each room with her presence. Then all were assembled in the hall for a dedicatory service. On the
floor were seated the pupils, a thousand girls; on the platform, teachers
20 and visitors; and in the centre, Miss Cushman. Here she made her "maiden
speech," as she smilingly said. Those upturned girlish faces were all the
inspiration she needed, and a flush of enthusiasm gathered on her pale
face. For their encouragement she told them she walked those very streets,
a school-girl as poor as the poorest among them. With rapid gestures of
25 her large, shapely hands, her eyes glowing with the fire of her own peculiar genius and her habitual intensity, she told them that whatever she had
attained had been by giving herself to her work.

A patience that tired not, an energy that faltered not, a persistence that
knew no flagging, principles that swerved not, and the victory was hers,
30 after long years of hard work. Higher than her intellectual strength, higher
than her culture or genius or graces of character, she ranked her ability for
work. This was the secret of her success, and the legacy she bequeathed
the girls of the Cushman School. They knew something of her history; that
she had educated herself; that she had stoutly resisted the shafts of disease;
35 that the great men of the age delighted to do her honor; that she was an
earnest, religious woman, upon whose fair name rested no shadow of
suspicion.

14. The primary focus of the passage is on the

(A) numerous appearances made by the celebrated actress Charlotte
Cushman.

(B) richness and complexity of Boston.

(C) events leading to and including the dedication of the Cushman
School.

(D) fact that many opposed the dedication.

(E) opening of a school for girls.

15. When referring to dedicating the school to a woman, the author

(A) is very much opposed since there were many who needed to be
recognized.

(B) expresses intense interest in the exact source of the choice.

(C) expresses enthusiastic approval.

(D) expresses appreciation to the mayor who made it all possible.

(E) concludes that there was no other choice since there was no mayor who needed recognition.

16. In lines 2–3 the words "vigilant eyes of the cockerel" mean most nearly

(A) the watchful eye of the one in charge—the mayor.

(B) the eye full of revenge belonging to the one in charge—the mayor.

(C) the eye full of revenge of the town dowager or cockerel or older woman.

(D) the constant eye of the weather cock.

(E) the constant eye of the storm or the hurricane.

17. Based on this passage, the author's reaction to suffrage for women would be

(A) enthusiastic approval of the right.

(B) objective assessment of suffrage.

(C) disdain for the entire idea.

(D) a careful study of the effect on male counterparts.

(E) appreciation for those opposing the idea.

18. The tone of the author is

(A) irony.   (D) enthusiasm.

(B) hostility.   (E) disdain.

(C) sarcasm.

Questions 19–26 are based on the following passage.

In the following passage, a nineteenth century historian examines the early period of American history.

1   In the history of men and nations, while we remain immersed in the study of personal incidents and details, as what such a statesman said or how many men were killed in such a battle, we may quite fail to understand what it was all about, and we shall be sure often to misjudge men's

5 characters and estimate wrongly the importance of many events. For this
reason we cannot clearly see the meaning of the history of our own times.
The facts are too near us; we are down among them, like the man who
could not see the forest because there were so many trees. But when we
look back over a long interval of years, we can survey distant events and
10 personages like points in a vast landscape and begin to discern the meaning of it all. In this way we come to see that history is full of lessons for
us. Very few things have happened in past ages with which our present
welfare is not in one way or another concerned. Few things have happened in any age more interesting or more important than the American
15 Revolution.

It is always difficult in history to mark the beginning and end of a
period. Events keep rushing on and do not pause to be divided into chapters; or, in other words, in the history which really takes place, a new
chapter is always beginning long before the old one is ended.

20 In telling the story of the American Revolution we must stop somewhere, and the inauguration of President Washington is a very proper
place. We must also begin somewhere, but it is quite clear that it will not
do to begin with the Declaration of Independence in July, 1776, or even
with the midnight ride of Paul Revere in April, 1775.

25 If we were going to take a very wide view of the situation, and try to
point out its relations to the general history of mankind, we should have
to go back many hundreds of years and not only cross the ocean to the
England of King Alfred, but keep on still further to the ancient market-
places of Rome and Athens, and even to the pyramids of Egypt; and in all
30 this long journey through the ages we should not be merely gratifying an
idle curiosity, but at every step of the way could gather sound practical
lessons, useful in helping us to vote intelligently at the next election for
mayor of the city in which we live or for president of the United States.

We are not now, however, about to start on any such long journey. It is
35 a much nearer and narrower view of the American Revolution that we
wish to get. There are many points from which we might start, but we
must at any rate choose a point several years earlier than the Declaration
of Independence. People are very apt to leave out of sight the "good old
colony times" and speak of our country as scarcely more than a hundred
40 years old. Sometimes we hear the presidency of George Washington spoken of as part of "early American history"; but we ought not to forget that
when Washington was born the commonwealth of Virginia was already
125 years old. The first governor of Massachusetts was born three centuries ago, in 1588, the year of the Spanish Armada. Suppose we take the
45 period of 282 years between the English settlement of Virginia and the
inauguration of President Benjamin Harrison, and divide it in the middle.

That gives us the year 1748 as the half-way station in the history of the American people. There were just as many years of continuous American history before 1748 as there have been since that date.

19. The author of the passage

    (A) does not attach much importance to the Revolutionary War time period.

    (B) believes from the facts of the past we can understand those events of the past.

    (C) believes we can understand the present and what it is all about.

    (D) believes that events in history are easy to compartmentalize.

    (E) believes that current events are difficult for us to see the meaning of today since we are too close to the events.

20. In looking for the very beginning of the American Revolution, according to the author

    (A) one should start with the Declaration of Independence.

    (B) one should use July 1776 as a starting point.

    (C) one should begin with the midnight ride of Paul Revere in April 1775.

    (D) one must go to events a century before the Revolution to find the start of the American Revolution.

    (E) one must go as far back as the pyramids of Egypt.

21. In looking at ancient history the author believes that

    (A) one can find accurate meaning in the facts of history.

    (B) one should be merely gratifying an idle curiosity.

    (C) one should find sound practical lessons to help us today.

    (D) one will find the starting place for which this writing on the American Revolution will begin and the view this writing will seek.

    (E) one would waste time and energy; there is no relation to modern events.

22. The author uses as the midpoint in his treatment of the American Revolution

   (A) the 1588 benchmark.

   (B) 141 years after the first permanent settlement of Virginia and 141 years before the inauguration of Harrison.

   (C) the time when the Commonwealth of Virginia was 125 years old.

   (D) the halfway point between the settlement of Virginia and the inauguration of President Washington.

   (E) the birthday of the first governor of Massachusetts.

23. The author's feelings about history can be best described as

   (A) enthusiastic.

   (B) unenthusiastic.

   (C) reserved since he does not believe in its accuracy and useful-ness.

   (D) negative.

   (E) neither positive nor negative.

24. To the author, the early American period in history

   (A) is during the presidency of George Washington.

   (B) begins with the American Revolution.

   (C) is the same as that of the pyramids in Egypt.

   (D) begins with the first permanent English settlement.

   (E) is recorded inaccurately and should be disregarded.

25. The author's opinion is that

   (A) few things have happened that are more important than the inauguration of President Washington.

   (B) few things have happened that are more important than the American Revolution.

   (C) historic events are easy to categorize and compartmentalize.

(D) "the lull" occurred after the American Revolution.

(E) the Aix-la-Chapelle puts an end to the American Revolution.

26. The author would advocate that a historian

    (A) become immersed in the study of personal incidents and details.

    (B) survey distant events and personages in order to get all the specifics.

    (C) survey distant events and try to get the meaning of it all.

    (D) is not important since very few things have happened in past ages with which our present welfare is concerned.

    (E) is not needed since they are too immersed in the past.

Section 2

TIME: 25 Minutes
20 Questions

DIRECTIONS: Solve each problem, using any available space on the page for scratch work. Then decide which answer choice is the best and fill in the corresponding oval on the answer sheet.

NOTES:

(1) The use of a calculator is permitted. All numbers used are real numbers.

(2) Figures that accompany problems in this test are intended to provide information useful in solving the problems. They are drawn as accurately as possible EXCEPT when it is stated in a specific problem that the figure is not drawn to scale. All figures lie in a plane unless otherwise indicated.

REFERENCE INFORMATION:

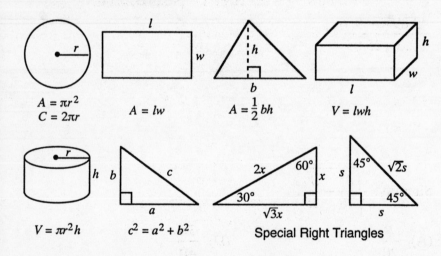

$A = \pi r^2$
$C = 2\pi r$

$A = lw$

$A = \frac{1}{2}bh$

$V = lwh$

$V = \pi r^2 h$

$c^2 = a^2 + b^2$

Special Right Triangles

The number of degrees of arc in a circle is 360.
The measure in degrees of a straight angle is 180.
The sum of the measures in degrees of the angles of a triangle is 180.

1. A rectangular wall has the dimensions F and G. A rectangular window in the wall has the dimensions K and L. Represent the shaded area of the wall.

    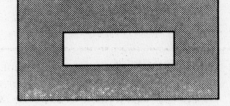

    (A) $FG + KL$

    (B) $FG - KL$

    (C) $KL - FG$

    (D) $(FG)^2 - (KL)^2$

    (E) None of these

2. If $A + B = C$ and $A - B = D$, then $A^2 - B^2 =$

    (A) C^2D^2.

    (D) $C^2 + D^2$.

    (B) $C - D$.

    (E) CD.

    (C) $C + D$.

3. Which of the following is the closest approximation of
    $$\frac{49.89 \times 489.76}{2.3 \times 25.05}?$$

    (A) .5

    (D) 500

    (B) 5

    (E) 5,000

    (C) 50

4. Simplify: $\sqrt{\dfrac{B^2}{16} - \dfrac{B^2}{25}}$.

    (A) $\dfrac{B}{20}$

    (D) $\dfrac{3B}{40}$

    (B) $\dfrac{3B}{20}$

    (E) $\dfrac{4B}{9}$

    (C) $\dfrac{B}{20}$

5. $5^{-2} + 5^{-1} + 5^0 =$

    (A) $1\dfrac{6}{25}$

    (B) $1\dfrac{1}{5}$

(C) 1

(D) $\dfrac{4}{5}$

(E) $\dfrac{3}{5}$

6. What time is it 110 hours after 9 a.m.?

(A) 10 a.m.   (D) 11 a.m.

(B) 10 p.m.   (E) 11 p.m.

(C) 12 noon

7. To obtain a final average of 85% in a certain subject, what grade must a student earn in a test after having an average of 83% in four examinations?

(A) 87   (D) 93

(B) 89   (E) 95

(C) 91

8. Each of the following sets of three numbers could represent the lengths of the side of a triangle EXCEPT:

(A) 5, 10, 6.   (D) 8, 3, 7.

(B) 4, 6, 13.   (E) 9, 6, 13.

(C) 7, 7, 10.

9. A rich landowner left half of his estate to his wife, one-fourth to his son, one-fifth to his daughter, and the remainder, $7,000, to his church. What is the total amount left by the landowner?

(A) $10,500   (D) $14,000

(B) $12,250   (E) $140,000

(C) $13,650

10. A rectangular solid is 10 cm long and 5 cm wide. How high must it be to have a volume of 200 cu cm?

(A) 1   (B) 2

(C) 3   (D) 4

(E) 5

11. If a garage can wash 5 cars in 30 minutes, how long would it take to wash 30 cars?

(A) 3 hours   (D) 6 hours

(B) 3 hours 5 minutes   (E) 30 hours

(C) 5 hours

12. $\dfrac{2^{-4}+2^{-1}}{2^{-3}} =$

(A) $\dfrac{9}{2^7}$ (D) 2^{-3}

(B) $\dfrac{9}{2^{-1}}$ (E) $\dfrac{9}{2}$

(C) $\dfrac{1}{2}$

13. Mr. Baker is 30 years old when his son is 4 years old. In how many years will Mr. Baker be five times as old as his son?

(A) 2   (D) $3\dfrac{1}{2}$

(B) $2\dfrac{1}{2}$ (E) 4

(C) 3

14. A typist can normally complete a task in four hours. What part of this task can be completed from 11:45 a.m. to 12:15 p.m.?

(A) $\dfrac{1}{8}$ (D) $\dfrac{1}{2}$

(B) $\dfrac{1}{6}$ (E) $\dfrac{3}{4}$

(C) $\dfrac{1}{4}$

15. A suede jacket was purchased at a cost of $96, after a 60% discount. What was the original price of the purchase?

(A) $134.40

(D) $250

(B) $153.60

(E) $144

(C) $240

16. By how much is $2/3$ larger than 30% of 2?

(A) $\dfrac{1}{3}$

(D) $\dfrac{3}{5}$

(B) $\dfrac{2}{3}$

(E) $\dfrac{1}{15}$

(C) $\dfrac{2}{5}$

17. In a class of x students there are y boys. The ratio of girls to boys is

(A) $x{:}y$.

(D) $\dfrac{y-x}{y}$.

(B) $y{:}x$.

(E) $\dfrac{y-x}{x}$.

(C) $\dfrac{x-y}{y}$.

18. A painting is 3 ft long and 2 ft wide. How long will a larger painting of the same proportions be if it is 5 ft wide?

(A) 6 ft

(D) 15 ft

(B) 7.5 ft

(E) 30 ft

(C) 10 ft

19. Five years ago James was x years old. How old will he be in y years from now?

(A) $x-y+5$

(D) $y+5$

(B) $y+x$

(E) $y+x+5$

(C) $x+y-5$

20. The area of a triangle whose legs are in the ratio of 3:4 is 96. The length of the hypotenuse is

(A) 12.

(D) 96.

(B) 16.

(E) 400.

(C) 20.

Section 3

TIME: 25 Minutes
           26 Questions

For each question in this section, select the best answer from among the given choices and fill in the corresponding oval on the answer sheet.

DIRECTIONS: Each sentence below has one or two blanks, each blank indicating that something has been omitted. Beneath the sentence are five lettered words or sets of words. Choose the word or set of words that **BEST** fits the meaning of the sentence as a whole.

EXAMPLE:

Although the critics found the book _____, many of the readers found it rather _____.

(A) obnoxious . . . perfect

(B) spectacular . . . interesting

(C) boring . . . intriguing

(D) comical . . . persuasive

(E) popular . . . rare

Ⓐ Ⓑ ⬤ Ⓓ Ⓔ

---

27. Many cultures have similar _____ of the same proverb, fable, or folk tale.

   (A) parts

   (B) assets

   (C) versions

   (D) traditions

   (E) translations

28. Because the book detailed the lives of early Greek philosophers, it was included in the _____ for the Western Civilization class.

   (A) bookshelf

   (B) syllabus

   (C) rhetoric

   (D) argumentation

   (E) debate

29. When a rat has been trained to press a lever to get a piece of cheese, it is displaying a(n) _____ response.

   (A) ordered

   (B) repetitious

(C) formed   (D) conditioned

(E) lazy

30. The audience showed its _____ with the performance by moving about and coughing restlessly during the second act.

(A) displeasure   (D) tirade

(B) criticism   (E) glee

(C) astonishment

31. The division manager told the employees that she was more interested in seeing the profit margin rise than in hearing praises of empty _____ .

(A) reproof   (D) cadences

(B) imagery   (E) aspirations

(C) flattery

32. The laboratory instructor explained that the liquid compound could easily _____ , so they were to leave the containers covered.

(A) coagulate   (D) suffocate

(B) eviscerate   (E) evaporate

(C) inundate

DIRECTIONS: Each question below consists of a related pair of words or phrases, followed by five lettered pairs of words or phrases. Select the lettered pair that best expresses a relationship similar to that expressed in the original pair.

EXAMPLE:

SMILE : MOUTH ::

(A) wink : eye   (D) tan : skin

(B) teeth : face   (E) food : gums

(C) voice : speech

33. ALIAS : IDENTITY ::

    (A) tourist : country   (D) signature : author

    (B) judgment : value   (E) illusion : perception

    (C) drawing : color

34. ORIGINAL : REPLICA ::

    (A) facade : mask   (D) importance : substance

    (B) puzzle : solution   (E) scheme : design

    (C) depth : gauge

35. GOOD : SUPERIOR ::

    (A) bleak : desolate   (D) morbid : death

    (B) rancid : spoiled   (E) enthusiasm : frenzy

    (C) mundane : worldly

36. TACITURN : WORDS ::

    (A) impoverished : money   (D) obdurate : energy

    (B) cunning : time   (E) stubborn : regret

    (C) overweight : fat

37. PERMIT : SANCTION ::

    (A) amateur : singer   (D) harangue : tirade

    (B) fanatic : cause   (E) microcosm : germ

    (C) glamour : model

38. EFFERVESCENT : BUBBLES ::

    (A) clean : uncontaminated   (D) exotic : country

    (B) taste : tongue   (E) old : newborn

    (C) new : price

39. ECCENTRIC : PECULIAR ::

(A) king : power

(B) bully : cowardly

(C) egocentric : shameless

(D) celebrity : distinct

(E) judge : impartial

DIRECTIONS: Read the passage and answer the questions that follow. Each question will be based on the information stated or implied in the passage or its introduction.

Questions 40–45 are based on the following passage.

This passage discusses the rise of the study of humanities and the classics in Italy and those responsible for its development.

1   The Italian cultivation of classical literature had attained its highest point, and was already verging towards decline. More than a century had passed since Petrarch had kindled the first enthusiasm. It requires some effort of the imagination for us to realise what that movement meant. The
5   men of the fourteenth century lived under a Church which claimed the surrender of the reason, not only in matters of faith, but in all knowledge: philosophy and science could speak only by the doctors whom she sanctioned. When the fourteenth century began to study the classics, the first feeling was one of joy in the newly revealed dignity of the human mind; it
10 was a strange and delightful thing, as they gradually came to know the great writers of ancient Greece and Rome, to see the reason moving freely, exploring, speculating, discussing, without restraint. And then those children of the middle age were surprised and charmed by the forms of classical expression,—so different from anything that had been familiar
15 to them. Borrowing an old Latin word, they called this new learning *humanity*; for them, however, the phrase had a depth of meaning undreamt of by Cicero. Now, for the first time, they felt that they had entered into full possession of themselves; nothing is more characteristic of the Italian renaissance than the self-asserting individuality of the chief actors; each
20 strives to throw the work of his own spirit into relief; the common life falls into the back-ground; the history of that age is the history of men rather than of communities.

In the progress of this Italian humanism three chief phases may be roughly distinguished. The first closes with the end of the fourteenth cen-
25 tury,—the time of Petrarch and his immediate followers,—the morning-time of discovery. Then, in the first half of the fifteenth century, the discovered materials were classified, and organized in great libraries;

Greek manuscripts, too, were translated into Latin,—not that the versions
might be taken as substitutes for the original, but to aid the study of Greek
30 itself. The men of this second period were gathered around Cosmo de'
Medici at Florence, or Nicholas V at Rome. The third stage was that in
which criticism, both of form and of matter, was carried to a higher level,
chiefly by the joint efforts of scholars grouped in select societies or academies, such as the Platonic academy at Florence, of which Ficino was the
35 centre. The greatest man of this time,—the greatest genius of the literary
renaissance in Italy,—was Angelo Poliziano; he died in 1494.

40. In line 1, the word "cultivation" most nearly means

(A) growth. (D) study.

(B) refinement. (E) enrichment.

(C) support.

41. In the sentence "philosophy and science could speak . . . sanctioned"
(lines 7–8), the author stresses the Church's

(A) commitment to education.

(B) absolute control of thought.

(C) growing sensitivity to new ideas.

(D) dependence upon Greek thought.

(E) freedom from political influence.

42. When the author states that "nothing is more characteristic . . . chief
actors" (lines 18–19), he implies that

(A) self-assertion is a sign of progress.

(B) the Middle Ages valued self-assertion.

(C) the Renaissance developed a clear sense of community.

(D) the Middle Ages valued community over the individual.

(E) the Church supported the growth of self-assertion.

43. In the sentence "each strives to throw" (lines 19–20), the author
creates an analogy to

(A) sculpture. (B) painting.

(C) architecture.   (D) film.

(E) music.

DIRECTIONS: Read the passages and answer the questions that follow. Each question will be based on the information stated or implied in the selections or the introduction, and may be based on the relationship between the passages.

Questions 44–52 are based on the following passages.

Each passage considers the proposition that all pleasures are morally good. Passage 2 offers a critique of the arguments offered in Passage 1.

Passage 1

1   It is widely held among those who engage in the study of morality that pleasure is good and pain is evil and that, consequently, any action is morally good whose results are more pleasant than painful.

To their credit, many proponents of this view take great pains to distin-
5 guish types and levels of pleasure. John Stuart Mill, for example, proposes that "It is better to be Socrates dissatisfied than a pig satisfied": since humans are capable of higher pleasures—intellectual pleasures, for example—than are lower forms of animal life, humans ought not to settle for the baser, merely physical pleasures.

10   Many proponents of the view also concern themselves with everyone affected by an action—it is not enough that the agent receives pleasure from her action, a majority of those affected by the action must receive pleasure too. As a proponent of *utilitarianism,* Mill argues this, on the grounds that if pleasure is good, then more pleasure is better.

15   Many are tempted by these qualifications—distinctions among plea-sures and concern about the welfare of the majority—to accept some form of the proposition that all pleasures are good. But one ought not to give into the temptation for at least two reasons. In the first place, the proposi-tion itself, "All pleasures are good," does not logically commit its propo-
20 nents to any distinctions among pleasures or to concern for the majority. A good old fashioned egoist—one who promotes only her own pleasure—could maintain this position consistently while taking the first pleasures that came along, regardless of who else might suffer. Yet such an attitude is arguably immoral.

25   In the second place, as Plato notes in his dialogue *Gorgias,* there obvi-ously are bad pleasures. The pleasure of overeating, for instance, is a harmful pleasure and to the extent it is harmful, it is bad. On the other

hand, it would be absurd to propose that goodness can be bad: "bad" and "good" are contradictory terms and each is defined in part by the absence
30 of the other. If pleasure can be bad and goodness cannot be bad, then it follows that pleasures are not necessarily good.

Given the moral shortcomings of egoism—the position that "If it pleases *me,* then it's good"—and the possibility of there being bad pleasures, we must conclude that the proposition "All pleasures are good," is
35 false.

Passage 2

Many moral theorists argue that all pleasures are good because it is natural for us to be drawn toward the pleasant and to be repelled by the painful.

Epicurus (341–271 B.C.) argues this point, adding that we should ac-
40 custom ourselves to the simplest pleasures so that we are easily satisfied.

Thomas Hobbes (1588–1679) holds that humans are basically automata—self-moving machines—whose principle sources of motion are pleasure, which attracts us, and pain, which repels us. To call something good, he insists, is to say we expect pleasure from it. Thus, all pleasures
45 are good (and all pains are evil).

Where Hobbes is concerned primarily with his own pleasure and pain, Jeremy Bentham (1748–1832) concludes that since pleasure is by nature good and pain by nature evil, it is important to promote as much pleasure as possible. This entails promoting the greatest good for the greatest num-
50 ber of people involved—the basic tenet of utilitarianism.

Contemporary philosopher Peter Singer argues that mistreatment of animals is wrong because it causes them to suffer and suffering is wrong because it causes pain. The implication here is that pain is evil and its opposite, pleasure, is good.

55 All this support notwithstanding, some still reject the proposition that all pleasures are good. One objection alleges that the proposition encourages selfish egoists who care only about their own pleasures. But even the egoistic Hobbes felt that to secure a pleasant life for oneself, one must see that others are happy too. Otherwise these others might attack him, which
60 would be very unpleasant indeed. So the proposition, properly understood, does not promote selfishness but at the worst "enlightened self-interest."

Another objection is that some pleasures are bad, which contradicts the proposition that they are all good. As proof, Plato offers the example of the pleasure of overeating. Eating too much could be pleasant, he agrees,
65 but since it is harmful, it must be bad. But Plato fails to distinguish sufficiently between what is actually bad and the pleasure itself. What is bad is the harm to the body which results from the overeating; but the

overeater might find the taste (for example), not the harm, pleasant. Thus Plato's example doesn't prove his point.

70   So there is plenty of historical and authoritative support to suggest that all pleasures are good and arguments to the contrary appear to be ill-founded.

44. Which of the following is true of the concept of utilitarianism as it appears in Passage 2?

(A) It is offered as a criticism of Hobbes' egoism.

(B) Its fundamental proposition is the same as it is in Passage 1.

(C) It is the basis of Epicurus' argument.

(D) It is consistent with Plato's view about the moral value of pleasure.

(E) It is the basis of Mill's argument.

45. Which of the following propositions is consistent with Mill's argument as it appears in Passage 1?

(A) Any pleasure is as good as any other, as long as there is more of it than there is pain.

(B) Each person is interested primarily in his own pleasure and should, therefore, avoid making enemies with others.

(C) The proposition that all pleasures are good encourages egoism.

(D) The greater the pleasure the better the act which caused it.

(E) There are bad pleasures.

46. Which of the following best expresses the point to including in Passage 2 the views of Epicurus, Bentham, Hobbes, and Singer?

(A) Hobbes and Bentham would have disagreed.

(B) They differed in their views about the extent to which pleasure should be realized.

(C) It is not only the pleasure of humans that counts, but also the pleasure of other animals.

(D) Singer was an Epicurean.

(E) If thinkers in different periods of history hold basically the same view, then this lends weight to the argument in favor of this view.

47. What is the point about egoism in lines 57–61 that challenges the comment about egoism in lines 32 and 33?

   (A) Nobody who agrees that all pleasures are good is an egoist.

   (B) To be egoistic is not necessarily to lack concern about the well-being of others.

   (C) No egoist is selfish.

   (D) Hobbes may actually have been a utilitarian.

   (E) The selfishness of the egoist does not disprove that all pleasures are good.

48. Which of the following, if true, would weaken the argument in Passage 2?

   (A) Singer was not a utilitarian.

   (B) Bentham did not make the distinction that Mill does between levels of pleasure.

   (C) More people over the years have disagreed than agreed that all pleasures are good.

   (D) Plato was a utilitarian.

   (E) Overeating is not the only example Plato offers of bad pleasures; he also regards the pleasure of drinking too much as a bad pleasure.

49. Based solely on the information about Epicurus in Passage 2, which of the following may we conclude?

   (A) Epicurus disagrees with Plato's claim that there are bad pleasures.

   (B) Epicurus was a utilitarian.

   (C) Epicurus was an egoist.

   (D) Passage 1 would have had a stronger argument, had it relied on Epicurus as an authority instead of Plato.

(E) Hobbes would disagree with Epicurus' claim that we should accustom ourselves to the simplest pleasures.

50. According to Passage 2, which arguments "appear to be ill-founded" (lines 71 and 72)?

   (A) The historical arguments in support of the proposition that all pleasures are good.

   (B) Only Plato's argument that there are bad pleasures and the argument that selfishness is consistent with the proposition that all pleasures are good.

   (C) All arguments whose conclusions are contrary to the proposition that all pleasures are good.

   (D) The authoritative arguments in support of the proposition that all pleasures are good.

   (E) The contrary arguments offered by egoism on the one hand and utilitarianism on the other.

51. Why, according to Passage 1, are some people tempted "to accept some form of the proposition that all pleasures are good" (lines 16–17)?

   (A) Because there are not obviously bad pleasures.

   (B) Because the proposition "All pleasures are good" does not logically commit its proponents to any distinctions among pleasures.

   (C) Because the proposition "All pleasures are good" does not commit its proponents to any concern for the majority.

   (D) Because of the distinctions made by Mill and others among the types and levels of pleasure and because of the concern of Mill and others about the welfare of the majority.

   (E) Because the arguments in defense of this proposition are strong arguments.

52. What does Passage 2 appear to mean by the phrase "enlightened self-interest" (line 61)?

   (A) The understanding that some pleasures may not be good.

   (B) Interest in the greatest good for the greatest number.

(C) Interest not only in the welfare of oneself but also in the welfare of animals.

(D) Recognition that, while one's pleasure is of primary importance, it will be difficult to achieve if others are unhappy.

(E) The same thing as selfishness, but couched in less negative terms.

Section 4

TIME: 25 Minutes
20 Questions

DIRECTIONS: Solve each problem, using any available space on the page for scratch work. Then decide which answer choice is the best and fill in the corresponding oval on the answer sheet.

NOTES:

(1) The use of a calculator is permitted. All numbers used are real numbers.

(2) Figures that accompany problems in this test are intended to provide information useful in solving the problems. They are drawn as accurately as possible EXCEPT when it is stated in a specific problem that the figure is not drawn to scale. All figures lie in a plane unless otherwise indicated.

REFERENCE INFORMATION:

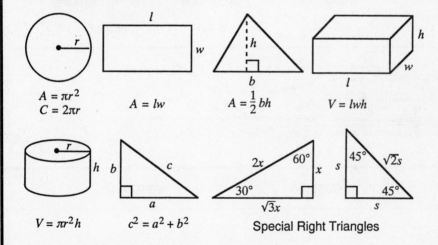

$$A = \pi r^2$$
$$C = 2\pi r$$

$$A = lw$$

$$A = \frac{1}{2}bh$$

$$V = lwh$$

$$V = \pi r^2 h$$

$$c^2 = a^2 + b^2$$

Special Right Triangles

The number of degrees of arc in a circle is 360.
The measure in degrees of a straight angle is 180.
The sum of the measures in degrees of the angles of a triangle is 180.

QUESTIONS 21–32 each consist of two quantities, one in Column A and one in Column B. You are to compare the two quantities and on the answer sheet blacken space

(A) if the quantity in Column A is greater;

(B) if the quantity in Column B is greater;

(C) if the two quantities are equal;

(D) if the relationship cannot be determined from the information given.

NOTES:

(1) In certain questions, information concerning one or both of the quantities to be compared is centered above the two columns.

(2) In a given question, a symbol that appears in both columns represents the same thing in Column A as it does in Column B.

(3) Letters such as x, n, and k stand for real numbers.

EXAMPLES:

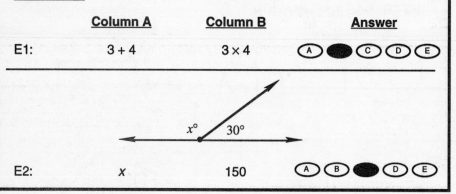

	Column A	**Column B**	**Answer**
E1:	$3 + 4$	3×4	Ⓐ ● Ⓒ Ⓓ Ⓔ
E2:	x	150	Ⓐ Ⓑ ● Ⓓ Ⓔ

Column A	**Column B**

21. The number of different prime factors of 18 | The number of different prime factors of 20

0 is the average of 10 and y.

22. y | 0

Column A	Column B

$ABCD$ is a rhombus;

$AD = \dfrac{2}{5}x$; $AB = y$.

23. x y

A car travels 40 m.p.h.

24.   How long it will take the car to travel 1 mile   1.5 minutes

---

$$2a = 3b$$
$$3b = 5c$$

25. $2a$ $5c$

Right triangles ABC and ACD share side AC.
$AB = 8$; $BC = 6$; $CD = 9$.

26. y $\sqrt{21}$

A bell rings every 3 minutes.
A buzzer buzzes every 5 minutes.
A light flashes every 4 minutes.

27.   If the 3 of them start at the same moment, the length of time before the 3 of them happen again together.   50 minutes

---

Given the 6-digit number 456,78M .

28.   In order for this 6-digit number to be divisible by 2 and 9, the number M must be equal to.   5

	Column A	**Column B**
29.	$\dfrac{9^4 \times 9 \times 9^5}{(9^5)^2}$	1

30. The area of rectangle *ABCD* — *A* is (0, 3) and *C* is (6, 7). — 22

31. The number of integers between 0 and 201 that are divisible by 2, 10, and 25 — 5

$$y = .8$$

32. $\dfrac{y^9 + y^7}{y^7}$ — 1.5

DIRECTIONS: Questions 33–40 require you to solve the problem and enter your answer in the ovals in the special grid:

Answer: $\frac{5}{12}$

Write answers here

Answer: 3.5

Answer: 525

Either position is correct

Fraction line

Decimal line

Grid in answer

- You may begin filling in your answer in any column, space permitting. Columns not needed should be left blank.

- Answers may be entered in either decimal or fraction form. For example, $^3/_{12}$ or .25 are equally acceptable.

- A mixed number, such as $4^1/_2$, must be entered either as 4.5 or $^9/_2$. If you entered 41/2, the machine would interpret your answer as $^{41}/_2$, not $4^1/_2$.

- There may be some instances where there is more than one correct answer to a problem. Should this be the case, grid only one answer.

- Be very careful when filling in ovals. Do not fill in more than one oval in any column, and make sure to completely darken the ovals.

- It is suggested that you fill in your answer in the boxes above each column. Although you will not be graded incorrectly if you do not write in your answer, it will help you fill in the corresponding ovals.

- If your answer is a decimal, grid the most accurate value possible. For example, if you need to grid a repeating decimal such as $0.66\overline{6}$, enter the answer as .666 or .667. A less accurate value, such as .66 or .67, is not acceptable.

33. A class of 24 students contains 16 males. What is the ratio of females to males?

34. A woman buys a dress on sale for $120. If she bought the dress at a 20% discount, find the actual price.

35. Find the value of x satisfying the equation $x \div 2 \times x \div x = 10$.

36. Consider a string 14 feet long which is cut into two equal parts. One part is used to form a circle and the other part is used to form a square. Find the sum of the areas of the circle and the square. (Use the approximation $\pi = {}^{22}/_7$.)

37. Consider the figure given below.

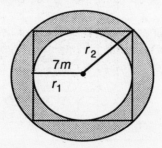

If the area of the square is 196 square meters, find the area of the shaded region. (Use $\pi = {}^{22}/_7$.)

38. Let $f(x) = x^2 - 1$ and $g(x) = 3x + 2$. Find the value of $g(f(3))$.

39. Evaluate the expression $\dfrac{x^2 y^{-1}}{3yz}$ for $x = 2$, $y = -1$, and $z = {}^1/_3$.

40. A ball is thrown up from the ground. The height of the ball is a function of time in feet which is given by the formula

$$h(t) = -16t^2 + 64t.$$

Find a time when the ball is 48 feet off the ground.

Section 5

TIME: 30 Minutes
              39 Questions

> **DIRECTIONS**: Each of the following sentences may contain an error in diction, usage, idiom, or grammar. Some sentences are correct. Some sentences contain one error. No sentence contains more than one error.
>
> If there is an error, it will appear in one of the underlined portions labeled A, B, C, or D. If there is no error, choose the portion labeled E. If there is an error, select the letter of the portion that must be changed in order to correct the sentence.
>
> **EXAMPLE:**
>
> He drove <u>slowly</u> and <u>cautiously</u> in order to <u>hopefully</u> avoid having an
>   **A**   **B**   **C**
>
> <u>accident</u>. <u>No error</u>.
>   **D**   **E**   

1. <u>Which</u> suspension bridge <u>is</u> the <u>longest</u>, the Verrazano-Narrows
   A   **B**   **C**
Bridge in New York City <u>or</u> the Golden Gate Bridge in San Fran-
                       D
cisco? <u>No error</u>.
      E

2. A main function <u>of proteins</u>, whether <u>they come</u> from <u>plant or animal</u>
              A   **B**   **C**
<u>sources, is</u> the building of body tissue. <u>No error</u>.
  D   **E**

3. <u>Recognizing</u> that we <u>had worked</u> very hard to complete our project,
     A   **B**
the teacher told Janice and <u>I</u> that we could give it to her <u>tomorrow</u>.
                    C   **D**
<u>No error</u>.
  E

4.   <u>According to</u> the United States Constitution, the legislative branch of
          A
     the government <u>has</u> powers <u>different than</u> <u>those</u> of the executive
                    B   **C**   **D**
     branch. <u>No error</u>.
              E

5.   After <u>being studied</u> for the <u>preceding ten years</u> by the National Heart,
           A   **B**
     Lung, and Blood Institute, the relationship of high levels of
     cholesterol in the blood to the possibility of <u>having</u> heart attacks
                                                    C
     <u>was reported</u> in 1984. <u>No error</u>.
      D   **E**

6.   The book *Cheaper By the Dozen* <u>demonstrates</u> that each of the chil-
                                      A
     dren of Frank and Lillian Gilbreth <u>was expected</u> <u>to use</u> <u>his or her</u> time
                                         B   **C**   **D**
     efficiently. <u>No error</u>.
                   E

7.   His aversion <u>with</u> snakes made camping an unpleasant activity
                  A
     <u>for him</u> and <u>one</u> <u>that</u> he tried diligently to avoid. <u>No error</u>.
      B   **C** **D**   **E**

8.   The story of the American pioneers, <u>those</u> who willingly left the
                                          A
     safety of <u>their</u> homes to move into unsettled territory, <u>show</u> <u>us</u> great
               B   **C** **D**
     courage in the face of danger. <u>No error</u>.
                                     E

9.   <u>Because of</u> the long, cold winters <u>and</u> short summers, farming in high
      A   **B**
     latitudes is <u>more difficult</u> <u>than low latitudes</u>. <u>No error</u>.
                   C   **D**   **E**

10. When my sister and <u>I</u> <u>were</u> in Los Angeles, <u>we</u> hoped that both of us
                 A **B**   **C**
could be <u>a contestant</u> on a quiz show. <u>No error</u>.
          D   **E**

11. After he <u>had broke</u> the vase <u>that</u> his mother <u>had purchased</u> in Europe,
           A   **B**   **C**
he tried to buy a new one for his father and <u>her</u>. <u>No error</u>.
                            D **E**

12. Some of the people <u>with whom</u> the witness <u>worked</u> <u>were engaged</u> in
                     A   **B**   **C**
covert activities <u>on behalf of</u> the United States government. <u>No error</u>.
           D   **E**

13. <u>Because of</u> their cold personalities and hot tempers, <u>neither</u> John
   A   **B**
Adams <u>nor</u> his son John Quincy Adams <u>were</u> especially successful in
       C   **D**
politics. <u>No error</u>.
         E

14. <u>Among</u> the reasons <u>for United States participation</u> in World War II
  A   **B**
<u>were</u> the Japanese attack on the <u>naval base</u> at Pearl Harbor on De-
C   **D**
cember 7, 1941. <u>No error</u>.
              E

15. Some parents make a <u>greater</u> attempt to frighten <u>their</u> children about
                   A   **B**
the dangers of driving <u>than</u> <u>teaching</u> them safe driving habits.
                  C   **D**
<u>No error</u>.
E

16. The high standard <u>of living</u> in Sweden <u>is shown</u> by <u>their</u> statistics
               A   **B**   **C**
<u>of life expectancy</u> and per capita income. <u>No error</u>.
  D   **E**

17. The snow leopard <u>is</u> a wild mammal in Central Asia <u>that has</u> large
                 A   **B**

    eyes, a four-foot body, <u>and</u> <u>white and bluish gray in color</u>. <u>No error</u>.
                              C   **D**   **E**

18. Selecting a lifetime vocation, <u>a young person</u> may have to choose
                                      A

    either a vocation that she enjoys <u>and</u> a vocation that will make <u>her</u>
                               B   **C**

    rich; that choice is perhaps the <u>most important</u> one she will ever
                                         D

    make. <u>No error</u>.
             E

19. Failing a test because the student <u>is</u> nervous <u>is</u> understandable; <u>to fail</u>
                                   A   **B**   **C**

    because <u>he or she</u> did not study is quite another matter. <u>No error</u>.
                D   **E**

20. Wealthy citizens often protest <u>about the building of</u> low-cost housing in the affluent communities where they reside.

    (A) about the building of

    (B) whether they should build

    (C) if builders should build

    (D) the building of

    (E) whether or not they should build

21. Siblings growing up in a family do not necessarily have equal opportunities to achieve, <u>the difference being their placement in the family, their innate abilities, and their personalities.</u>

    (A) the difference being their placement in the family, their innate abilities, and their personalities.

(B) because of their placement in the family, their innate abilities, and their personalities.

(C) and the difference is their placement in the family, their innate abilities, and their personalities.

(D) they have different placements in the family, different innate abilities, and different personalities.

(E) their placement in the family, their innate abilities, and their personalities being different.

22. Two major provisions of the United States Bill of Rights <u>is freedom of speech and that citizens are guaranteed a trial by jury</u>.

(A) is freedom of speech and that citizens are guaranteed a trial by jury.

(B) is that citizens have freedom of speech and a guaranteed trial by jury.

(C) is freedom of speech and the guarantee of a trial by jury.

(D) are freedom of speech and that citizens are guaranteed a trial by jury.

(E) are freedom of speech and the guarantee of a trial by jury.

23. Poets of the nineteenth century tried <u>to entertain their readers but also with the attempt of teaching them</u> lessons about life.

(A) to entertain their readers but also with the attempt of teaching them

(B) to entertain their readers but also to attempt to teach them

(C) to both entertain their readers and to teach them

(D) entertainment of their readers and the attempt to teach them

(E) both to entertain and to teach their readers

24. The city council decided to remove parking meters <u>so as to encourage</u> people to shop in Centerville.

(A) so as to encourage

(B) to encourage

(C) thus encouraging

(D) with the desire

(E) thereby encouraging

25. Visiting New York City for the first time, <u>the sites most interesting to Megan were</u> the Statue of Liberty, the Empire State Building, and the Brooklyn Bridge.

(A) the sites most interesting to Megan were

(B) the sites that Megan found most interesting were

(C) Megan found that the sites most interesting to her were

(D) Megan was most interested in

(E) Megan was most interested in the sites of

26. Although most college professors have expertise in their areas of specialty, <u>some are more interested in continuing their research than in teaching undergraduate students</u>.

(A) some are more interested in continuing their research than in teaching undergraduate students.

(B) some are most interested in continuing their research rather than in teaching undergraduate students.

(C) some prefer continuing their research rather than to teach undergraduate students.

(D) continuing their research, not teaching undergraduate students, is more interesting to some.

(E) some are more interested in continuing their research than to teach undergraduate students.

27. <u>Whether adult adoptees should be allowed to see their original birth certificates or not</u> is controversial, but many adoptive parents feel strongly that records should remain closed.

(A) Whether adult adoptees should be allowed to see their original birth certificates or not

(B) Whether or not adult adoptees should be allowed to see their original birth certificates or not

(C) The fact of whether adult adoptees should be allowed to see their original birth certificates

(D) Allowing the seeing of their original birth certificates by adult adoptees

(E) That adult adoptees should be allowed to see their original birth certificates

28. <u>Having studied theology, music, along with medicine</u>, Albert Schweitzer became a medical missionary in Africa.

(A) Having studied theology, music, along with medicine

(B) Having studied theology, music, as well as medicine

(C) Having studied theology and music, and, also, medicine

(D) With a study of theology, music, and medicine

(E) After he had studied theology, music, and medicine

29. When the Mississippi River threatens to flood, sandbags are piled along its banks, <u>and they do this to keep its waters from overflowing</u>.

(A) and they do this to keep its waters from overflowing.

(B) to keep its waters from overflowing.

(C) and then its waters won't overflow.

(D) and, therefore, keeping its waters from overflowing.

(E) and they keep its waters from overflowing.

30. <u>Because of the popularity of his light verse</u>, Edward Lear is seldom recognized today for his travel books and detailed illustrations of birds.

(A) Because of the popularity of his light verse

(B) Owing to the fact that his light verse was popular

(C) Because of his light verse, that was very popular

(D) Having written light verse that was popular

(E) Being the author of popular light verse

31. Lincoln's Gettysburg Address, <u>despite its having been very short and delivered after a two-hour oration by Edward Everett,</u> is one of the greatest speeches ever delivered.

    (A) despite its having been very short and delivered after a two-hour oration by Edward Everett

    (B) which was very short and delivered after a two-hour oration by Edward Everett

    (C) although it was very short and delivered after a two-hour oration by Edward Everett

    (D) despite the fact that it was very short and delivered after a two-hour oration by Edward Everett

    (E) was very short and delivered after a two-hour oration by Edward Everett

32. China, <u>which ranks third in area and first in population among the world's countries</u> also has one of the longest histories.

    (A) which ranks third in area and first in population among the world's countries

    (B) which ranks third in area and has the largest population among the world's countries

    (C) which is the third largest in area and ranks first in population among the world's countries

    (D) in area ranking third and in population ranking first among the world's countries

    (E) third in area and first in the number of people among the world's countries

33. <u>Leonardo da Vinci was a man who</u> was a scientist, an architect, an engineer, and a sculptor.

    (A) Leonardo da Vinci was a man who

    (B) The man Leonardo da Vinci

    (C) Being a man, Leonardo da Vinci

    (D) Leonardo da Vinci

    (E) Leonardo da Vinci, a man who

Questions 34–39 are based on the following passage.

(1) Using Indians to track down and fight other Indians was not a new idea during the conflict between the Whites and the Indians during the mid-1800 Indian Wars during the conquest of the Apaches. (2) The English and the French from early colonial times had exploited traditional intertribal rivalries to their own advantage.

(3) What was a novel idea of the U.S. Army during its war against the Apaches was using an Indian against members of his own tribe. (4) Gen. George Crook believed that the best work would be done by an Indian who had only just been fighting him. (5) Crook had learned that such a

scout would know alot because he would know the fighting habits, the hiding places, and the personalities of the Indians being pursued. (6) This method worked well for Crook and by the end of his career he had used about 500 Apache scouts.

(7) Crook demanded trust from all his troops and, in turn, he gave them his trust. (8) He paid his scouts well and on time, a very important factor. (9) Most importantly, Crook treated all the personnel under his command with dignity and respect. (10) These were good qualities. (11) These qualities no doubt earned Crook the admiration and loyalty of his Indian soldiers. (12) Though, the man himself won their respect. (13) Crook was like few West Point trained officers, for he understood his enemy well. (14) He learned to fight the Indians on their terms, to use the land and terrain to his advantage, and to abandon the textbook examples. (15) He got on a trail, and with his Apache scouts to guide him, he followed his quarry relentlessly.

(16) Crook's faith in his scouts never wavered. (17) Moreover, they gave him no grounds for worry. (18) In the annals of the Indian Wars, the story of Crook and his scouts is unique.

34. Which of the following is the best revision of the underlined portion of sentence 1 below?

    Using Indians to track down and fight other Indians was not a new idea <u>during the conflict between Whites and the Indians during the mid-1800 Indian Wars during the conquest of the Apaches</u>.

    (A) during the mid-1800 Indian Wars between Whites and Apaches.

    (B) during the long years of conflict between Whites and Indians.

    (C) during the mid-1800s when Indians and Whites came into conflict in the Indian Wars.

    (D) when the Apaches and Whites were engaged in conflict.

    (E) when, during the mid-1800 Indian Wars, Whites and Apaches engaged in fighting in the Indian Wars.

35. Which of the following is the best revision of the underlined portion of sentence 3 below?

    <u>What was a novel idea of the U.S. Army during its war</u> against the Apaches was using an Indian against members of his own tribe.

    (A) The U.S. Army's novel idea during this war

(B) What the U.S. Army had as a novel idea during its war

(C) The U.S. Army had the novel idea during this war

(D) During its war the U.S. Army's novelty

(E) A novelty of the U.S. Army's war during this time

36. Which of the following is the best revision of the underlined portion of sentence 5 below?

Crook had learned that such a scout <u>would know alot because he would know</u> the fighting habits, the hiding places, and the personalities of the Indians being pursued.

(A) would know alot about

(B) would know a lot about

(C) would know

(D) would have a great deal of useful knowledge concerning

(E) would have knowledge of

37. Which of the following is the best way to combine sentences 10, 11, and 12?

(A) Admiring and loyal because of Crook's good qualities, the Indian soldiers gave him their respect.

(B) Although earning the loyalty and admiration of the Indian soldiers, Crook won their respect.

(C) Crook won the Indian soldiers' respect, admiration, and loyalty because of his good qualities.

(D) Although these good qualities no doubt earned Crook the admiration and loyalty of his Indian soldiers, the man himself won their respect.

(E) Although the man himself earned respect, these good qualities earned Crook the Indian soldiers' admiration and loyalty.

38. In relation to the passage as a whole, which of the following best describes the writer's intention in paragraph 4?

(A) To narrate an important event

(B) To describe the best features of the subject

(C) To persuade readers to take a certain course of action

(D) To provide a conclusion

(E) To provide a summary of the passage

39. Which of the following would be the best way to revise sentence 15?

(A) He got on a trail, with his Apache scouts to guide him, he followed his quarry relentlessly.

(B) He got on a trail, and his Apache scouts guiding him, he followed his quarry relentlessly.

(C) He would get on a trail, and with his Apache scouts to guide him, he followed his quarry relentlessly.

(D) He got on a trail and he followed his quarry relentlessly, with his Apache scouts to guide him.

(E) He would get on a trail, and with his Apache scouts to guide him, would follow his quarry relentlessly.

TEST 3

ANSWER KEY

Section 1—Verbal

1.	(B)	9.	(C)	17.	(A)	25.	(B)
2.	(C)	10.	(A)	18.	(D)	26.	(C)
3.	(C)	11.	(A)	19.	(E)		
4.	(B)	12.	(D)	20.	(E)		
5.	(E)	13.	(E)	21.	(C)		
6.	(B)	14.	(C)	22.	(B)		
7.	(D)	15.	(C)	23.	(A)		
8.	(A)	16.	(D)	24.	(D)		

Section 2—Math

1.	(B)	8.	(B)	15.	(C)
2.	(E)	9.	(E)	16.	(E)
3.	(D)	10.	(D)	17.	(C)
4.	(B)	11.	(A)	18.	(B)
5.	(A)	12.	(E)	19.	(E)
6.	(E)	13.	(B)	20.	(C)
7.	(D)	14.	(A)		

Section 3—Verbal

27.	(C)	35.	(E)	43.	(B)	51.	(D)
28.	(B)	36.	(A)	44.	(B)	52.	(D)
29.	(D)	37.	(D)	45.	(D)		
30.	(A)	38.	(A)	46.	(E)		
31.	(C)	39.	(E)	47.	(B)		
32.	(E)	40.	(C)	48.	(C)		
33.	(E)	41.	(B)	49.	(A)		
34.	(B)	42.	(D)	50.	(C)		

Section 4—Math

21.	(C)	28.	(A)	35.	20
22.	(B)	29.	(C)	36.	6.96
23.	(A)	30.	(A)	37.	154
24.	(C)	31.	(B)	38.	26
25.	(C)	32.	(A)	39.	4
26.	(B)	33.	1/2	40.	1 or 3
27.	(A)	34.	150		

Section 5—Writing Skills

1.	(C)	11.	(A)	21.	(B)	31.	(C)
2.	(E)	12.	(E)	22.	(E)	32.	(A)
3.	(C)	13.	(D)	23.	(E)	33.	(D)
4.	(C)	14.	(C)	24.	(B)	34.	(A)
5.	(A)	15.	(D)	25.	(D)	35.	(A)
6.	(E)	16.	(C)	26.	(A)	36.	(C)
7.	(A)	17.	(D)	27.	(E)	37.	(D)
8.	(C)	18.	(B)	28.	(E)	38.	(D)
9.	(D)	19.	(C)	29.	(B)	39.	(E)
10.	(D)	20.	(D)	30.	(A)		

DETAILED EXPLANATIONS
OF ANSWERS

Section 1 — Verbal

1. **(B)**   The answer, "bibliography" (B), is a list of sources used in a report or other work which appears at the end of the piece. Students don't compile (put together) a "library" (A) when they do a report; they use the library. An "index" (C) tells what subjects are included in a long work, like a book, and doesn't include the sources used. An "abstract" (D) is a short summary telling what an article or other work will be about, which appears at the beginning of the work; it also does not include sources. A "depository" (E) is where books are kept.

2. **(C)**   It is logical that Bill and Mary would want to "return" (C) the favor the Browns had extended to them, and "invite" the Browns to their house, just as they had been invited, to have dinner in the future. To "extend" (A) is to make an extension of, and Bill and Mary could not make an extension of the Browns' hospitality—only the Browns could do that. "Propel" means push, and that does not describe this situation. To "reveal" (B) is to uncover, which does not make sense here; "restore" means put back; again this would not be logical. To "classify" (D) is to categorize, and to "revolve" is to turn around, again, not meaningful within the context of this sentence. To "represent" (E) is to stand for, which does not make sense, although they could "drive" the Browns to dinner at their house in the future; however, one possible answer will not complete the sentence, which calls for two.

3. **(C)**   "Previously" (C) is the answer because it means beforehand, and it is logical that if people know beforehand that a book is available, that will enable them to look for it when it comes out on the shelves of bookstores, so they can promptly buy it. "Primordially" (A) means prehistorically, which would be impossible! "Primarily" (B) would imply that there is something about television over other means of advertising which causes the popularity of a book; nothing else in the sentence indicates this. "Protectively" (D) means in a manner which protects something, and this does not make sense in the context of this sentence. "Pretentiously" (E)

means ostentatiously, or in a showing-off way, and this also does not have any bearing on why a book would sell out.

4. **(B)** The answer is (B), because there is a tension in the world between preserving the environment and doing so in a way which does not damage countries' economies. "Paleontological" (A) means pertaining to the time on earth before human beings existed, so there could be no "households" then. The sentence does not make clear any particular relationship between a "forest" (C) and "geographic" factors, so this cannot be the correct answer either. The problem with (D), "farm" . . . "universal," is similar, in that no relation between these two has been indicated by the context. A "nebula" (E) is a huge cloud of hydrogen in outer space, and people have not initiated committees to alter these phenomena, nor to take into account "galactic" (relating to galaxies, or huge clusters of stars, also in space) factors while doing so.

5. **(E)** The answer is (E), because it makes sense that if the delivery schedule is random (not according to a set pattern), then no one could predict when shipments would "arrive." If something "devolves" (A), it is transferred, and "harassment" is irritation. Neither of these terms fit within the context of the sentence. In (B), it is illogical that "taxation" would cause shipments to "cease." Similarly, if a delivery schedule is propitious (has propitiousness (C)), then it has the quality of being favorable, which has no logical connection with the shipments overlapping. In (D), for the shipments to "splatter" (sprinkle) would be unfortunate, but "sparseness" (infrequency) of delivery has no relevancy to this.

6. **(B)** The best choice is "safety" (B), and many ethologists (scientists who study the behavior of animals) say that some animals travel in packs to ensure their own safety. "Comfort" (A) is not as compelling a reason for animals to move around together as another one of the choices here. No one knows if animals want "adventure" (C) either, since that is a term human beings use for their own activities. If we say "leeway" (D), we must ask, "leeway for what?" (leeway is similar in meaning to liberty). While traveling in groups may provide for "rapidity" of movement, (E), again, that is not as good a reason as choice (B) presented in this question.

7. **(D)** A "precursor" (D) is something which comes before something else, and the Wright brothers did invent, or create, the first successful airplane in the early twentieth century. A "successor" (A) is a follower, so chronologically, the sentence would not make sense if this were the

answer. "Precedents" are events which occur for the first time, but an airplane cannot be "inaugurated" (B); presidents taking office are. An "expiration" (C) is an ending, so this is also not logical. "Exigencies" (E) are events which impinge in some way on other events, but to be "destabilized" means to be thrown off-balance, which would not imply success, as the sentence states.

8. **(A)** The relationship between THERMOMETER and TEMPERATURE can be described as: "A THERMOMETER is used to measure TEMPERATURE." The best choice is (A) because an ODOMETER is used to measure DISTANCE. Choice (B) is wrong because "a YARDSTICK is used to measure SPACE," makes no sense. A YARDSTICK is used to measure length. Choice (C) is wrong because "a BAROMETER is used to measure RAIN," is incorrect. A BAROMETER is used to measure atmospheric pressure. Choice (D) is incorrect because "a HYPOTHESIS is used to measure PROOF," is semantically inaccurate. A HYPOTHESIS is used to test a theory. Choice (E) says that "a COMPASS is used to measure FABRIC." This is incorrect. A COMPASS is used to measure circumference.

9. **(C)** The relationship between the given words can be described as: "A COMEDY will AMUSE you." Choice (C) says that "A TRAGEDY will SADDEN you." Choice (A) is wrong because "a DRAMA will SAVE you," makes no sense. Choice (B) is incorrect because "a FARCE (satirical comedy) will ENLIGHTEN you," is only partially correct. Not all FARCES are ENLIGHTENING. Choice (D) is wrong because "a MOVIE will PRAISE you," is not semantically meaningful. Choice (E) is wrong because "a PLAY will THANK you," is a ridiculous concept.

10. **(A)** The relationship between INPUT and COMPUTER can be described as follows: "You put INPUT (data) into a COMPUTER to make it run (do the work it was designed to do)." Choice (A) is the best choice because "you put FUEL into an ENGINE to make it run." Choice (B) is wrong because "you put UNIFORM into a SOLDIER to make him run," makes no sense. Choice (C) is wrong because "you put OPPORTUNITY into EXPERIENCE to make it run (work)," is not semantically meaningful. Choice (D) is incorrect because "you put DATA into PRODUCTION to make it run (work)," makes no sense. Choice (E) is wrong because "you put ABODE into a DWELLING to make it run," is a ridiculous sentence. ABODE and DWELLING are synonyms.

11. **(A)** The relationship between the given words should indicate that the words are synonyms. If you GARNISH something, then you DECORATE it. The best choice is (A) because "if you DEFACE (destroy the surface of) something, you MAR it." (B) is wrong because "if you SCRUTINIZE (study closely) something, you TEXT it," makes no sense. (C) is incorrect because "if you FIX something, you FURNISH it," is a meaningless sentence. (D) is wrong because "if you CHART something, you BRIDGE it," is a sentence that doesn't mean anything. (E) is incorrect because "if you EXTOL (praise) something, you HELP it," doesn't express the stated relationship.

12. **(D)** The relationship between the two given words is best expressed as: "If you SOOTHE something, you CALM it." The correct answer is (D) because "If you ENERGIZE (give energy to) something, you EXCITE (stimulate) it." (A) is incorrect because "if you ASSESS (evaluate) something, you PROPOSE (plan) it," makes no sense. (B) is wrong because "if you DEFAME (destroy the reputation of) something, you DOUBLE it," is a meaningless sentence. (C) is incorrect because "if you OUTLINE something, you PAPER it," is an erroneous analogy. You can OUTLINE something on PAPER. (E) is wrong because "if you MOISTEN something, you DESTROY it," isn't always correct. If you MOISTEN a silk dress, you may DESTROY it, but if you MOISTEN a plant, you won't.

13. **(E)** The relationship between BRAGGART and BOASTER can best be described in the following sentence: "A BRAGGART is a BOASTER." The best choice to characterize the same relationship is (E). "A CHARLATAN is a FRAUD." Choice (A) is wrong because "a CONSUMER is GULLIBLE," is not always correct. Sometimes CONSUMERS are GULLIBLE. Choice (B) is wrong because "a POLITICIAN is ZEALOUS (enthusiastic), is not always correct. Choice (C) is incorrect because "a COWARD is HILARIOUS," is not a semantically accurate sentence. Choice (D) is incorrect because "a LIAR is VIGILANT (alertly watchful)", does not make any sense.

14. **(C)** The primary focus of the passage is on the events leading to and including the dedication of the Cushman School. (C) is the best answer. The article *mentions in passing* the richness and complexity of Boston (B) and the fact that the conservatives opposed the dedication (D); neither (B) nor (D) are the primary focus of the passage. The passage mentions that Charlotte was a celebrated actress (A) but that is not the

primary focus. The passage is more than just about the opening of a school. Some of the events leading to that opening are given. (E) should not be chosen.

15. **(C)**   When referring to dedicating the school to a woman, the author expresses enthusiastic approval. (C) is the best choice. The conservatives—not the writer—were opposed; (A) should not be selected. The author does not seem to be concerned with who made the choice; she is just pleased with the choice itself. (B) is not the best choice. The writer does not actually "express appreciation to the mayor who made it all possible"; she merely mentions in passing that had there been a mayor who needed recognition, Cushman School might not be in existence. (D) is not the correct choice. She does not indicate that there was really no other choice; she merely mentions that no mayor needed recognition. (E) should not be chosen.

16. **(D)**   In lines 2–3 the words "vigilant eyes of the cockerel" mean most nearly the constant eye of the weather cock. (D) is the best choice. Since the cockerel is a bird—not a mayor—neither (A) nor (B) should be chosen. A cockerel is not an older woman; (C) is not a good selection. A hurricane or storm does often have an eye, but the words cockerel are in direct reference to the weather vane with the rooster; (E) is not a good choice.

17. **(A)**   Based on this passage, the author's reaction to suffrage for women would be enthusiastic approval of the right. (A) is the best selection. The writer would probably show enthusiasm for—not total objectivity—to suffrage for women; (B) is not a good choice. The writer seems to value women and would likely not show complete disdain for the entire idea. (C) is not the best choice. It is not likely that the author would engage in a careful study of the effect on male counterparts. (D) is not the most likely choice for her. It is not likely that the writer would show appreciation for those opposing the idea—just as she did not show appreciation for those who opposed a school with a woman's name.

18. **(D)**   The tone of the author is enthusiasm. In fact, the writer is very open about her enthusiasm. (D) is the best choice. The writer does not use irony—a happening contrary to the expected. (A) is not the best choice. The author does not employ hostility (B) or animosity; neither does she use sarcasm (C) or disdain (E).

19. **(E)**   The author of the passage believes that current events are difficult for us to see the meaning of today since we are too close to the events. (E) is the best choice. Since the writer attaches much importance to the Revolutionary War time period, choice (A) which states that the writer does *not* attach much importance to the Revolutionary War time period should not be chosen. The writer does not believe the facts alone can give us a true understanding of the past; choice (B) which states that the writer believes from the facts of the past we can understand those events of the past should not be chosen. The writer thinks we are too close to the events of the present to understand them; choice (C) says the writer believes we can understand the present and what it is all about. (C) is not true. The writer does not believe that history is easy to understand since events overlap. (D) is not a good selection.

20. **(E)**   In looking for the very beginning of the American Revolution, according to the author, one must go as far back as the pyramids of Egypt. (E) is the best choice. The true beginning came before the Declaration of Independence (A), July 1776 (B), the midnight ride of Paul Revere in April 1775 (C), and even further back than a century before the Revolution (D).

21. **(C)**   In looking at ancient history, the author believes that one should find sound practical lessons to help us today. (C) is the best choice. Since the writer does not advocate using facts alone, (A) is not the best choice. The writer believes there is more to history than merely gratifying an idle curiosity. (B) should not be chosen. This writing does not begin with ancient history so (D) is not the best choice. Since the writer believes that history relates to modern events, (E) should not be marked as the correct choice.

22. **(B)**   The author uses as the midpoint in his treatment of the American Revolution 141 years after the first permanent settlement of Virginia and 141 years before the inauguration of Harrison. (B) is the correct answer. (A) is not the best choice. The date 1588 is the date of the Spanish Armada. Since Virginia was settled in 1607, the date when the Commonwealth of Virginia would be 125 years old is 1732. (C) is incorrect. The author uses as the midpoint the halfway point between the settlement of Virginia and the inauguration of *Harrison*, not President Washington. (D) is wrong. The author does not use the birthday of the first governor of Massachusetts as the midpoint. (E) is incorrect.

23. **(A)** The author's feelings about history can be best described as enthusiastic. (A) is the best choice. The author, himself a historian, is certainly not unenthusiastic; (B) should not be chosen. The author mentions in this writing the lessons of history for today, he is certainly not reserved; (C) should not be selected. The writer is not negative toward history and its lessons; (D) should not be chosen. The writer is not positive, negative, or ambivalent toward history. (E) should not be chosen.

24. **(D)** To the author, the early American period in history begins with the first permanent English settlement. (D) should be selected. The presidency of George Washington, in his opinion, is after the important colonial period. (A) should not be chosen. Beginning with the American Revolution would omit the important colonial period. (B) should not be chosen. Although the beginning of the American Revolution begins as early as the Egyptian pyramids, this is not the early American period to the author. (C) is incorrect. The author does not believe that history should be disregarded; (E) is incorrect.

25. **(B)** The author's opinion is that few things have happened that are more important than the American Revolution. (B) is the correct answer. Although the inauguration of Washington may be important, the writer does not attach great importance to it. (A) should not be chosen. The author does not believe that historic events are easy to categorize and compartmentalize. He thinks they overlap; (C) should not be chosen. The "lull" the writer refers to occurred before the American Revolution. (D) is not a good choice. The Aix-la-Chapelle put an end to the war between England and France that had lasted five years, not to the American Revolution; (E) should not be used.

26. **(C)** The author would advocate that a historian survey distant events and try to get the meaning of it all. (C) is the best choice. Since the author cautions against becoming lost in details, choice (A), which recommends becoming immersed in the study of personal incidents and details, and choice (B), which suggests surveying distant events and personages in order to get all the specifics, should both be avoided. The author believes the past is important so neither (D)—which states that history is not important since very few things have happened in past ages with which our present welfare is concerned—nor (E)—which states that a study of history is not needed since they are too immersed in the past—should be chosen.

Section 2 — Math

1. **(B)** The shaded area is the outside rectangle minus the inside rectangle.

$$(F)(G) - (K)(L)$$

2. **(E)** Use the rule for the difference of 2 squares.

$$A^2 - B^2 = (A + B)(A - B).$$

So, if

$$A + B = C \qquad (1)$$

and $\quad A - B = D,$ $\qquad (2)$

multiply the left side of (1) with the left side of (2) getting $A^2 - B^2$.

Then multiply the right side of (1) with the right side of (2), getting CD.

3. **(D)** Round-off each number. For example,

$$\frac{50 \times 500}{2 \times 25}.$$

You may cancel, and the approximate answer is 500.

4. **(B)** Since 16 and 25 are perfect squares, use their product as your common denominator.

$$\sqrt{\frac{25B^2 - 16B^2}{16 \times 25}} = \sqrt{\frac{9B^2}{16 \times 25}}$$

Now take the square root of the top and the square root of the bottom.

$$\frac{3B}{4 \times 5} = \frac{3B}{20}$$

5. **(A)**

$$5^{-2} = \frac{1}{5^2} = \frac{1}{25}$$

$$5^{-1} = \frac{1}{5}$$

$$5^0 = 1$$

$$\frac{1}{25} + \frac{1}{5} + 1 = \frac{31}{25} = 1\frac{6}{25}$$

6. **(E)** Every 24 hours the clock will be back to where it started. Divide 110 by 24, which gives 4 and a remainder of 14. This means the clock goes around 4 times and back to where it started (9 a.m.) plus 14 hours, which gives you 11 p.m.

7. **(D)** Sum of four exams = (83) (4) = 332. Sum required for average of 85% after five exams = (85) (5) = 425. Difference (grade required on fifth exam) = 93.

8. **(B)** The sum of two sides of a triangle must be greater than the third side. In (B), 4 + 6 < 13.

9. **(E)**

$$\frac{1}{2} + \frac{1}{4} + \frac{1}{5} = \frac{19}{20}$$

$1/20$ is left for the church. Let x = amount left by landowner.

$$\frac{1}{20}x = \$7,000$$

$$x = \$7,000 \times 20$$

$$x = \$140,000$$

10. **(D)** $V = LWH$

$$200 = 10 \times 5 \times H$$

$$200 = 50H$$

$$\frac{200}{5} = H$$

$$4 = H$$

11. **(A)** It takes 6 minutes to wash one car. $30 \div 5 = 6$. Therefore, $30 \times 6 = 180$ minutes $= 3$ hours.

12. **(E)**

$$\frac{2^{-4} + 2^{-1}}{2^{-3}} = \frac{\frac{1}{2^4} + \frac{1}{2}}{\frac{1}{2^3}}$$

$$= \frac{2^4\left(\frac{1}{2^4} + \frac{1}{2}\right)}{2^4 \frac{1}{2^3}}$$

$$= \frac{1 + 2^3}{2} = \frac{9}{2}$$

13. **(B)** Let $x =$ time needed to reach the desired age ratio. At that time the son will be $4 + x$ years old and Mr. Baker will be $30 + x$ years old.

$$5(4 + x) = 30 + x$$

$$20 + 5x = 30 + x$$

$$5x - x = 30 - 20$$

$$4x = 10$$

$$x = 2\frac{1}{2}$$

Son's age

$$4 + x = 4 + 2\frac{1}{2}$$

$$= 6\frac{1}{2}$$

Mr. Baker's age

$$30 + x = 30 + 2\frac{1}{2}$$

$$= 32\frac{1}{2}$$

14. **(A)** 4 hours = 240 minutes. Time elapsed between 11:45 a.m. and 12:15 p.m. = 30 minutes.

$$\frac{30}{240} = \frac{1}{8}$$

of task completed in 30 minutes.

15. **(C)** Let x = original price of purchase.

$$x - .60x = \$96$$

$$.40x = \$96$$

$$x = \frac{\$96}{.40}$$

$$x = \$240$$

16. **(E)** 30% of 2 = 0.6 or $\frac{3}{5}$

$$\frac{2}{3} - \frac{3}{5} = \frac{10}{15} - \frac{9}{15} = \frac{1}{15}$$

17. **(C)**

Number of girls = $x - y$

Ratio of girls to boys = $\dfrac{x - y}{y}$

18. **(B)** The width of the larger frame is 5 feet wide, as compared with 2 feet of the smaller frame. Using ratio and proportion:

$$\frac{2}{5} = \frac{3}{x}$$

$$2x = 15$$

$$x = 7.5 \text{ feet}$$

19. **(E)** Today James is $5 + x$ years old. In y years he will be $5 + x + y$ years old.

20. **(C)**   Let legs $= 3x$ and $4x$.

$$\text{Area} = \frac{(3x)(4x)}{2} = 96$$

$$\frac{12x^2}{2} = 96$$

$$6x^2 = 96$$

$$x^2 = \frac{96}{6}$$

$$x^2 = 16$$

$$x = 4$$

Let legs $= 12$ and 16. Apply the Pythagorean Theorem.

$$h^2 = (12)^2 + (16)^2$$

$$h^2 = 144 + 256$$

$$h^2 = 400$$

$$h = \sqrt{400}$$

$$h = 20$$

Section 3 — Verbal

27. **(C)**   The answer is (C), because there are many "versions" (similar accounts) of the same stories in many different cultures. While many cultures' stories have "parts" (A) which are similar, this would not be as inclusive as choice (C), so it would not be as accurate. An "asset" (B) is a positive point, and that would require attaching value judgments to the relative value of different cultures' fables, etc., which this sentence fails to establish the validity of doing. A "tradition" (D) is a custom, which does not make sense in the context of this sentence. While there exist many "translations" (E) of the same folk tales, the sentence would mean that these translations exist within many cultures, and the sentence has not provided proof for a statement such as this one, either.

28. **(B)**   A "syllabus" is a course of study. In this sentence, the works of those philosophers, and their lives, was on the syllabus for a class in Western Civilization, so (B) is the answer. Anyone who has visited a college campus around the beginning of a semester knows that the "book-shelf" carries the texts for classes on its shelves. However, the bookshelf (A) is not a part of the class itself, so the sentence would make no sense if this were chosen as the answer. Although "rhetoric" (C), "argumentation" (D), and "debate" (E) were introduced by the Greek philosophers about 3,000 years ago, the sentence speaks of something in relation to a current class, not in relation to their accomplishments.

29. **(D)**   The answer is (D) "conditioned," which means trained, and these rats are trained to get the cheese they want by learning to press the lever for it. A rat cannot be "ordered" (A) to do something, since an order is given in language, which rats have not been shown to understand. Although rats may achieve getting a piece of cheese through "repetitious" behavior (B), experiments of this type are not interested in training the rats for repetition, which the context of the sentence would imply, but for something else. "Formed" (C) would be redundant (repetitive) in the context of this sentence. One cannot say, either, that rats are "lazy" (E), since this is a label for behavior that can only be applied with any certainty to people, not to animals.

30. **(A)**   Only if an audience were displeased (A) would it show the rude behaviors described in the sentence. While "criticism" (B) can mean a negative reaction, it can also simply mean a commentary on something,

so this would not be specific enough a term in the context of this sentence. "Astonishment" (C), or great surprise, would not account for the kinds of behavior exhibited by this audience, which would be considered rude. A "tirade" (D) is an angry discourse on something, and the behaviors of the audience did not fall within this definition. "Glee" (E), or great happiness, would also not account for this audience's reactions to the performance, so this is not the answer, as glee would lead to applause, not the behaviors described.

31. **(C)**   The correct choice is "flattery" (C) because it stands to reason that the division manager would be more interested in the employees making money for the company than telling her flattering things. A "reproof" (A) is a rebuke, or a chiding, so it would not be in keeping with the word "praise" which would precede it. "Imagery" (B) is the evocation, or calling up, of pictures and images, so this has little bearing on the meaning of this sentence. "Cadences" (D) are styles of speaking, and while this could have meaning within the context of this sentence, it would not be as precise a meaning as choice (C). "Aspirations" (E) are hopes, which would never be "empty" (the adjective preceding the blank), so this could not be the correct answer either.

32. **(E)**   The answer is (E), "evaporate," because this teacher warned the class not to let the liquid in the lab dishes be released into the air (evaporate) by leaving the lab dishes with the compound uncovered. To "coagulate" (A) means to clot. Even though this could fit into the context of the sentence, a liquid is more likely to evaporate than to coagulate when exposed to the air. To "eviscerate" (B) means to disembowel, as a fish is eviscerated before broiling, so that has no meaning in this context. To "inundate" (C) is to overcome by superior force, so this word, also, does not apply to this sentence. To "suffocate" (D) means to cause someone or something to experience a lack of air, which was the opposite of what this instructor warned the class about.

33. **(E)**   An ALIAS is a false IDENTITY. The best choice that measures the same relationship as the given words is (E). An ILLUSION is a false PERCEPTION. Choice (A) is wrong because a "TOURIST is a false COUNTRY," makes no sense. Choice (B) is incorrect because "a JUDGMENT is a false VALUE," is not a meaningful relationship. Choice (C) is wrong because "a DRAWING is a false COLOR," has no meaning. A DRAWING can be composed of COLOR. Choice (D) is wrong because "a SIGNATURE is a false AUTHOR," is a statement that makes no sense.

34. **(B)** The relationship between the given words can be described as: "An ORIGINAL is the opposite of REPLICA (duplicate)." (B) is the answer because "a PUZZLE is the opposite of SOLUTION." If you have the SOLUTION, you no longer have a PUZZLE. (A) is wrong because "a FACADE (something that's false, superficial) is the opposite of MASK," is wrong. Sometimes a FACADE is a MASK. (C) is incorrect because "a DEPTH is the opposite of GAUGE," makes no sense. A GAUGE can be used for measuring DEPTH. (D) is wrong because "an IMPORTANCE is the opposite of SUBSTANCE," is meaningless. (E) is incorrect because "a SCHEME is the opposite of DESIGN," is false. A SCHEME can be a DESIGN. The words are synonyms.

35. **(E)** The relationship between the two given words can be described as: "GOOD is a lesser condition than SUPERIOR," or "SUPERIOR is a stronger word than GOOD." (E) is the answer because "ENTHUSIASM (strong warmth of feeling) is a lesser condition than FRENZY (violently agitated)." (A) is incorrect because "BLEAK is a lesser condition than DESOLATE," is semantically incorrect. BLEAK and DESOLATE are synonyms, and therefore one word is not stronger than the other. (B) is wrong because. RANCID (having a bad smell, rotten) is a lesser condition than SPOILED," is not accurate. RANCID and SPOILED are similar in meaning, and are synonyms. (C) is wrong because "MUNDANE (concerned with the practical details of everyday life) is a lesser condition than WORLDLY," is inaccurate. The two words are synonyms. Choice (D) is incorrect because "MORBID (gruesome) is a lesser condition than DEATH," is not a meaningful sentence.

36. **(A)** The relationship between the given words can be described as: "A TACITURN (reserved, reticent) person has few (little amount) WORDS." Choice (A) expresses the same relationship. "An IMPOVERISHED person has little MONEY." Choice (D) is wrong because "an OBDURATE (stubborn) person has little ENERGY," makes no sense. Choice (B) is wrong because "a CUNNING (shrewd) person has little TIME," is not meaningful. Choice (E) is incorrect because "a STUBBORN person has little REGRET," makes no sense. Choice (C) is wrong because "an OVERWEIGHT person has little FAT," is not necessarily accurate.

37. **(D)** The relationship between the given words can be described as: "A PERMIT (written permission) is a SANCTION (authoritative approval)." The words are synonyms. Choice (D) says that "a HARANGUE

(loud verbal attack) is a TIRADE (prolonged speech of abuse)." HARANGUE and TIRADE are also synonyms. Choice (A) is wrong because "an AMATEUR (somebody with little skill) is a SINGER," makes no semantic sense. Choice (B) is incorrect because "a FANATIC is a CAUSE," is not correct. A FANATIC has a CAUSE. Choice (C) is wrong because "a GLAMOUR is a MODEL," is not accurate. These words are not synonyms. A MODEL may have GLAMOUR. Choice (E) is wrong because "a MICROCOSM (small world) is a GERM," makes no sense.

38. **(A)**   The relationship between the given words can be expressed as: "If something is EFFERVESCENT, it has BUBBLES." The best choice is (A). "If something is CLEAN, it is UNCONTAMINATED (clean, has no germs)." (B) is incorrect because "if something is TASTE, it has TONGUE," makes no sense. (C) is wrong because "if something is NEW, it has PRICE, "is a semantically meaningless sentence. (D) is incorrect because "if something is EXOTIC (foreign, strange), it has COUNTRY," makes no sense. (E) is wrong because "if something is OLD, it is NEWBORN," is incorrect. If something is OLD, it is the opposite of NEWBORN.

39. **(E)**   Someone who is ECCENTRIC has PECULIAR tendencies. "An ECCENTRIC is PECULIAR." The answer is (E), "A JUDGE is IMPARTIAL (shows no favoritism)." (A) is wrong because "a KING is POWER," tells you what a KING has as a result of his station in life. POWER is not an intrinsic quality of being a KING. (B) is incorrect because "a BULLY is COWARDLY," is not a semantically accurate statement. Some BULLIES may be COWARDLY, but others are not. (C) is wrong because "an EGOCENTRIC (self-centered) is SHAMELESS," may or may not always be true. (D) "a CELEBRITY is DISTINCT (one of a kind, separate)," is not an accurate statement. Because a person is a CELEBRITY, that doesn't make them DISTINCT.

40. **(C)**   The active support or patronage is usually tied up in the metaphorical usage. The growth or fruition is encouraged (A). Such encouragement may lead to a refined product or strain (B). The study itself is subject to support (D). The ground may be enriched through such nourishment (E).

41. **(B)**   These subjects can be examined only by approved authorities. The Church's commitment to broad education (A) is dubious. The "surrender of reason" hardly fastens new ideas (C). Greek thought enters the

discussion only several lines later (D). The Church's connection with civil authority does not arise in this passage (E).

42. **(D)**   The Middle Ages, by implied contrast to the Renaissance, valued community over the individual. The author here (A) attaches no explicit value to this shift. Quite the opposite of self-assertion, the Middle Ages, according to the author, valued denial of the individual (B). The Renaissance sense of community is not central to this analogy (C). Although its role goes unnoticed here, the Church would not be viewed as friendly to the growth of individuality (E).

43. **(B)**   The analogy is to painting, evident in the terms "relief" and "background." It is not three-dimensional (A). The author stresses depiction of human beings (C). The art form is visual, not based in sound (E). It does predate the development of film (D), although a modern reader may neglect that fact.

44. **(B)**   Both passages identify as the characteristic conclusion of utilitarianism that we should promote the greatest good for the greatest number and that this good is pleasure. While Hobbes' egoism (A) and utilitarianism may disagree on this point, neither view is discussed as a criticism of the other in Passage 2. Passage 2 says nothing about whether Epicurus (C) was a utilitarian. Plato's view about the moral value of pleasure (D), that it can be bad, is *inconsistent* with the utilitarian view that all pleasure is good. Although Mill's argument (E) is utilitarian, only Bentham's utilitarianism is mentioned in Passage 2.

45. **(D)**   This is consistent with the premise noted in line 14 that if pleasure is good, then more pleasure is better. Contrary to choice (A) the passage notes that Mill distinguishes types and levels of pleasure and that some pleasures are worthier of pursuit than others. Mill's suggestion that we should promote the greatest good for the greatest number is not consistent with the proposition that each person is primarily interested in his own pleasure (B), nor, therefore is it consistent with egoism (C). While Mill acknowledges that some pleasures are more worthy of pursuit than others, he never says that there are bad pleasures (E), and Passage 1, especially line 14, implies that he thinks all pleasures are good.

46. **(E)**   Passage 2 explicitly appeals to historical and authoritative support in its defense of the proposition that all pleasures are good and uses these four authorities as examples of such support. Although Passage 2

notes a disagreement between Hobbes and Bentham (A), its reason for including them is that they both support the passage's argument. Whether or not these four disagreed concerning the extent to which pleasure is realized (B) is secondary to the point that they all agreed on the inherent goodness of pleasure. Passage 2 acknowledges Singer's interest in animals (C), but it is not the point of the passage either to prove or to disprove this. There is nothing in Passage 2 to indicate whether or not Singer was an Epicurean (D).

47. **(B)** While Passage 1 suggests that the egoist is concerned only with herself, Passage 2 claims that interest in the well-being of others is consistent with egoism. Passage 2 *acknowledges* that Hobbes, who is an egoist (A), believes that all pleasures are good. It suggests only that egoists *may* not be selfish (C). It does not suggest that Hobbes may have been a utilitarian (D). The point in lines 57–61 is not about selfish egoists (E), but about an egoist that may not be selfish.

48. **(C)** One of the key premises to the argument in Passage 2 is that many people *have* agreed that all pleasures are good. But if more have disagreed, this argument is weak. Whether Singer was a utilitarian (A) is irrelevant to Passage 2. Passage 2 acknowledges this difference between Bentham and Mill (B), but the argument depends on Bentham only for his view that all pleasures are good. Passage 2 says nothing about whether Plato was a utilitarian (D), but if he were, this would hurt his own position, and thus strengthen the position of Passage 2. The example of over-drinking (E) would be subject to the same criticism as the example of overeating, so it wouldn't help Plato's argument or hurt the argument in Passage 2.

49. **(A)** Passage 2 makes clear that Epicurus thinks all pleasures are good, even if the simplest pleasures are the best. It does not discuss whether Epicurus was a utilitarian (B) or an egoist (C). Had Passage 1 relied on Epicurus as an authority (D), it would have weakened the argument since it is arguing *against* Epicurus' position. We can't tell from Passage 2 whether Hobbes (E) would have agreed or disagreed with Epicurus' plea for the simple life.

50. **(C)** The passage refers to *all* arguments to the contrary. It indicates that these historical arguments (A) are *well*-founded. It does not single out Plato's argument or the argument about selfishness (B). It indicates that

these authoritative arguments (D), as well as the egoistic and utilitarian positions (E) are *well*-founded.

51. **(D)** These lines refer to the distinctions made by Mill and others. Eventually Passage 1 supports the proposition that there are bad pleasures (A). It acknowledges that the proposition "All pleasures are good" does not commit its proponents to any distinction among pleasures (B) or to any concern for the majority (C), but far from tempting people to accept this argument the Passage suggests that this should tempt people to accept the contrary. The Passage denies that arguments in defense of this proposition are strong arguments (E).

52. **(D)** It attempts to address the criticism of egoism's alleged selfishness by showing that Hobbes's egoism leads him to care about others—a result of his enlightened self-interest. The passage denies that Hobbes, in his enlightened self-interest, thinks that some pleasures are not good (A). It admits to Hobbes's egoism which precludes his promoting the greatest good for the greatest number (B). It says nothing about whether Hobbes was interested in the welfare of animals (C). The point of addressing this issue is to show that egoism does *not* necessarily entail selfishness, contrary to answer (E).

Section 4 — Math

21. **(C)**   A prime number is a number greater than 1, which only has 2 factors; itself and 1. 2 is the only even prime number.

The prime factors of 18 are 2 and 3.

The prime factors of 20 are 2 and 5.

22. **(B)**

$$\frac{10+y}{2}=0$$
$$10+y=0$$
$$y=-10$$

23. **(A)**   Since a rhombus is equilateral,

$$\frac{2}{5}x=y$$

$$2x=5y$$

24. **(C)**   40 m.p.h. is the same as 40 miles in 60 minutes.

$$\frac{60}{40}=\frac{3}{2}=1.5$$

25. **(C)**   If the first quantity is equal to the second quantity, and the second quantity is equal to the third quantity, then the first quantity *must* be equal to the third quantity.

$$2a=3b \text{ and } 3b=5c, \text{ then } 2a=5c$$

26. **(B)**   In triangle ABC,

$$6^2+8^2=AC^2$$

$$36+64=AC^2$$

$$100=AC^2$$

$$10=AC$$

In triangle ADC,

$$y^2 + 9^2 = 10^2$$

$$y^2 + 81 = 100$$

$$y^2 = 19$$

$$y = \sqrt{19}$$

27. **(A)**   If 2 or more things occur at different times, and they start together, they will occur again at their least common multiple (LCM). The LCM of 3, 5, and 4 is 60.

28. **(A)**   For the number to be divisible by 2, M must be an even number. For the original number to be divisible by 9, the sum of the digits must be a number that is divisible by 9. Therefore, M must equal 6.

$$(4 + 5 + 6 + 7 + 8 = 30; 36 - 30 = 6)$$

29. **(C)**   In multiplication of exponents, if the bases are the same, keep the base and add the exponents.

$$9^4 \times 9 \times 9^5 = 9^{10}$$

$$(9^5)^2 = 9^5 \times 9^5 = 9^{10}$$

So
$$\frac{9^{10}}{9^{10}} = 1$$

30. **(A)**   The length of AB is $(6 - 0) = 6$.

The length of CB is $(7 - 3) = 4$.

Area of rectangle $= 6 \times 4 = 24$

31. **(B)**   Any number divisible by 2, 10, and 25 must be divisible by their least common multiple, which is 50. The integers between 1 and 201 which are divisible by 50 are 50, 100, 150, and 200.

32. **(A)**   Either cancel each term by y^7, leaving $y^2 + 1$ or factor:

$$\frac{y^7(y^{2+1})}{y^7}$$

The y^7 cancels out leaving $y^{2}+1$.

Since $y = .8$, $(.8)^2 + 1 = .64 + 1 = 1.64$

33. The correct response is:

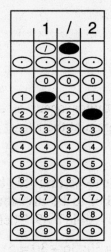

It is given that there are 24 students in all and 16 are male. By subtracting 16 from 24, we find that there are 8 females in the class. Setting up a ratio of females to males we get 8 to 16. Simplifying this we get 1 to 2, or written differently, 1/2.

Note: Because this is a ratio, there is no other way to grid this response beside the one shown. Gridding .5 would not be acceptable in this case.

34. The correct response is:

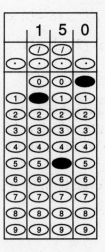

We have

(Actual price) – 20% (Actual price) = Discount price

$$x - 20\%x = 120$$

This yields

$$.8x = 120$$

$$x = \$150$$

35. The correct response is:

The key here is to recall that the order of operations is performed from left to right when the operations involved (in this case division and multiplication) have the same level of precedence. We have

$$\left(\frac{x}{2}\right) \times x \div x = 10$$

$$\left(\frac{x^2}{2}\right) \div x = 10$$

$$\frac{x}{2} = 10$$

$$x = 20$$

36. The correct response is:

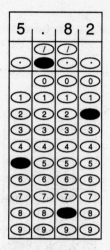

The total circumference of the square is 7 feet making the side of the square $7/4$ feet; thus, the area of the square is

$$A_{\text{square}} = \left(\frac{7}{4}\right)^2 = \frac{49}{16} \text{ square feet.}$$

As the total circumference of the circle is also 7 feet, we find the radius from the equation

$$2\pi r = 7$$

$$2\left(\frac{22}{7}\right)r = 7$$

yielding $\qquad r = \dfrac{49}{44}.$

This gives the area of the circle as

$$A_{\text{circle}} = \pi r^2$$

$$= \frac{22}{7}r^2$$

$$= \frac{22}{7}\left(\frac{49}{44}\right)^2$$

$$= \frac{343}{88} \text{ square feet}$$

The total area is given by

$$A_{\text{square}} + A_{\text{circle}} = \frac{49}{16} + \frac{343}{88} = 6.96 \text{ square feet.}$$

37. The correct response is:

Let

r_1 = radius of the inner circle

and r^2 = radius of the outer circle.

As $r_1 = 7$ meters we can calculate r_2 since it is the diameter of the square. From the Pythagorean Theorem we get

$$r_2 = \sqrt{7^2 + 7^2} = \sqrt{98} \text{ meters.}$$

The area of the shaded region is the difference between the areas of the two circles, i.e., area of shaded region equals

$$\pi r_2^2 - \pi r_1^2 = \left(\frac{22}{7}\right)r_2^2 - \left(\frac{22}{7}\right)r_1^2$$
$$= \left(\frac{22}{7}\right)98 - \left(\frac{22}{7}\right)49$$
$$= (22)(14) - (22)(7)$$
$$= (22)(7)$$
$$= 154 \text{ square meters}$$

38. The correct response is:

First we find the value of $f(3)$. This is given by

$$f(3) = 3^2 - 1 = 8;$$

thus $\quad g(f(3)) = g(8)$

$$= 3(8) + 2 = 26.$$

39. The correct response is:

Plugging in these values we obtain

$$\frac{2^2(-1)^{-1}}{3(-1)\left(\frac{1}{3}\right)} = \frac{-4}{-1} = 4.$$

40. The correct response is:

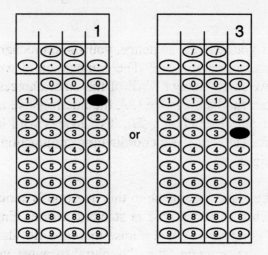

or

Using the formula given we have

$$48 = -16t^2 + 64t$$
$$0 = -16t^2 + 64t - 48$$

After factoring, we get

$$0 = (t - 1)(t - 3)$$

This yields $t = 1$ and $t = 3$ as the possible solutions.

Section 5 — Writing Skills

1. **(C)**   As you read the sentence, you should recognize the choice (C) presents an error in comparison. The comparison of two bridges requires the comparative form "longer." All of the other choices are acceptable in standard written English. Choice (A), the interrogative adjective "Which," introduces the question; choice (B), "is," agrees with its singular subject "bridge"; choice (D), "or," is a coordinating conjunction joining the names of the two bridges.

2. **(E)**   The correct response to this question is choice (E). All labeled elements are choices acceptable in standard written English. Choice (A), "of proteins," is a prepositional phrase that modifies the word "function"; in choice (B), the pronoun "they "is plural to agree with its antecedent, "proteins," and the verb "come" is also plural to agree with its subject, "they"; choice (C), "plant or animal sources," is idiomatic; and Choice (D), "is," is singular to agree with its singular subject, "function."

3. **(C)**   The error is choice (C), "I," which is in the nominative case. Because the words "Janice" and "I" serve as indirect objects in the sentence, the correct pronoun is the first person objective form, "me." Choice (A), "Recognizing," is a participle introducing an introductory participial phrase modifying "teacher;" choice (B), "had worked," is a verb in the past perfect tense because the action in the phrase was completed before the action in the main clause occurred; choice (D), "tomorrow," is an adverb modifying the verb "could give."

4. **(C)**   The error occurs at choice (C), where the preposition "from" is idiomatic after the word "different." Although some experts insist upon the use of "from" after the adjective "different," others accept the use of "different than" in order to save words. An example would be "different than you thought"; the use of "from" would require the addition of the word "what." Choice (A), "According to," is a preposition correctly introducing a prepositional phrase; choice (B), "has," is third person singular to agree with its subject "branch"; and choice (D), "those," is a plural pronoun to agree with its antecedent "powers."

5. **(A)**   Choice (A) should be a gerund in the present perfect form (having "been studied") to indicate that the action expressed by the gerund

occurred before the relationship was reported. Choice (B), "preceding ten years," is idiomatic. Choice (C), "having," is a gerund introducing the phrase "having heart attacks" which is the object of the preposition "of"; choice (D), the past tense passive verb "was reported," is singular to agree with its subject, "relationship."

6. **(E)** Your answer should be choice (E), indicating that this sentence contains no error in standard written English. Choice (A), "demonstrates," is present tense third person singular to agree with its subject, "book"; choice (B), "was expected," uses the third person singular form of "to be" to agree with its subject "each;" choice (C), the infinitive "to use," is idiomatic after the passive verb "was expected"; and choice (D), "his or her," is singular to agree with its antecedent, the indefinite pronoun "each," and provides gender neutrality.

7. **(A)** You should recognize in choice (A) that the idiomatically acceptable preposition to follow "aversion" is "to." The other choices in the sentence are acceptable in standard written English. Choice (B), "for him," is a prepositional phrase modifying "activity;" choice (C), "one," is a pronoun appropriate to refer to its antecedent "activity;" and choice (D), "that," is a relative pronoun introducing a restrictive adjective subordinate clause modifying "one."

8. **(C)** Choice (C) contains the error because the subject of the verb "show" is "story," a singular noun that calls for the third person singular verb, "shows." The rest of the sentence represents correct usage. Choices (A) and (B), "those" and "their," are plural pronouns that agree with the antecedent "pioneers"; choice (D), "us," is in the objective case because it is the indirect object in the sentence.

9. **(D)** Choice (D) presents an error in comparison, appearing to compare "farming" with "low latitudes" when what is intended is a comparison of "farming in high latitudes" with "farming in low latitudes." The corrected sentence reads: "Because of the long, cold winters and short summer growing season, farming in high latitudes is more difficult than farming in low latitudes." The other choices all represent appropriate usage in standard written English. Choice (A), "Because of," is idiomatically correct as a preposition; choice (B), "and," is a coordinating conjunction joining the nouns "winters" and "summers." Choice (C), "more difficult," is the comparative form appropriate to compare two items.

10. **(D)**   The error is in choice (D). The word "contestant" is a predicate nominative in the subordinate noun clause, and it must agree in number with the plural subject of the clause, the pronoun "both," to which it refers. The noun clause should, therefore, read: "that both of us could be contestants on a quiz show." Choice (A), "I," is part of the compound subject of the introductory adverb clause and is, correctly, in the nominative case. Choice (B), "were," is plural to agree with its compound subject. Choice (C), "we," is plural to agree with its compound antecedent, "sister and I," and is in the nominative case because it is the subject of the verb "hoped."

11. **(A)**   The error is in choice (A). The auxiliary verb "had" calls for the past participle form of the verb "break," which is "broken." All of the other choices are acceptable in standard written English. Choice (B), "that," is the correct relative pronoun to follow "vase" and introduce the subordinate adjective clause; choice (C), "had purchased," is the past perfect form of the verb to indicate action completed in the past before the action of the verb in the main clause; choice (D), "her," is the object of the preposition "for."

12. **(E)**   This sentence contains no error in standard written English. Choice (A), the prepositional phrase "with whom," introduces an adjective clause modifying the word "people." The relative pronoun "whom" is in the objective case because it serves as the object of the preposition "with." The simple past tense "worked" is appropriate for choice (B); choice (C), "were engaged," is plural to agree with its subject "some"; choice (D) is an idiomatic expression replacing the preposition "for."

13. **(D)**   Your reading of the sentence should indicate that choice (D), "were," presents an error in subject-verb agreement. A compound subject joined by "or" or "neither . . . nor" calls for a verb that agrees in number with the second part of the compound subject, which is, in this case, singular. The correct choice is the verb "was." The other answers represent correct usage. Choice (A), "Because of," is idiomatic; choices (B) and (C) are correlative conjunctions.

14. **(C)**   Again the error is one of agreement of the subject and verb. Choice (C), "were," is plural; because its subject is "attack," not "reasons," which is the object of the preposition "among" and therefore cannot be the subject of the sentence, the verb should be the singular "was." Choice (A), "Among," introduces a prepositional phrase; choice (B) is an

idiomatically acceptable prepositional phrase to modify the noun "reasons;" choice (D), "naval base," poses no error in usage.

15. **(D)**   Your analysis of this sentence should disclose an error in parallelism in choice (D). "Teaching" should be replaced by "to teach," an infinitive parallel with "to frighten." Both infinitives modify the noun "attempt." The other choices all represent standard usage in written English. Choice (A), "greater," is the comparative form of the adjective, correctly used to compare two items; choice (B), "their," is a plural possessive pronoun agreeing in number with its plural antecedent, "parents"; and choice (C), "than," is idiomatic to introduce the second part of the comparison.

16. **(C)**   You should recognize that the possessive pronoun in choice (C), "their," is not the appropriate pronoun to use in referring to a country. Choice (A), "of living," and choice (D), "of life expectancy," are both idiomatically acceptable prepositional phrases; choice (B), "is shown," is passive and agrees in number with its singular subject, "standard."

17. **(D)**   Choice (D), "white and bluish gray in color," is the third in a series of objects of the verb "has." The error lies in its lack of parallelism with the other two objects, "eyes" and "body." Corrected, the sentence reads: "The snow leopard is a wild mammal in Central Asia that has large eyes, a four-foot body, and a white and bluish gray color." The other choices are all acceptable in standard written English. Choice (A), "is," is singular to agree with its subject "leopard." Choice (B), "that has," is composed of the relative pronoun "that" referring to the noun "mammal," and the verb "has," that agrees with its subject in number. Choice (C), "and," is a coordinating conjunction correctly used to join the three objects of the verb.

18. **(B)**   You should recognize that choice (B), "and," is not the correct correlative conjunction to follow "either." The correct word is "or." The other choices all represent acceptable choices in standard written English. Choice (A), "a young person," is correctly placed immediately after the introductory participial phrase that modifies it; choice (C), "her," is singular to agree with its antecedent "person" and objective because it is the object of the verb "make." Choice (D), "most important," is in the superlative form because the comparison involves more than two choices.

19. **(C)**   Choice (C), "to fail," is incorrect in standard written English.

The sentence contains two parallel ideas that should be expressed with the same grammatical form. Because "Failing" is a gerund, the "infinitive" to "fail" should be replaced with "failing" to make the construction parallel. Choice (A), "is," agrees in number with its subject, "student"; choice (B), "is," agrees in number with its subject, "Failing"; choice (D) is singular to agree with its antecedent, "student," and indicates no gender preference.

20. **(D)**   Because the verb "protest" can be transitive and have a direct object, choice (D) avoids awkward wordiness and use of the unnecessary preposition "about." Choices (B) and (E) include unnecessary words and uses the pronoun "they" that has no clear antecedent; choice (C) is also unnecessarily wordy and contains the repetitious words, "builders should build."

21. **(B)**   Choice (B) best shows the causal relationship between sibling opportunities and their placement in the family, their abilities, and their personalities, and retains the subordination of the original sentence. Choices (A) and (E) provide dangling phrases. Choice (C) with its use of the coordinating conjunction "and" treats the lack of opportunity and its cause as if they are equal ideas and does not show the causal relationship between them, and choice (D) results in a run-on sentence.

22. **(E)**   Only choice (E) corrects the two major problems in the sentence, the lack of subject-verb agreement and the lack of parallelism. In choices (A), (B), and (C), the verb "is" does not agree with its plural subject, "provisions." Choices (A) and (D) have unlike constructions serving as predicate nominatives, the noun "freedom" and the clause "that citizens are guaranteed a trial by jury." Choice (E) correctly uses the plural verb "are" to agree with the plural subject, and the predicate nominative is composed of two parallel nouns, "freedom" and "guarantee."

23. **(E)**   The errors found in the original sentence, choice (A), involve parallelism and redundancy. Choice (E) uses the parallel infinitives "to entertain" and "to teach" as direct objects and eliminates the repetition created in use of both "tried" and "attempt" in the original sentence. Choices (B) and (C) provide parallel construction, but choice (B) retains the redundancy and choice (C) incorrectly splits the infinitive "to entertain;" although choice (D) provides parallelism of the nouns "entertainment" and "attempt," the redundancy still remains, and the word order is not idiomatic.

24. **(B)**   Choice (B) adequately conveys the reason for removal of the parking meters with the least wordiness. Choices (A) and (D) contain unnecessary words; choices (C) and (E) have dangling participial phrases.

25. **(D)**   Choice (D), in which "Megan" correctly follows the phrase, conveys the meaning with the least wordiness. The problem with choice (A) is the introductory participial phrase; it must be eliminated or followed immediately by the word modified. Choice (B) does not solve the problem of the dangling phrase; choices (C) and (E) add words unnecessary to the meaning of the sentence.

26. **(A)**   The given sentence is acceptable in standard written English. Each of the alternate choices introduces a problem. Choice (B) uses the superlative form of the adjective, "most interested," when the comparative form "more interested" is correct for the comparison of two options; choices (C) and (E) introduce a lack of parallelism and choice (D) is not idiomatic.

27. **(E)**   The noun clause in choice (E) is idiomatically acceptable. The use of "Whether" in choices (A) and (B) leads the writer to add "or not," words that contribute nothing to the meaning and result in awkwardness of construction. In choice (C), "the fact of whether," is not idiomatic, and choice (D) with its awkward gerund phrase is also not idiomatic.

28. **(E)**   This sentence presents two problems, namely use of a preposition instead of a coordinating conjunction to join the objects of the participle "having studied" and failure to show a time relationship. Choice (E) corrects both problems. Choice (B) simply replaces the preposition "along with" by "as well as"; choice (C) unnecessarily repeats the conjunction "and" rather than using the quite appropriate series construction. None of the choices (A), (B), (C), or (D) correctly shows the time relationship.

29. **(B)**   This sentence contains the ambiguous pronoun "they," for which there is no antecedent and fails to show the relationship of the ideas expressed. Choice (B) eliminates the clause with the ambiguous pronoun and correctly expresses the reason for the sandbag placement. Choice (C) suggests that the two clauses joined by "and" are equal and does not show the subordinate relationship of the second to the first. Choice (D) introduces a dangling phrase with a coordinating conjunction, "and," that suggests the joining of equals, and choice (E) retains both errors from the original sentence.

30. **(A)**   This sentence is correct in standard written English. Choices (B) and (C) introduce unnecessary words that add nothing to the meaning and make the sentence awkward and wordy; choices (D) and (E) do not correctly show relationship.

31. **(C)**   Choice (C) shows the relationship accurately and eliminates the awkward gerund construction as the object of the preposition "despite." The adjective clause in choice (B) fails to show the relationship of the original sentence; choice (D) introduces the superfluous words "the fact that." Choice (E) inappropriately places the qualifying information in equal and parallel construction to the main idea of the sentence.

32. **(A)**   This sentence is correct in standard written English. Choices (B) and (C) lose the strength of the parallelism in choice (A). Choice (D), although containing parallel construction, is idiomatically awkward with its participial phrases. Choices (B), (C), and (E) all exhibit wordiness.

33. **(D)**   The original sentence, choice (A), contains the obvious and redundant words "was a man who." Choices (B), (C), and (E) are also unnecessarily verbose. Choice (D) makes the statement in the most direct way possible and represents correct standard usage.

34. **(A)**   Choice (A) is the best condensation of the wordy portion. Choice (B) and choice (D) omit the time period. Choice (C) is redundant, repeating the "conflict" idea twice. Choice (E) is almost as wordy and repetitive as the original.

35. **(A)**   Choice (A) reduces wordiness through two means: deleting a subordinate clause by eliminating "What" and deleting a prepositional phrase by converting it to a possessive. Choice (B) keeps the subordinate clause. Choice (C) creates an incorrect sentence structure. Choice (D) trivializes the serious conflicts by using the word "novelty," which has light connotations. Choice (E) changes the focus of the action from the Army.

36. **(C)**   Choice (C) is the best reduction of the wordy original. Choice (A) uses "alot" and choice (B) uses "a lot," both of which are not formal usage to mean "much." Choice (D) is almost wordier than the original. Choice (E) is a bit stiff for the tone of the article.

37. **(D)**   Choice (D) presents the ideas correctly and concisely. Choices

(A) and (C) use the awkward phrase "because of." Choice (B) sounds as if the first part of the sentence is unrelated to the last part. Choice (E) repeats the verb "earned" twice.

38. **(D)** Paragraph 4 is a conclusion (D), winding up the main idea, the good relationship between Crook and Indian soldiers. Choice (A) is not correct as there is no specific incident given. Choice (B) could be a second choice, but the best features of the subject are more fully discussed earlier in the paper. Choice (C) has no bearing on this essay. Choice (E) could be a choice if there were a recounting of the main points, but the major ideas of the last paragraph are the faith Crook and the Apaches had in one another and the uniqueness of their relationship.

39. **(E)** The past progressive tense is best, as it expresses Crook's use of the scouts as a common occurrence, not as a single event, which may be implied by the past tense in the original. (A) eliminates "and" which further confuses the sentence and does not help the verb problem. (B) makes it sound even more like a singular occurrence. (C) changes only the first verb to the progressive. (D) is not grammatically incorrect, but does not clarify the sentence any, and lets the verb tense stand.

PSAT/ NMSQT

Answer Sheets

PSAT/NMSQT – Diagnostic Test
ANSWER SHEET

SECTION 1

1. Ⓐ Ⓑ Ⓒ Ⓓ Ⓔ
2. Ⓐ Ⓑ Ⓒ Ⓓ Ⓔ
3. Ⓐ Ⓑ Ⓒ Ⓓ Ⓔ
4. Ⓐ Ⓑ Ⓒ Ⓓ Ⓔ
5. Ⓐ Ⓑ Ⓒ Ⓓ Ⓔ
6. Ⓐ Ⓑ Ⓒ Ⓓ Ⓔ
7. Ⓐ Ⓑ Ⓒ Ⓓ Ⓔ
8. Ⓐ Ⓑ Ⓒ Ⓓ Ⓔ
9. Ⓐ Ⓑ Ⓒ Ⓓ Ⓔ
10. Ⓐ Ⓑ Ⓒ Ⓓ Ⓔ
11. Ⓐ Ⓑ Ⓒ Ⓓ Ⓔ
12. Ⓐ Ⓑ Ⓒ Ⓓ Ⓔ
13. Ⓐ Ⓑ Ⓒ Ⓓ Ⓔ
14. Ⓐ Ⓑ Ⓒ Ⓓ Ⓔ
15. Ⓐ Ⓑ Ⓒ Ⓓ Ⓔ
16. Ⓐ Ⓑ Ⓒ Ⓓ Ⓔ
17. Ⓐ Ⓑ Ⓒ Ⓓ Ⓔ
18. Ⓐ Ⓑ Ⓒ Ⓓ Ⓔ
19. Ⓐ Ⓑ Ⓒ Ⓓ Ⓔ
20. Ⓐ Ⓑ Ⓒ Ⓓ Ⓔ
21. Ⓐ Ⓑ Ⓒ Ⓓ Ⓔ
22. Ⓐ Ⓑ Ⓒ Ⓓ Ⓔ
23. Ⓐ Ⓑ Ⓒ Ⓓ Ⓔ
24. Ⓐ Ⓑ Ⓒ Ⓓ Ⓔ
25. Ⓐ Ⓑ Ⓒ Ⓓ Ⓔ
26. Ⓐ Ⓑ Ⓒ Ⓓ Ⓔ

SECTION 2

1. Ⓐ Ⓑ Ⓒ Ⓓ Ⓔ
2. Ⓐ Ⓑ Ⓒ Ⓓ Ⓔ
3. Ⓐ Ⓑ Ⓒ Ⓓ Ⓔ
4. Ⓐ Ⓑ Ⓒ Ⓓ Ⓔ
5. Ⓐ Ⓑ Ⓒ Ⓓ Ⓔ
6. Ⓐ Ⓑ Ⓒ Ⓓ Ⓔ
7. Ⓐ Ⓑ Ⓒ Ⓓ Ⓔ
8. Ⓐ Ⓑ Ⓒ Ⓓ Ⓔ
9. Ⓐ Ⓑ Ⓒ Ⓓ Ⓔ
10. Ⓐ Ⓑ Ⓒ Ⓓ Ⓔ

11. Ⓐ Ⓑ Ⓒ Ⓓ Ⓔ
12. Ⓐ Ⓑ Ⓒ Ⓓ Ⓔ
13. Ⓐ Ⓑ Ⓒ Ⓓ Ⓔ
14. Ⓐ Ⓑ Ⓒ Ⓓ Ⓔ
15. Ⓐ Ⓑ Ⓒ Ⓓ Ⓔ
16. Ⓐ Ⓑ Ⓒ Ⓓ Ⓔ
17. Ⓐ Ⓑ Ⓒ Ⓓ Ⓔ
18. Ⓐ Ⓑ Ⓒ Ⓓ Ⓔ
19. Ⓐ Ⓑ Ⓒ Ⓓ Ⓔ
20. Ⓐ Ⓑ Ⓒ Ⓓ Ⓔ

SECTION 3

27. Ⓐ Ⓑ Ⓒ Ⓓ Ⓔ
28. Ⓐ Ⓑ Ⓒ Ⓓ Ⓔ
29. Ⓐ Ⓑ Ⓒ Ⓓ Ⓔ
30. Ⓐ Ⓑ Ⓒ Ⓓ Ⓔ
31. Ⓐ Ⓑ Ⓒ Ⓓ Ⓔ
32. Ⓐ Ⓑ Ⓒ Ⓓ Ⓔ
33. Ⓐ Ⓑ Ⓒ Ⓓ Ⓔ
34. Ⓐ Ⓑ Ⓒ Ⓓ Ⓔ
35. Ⓐ Ⓑ Ⓒ Ⓓ Ⓔ
36. Ⓐ Ⓑ Ⓒ Ⓓ Ⓔ
37. Ⓐ Ⓑ Ⓒ Ⓓ Ⓔ
38. Ⓐ Ⓑ Ⓒ Ⓓ Ⓔ
39. Ⓐ Ⓑ Ⓒ Ⓓ Ⓔ
40. Ⓐ Ⓑ Ⓒ Ⓓ Ⓔ
41. Ⓐ Ⓑ Ⓒ Ⓓ Ⓔ
42. Ⓐ Ⓑ Ⓒ Ⓓ Ⓔ
43. Ⓐ Ⓑ Ⓒ Ⓓ Ⓔ
44. Ⓐ Ⓑ Ⓒ Ⓓ Ⓔ
45. Ⓐ Ⓑ Ⓒ Ⓓ Ⓔ
46. Ⓐ Ⓑ Ⓒ Ⓓ Ⓔ
47. Ⓐ Ⓑ Ⓒ Ⓓ Ⓔ
48. Ⓐ Ⓑ Ⓒ Ⓓ Ⓔ
49. Ⓐ Ⓑ Ⓒ Ⓓ Ⓔ
50. Ⓐ Ⓑ Ⓒ Ⓓ Ⓔ
51. Ⓐ Ⓑ Ⓒ Ⓓ Ⓔ
52. Ⓐ Ⓑ Ⓒ Ⓓ Ⓔ

SECTION 4

21. Ⓐ Ⓑ Ⓒ Ⓓ Ⓔ
22. Ⓐ Ⓑ Ⓒ Ⓓ Ⓔ
23. Ⓐ Ⓑ Ⓒ Ⓓ Ⓔ
24. Ⓐ Ⓑ Ⓒ Ⓓ Ⓔ
25. Ⓐ Ⓑ Ⓒ Ⓓ Ⓔ
26. Ⓐ Ⓑ Ⓒ Ⓓ Ⓔ
27. Ⓐ Ⓑ Ⓒ Ⓓ Ⓔ
28. Ⓐ Ⓑ Ⓒ Ⓓ Ⓔ
29. Ⓐ Ⓑ Ⓒ Ⓓ Ⓔ
30. Ⓐ Ⓑ Ⓒ Ⓓ Ⓔ
31. Ⓐ Ⓑ Ⓒ Ⓓ Ⓔ
32. Ⓐ Ⓑ Ⓒ Ⓓ Ⓔ

See grids on the
following page
for nos. 33–40

SECTION 5

1. Ⓐ Ⓑ Ⓒ Ⓓ Ⓔ
2. Ⓐ Ⓑ Ⓒ Ⓓ Ⓔ
3. Ⓐ Ⓑ Ⓒ Ⓓ Ⓔ
4. Ⓐ Ⓑ Ⓒ Ⓓ Ⓔ
5. Ⓐ Ⓑ Ⓒ Ⓓ Ⓔ
6. Ⓐ Ⓑ Ⓒ Ⓓ Ⓔ
7. Ⓐ Ⓑ Ⓒ Ⓓ Ⓔ
8. Ⓐ Ⓑ Ⓒ Ⓓ Ⓔ
9. Ⓐ Ⓑ Ⓒ Ⓓ Ⓔ
10. Ⓐ Ⓑ Ⓒ Ⓓ Ⓔ
11. Ⓐ Ⓑ Ⓒ Ⓓ Ⓔ
12. Ⓐ Ⓑ Ⓒ Ⓓ Ⓔ
13. Ⓐ Ⓑ Ⓒ Ⓓ Ⓔ
14. Ⓐ Ⓑ Ⓒ Ⓓ Ⓔ
15. Ⓐ Ⓑ Ⓒ Ⓓ Ⓔ
16. Ⓐ Ⓑ Ⓒ Ⓓ Ⓔ
17. Ⓐ Ⓑ Ⓒ Ⓓ Ⓔ
18. Ⓐ Ⓑ Ⓒ Ⓓ Ⓔ
19. Ⓐ Ⓑ Ⓒ Ⓓ Ⓔ
20. Ⓐ Ⓑ Ⓒ Ⓓ Ⓔ

SECTION 5 (CONT'D)

21. Ⓐ Ⓑ Ⓒ Ⓓ Ⓔ
22. Ⓐ Ⓑ Ⓒ Ⓓ Ⓔ
23. Ⓐ Ⓑ Ⓒ Ⓓ Ⓔ
24. Ⓐ Ⓑ Ⓒ Ⓓ Ⓔ
25. Ⓐ Ⓑ Ⓒ Ⓓ Ⓔ
26. Ⓐ Ⓑ Ⓒ Ⓓ Ⓔ
27. Ⓐ Ⓑ Ⓒ Ⓓ Ⓔ
28. Ⓐ Ⓑ Ⓒ Ⓓ Ⓔ
29. Ⓐ Ⓑ Ⓒ Ⓓ Ⓔ
30. Ⓐ Ⓑ Ⓒ Ⓓ Ⓔ

31. Ⓐ Ⓑ Ⓒ Ⓓ Ⓔ
32. Ⓐ Ⓑ Ⓒ Ⓓ Ⓔ
33. Ⓐ Ⓑ Ⓒ Ⓓ Ⓔ
34. Ⓐ Ⓑ Ⓒ Ⓓ Ⓔ
35. Ⓐ Ⓑ Ⓒ Ⓓ Ⓔ
36. Ⓐ Ⓑ Ⓒ Ⓓ Ⓔ
37. Ⓐ Ⓑ Ⓒ Ⓓ Ⓔ
38. Ⓐ Ⓑ Ⓒ Ⓓ Ⓔ
39. Ⓐ Ⓑ Ⓒ Ⓓ Ⓔ

SECTION 4 GRIDS

33. 34. 35. 36.

37. 38. 39. 40.

Drill: Student-Produced Response

13. [grid-in answer bubble: 4 columns with fraction slashes, decimal points, digits 0-9]

14. [grid-in answer bubble: 4 columns with fraction slashes, decimal points, digits 0-9]

15. [grid-in answer bubble: 4 columns with fraction slashes, decimal points, digits 0-9]

16. [grid-in answer bubble: 4 columns with fraction slashes, decimal points, digits 0-9]

17. [grid-in answer bubble: 4 columns with fraction slashes, decimal points, digits 0-9]

18. [grid-in answer bubble: 4 columns with fraction slashes, decimal points, digits 0-9]

19. [grid-in answer bubble: 4 columns with fraction slashes, decimal points, digits 0-9]

20. [grid-in answer bubble: 4 columns with fraction slashes, decimal points, digits 0-9]

21. [grid-in answer bubble: 4 columns with fraction slashes, decimal points, digits 0-9]

22. [grid-in answer bubble: 4 columns with fraction slashes, decimal points, digits 0-9]

23. [grid-in answer bubble: 4 columns with fraction slashes, decimal points, digits 0-9]

24. [grid-in answer bubble: 4 columns with fraction slashes, decimal points, digits 0-9]

25.

	/	/	
.	.	.	.
	0	0	0
1	1	1	1
2	2	2	2
3	3	3	3
4	4	4	4
5	5	5	5
6	6	6	6
7	7	7	7
8	8	8	8
9	9	9	9

26.

	/	/	
.	.	.	.
	0	0	0
1	1	1	1
2	2	2	2
3	3	3	3
4	4	4	4
5	5	5	5
6	6	6	6
7	7	7	7
8	8	8	8
9	9	9	9

27.

	/	/	
.	.	.	.
	0	0	0
1	1	1	1
2	2	2	2
3	3	3	3
4	4	4	4
5	5	5	5
6	6	6	6
7	7	7	7
8	8	8	8
9	9	9	9

28.

	/	/	
.	.	.	.
	0	0	0
1	1	1	1
2	2	2	2
3	3	3	3
4	4	4	4
5	5	5	5
6	6	6	6
7	7	7	7
8	8	8	8
9	9	9	9

29.

	/	/	
.	.	.	.
	0	0	0
1	1	1	1
2	2	2	2
3	3	3	3
4	4	4	4
5	5	5	5
6	6	6	6
7	7	7	7
8	8	8	8
9	9	9	9

30.

	/	/	
.	.	.	.
	0	0	0
1	1	1	1
2	2	2	2
3	3	3	3
4	4	4	4
5	5	5	5
6	6	6	6
7	7	7	7
8	8	8	8
9	9	9	9

31.

	/	/	
.	.	.	.
	0	0	0
1	1	1	1
2	2	2	2
3	3	3	3
4	4	4	4
5	5	5	5
6	6	6	6
7	7	7	7
8	8	8	8
9	9	9	9

32.

	/	/	
.	.	.	.
	0	0	0
1	1	1	1
2	2	2	2
3	3	3	3
4	4	4	4
5	5	5	5
6	6	6	6
7	7	7	7
8	8	8	8
9	9	9	9

33.

	/	/	
.	.	.	.
	0	0	0
1	1	1	1
2	2	2	2
3	3	3	3
4	4	4	4
5	5	5	5
6	6	6	6
7	7	7	7
8	8	8	8
9	9	9	9

34.

	/	/	
.	.	.	.
	0	0	0
1	1	1	1
2	2	2	2
3	3	3	3
4	4	4	4
5	5	5	5
6	6	6	6
7	7	7	7
8	8	8	8
9	9	9	9

35.

	/	/	
.	.	.	.
	0	0	0
1	1	1	1
2	2	2	2
3	3	3	3
4	4	4	4
5	5	5	5
6	6	6	6
7	7	7	7
8	8	8	8
9	9	9	9

36.

	/	/	
.	.	.	.
	0	0	0
1	1	1	1
2	2	2	2
3	3	3	3
4	4	4	4
5	5	5	5
6	6	6	6
7	7	7	7
8	8	8	8
9	9	9	9

37.

	⊘	⊘	
⊙	⊙	⊙	⊙
	⓪	⓪	⓪
①	①	①	①
②	②	②	②
③	③	③	③
④	④	④	④
⑤	⑤	⑤	⑤
⑥	⑥	⑥	⑥
⑦	⑦	⑦	⑦
⑧	⑧	⑧	⑧
⑨	⑨	⑨	⑨

38.

	⊘	⊘	
⊙	⊙	⊙	⊙
	⓪	⓪	⓪
①	①	①	①
②	②	②	②
③	③	③	③
④	④	④	④
⑤	⑤	⑤	⑤
⑥	⑥	⑥	⑥
⑦	⑦	⑦	⑦
⑧	⑧	⑧	⑧
⑨	⑨	⑨	⑨

39.

	⊘	⊘	
⊙	⊙	⊙	⊙
	⓪	⓪	⓪
①	①	①	①
②	②	②	②
③	③	③	③
④	④	④	④
⑤	⑤	⑤	⑤
⑥	⑥	⑥	⑥
⑦	⑦	⑦	⑦
⑧	⑧	⑧	⑧
⑨	⑨	⑨	⑨

40.

	⊘	⊘	
⊙	⊙	⊙	⊙
	⓪	⓪	⓪
①	①	①	①
②	②	②	②
③	③	③	③
④	④	④	④
⑤	⑤	⑤	⑤
⑥	⑥	⑥	⑥
⑦	⑦	⑦	⑦
⑧	⑧	⑧	⑧
⑨	⑨	⑨	⑨

PSAT/NMSQT – Test 1
ANSWER SHEET

SECTION 1

1. Ⓐ Ⓑ Ⓒ Ⓓ Ⓔ
2. Ⓐ Ⓑ Ⓒ Ⓓ Ⓔ
3. Ⓐ Ⓑ Ⓒ Ⓓ Ⓔ
4. Ⓐ Ⓑ Ⓒ Ⓓ Ⓔ
5. Ⓐ Ⓑ Ⓒ Ⓓ Ⓔ
6. Ⓐ Ⓑ Ⓒ Ⓓ Ⓔ
7. Ⓐ Ⓑ Ⓒ Ⓓ Ⓔ
8. Ⓐ Ⓑ Ⓒ Ⓓ Ⓔ
9. Ⓐ Ⓑ Ⓒ Ⓓ Ⓔ
10. Ⓐ Ⓑ Ⓒ Ⓓ Ⓔ
11. Ⓐ Ⓑ Ⓒ Ⓓ Ⓔ
12. Ⓐ Ⓑ Ⓒ Ⓓ Ⓔ
13. Ⓐ Ⓑ Ⓒ Ⓓ Ⓔ
14. Ⓐ Ⓑ Ⓒ Ⓓ Ⓔ
15. Ⓐ Ⓑ Ⓒ Ⓓ Ⓔ
16. Ⓐ Ⓑ Ⓒ Ⓓ Ⓔ
17. Ⓐ Ⓑ Ⓒ Ⓓ Ⓔ
18. Ⓐ Ⓑ Ⓒ Ⓓ Ⓔ
19. Ⓐ Ⓑ Ⓒ Ⓓ Ⓔ
20. Ⓐ Ⓑ Ⓒ Ⓓ Ⓔ
21. Ⓐ Ⓑ Ⓒ Ⓓ Ⓔ
22. Ⓐ Ⓑ Ⓒ Ⓓ Ⓔ
23. Ⓐ Ⓑ Ⓒ Ⓓ Ⓔ
24. Ⓐ Ⓑ Ⓒ Ⓓ Ⓔ
25. Ⓐ Ⓑ Ⓒ Ⓓ Ⓔ
26. Ⓐ Ⓑ Ⓒ Ⓓ Ⓔ

SECTION 2

1. Ⓐ Ⓑ Ⓒ Ⓓ Ⓔ
2. Ⓐ Ⓑ Ⓒ Ⓓ Ⓔ
3. Ⓐ Ⓑ Ⓒ Ⓓ Ⓔ
4. Ⓐ Ⓑ Ⓒ Ⓓ Ⓔ
5. Ⓐ Ⓑ Ⓒ Ⓓ Ⓔ
6. Ⓐ Ⓑ Ⓒ Ⓓ Ⓔ
7. Ⓐ Ⓑ Ⓒ Ⓓ Ⓔ
8. Ⓐ Ⓑ Ⓒ Ⓓ Ⓔ
9. Ⓐ Ⓑ Ⓒ Ⓓ Ⓔ
10. Ⓐ Ⓑ Ⓒ Ⓓ Ⓔ

11. Ⓐ Ⓑ Ⓒ Ⓓ Ⓔ
12. Ⓐ Ⓑ Ⓒ Ⓓ Ⓔ
13. Ⓐ Ⓑ Ⓒ Ⓓ Ⓔ
14. Ⓐ Ⓑ Ⓒ Ⓓ Ⓔ
15. Ⓐ Ⓑ Ⓒ Ⓓ Ⓔ
16. Ⓐ Ⓑ Ⓒ Ⓓ Ⓔ
17. Ⓐ Ⓑ Ⓒ Ⓓ Ⓔ
18. Ⓐ Ⓑ Ⓒ Ⓓ Ⓔ
19. Ⓐ Ⓑ Ⓒ Ⓓ Ⓔ
20. Ⓐ Ⓑ Ⓒ Ⓓ Ⓔ

SECTION 3

27. Ⓐ Ⓑ Ⓒ Ⓓ Ⓔ
28. Ⓐ Ⓑ Ⓒ Ⓓ Ⓔ
29. Ⓐ Ⓑ Ⓒ Ⓓ Ⓔ
30. Ⓐ Ⓑ Ⓒ Ⓓ Ⓔ
31. Ⓐ Ⓑ Ⓒ Ⓓ Ⓔ
32. Ⓐ Ⓑ Ⓒ Ⓓ Ⓔ
33. Ⓐ Ⓑ Ⓒ Ⓓ Ⓔ
34. Ⓐ Ⓑ Ⓒ Ⓓ Ⓔ
35. Ⓐ Ⓑ Ⓒ Ⓓ Ⓔ
36. Ⓐ Ⓑ Ⓒ Ⓓ Ⓔ
37. Ⓐ Ⓑ Ⓒ Ⓓ Ⓔ
38. Ⓐ Ⓑ Ⓒ Ⓓ Ⓔ
39. Ⓐ Ⓑ Ⓒ Ⓓ Ⓔ
40. Ⓐ Ⓑ Ⓒ Ⓓ Ⓔ
41. Ⓐ Ⓑ Ⓒ Ⓓ Ⓔ
42. Ⓐ Ⓑ Ⓒ Ⓓ Ⓔ
43. Ⓐ Ⓑ Ⓒ Ⓓ Ⓔ
44. Ⓐ Ⓑ Ⓒ Ⓓ Ⓔ
45. Ⓐ Ⓑ Ⓒ Ⓓ Ⓔ
46. Ⓐ Ⓑ Ⓒ Ⓓ Ⓔ
47. Ⓐ Ⓑ Ⓒ Ⓓ Ⓔ
48. Ⓐ Ⓑ Ⓒ Ⓓ Ⓔ
49. Ⓐ Ⓑ Ⓒ Ⓓ Ⓔ
50. Ⓐ Ⓑ Ⓒ Ⓓ Ⓔ
51. Ⓐ Ⓑ Ⓒ Ⓓ Ⓔ
52. Ⓐ Ⓑ Ⓒ Ⓓ Ⓔ

SECTION 4

21. Ⓐ Ⓑ Ⓒ Ⓓ Ⓔ
22. Ⓐ Ⓑ Ⓒ Ⓓ Ⓔ
23. Ⓐ Ⓑ Ⓒ Ⓓ Ⓔ
24. Ⓐ Ⓑ Ⓒ Ⓓ Ⓔ
25. Ⓐ Ⓑ Ⓒ Ⓓ Ⓔ
26. Ⓐ Ⓑ Ⓒ Ⓓ Ⓔ
27. Ⓐ Ⓑ Ⓒ Ⓓ Ⓔ
28. Ⓐ Ⓑ Ⓒ Ⓓ Ⓔ
29. Ⓐ Ⓑ Ⓒ Ⓓ Ⓔ
30. Ⓐ Ⓑ Ⓒ Ⓓ Ⓔ
31. Ⓐ Ⓑ Ⓒ Ⓓ Ⓔ
32. Ⓐ Ⓑ Ⓒ Ⓓ Ⓔ

See grids on the
following page
for nos. 33–40

SECTION 5

1. Ⓐ Ⓑ Ⓒ Ⓓ Ⓔ
2. Ⓐ Ⓑ Ⓒ Ⓓ Ⓔ
3. Ⓐ Ⓑ Ⓒ Ⓓ Ⓔ
4. Ⓐ Ⓑ Ⓒ Ⓓ Ⓔ
5. Ⓐ Ⓑ Ⓒ Ⓓ Ⓔ
6. Ⓐ Ⓑ Ⓒ Ⓓ Ⓔ
7. Ⓐ Ⓑ Ⓒ Ⓓ Ⓔ
8. Ⓐ Ⓑ Ⓒ Ⓓ Ⓔ
9. Ⓐ Ⓑ Ⓒ Ⓓ Ⓔ
10. Ⓐ Ⓑ Ⓒ Ⓓ Ⓔ
11. Ⓐ Ⓑ Ⓒ Ⓓ Ⓔ
12. Ⓐ Ⓑ Ⓒ Ⓓ Ⓔ
13. Ⓐ Ⓑ Ⓒ Ⓓ Ⓔ
14. Ⓐ Ⓑ Ⓒ Ⓓ Ⓔ
15. Ⓐ Ⓑ Ⓒ Ⓓ Ⓔ
16. Ⓐ Ⓑ Ⓒ Ⓓ Ⓔ
17. Ⓐ Ⓑ Ⓒ Ⓓ Ⓔ
18. Ⓐ Ⓑ Ⓒ Ⓓ Ⓔ
19. Ⓐ Ⓑ Ⓒ Ⓓ Ⓔ
20. Ⓐ Ⓑ Ⓒ Ⓓ Ⓔ

SECTION 5 (CONT'D)

21. Ⓐ Ⓑ Ⓒ Ⓓ Ⓔ   31. Ⓐ Ⓑ Ⓒ Ⓓ Ⓔ
22. Ⓐ Ⓑ Ⓒ Ⓓ Ⓔ   32. Ⓐ Ⓑ Ⓒ Ⓓ Ⓔ
23. Ⓐ Ⓑ Ⓒ Ⓓ Ⓔ   33. Ⓐ Ⓑ Ⓒ Ⓓ Ⓔ
24. Ⓐ Ⓑ Ⓒ Ⓓ Ⓔ   34. Ⓐ Ⓑ Ⓒ Ⓓ Ⓔ
25. Ⓐ Ⓑ Ⓒ Ⓓ Ⓔ   35. Ⓐ Ⓑ Ⓒ Ⓓ Ⓔ
26. Ⓐ Ⓑ Ⓒ Ⓓ Ⓔ   36. Ⓐ Ⓑ Ⓒ Ⓓ Ⓔ
27. Ⓐ Ⓑ Ⓒ Ⓓ Ⓔ   37. Ⓐ Ⓑ Ⓒ Ⓓ Ⓔ
28. Ⓐ Ⓑ Ⓒ Ⓓ Ⓔ   38. Ⓐ Ⓑ Ⓒ Ⓓ Ⓔ
29. Ⓐ Ⓑ Ⓒ Ⓓ Ⓔ   39. Ⓐ Ⓑ Ⓒ Ⓓ Ⓔ
30. Ⓐ Ⓑ Ⓒ Ⓓ Ⓔ

SECTION 4 GRIDS

33. [grid]   34. [grid]   35. [grid]   36. [grid]

37. [grid]   38. [grid]   39. [grid]   40. [grid]

PSAT/NMSQT – Test 2
ANSWER SHEET

SECTION 1

1. (A) (B) (C) (D) (E)
2. (A) (B) (C) (D) (E)
3. (A) (B) (C) (D) (E)
4. (A) (B) (C) (D) (E)
5. (A) (B) (C) (D) (E)
6. (A) (B) (C) (D) (E)
7. (A) (B) (C) (D) (E)
8. (A) (B) (C) (D) (E)
9. (A) (B) (C) (D) (E)
10. (A) (B) (C) (D) (E)
11. (A) (B) (C) (D) (E)
12. (A) (B) (C) (D) (E)
13. (A) (B) (C) (D) (E)
14. (A) (B) (C) (D) (E)
15. (A) (B) (C) (D) (E)
16. (A) (B) (C) (D) (E)
17. (A) (B) (C) (D) (E)
18. (A) (B) (C) (D) (E)
19. (A) (B) (C) (D) (E)
20. (A) (B) (C) (D) (E)
21. (A) (B) (C) (D) (E)
22. (A) (B) (C) (D) (E)
23. (A) (B) (C) (D) (E)
24. (A) (B) (C) (D) (E)
25. (A) (B) (C) (D) (E)
26. (A) (B) (C) (D) (E)

SECTION 2

1. (A) (B) (C) (D) (E)
2. (A) (B) (C) (D) (E)
3. (A) (B) (C) (D) (E)
4. (A) (B) (C) (D) (E)
5. (A) (B) (C) (D) (E)
6. (A) (B) (C) (D) (E)
7. (A) (B) (C) (D) (E)
8. (A) (B) (C) (D) (E)
9. (A) (B) (C) (D) (E)
10. (A) (B) (C) (D) (E)

11. (A) (B) (C) (D) (E)
12. (A) (B) (C) (D) (E)
13. (A) (B) (C) (D) (E)
14. (A) (B) (C) (D) (E)
15. (A) (B) (C) (D) (E)
16. (A) (B) (C) (D) (E)
17. (A) (B) (C) (D) (E)
18. (A) (B) (C) (D) (E)
19. (A) (B) (C) (D) (E)
20. (A) (B) (C) (D) (E)

SECTION 3

27. (A) (B) (C) (D) (E)
28. (A) (B) (C) (D) (E)
29. (A) (B) (C) (D) (E)
30. (A) (B) (C) (D) (E)
31. (A) (B) (C) (D) (E)
32. (A) (B) (C) (D) (E)
33. (A) (B) (C) (D) (E)
34. (A) (B) (C) (D) (E)
35. (A) (B) (C) (D) (E)
36. (A) (B) (C) (D) (E)
37. (A) (B) (C) (D) (E)
38. (A) (B) (C) (D) (E)
39. (A) (B) (C) (D) (E)
40. (A) (B) (C) (D) (E)
41. (A) (B) (C) (D) (E)
42. (A) (B) (C) (D) (E)
43. (A) (B) (C) (D) (E)
44. (A) (B) (C) (D) (E)
45. (A) (B) (C) (D) (E)
46. (A) (B) (C) (D) (E)
47. (A) (B) (C) (D) (E)
48. (A) (B) (C) (D) (E)
49. (A) (B) (C) (D) (E)
50. (A) (B) (C) (D) (E)
51. (A) (B) (C) (D) (E)
52. (A) (B) (C) (D) (E)

SECTION 4

21. (A) (B) (C) (D) (E)
22. (A) (B) (C) (D) (E)
23. (A) (B) (C) (D) (E)
24. (A) (B) (C) (D) (E)
25. (A) (B) (C) (D) (E)
26. (A) (B) (C) (D) (E)
27. (A) (B) (C) (D) (E)
28. (A) (B) (C) (D) (E)
29. (A) (B) (C) (D) (E)
30. (A) (B) (C) (D) (E)
31. (A) (B) (C) (D) (E)
32. (A) (B) (C) (D) (E)

> See grids on the
> following page
> for nos. 33–40

SECTION 5

1. (A) (B) (C) (D) (E)
2. (A) (B) (C) (D) (E)
3. (A) (B) (C) (D) (E)
4. (A) (B) (C) (D) (E)
5. (A) (B) (C) (D) (E)
6. (A) (B) (C) (D) (E)
7. (A) (B) (C) (D) (E)
8. (A) (B) (C) (D) (E)
9. (A) (B) (C) (D) (E)
10. (A) (B) (C) (D) (E)
11. (A) (B) (C) (D) (E)
12. (A) (B) (C) (D) (E)
13. (A) (B) (C) (D) (E)
14. (A) (B) (C) (D) (E)
15. (A) (B) (C) (D) (E)
16. (A) (B) (C) (D) (E)
17. (A) (B) (C) (D) (E)
18. (A) (B) (C) (D) (E)
19. (A) (B) (C) (D) (E)
20. (A) (B) (C) (D) (E)

SECTION 5 (CONT'D)

21. Ⓐ Ⓑ Ⓒ Ⓓ Ⓔ   31. Ⓐ Ⓑ Ⓒ Ⓓ Ⓔ
22. Ⓐ Ⓑ Ⓒ Ⓓ Ⓔ   32. Ⓐ Ⓑ Ⓒ Ⓓ Ⓔ
23. Ⓐ Ⓑ Ⓒ Ⓓ Ⓔ   33. Ⓐ Ⓑ Ⓒ Ⓓ Ⓔ
24. Ⓐ Ⓑ Ⓒ Ⓓ Ⓔ   34. Ⓐ Ⓑ Ⓒ Ⓓ Ⓔ
25. Ⓐ Ⓑ Ⓒ Ⓓ Ⓔ   35. Ⓐ Ⓑ Ⓒ Ⓓ Ⓔ
26. Ⓐ Ⓑ Ⓒ Ⓓ Ⓔ   36. Ⓐ Ⓑ Ⓒ Ⓓ Ⓔ
27. Ⓐ Ⓑ Ⓒ Ⓓ Ⓔ   37. Ⓐ Ⓑ Ⓒ Ⓓ Ⓔ
28. Ⓐ Ⓑ Ⓒ Ⓓ Ⓔ   38. Ⓐ Ⓑ Ⓒ Ⓓ Ⓔ
29. Ⓐ Ⓑ Ⓒ Ⓓ Ⓔ   39. Ⓐ Ⓑ Ⓒ Ⓓ Ⓔ
30. Ⓐ Ⓑ Ⓒ Ⓓ Ⓔ

SECTION 4 GRIDS

33.
34.
35.
36.
37.
38.
39.
40.

PSAT/NMSQT – Test 3
ANSWER SHEET

SECTION 1

1. Ⓐ Ⓑ Ⓒ Ⓓ Ⓔ
2. Ⓐ Ⓑ Ⓒ Ⓓ Ⓔ
3. Ⓐ Ⓑ Ⓒ Ⓓ Ⓔ
4. Ⓐ Ⓑ Ⓒ Ⓓ Ⓔ
5. Ⓐ Ⓑ Ⓒ Ⓓ Ⓔ
6. Ⓐ Ⓑ Ⓒ Ⓓ Ⓔ
7. Ⓐ Ⓑ Ⓒ Ⓓ Ⓔ
8. Ⓐ Ⓑ Ⓒ Ⓓ Ⓔ
9. Ⓐ Ⓑ Ⓒ Ⓓ Ⓔ
10. Ⓐ Ⓑ Ⓒ Ⓓ Ⓔ
11. Ⓐ Ⓑ Ⓒ Ⓓ Ⓔ
12. Ⓐ Ⓑ Ⓒ Ⓓ Ⓔ
13. Ⓐ Ⓑ Ⓒ Ⓓ Ⓔ
14. Ⓐ Ⓑ Ⓒ Ⓓ Ⓔ
15. Ⓐ Ⓑ Ⓒ Ⓓ Ⓔ
16. Ⓐ Ⓑ Ⓒ Ⓓ Ⓔ
17. Ⓐ Ⓑ Ⓒ Ⓓ Ⓔ
18. Ⓐ Ⓑ Ⓒ Ⓓ Ⓔ
19. Ⓐ Ⓑ Ⓒ Ⓓ Ⓔ
20. Ⓐ Ⓑ Ⓒ Ⓓ Ⓔ
21. Ⓐ Ⓑ Ⓒ Ⓓ Ⓔ
22. Ⓐ Ⓑ Ⓒ Ⓓ Ⓔ
23. Ⓐ Ⓑ Ⓒ Ⓓ Ⓔ
24. Ⓐ Ⓑ Ⓒ Ⓓ Ⓔ
25. Ⓐ Ⓑ Ⓒ Ⓓ Ⓔ
26. Ⓐ Ⓑ Ⓒ Ⓓ Ⓔ

SECTION 2

1. Ⓐ Ⓑ Ⓒ Ⓓ Ⓔ
2. Ⓐ Ⓑ Ⓒ Ⓓ Ⓔ
3. Ⓐ Ⓑ Ⓒ Ⓓ Ⓔ
4. Ⓐ Ⓑ Ⓒ Ⓓ Ⓔ
5. Ⓐ Ⓑ Ⓒ Ⓓ Ⓔ
6. Ⓐ Ⓑ Ⓒ Ⓓ Ⓔ
7. Ⓐ Ⓑ Ⓒ Ⓓ Ⓔ
8. Ⓐ Ⓑ Ⓒ Ⓓ Ⓔ
9. Ⓐ Ⓑ Ⓒ Ⓓ Ⓔ
10. Ⓐ Ⓑ Ⓒ Ⓓ Ⓔ

11. Ⓐ Ⓑ Ⓒ Ⓓ Ⓔ
12. Ⓐ Ⓑ Ⓒ Ⓓ Ⓔ
13. Ⓐ Ⓑ Ⓒ Ⓓ Ⓔ
14. Ⓐ Ⓑ Ⓒ Ⓓ Ⓔ
15. Ⓐ Ⓑ Ⓒ Ⓓ Ⓔ
16. Ⓐ Ⓑ Ⓒ Ⓓ Ⓔ
17. Ⓐ Ⓑ Ⓒ Ⓓ Ⓔ
18. Ⓐ Ⓑ Ⓒ Ⓓ Ⓔ
19. Ⓐ Ⓑ Ⓒ Ⓓ Ⓔ
20. Ⓐ Ⓑ Ⓒ Ⓓ Ⓔ

SECTION 3

27. Ⓐ Ⓑ Ⓒ Ⓓ Ⓔ
28. Ⓐ Ⓑ Ⓒ Ⓓ Ⓔ
29. Ⓐ Ⓑ Ⓒ Ⓓ Ⓔ
30. Ⓐ Ⓑ Ⓒ Ⓓ Ⓔ
31. Ⓐ Ⓑ Ⓒ Ⓓ Ⓔ
32. Ⓐ Ⓑ Ⓒ Ⓓ Ⓔ
33. Ⓐ Ⓑ Ⓒ Ⓓ Ⓔ
34. Ⓐ Ⓑ Ⓒ Ⓓ Ⓔ
35. Ⓐ Ⓑ Ⓒ Ⓓ Ⓔ
36. Ⓐ Ⓑ Ⓒ Ⓓ Ⓔ
37. Ⓐ Ⓑ Ⓒ Ⓓ Ⓔ
38. Ⓐ Ⓑ Ⓒ Ⓓ Ⓔ
39. Ⓐ Ⓑ Ⓒ Ⓓ Ⓔ
40. Ⓐ Ⓑ Ⓒ Ⓓ Ⓔ
41. Ⓐ Ⓑ Ⓒ Ⓓ Ⓔ
42. Ⓐ Ⓑ Ⓒ Ⓓ Ⓔ
43. Ⓐ Ⓑ Ⓒ Ⓓ Ⓔ
44. Ⓐ Ⓑ Ⓒ Ⓓ Ⓔ
45. Ⓐ Ⓑ Ⓒ Ⓓ Ⓔ
46. Ⓐ Ⓑ Ⓒ Ⓓ Ⓔ
47. Ⓐ Ⓑ Ⓒ Ⓓ Ⓔ
48. Ⓐ Ⓑ Ⓒ Ⓓ Ⓔ
49. Ⓐ Ⓑ Ⓒ Ⓓ Ⓔ
50. Ⓐ Ⓑ Ⓒ Ⓓ Ⓔ
51. Ⓐ Ⓑ Ⓒ Ⓓ Ⓔ
52. Ⓐ Ⓑ Ⓒ Ⓓ Ⓔ

SECTION 4

21. Ⓐ Ⓑ Ⓒ Ⓓ Ⓔ
22. Ⓐ Ⓑ Ⓒ Ⓓ Ⓔ
23. Ⓐ Ⓑ Ⓒ Ⓓ Ⓔ
24. Ⓐ Ⓑ Ⓒ Ⓓ Ⓔ
25. Ⓐ Ⓑ Ⓒ Ⓓ Ⓔ
26. Ⓐ Ⓑ Ⓒ Ⓓ Ⓔ
27. Ⓐ Ⓑ Ⓒ Ⓓ Ⓔ
28. Ⓐ Ⓑ Ⓒ Ⓓ Ⓔ
29. Ⓐ Ⓑ Ⓒ Ⓓ Ⓔ
30. Ⓐ Ⓑ Ⓒ Ⓓ Ⓔ
31. Ⓐ Ⓑ Ⓒ Ⓓ Ⓔ
32. Ⓐ Ⓑ Ⓒ Ⓓ Ⓔ

See grids on the
following page
for nos. 33–40

SECTION 5

1. Ⓐ Ⓑ Ⓒ Ⓓ Ⓔ
2. Ⓐ Ⓑ Ⓒ Ⓓ Ⓔ
3. Ⓐ Ⓑ Ⓒ Ⓓ Ⓔ
4. Ⓐ Ⓑ Ⓒ Ⓓ Ⓔ
5. Ⓐ Ⓑ Ⓒ Ⓓ Ⓔ
6. Ⓐ Ⓑ Ⓒ Ⓓ Ⓔ
7. Ⓐ Ⓑ Ⓒ Ⓓ Ⓔ
8. Ⓐ Ⓑ Ⓒ Ⓓ Ⓔ
9. Ⓐ Ⓑ Ⓒ Ⓓ Ⓔ
10. Ⓐ Ⓑ Ⓒ Ⓓ Ⓔ
11. Ⓐ Ⓑ Ⓒ Ⓓ Ⓔ
12. Ⓐ Ⓑ Ⓒ Ⓓ Ⓔ
13. Ⓐ Ⓑ Ⓒ Ⓓ Ⓔ
14. Ⓐ Ⓑ Ⓒ Ⓓ Ⓔ
15. Ⓐ Ⓑ Ⓒ Ⓓ Ⓔ
16. Ⓐ Ⓑ Ⓒ Ⓓ Ⓔ
17. Ⓐ Ⓑ Ⓒ Ⓓ Ⓔ
18. Ⓐ Ⓑ Ⓒ Ⓓ Ⓔ
19. Ⓐ Ⓑ Ⓒ Ⓓ Ⓔ
20. Ⓐ Ⓑ Ⓒ Ⓓ Ⓔ

SECTION 5 (CONT'D)

21. Ⓐ Ⓑ Ⓒ Ⓓ Ⓔ   31. Ⓐ Ⓑ Ⓒ Ⓓ Ⓔ
22. Ⓐ Ⓑ Ⓒ Ⓓ Ⓔ   32. Ⓐ Ⓑ Ⓒ Ⓓ Ⓔ
23. Ⓐ Ⓑ Ⓒ Ⓓ Ⓔ   33. Ⓐ Ⓑ Ⓒ Ⓓ Ⓔ
24. Ⓐ Ⓑ Ⓒ Ⓓ Ⓔ   34. Ⓐ Ⓑ Ⓒ Ⓓ Ⓔ
25. Ⓐ Ⓑ Ⓒ Ⓓ Ⓔ   35. Ⓐ Ⓑ Ⓒ Ⓓ Ⓔ
26. Ⓐ Ⓑ Ⓒ Ⓓ Ⓔ   36. Ⓐ Ⓑ Ⓒ Ⓓ Ⓔ
27. Ⓐ Ⓑ Ⓒ Ⓓ Ⓔ   37. Ⓐ Ⓑ Ⓒ Ⓓ Ⓔ
28. Ⓐ Ⓑ Ⓒ Ⓓ Ⓔ   38. Ⓐ Ⓑ Ⓒ Ⓓ Ⓔ
29. Ⓐ Ⓑ Ⓒ Ⓓ Ⓔ   39. Ⓐ Ⓑ Ⓒ Ⓓ Ⓔ
30. Ⓐ Ⓑ Ⓒ Ⓓ Ⓔ

SECTION 4 GRIDS

33. 34. 35. 36.

37. 38. 39. 40.